A Critical History of Philosophy

(Volume I)

Asa Mahan

Alpha Editions

This edition published in 2019

ISBN : 9789389265149

Design and Setting By
Alpha Editions
email - alphaedis@gmail.com

This book is a reproduction of an important historical work. Alpha Editions uses the best technology to reproduce historical work in the same manner it was first published to preserve its original nature. Any marks or number seen are left intentionally to preserve its true form.

A CRITICAL HISTORY OF PHILOSOPHY.

BY

REV. ASA MAHAN, D.D., LL.D.,

AUTHOR OF

'THE SCIENCE OF INTELLECTUAL PHILOSOPHY,' 'THE SYSTEM OF MENTAL PHILOSOPHY,' 'THE SCIENCE OF LOGIC,' 'THE SCIENCE OF NATURAL THEOLOGY,' ETC.

IN TWO VOLUMES.

VOL. I.

> 'How charming is divine Philosophy;
> Not harsh and crabbed, as dull fools suppose,
> But musical as is Apollo's lute,
> And a perpetual feast of nectar'd sweets,
> Where no crude surfeit reigns.'

NEW YORK:
PHILLIPS & HUNT.
CINCINNATI:
WALDEN & STOWE.
1883.

PREFACE.

THE following fact, which occurred more than twenty years since, was the prime occasion of the preparation and publication of the following Treatise. A distinguished German scholar who was then the president of the leading Lutheran College in the United States, after having read a work of mine entitled 'The Science of Intellectual Philosophy,' a work in which I gave a specific statement of the character of the different systems of Philosophy which in the present and past ages have been commended to world-thought —this scholar, after having read that work, remarked to a friend of mine 'that President Mahan ought to write a History of Philosophy.' The reason assigned for that judgment was this: 'He *understands* the diverse systems which the history of Philosophy presents to our regard.' As I revolved the subject in thought, the plan of the following Treatise opened at once, with perfect distinctness, upon my mind—a plan which, as I clearly perceived, remedied fully the essential defects which characterize all Histories of Philosophy which have hitherto been written. The defect referred to is this—in such histories there is no clear and distinct *classification* of the diverse systems presented. In reading, consequently, the mind becomes confused, rather than instructed, as the diverse, and contradictory, and undefined solutions of world-problems become subjects of thought and reflection. The plan suggested, on the other hand, enables the author to define and classify beforehand all such systems which ever have appeared, or ever can appear, and to do this with such perfect distinctness and definiteness that, when any such system is presented, the reader will at once perceive to what class it belongs, what are its essential characteristics, what are its constituent elements, upon what basis it rests, what are its real merits or defects, and, consequently, what place it should occupy in his regard.

When the plan had assumed a full and mature form in my own mind, and before I put pen to paper upon the subject, I presented it verbally to a large number of the best thinkers and judges on such subjects that I met with. From every one of these I received an earnest exhortation to make it my first business to fill out the plan presented, and to publish it for the benefit of the world. After such a presentation to Bishop Simpson, for example, who had had a large experience as a professor of mental and moral science, he thus expressed himself to me : President Mahan, my earnest advice to you is to prepare that work as soon as practicable, and to publish it, not only for the benefit of science, but as a fundamental vindication of the central truth of Christianity, the doctrine of a personal God. Your plan, as I clearly perceive, not only lays bare the banks of sand on which all false and godless systems are based, but reveals, with perfect distinctness, the Theistic system as resting upon the rock of truth itself. This plan also perfectly remedies the fundamental defects manifest in all the Histories of Philosophy which I have ever met with. I do not put the above in quotations, because I can give, not the words, but only the thoughts, the thoughts of encouragement, expressed by the venerable Bishop.

Thus encouraged and admonished, the work was commenced. When I had finished the Introduction, knowing very well that it was a complete treatise in itself—that if it was a marked success, such would be that of the whole work ; and that if it was a failure, the whole Treatise would be an abortion—I submitted the manuscript containing said Introduction to quite a sufficient number of the best thinkers and judges I could select, earnestly requesting them to carefully read, and then give in writing their candid judgment of the real merits of the work. From every one of these I received the same expressions of approbation and encouragement which I had previously received from a verbal presentation of the plan of the work.

Among these written testimonials, and as fair examples of all the others, I present but the three following. The first, and that which, on account of its completeness, as well as for the known reputation of the author, deserves very special attention, is from the Right Reverend the Dean of Canterbury, D.D. The second is from the late Bishop E. O. Haven and two of his leading associate professors in the North-Western University, of which the Bishop was then Chancellor. The third and last is from the late Rev. Leonard Bacon, D.D., a name not only known in Europe, but held in universal honour in the United States.

DEANERY, CANTERBURY, 23rd *February*, 1880.

MY DEAR SIR,—

I have read with great interest the Introduction, which you sent me, to your 'Critical History of Philosophy.' I like it exceedingly. Usually a history of Philosophy gives at best a fair statement of what others have held, and after reading of system after system, the mind is left in a state of utter confusion, not knowing what to believe, and wondering how, upon every conceivable subject, thinkers have held the very reverse of one another. You propose to take your readers through all these philosophies with the lamp of real science in your hand. As you show, only four systems of Philosophy are really possible, Materialism, Idealism, Scepticism, and Realism. Of these you demonstrate, that while the three former are based upon assumptions 'begged' by their upholders, the latter rests upon data and facts intuitive and connatural. The charm of the former consists often in the logical exactness with which the system is deduced from the assumed principles, and while following admiringly the chain of deductions growing in orderly sequence out of one another, we forget that the assumption rests solely upon an act of the will with no external validity. Your criteria are all facts or deductions which follow necessarily from these facts.

Your work, I venture humbly to think, will have a twofold value. First, it will show how, under an endless apparent variety, there lie a limited number of principles at the root, appearing again and again, in changing forms, but really the same. And secondly, it will examine each system of thought by criteria of which you have proved the soundness of truth. And so a student, who has read your 'History of Philosophy' with fair attention, will, when he lays it down, find that all these varying systems have arranged themselves in his mind under their proper heads, and that he has seen hence their weakness and their strength. Instead of burdening his memory, it will guide his judgment.

Believe me, my dear sir,
Very truly yours,
N. PAYNE SMITH.

Rev. Asa Mahan, D.D.

NORTH-WESTERN UNIVERSITY, EVANSTON, ILLINOIS,
25th April, 1872.

We have listened to some passages from a manuscript, 'Critical History of Philosophy,' by Rev. Dr. Asa Mahan, together with a general description of his plan and method in the work. The plan strikes us as admirable, and the purpose to present the history of Philosophy critically, rather than chronologically, is good. Judging from what we have heard, the object of the book is, not to mention and describe critically all prominent writings on Philosophy, but positively to establish its fundamental principles, and to show the relations of all leading systems to these principles. A good work, well wrought out on this plan, must be of very great value. We think the book will meet an acknowledged want.

E. O. HAVEN.
M. RAYMOND.
J. S. JEWELL.

NEWHAVEN, 20*th June*, 1872.

DEAR SIR,

I regret that I have not had time for a thorough study of your manuscript, placed in my hands by Dr. White. But I have examined a portion of it with careful attention; and though such inquiries have been to me of late less fascinating than they once were, my own studies having led me in other directions, I have found my interest in your great theme renewed and freshened by the study of that portion.

I trust you will complete the work and publish it. For my own part, I profess no philosophy but common-sense; and I like your philosophy because it seems to be about the same thing—common-sense analyzing and defining itself. In these days, when popular literature is so widely infected with the scepticism of scientific Materialism, on the one hand, and fantastic Idealism, on the other, you have undertaken the task of teaching thinkers how to think, and of affirming and maintaining, in the face of all Pyrrhonism, the validity of those primary intuitions which are essential to all thought. 'Fit audience' may you find, and not 'few.' You do not address yourself directly to the million, but if you can rectify the thinking of those who guide the million—authors, teachers, preachers—you will do a great work for your own and the coming generations. Fully aware that my judgment is not worth much, I will nevertheless venture to express the opinion that the work you have now in hand is better than anything you have yet done, and that your History of Philosophy will be a substantial contribution to the progress of Philosophy.

Yours truly,
LEONARD BACON.

Rev. A. Mahan, D.D.

Thus encouraged, I entered with a will upon the details of the Treatise itself. At every step, as I progressed, I became more and more deeply impressed with the importance of the work in which I was engaged; and when I had carefully reviewed the work after my task was completed, I became fully assured that what I had written did, what had never been done before, meet fully a central want of the present age. What is now imperiously needed is a clear and distinct understanding of the real nature and character of the imposing systems of Idealism, Materialism, and Scepticism, which are being commended to public regard. While these systems are not thus understood, the great names by which they are represented impart to them an overshadowing influence with the public. When distinctly unmasked, and revealed to the world as they are in themselves, one impression will be permanently left upon the public mind—namely, that not a few of the greatest thinkers the world has known have expended their great powers in developing and systematizing the greatest conceivable errors and absurdities, and that the utterance of an ancient wise man is true, that the mass of 'philosophers are a race mad with logic, and feeding the mind on chimeras.' Whether such utterances are true or not, the intelligent reader of the following Treatise will not fail to *know* Idealism in all its forms, Materialism, and Scepticism, as they are, and that in distinct contrast with the only remaining system, Realism, which embodies and scientifically verifies the doctrine of Theism, the only true hypothesis of Ultimate Causation.

To the following statement we would invite special attention. In reading the following Treatise, the reader will not fail to notice that, in our expositions of the same systems as developed in different ages, thoughts before expressed are often repeated. The reason for such repetition was this: the Author was desirous that the reader, instead of being necessitated to refer back to what had before been written, should in every case have truth and error directly and distinctly before his mind, and thus be able to form a more distinct and ready judgment of their respective claims. With the above statements and explanations, the Treatise is commended to the impartial judgment of the public.

CONTENTS.

GENERAL INTRODUCTION.

SECTION I.
	PAGE
THE DESIGN AND PLAN OF THE WORK	1
What we purpose to Accomplish, and by what Method	2

SECTION II.

PHILOSOPHY—ITS NATURE AND TRUE AND PROPER SPHERE IN THE EMPIRE OF WORLD THOUGHT	3
What does Philosophy imply?	5
Relations of these two Forms of Knowledge to each other	5
Criteria of True and False Systems of Science	6
Principles and Facts of True Science, as distinguished from Assumptions, Opinions, Conjectures, etc.	7
Principles as distinguished from mere Assumptions	7
Opinions, Beliefs, Conjectures, etc., as distinguished from Facts of Real Knowledge	9
Intuitions and Forms of Belief which take rise from Intuitions	9
Condition of Real Knowledge	10
The Question, What can we Know?—how Answered	10
Conditions, Extent, and Limits of Valid Knowledge as Affirmed in all Systems of Materialism and Idealism	11
Remarks on these Hypotheses	11

SECTION III.

FOUR, AND BUT FOUR REALITIES, VIZ., SPIRIT, MATTER, TIME, AND SPACE, ARE REPRESENTED, OR ARE REPRESENTABLE, IN HUMAN THOUGHT	13
Nature, Character, and Mutual Relations of these Four Realities	14
All these Realities are distinctly represented in Human Thought	15
No other Reality is or can be represented in Human Thought	15
These Realities wholly unlike each other	15
These Realities differ equally relatively to our Manner of Perceiving and Apprehending them	16
These Realities sustain to each other fixed and definable Relations	17
These Apprehensions not Self-contradictory	18
Necessary Deductions from the Principles and Facts just evinced as True	21

xii   CONTENTS.

	PAGE
These Four Realities are apprehended by Universal Mind as actually Known Realities, nor can our Apprehensions of any one of them be changed, modified, or displaced from Human Thought	22
Our Apprehensions of these Realities have all the Fundamental Characteristics of Forms of Valid Knowledge, Characteristics which True Science must and will Acknowledge	26
I. The Validity of these Apprehensions cannot be Disproved, or rendered Doubtful	26
1. Such Forms of Knowledge not Naturally Impossible	27
2. Facts in Disproof cannot be found outside of the Sphere of these Apprehensions	27
3. Facts in Disproof cannot be found in the Relations of these Apprehensions to one another	28
4. Such Facts cannot be found in what is Intrinsic in any of these Apprehensions	28
II. Our Apprehensions of Space, Time, Matter, and Spirit are, in all their essential elements and characteristics, distinct, separate, and dissimilar from all Assumptions, Beliefs, and Opinions, which may or may not be true	31
III. These Apprehensions have all Possible Positive Characteristics of Real Absolute Knowledge	32
Necessary Ideas	32
Contingent Ideas—Matter and Spirit	33

SECTION IV.

ORIGIN, GENESIS, AND CHARACTER OF ALL ACTUAL AND CONCEIVABLE SYSTEMS OF PHILOSOPHY 37

The Diverse Systems Defined	37
Materialism	38
Necessary Problems which this Hypothesis involves	39
Idealism—Doctrine Explained	42
The Theory of External Perception	42
Problems common to Idealism in all its Forms	43
Ideal Dualism	45
Problems specially pertaining to Ideal Dualism	45
Idealism Proper	46
Subjective Idealism	46
Problems of Subjective Idealism	47
Pantheism Proper	48
Special Assumptions of Pantheism and Pure Idealism	48
Necessary Problems of Pantheism	51
Pure Idealism	52
General and Particular Problems of Pure Idealism	52
Relations to each other of the Hypotheses of Materialism and Idealism	54
Scepticism—The Doctrine Defined	57
Doctrine common to this and other Systems	58
The Grand Problem of this System	58
The Condition on which this Problem can be Solved	59
The Sceptical Assumption Refuted	59
Realism—The System Defined	60
The General Problem of this System	61
Particular Special Problems of the System	61
Realism Verified	62
Postulates common to all Systems	63
Criteria of Forms of Valid Knowledge as already Stated	63
Our Knowledge of Space and Time Verified	64
Our Apprehensions of Matter and Spirit Verified	65

SECTION V.

MISCELLANEOUS TOPICS AND SUGGESTIONS.

	PAGE
Materialism, Idealism, and Scepticism all constructed throughout after one and the same Method—Begging the Question	65
The proper place and influence of the different Mental Faculties in the Constitution of Systems of Knowledge	69
Secret of the Power of Scepticism	73
The Secret of the Power of Systematized Thought, and the only Proper Method of Examining such Systems	75
The True Philosopher and Pedant distinguished	77
When should the Deductions and Opinions of Philosophers have Weight with us?	78
Prudential Considerations	79
Plan of our Future Inquiries	80

PART I.

THE ORIENTAL PHILOSOPHY.

CHAPTER I.

THE HINDU PHILOSOPHY.

Sources of this Philosophy	81

SECTION I.

EXPOSITION OF THE GENERAL DOCTRINE OF THE VEDAS	82
General Reflections on the Hindu Doctrine	83
Philosophers and Religionists of India	86

SECTION II.

THE MIMANSA AND VEDANTA SYSTEMS	87
The Vedanta System	88
Specific Expositions of the Vedanta System	90
Ancient and Modern Pantheism	93
The Fixed Method of Pantheism as seen in the Light of the Immutable Principles of True Science	97
Conditions on which the Race can enjoy the Benefits of 'the Revelation of Absolute Science'	99

SECTION III.

THE SEMI-ORTHODOX SYSTEMS	100
The Sankhya of Kapila	100
The Sankhya and Vedanta Systems compared	102
Hindu and Modern Dualism	103

SECTION IV.

The Yoga Shastra of Patandjali — 106

SECTION V.

The Vaieschika System of Kanada — 107

SECTION VI.

The Hindu Logic — 108

SECTION VII.

The Heterodox Systems.

The Djainas and Buddhists — 111
   I. The System of the Djainas — 111
   II. The Buddhists — 112
Buddhist Systems of Philosophy — 115
Pure Idealism — 115
Subjective Idealism — 116
The Buddhist Material Systems — 116
Relations of the Buddhist and Hindu Systems to each other — 117

SECTION VIII.

General Remarks upon the Indian Philosophy — 117

SECTION IX.

The Chinese Philosophy — 119

SECTION X.

The Persian System — 120

Zoroaster as a Teacher of Morals and Philosophy — 121
The Cosmology of the 'Boundehesch' — 121

SECTION XI.

The Egyptian System — 123

SECTION XII.

General Remarks upon the Oriental Systems — 125

1. The Connection of these Systems with Religion — 125
   Relation of Oriental Religions to the Primitive Religion of the Race — 127
   Monotheism the Original Faith of the Race — 127
2. Relations of these Systems to the Doctrine of the Soul as Distinct from all Material Existences, and as Immortal — 130
3. The Relations of these Systems to the Doctrine of Right and Wrong, of Moral Obligation, Moral Desert, and Retribution — 131

CONTENTS.

	PAGE
4. Relations of these Systems to the Doctrine of Human Sinfulness	131
5. The Idea of Salvation from Sin the common Element of all these Religious Systems	132
6. The Idea of Human Existence and Salvation, as it Appears in the Light of all these Systems	133
7. What has the Race Reason to Expect from the Anti-Theistic Philosophies which are being Commended to Human Regard?	134

PART II.

THE GRECIAN PHILOSOPHY.

INTRODUCTION.

SECTION I.

THE RELATIONS OF THE GREEKS TO THE ORIENTAL NATIONS	137
Correspondences and Differences between the Grecian and the Oriental Systems	138

SECTION II.

THE RELIGION OF THE GREEKS	139
Grecian Polytheism	139
The Monotheism of Greece	140

SECTION III.

NATURE, CHARACTER, AND MUTUAL RELATIONS OF KNOWLEDGE À PRIORI AND À POSTERIORI. THESE FORMS OF KNOWLEDGE DISTINGUISHED AND DEFINED	144
Relations between Knowledge *à priori* and *à posteriori*	146
Necessary Deductions from the Preceding Analysis	148
All Questions Pertaining to Ontology belong exclusively to the *à posteriori*, or Mixed Sciences	153
By no possibility can the Knowledge affirmed be obtained of any such Substances or Causes	153

SECTION IV.

MYSTERY AND ABSURDITY DEFINED AND DISTINGUISHED	159
Existence involves a Mystery	161
Bearing of these Conclusions upon our former Deductions	162
The Existence of a Power of Knowledge involves a Mystery equally profound	163

SECTION V.

IN WHAT SENSE AND FORM IS HUMAN KNOWLEDGE RELATIVE AND PHENO-
MENAL? — 164

In Phenomena, Objects are Manifested as they are, and not as they are not — 165
The Dogma that all our World-Knowledge is mere Illusory Appearance — 166
The Real Relativity of Knowledge — 167

SECTION VI.

PHYSIOLOGY AND METAPHYSICS — 169

SECTION VII.

FORMS OF PROGRESSION COMMON TO ANTI-THEISTIC SYSTEMS OF PHILOSOPHY — 171

SECTION VIII.

THE SCHOOLS OF PHILOSOPHY IN GREECE — 173

CHAPTER I.

THE PRE-SOCRATIC EVOLUTION IN PHILOSOPHY. 175

SECTION I.

THE IONIC SCHOOL—THALES OF MILETUS — 175

Exposition of the Doctrines of Thales — 175
The Cosmological Doctrine and Teachings of Thales — 176
The Theistic Doctrine and Teachings of Thales — 176
Anaximander and Anaximenes — 179
Anaxagoras — 180
Mr. Lewes corrected — 183
Observations upon the Teachings and Doctrines of the Ionic School — 184

SECTION II.

THE ITALIC SCHOOL — 185

Pythagoras — 185

SECTION III.

THE ELEATIC SCHOOL — 188

The Eleatic Metaphysical School — 188
Mr. Lewes' Vindication of Zeno's Argument — 193
The Method of this School — 194
The Physical School of Elea — 195
Exposition of the System of these Philosophers — 195
General Reflections upon this System — 197

SECTION IV.

	PAGE
THE INTERMEDIATE SCHOOL	201
Heraclitus and Empedocles	201

SECTION V.

THE SOPHISTS	203
Common Doctrine of the Sophists	204
The Method of the Sophists	205
The Sources of the wide-spread Influence of the Sophists	205
General Reflections suggested by the Preceding Analysis of the Pre-Socratic Systems of Philosophy	206

CHAPTER II.

THE SOCRATIC EVOLUTION IN PHILOSOPHY.   212

INTRODUCTION.

PSYCHOLOGY AND PHILOSOPHY	212
The Object of Philosophy	212
The Immutable Characteristics of all Explicable Facts and Relations	213
The Great Problem of Philosophy	214
The Relations of Psychology to Philosophy	215
Intellectual Faculties, Primary and Secondary	215
Relations of these Faculties to Science	217
Comparative Validity and Authority of these Faculties	218

SECTION I.

SOCRATES	219
Common-Sense	222
The Era of the Public Teaching of Socrates	224
The Method of Socrates	225
Special Doctrines Taught by Socrates	229
The Dæmon of Socrates	231

SECTION II.

PLATO	232
Plato as Contrasted with Socrates, Aristotle, and Anaxagoras	232
Plato's Method	234
General Characteristics of Plato as a Thinker	235
Doctrines which, as all Authorities admit, Plato did hold and teach	236
The Psychology of Plato	239
Reason and Judgment	241
Sensation, or Sense-Perception	242
General Remarks upon this Psychology	243

CONTENTS.

	PAGE
Plato's Doctrine of Ideas	249
In what Language and Form Plato has stated his own Doctrine	249
Plato's Real Doctrine of Ideas	251
Consequences which follow from each Exposition which has been given of Plato's Doctrine of Ideas	253
Consequences resulting from the Exposition which affirms Plato's Ideas to be 'the Eternal Thoughts of the Divine Intellect'	253
Consequences resulting from the Doctrine that Plato's Ideas are Real Separate Existences	255
General Remarks upon Plato as a World-Thinker	255
Plato, when in the Sphere of Socratic Thought, and when Philosophizing	256
Plato, as furnishing another example of the validity of *à priori* insight and of the *à priori* method of Philosophizing	257
The Faculty, or Faculties, actually employed by Plato and other Philosophers who adopt the *à priori* method when Philosophising	259
Plato as a Logician	260
The Doctrine of Innate Ideas	261
The Idea of Reason as a Faculty possessed only by Philosophers	263
Three great Central Truths, for the first scientific Enunciation of which the World is indebted to Plato	264

SECTION III.

ARISTOTLE	265
Aristotle's Classification of the Sciences	266
Questions at Issue between Aristotle and Plato	266
The Doctrine of Individual Existence as Opposed to that of Ideas	267
The Validity of Sensation, or Sense-Perception	268
The Summum Bonum	269
Doctrine of Reminiscence	271
The Universe as an External Existence, and as Organized in Time	271
Aristotle's Logic	271
Fundamental Error of Mill in his Logic	275
Aristotle's Formula pertaining to the Origin, Source, and Consequent Elements, of all our Knowledge	277
Aristotle's Ethics	279
'The First Philosophy,' or Metaphysics of Aristotle	280
Aristotle's Proof of the Divine Existence	281
Evidence of the Being, Perfections, and Providence of a Personal God, as deducible from the Platonic, Aristotelian, and the only other conceivable standpoint	282
Argument in the most general Form	283
The Argument as Deducible from the Platonic Standpoint	285
Argument from the Aristotelian Standpoint	285
The Argument as Deducible from the only remaining Standpoint, no other Hypothesis being Conceivable	286

SECTION IV.

THE EPICUREANS	288
Perceived and Implied Forms of Knowledge	289
Test of Valid Knowledge	290
The General Psychology of Epicurus	291
Epicurean Doctrine of Creation	292

SECTION V.

	PAGE
THE STOICS	295
Criteria of Truth according to the Stoics	295
The Physics of the Stoics	296
Some of the Special Doctrines of the Stoics	297
The Ethics of the Stoics	298

CHAPTER III.

THE DECLINE OF THE GRECIAN PHILOSOPHY.

INTRODUCTION.

SECTION I.

CAUSES OF THIS DECLINE	300
Incidental Causes of the Decline of the Grecian Philosophy	302

SECTION II.

THE SCEPTICAL PHILOSOPHY	304
The Issue as Stated by Mr. Lewes	305
What Criterion is there of the Truth of our Knowledge?	305
Erroneous Statements and Expositions of Mr. Lewes	305
Criteria of Valid Knowledge	308
Necessary Deductions from a Rigid Application of these Criteria	310
The Sceptical Doctrine Self-contradictory	313
The Sceptical Distinction between Phenomena and Noumena	313
Observations upon the Sceptical Doctrine on these Subjects	314
Positive Sides of the Sceptical Philosophy	317
Necessary Deductions from Fundamental Principles of this System	317

DECLINE OF THE GRECIAN PHILOSOPHY.

SECTION I.

THE PYRRHONISTS	321
The Peculiar Form of the Pyrrhonic Scepticism	324
The Consummation sought by the Pyrrhonists through their Philosophy	325

SECTION II.

THE OLD, MIDDLE, AND NEW ACADEMY	326
The Probable Substituted for the Absolute	327

SECTION III.

CONTINUATION OF THE ARISTOTELIAN SCHOOLS - 330

SECTION IV.

NEO-PLATONISM - 331

General Reflections on the Grecian Evolution in Philosophy - 335
Verification of our Statement in Regard to the Number and Character of all Possible and Actual Systems of Philosophy - 335
The Systems present or wanting in the Grecian, and common or peculiar to Oriental and Modern Schools - 336
In what Sense and Form was Grecian Philosophy Introductory to Christianity? 339

PART III.

BOOK I.

THE CHRISTIAN EVOLUTION IN PHILOSOPHY.

SECTION I.

DOCTRINE, OR HYPOTHESIS, OF ULTIMATE CAUSATION - 341

The Doctrine of Providence - 343
Relations of the above Doctrines to Science - 343

SECTION II.

ONTOLOGY OF THE BIBLE - 346

Relations of Science to the Doctrines of Scriptural Ontology - 347

SECTION III.

THE MORALITY OF THE SCRIPTURES - 350

SECTION IV.

SPECIAL AND PECULIAR DOCTRINES OF CHRISTIANITY - 352

The Tri-Unity of the Godhead - 352
Revealed Relations of these Tri-Personalities to one Another - 353
Considerations which Commend this Doctrine to our Reason and Judgment - 355
The Doctrine of Incarnation and Atonement - 356
Relations of the Doctrine of Incarnation to Reason and Science - 357

ATONEMENT.

Relation of this Doctrine to Reason and Science - 358
Relations of God to Believers as a Hearer of Prayer - 359
Relations of this Doctrine to the Teachings of Science - 359

BOOK II.

PHILOSOPHY OF THE EARLY CHRISTIAN ERA.

SECTION I.

	PAGE
RELATIONS BETWEEN THEISM PROPER AND CHRISTIAN THEISM	364
Christian Theism renders infinitely more distinct and impressive the Real Verities apprehended through Natural Theism	364
Christian Theism extends our Vision of Truth beyond the possible reach of Natural Theism	365
Christian Theism confirms and reaffirms the Validity of the Doctrine of God as taught by Natural Theology	366

SECTION II.

THE RELATIONS OF CHRISTIAN THEISM TO THE SCIENCE OF COSMOLOGY	368
The Question of the Reality of these Facts, to be determined, first of all, wholly irrespective of their bearing upon the Claims of the Christian Religion	369

SECTION III.

RELATIONS OF SUPERNATURAL EVENTS, AND THE ACTIONS OF A SUPERNATURAL POWER IN NATURE, TO THE SO-CALLED LAWS OF NATURE	369

SECTION IV.

SUPERNATURAL OR MIRACULOUS EVENTS DEFINED—THEIR POSSIBILITY AND PROBABILITY—THEIR BEARING UPON THE CLAIMS OF CHRISTIAN RELIGION, ETC.	370
Such Events Defined	370
Conditions of the Possibility or Probability of the Occurrence of Supernatural Events	371
The Knowledge which all who affirm the Impossibility, Improbability, or Non-actuality of Supernatural Events do, in reality, assume the possession of	371
Conditions on which we are Absolutely Bound to admit the Actual Occurrence of Supernatural Events	372
Conditions on which we may Properly withhold Assent to the Actuality of Supernatural Events affirmed to have occurred	373
Relations of these Events to the Christian Religion	374
Relations of these Events to the Christian Scriptures	375

SECTION V.

REVELATION AND INSPIRATION	377
Terms Defined	377

SECTION VI.

	PAGE
NEEDFUL EXPLANATIONS	381
Special Explanations	382

SECTION VII.

OBJECTIONS ANSWERED	385

SECTION VIII.

THE PHILOSOPHY OF THE EARLY CHRISTIAN CHURCH	392
An Example of the Philosophic Teachings of the Leading Doctors of the Primitive Church	394

SECTION IX.

ANTI-CHRISTIAN SPECULATIONS	397
Oriental Doctrines	397
The Græco-Oriental Philosophy	399

SECTION X.

CHRISTIAN DOCTRINE AS CORRUPTED BY 'SCIENCE FALSELY SO-CALLED'	400

CHAPTER III.

THE MEDIÆVAL EVOLUTION IN PHILOSOPHY.

The Rise of Scholasticism	401
Scholasticism in its Primal Form	402
This Doctrine Verified	403
Scholasticism in its Final Form	405
The Nominalism and Realism of the Middle Ages	406
The Mysticism of the Middle Ages	409
The Teachings of Thomas Aquinas	416
Decline and Fall of Scholasticism	418
The Dogma that Doubt is a Pre-requisite Condition of Knowledge	419
The Real Place of 'Prudential Doubt' in Science	423
Heterodox Teachings and Systems of the Middle Ages	424
Scientific Problems discussed in the Middle Ages	427
Puerility of the Questions agitated by the Schoolmen compared with those common in other Eras	428
The Main Problems agitated by the Schoolmen not Puerile	429

A
CRITICAL HISTORY OF PHILOSOPHY.

GENERAL INTRODUCTION.

SECTION I.

THE DESIGN AND PLAN OF THE WORK.

I PROPOSE, from a standpoint entirely new, in conformity with a plan, and for an end hitherto unattempted, to write a History of Philosophy. In the productions of this character which occupy places in the libraries of world-thinkers, we have, for the most part, a mere chronology of men and their systems, systems more or less distinctly exhibited. We are not, first of all, as we should be, put in full possession of the nature and character of Philosophy itself, of its appropriate and exclusive sphere in the empire of world-thought, and of the great problems of being and its laws, and of causes proximate and ultimate, which it is its province to solve, and which it must solve before its mission is ended. Nor are we informed of the *principles* and *facts* which must be laid down and adduced as the basis of all our deductions, and that as the immutable condition of a true solution of the problems under consideration. Last of all, no consciously valid *tests* or *criteria* are given by which we may distinguish the true from the false methods of philosophizing, valid from invalid principles in science, or real from assumed facts which may be adduced, as the basis of scientific deduction.

On the other hand, we are informed, when any particular system is presented, that such an individual, in such an age, thought out that system. We are not rendered conscious of the real relations of the system to the true and proper system of Philosophy, what was the actual world-problem which the author attempted to solve, what was his actual method of philosophizing, what were the principles he laid down, and what were the facts which he adduced as the basis of his deductions, and wherein and why he succeeded or failed in accomplishing the end proposed.

Hence it is that, in the study of such productions, the reader finds, at length, a confused panorama of multitudinous contradictory systems passing before his mind, systems none of which he very clearly apprehends, until at last he comes to feel that 'chaos has come again.' He accordingly lays down the volume in which these systems are presented, with the consciousness that he has been rather confused than instructed by what he has read. In short, histories of philosophy have not, for the most part, to say the least, been what such productions should be, to wit, not mere chronologies of systems and men who have appeared and disappeared in the sphere of world-thought, but in the true and proper sense of the words, *critiques* of systems and men of the former ages especially, critiques which shall not only disclose to the thoughtful inquirer the mazes of 'science falsely so-called,' the deceptions of sophistry, the false assumptions and deductions of unbelief, and the hiding-places of error in all its assumed scientific forms, but shall open upon his vision the realm of truth itself, and 'the highway' of true science to that realm.

WHAT WE PURPOSE TO ACCOMPLISH, AND BY WHAT METHOD.

What we purpose to accomplish in the following treatise, together with the method by which we shall attempt to realize that purpose, has been indicated, though not fully developed, in what we have already stated. It is by no means certain that he who is able to point out the errors of others will succeed in remedying the evils of which he complains. Nor does the ability to show where and why others have deviated from the right path imply the possession of that higher wisdom by which the track of truth is revealed to universal mind. Our purpose is to attempt, at least, the accomplishment of both these results. We shall attempt, not only to expose the errors of 'science, falsely so-called,' but at the same time to render plain the track on which real science conducts to the domain of truth itself. Truth, when fully apprehended, not only demonstrates to the mind its own validity as truth, but at the same time makes equally manifest error as it is, error as constituted wholly of 'vain imaginings,' wild assumptions, and false deductions. Naked error is powerless to deceive, and borrows all its effectiveness from the fragments of truth with which it is associated. Error always starts upon the track of truth, and at particular points takes its departure from that path. Philosophy will never have completed its heaven-appointed mission until it shall have fully disclosed, not only the line on which truth leads, but shall have shown, with equal distinctness, *where* and *why* error, in all its forms, takes its departure from that line.

We shall, therefore, in this our introduction, stop for a while to disclose and determine the real nature and exclusive sphere of Philosophy itself, the great problems which it is its exclusive province to solve, the principles and facts which lie at the basis of valid deductions in this science, the *criteria* by which we may distinguish valid from invalid principles, and real from assumed or improperly adduced facts—the true and only true *method* of conducting our inquiries in this science—and this as distinguished from those which obtain in systems of error, the possible hypotheses of *ontology* and ultimate causation, and the tests by which we may distinguish among these the true from the false. We shall then be fully prepared, not only for a specification, but critical examination of the various systems which, in the present and past eras of the world's history, have been developed and commended to the regard of mankind.

SECTION II.

PHILOSOPHY—ITS NATURE AND TRUE AND PROPER SPHERE IN THE EMPIRE OF WORLD-THOUGHT.

SCIENCE has been rightfully defined as *knowledge systematized.* According to Webster, it is 'certain knowledge' or 'leading truths relating to any subject arranged in systematic order.' Pure science, such as the mathematics, is based exclusively upon self-evident principles and facts. The mixed sciences, such as physics and metaphysics, are built upon principles absolutely known as having universal and necessary validity, and facts of perception external or internal, facts known with equal certainty to be real. Knowledge pertaining to self-evident principles and facts is denominated knowledge *à priori.* Knowledge pertaining to facts of perception is called knowledge *à posteriori.* This distinction should be kept distinctly in mind, inasmuch as these two forms of knowledge will hereafter be frequently referred to under the above designations. Knowledge of the former kind is denominated *necessary,* and that of the latter *contingent* knowledge. Objects of the former class are apprehended as real, with the absolute impossibility of conceiving them as not existing, or as being in any respects different from, or opposite to, what we apprehended them to be. Objects of the latter class are conceived to be real, with the possibility of *conceiving* of their non-reality, or of their being different from what we apprehended them to be. While I know space, for example, to be a reality in itself, I find it to be an absolute impossibility for me even to conceive of its non-existence, or as being, in any respect, different from what I apprehend it to be. The idea of space, therefore, is denominated a *necessary* idea. I know myself and body, on the other hand, as realities, and that with the same absoluteness that I know space to be a reality. Self and body, however, are conceived of as realities, with the possibility of conceiving that they do not exist, or that they might be, in themselves, other than they are. Our conceptions of self and body, therefore, are denominated *contingent* ideas. As far as absoluteness of validity is concerned, real knowledge in one form is just as valid for the reality and character of its object as in the other. Knowledge, in its necessary and contingent forms, differs merely and exclusively in regard to the nature of its objects and our modes of conceiving of the same, but not at all as far as *validity* is concerned. I know myself, for example, as a real self-conscious personality, with the same absoluteness that I know space as a reality. The difference pertains exclusively to my modes of conceiving of these realities. The same holds equally of real knowledge in all its forms, as far as absoluteness of validity is concerned.

Science, in constructing systems of truth, has to do with nothing but real knowledge; that is, with principles known to possess absolute and necessary validity, and with facts known, with equal certainty, to be real. Should any principle or fact whose validity or certainty is not thus known be taken up as a part of such system, the whole process would thereby be vitiated. In the sphere of human thought we meet, not only with forms of real knowledge, but with those of assumptions, beliefs, opinions, and conjectures. Systems based upon, or constructed out of the forms last noticed, are logical fictions, probabilities, or mere fancies, and not creations of science. To impose upon the public deductions based upon mere assumptions, conjectures, beliefs, or opinions, as truths of science, is sophistry. Real science never attempts to systematize or elucidate the unknowable, or the unknown. Realities discovered and brought within the sphere of actual knowledge, these are the exclusive objects of its authoritative teachings. Realities admitted to be located within the domain of the unknowable, or unknown, are thereby, in fact and form, wholly absent from the sphere of true science. Upon assumptions, nothing but logical fictions can be constructed. From mere beliefs, opinions, or conjectures, nothing but probabilities, possibilities, or guesses can be deduced.

Philosophy differs from science only as being less general and more specific and circumscribed in its sphere of inquiry and deduction. Science systematizes knowledge in *all* its forms. Philosophy, distinguished from science as a part from the whole, attempts 'an explanation of the *reason* of things,' or the *causes* of facts and events—ultimate causes especially. The grand problem of Philosophy pertains to the *ultimate reason*, the finally all-determining cause which reveals the reason why the facts of universal nature are as they are, and not otherwise. The problems of *ontology*, the inquiry what realities do exist, what are their nature and essence, qualities and attributes, what are the laws which govern them, and what is the ultimate reason or cause of the facts under consideration, these are problems with which Philosophy, in its true and proper sphere, concerns itself. In studying the history of Philosophy, we shall find that these are the main problems professedly solved in all the systems which we shall have occasion to investigate. Germany in former years claimed for itself the honour of being the home of Philosophy. Thinkers in other nations were occupied mainly in the sphere of psychology and kindred sciences, while German thought was devoted to the solution of the great problems pertaining to the conditions of valid knowledge, of ontology, of being, its nature and laws, and especially of ultimate causation. This claim was just as far as the true and proper idea of Philosophy itself, its real sphere in the empire of thought, and its great problems are concerned. Germany, as we shall see hereafter, erred fundamentally, as far as *method* is concerned, and, consequently, as utterly failed in the solution of the problems of world-thought.

What does Philosophy imply?

Philosophy is not a *primary*, but an ultimate form of thought. Science, as we have seen, is knowledge reduced to system. Philosophy is science in its ultimate form. Science as Philosophy, and in all other forms, implies the pre-existence of real knowledge. Knowledge must exist before it can be systematized or explained and elucidated. Neither science nor Philosophy can create knowledge. They can, we repeat, but systematize and elucidate the previously known. Real knowledge exists in the Intelligence in two forms, the systematized and elucidated, as in science and Philosophy, and in those primordial forms which precede science.

Relations of these two Forms of Knowledge to each other.

A very important inquiry here presents itself—to wit, what are *the relations* of these two forms of knowledge, the primordial and the systematized and elucidated, to each other? The former, we remark in general, must contain, in an unreflective and unsystematized form, *all* that is found in the reflective and systematized form. All systems of science and Philosophy are constituted wholly of principles and facts, the former organizing and elucidating the latter. These principles and facts must have been previously known, that is, in their primordial forms, or they could not have been employed in the construction of systems of knowledge. When we recur to the action of the Intelligence, and contemplate its states prior to all proper scientific movements, we shall discover two distinct forms of activity, the *primal proper*, or the purely intuitional, and what is denominated the *practical*, a state intermediate between intuition and science. By intuition all the elements which constitute systems of knowledge are given. In this primal action of the Intelligence, we have real knowledge with no intermixture of error. The reason is obvious. We have here the pure and exclusive action of the Intelligence uninfluenced by that of any of the other faculties. If the Intelligence should err here, it would be because it is its nature, or the necessary law of its activity, to err, and knowledge proper in any form would be impossible.

In the intermediate procedure of the Intelligence, the procedure denominated practical, we have, in their concrete and particular forms, all the *principles* and *facts* which constitute systems of knowledge. The child and the peasant, for example, when they perceive that two given objects are each equal to one and the same third object, know, with the same absoluteness that the philosopher does, that the two objects first designated are equal to one another. While all in common draw the same conclusions in view of the same facts, and all are guided in doing so by the same principles—to wit, things equal to the same things are equal to one another, the true philosopher only understands clearly the reason why he makes such deductions in view of the facts referred to. The reason is that he only knows this principle in its abstract and universal form, and in its light *reflectively* contemplates these facts. Knowledge, in its original, concrete, and particular forms, cannot be systematized. It is only when principles are evolved and presented in their necessary and universal forms, and facts are set in the clear light of such principles, that we have science or knowledge systematized, that is, truth in its scientific forms.

While in pure intuition we meet with nothing but the elements of real knowledge, in the practical forms of thought we find truth intermingled with error. The reason is that here, what does not occur in the primal intuitional state, we have the action of the Intelligence in connection with that of other faculties. As a consequence, we have forms of real knowledge intermingled with assumptions, opinions, beliefs, conjectures, and guesses, judgments, some of which are and some of which are not true, while others may or may not be true.

Criteria of Truth and False Systems of Science.

When systems are constructed exclusively from principles and facts which are the objects of intuitional knowledge, and from deductions necessarily implied by such principles and facts, we then, and only then, have true science. When, on the other hand, mere assumptions, opinions, beliefs, conjectures, or guesses, with deductions from the same, pass over and lie at the foundation, or enter as constituent elements into the structure of systems of affirmed knowledge, we then have 'science, falsely so-called.' We have here undeniably universal and infallible tests or criteria, by which, of affirmed systems of knowledge or science, we are to distinguish the valid from the invalid, the true from the false. Systems of the former classes are to be esteemed as rightfully having place in the sphere of true science. Those of the latter class are to be regarded as having place nowhere but within the circle of logical fiction. Deductions of the former class are to be regarded as truths of science; those of the latter, as the lawless sophisms or wild guesses of false science.

PRINCIPLES AND FACTS OF TRUE SCIENCE, AS DISTINGUISHED FROM ASSUMPTIONS, OPINIONS, CONJECTURES, ETC.

A question of fundamental importance here arises—to wit, how shall we distinguish principles and facts of real science from mere assumptions, opinions, beliefs, conjectures, or guesses, which may be employed as principles or facts in the construction of systems of science? A ready answer can now be given to this inquiry, an answer the universal and absolute validity of which must be admitted as soon as the subject is understood. We begin with

Principles as distinguished from mere Assumptions.

Affirmed systems of science may, undeniably, be based either upon valid principles, or upon mere assumptions, that is, unauthorized judgments employed as principles in the construction of such systems. How shall we distinguish the former from the latter? Every judgment of the former class has, undeniably, and as all thinkers admit, these immutable and inseparable characteristics, *absolute universality* and *necessity.* In other words, it is absolutely impossible for the mind to conceive that they are not, and must not be, valid in themselves, and do not and must not hold true in respect to all objects and events to which they are applicable. Take as example such judgments as these: Things equal to the same things are equal to one another; A whole is greater than any of its Parts; Body implies space; Succession implies time; Events imply a cause; Phenomena imply substance; In every appearance some reality appears; The conditioned implies the unconditioned; and, It is impossible for the same thing at the same moment to exist and not exist. If we consider any one of these judgments, or all of them together, we shall perceive absolutely that they, one and all, have self-evident validity, and that universally; that they not only are true, but that they cannot be false, and cannot but hold true relatively to all objects and events to which they are applicable. Systems of knowledge resting upon such principles must have a strictly scientific basis. There are four, and only four, conditions on which any proposition or judgment can have self-evident validity. They are the following: 1. When the subject and predicate are identical, as in the judgment, A is A; these are mere *tautological* judgments, and, of course, are of no use in science. 2. When the predicate represents an essential element of our conception of the subject, as in the judgment, All bodies have extension; these are *explicative* judgments, and, as such, have important uses in science. 3. When the subject *implies* the predicate, as in the judgment, Body implies space; as in all such cases it is impossible to conceive of the reality of the object represented by the subject without affirming the same of that represented by the predicate, all such judgments do and must have universal and necessary validity. These are called *implied* or *implicative* judgments, and may be and are employed as principles in all the sciences. 4. When the subject sustains to the predicate the relation of absolute and intuitive incompatibility, and the judgment affirms that relation, as in the judgments, It is impossible for the same thing at the same time to exist and not to exist; and, A strait line cannot enclose a space. All the axioms and principles in all the sciences belong to one or the other of the two classes last named, the positive to the former, and the negative to the latter. No judgment can have universal and necessary validity, but upon one of the four conditions above specified, for the reason that it is utterly impossible for the mind even to conceive of any other condition on which any judgment can possess self-evident, universal, and necessary validity. We thus have an absolutely valid test by which we can infallibly determine the character and claims of any proposition or judgment which may be employed as a first principle in science. Any judgment not having any one of these characteristics is to be rejected, together with the system based upon it, as utterly void of validity.

What, as distinguished from valid principles in science, are assumptions? They are, we answer, judgments having no self-evident validity in themselves, which have not, if true, been verified as true, or which may be false in fact; judgments which are, nevertheless, employed as principles in the construction of systems of science. All systems resting upon assumptions instead of valid principles, whatever their characteristics in other respects, and whatever names they may represent, are nothing but logical fictions. When any system has been ascertained and shown to rest on such a basis, no further examination of its claim is required. It is to be esteemed and treated as an unsubstantial creation of false science.

Opinions, Beliefs, Conjectures, etc., as distinguished from Facts of real Knowledge.

But how shall we distinguish real knowledge pertaining to realities and facts from mere opinions, beliefs, and conjectures pertaining to the same objects? Phenomena of the class last named, we answer, may be and often are changed, varied, or utterly and for ever displaced from human regard. We may hold one opinion or form of belief to-day, and its opposite to-morrow. Forms of belief which for ages, it may be, have had absolute authority in human regard, may, by increase of knowledge, be utterly displaced from human thought and regard. Real knowledge, on the other hand, has the character of absolute *immutability*. So far as we really and truly *know* an object, our convictions pertaining to it can never by any possibility be either changed or modified.

Mutability, then, is the fixed characteristic which reveals and distinguishes all mental apprehensions and judgments as mere opinions, beliefs, conjectures or guesses. Absolute *immutability*, on the other hand, as absolutely reveals, characterizes, and distinguishes from all other phenomena real knowledge in all its forms. When we have apprehensions and convictions relatively to any objects or facts, apprehensions and convictions which neither reasoning, nor sophistry, nor any increase of knowledge or forms of experience can displace, change, or modify, here we find ourselves in the presence of real knowledge, or knowledge in no form has place in human thought. Who will question the validity of the above distinctions and criteria? All systems of error, then, have their basis in assumptions, or are constituted in their superstructure of mere beliefs, opinions, conjectures, or guesses at truth. All systems of real science have for their basis universal and necessary principles, and in their superstructure are constituted exclusively of the forms and elements of real knowledge.

Intuitions and Forms of Belief which take rise from Intuitions.

We can now understand how it is that real intuitions are often confounded with forms of belief which are sometimes connected with and take rise from the former, and how it is that the validity of the former is called in question from the fact that the latter is found to be false. From the appearance of the earth as visible to the eye, the race once held that our globe is a vast plane, dotted with mountains, hills, valleys, lakes and oceans. The visible is the object of intuition. The judgment that the earth is a plane, and not a globe, is an unauthorized inference deduced from the intuition, an opinion which a wider induction of facts proved to be false. From the actual visibilities of the earth, as related to the sun, the moon, and the stars, men once inferred that all the heavenly bodies moved daily round the earth. What was actually seen is one thing; an inference deduced from visible facts is quite another. In what was really seen we have facts of actual intuitive knowledge. In what was inferred we have opinions, beliefs, conjectures, in all of which there is a liability to error. The same holds true in all similar cases. In all appearances, even in what are called the optical illusions of mirage, *some* reality appears. In what actually appears we have facts of intuition, and here is real knowledge. In what is inferred from such facts, here, and only here, is the illusion. Such discriminations must be made everywhere; otherwise we shall confound truth with error.

CONDITION OF REAL KNOWLEDGE.

Science, as we have seen, is knowledge systematized. A question of fundamental importance here presents itself—to wit, What is the immutable condition of real knowledge? To this question but one answer can be given: *Knowledge implies a subject possessed of the capacity or power to know, and an object so correlated to this faculty, that when the proper conditions are fulfilled, knowledge of said object necessarily arises, in consequence of that reciprocal relation.* On no other condition is it possible for us even to conceive of the *existence* or *possibility* of knowledge. If knowledge exists at all, it must be, we repeat, because there exists a faculty which is, relatively to some object, a *power* of knowing, and an object which is, relatively to such power, an *object* of knowledge; and the power and object in such relations to each other, that real knowledge arises in consequence of this relation. Let anyone attempt to conceive of the fact or possibility of a knowledge of any object whatever on any other condition than the one before us, and he will find himself utterly unable to form such a conception. We have here, then, the one absolute condition of real knowledge—a condition which properly takes rank as a principle of science.

THE QUESTION, WHAT CAN WE KNOW?—HOW ANSWERED.

The question, What can we know? can be correctly answered but by a valid answer to another—to wit, What *do* we know, and what is *implied* by facts of actual knowledge? *À priori*, we cannot determine whether any or what faculties or objects of knowledge do, or do not, exist. The existence and nature of all powers and causes of every kind are revealed and determined, not *à priori*, but exclusively, by the known effects which they produce, and through what is implied by such effects. So of a power of knowledge. The existence and nature of said power can, by no possibility, be determined but through facts of actual knowledge. The question, What can we know? together with the other question, What are the extent and limits of valid knowledge? is determinable, we repeat, only through a valid determination of the *facts* and *objects* of actual knowledge, and what is implied by the same. We have in the answer now given to the question, What can we know? another immutable principle of universal science. Any other answer to this question conducts us, not in the direction of true, but of false science. The fundamental postulate of all the sciences, is the existence of the intelligence as a faculty with correlated objects of valid knowledge. Take away this one postulate, and we have undeniably no basis for scientific induction or deduction in any direction whatever. If no reality is known and recognizable as known, we have self-evidently nothing, not even knowledge itself, to systematize, explain, or elucidate. No principles are, or can be, of more fundamental importance and authority in science than those just defined, together with the criteria previously given—criteria by which we can infallibly distinguish, in respect to principles and facts of science, all forms of valid knowledge from assumptions, beliefs, opinions, and conjectures which enter, as constituent elements, into all systems of 'science falsely so-called.'

Conditions, Extent, and Limits of Valid Knowledge as Affirmed in all Systems of Materialism and Idealism.

The conditions, extent, and limits of valid knowledge as affirmed by the founders and advocates of Materialism on the one hand, and Idealism on the other, now claim a moment's attention. Materialism, as taught by all its advocates, affirms the absolute impossibility of valid knowledge, but upon one exclusive condition—that the object shall be *external* to the faculty of knowledge. In other words, we can have no real knowledge of any realities but such as are external to us. Idealism, on the other hand, denies absolutely the possibility of all knowledge of outward objects. In the different schools of idealism, the condition of valid knowledge is expressed in two forms : 1. That there must be a 'synthesis of being and knowing;' that is, that the subject and object of knowledge must be one and identical. This is the condition on which, as a principle, pantheism and subjective idealism are in fact and form based. 2. 'An absolute *identity* of being and knowledge;' that is, that knowledge itself and the object of knowledge must be one and identical. It is a question in dispute among German thinkers whether Schelling or Hegel first announced this condition as a principle in science.

Remarks on these Hypotheses.

On these hypotheses we have the following fundamental remarks to offer :

1. The condition of valid knowledge, in neither of the forms above announced, has even the appearance of self-evident certainty, and con-

sequently has no claim whatever to the place in the sphere of thought assigned to said condition by its advocates—to wit, that of a principle in science—a principle which has universal and necessary validity. Knowledge not merely in one, but in three distinct forms, and the consequent existence of corresponding powers of knowledge, are equally conceivable, and, therefore, in themselves possible. We can conceive of an intelligence to which nothing but a knowledge of external objects is possible. Equally conceivable is an intelligence capacitated exclusively for subjective knowledge, or of one which shall know its own knowledge. Finally, we can with equal facility conceive of a power of intelligence to which knowledge in all these three forms shall be both possible and actual. All this is undeniable. How, then, can we determine under which of the above conceptions the human intelligence shall be classed? Not *à priori*, as is attempted in each of the schools under consideration. A penny is about to be thrown into the air. We should regard an individual as demented who should affirm himself possessed of the power to determine by *à priori* insight, and that with absolute certainty, which side will fall uppermost. Equally removed from such insight are the three cases under consideration. The possibility of knowledge in any one form designated is just as conceivable, and, therefore, as probable in any given case as in any of the others. *À priori*, it is just as possible and probable in itself that the human intelligence is capacitated for real knowledge in all these forms, as in any one of them.

The question before us, then, is to be determined wholly and exclusively *à posteriori;* that is, by reference to actual facts of consciousness. If we are actually conscious of knowledge, but in one exclusive form, the objective or subjective, or of actually knowing no other object but the mere act of knowing itself, such, we are to affirm, are the nature, extent, and limits of our faculty of knowledge. If, on the other hand, we are absolutely conscious of actual knowledge in all these forms, upon this adamantine fact we are to base our deductions in regard to the nature, extent, and limits of the human intelligence as a faculty of knowledge. The hypothesis of Materialism, and those of Idealism in all its forms, stand revealed as mere lawless assumptions, and nothing else.

2. While the hypothesis of Materialism on the one hand, and those of Idealism on the other, are utterly incompatible the one with the other, the evidence in favour of the claims of the former is absolutely equal to that in favour of the latter. The possibility of knowledge in its objective is just as conceivable as in its subjective forms. No *à priori* proof, evidence, or antecedent probability, can be adduced in favour of one as against the other. The evidence *à posteriori*, also, is balanced with equal absoluteness. We are as perfectly conscious of actual knowledge in one form as in the other. No possible argument can be adduced in favour of

one hypothesis, *an argument* which does not bear with equal absoluteness in favour of the other.

3. In the clearest possible testimony of universal consciousness we have absolute disproof of both these hypotheses. If we are conscious of anything, we are conscious, and equally so, of actual knowledge, both in its subjective and objective forms. In every act of external perception, for example, we are just as absolutely conscious of knowing 'things without us,' as we are of knowing facts of internal experience. To deny this is, in the language of Sir William Hamilton, to affirm 'consciousness to be a liar from the beginning.'

4. Each of these hypotheses, by impeaching the validity of consciousness in one form, implies the absolute impossibility of real knowledge in any form. Each hypothesis denies absolutely the validity of consciousness in one of its known forms. If this faculty, as is affirmed, fundamentally deceives us in one form, it is to be trusted nowhere. Each of these hypotheses actually saps the foundation of knowledge in every sphere, actual and conceivable.

5. The hypothesis of Pure Idealism, that of 'absolute identity of being and knowing'—that is, that knowledge itself and the object of knowledge are always one and identical—is of utterly inconceivable and impossible validity. Thought without a thinker, ideas existing nowhere and in no time, and existing as the attributes of no real being, phenomena without substance, events without causes, and knowledge without a subject or object, except knowledge itself—can a greater absurdity have place in this or any other world? It was well said by a great German philosopher that the system of Hegel, which was based upon this hypothesis, was 'nothing in itself nor of itself; nor was its author in himself, but beside himself.' We can affirm with perfect safety that any professed system of science which has its basis in either of the above hypotheses must be void of all claims to truth, if that hypothesis is not and cannot be verified.

SECTION III.

FOUR, AND BUT FOUR, REALITIES ARE REPRESENTED, OR ARE REPRESENTABLE, IN HUMAN THOUGHT.

We now advance to a consideration of the hypothesis which lies at the foundation of this entire Treatise, the hypothesis about which all the inductions, deductions, expositions, and elucidations of said Treatise revolve. The hypothesis is this: *Four, and but four, realities ever have been, or by any possibility can be, represented as realities in human thought.* We refer, of course, to *spirit* and *matter, time* and *space.* Whatever is represented or representable as real, must of necessity be apprehended as one or the other of these realities, or as a property, attribute, state or effect of the same. The reason is obvious and undeniable. *Nothing else is the object of perception external or internal, and no other reality is implied by what we perceive.*

Body and its qualities, of which we become conscious through external, and mind with its operations, of which we become conscious in internal, perception, do imply the reality of time and space, and imply nothing else. *Time* and *space* by themselves do not imply the reality of either matter or spirit, much less, if possible, do they imply any other reality. Undeniably, no reality is or can be representable in human thought but objects of external and internal perception, and such as are implied by what we perceive. All must admit that no other realities are the conscious objects of perception, external or internal, but matter and spirit, with their phenomena, and that these imply no other realities but time and space. These realities are, undeniably, represented in human thought, and it is equally manifest that none others can be thus represented.

Let anyone attempt to form a positive conception of some reality which is neither matter, spirit, time, nor space, and he will find that he has attempted an utter impossibility. The reason is obvious. No elements of thought exist, elements out of which such a conception can by any possibility be constructed. All ideas in the mind, and all language also, take exclusive form from our apprehensions of these four realities, and of their apprehended attributes, properties or phenomena. Whatever is apprehended as not being one or the other of these realities, or their properties or phenomena, is, of necessity, apprehended as nothing —as no reality at all. Thoughts of such realities must be utterly objectless, and as wholly void of content in themselves; while the words representing such ideas must be totally void of meaning. Human thought is necessarily limited to these four realities, their nature, attributes, properties, phenomena, and mutual relations included.

NATURE, CHARACTER, AND MUTUAL RELATIONS OF THESE FOUR REALITIES.

Questions of fundamental importance here arise; namely, What are the essential characteristics, as represented in human thought, of these four realities? What are their mutual relationships, the one to each of the others? and what are their relations as objects of knowledge to the human intelligence? These questions, as we believe, admit of definite answers, and may be settled upon purely scientific grounds. Let us proceed to the accomplishment of these objects.

All these Realities are distinctly represented in Human Thought.

Our first position is this, all these realities are, in fact, distinctly represented in human thought. No individual, young or old, learned or unlearned—an individual of common understanding—misapprehends us when we speak to him of matter or spirit, time or space. Nor does he ever confound any one of these realities with any other. In all languages, also, specific terms are employed to represent each of these realities. In all systems of Philosophy, too, the existence of all these realities, and the validity of our knowledge of the same, are affirmed or denied, and that in forms which imply the absolute universality and identity of human apprehension of all these existences. When philosophers, for example, deny the existence of any one of these realities, or impeach the validity of our knowledge of the same, no one misunderstands them. Such facts absolutely evince the existence in all minds of the apprehensions, clear and distinct, of all these four realities. Nor will real thinkers of any school deny the validity of these statements.

No other Reality is or can be represented in Human Thought.

Nor is any other reality represented in human thought; nor can we receive any such representation until some fifth entity, having none of the properties of any of these, is distinctly manifested to us. *A priori*, we cannot determine what realities do or do not exist in time and space. *A posteriori*, we perceive, and consequently know of none but material or mental entities, together with their attributes, properties, and relations. Nor of any effects ever perceived by us, are we able to affirm absolutely that they are not the phenomena of material or spiritual entities. No philosopher has ever witnessed a single phenomenon not connected with one or other of these substances. Pure idealists give us a system which has no material or spiritual substance in it. Every constituent element of that system, however, is taken, body and soul, from one of the known attributes of one of these substances—to wit, thought. Suppose that all of these realities, with all their attributes, properties, and mutual relations, were left out. Where would be our material for the construction of any system, or for the formation of any conception of any reality whatever? The fact that, in such circumstances, we can have no thought-representations of any realities of any kind, evinces absolutely that the elements of all our conceptions and ideas are derived wholly from these four realities.

These Realities wholly unlike each other.

We remark, in the next place, that as represented in human thought, each of these realities is wholly unlike every other. There is not an essential property or attribute of any one of them that, in any form, resembles any property or attribute which, as represented in human thought, pertains to either of the others. When we have fully analyzed our apprehensions of space, for example, we cannot find in the idea a single element which can be found in our apprehension of either of the other realities. So in all other cases. When we compare our conceptions of matter and spirit, we find in these conceptions no common elements. What is there in thought, feeling, and acts of will, which include all the attributes of mind, that in any sense resembles extension and form, essential properties of matter—that is, whenever we compare these realities as actually represented in human thought? We sometimes, but never in the same sense, employ the same term to represent certain properties of each of these realities. We speak, for example, of body, space, and time, as having extension. But neither, as represented in thought, has extension in the same sense and form that either of the others has. The fact is undeniable that, as represented in our apprehensions, each of these realities is wholly unlike every other. We may, by assumption, resolve matter into spirit, and spirit into matter, and time and space into mere laws of thought. In our actual apprehensions, however, they are still the same distinct, separate, and dissimilar realities that they were before. We may assume that certain movements of matter eliminate thought and other mental acts and states, and that the content of all objects of external perception is sensation, a mere feeling of the mind. But we can no more conceive matter as exercising the functions of spirit, or as identical with any mental state, than we can conceive of the annihilation of time or space. We can as readily conceive of empty space as actually thinking, feeling, and willing, or as possessed of the properties of solidity and form, as in thought to affirm the former class of phenomena to be functions of matter, or the latter to be attributes of mind. Some scientists have assured us that in dissecting and analyzing a dead man's brains, they have discovered the identical process by which matter eliminates thought. With just as great a show of wisdom they might affirm that they had discovered and demonstrated that the powers of thought, feeling, and willing, together with that of gravitation, necessarily inhere as essential properties in a circle or square. Thought, with all the other functions of mind, is not at a greater remove from our apprehensions of a triangle than it is from that of matter. Of the validity of all these statements every mind must be absolutely conscious.

These Realities differ equally relatively to our Manner of Perceiving and Apprehending them.

If we contemplate these realities with reference to our manner of perceiving and apprehending them, we shall find them in forms equally fundamental, distinguished and peculiarized, the one from each of the others. Matter, we consciously perceive, in all its properties, as an exterior object distinct and separate from ourselves. Of mind, in all its functions and operations, we are conscious as the object of internal perception. As thus perceived, these realities are never in thought confounded, but for ever separated, the one from the other. Space we are conscious of apprehending as implied by body, which we perceive, and as the place of the same. Time we apprehend as implied by successive events of which we are conscious, and as the place of such events. As related to our manner of perceiving and apprehending them, each of these realities thus stands at an infinite remove from every other.

There are two peculiarities which separate time and space, with their properties, from spirit and matter, with their phenomena. The former we apprehend as existing, with the impossibility of conceiving of their non-existence, or as being in any respects different from our apprehensions of them. Matter and spirit we apprehend as realities, with the possibility of conceiving of their non-being. While we cannot conceive of space or time as not existing, we can conceive of them as unoccupied by substances and events. We therefore classify our ideas of the former realities as necessary, and those of matter and spirit as contingent, ideas. Time and space, also, are, though in different senses, apprehended as absolutely infinite and unlimited; the former in the past and future, and the latter in all directions. Matter and our own spirits, in senses equally special and peculiar, are apprehended as finite and limited; the former as existing in and occupying space, and the latter in the range of its faculties. Thus distinct and separated in human thought and apprehension is each of these realities from every other. In this light true science must and will recognize them.

These Realities sustain to each other fixed and definable relations.

While these realities, as universally represented in human thought, are thus unlike, distinct, and dissimilar, each from every other, they all sustain to each other fixed and definable relations. Some of these we have already specified. Space and time are apprehended as the *places* of substances and events, and as the necessary *conditions* of their existence and occurrence. We cannot conceive of substances and events without apprehending them as existing somewhere, that is, in space, and as occurring in definite periods of time. The ideas of space and time also render conceivable the *possibility* of the existence and occurrence of substances and events. If the former are not real, the latter cannot be.

While our ideas of space and time, that is, necessary ideas, are thus universally given as the logical antecedents of contingent ideas, those of matter and spirit, and in the order of origination in the mind, that is, contingent ideas, as universally *precede* necessary ones. Space and time are apprehended but as the places of substances and events, and as implied by the same. In no other forms can the former be defined. It is self-evident that a reality which is and can be apprehended, but as the place of, and as implied by, some other reality, cannot have been apprehended before the latter. Contingent ideas, then, must have been originated in the mind before necessary ones could have been. These relations, the logical and chronological order of these ideas, should be clearly apprehended and kept distinctly in mind, as they will hereafter be found to be of fundamental importance in the explanation of different systems of Philosophy.

Another relation of equal importance between our apprehensions of these realities here claims special attention. We refer to the relation of *absolute compatibility*. There is absolutely nothing in our ideas of any one of these realities in the remotest degree incompatible with our apprehensions of either of the others. The idea that space is a reality in itself is in no sense or form incompatible with the idea that time is also, and in the same sense, real. The idea that space and time are realities in themselves is equally compatible with the conception that matter and spirit are also realities in themselves. Nothing is or can be more self-evident than this, that an implied reality cannot be incompatible with the reality by which the former is implied, and that the latter cannot be incompatible with the former. The same relation of absolute compatibility exists between our apprehensions of matter and spirit. Matter is apprehended as relatively to spirit an *object*, and the latter as a *faculty*, of knowledge. The conception of the reality of one is in no sense or form incompatible with that of the other. Matter is apprehended as a substance existing in and occupying space, and, consequently, as possessed, among others, of the qualities of real extension and form. Mind is apprehended as an immaterial substance exercising the functions of thought, feeling, and willing. The idea that the object of the former apprehension exists as a reality in itself in no sense whatever contradicts the idea that the object of the latter exists as a similar reality. Nor can we find, on the most rigid scrutiny, in one of these apprehensions, a single element in the remotest degree contradictory to any element existing in the other. How, for example, can extension, form, colour and attraction, existing as qualities in one substance, be in the remotest degree incompatible with any form of thought, feeling, and willing, existing as attributes of another substance?

These Apprehensions not Self-contradictory.

Nor, we remark finally, can any self-contradictory elements be found in our apprehensions of any one of these realities, elements which prove such apprehension to be invalid for the reality and character of its object.

As we here encounter the only formal argument ever adduced against the validity of our knowledge of the realities under consideration, very special attention is requested to what we have now to offer. Our apprehensions of each of these realities are, it is affirmed, self-contradictory, and, therefore, invalid. Let us see if any such contradictions do indeed exist in these apprehensions. Our ideas of space and time are undeniably absolutely simple ideas, and can, therefore, by no possibility, be either of them self-contradictory. The fundamental elements of contingent ideas are substance and attribute, the latter implying the former. Here, undeniably, is not the remotest appearance of self-contradiction. The implied, and that by which the former is implied, cannot be incompatible the one with the other. The same holds true of all the constituent elements relating to each other, elements of each of these apprehensions. There can be nothing, for example, in any form of thought that is incompatible with the existence of any feeling or act of will, facts which exist or occur in the mind. Nor is there the remotest appearance of incompatibility between any one of these classes of phenomena and any other. The idea of mind as possessed of threefold capacities, those of thought, feeling, and willing, is just as self-consistent as any idea can be. Analyze the facts of mind as carefully and fully as may be, and we shall find between every one and every other of them the fixed relation of absolute compatibility.

In respect to what is intrinsic in our apprehensions of matter, but one seeming contradiction is found, and this not in the idea as it actually exists in the mind, but in another substituted for this, and constituted for the occasion. The apprehension actually existing in the mind is this: all objects of external perception are apprehended as compound substances constituted of simple parts, the former being divisible, and the latter wholly incapable of being divided, the simple, also, being given not as perceived, but as implied by the compound which is an object of perception. Here, again, we have the perceived and the implied, between which there can by no possibility be any real nor even apparent contradiction. The *seeming* contradiction is thus rendered plausible. Take any material object we please. We apprehend it as a whole, made up of parts. Conceive this object divided, and then form a conception of either of the parts. The result will be that this new conception will be found to be like the first, constituted of the idea of a whole made up of parts. Repeat the operation as long and often as we please, and the same result will be obtained—the conception of a whole made up of parts. Hence the deduction that all our apprehensions of material objects are those of compounds constituted of compounds, which is self-contradictory. Our apprehensions of material objects being thus self-contradictory, the further inference is deduced that such apprehensions cannot be valid for the reality and character of their objects. The fallacy involved in such reasoning is obvious. A fiction is here substituted for a reality. The actually existing apprehension of material objects is, as we have seen, not that of a compound made up of parts which are themselves compounded, and capable of being divided, but of a compound constituted of absolute simples, simples which cannot be separated into parts. To prove the existence of contradictory elements in any conception, we must take that conception as actually given, and not as it is not given, in consciousness. The conception of material objects actually given is wholly void of real or apparent contradiction. The fiction substituted for what is real has in it incompatible elements. The manner in which this self-contradictory fiction is formed may be readily explained. When we form a conception of any material object, we employ a secondary intellectual faculty, the understanding, or notion-forming power of the mind: All such objects apprehended through this faculty must be conceived of as wholes constituted of parts. If we conceive an object to be divided, and then, through this secondary faculty, form a conception of either of the divided parts, we shall obtain the same result as before, the conception of a compound constituted of parts. Continue the process of division and of conception as long as we please, and the same result follows, the conception of a compound made up of parts. Now, it is not through such a process, or by means of this conceptive faculty, that we obtain our idea of the simple which cannot be divided. This idea, on the other hand, is furnished wholly through a primary faculty, the reason, the organ of implied knowledge, the faculty which gives us the necessary elements which enter into all our conceptions. We perceive body, succession and events. Reason, on occasion of such perceptions, apprehends space, time, substance, and cause, as necessarily implied by what we perceive. So, when we perceive the compound, reason apprehends the simple as implied by the perceived. The understanding blends the perceived and implied elements into the conception represented by the term body.

Between the perceived and implied elements constituting this conception, as in all other cases of perceived and implied knowledge, even the appearance of incompatibility or self-contradiction is impossible. It is thus demonstrably evident that our apprehensions of no one of the realities under consideration are in any sense or form incompatible with those of any other, and that our actual apprehension of each one of them is equally void of contradictory elements.

An argument against the validity of our knowledge of all material objects is also drawn from our affirmed apprehensions of the infinite divisibility of matter. On the one hand, it is affirmed that it is impossible for us to conceive of matter as real without conceiving of it as being infinitely divisible. On the other hand, infinite divisibility cannot be represented in thought. Hence the inference that our ideas of this substance cannot be valid. Such is the argument of Kant, and from him as given by Herbert Spencer. In our actual apprehension of this substance, as we have seen, it is not conceived at all as being, in itself, infinitely divisible, but the opposite. Suppose, now, that we can or cannot *conceive* of it as being thus divisible. From this fact we cannot infer that it does not exist in the form in which we actually conceive it to exist. Who doubts the actual existence in space of a straight line one inch long? Yet all that Kant and Spencer have said about the divisibility of matter apply in fact and form, as shown in 'The Science of Natural Theology,' pp. 272, 273, to our apprehensions of every such line. We should subject ourselves to the just charge of infinite stupidity if we should infer from such quibbling that no such lines do or can exist. So of the same identical argument against the validity of our idea of matter. Matter in any form, as conceived by the understanding, is divisible. Not so of its constituent elements as apprehended by the reason.

Necessary Deductions from the Principles and Facts just evinced as True.

1. Any systems of science or Philosophy, systems built upon the hypothesis that the relation of incompatibility exists between our apprehensions of any one and any other of the four realities under consideration, or that any of these apprehensions are, in themselves, self-contradictory —any such systems, we say, have place nowhere but in the sphere of 'science falsely so-called.' They can have no claims whatever to our regard as ' knowledge systematized.'

2. Equally void of all claims to our regard, as a principle in science, is the hypothesis that lies at the basis of Materialism on the one hand, and of Idealism on the other, to wit, *that there exists but one substance or principle of all things.* It is demonstrably evident that no form of proof, positive evidence, or even antecedent probability, can be adduced in favour of this hypothesis. No one will have the effrontery to claim for it the prerogative of a self-evident judgment. The predicate, in this case, is, undeniably, neither identical with, nor does it represent an essential element of, the subject, nor is it implied by the subject. In short, this hypothesis has not one of the immutable characteristics of a self-evident proposition or principle in science. *À priori*, we have just as much authority for the hypothesis that two substances exist, as we have, or can have, that but one exists. Nor can we find, in the whole range of human thought, a single principle or fact which renders it, in the remotest degree, certain, or even probable, that this hypothesis is true. On the other hand, we have the same evidence that two substances, matter and spirit, exist, that we have, or can have, that one or the other of them does exist. The deduction which lies at the basis of

the two systems under consideration, the hypothesis which must be true, or each of them must be false, is nothing but a mere bald, naked, and lawless assumption, an assumption which has no more claims to our regards as a principle or fact in science than can be claimed for the greatest absurdity that was ever intruded into the sphere of human thought.

3. Our next deduction is this: no form nor degree of disproof, positive evidence, or antecedent probability can, by any possibility, be adduced against the validity of our apprehensions of any one, or all of the four realities under consideration. In itself, as we have seen, it is just as possible and probable that the objects of all these apprehensions exist together, as that any one of them exists alone. Nor can anything, as we have further seen, be shown to exist intrinsically in any one of these apprehensions, anything, in any form or degree, disproving or rendering improbable the validity of such apprehension for the reality and character of its object. Nowhere, in the wide range of human thought, can a solitary principle or fact be adduced, a principle or fact on the authority of which the absolute validity of our apprehension of any one of those realities can be justly impeached.

4. The validity of our last deduction is rendered self-evident by what has just been proven. The deduction may be thus stated: any form of positive proof or valid evidence in favour of the validity of any one or all of our apprehensions of matter, spirit, space, and time, for the reality and character of their objects, verifies for such apprehensions a place in the sphere of true science. Whenever two hypotheses are present, one of which must be true and the other false, the total absence of all evidence in favour of one, and positive evidence in favour of the other, vindicates for the latter a claim in our regard as a valid principle or real fact of science. The same holds true of a given hypothesis, against which no form or degree of disproof, positive evidence, or antecedent probability can be adduced, and in favour of which real proof or valid evidence does exist. Such, undeniably, are the real relations of science to each of the four apprehensions under consideration. Whether such forms of proof and valid evidence in their favour do exist, is hereafter to be shown. The bearing of such proof or evidence, when adduced, is undeniable. To render perfectly distinct the true state of the case, is the object of the present presentation.

THESE FOUR REALITIES ARE APPREHENDED BY UNIVERSAL MIND AS ACTUALLY KNOWN REALITIES, NOR CAN OUR APPREHENSIONS OF ANY ONE OF THEM BE CHANGED, MODIFIED, OR DISPLACED FROM HUMAN THOUGHT.

Our next position in regard to these four realities, space, time, matter, and spirit, and in regard to our apprehensions of the same, claims very special attention on account of its fundamental bearings upon our present and future inquiries. Our position is this : these four realities, all in common, are apprehended by universal mind as actually *known* realities, and our apprehensions of them, in all their essential characteristics, can, by no possibility, be changed or modified or displaced from human thought.

We think of space as the place of substances, of time as the place of events, and of space and time as the necessary condition of the possibility of the existence of substances and the occurrence of events. We then think of body as existing in and occupying space, and consequently, as possessed of real extension and form. We finally think of ourselves, our minds, as real, substantial personalities exercising the functions of thought, feeling, and willing. Not a shadow of doubt exists in our minds that all these objects of thought are realities in themselves, and that we actually apprehend them as they are. In other words, all these realities are consciously represented in universal thought as absolutely *known* realities. Our apprehensions of them do not lie under the eye of consciousness as mere assumptions, opinions, beliefs, imaginings, or guesses, which may or may not be true, but as forms of absolute knowledge. In the interior of his own mind, no one is ever conscious of himself as merely thinking, supposing, imagining, or guessing what he thinks, feels, and wills, but as absolutely knowing himself as the subject of all these operations. We are not conscious of matter as an object of doubtful belief, imagining, or of 'prudent guessing,' but as a directly perceived, and, therefore, *known* reality. The certainty of the self and the not-self, as given in universal consciousness, is equal and absolute. While we thus *know* mind and matter as realities in themselves, we do and must know with the same absoluteness that they do and must exist and act in time and space. Time and space, therefore, must be recognized in the consciousness, not only as *actual*, but as *known* realities. No one can honestly interpret the facts of his own consciousness and doubt the perfect validity of the above statements.

This leads us to remark, in the next place, that in all essential particulars, and in certain fundamental respects, our apprehensions of each and every one of these realities can, by no possibility, be displaced from human thought, nor can they, in any form, be changed or modified. As far as our apprehensions of space and time are concerned, we have already seen that it is absolutely impossible for us to conceive of the non-existence of these realities, or of their being, in any respects, different from what we apprehend them to be. In the absolute validity of these statements all thinkers of all schools agree. So far, then, the apprehensions under consideration must be admitted to have an immutably fixed place and character in human thought.

An equally immutable fixedness of place and character, in all essential particulars, is possessed, in universal thought, by our apprehensions of mind and matter. We are ever immutably conscious of ourselves, and cannot but be thus conscious, as real, substantial personalities possessing the powers and exercising the functions of thought, feeling, and willing. Nor can we possibly change or modify our apprehensions of ourselves as such personalities. We may *assume* and affirm matter to be the only reality, and that thought, feeling, and willing are nothing but phenomena of this one substance. Or we may *assume* and affirm that neither matter nor spirit exist as real substances, and resolve all realities into pure thought. In the very midst of all such assumptions and reasonings, and despite of all such deductions to the contrary, we are, and cannot but be, present to ourselves as the identical personalities above defined. While Messrs. Hill, Huxley, Spencer and Emerson, for example, stand out to themselves, in their systems, as demonstrated nonentities, they are, like all the rest of the race, ever present to themselves as real substantial personalities—yes, more than this, as real substantial thinkers of great eminence. They have never for a moment doubted, or can doubt, of themselves, or changed or modified their apprehensions of themselves in the particulars above stated. Conscious thinkers attempting to demonstrate to themselves, and to all mankind, that they themselves do not think at all? This is the scientific farce which such thinkers are perpetually acting and re-acting before themselves and before the world, and all this with the eye of their own consciousness ever fixed with direct, distinct, and clear vision upon their own substantial selves as stultifying themselves. We can no more, in the interior of our own minds, doubt the absolute validity of our knowledge of ourselves, or change or modify our apprehensions of ourselves, that is, in the fundamental particulars under consideration, than we can doubt the validity of our knowledge of a circle or square, or change or modify our apprehensions of these figures. In our interior apprehensions and convictions, we no more, and can no more, confound our conscious selves with material existences around us, our minds with our bodies, or our souls with our brains, than we do or can confound a circle with a triangle. In all minds in common, all reasonings and affirmed demonstrations to the contrary notwithstanding—in all minds in common, we say, spirit and matter are as distinctly separated and distinguished, the one from the other, as are the two figures above named from each other.

The same remarks are equally applicable to our apprehensions of matter. All men are distinctly and absolutely conscious of a direct and immediate perception of this substance as a reality exterior and objective to the mind, and as possessed, among others, of the essential qualities of extension and form. This apprehension which we have of this substance, together with our absolute conviction of its real existence as such a substance, can no more be displaced from human thought, or in any sense or form be changed or modified, than can our apprehensions and convictions in respect to any mathematical figures whatsoever. In the absolute validity of these statements, all men, philosophers among the rest, perfectly agree. Kant, for example, while he denies absolutely the validity of all our apprehensions of both matter and spirit, affirms, as absolutely, that it is impossible for reasoning or philosophy to displace these apprehensions from human thought, to change or modify the same, or to banish the conviction which is omnipresent in universal mind, that these apprehensions have absolute validity for the reality and character of their objects. The reason which he assigns for this undeniable fact, is this: 'We have to do with *natural and unavoidable illusion,* which reposes upon subjective principles.' This 'natural and unavoidable illusion,' he adds, 'is not one in which, for instance, a blockhead, from want of knowledge, involves himself, or which a trickster has artfully imagined in order to torment reasonable people, but one which irresistibly adheres to human reason, and even when we have discovered its delusion, still will not cease to play tricks upon reason and to push it continually into momentary errors, which always require to be corrected.' We have, undeniably, in all such cases, not reason through laws 'irresistibly inhering' in itself, imposing upon itself 'natural and unavoidable illusion,' and as necessarily 'playing tricks' upon itself. We have, on the other hand, reason itself, through its inherent and immutable laws, correcting the illusions and tricks which false science is endeavouring to impose, as truths of real science, upon the universal human intelligence. In accordance with the teaching of Kant, Coleridge affirms that our apprehension of external material substances, together with our absolute belief of the validity of such apprehension, is 'innate, indeed, and con-natural,' that it 'remains proof against all attempts to remove it by grounds or arguments,' and 'lays claim to IMMEDIATE certainty as a position at once indemonstrable and irresistible.' Yet he affirms this belief to be 'nothing but a prejudice, innate, indeed, and con-natural, but still a prejudice.' No philosopher of any age or school, a philosopher who denies the validity of our knowledge of the nature of matter especially, ever did deny, or will deny, the above statements of Kant and Coleridge. All agree that our apprehensions and beliefs in respect to the essential characteristics of spirit and matter are 'natural and unavoidable,' 'innate, indeed, and con-natural,' that they cannot be eradicated, changed, or modified, but 'remain proof against all attempts to remove them by grounds or argument,' and 'lay claim to immediate certainty as a position at once indemonstrable and irresistible.' 'This faith,' that is, this natural, unavoidable, irresistible, and immovable conviction, 'the philosopher,' that is, philosopher of his school, Mr. Coleridge tells us, '*compels* himself to *treat* as nothing but a prejudice,' an 'illusion,' as Kant calls it. We fully confess that we regard an assumption forced upon the mind by an act of will, and that in opposition to 'a natural and immovable intellectual intuition,' which 'remains proof against all attempts to remove it by grounds or arguments'—we regard such a forced assumption, we say, 'as nothing but a prejudice,' 'an illusion' of false science. On the other hand, we regard an intuitive conviction, which no system of philosophy can change, modify, or displace from human thought, as itself a truth of real science. The fact is undeniable, that all these realities are distinctly revealed in the universal consciousness as objects of valid knowledge, that in all essential particulars our apprehensions of these realities can, by no possibility, be changed, or modified, or displaced from human thought, and that the validity of these apprehensions can be impeached, not by any principle or fact given as valid, or real, by the intelligence, but by a mere assumption forced into the sphere of thought by a lawless act of will, an assumption in which we compel ourselves to '*treat* as nothing but a prejudice,' an 'illusion,' apprehensions which the intelligence does and must regard as forms of absolute knowledge. We shall have occasion to speak, more at length, upon this great central fact hereafter.

OUR APPREHENSIONS OF THESE REALITIES HAVE ALL THE FUNDAMENTAL CHARACTERISTICS OF FORMS OF VALID KNOWLEDGE, CHARACTERISTICS WHICH TRUE SCIENCE MUST AND WILL ACKNOWLEDGE.

We now advance to our great central and final position in regard to these realities, and to our apprehensions of the same. These apprehensions, we remark, possess all actual and conceivable characteristics of real absolute knowledge, and hence, true science must, and will, accept of the objects of these apprehensions, as realities in themselves, and as being in themselves what we apprehend them to be. The validity of this position we argue from the following considerations:

I. The Validity of these Apprehensions Cannot be Disproved, or Rendered Doubtful.

We affirm, then, in the first place, that by no possibility can the validity of these apprehensions be disproved or rendered, in the remotest degree, doubtful. To accomplish such a result, we *must find forms of knowledge of the validity of which we are, and must be, more certain than we are of that of these apprehensions,* forms *which if true, the latter must be false.* The only conceivable conditions on which such incompatible forms of knowledge can be discovered and adduced are the following: 1. An attempt may be made to show that such forms of knowledge are naturally impossible. 2. Or that facts exist outside of the sphere of these apprehensions, facts incompatible with the validity of said apprehensions.

3. Or such facts may be sought in the relations of these apprehensions to one another. 4. Or, finally, these facts may be sought in what is intrinsic in one or more of the apprehensions themselves. We propose to consider, in the order designated, these, the only conceivable forms of disproof that can be adduced.

1. *Such Forms of Knowledge not Naturally Impossible.*

Valid knowledge, in all these forms, cannot be shown to be impossible in itself. Nor is there any form or degree of antecedent probability against the actual existence of such knowledge. Knowledge in its exterior is just as conceivably possible as in its interior form. If we should, as philosophers of a certain school do, deny the possibility of knowledge in any one form, because we cannot show *how* such knowledge is possible, we should be compelled to deny its possibility in every form. Suppose the transcendental philosopher were required to show us *how* and *why* thought becomes its own object, and knows itself? He assures us, that in all acts of external perception, an exclusively mental state is made to appear to the mind, as the exclusive quality of an object exterior to, and separate from, the perceiving subject. He would find the *how* and the *why* quite as inexplicable in all such cases, and indeed in all cases, as in that of actual external perception. The real question for science to determine is not *how* and *why* we know in any case, but *what* we do know. No one can affirm *à priori* that God does not possess actual knowledge in all these forms, and that He cannot create an intelligence capacitated for such knowledge. We cannot, therefore, affirm *à priori*, that the human intelligence is not such a power. If such knowledge is not, and it undeniably is not, self-evidently impossible in itself, then there is, and can be, no antecedent probability against the actual existence of such a power; and the question whether the human intelligence is, or is not, such a power, is simply a question of fact, and is to be determined, like all other questions pertaining to mental facts, by an appeal to consciousness. The question for science is simply this: Are we, in fact, conscious of knowing our own mental states, and also 'things without us,' and also time and space as necessary existences, and as necessarily implied by what we perceive? If such is found to be the real state of our consciousness, science demands that we shall recognize the human intelligence as such a power.

2. *Facts in Disproof cannot be found outside of the Sphere of these Apprehensions.*

We may go wholly *out of the spheres of all these apprehensions*, and seek for real facts there, facts of the reality of which we are, and must be, more assured than we are of the existence of the realities under consideration, facts which absolutely imply the invalidity of said apprehensions. Now, outside of this sphere, undeniably no facts exist of which we can form the remotest apprehension. As far as human thought can reach, or divine, we are here in the region of absolute nonentity, in the midst of total vacancy, where nothing is revealed as the basis of any deductions whatever. In the midst of this 'palpable obscure,' nothing, surely, is, or can be revealed, to invalidate our knowledge of space, time, matter, or spirit.

3. *Facts in Disproof cannot be found in the Relations of these Apprehensions to one another.*

Or, we may seek for the form of knowledge after which we are inquiring, in the *relations* to one another of our apprehensions of the four realities under consideration, and may look for the object we seek in that direction. But here our researches will be found to be as vain and fruitless as before. Each of these apprehensions, as we have seen, sustains the relation of absolute compatibility with every other. There is the utter absence of all appearance of contradiction between our ideas of space and time, and between those and our apprehensions of matter and spirit. Nor is there a solitary element in our apprehensions of either of these substances, in the remotest degree, incompatible with, or contradictory to, any element existing in the other. No one professes to find here anything whatever to disprove or render improbable the validity of our knowledge of any one of these realities.

4. *Such Facts cannot be found in what is Intrinsic in any of these Apprehensions.*

Or, finally, we may look for the object we seek in the only remaining direction, in what is *intrinsic* in one or more of these apprehensions themselves. We have already anticipated nearly, or quite, all that can be found here bearing upon our inquiries. Ever since the days of Zeno, of the Italic School of Greece, philosophers of the same school have affirmed that none of our world-conceptions, or necessary ideas, can be valid for the reality and character of their objects, because all such apprehensions contain, within themselves, the elements of absolute self-contradictions. Here the following fundamental questions at once present themselves. Are we, or can we be, as absolutely assured, or more so, of the actual existence of such contradictions, than we are of the reality of time and space, on the one hand, and of our personal existence as exercising the functions of thought, feeling and willing, and of matter, as having real extension and form, on the other? Can I be so absolutely certain that these philosophers are right, as I am that I am now thinking upon the subject? Can I be so certain of the validity of their argument to prove the existence of these contradictions, as I am that I think, I feel, and I will, and that matter is immediately and directly before me, as possessed of the qualities of real extension and form? These philosophers themselves admit and affirm that in their own minds the conviction of the absolute validity of these conceptions and ideas 'remains proof against all their attempt to remove it, by the grounds and arguments' which they themselves adduce. Why, then, should *we* admit the validity of such grounds and arguments? We may ask, further, whether the same, or precisely similar, perplexities and seeming contradictions do not connect themselves with absolutely known truths? *Something is real.* This is undeniable, and will be admitted by the class of philosophers under consideration. Against the validity of this undeniable proposition, there exist, in all their force, all the difficulties, perplexities, and arguments, ever adduced against the validity of all our world-conceptions, and necessary ideas. If anything, be it spirit or matter, exists, it must exist somewhere and in some time, that is, in time and space. This implies the real existence, as realities in themselves, of time and space, and that in absolute accordance with our apprehensions of these realities. But time and space, these philosophers assure us, are not, and cannot be, the realities which we apprehend them to be, because such apprehensions have in them the elements of absolute contradiction. Now, reasoning which, if its validity be admitted, would prove absolutely that no form of being does, or can exist, can have validity in no sphere of human thought, much less against our world-conceptions and necessary ideas.

But we are fully able to see through and expose the sophistry and false deductions of these philosophers. All the contradictions which they adduce are, as we have already seen, undeniably found to exist exclusively, not in our world-conceptions, which actually exist in human thought, but in *fictions* manufactured for the occasion, and substituted for realities as they are. A compound constituted of compounds, and represented as such in thought, is self-contradictory, and cannot be real. Such, it is affirmed, are all our world-conceptions. On the other hand, the conception of a compound constituted of absolute simples is an idea void of all appearance even of self-contradiction. Such, as we have seen, are, without exception, all our world-conceptions, as they actually exist in human thought. Taken as they actually exist in the universal consciousness, no element can be found in any of these apprehensions—no element in the remotest degree incompatible with any other found in the same conception.

The argument of Mr. Spencer to prove that our ideas of space and time are self-contradictory, and that space and time cannot, therefore, be in themselves the realities which we apprehend them to be—his argument on this point, we say, is based wholly, in fact and form, upon the assumption that, if they exist at all, space and time both must exist as 'entities or the attributes of entities,' as 'things having or not having attributes,' facts utterly incompatible with our actual apprehensions of these realities. Here, again, we undeniably have a *fiction* substituted for a reality, and imposed upon the mind as that reality. Space and time are actually apprehended as the *places* of 'entities and their attributes,' and of 'things having attributes,' and not as entities, things, or attributes of entities; and nowhere but in the brain of a *bewildered* philosopher are our ideas of these realities confounded with our conceptions of 'entities' and 'things' and 'their attributes,' substances and attributes existing in time and space. If by the terms 'entity' and 'thing' Mr. Spencer means not *substances*, but *realities*, then his argument has no other characteristic than that of senseless tautology. It stands thus : 'If space and time are real substances in themselves—that is, realities—they must be realities or the attributes of realities.' If by these terms he means *substances* or *their attributes*, he has undeniably confounded the implied with that by which the former is implied, and stands openly convicted of a gross sophism. Neither substances nor their attributes are or can be time or space, but, as the immutable condition of the possibility of their existence, imply time and space. Time and space, as actually represented in human thought, therefore, are not substances or entities, but yet realities in themselves, and such realities as we apprehend them to be; and our apprehensions of them have not, as Mr. Spencer affirms, a 'purely relative,' but an absolute validity.

In his chapter on 'Ultimate Scientific Ideas,' Mr. Spencer has fully demonstrated the validity of our ideas of these realities. Against the monstrous absurdity of Kant, that space and time are nothing in themselves but '*à priori* laws or conditions of the conscious mind,' Mr. Spencer urges the following demonstrative argument: 'If space and time, present to our minds, belong to the *ego*, then of necessity they do not belong to the *non-ego*. Now, it is absolutely impossible to think this' (that they do belong to the *ego*). Again, 'The direct testimony of consciousness is, that time and space are not within but without the mind, and so absolutely independent of it that they cannot be conceived to become non-existent, even were the mind to become non-existent.' No reasonable man will or can question the demonstrative validity of this argument. If the 'direct testimony of consciousness' is to be admitted as of absolute validity in one, it must be in all cases. This is self-evident. 'Now, the direct testimony of consciousness is' not only that 'space and time cannot be conceived to become non-existent, even were the mind to become non-existent,' but that, as realities, they cannot be conceived to be, in any respects whatever, different from what we apprehend them to be. The testimony of consciousness is just as absolute in one case as in the other. Our apprehensions of space and time, therefore, have in all respects absolute validity for the reality and character of their objects. From all that has been shown above, the deduction is absolute that the invalidity of our apprehensions of time and space, matter and spirit, cannot by any possibility be disproved or rendered in the remotest degree improbable.

II. Our Apprehensions of Space, Time, Matter, and Spirit are, in all their essential elements and characteristics, distinct, separate, and dissimilar from all Assumptions, Beliefs, and Opinions, which may or may not be true.

Our apprehensions of the four realities under consideration are, we remark in the next place, in all their essential elements and characteristics, most obviously distinguishable from and dissimilar to all forms of *assumptions, opinions, beliefs,* and *conjectures,* which may or may not be true. Phenomena of the latter class, all in common, as we have seen, have these fixed characteristics, that they are subject to change, modification, and displacement from human thought and regard. Our apprehensions of the realities under consideration, as we have also seen, have, all in common, characteristics of a distinct and opposite nature—characteristics equally and absolutely fixed and immutable—the utter impossibility of being changed, modified, or displaced from human thought and regard.

The elements also which enter into and constitute our fundamental apprehensions of space and time, matter and spirit, have all the characteristics of original intuition, while assumptions, beliefs, and opinions have all the characteristics of secondary operations—operations in which acts of the intellect are, to a greater or less degree, modified or determined by impulsions of the sensibility, or volitions of the will. How often do men think so-and-so because they desire or determine thus to think! Thus, consequently, we have assumptions, beliefs, opinions, conjectures, and guesses—that is, ever-changing phenomena, in which error and truth are lawlessly intermingled. In original intuition, which precedes such impulsions and determinations, we have pure intellection—the direct, immediate, and open vision of truth itself. Assumptions, beliefs, and opinions consequently come and go, appear and disappear, and take on an endless diversity of modifications. Original intuition, however, never changes. By every law and principle of correct classification our fundamental apprehensions of space and time, and spirit and matter, take rank, not among changeable and ever-changing assumptions, opinions, or beliefs, but among the immutable facts of original intuition. In the universal consciousness the essential elements of all these apprehensions are distinctly recognized, not as belonging to the former class of phenomena, but as facts of original intuition. We regard ourselves as self-conscious personalities, exercising the functions of thought, feeling, and will, and matter as an exterior substance having extension and form, not because we desire or choose thus to regard ourselves or it, but because we are absolutely conscious of a direct and immediate intuition of ourselves as such personalities, and of it as such a substance. By conscious intuition similarly direct and immediate we recognize space and time as the places of substances and events, realities implied by what we perceive, and the conscious objects of necessary ideas. In all systems of true science, therefore, these essential apprehensions will be distinguished and separated from all the variable and ever-varying phenomena above designated, and ranked among the adamantine facts of original intuition.

III. These Apprehensions have all Possible Positive Characteristics of Real Absolute Knowledge.

Having shown incontrovertibly that the validity of these apprehensions can, by no possibility, be disproved, or, in any form or degree, rendered improbable, and having as incontestably proven that they are to be distinguished and separated from all forms of assumption, opinion, and belief, which may or may not be true, we now proceed to demonstrate, by the most rigid application of scientific criteria, that these apprehensions possess, in their most perfect forms, all conceivable characteristics of real knowledge. The facts already established evince this beyond all reasonable doubt, if they do not render it demonstrably evident. Apprehensions existing in all minds in common; apprehensions which can by no possibility be in the remotest degree changed, modified, or displaced from human thought and regard, and which, by fundamental characteristics, stand utterly distinguished and separated from all forms of assumptions, opinions, and beliefs which are continually subject to change and modification, and are often wholly displaced from human thought and regard—if such facts do not verify apprehensions as forms of actual knowledge, we can have no evidence that real knowledge, in any form, has a dwelling-place in the mind of man. Let us, however, enter at once upon a careful scrutiny of these apprehensions in the light of scientific tests, or criteria which absolutely verify, as such, all forms of real knowledge—knowledge which has place in systems of true science.

Necessary Ideas.

We commence with our necessary ideas of space and time. We have precisely the same evidence that these objects are realities in themselves, and, in all respects, such realities as we apprehend them to be, that we have of the truth of the axioms, Things equal to the same things are equal to one another, and It is impossible for the same thing, at the same time, to exist, and not to exist. Why do we, and all men, hold these propositions to be true? But one answer can be given. It is absolutely impossible for us even to conceive them not to be true. We, therefore, rightly affirm that we know absolutely that they are and must be true.

The validity of such forms of knowledge cannot be doubted. For the same identical reasons for which we affirm that these axioms are and must be true, we affirm space and time to be realities in themselves, and in all respects such realities as we apprehend them to be. We can no more conceive that space and time are not realities in themselves, and the identical realities which we conceive them to be, than we can conceive that things equal to the same things are not equal to one another, and that it is possible for the same thing, at the same moment, to exist and not exist. That our apprehensions of space and time are, in the sense explained, necessary ideas, all thinkers of all schools admit and affirm. 'We can never,' says Kant, 'make to ourselves a representation of this, that there is no space, although we may very readily think' (conceive) 'that no objects therein are to be met with.' 'Time,' he says, 'is a necessary representation.' 'Space and time,' says Mr. Herbert Spencer, as already cited, 'cannot be conceived to become non-existent.' No thinker was ever known to deny the validity of the expositions here given. We must hold, then, that time and space are realities in themselves, or deny the validity of all the principles and axioms of all the sciences, the mathematics among the rest.

Contingent Ideas—Matter and Spirit.

Let us now turn our attention to contingent ideas, and consider the relations of said ideas to their objects, matter and spirit. These ideas, we affirm, as seen in the clearest light of all absolute scientific criteria applicable to such cases, have all the characteristics of real, valid knowledge. This we affirm from the following considerations:

1. There are no other forms of knowledge which have, or can have, in them the elements of more *absolute certainty*. We are just as distinctly and absolutely conscious of *knowing* these realities as they are, as we are of knowing time and space as they are in themselves. The conscious *certainty* of knowledge is just as absolute in one case as in the other. This certainty also admits of no *degrees*. Whenever we think of time and space, we are at one time just as certain that we *know* them, as we are at any other. With the same changeless certainty, we *know* ourselves as personalities exercising the functions of thought, feeling, and willing and matter as directly and immediately before us, and as possessed of extension and form; we thus know ourselves and matter, we say, whenever we think of ourselves and it. This omnipresent and changeless conscious certainty is one of the fixed and immutable tests of real knowledge. Some individuals do, indeed, deny the validity of our knowledge of these realities. The same individuals, however, all in common, deny the validity of knowledge, even in its necessary forms. On one condition only can the validity of our knowledge of either of these realities be

denied, to wit, a universal and absolute impeachment of the intelligence itself, as a faculty of knowledge in every form.

2. Another infallible, scientific criterion of valid knowledge is the direct, immediate, and absolute testimony of the universal consciousness. If we apply this test with the utmost scrutiny, we shall be compelled to rank our fundamental apprehensions of matter and spirit among the most clearly marked forms of real knowledge. Of nothing can we be more distinctly and absolutely conscious than we are of our personal selves, as thinking, feeling, and willing, and absolutely perceiving, or knowing, matter as an exterior reality having real extension and form. If we think of the *qualities* of matter, we find most clearly and definitely marked forms of real knowledge. We need to refer here but to two classes of qualities, the primary and the secondary. The latter are, in universal mind, recognized as the unknown *causes* of known states of the *sensibility*, sensations, of which we are directly and absolutely conscious. The primary qualities, on the other hand, are as universally recognized as the equally known *objects* of known states of the *intelligence*, external perception, of which we are as directly and absolutely conscious. The secondary quality is given in consciousness as *felt*, and, therefore, *inferred*. The primary, on the other hand, is given as directly and immediately *perceived*, and, therefore, *affirmed*. We are conscious of a medium, sensation, between us and the unknown cause of the sensation. We are as absolutely conscious of direct and immediate knowledge in respect to the known object of perception. There is no more obvious and dangerous error in science than the hypothesis that *all* our knowledge of matter is indirect and mediate, through sensation. We must affirm, then, that our knowledge of mind, on the one hand, and of matter, on the other, is, in its fundamental characteristics, of absolute validity for the reality and character of its object, or, in the language of Sir William Hamilton, 'affirm consciousness to be a liar from the beginning.'

3. The fundamental elements which constitute our apprehensions of these substances have all the characteristics of original and *direct intuition.* We are absolutely conscious that our *present* fundamental perceptions, external and internal, are intuitional, and the apprehensions thus originated have all the characteristics of perfect immutability. This evinces, undeniably, that the elements constituting these apprehensions have, from the beginning, been of the same character. On no other hypothesis, also, can we account for the *origin* of these apprehensions. We apprehend ourselves as self-conscious personalities, exercising the functions of thought, feeling and willing. But one account can be given of the origin of such an apprehension—the consciousness of self as the subject of such phenomena. The immutable condition of the origination in the intelligence, of the apprehension of an exterior object, having extension and

form, is the actual conscious perception of such object. There is nothing in mere sensation, an exclusively sensitive and subjective state—a state utterly void of extension, form, colour, solidity, or attraction, even to suggest an exterior object, much less one having these specific qualities. How could a mere subjective state, void of all these qualities, be consciously perceived as an exclusively exterior object having these specific qualities? How can different sensations, all absolutely agreeing in this, that they are exclusively subjective, and as such, all in common, utterly void of the element of extension—how, we ask, can such sensitive states be perceived, not only as exclusively exterior objects, but as such, all having this element in different *degrees*, one being, for example, ten or an hundred times as large as the other? Of two exclusively subjective states, how, we ask again, can one of these sensations be perceived in consciousness as wholly a subjective state, and thus originate the idea of a *secondary* quality of matter, and the other subjective state be perceived in the same consciousness as a quality of an object wholly exterior to and separate from the mind, and thus originate the idea of a *primary* quality of the same subject? Of two sensations both in common exclusively phenomena of the self, how can we be conscious of one as an exclusive quality of the self, and of the other as, with equal exclusiveness, a quality of the not-self? If the sensational hypothesis is true, we have, undeniably, an absolute refutation of the axiom, Things equal to the same things are equal to one another.

But one rational account can be given of the origin of our fundamental apprehensions of matter and spirit, viz., that those apprehensions must, from the beginning, have been constituted wholly of original intuition, and must, therefore, be regarded as forms of real knowledge. No deduction can have higher claims to absolute validity than this.

4. *Immutability*, as we have seen, is another all-authoritative criterion which characterizes and peculiarizes all forms of absolute knowledge. As we have also seen, we can no more change, modify, or displace our essential apprehensions of space and time, matter and spirit as realities in themselves, and the identical realities which we apprehend them to be, than we can change, modify, or displace our apprehensions of a circle or a square. Do what we will, reason upon the subject as we may, space and time, matter and spirit are before us as known realities, and by no possibility can we change, modify, or displace our apprehensions of them as such realities. Assumptions, opinions, beliefs, and conjectures may 'appear for a little while, and then vanish away.' While they remain they are subject to perpetual changes and modifications. But here are apprehensions which have absolute fixedness of form and place in human thought. Nothing but real knowledge can be even conceived to possess such immutably fixed characteristics. These apprehensions, then, do, and must, take

rank as forms of real knowledge. Nothing but 'science, falsely so-called,' can place them under any other category.

5. The reasons, we remark again, for which philosophers of certain schools have impeached the validity of one or more of these apprehensions, vindicate most absolutely their claims to our regard as forms of real knowledge. These reasons take on two, and only two, forms : (1) that which we have already considered, the elements of contradiction said to be found in the apprehensions themselves. These contradictions we have already shown to be wholly imaginary, and that the deduction based upon them is void of validity. On this topic nothing more need be adduced. (2) The only remaining reason is based upon the difficulty which philosophers find in accounting for the possibility of knowledge, either in its subjective or objective form. One class cannot see *how* knowledge is possible but of 'things without us,' and the other but of mental states. The Idealist, as a consequence, in the language of Coleridge, 'compels himself to treat' what all admit to be the universal faith of mankind, 'that there exist things without us,' as 'nothing but a prejudice.' Suppose that we cannot account for the possibility of real knowledge in any form. Shall we, for such a reason, deny the *facts* of actual knowledge, the facts of the reality of which we are absolutely conscious? Did ever a greater absurdity have place in the brain even of a crazy philosophy? In the case before us, it should be borne in mind that we have nothing but a few self-styled philosophers against the world, philosophers themselves of all schools included. While the philosopher is 'compelling himself,' in the construction of his system, to treat 'as nothing but a prejudice' this universal faith, in his inward immovable convictions, as he himself acknowledges, he believes, as absolutely as do the rest of mankind, in space and time, matter and spirit, as knowable and actually known realities. No philosopher of any school will deny the perfect truthfulness of these statements. Apprehensions distinctly revealed in the universal consciousness as having undeniable validity for the reality and character of their objects, apprehensions, also, which can by no possibility be impeached but for the reason above stated, such apprehensions, we say, science must and will recognize as forms of absolute knowledge.

6. One reason more, and we close the present argument. The validity of our apprehension of no one of these realities can be impeached but for 'grounds and arguments' which, if admitted, would utterly annihilate the validity of the Intelligence itself, as a faculty of knowledge in every form whatever. If apprehensions, the validity of which cannot be disproved or rendered improbable, which, by fundamental characteristics, are distinguished and separated wholly from all assumptions and beliefs which may be true or false, which cannot be in the least degree changed,

modified, or displaced from human thought, which co-exist in universal mind with an absolute certainty of their truthfulness, which are consciously constituted of the elements of original intuition, which the universal consciousness distinctly and positively recognizes as pertaining to their objects as directly and immediately perceived, or as necessarily implied by what is thus perceived, which can be 'treated as a prejudice,' but for reasons of which science has just cause to be ashamed, and which finally can be impeached but 'for grounds and arguments' which, if their validity be admitted, would imply the universal and utter falseness of the Intelligence itself as a faculty of knowledge, if such apprehensions are not verified as forms of absolute knowledge, knowledge, we repeat, in no form has or can have place in the human mind. We have, then, real valid knowledge of the four realities under consideration.

SECTION IV.

ORIGIN, GENESIS, AND CHARACTER, OF ALL ACTUAL AND CONCEIVABLE SYSTEMS OF PHILOSOPHY.

THE DIVERSE SYSTEMS DEFINED.

WE are now fully prepared to explain distinctly the origin, genesis, and character, of all actual and conceivable systems of Philosophy, systems which demand the investigation, elucidation, and criticism of the individual who writes a critical History of Philosophy. All such systems have their origin and genesis in, and take definite and fixed forms from, certain *postulates* pertaining to affirmed necessary relations of the human Intelligence, as a faculty of knowledge to these four realities. As the number of these relations is fixed and definite, but a certain fixed and definite number of systems of Philosophy ever have arisen, or can arise. They are the following: 1. It may be postulated that knowledge is possible but in its *objective* form, that is, relatively to 'things without us,' and that it is actual in this exclusive form. This postulate gives us Materialism, the system which affirms matter to be the only existing substance. 2. It may be assumed, on the other hand, that knowledge is possible but in its *subjective* form, that is, relatively to mind, or its operations, and is actual in this form. Hence Idealism, with its varied systems, Idealism which resolves all realities into mind, or its operations. 3. We may, in the next place, deny the validity of knowledge, both in its *objective* and *subjective* forms, affirming all our knowledge to be exclusively phenomenal, mere appearance in which no reality, as it is in itself, appears, and, in the language of Mr. Herbert Spencer, 'that the reality existing behind all appearance is, and ever must be, unknown.' This gives us the hypotheses Scepticism, which denies the possibility of any positive system of knowledge. Of all such systems, Scepticism affirms that each may, or may not, be true, and that by no possibility can we determine which is and which is not true. 4. We may, finally, affirm knowledge to be possible and actual in both forms, and hence include in our theory of existence spirit and matter, and space and time, as knowable and known realities. Here we have the hypotheses of Realism. As these four include all possible systems, and as each is perfectly incompatible with every other, one of these must be true, and all the rest false. The grand problem in philosophy is this, to determine absolutely which, of all these conflicting hypotheses, is true. How can this question be answered? We have the answer, we judge, in the preceding discussions, in which it has been incontestably proven that we have a valid knowledge of all the four realities under consideration, and, consequently, that the Intelligence is, in fact, a faculty of real knowledge, in its objective, subjective, and implied forms. In all these respects the verdict of the universal consciousness is perfectly clear, distinct, and absolute. The self, the not-self, and space and time, as implied by the self and not-self, of all these we are distinctly conscious as objects of real knowledge. Nor is there any distinction in the distinctness or absoluteness of the testimony of consciousness in respect to the existence or character of the self and not-self, or in respect to the reality of space and time as implied by the known facts of matter and spirit. The validity of consciousness is to be admitted or denied universally in respect of all these realities in common. Some special remarks, however, are required in respect to each of the hypotheses before us. We commence with

MATERIALISM.

Materialism, as we have said, affirms the possibility of knowledge in the objective form exclusively, and its actuality in this one exclusive form. As nothing but the known can have place in a system of science, matter as the only substance, and with it Atheism, is the necessary deduction from this hypothesis.

The doctrine of Materialism is set forth in two forms by its various advocates, each having a special hypothesis pertaining to the *mode* of our knowledge of matter: (1) Our knowledge of this substance is affirmed to be *direct* and *immediate*, and therefore of absolute validity; (2) our knowledge of this same substance is affirmed to be *indirect* and *mediate*—that is, through sensation. No other cause, however, it is assumed, but an external, material one can by any possibility account for the existence of sensation. On both hypotheses, therefore, our knowledge of this substance is to be regarded as having absolute validity. Matter being thus assumed to be the only existing substance, and the exclusive principle of all things, certain problems, nearly or quite definite in number and character, present themselves, and that with corresponding solutions of said problems. These problems and solutions, in nearly the same forms, will present themselves among all peoples, and be repeated over and over again in every age, among whom and in which the doctrine itself shall be avowed. The Materialism of the present century has, in no essential particulars, changed the forms, the problems, and the expositions and solutions of the same which, in the earliest eras of philosophy, presented themselves to the Oriental and Grecian mind. The present state of thought and inquiry, however, forces upon the advocates of this hypothesis certain special problems which must be solved, or the hypothesis itself must be abandoned. Let us consider some of these problems.

Necessary Problems which this Hypothesis involves.

1. The general assumption that lies at the basis of this hypothesis is this, that *but one substance or principle of all things does or can exist.* Unless this assumption can be proved to have absoute validity, Materialism must be regarded as nothing but a logical fiction. How can the Materialist verify this assumption as a truth of science? This is the first problem devolved upon him by the exigencies of his system. Has this assumption self-evident validity? No one will pretend that it has. How can its validity be demonstrated as a deductive verity? It is equally undeniable that no grounds or arguments can be adduced to verify it as such a truth. The whole system of Materialism has, undeniably, no other basis than a mere naked, lawless assumption, and can have no more claim to our regard than the empty assumption on which the system rests.

2. The special assumption that lies at the basis of Materialism in both its forms is this, that knowledge is possible but in its external form, and is actual in this form. One of the great problems devolved upon the advocates of this hypothesis is the verification of this assumption. It is, undeniably, not self-evidently true; nor can the remotest degree of antecedent probability be adduced in its favour. Real knowledge in its subjective form is just as conceivably possible, and therefore as antecedently probable, as in this. Equally impossible is it, by any process of logical deduction, to prove it true. Consciousness does, indeed, affirm knowledge to be actual in respect to 'things without us.' Its verdict, on the other hand, is equally absolute in respect to the fact of subjective knowledge. How, then, can this assumption be verified as a truth of science? The thing is undeniably impossible. Yet this assumption must be absolutely verified, or the system based upon it must be regarded as a logical fiction.

3. A third problem is this—to explain, in consistency with the principle of the system, the conscious facts of subjective knowledge just as

they exist in universal mind. If knowledge is possible and actual but in respect to things without us—that is, in its objective form—then the words *subject* and *object*, *I* and *thou*, the *me* and the *not-me*, are words without meaning. If this assumption is valid, no philosopher can distinguish between himself and the beast on which he rides; nor could Mr. Compte, while living, have known himself to have been the author of 'The Positive Philosophy.' Here is the fatal rock that lies in the necessary course of Materialism. Upon that rock the system must fall, or be fallen upon by it. In the one case his system will 'be broken; in the other, it will' be ground to powder.

4. Another problem devolved upon the advocates of Materialism by the exigencies of their system is this—to demonstrate the fact that the fundamental elements of subjective and objective knowledge are perfectly identical in their nature. The fundamental characteristic of the object of subjective knowledge is the personal self exercising the functions of thought, feeling, and voluntary determination. The equally fundamental characteristic of the object of objective knowledge is an impersonal not-self possessed, among others, of the essential qualities of extension and form. Unless the Materialist can demonstrate that these two classes of conscious facts are absolutely identical in their nature, and necessarily imply a corresponding identity in the nature of the subject and object, and that nature an undeniably material one, the system itself stands revealed as a fiction of a crazy Philosophy.

Can the Materialist solve such a problem as this? We have but two scientific criteria by which to judge of the nature of substances through their fundamental phenomena. They are these: Phenomena in their essential characteristics alike are to be referred to the same substances; Phenomena in their equally essential characteristics unlike are to be referred to distinct and separate substances. These are the immutable and exclusive principles of all correct classification and deduction. Now when, and only when, the Materialist will demonstrate the fact that thought, feeling, and willing are identical in nature with extension and form, and that all these in common are and must be the exclusive phenomena of external material substances, then we will agree with him in affirming matter to be the only existing substance.

5. Another fundamental problem forced upon the Materialist by the exigencies of his system is, to verify the logical connection between the fact or facts which he adduces, and the deduction which he draws from these facts. We are conscious, he affirms, of a direct and immediate knowledge of matter as an exterior substance having extension and form. This is his fact. The deductions drawn from this fact are the following: that matter, as possessed of these qualities, really exists; that no substance but matter does exist; and that thought, feeling, and voluntary deter-

mination are material phenomena. We grant the validity of his first deduction; but where is the logical connection between this admitted fact and his second and third deductions? The fact that matter is real does not present the shadow of a reason for the deduction that no other substance does exist, much less that thought, feeling, and willing are material phenomena. But this, undeniably, is all the basis which the Materialist has for his ultimate deductions.

6. The problems above presented are based upon the first hypothesis of Materialism, the hypothesis above stated—to wit, that our knowledge of matter is direct and immediate. The problem devolved upon those who affirm our knowledge of this substance to be indirect and mediate—that is, through sensation—is this, to prove that the cause of sensation must be an external material one. We are conscious of the sensation itself, not of its cause. It is by no means a self-evident truth that the cause of this mental state *must* be either external or material; nor is there in the nature of this state any 'grounds or arguments' for the deduction that this state is the product of such a cause. For aught that appears in the fact itself, this cause may be wholly internal, or may be the resultant of a spiritual cause *ab extra*. No grounds whatever can be vindicated for the materialistic hypothesis in the fact under consideration.

7. The next problem that we notice, as devolved upon the Materialist by the exigencies of his system, is, to meet and invalidate the counter-arguments of Idealism against his theory. Idealists adduce the direct and absolute testimony of consciousness to the fact of subjective knowledge, and to the fundamental difference between phenomena given by internal and external perception. The Materialist cannot deny either of these conscious facts. Where is his ground for the assumption that knowledge is possible and actual only in its external form, and that phenomena, absolutely incompatible in their nature, are to be referred to one and the same substance, and that that substance is an external, material one? Has not the Idealist the same reason, to say the least, to affirm mind, or its operations, to be the only reality, as the Materialist has, or can have, to affirm the same thing of matter? Have we not the same reasons for referring the phenomena of external perception to mind that we can have for referring thought, feeling, and willing to matter? When the Materialist has demonstrated the invalidity of the axiom—things equal to the same things are equal to one another—he may hope to present a satisfactory solution of the problem under consideration.

8. The last problem which meets the materialistic hypothesis, face to face, is the counter-facts and demonstrations of Realism. This theory affirms knowledge, in both its exterior and interior forms, to be actual, and therefore, in itself, possible. The evidence adduced in favour of this affirmation is the direct, immediate, and absolute testimony of universal

consciousness, and the equally absolute incompatibility with each other of the facts of external and internal perception. That such is the nature of the testimony of consciousness, the Materialist cannot deny. How can he invalidate the evidence furnished by this testimony? No dream of false science ever was, or can be, more visionary and baseless than is the hypothesis of Materialism.

IDEALISM—*Doctrine Explained.*

The *general* assumption of Idealism is that knowledge is possible only in its *subjective* form. In connection with this assumption, the system in all its forms assumes also that the object of external perception is not any reality exterior to the mind, but a certain sensitive or ideal state denominated *sensation*. In accounting for sensation, as an effect, two causes are assigned by different idealistic schools. According to one, this cause is wholly subjective. According to the second school, this cause is an unknown and unknowable entity exterior to, and separate from, the subject of the sensation. This last hypothesis gives rise to the system of Ideal Dualism, of which Kant is the leading modern advocate and expounder. According to this school, not one, but two substances exist as the principles of all things—the unknown and unknowable *cause*, and the equally unknown and unknowable *subject* of sensation. This hypothesis is repudiated by all the other idealistic schools, for the reason that it is incompatible with the doctrine of the *unity of science*, a doctrine which it is affirmed must be true, and which immutably demands that there shall be but *one* substance, or principle, of all things.

The Theory of External Perception.

As the doctrine of external perception, as expounded by Kant, has been, in fact and form, adopted by all schools of modern Idealism, we will first of all give a specific exposition of this doctrine. A seemingly exterior object is before us, a mountain for example. As given in the universal consciousness, that object exists exterior to and separate from the mind, and the mind is conscious of it, as an object of direct and immediate perception, or of real knowledge. In this fact, viz. the nature of the testimony of the universal consciousness, all schools agree. According to Idealism, however, no such object, no object of any kind exterior to the mind, exists. What is in reality perceived is an exclusively mental state denominated sensation, a sensitive or ideal state, made to *appear* as an exterior object by laws of thought in the subject itself. Neither the self, nor the not-self, is the reality which we apprehend it to be. Neither has anything more than a phenomenal, or ideal, existence. How is this sensitive or ideal state made to appear as an object exterior to the mind, and as such a specific object? A sensation or its idea is induced, all consideration of its cause being now left out of the account. On occasion of the sensation two ideas arise, those of time and space. Through these ideas, this subject state, the sensation, is made to appear as an external object, and as possessed of this one specific form. The only object perceived, 'the content of the perception,' is the sensation. The reason why the sensation *appears* as having exteriority and form is the ideas of time and space. 'Space and time,' says Kant, 'are the pure forms of them' (objects of external perception), 'sensation in general the matter.'

The necessary deduction from this doctrine is thus given by Kant: 'We have therefore intended to say that all our intuition is nothing but the representation of phenomenon—that the things which we envisage are not that in themselves for which we take them, neither are their relationships so constituted as they appear to us, and that if we do away with our subject, or even only the subjective quality of our senses in general, every quality or relationship of objects in space and time, nay, even time and space themselves, would disappear, and cannot exist as phenomena in themselves, but only in us.' We have here the common doctrine, and the common consequence of the same, as set forth in the systems of Idealism in all their forms. The systems differ but in respect to the *cause* of sensation. In regard to the subsequent developments of thought, they all agree. Certain problems here present themselves, problems which must be satisfactorily solved, or Idealism, in none of its forms, can be true. Certain other problems present themselves which must be solved, or Ideal Dualism must take rank as a system of false science.

Problems Common to Idealism in all its Forms.

Among these common problems, we direct special attention to the following:

1. Space and time appear, in all these systems, in two forms—as realities in themselves, realities exterior to the mind, realities the non-being of which is affirmed to be absolutely inconceivable and impossible—and then as no exterior realities at all, but simply and exclusively as regulative *ideas* in the mind itself. As given in the universal intelligence, 'regulative ideas' are one thing, and space and time quite others. As given in these systems, they are one and identical. Their identity is, undeniably, not self-evident. Can it be established by proof? No philosopher of any school will attempt such a form of demonstration as that. Yet the absolute identity of time and space, with ideas in the mind, must be demonstrated, or Idealism, in all its forms, will, and must stand revealed, as resting upon nothing but one of the most absurd assumptions that was ever introduced into the realm of science.

2. Sensation, in all its forms, is not only a subjective state, but as such, is absolutely void of extension and form. The ideas of time and space

pertain to their objects, not only as exterior realities, but as strictly *infinite* in extent. How can ideas which pertain to their objects, as exterior and infinite, make a purely subjective state which is utterly void, in itself, of all extension and form, *appear* as being not only exterior to the mind, and independent of it, but as possessed of *definite* extension and form, and this in a *finite* degree? If the idea of infinite extension imparts to that which has no extension at all the appearance of extension in any form, should not such a cause impart the appearance of *infinite* extension? As related to extension and form, all sensations possess absolute identity of character, that is, the total absence of these qualities in all degrees. How can the same ideas, acting upon the same identical characteristics, make one sensation appear, as an exterior object, incomparably larger or smaller than another absolutely similar object? Can the same identical cause, operating upon the same identical characteristics, produce results utterly diverse from one another? Idealism must satisfactorily answer all these questions, or take rank as 'science falsely so-called.'

3. No psychological fact can be rendered more demonstrably evident than this, that in the order of origination in the mind, perception external and internal *precedes* the ideas of time and space. Space and time are apprehended but as the *places* of substances and events, as *implied* by the same, and as the immutable *condition* of their existence and occurrence. We perceive body, succession, and events, and, as a consequence, apprehend space, time, and cause as implied by what we perceive. That which is known but as the place of another, and as implied by it, can by no possibility have been originated in the mind prior to the latter, and have given character and form to it. The actual perception of body, succession, and events, must have preceded in the mind the ideas of time and space. No psychological fact can, we repeat, have more demonstrative proof than this. Now in all systems of Idealism in common, the ideas of time and space are affirmed to have existed in the mind prior to perception in any form, and that these ideas determine, as causes, the forms of perception as effects. Here is a fundamental pyschological error on which all these systems must inevitably fall to pieces, unless this fatal rock can be removed, the removal of which is undeniably impossible.

We will now enter upon a direct consideration of the diverse systems of Idealisms, systems all of which, as developed in all ages, take rank in one or the other of the following forms, each of which will be specifically defined and elucidated in the order designated, namely, Ideal Dualism, Subjective Idealism, Pantheism, and Pure Idealism.

IDEAL DUALISM.

The system of Ideal Dualism has been already defined. We will proceed, at once, to consider the special problems in the full solution of which the destiny of the system is involved.

Problems especially pertaining to Ideal Dualism

1. To account for the existence of sensation, two *unknown* and *unknowable* realities, as we have seen, are postulated as real—the *subject* and the *exterior cause*. In the universal intelligence, two *knowable* and *known* substances are given—substances whose action and reaction upon each other readily and intelligibly account for the existence of sensation, namely, the mind which experiences, and the external material cause which induces, the sensation. Why this substitution of these unknowable and unknown realties to account for a known effect, when the same effect can be more readily accounted for by reference to what is given in the universal intelligence as actually knowable and known? Why go outside of the Intelligence to find 'imaginary substrata,' to account for a known effect, when, within the proper sphere of the Intelligence, there exist consciously known causes abundantly adequate to account for the same effect? How can the ideal dualist answer such questions as these?

2. Two unknown and unknowable entities are assumed as real, and assumed to account for a single known effect, sensation. Why assume *two* such realities? As both are unknown, how can it be known that sensation is not the result of principles intrinsic, and acting potentially, in one of them? We have, by hypothesis, a known effect, and an unknown cause of the same. As the cause is wholly unknown, we have no means of determining whether it is one or many, *ab extra* or *ab intra*. Does not Ideal Dualism undeniably rest upon a mere lawless assumption?

3. In the universal intelligence, two realities are given as the conscious objects of direct and immediate and absolute knowledge—the mind as the subject of sensation, and the exterior material cause of the same. Ideal Dualism impeaches the validity of our knowledge of both of these entities. In this impeachment, this system is itself impeached by the absolute testimony of the universal consciousness, on the one hand, and by the equally absolute deductions of Materialism, Idealism proper, and Realism on the other. All these systems unite with the universal consciousness in affirming the validity of our knowledge in one or the other, or both these forms. Nor can Ideal Dualism confront this affirmation with any form or degree of proof, or positive evidence. Our knowledge of these realities is, undeniably, not self-evidently invalid. Nor can any

form of proof be adduced against its validity, proof whose validity is more obvious and absolute than is that of the forms of knowledge which are impeached. This the advocates of the system must do, or it must fall to pieces upon the absolute evidence before us. Nothing, we are quite safe in affirming, can save this system from the doom which awaits it.

IDEALISM PROPER.

While it is assumed, in common with the teachings of Materialism, that but one reality, or principle, of all things does, or can exist, it may be postulated, in opposition to Materialism, that knowledge is possible only in its subjective form, and is actual in this form. It follows, as a necessary deduction from this assumption and postulate, that mind, or its operations, and nothing else, has real being. We have here the system of Idealism, which, by different schools of the same system, is based upon two distinct and opposite assumptions, and under these, assumes two forms. It is assumed, in the first place, that the exclusive condition of the possibility of knowledge is 'a synthesis of being and knowledge in the I,' that is, that the *object* and *subject* of knowledge must be, in substance, one and identical. We give the assumption in the words of its advocates. From this assumption, as a principle, two systems have been deduced—Subjective Idealism and Pantheism proper. We will proceed at once to elucidate these two systems in the order designated, and will then consider Idealism in its final form, and as announced under another assumption.

SUBJECTIVE IDEALISM.

The first system assumes that the only existing reality is the self-conscious subject, the I; and that all apparent realities within and around us are only ideal forms of being and life, forms made real by the I to the I, in its process of necessary self-development. According to this system, all seeming realities, 'the me and the not-me,' the universe of matter and spirit, with God as their Author, are nothing in themselves but pure ideal existences, and as such generated for 'the self' by 'the self,' that is, for and by the I of consciousness. God, as this system teaches, it should be borne in mind, does not create the self-conscious subject, or the external universe; but the I generates these, and God as their ideal Author. Hence, learned professors of this school in the German universities were accustomed to make such announcements as this to their pupils: 'Having completed our genesis of the universe, to-morrow, gentlemen, I will generate God.'

Problems of Subjective Idealism.

The problems forced, by the exigencies of this system, upon its advocates are such as the following:

1. An absolute verification of the general assumption that lies at the basis of Materialism, on the one hand, and of Idealism in all its forms, on the other, the assumption that but *one substance or principle of all things exists*. We have already said all that is required in respect to this assumption. We simply restate here what we have proved before, that this assumption must be absolutely verified as a principle in science, or not only Materialism, but also Idealism in all its forms, must be regarded as systems of false science. But this assumption, as we have already demonstrated, cannot be thus verified, and Idealism, in all its forms, stands revealed as resting upon no scientific basis whatever.

2. The next problem, the solution of which is required of Subjective Idealism, is a similar verification of the particular assumption that lies, with that just referred to, at the basis of Idealism, in all its forms, the assumption that knowledge is possible but in its subjective form, and is actual only in this form. This assumption, as we have shown, has no self-evident validity, and cannot, by any possibility, be verified 'by grounds and arguments' as a truth of science. Yet this impossible end must be absolutely realized, or Idealism, in all its forms, must stand demonstrated as having no other basis but two empty and lawless assumptions, and must fall to pieces upon these fatal rocks.

3. The third problem devolved upon the Subjective Idealist is this: To answer the question, *How* does this sole reality, 'the me' existing nowhere and in no time, time and space being only laws of thought, according to the system—how does this sole reality, we say, first of all originate by itself and for itself the identical thought representations which it actually has of the self and the not-self, the I, the universe, and God? Unless the advocate of the system can show us just *how* the thing is done, and prove to us absolutely, that it was, and must have been, done in that one exclusive form, we can have no evidence whatever that we are not being imposed upon by fictions, instead of facts. Can the Subjective Idealist give the explanation and furnish the demonstration required? Not unless he is omniscient.

4. How does this single 'I,' in the next place, absolutely recognize the self and the not-self, 'the I,' the universe, and God, time and space, as real, distinct, and absolutely separate existences, and thus image to itself a great lie?

5. How does this lying 'I' *then* recognize the self as the only reality, and the not-self, the universe, and God, together with time and space, as mere ideal generations of 'the I myself I'? It is not sufficient for the

advocate of the system to affirm that 'the I' does make these successive summersets. He must render the process itself demonstrably evident to our minds, and equally demonstrate its validity, or we dementate ourselves when we credit his revelations.

6. The advocates of this system must also furnish absolute criteria by which we can determine, with perfect certainty, which of these processes conducts us to real truth. To demand less than this, is to put out our own eyes, and surrender ourselves, as blind dupes, it may be, to philosophic jugglery. Can the advocate of the system furnish the required criteria? Can he solve all the problems forced upon him by the absolute exigencies of his own system? He can no more do it than he can systematize chaos.

Pantheism Proper.

Subjective Idealism affirms the 'I of consciousness' to be the only reality, and deduces from this individual subject 'the me and the not-me,' the universe and God, space and time, as they are represented in thought. Pantheism, the second form of Idealism, assumes the Infinite and Absolute to be alone real, and deduces from this sole reality time and space and all substances represented in thought as existing in time and space. The Infinite, according to the first system, is, by a process of self-development, deduced from the Finite. The Finite, according to the second system, is by a similar process deduced from the Infinite. Each system rests upon the common assumption already refuted, and borrows all its claims from that assumption, viz., that but one substance, or principle of all things, exists. Each system, also, rests upon the particular assumption, which we have also refuted, that knowledge is possible only in the subjective form, and is actual but in this form. Unless both these assumptions are absolutely verified, Idealism, in all its forms, must be ranked among the fictions of false science.

Special Assumptions of Pantheism and Pure Idealism.

There is a special assumption peculiar to Pantheism and Pure Idealism, an assumption which demands special attention in this connection. The special assumption of Idealism is, as we have stated, that knowledge is possible only in its subjective form, and is actual in this form. It is undeniable that the exclusive object of self-consciousness is the personal self, the individual mind as endowed with the functions of thought, feeling, and willing. If but one substance or principle of all things does exist, and we are conscious of the self as a real existence, the necessary deduction would be, that the self only is real. But this destroys the unity of science, as it does, in fact, admit that there may be as many selfs, as there are individual consciousnesses. To the existence of but one actual substance, or principle of all things, the conscious self must be regarded as, and must be, in fact, an attribute of a higher unity, the Infinite and Absolute. How can we know that such an infinite and absolute form of being exists, and constitutes of itself the whole real essence of the universe? Not surely through the consciousness, as it exists in the universal mind. We are, as we have said, as far as subjective knowledge is concerned, conscious only of the individual and personal self. Much less are we conscious of the self as not being a distinct, separate, and individual existence, but a part of the essence of the Absolute, and of the latter as the only real existence. This knowledge, according to the teachings of Pantheism, in all ages, is attained wholly by means of a special faculty of 'intellectual intuition,' a faculty called by the Germans 'intellectual anschauung,' a faculty of which philosophers of special endowments are exclusively possessed. Coleridge calls this faculty 'the philosophic faculty,' and affirms that those only who are endowed with this special scientific insight take rank as philosophers. All but this favoured few are necessitated to rely wholly upon their own native intuitions and necessary deductions from the same. If they would enjoy the results of the higher insight, they must implicitly accept, 'asking no questions for conscience' sake,' the sovereign dicta of the philosophers. 'These original and innate prejudices, which nature herself has implanted in all men, are, to all but the philosopher,' Coleridge adds, 'the first principles of knowledge and the final test truth.' That he may enjoy the functions of the higher insight, 'the philosopher,' he adds, '*compels* himself to treat this faith' (the intuitions of the universal intelligence) 'as nothing but a prejudice, innate, indeed, and connatural, but still a prejudice.' All our intuitive forms of knowledge and belief are *assumed* to be wholly illusory and false. 'This purification of the mind,' says Coleridge, 'is affected by an absolute and scientific scepticism to which the mind *voluntarily* determines itself for the specific purpose of future certainty.' 'This intellectual intuition,' in the language of Mr. Morrell, 'is a kind of higher and spiritual sense, through which we feel the presence of the Infinite both within and around us; moreover, it affords us a species of knowledge which does not involve the relation of subject and object, but enables us to gaze at once by the eye of the mind upon the eternal principle itself from which both proceed, and in which thought and existence are absolutely identical. Before the time when creation began, we may imagine that an infinite mind, an infinite essence, or an infinite thought (for here all these are one), filled the universe of space. This, then, as the self-existent *One*, must be the only absolute reality; all else can be but a developing of the one original and eternal being, and intellectual intuition is the faculty by which we rise to the perception of this, the sole ground and realistic basis of all things.'

'Unless by this spiritual vision we can realize the presence of the Infinite, as the only real and eternal existence, we have not the capacity,' Schelling affirms, 'to take the very first step into the region of the speculative philosophy.'

The above citations and explanations clearly evince the fact that we have rightly apprehended and expounded the real doctrine of Pantheism, together with its method of procedure throughout. The following, as given by these philosophers themselves, is a true statement of the Pantheistic teachings and principles:

1. All our fundamental apprehensions pertaining to spirit, matter, space, time, the universe, and God are intuitive, innate, connatural, irresistible, unchangeable, and irradicable, forms of thought and belief—intuitive convictions which necessarily arise in the mind from principles inhering in the Intelligence itself. On no subject are the teachings of these philosophers more distinct and absolute than on this.

2. It is not on the *professed* authority of intellectual convictions, but upon the avowed authority of a purely acknowledged *assumption*, that these intuitive, necessary, and irradicable convictions are '*treated* as nothing but a prejudice or illusions' in the Pantheistic Philosophy. On this subject its advocates practise no deceptions upon us; they themselves affirm their assumption to have no other basis but a sentiment of will, a sentiment to which 'the mind *voluntarily* determines itself.'

3. The existence and absolute authority in science of this faculty of intuition is also an exclusive *matter of assumption*. It is not professed that the existence and authority of this faculty are intuitive truths, nor are any arguments in proof to that effect adduced. On the other hand, we must *assume* all this, as the immutable condition of 'taking the very first step into the region of the speculative Philosophy.'

4. Another equally absolute assumption of Pantheism is this—that as a principle in science, naked assumptions, mere sentiments of will, have, and should have, higher place and authority than original, irresistible, and irradicable intuitions of the Intelligence. It is upon the openly avowed authority of the former that that of the latter is set aside and 'treated as a prejudice.'

5. If we accept the teachings of Pantheism, we adopt a system which openly ignores and repudiates acknowledged principles and facts of original intuition, and is openly founded upon admitted assumptions and nothing else. We must also denounce as vulgar prejudice all methods in science which have for their basis admitted principles and facts of original intuition, and treat as the only scientific method that which constructs systems upon nothing but mere assumptions. Coleridge admits that Idealism, in all its forms, rests upon nothing but assumptions; but science in every form, he adds, has in fact no other basis. We must assume

something, or we cannot reason at all. This is all true, but not at all in the sense in which he affirms it. True science assumes original intuitions of the *Intelligence* as valid for scientific deduction; false science adopts and treats mere assumptions, or sentiments of will, as having even higher authority than real intuition. And here, undeniably, is the real difference between Materialism, Pantheism, and Idealism in all its forms, and real science.

Necessary Problems of Pantheism.

The necessary problems devolved by the immutable exigencies of this system upon its advocates are such as the following. We must also insist upon a full demonstrative solution of all these problems, provided we would not put out our own eyes, and then give ourselves up to the guidance of self-styled philosophers as totally blind, it may be, as ourselves. But what are the necessary problems under consideration? They are such as the following:

1. After giving absolute demonstration of the validity of the assumption that but one substance or principle of all things does exist, and also of the impossibility of knowledge but in its subjective form, the Pantheist must absolutely demonstrate the existence and supreme authority of this 'faculty of intellectual intuition.' The existence and authority of this faculty are not, as we have seen, intuitive truths; neither can they be admitted, without infinite folly on our part, but as absolutely demonstrated truths. This is what the Pantheist is bound to require of himself, and what we are bound to demand of him, as the immutable condition of admitting the validity of his system. Will he, can he, give us the required demonstration? Because *he* cannot see *how* a certain form of knowledge is possible, must we deny its *actual* existence, when we and all the world are absolutely conscious of its presence in our own minds? This faculty, if it exists, is admitted not to be a faculty of primary, but wholly of secondary, forms of intuitive knowledge. Can the Pantheist give us demonstrative reasons for the assumption that secondary and derivative intuitions, supposing them to exist, should have sovereign authority above and against the primary? Are not the latter the source and test of all valid knowledge? We prudently wait for the required demonstration.

2. Another necessary problem of Pantheism is this—to furnish demonstrative reasons why mere and admitted *assumptions* should have, in science, supreme authority over and against real and admitted original, immutable, and irradicable *intuitions*. Nothing, we judge, but a reckless and lawless assumption can cut this 'Gordian knot.'

3. The Pantheist himself will admit that *all* assumptions do not have, and should not have, this sovereign authority. Before we can, without

stultifying ourselves, admit the sovereign validity and authority of assumptions of any kind, we must require our self-styled philosopher to give us tests of demonstrative validity—tests by which we can infallibly distinguish between assumptions which have this sovereign authority and those which have no authority at all. Will he furnish us with the required criteria?

4. We may, and we shall, if we reason as wise and prudent men, we remark finally, require our philosopher to render demonstrably evident to our minds *why* we should not regard and treat as logical fictions all systems of every kind—systems which manifestly have, and which are admitted and affirmed by their advocates to have, no other basis than mere assumptions. The reason why Philosophy has so often run mad in this crazy world is this—that philosophers, as well as others, have not been rigidly required to give, 'with meekness and fear, a *reason* of the hope that is in them.'

Pure Idealism.

The necessary condition of valid knowledge is stated in another form by another school of Idealists, and is denominated the principle of ABSOLUTE IDENTITY. This condition is thus announced by Schelling and Hegel, the question, as we have stated before, which of the two originated the idea being yet a matter of dispute; the condition, we say, is thus announced by these individuals, and universally adopted by Pure Idealists, to wit: Real knowledge is possible but upon the condition that 'being and knowing shall be one and identical,' that is, that *knowledge itself* and the *object* of knowledge shall be absolutely one and identical. Coleridge announces the same principle in this form, 'a perfect identity between the subject and object, that is, between the self, the intelligence which knows, and the object known.' The system resulting from this principle is that of Pure Idealism. According to the fundamental deductions of this system, no *substances*, material or mental, finite or infinite, exist. Nor are space and time realities in themselves, any more than matter and spirit which we apprehend as existing and acting in space and time. Ideas, knowledge itself, ideas without subjects or objects, ideas alone are real. All else is illusion, creation is nothing but a process of pure thought, and time and space, matter and spirit, have being only as ideas, and God is nothing but the central idea about which others revolve, and from which they take form.

General and Particular Problems of Pure Idealism.

The general problem which the exigencies of this system forces upon its advocates is this, to deduce from this one 'principle of absolute identity' all our apprehensions and experiences just as they are, to assume nothing not real, to admit and explain all that is real, and so to elucidate and explain all of our actual apprehensions and experiences, as to render it demonstrably evident that this one exclusive system is and must be true, and that all others must be false. Until all this is fully accomplished, science absolutely requires us to regard and treat our fundamental world-conceptions and necessary ideas as having real validity for the reality and character of their objects. In their endeavours to accomplish their object, the advocates of this system are necessarily met by particular problems such as the following, problems all of which they must fully and absolutely solve, or stand revealed to the world as the abettors of 'science falsely so-called :'

1. A demonstration of the validity of the principle of absolute identity itself. This principle undeniably is not self-evidently true, nor is there, in the remotest degree, any antecedent probability in its favour, actual knowledge in other forms, and on other conditions, being just as conceivably possible as in this one exclusive form, and on this one exclusive condition. To prove the validity of this principle, they must find a form of thought of the validity of which we are and must be more certain than we are, or can be, of that of our necessary ideas and world-conceptions, a form of thought utterly incompatible with our apprehensions of time and space, mind and matter. Can such a form of thought be found? We apprehend time and space, for example, with the conscious impossibility of conceiving of them as not existing, or as being in any respects different from what we apprehend them to be. Can a form of thought be found to which a greater certainty attaches than this? Our apprehensions of matter and spirit are attended with a conscious certainty of their validity, a conscious certainty which utterly excludes all doubt. Can there be adduced a form of thought which is attended with a conscious certainty more absolute?

2. The second particular problem imposed upon Pure Idealists, by the exigencies of their systems, is this, to show *how* and *why* pure thought, existing as the sole reality, first of all absolutely attaches itself as an *attribute* to a self-conscious personal intelligence who is consciously possessed of other attributes than thought, to wit, feeling and voluntary determination ; how and why it is that it affirms it to be absolutely impossible for itself to exist but as the attribute of a real personal thinker, that all events imply a cause, and all phenomena substance, or real being ; how and why it is that thought then becomes directly and absolutely conscious to itself of exterior material, realities, and thus apprehends, as thus perceived, a scientifically organized universe, created and controlled by an infinite and perfect personal God ; and how and why, finally, thought apprehends this universe as existing in time and space, and attaches to these realities the attributes of absolute and necessary existence.

3. The third particular problem devolved upon pure Idealists by the necessary exigencies of their system is to demonstrate the possibility of the existence of thought itself without a thinker, of phenomena without substance, of events without causes, of the possibility of that which thought affirms to be impossible, the invalidity of necessary ideas for example, and finally the possibility of thought existing and developing itself nowhere and in no time.

4. Another problem is this: to show how and why it is that thought, pure knowledge, after having originated from laws necessarily inhering in itself all the above apprehensions and experiences, finally from laws also inhering in itself, lifts the vail and stands revealed to itself as the sole reality, and by self-compulsion repudiates all its prior apprehensions and experiences as mere 'illusions.'

5. The last problem is to render demonstrably evident to our minds *why* we should regard this last and compulsory form of thought as having exclusive validity, and 'compel ourselves to treat' all our necessary and absolute ideas and world-knowledge as 'nothing but a prejudice.' All the above problems the advocates of this system must fully and satisfactorily solve, or stand convicted before the world as exercising the worthy functions, in the language of Kant, of 'playing tricks upon reason.'

Relations to each other of the Hypotheses of Materialism and Idealism.

Before closing our criticisms upon the two general systems above considered, those of Materialism and Idealism, we deem it important to direct special attention to the relations which, as rival and contradictory systems, they sustain to each other. A careful consideration of these relations will absolutely evince the fact that they are not only contradictory, but mutually destructive systems, and that, as a consequence, neither of them can be true. To set this department of our subject in distinct visibility before the mind, we shall be necessitated to repeat a few statements formerly made. On these hypotheses, then, we remark:

1. That both in common rest primarily upon one and the same assumption, and from it borrow all their claims to validity, an assumption not self-evidently true, which has no antecedent probability in its favour, and which is demonstrably false. We refer, of course, to the assumption that there does, in fact, 'exist but one system or principle of all things.' That this assumption is not of self-evident validity is undeniable, as we have already shown. The existence of two substances, matter and spirit, is just as conceivable, and, therefore, possible in itself, as that of one. The idea that one of them exists renders it in no degree whatever probable even that the other does not exist. It is just as conceivable, and, therefore, possible and probable in itself, that all four of the realities to

which we have so often referred exist together, as that any one of them exists alone.

On the other hand, we have absolute proof, as we have abundantly shown, of the actual co-existence of all these realities, of matter and spirit as the conscious objects of direct, immediate, and intuitive knowledge, and of space and time, as necessarily implied by the conscious objects of direct and immediate external and internal perception. This assumption, therefore, stands revealed as a demonstrated error.

What infinite presumption, also, does the presentation of this assumption, as a principle in science, imply ! Permit us, in the name of science, to ask the disciples and leaders of each of these schools whether they have actually traversed infinite space, and can affirm from personal knowledge that throughout this boundless domain but one single substance exists ? If but one substance does, in fact, exist, none but absolute omniscience has the remotest right to affirm it as a theory of universal being and its laws, and finally impose that theory upon the world as a system of science. Philosophers, those of certain schools especially, need to be reminded that with them, in common with the rest of mankind, knowledge has, and presumption should have, its limits ; and that when, as in each of the cases before us, they construct, upon mere assumptions, proud superstructures of affirmed knowledge systematized, they are, in fact, building up nothing but logical fictions.

2. Each of these hypotheses, we remark, in the next place, rests directly upon a particular assumption identical, in character, with the general one which we have just exposed. Each system assumes and affirms, as we have seen, the one that knowledge is possible and actual but in its exterior, or objective, and the other only in its interior, or subjective, form. Take from both the general, and from each its special and peculiar assumption, and no systems can stand revealed, as being mere and exclusive logical fictions, than is undeniably true of each of the hypotheses under consideration. Knowledge is possible but in respect 'to things without us,' postulates Materialism, and is actual in this exclusive form. Matter, therefore, and that alone, is real. Knowledge is possible, replies Idealism, but upon the exclusive condition of an absolute 'synthesis,' or 'identity' 'of being and knowing,' that is, in its subjective form, and is actual in this form. Mind or thought, therefore, and it alone, is real. One or the other, or both of these hypotheses, must be false. This is undeniable. As each, as compared with the other, is just as conceivably true as the other, neither can lay any claims whatever to intuitive, or necessary, certainty ; nor can one be regarded, as in itself, more probably true than the other. The positive evidence in favour of each, as against the other, is absolutely balanced. We are, undeniably, just as conscious of actual knowledge, in one form, as in the other. The argument of each, as

against the exclusive claims of the other, has, therefore, demonstrative validity. What, then, is the undeniable character of the assumption on which, as a principle, each of these systems immediately rests? It is, undeniably, nothing but a mere assumption, with none whatever of the characteristics of a principle in science, an assumption which is not intuitively true, in favour of which no form, or degree, of even antecedent probability can be adduced, and against the validity of which the most absolute forms of positive proof may be adduced. Now a system can, in no form or degree, be more substantial than the principle on which it is based.

3. Each of these incompatible assumptions has absolute omnipotent power in its assaults upon the other, and is the perfection of *impotence* against the blows of its antagonist. Each presents arguments against the exclusive claims of the other—arguments which the latter can, by no possibility, invalidate, and which must be invalidated, or these claims will stand revealed as demonstrated *abortions*. Neither can present a solitary argument, or form of proof, in its own favour, which the other cannot counterbalance by arguments and forms of proof of the same identical character and force in favour of its own validity. Does one appeal to consciousness, the other can, with equal force, make the same appeal, we being just as absolutely conscious of real knowledge in one form as we are, or can be, in the other. Does one *assume* knowledge to be possible but in one form, the other can *assume*, with the same assurance, and with equal reason, that knowledge is possible but in the opposite form.

4. Each of these assumptions, we remark once more, is confronted by the absolute claims of a third hypothesis, one whose impregnable 'grounds and arguments' are absolutely destructive of the claims of the material assumption, on the one hand, and the ideal, on the other. We refer, of course, to the hypothesis of Realism. While this hypothesis denies the validity of each of these assumptions, in its exclusive form, it affirms its full validity as far as the fact of knowledge in that form is concerned. This affirmation is based upon the equal and absolute testimony of consciousness to the fact and validity of actual knowledge in both its subjective and objective forms. 'In our perceptive consciousness,' says Sir William Hamilton, 'there is revealed, as an ultimate fact, a *self* and a *not-self*, each given as independent, each known only in antithesis to the other. No belief is more *intuitive, universal, immediate*, or *irresistible* than that this antithesis is real and known to be real; no belief is, therefore, more true. If the antithesis be illusive, *self* and *not-self, subject* and *object, I* and *thou* are distinctions without a difference, and consciousness, so far from being 'the internal voice of our Creator,' is shown to be, like Satan, 'a liar from the beginning.' The testimony of consciousness is,

undeniably, just as direct, immediate, and absolute to the existence of matter as an exterior substance distinct and separate from the knowing subject, and as possessed of real extension and form, as it is to our own personal existence, as exercising the functions of thought, feeling, and voluntary determination, and in no case is its testimony more distinctly and absolutely pronounced than it is in each of these. If this faculty is to be regarded as deceiving us, in respect to either of these forms of knowledge, it is to be deemed a lying witness everywhere. What must we think of professed systems of knowledge—systems which take exclusive form, and borrow all their claims, from such shadowy assumptions as these? In the light of impartial science, such systems can take no higher rank than logical fictions. One of the great mysteries of the past is the fact that such baseless and insubstantial forms of thought could, for such long ages, command the regard of great thinkers. Pure Idealism, as we have seen, cannot be true unless the axioms—body implies space, succession, time, events, causes, and things equal to the same things are equal to one another—are false. No axiom is, or can be of more absolute validity than is the affirmation of universal mind, that thought implies a thinker, and the reality of thought the prior existence of a real *faculty* and *object* of knowledge. We *know*, and cannot but know, that this system cannot be true. Yet this system does not rest upon assumptions more obviously invalid, than does Materialism, on the one hand, and Idealism, in its other forms, on the other.

III.—SCEPTICISM.

The Doctrine Defined.

A third position may be postulated in regard to the relations of our intelligence to these realities. It may be assumed that real knowledge, both in its objective and subjective forms, is impossible; that all our perceptions, both external and internal, are illusory, and void of objective validity; that knowledge, in all its forms, is exclusively phenomenal, mere appearance in which no reality appears, or is manifested as it is in itself, and that, consequently, in the language of Mr. Herbert Spencer, 'the reality existing behind all appearance is, and ever must be, unknown,' 'matter and spirit' being, in the language of Mr. Huxley, 'nothing but imaginary substrata to which we refer certain facts of which we are conscious.' Nothing whatever is really, but only *relatively*, known. This relativity, and real non-validity, pertain, not merely to matter and spirit, but equally to time and space, and all necessary ideas and principles. In his 'Logic,' and in his reply to Sir William Hamilton, Mr. Mill formally combats the doctrine that *inconceivability* is an evidence of truth or untruth, that is, that the fact that we cannot conceive a proposition to be false is evidence of its truth, or that we cannot conceive a judgment to be true is evidence of its untruth. We cannot, for example, even conceive that the proposition, things equal to the same things are not equal to one another, is true, or that the proposition, a strait line cannot enclose a space, is false. Inconceivability, even in such cases, Mr. Mill, in fact and form, maintains is no valid evidence of truth or untruth. God, according to this system, is the unknowable and unknown ultimate cause of the facts of an unknown and unknowable universe. 'The religious sentiment,' says Mr. Herbert Spencer, 'must ever continue to occupy itself with a universal causal agent posited as not to be known at all.' This system, which absolutely impeaches the Intelligence itself, and that universally, as a faculty of knowledge, in respect to all realities in common, is called Scepticism. Scepticism proper proposes no positive hypothesis in regard to being, or its laws, but denies absolutely the possibility of any hypothesis, which can be *verified*, as true or false. Of each of the hypotheses of Materialism, Idealism, and Realism, it affirms that it may or may not be true, and that it is absolutely impossible to determine which is, and which is not, true. Such is the Sceptical Philosophy.

Doctrines Common to this and Other Systems.

In common with all other systems, Scepticism admits and affirms that, by a necessary law of the Intelligence, in its intuitive procedure, space and time, matter and spirit, are apprehended as knowable and known realities, and that our apprehensions of them as such realities can by no possibility be changed, modified, or displaced from human thought. Notwithstanding all this, it professes to find full proof that these apprehensions are 'nothing but a prejudice.'

The Grand Problem of this System.

The grand problem devolved, by the exigencies of this system, upon its advocates is an absolute demonstration of the validity of their universal impeachment of the Intelligence as a faculty of knowledge. They must demonstrate the fact that 'mind and matter are nothing but imaginary substrata,' that space and time are no realities in themselves, or that they are not the realities which we necessarily apprehend them to be. In short, they must render it demonstrably evident that, of all realities as they are, we do know, and can know, just nothing at all; or, in the language of an old Grecian Sceptic, that 'we don't know, that we don't know anything at all.' This they must fully accomplish, or stand revealed as acting the sophist before the world.

The Condition on which this Problem can be Solved.

To attain their purpose these men *must adduce some form of knowledge of the validity of which we are, and must be, more absolutely certain than we are of our own personal existence, of that of material substances around us, and of the reality of time and space, a form of knowledge wholly incompatible with the validity of our apprehensions of these realities.* Science demands all this as the immutable condition of admitting the possible validity of the Sceptical hypothesis. Who need to be told that Sceptics can never accomplish the end demanded of them by the exigencies of their system, that they can by no possibility adduce the form of knowledge referred to, that of nothing can we be more certain than we are of our own personal existence, as real beings who actually think, feel, and will, of the reality of matter which is directly and immediately present before us, as possessed of extension and form, and of that of space and time which we *know* as being of necessity the realities which we apprehend them to be ?

The Sceptical Assumption Refuted.

The fundamental assumption of Scepticism, as we have seen, is this: that the human intelligence, from its nature and laws, is a faculty of knowledge relatively to but one reality, to wit, its own utter incapacity to know anything of mind, matter, space, and time, as they are in themselves, if they exist at all, or of any other form of being, if it is real. To this absolute conscious ignorance Mr. Huxley informs us that scientists of his school 'have attained by their wisdom.'

What is the character of this assumption ? It has, undeniably, no self-evident validity. Equally manifest is it that this assumption stands in open opposition to the intuitive convictions of the race, as well as to the direct, immediate, and absolute testimony of universal consciousness. All men, Sceptics among the rest, intuitively and absolutely believe that they *know* mind and matter, space and time, as realities in themselves. Of the presence of such knowledge *now* in the mind, all men are absolutely conscious. To justify himself to himself, and to the world, of whom he professes to know nothing, the Sceptic must, we repeat, give us an absolute demonstration of the validity of his fundamental assumption, a demonstration of the validity of which we are, and must be, more absolutely certain than we are, or can be, of our own existence, and of that of the universe around us, together with that of space and time. This is the least that can be demanded of him. We know absolutely that he can never accomplish such an end as that; that he can never induce the Intelligence to perpetrate upon itself such a *felo de se*.

The Sceptic has no expectation or desire that his hypothesis shall be accepted anywhere but in the sphere of morals and religion. In all other departments of belief and action his inward choice is that men shall think and act as they would were his monstrous absurdities never obtruded into the realm of science. We have already fully exposed the utter emptiness and sophistry of the reasonings by which the validity of this hypothesis is affirmed to have been established. On this point nothing need be added in this connection. Sceptics universally admit that their hypothesis is utterly opposed to the intuitive convictions of the race, and that these convictions 'remain proof against all grounds and arguments' which they can adduce for their subversion. Yet they maintain that on account of their 'grounds and arguments,' which have no power to change, modify, or displace these convictions, we ought, as far, at least, as morals and religion are confirmed, to 'compel ourselves to *treat*' this 'innate and connatural,' this unchangeable and irradicable 'faith, as nothing but a prejudice.' What shall we do? We cannot, if we would—and the Sceptic is here in the same limbo as ourselves—we cannot, if we would, we say, change, modify, or displace the direct, immediate, and absolute consciousness which we have both of the self and of the not-self, and of the necessary existence of time and space. If we attempt to compel ourselves to treat our apprehensions and convictions in regard to them as mere illusions, matter and spirit are immediately before us as the same consciously known entities that they previously were, and we find it just as impossible as ever even to conceive of the non-existence of time and space, any more than we can affirm that it is possible for the same thing at the same moment to exist and not to exist. We choose, therefore, to receive, as truths of science, undeniably intuitive and necessary, convictions of our own and the universal intelligence, rather than 'compel ourselves to treat,' as such, mere assumptions of scientists, assumptions for the validity of which no good reasons whatever can be offered, and no 'grounds or arguments' adduced which do not characterize those who adduce them as sophists who are employing their philosophical talents for no higher end than, in the language of Kant, which we have before cited, 'playing tricks upon reason.'

IV. Realism.

The System Defined.

The last position, which may be taken in regard to the relations of the Intelligence to the four realities under consideration, now claims our attention. It may be postulated, as we have said, that the Intelligence, relatively to all these realities, is a faculty of valid knowledge, and that, as far as their essential characteristics are concerned, they consequently are knowable and known objects.

This system is properly denominated Realism, because it affirms real valid knowledge to be possible and actual in its subjective, objective, and implied forms, and presents for scientific systematization spirit and matter, space and time, as realities in themselves, and as, in all their fundamental characteristics, knowable and known as such realities. In its theory of universal knowledge it professedly gives us a scientifically systematized whole including, as its essential parts, space and time as the real places of substances and events, finite mind with its powers of thought, feeling, and voluntary determination, matter with its directly and intuitively known primary, and its indirectly and relatively known secondary, qualities, the universe material and mental organized and operating throughout in absolute accordance with scientific ideas and principles, and finally an infinite and perfect self-conscious personal God, 'clearly seen by the things that are made' as the Creator and Governor of all conditional existences, and these realities as verified facts and truths of science; in other words, A PHILOSOPHY OF UNIVERSAL EXISTENCE AND ITS LAWS. This system also professedly explains and elucidates the origin and genesis of all the sciences, pure and mixed, and vindicates for them all not only a *relative*, but *absolute* validity.

The General Problem of this System.

The general problem devolved, by the necessary exigencies of this system upon its advocates, is a verification, as a fact and truth of science, of the absolute validity of the general postulate of this system in regard to the *extent* and *limits* of *valid* knowledge. This end being accomplished, all the subsequent deductions of the system follow by logical necessity. The truth of this statement is undeniable, and has, in fact, never been denied. The claims of the deductions of Theism to take rank as truths of science have never been denied, in any age or in any school of Philosophy, but upon one exclusive ground—to wit, a formal impeachment of the validity of human knowledge in some one or all of the specific forms in which that knowledge is impeached in the system of Materialism, Idealism, or Scepticism. Hence the perfect necessity of verifying, as a truth of science, the validity of the postulate under consideration. In accomplishing this result, the following particular problems must be fully solved:

Particular Special Problems of the System.

1. A specific answer to the question, 'What is the necessary, immutable, and exclusive condition of the possibility of valid knowledge in any form? and in what form, and upon what conditions, can the question, What can *we* know? receive a valid answer?' This problem has been already solved.

2. A similar demonstration, which has already been given, of the specific scientific criteria which characterize and distinguish all forms of

valid knowledge, in opposition to all forms of thought which are not valid for the reality and character of their objects, criteria especially which peculiarize and separate *basis* principles from *assumptions* in science, and facts of real knowledge as distinguished from objects of opinion, belief, and conjecture—objects not known to be real, facts which may, and those which cannot, have place as constituent elements in systems of real science.

3. By a rigid application of the above condition and criteria, the human intelligence must be demonstrated to be, relatively to spirit and matter, space and time, a *faculty*, and that they are to it *objects* of real knowledge; that they consequently are realities in themselves, and knowable and known as they are in themselves; that Realism is based exclusively upon principles having necessary validity, and facts of valid knowledge; and that its deductions are the necessary consequents of such principles and facts, and as a system it consequently has the absolute characteristics of 'knowledge systematized.'

4. It must be rendered equally evident that all the sciences, pure and mixed, are fully explicable on the principles of this system, and in their light stand fully revealed and vindicated as the interpreters, not of relative, but real truth.

5. It must be rendered demonstrably evident, we remark finally, that all opposite systems, Materialism, Idealism in all its forms, and Scepticism, are based wholly, not upon principles of science, but upon mere assumptions employed as principles; and that their constituent elements are either a partial induction of facts of valid knowledge, or objects of opinions and beliefs which are subject to continuous changes and modifications, and displacement from human thought; and, consequently, that the deductions of these systems have all the characteristics of errors of false science.

REALISM VERIFIED.

As Materialism, Idealism in its various forms, Scepticism, and Realism embrace all conceivable and possible systems, and one of them must be true, and all the others false, each being utterly incompatible with every other, when all the five problems just named have been fully solved, the entire deductions of Realism will stand revealed as absolutely verified truths of science. Most of the above-designated problems have already been solved, and all others will be in future departments of this Treatise.

As Materialism, Idealism, and Scepticism have also been proven to be systems of false science, we might close the argument here, and assume, as already verified, Realism as 'knowledge systematized.' The importance of the subject, however, demands a special verification of the claims of this system. We shall confine our remarks in this connection to one point exclusively, as the whole issue turns here. We refer to the question already determined—to wit, the validity of our knowledge of the four realities under consideration.

Postulates Common to All Systems.

The postulate strictly common to all these systems is this—that the *human intelligence is, relatively to some realities, a faculty of valid knowledge.* If this postulate is not granted, nothing is or can be given to reason about, and there is no intelligence given to reason about realities if they do exist. Something must be given—universal doubt, if you please—as real, and really known. All agree in, then, and none profess to doubt, the strict validity of the postulate under consideration.

With the same strictness of unanimity all agree that there exist in the mind a great variety and diversity of forms of thought—forms some of which pertain to their objects as verily known realities, while others pertain to their objects not as really known, but as of conceivable or inconceivable, possible or impossible, probable or improbable, or even conjectural realities. All agree, also, in the facts that in the mind there exist *assumptions* in which forms of thought of some of the classes last named, forms not known to be valid, are introduced as principles or facts in the construction of systems of affirmed science. So far, no difference of opinion does or can obtain among *real* thinkers. From these common convictions and admissions it follows by logical necessity that the distinction between systems of real and false science lies here. The former are constituted exclusively of principles, facts, and deductions which exist in the mind as forms of valid knowledge, and which, when clearly apprehended, must be recognized by the universal intelligence as such forms. Systems of false science, on the other hand, are constituted, in whole or in part, of forms of thought not really valid for the reality and character of their objects—that is, of mere assumptions employed as principles—and facts of merely conceivable, possible, probable, or conjectural, and of not *known* reality, or fallacious deductions.

Criteria of Forms of Valid Knowledge as already Stated.

How especially shall we distinguish valid principles from mere assumptions, and facts of real knowledge from those which have nothing but a conceivable, possible, probable, or conjectural reality ? In other words, what are the fixed, immutable, and infallible criteria by which we can certainly distinguish forms of valid, from those of invalid, knowledge ? This is the fundamental question which lies at the threshold of our investigations, and must be validly solved, or we shall advance blindly forward in all our inquiries throughout the whole sphere of thought. We have adduced this as one of the criteria after which we are inquiring, to wit, absolute *fixedness* and *immutability*. Real knowledge, of course, must have these characteristics. When we really and truly *know* an object, our apprehensions of it must have these characteristics, that they cannot be changed, modified, or displaced from human thought. Assumptions and all forms of thought, which have only a conceivable, possible, probable, or conjectural validity, are of course subject to perpetual changes and modifications, and may be displaced from human thought and regard. *Principles* in science and forms of necessary knowledge have this immutable characteristic, that we cannot even *conceive* of their non-validity. Facts of science are objects which may be *conceived* to be real or unreal, but cannot be *apprehended* as unreal, or as being different from what we apprehended them to be.

Our Knowledge of Space and Time Verified.

In view of these self-evident criteria of valid knowledge, Realism affirms, as objects of necessary knowledge, first of all, the reality of space and time, and that they are in themselves such realities as we apprehend them to be. The reason is obvious. We can by no possibility even represent them in thought as not existing, or as being in any respects different from what we apprehended them to be. For these reasons our apprehensions of them cannot in the least form or degree be changed, modified, or displaced from human thought. Compare now these apprehensions with the general assumption which, as a principle, lies at the basis of Materialism on the one hand, and of Idealism on the other, to wit, that but one substance or principle of all things does exist. It is undeniable that the actual existence of two substances is just as conceivable, and therefore as possible in itself, as one. Nor, as we have shown, can any being, but one absolutely omniscient, have any right to affirm that but one substance does, in fact, exist. We have finally absolute, intuitive proof that two distinct and separate substances do exist. Compare once more our apprehensions of space and time with the two particular assumptions that lie at the basis of the Materialistic, and of the Idealistic hypotheses, the one affirming that knowledge is possible and actual but in its objective, and the other, but in its subjective, form. No fact of consciousness is more undeniable than this, that the possibility of knowledge is just as conceivable, and as consciously actual in one form as in the other, and in both forms as in either. What right, then, has either of these assumptions to the place they occupy in these systems, that of a principle in science? No more, we reply, than the assumption that a strait line may enclose a space. In what light must true science regard systems which cannot be true unless those assumptions have absolute validity? As logical fictions, and nothing else. Our apprehensions of time and space, on the other hand, stand revealed as undeniable forms of valid knowledge, and as having, of absolute right, their places in forms of 'knowledge systematized.'

Our Apprehensions of Matter and Spirit Verified.

On the authority of the same criteria, Realism affirms our apprehensions of spirit and matter to be forms of contingent but absolutely valid knowledge. The reason is that while in external and internal perception, we have a direct, immediate, and absolute consciousness of them as actually existing, and as such as distinct and separate realities, the fundamental apprehensions of them which we thus obtain can no more be changed, modified, or displaced from human thought, than can our apprehensions of a circle or a square. While we have many variable and shadowy assumptions, opinions, and conjectures in regard to these substances, our apprehensions of the self as a thinking, feeling, willing, personal existence, and of the not-self as a real exterior substance, having extension and form, never change, and cannot be displaced. Space, time, spirit, and matter, then, are realities in themselves, and as such are knowable and known realities. Our apprehensions of them also have all possible characteristics of forms of valid knowledge, of verities of science, and Realism rests upon no other basis than the rock of truth.

SECTION IV.

MISCELLANEOUS TOPICS AND SUGGESTIONS.

MATERIALISM, IDEALISM, AND SCEPTICISM, ALL CONSTRUCTED THROUGHOUT AFTER ONE AND THE SAME METHOD—BEGGING THE QUESTION.

We have reserved for a separate consideration a very important characteristic of the systems above named, the systems whose claims we have already, it may be thought, sufficiently investigated. There is no more vicious form of scientific and logical error known to the human mind, than that, which goes by the name of begging the question an error which consists, not only in the substitution of assumptions in the place of principles, and the induction of false, instead of real facts, but in the adoption of mere assumptions which are really identical with the conclusion desired to be reached. Here lies the fundamental vice of Materialism, of Idealism in all its forms, and finally of Scepticism. The basis principles of all these systems are assumptions which are identical with their proximate and final deductions, a fact which marks them, all in common, as systems of seductive error. This charge we will now proceed to verify.

The fundamental issue between Realism, and with it Theism, and Materialism, on the one hand, and Idealism on the other, is this: Whether one, and but one substance or principle of all things does exist. Unless this one issue be granted, or verified by proof against Realism, not one step can be taken in the direction of either of the other systems. This issue is openly begged by the assumption, that but one substance and principle of all things do exist, an assumption not even professedly self-evident, and for the verification of which by proof no attempt is made. The validity of the assumption, on the other hand, is taken for granted, and upon it, as an admitted principle, a system is at once reared up. This assumption being granted, every issue with Realism is settled at once, for if but one substance does or can exist, matter and spirit cannot both be real. But who does not perceive that the issue with Realism is begged, and begged by a mere assumption which is identical with the deduction desired? Thus, the first step is taken in exclusive conformity to one of the most vicious principles known to science.

As soon as this first step has been thus taken, a fundamental issue arises between the two rival systems, Materialism, on the one hand, and Idealism on the other. One of these, the previous assumption being granted, must be true, and the other false. How can it be known which is true, and which false? Not by intuition, or by deduction, the claims of each, as against the other, being absolutely balanced. Mr. Huxley is undeniably right when he affirms that 'our knowledge of what we call the material world is, to begin with, at least as certain and definite as that of the spiritual world.' On what basis, then, can an advance be made in the direction of either of these systems? By a naked assumption which begs the issue, and by nothing else. This advance the Materialist makes by the assumption that knowledge is possible but in its exterior form, or in respect to 'things without us,' and is real in this form. This involves, on the principle of identity, the validity of the material hypothesis in all its forms and deductions. This step the Materialist takes, we repeat, not by showing that his hypothesis has self-evident validity, or is a demonstrated truth, nor after he has invalidated the assumption of the Idealist, but by viciously begging the question at issue. Having *assumed* the validity of his principle, he goes on and rears up the whole superstructure of his system.

As against the Materialist, the Idealist begs the question, not on 'grounds or arguments,' but by the naked assumption that knowledge is possible only in its interior form, and is actual in that form. The condition of valid knowledge, he affirms without proof or argument, is 'a synthesis of being and knowing.' This assumption not only begs the question against the Materialist, but involves, on the validity of a series of identical propositions, the whole system of Idealism.

But here two contradictory systems present themselves, Subjective Idealism and Pantheism. Advocates of the former system assume the fact, that we are conscious of 'the me,' and of nothing else. As but one substance does exist, and 'the me' is known, in consciousness, to exist, 'the me' must be the sole existence and principle of all things. This argument, on the authority of the common consciousness, has against the Pantheist absolute validity. We are directly and immediately conscious of 'the me,' and in no sense or form are we thus conscious of the Infinite and Absolute. The Pantheist gets over this difficulty by the naked assumption which undeniably begs the question at issue between him and the Subjective Idealist, the assumption of 'a special faculty of intuition,' a faculty by which the Infinite and Absolute is directly known as the only substance, and 'the me' as a development of that one substance. The Pantheist does not profess that his special faculty has self-evident reality. Nor does he offer any arguments to prove its existence and supreme authority. This is simply assumed, and with it is begged the validity of the whole system of Pantheism. If but one substance does exist, and the Infinite and Absolute, as the substance and principle of all things, is directly and immediately perceived to be that substance, this is identical with all that is in the system.

The two systems just considered admit this in common, that *substance* is real. But here another issue arises. The doctrine of substance is denied, and that upon the authority of the general principle admitted as valid by Materialists and Idealists in common, that but one principle of all things does, or can exist. Knowledge, or thought, is real. This must be admitted. Must not thought, then, be the only reality, the real substance and principle of all things? This issue the Pure Idealist begs, by the assumption that the condition of valid knowledge is this, that 'being and knowing must be one and identical.' This assumption involves, on the principle of identity, the validity of the system of Pure Idealism throughout. All comes under the vicious principle of begging the question.

When the Idealist comes to construct his system in detail, the same method as before is still pursued. The common assumption of the system is, that in external perception, the real object perceived is not without, but within us, and that sensation, as an ideal or sensitive state, is that object. Each system has to account for the existence or origination of the sensation in the one or the other of these forms. To account for the origination of this phenomenon, Kant assumed, or begged, the existence of two unknowable entities, *noumena*, and referred sensation, as an effect, to the action and reaction of these two substances upon each other, as causes

This, according to Fichte, destroyed the unity of science, which demands that there shall be but one substance, or principle, of all things. To account for sensation in the one substance, 'the me,' this philosopher assumed, that is, begged, the existence in 'the me' of two distinct and opposite principles—that of spontaneous self-activity and expansion, and that of certain 'inexplicable limitations.' Of the existence and action of these principles we have, as Fichte admitted, no consciousness. They exist below, and act prior to consciousness, if they exist and act at all. We are conscious only of the result of their mutual action and reaction, that is, of the sensation which they induce. It is undeniable that the existence and action of these principles are simply *begged*, or *assumed*, to meet an exigency of the system—to wit, to account for sensation.

To account for sensation and all other mental operations, the Pantheist assumes, or begs, for his system the existence in the Infinite and Absolute of two similar principles. For a similar purpose, the Pure Idealist begs for his system the existence of similar principles in pure thought. Nothing is proven—all is begged as the exigences of any system require, and always what is begged is identical with the deduction sought to be reached. Fichte begged, as the fundamental condition of the existence of a system of knowledge, scientifically developed, that all the parts must involve each other on the principle of absolute identity. All must conform to the proposition, A is A. In formal conformity to this principle, all the forms of Idealism are developed. All the deductions are, in fact and form, identical with the basis assumption. In other words, none of these systems have any place whatever within the circle of the sciences. The axioms, or principles, of all the real sciences do not imply the existence, or character, of any facts whatever. Those principles imply simply what will, and must, be true, if facts of a given character shall be *found* to exist. Take, as an example, the axiom, 'Things equal to the same things are equal to one another.' This axiom has, in the first place, self-evident validity. In the next place, it determines nothing whatever about the question what things do, or do not exist. This is true of all the principles, or axioms, of all the sciences. What should we think, if all the so-called sciences were constructed upon principles, or assumptions, not of self-evident validity, and which have not been, or cannot be, proven true, but which, on the naked principle of identity, imply all the facts and deductions of which said systems are constructed? We should stultify ourselves, if we should call them systems of real science. We do, in fact and form, stultify ourselves when we locate any of the systems of Materialism, or Idealism, within the circle of real science. We might, with the same propriety, affirm that an individual who has repeated a hundred times in succession the proposition, A is A, has constructed a system of real science as to call any of the systems under consideration a system of science.

All that has been said above has a direct application to the system of Scepticism. Its basis principle, that 'all our knowledge is mere appearance, and that the realities existing behind all appearances, are, and ever must be unknown,' is, as we have already shown, not self-evidently true; nor is it capable of being verified by proof. Yet that assumption is absolutely identical with the final deduction of the system—to wit, that all *positive* systems are foundationless. In other words, Scepticism, in none of its forms, has any other basis than a vicious assumption which begs all questions at issue between it and all other systems. We shall have frequent occasion to recur to the undeniable facts above presented and elucidated, as we enter upon our future expositions and criticisms.

THE PROPER PLACE AND INFLUENCE OF THE DIFFERENT MENTAL FACULTIES IN THE CONSTITUTION OF SYSTEMS OF KNOWLEDGE.

It is self-evident that if we would have systems of science or philosophy —systems which may, with any show of truth, take rank as 'knowledge systematized,' the pure intelligence, unperverted, and not determined in its proper activity by the impulsions of the sensibility, or will, must furnish all the principles, facts, and deductions which constitute the system, and must determine the place and relations of all the facts of the same. Will must have place but in determining attention to principles, facts, and deductions, and finally to the proper place of each fact in the system, and all for the fixed purpose of *knowing* truth as it is. All promptings of desire must be ignored and suppressed but those in which there is a 'cry after *knowledge*,' and 'a lifting up of the voice for *understanding*'—a cry through which '*wisdom* enters into the heart and *knowledge* is pleasant to the soul.' There must be a fixed determination of will that *assumptions*, together with mere opinions and conjectures, shall have no place in the system, and that there shall be absolute integrity in the induction of principles and facts, and in all deductions from the same. Whatever judgments the Intelligence gives forth as self-evidently true, these, and these only, must have place as principles. Whatever the Intelligence, in its integrity, affirms to be real, must be accepted as actual facts. And finally, whatever deductions the Intelligence gives forth as the necessary consequents of such principles and facts must be rigidly accepted as truths of science. Nothing but what the Intelligence gives forth in the form of necessary and intuitive principles, actual facts, and necessary deductions from said principles and facts, must have place in the system. Here, and here only, is real integrity in scientific induction and deduction.

It is equally evident that systems may be constructed in conformity with other and opposite methods—methods in which principles, facts, and deductions shall be wholly, or for the most part, determined by fiats of will, or prompting of desire. A merchant, we will suppose, is about to send a cargo of goods from New York to Liverpool, and wishes to determine the time of their passage. He requires his clerk to give the time, and to give it from the following data: Distance from New York to Halifax, 300 miles; from thence to the coasts of Newfoundland, 200; and from thence to Liverpool, 500 miles. Distance sailed over, each day, 200 miles. The clerk can as readily give the result from these data as from data furnished by the most approved records of facts. He informs his employer, however, that the data assigned do not accord with those furnished by the records referred to. 'No matter,' replies the merchant; 'compel yourself to treat the data furnished by these records as nothing but a prejudice,' 'innate, indeed, and connatural, yet nothing but a prejudice,' and give the deduction from the data which I have furnished. When you have done so, call the latter calculations science, and calculations as commonly made, forms of old superstition. The world would know at once that if the man is serious, he has become demented. The reason is obvious. He has determined his data, and as a consequence his deductions, wholly by his will, and not by his intelligence.

A system of affirmed world-knowledge is before us, a system commended to our regard as 'knowledge systematized.' On examination, we find it to be constructed wholly, not of principles and facts furnished by the Intelligence when acting in its pure integrity, but from will-data—data in which the ultimate deductions are all begged. We find mere naked assumptions substituted for known principles of science, and facts of absolute conscious intuition ignored or forcibly 'treated as nothing but a prejudice,' and facts of false or partial induction introduced just as the exigencies of the system, and not as the absolute dicta of the Intelligence require. What shall we think of such systems? We must regard them as false systems, of course, and repudiate their deductions as we would those secured by the merchant referred to. We must also judge of the framers of these systems as we would of such individual. We must affirm them to be demented, or false to moral integrity, in the sphere of scientific thought and deduction. We must bear in mind that a philosopher may be as really dishonest and criminal in his study and books, as the merchant in his store, or the politician in handling the public treasures. The philosopher may be as dishonest and criminal in imposing upon the public the deductions of false science through deceptive will-data, as the citizen is who imposes upon the community deceptive wares, or counterfeit money. The distinction is so manifest between assumptions and principles, and false and valid inductions of facts, that without moral dishonesty fundamental errors in respect to being and its laws, to the soul and its destiny, to moral principle and ultimate causation are hardly possible. The wide gulf which separates systems of true, from those of false, science has been made sufficiently plain, perhaps, in the above presentations. We will now adduce, in further elucidation of the distinction under consideration, some palpable facts of actual experience in this business of world-making.

Suppose that a so-called philosopher requires his intelligence to construct a system of world-knowledge from the following data: Assumption first, But one substance or principle of all things does exist. Assumption second, Knowledge is possible only in its subjective form, and is actual in that form. Assumption third, Being and knowing are one and identical. Give the necessary deduction from such data; in other words, give us from these data the only possible system of existence, and the implied laws of the same. But one answer can be given, to wit, thought with its inhering laws is real, and nothing else can exist. Our philosopher is reminded of the fact that it is impossible for us to conceive of thought without a thinker, of phenomena without substance, and of events without real causes. He is also reminded of the fact that the possibility of knowledge in its exterior is just as conceivable as in its subjective form, and that we are as absolutely conscious of its actuality in the former, as we are in the latter form. All this is freely granted, replies our philosopher. Yet 'you must compel yourselves to *treat*,' in the construction of your system of knowledge, all such unavoidable and irradicable intuitions and convictions 'as a prejudice, innate, indeed, and connatural, yet nothing but a prejudice.' You must construct your system from the exclusive data furnished. When you have done so, you must call your system the only true science, and repudiate all opposite ones as the creations of old superstition and prejudice. You may then regard yourself as having an honourable place in the realm of 'Divine Philosophy.'

Suppose, on the other hand, that another philosopher requires his intelligence to construct a system from the following data: Assumption first, But one substance or principle of all things does, or can, exist. Assumption second, Knowledge, only in reference to 'things without us,' is possible, and is actual in this form. What, and what alone from such data is to be regarded as real, and what must be the laws of its existence and activity? What especially must thought, feeling, and willing pertain to as phenomena? But one answer can be given. Matter with its inhering laws, and that only, is real, and is the exclusive principle of all things. Mental phenomena are nothing but facts of material development, and all ideas of God, duty, and immortality, are chimeras. Our philosopher is reminded of the fact that his fundamental assumption is not a self-evident truth, and that it has not been, and cannot be, verified by proof. He is also reminded that we are as absolutely conscious of the possibility and reality of knowledge in its subjective, as in its exterior form. 'Granted,' replies our philosopher, 'yet you must compel yourselves to treat,' all forms of subjective knowledge, 'as a prejudice, innate, indeed, and connatural, yet as nothing but a prejudice.' You must construct your theory of being and its laws with rigid conformity to the data given. When you have completed the superstructure, you must compel yourself to regard it as 'knowledge systematized,' and denounce all opposite systems as illusions. You may then regard yourself as a full fledged philosopher.

One more example. A philosopher requires his intelligence to give the true theory of knowledge systematized, and to give the same from the following data: Assumption—All our world-knowledge is of mere relative validity, mere appearance or illusion, and 'the reality existing behind all appearance is, and ever must be, unknown.' What is the necessary deduction from such data? The absolute impossibility of developing any valid system of being and its laws. We remind our philosopher that his assumption has none of the characteristics of a principle in science, and that it cannot be verified as a deductive truth, it being impossible for us to be as absolutely assured of the validity of any deduction from any reasoning process which he may adduce to prove his assumption, as we are of the reality of our personal existence, and of that of 'things without us.' All this is true, our philosopher replies; 'yet you must compel yourselves to treat' all your subjective and objective intuitions 'as nothing but a prejudice, innate, indeed, and connatural, yet nothing but a prejudice.' You must compel yourself to treat, as the sole truth of science, the necessary deduction yielded by the data given.

Suppose now that our philosopher, after having affirmed the absolute validity of the sceptical hypothesis as above given, after having affirmed that 'matter and spirit are but names for an imaginary substrata of groups of natural phenomena,' should then pledge himself to *demonstrate* to and for us 'a *physical* basis for life' in all its forms—should then infer, from such affirmed demonstration, that all mental facts are but forms of material development—'molecular changes in protoplasm, or the matter of life'—that man, in his material and mental structure, is constituted wholly of an organized mass of living protoplasm, which may have been developed out of the dead protoplasm of a dead sheep, "matter"'—that 'as surely as every future grows out of the past and present, so will the physiology of the future extend the realm of *matter* and *law*, until it is co-extensive with knowledge, with feeling, and with action'—that all inquiries pertaining to religion and immortality are as vain as 'lunar politics'—'that matter may be regarded as a property of thought,' and 'thought may be regarded as a property of matter'—and finally, that 'it is certain that we have no knowledge of the nature of either matter or spirit.' When our scientist has carried us through all these labyrinths of contradictory statements, what is he in self-regard, and what is he in the regard of his school of thinkers? A great central light in the high realm of the 'New Philosophy.'

No honest thinker will deny the strict validity of the above statements of the exclusive methods in conformity to which all the systems presented are constructed. What, then, are the fundamental characteristics of all the principles, facts, and deductions which constitute the material and form of said systems? Those principles and facts are all undeniably given and furnished by arbitrary fiats of will. No other rational account can by any possibility be given of the fixed methods of development adopted and immutably adhered to in the construction of these systems, and consequently of the systems themselves. Mere assumptions are substituted for known principles of science and conscious facts; facts of innate, connatural, unavoidable, and irrepressible intuition are ignored, or compulsorily *treated* as creations of prejudice; and a part of real facts are adduced just as the exigencies of the system demand. What, then, are these systems but arbitrary creations of will and desire, instead of structures of systematized knowledge, whose principles, facts, and deductions are furnished and harmonized by the intelligence? We shall find, in our future examinations of actual systems of Philosophy, that will has, in fact, had far more influence and control in the construction of most systems than the intelligence has.

Secret of the Power of Scepticism.

Scepticism, as a mental state, is so opposite to the instinctive desires and conscious wants of universal mind, and as a form of belief is so contradictory to all the intuitive convictions of the race, that it would seem, at first thought, that such a system could never gain influence with any considerable portion of mankind, and especially with any class of world-thinkers. All mankind have a quenchless thirst for knowledge, and the profession of world-thinkers is to furnish food for thought, to put into the hand of the inquirer the lamp of truth, and to furnish the race with 'knowledge systematized.' Scepticism professedly takes from the race 'the key of knowledge' itself, affirming that truth is impenetrably veiled, not only from the unlearned and ignorant, but from the truly 'wise and prudent'—even from those who 'seek for her as silver, and search for her as for hid treasures.' Yet there are two mental states—godless ignorance and learned pedantry—over which this soulless, blind, and self-induced idiotic system, this Philosophy which is adapted but to the vision of 'Chaos and Old Night,' has omnipotent power. When an ignorant mind has, for any cause, acquired an inward prejudice and repellancy against the claims of morality and religion, there is no sentiment so genial to the mental state thus induced as Scepticism—the sentiment of universal doubt—the sentiment which assumes, at once, all moral and religious thought and inquiry to be fruitless and void. So when an individual in whom the organ of self-esteem and self-veneration is largely developed has made observations somewhat extensive in some one or two of the natural sciences, how genial to the sentiment of such a mind is the idea that he now fully comprehends, and is as fully able to expound, the problem of universal being and its laws! Nor is there any highway so straight and so direct to the consciousness of this lofty pre-eminence as that revealed by the dogma of Scepticism. Let an individual simply assume that all knowledge is 'exclusively phenomenal, and that the reality existing behind all appearance is, and ever must be, unknown,' and he has, by a single stroke, sundered 'the Gordian knot'—universal being and its laws—and stands revealed to himself as the wisest of men, self-elevated far above the low realm in which grovelled such low thinkers as Thales, Socrates, Plato, Aristotle, Cicero, Newton, Locke, and La Place—self-elevated to a place as a fixed star among all the world-renowned world-thinkers 'from Protagoras to Kant,' and from Kant to Huxley.

Nor is there any path so straight and direct to, at least, a temporary notoriety. If an individual desires to be known and talked about, he need not set fire to the 'Temple of the Great Goddess Diana,' or discover a new asteroid. Let him, on the other hand, magnify Physiology, and one or two other kindred sciences, and then denounce all moral and religious thought and inquiry as 'Lunar Politics,' affirming that 'matter and law have devoured spirit and spontaneity,' and with these God, duty, and immortality. Let him boldly affirm that, 'as surely as every future grows out of the past and present, so surely will the physiology of the future gradually extend the realm of matter and law until it is co-extensive with knowledge, with feeling, and with action.' Such a man will not fail to be talked about on both sides of the Atlantic. Most, if not all, will inwardly regard him as a kind of moral and intellectual monster, and will instinctively tremble at his terrible temerity. Yet they have an irresistible curiosity for monstrosities, and will go as far to see and hear such a man as they would to see another individual whose small skeleton is covered with five or six hundred pounds of fat.

But this sentiment has, at the present time, not a little influence even among thoughtful minds, both in America and Great Britain. The argument, as far as Theism and Christianity are concerned, is claimed, with much show of truth, to be with Messrs. Mill, Spencer, and their associates. Where lies the secret of the *intellectual* power of Scepticism at the present time? The deductions of the individuals above referred to are to a great extent *ex concesis*. They argue mainly from premises furnished them and admitted as valid by their opponents. It is admitted by leading theologians, and definitely taught in not a few of our leading institutions, that our world-knowledge has, in all fundamental respects, only a relative, and not a real validity; that our necessary and theistic ideas have in them the elements of self-contradiction, and, therefore, do not and cannot represent their objects as they are in themselves. Messrs. Mill and Spencer simply deduce from these conceded principles and facts the conclusions to which said principles and facts undeniably conduct us, and present their deductions to the world as truths of science. As far as their deductions are concerned, these men are undeniably right. If our world-knowledge has not a real, but only a relative validity, where is our basis for any *positive* deductions on any subject? If we do not and cannot know 'the things that are made,' or whether they are or are not created objects at all, what can we know about the ultimate cause of all things? If all our necessary and theistic ideas are, in fact, self-contradictory, we are bound, in logical consistency, to reject them as absurd. If all positive conceptions have these characteristics, we are bound to repudiate the whole of them as invalid or false. When we yield to the Sceptic, or Anti-Theist, these premises, we convict ourselves of logical dishonesty if we deny his deductions. Wherein lies the error of the Sceptic? It lies here: in putting forth these deductions, not as following from the principles and facts under consideration, but in imposing said deductions upon the world as truths of science. The relation of necessary connection between given principles and the conclusion deduced from them is no proof at all that that conclusion is a truth of science. Such proof depends upon the validity of the premises. The strength of Scepticism over thoughtful minds lies in the necessary connection between his deductions and his premises, premises admitted to be correct. The weakness of the system lies in the falseness of its premises. When assaulted here, Scepticism is the perfection of impotency. Here lies the fundamental error of the friends of truth, the conceding to unbelief all the grounds she asks to sustain her deductions.

The Secret of the Power of Systematized Thought, and the only Proper Method of Examining such Systems.

Almost any form of thought, when presented in a *systematized form*, a form in which all the deductions have a fixed logical connection with the premises laid down, and in which all the constituent elements appear as essential parts of a grandly harmonized whole, thought thus systematized, whatever its intrinsic character, is almost certain to have weight and power with multitudes of thinkers; while truth, of the greatest moment in itself, but presented in a confused and fragmentary form, is very likely to be rejected. Many reasons might be assigned for such a fact, reasons not altogether dishonourable to human nature. We naturally delight in systematized order, and in logical consecutiveness of thought. Most of our important forms of belief also are deductive rather than intuitive. Hence it is that when a deduction has a necessary connection with the premises presented, and especially when such deduction constitutes an essential part of a harmoniously systematized form of thought, we naturally accept it as a truth of science, and that without inquiry into the foundation on which said deduction is based. Here lies one of the main secrets of the power of false science in all its forms. It most commonly commends itself to the human mind as a harmoniously systematized whole, all the parts being logically connected together by bands of resistless strength. Any deduction having such connections almost forces belief. If refutation is attempted by an attack upon the deduction itself, or by an endeavour to break its logical connection with the premises on which it rests, we are almost sure of an inglorious defeat. The reason is that we attack error just where its power is often omnipotent. On the other hand, when we descend to a rigid examination of the essential character of the *principles* and *facts* on which the deductions of false science repose, we shall almost invariably find absolute refutation to be the easiest thing imaginable, and shall as readily render the advocates of error ashamed of their own logic.

We have here not only indicated the grand secret of the power of the deductions of false science, but have as clearly suggested the almost exclusive method of correct examination of such systems, and of refuting their seductive deductions. Systematized error should always be primarily examined with *reference to the nature of its basis principles and essential facts*. Here lies the secret, not of its strength, but of its weakness. Nothing can be more imbecile than error when thus assaulted. Nothing has greater strength than many of the most pernicious forms of error when assaulted, as they too commonly are, by direct attacks upon the character of its deductions, their connection especially with the assumed principles and facts on which said deductions are based. Systematized error almost always reposes upon mere assumptions instead of valid scientific principles, or a partial or false induction of facts, or upon both combined. In almost all instances there is a necessary connection between the final deductions and the principles and facts referred to.

When we contemplate the varied systems of Materialism and Idealism, as developed by the great thinkers of the present and past ages, what imposing superstructures rise up before us? What perfection of logic commends itself to our regard, as far as connection between assumed principles and facts, and proximate and remote deductions, are concerned? In such systems there is a scientifically determined place for every part, and every part is in its place. How can such systems be scientifically examined and refuted? By one method almost exclusively, that which we have adopted—to wit, a fundamental examination and exposure of their false *basis principles* and *essential facts*. In very many, and perhaps a majority of, instances refutation of these systems has been attempted in connection with a distinct *admission* of the validity of the assumptions on which, as principles and facts, the deductions of these systems are based, an attempt in which an inglorious defeat is inevitable. Others assault the deductions of these systems while they wholly *ignore* all examination of the assumed principles and facts from which these deductions are drawn—assaults, of course, just as void of consequence as the former. If these systems are based upon valid principles, and a scientific induction of facts, we involve ourselves in the just charge of logical infidelity if we do not grant their entire deductions. A rigid examination of the assumed principles and facts on which these systems are founded, on the other hand, absolutely evinces that they are mere fictions of a crazy philosophy.

THE TRUE PHILOSOPHER AND PEDANT DISTINGUISHED.

Sir Isaac Newton remarked that the real difference between himself and the world around him appeared to him to be mainly of this character. All were standing together upon the shore of an ocean, as yet unfathomed and untraversed. He had gathered a larger number of bright and shining pebbles than the rest, while he was as ignorant as his associates of the chief mysteries of that unfathomed and untraversed ocean that lay out before them. Himself, as well as all around him, was yet but a child in knowledge. Here towers up before us the true philosopher. Such an individual has an omnipresent apprehension of his limited knowledge and liability to error. In the construction of systems of knowledge, he is very cautious and careful in laying down principles and in the induction of facts, and equally so in his deductions from said principles and facts. He never sets forth mere assumptions, opinions, or conjectures, as principles, facts, or deductions in science. If he puts forth any of these, he claims for them no *positive* authority whatever. On the other hand, he characterizes them as mere assumptions, opinions, or conjectures. When he has thoroughly explored any one sphere of thought and inquiry, he is very modest in the expression of opinions in respect to the great truths which lie hid in mines which he has not explored, and never sets up such opinions as truths of science. Hence the deductions of such men have permanent weight with mankind, while their mere opinions, though respected, are never cited as of sovereign authority. Such is the divine character and mission of the true philosopher.

What, then, is the pedant in science as distinguished from the true philosopher? The former having acquainted himself more or less perfectly with the problems of one or more of the sciences, the natural sciences particularly, at once apprehends himself as having attained to a full knowledge of universal being and its laws, particularly in respect to all problems pertaining to matter, spirit, time, space, God, duty, and immortality. His opinions on all these infinite themes are set forth as immutable truths of science. Has he not profoundly studied a dead man's brains? Can he not name every bone in the skeleton of the iguanadon, the magatherion, and the monkey by whom, as he imagines, man was begotten? Has he not looked through our largest telescopes and most powerful microscopes? Can he not tell us how many lenses there are in the eye of the common fly? Is he not consequently possessed of '*all* wisdom and *all* knowledge'? Does he not know that the idea that creation was originated by an infinite and perfect mind is 'the carpenter theory'—that 'it is possible that there is a mode of being as much transcending intelligence and will as these transcend mechanical motion;' that 'the religious sentiment in man must ever continue to occupy itself with a universal causal agent posited as not to be known at all;' that matter alone is real, and that all events, thought, feeling, and voluntary determination included are the results of material organization; that all known events are the results of the counter-agency of two unknown and unknowable entities existing and acting nowhere and in no time, space and time being only laws of thought; that 'the I myself I' alone is real; that the Infinite and Absolute is the exclusive existing substance and principle of all things; that being and thought are absolutely one and identical; that 'vice and crime are normal states of human nature;' that 'the inmates of our prisons and brothels are advancing toward eternal life;' that true science 'places our feet upon the first rung of a ladder which is the reverse of Jacob's, and leads to the antipodes of heaven,' that is, down to the abyss of annihilation; that matter is a form of thought, and that thoughts 'are the expression of molecular changes in the matter of life'— in short, that the same thing can, in the same moment, exist and not exist? One great central form of knowledge such philosophers appear not to have acquired—the undeniable fact that, in the sphere of scientific thought, they themselves are pedants.

When should the Deductions and Opinions of Philosophers have Weight with us?

A very important question here arises—to wit, when should the deductions and opinions of philosophers have weight with us? Their deductions should have weight when, and only when, they are visibly deduced, as necessary consequences, not from assumptions, or partial, or false, inductions of facts, but from necessary principles, and a full and real induction of knowable and known facts. Here thinkers should be held to the strictest account. Their opinions should have weight when, and only when, they lie in the line of known truths, and are rendered undeniably probable by facts already ascertained.

When, on the other hand, a so-called philosopher requires our assent to dogmas based upon mere assumptions, or partial, or false, inductions of facts—when he sets forth mere opinions as truths of science—and especially when he passes beyond his proper sphere of thought and inquiry, and on the basis of a reputation previously acquired, imposes his *opinions* upon the world as deductions of science, such thinkers deserve, and should receive, the reprobation of the universe. If an individual, for example, who has had great experience in respect to certain metals, first judging their weight from sight, and then correcting such judgments by the decision of the scales, should tell us that he believed that a given mass would weigh about so much, his opinion, though not infallible, should have great weight with us. Suppose, now, that a mass of matter is before us, a mass of a kind of which he has no knowledge whatever, and that he should, on the ground of his experience of known substances, obtrude upon us, as truths of science, his opinions about the weight of this object. If we should judge wisely, we should say that the period of his inane pedantry had arrived. So when individuals, on the ground of their attainments in the science of chemistry, physiology, or anatomy, and other kindred sciences, begin to dogmatize about the agency of God in nature, about great problems in the sphere of metaphysics, revelation, or theology, their opinions should have no more weight with us than those of mere children, or savages. If these men, in the true and proper sense of the word, were scientists, they would never dogmatize anywhere, especially in spheres of thought and inquiry which they have never traversed.

Prudential Considerations.

Idealists, Materialists, and Sceptics, all in common, in law, in politics, in history, in all experimental sciences, and, in fact, in all civil and social questions of general and everyday life, religion only excepted, *act* upon the exclusive postulate, that Realism, in all its principles and deductions, is absolutely true, and all opposite principles and deductions are utterly false. The Pure Idealist, for example, while he absolutely denies the existence of all things without the circle of pure thought, is just as anxious for his breakfast, is as indignant at fancied wrongs from non-real beings around, as prompt to appeal to non-real society for the protection of unreal rights, and as anxious about his reputation among men whom he holds not to exist at all, as any Realist in existence. All is practically real, and is treated as such, until we enter the single sphere of religious thought and activity. Why this solitary exception in the whole range of human thought and action? Religious thought and activity is as immutable a demand of our moral and spiritual nature, as is any other that can be designated. Why are the facts, principles, and deductions of Realism, all with this one single exception, regarded and treated as absolute verities? We leave this question for the thoughtful consideration of every prudent and reflective mind.

PLAN OF OUR FUTURE INQUIRIES.

We have now completed our preliminary discussions, all of which will hereafter be found necessary and conducive to our great purpose—an exposition, elucidation, and criticism, of the various systems of Philosophy which have hitherto occupied the attention of the thoughtful portion of our race. In the systems of Oriental Philosophy, we find the *original* types, as well as the *sources*, of all other systems which have since arisen, the sceptical and proper theistic forms excepted. We shall, therefore, first of all, examine these oriental systems in the order of their apparent origination—to wit, the Hindu, the Buddhist, the Chinese, the Persian, and the Egyptian systems. We shall then consider Philosophy, as developed in successive ages, by the Grecian mind. Having presented the varied forms of philosophic thought which prevailed during the early centuries of the Christian era, and through the Middle Ages, we shall devote *special* attention to what is properly denominated Modern Philosophy.

PART I.
THE ORIENTAL PHILOSOPHY.

CHAPTER I.
THE HINDU PHILOSOPHY.

SOURCES OF THIS PHILOSOPHY.

ALL forms of the Hindu Philosophy are professedly drawn from the sacred books of the Hindu people—books denominated 'Vedas,' a Sanscrit form of the word *vidya*, which means *science*, or *law*. The original compilation of these books is attributed by the legends of the Hindus to an individual named Vyasa. The Vedas are distributed into four books: the Rig-Veda, which is constituted of prayers and hymns in verse; Yadjour-Veda, of prayers in prose; the Sama-Veda, of prayers to be chanted; and the Atharvun, of liturgical formulas.

In addition to the Vedas, there are three other works: the Pouranas, comprised in eighteen poetical productions, designed to reveal and elucidate the doctrine of a mythological Theogony and Cosmogony; the Rawayan, which contains a history of the exploits of the gods; and, lastly, Manava-Daharma-Shaster, which contain a collection of the laws of Menu. The special doctrines of the later books of the Hindus are professedly drawn, for the most part, from the Vedas.

The productions last referred to are divided into three classes: the Orthodox, or those fully conformed to the Vedas; the Semi-orthodox, or those conformed in part, and in part not conformed, to the Vedas; and the Heterodox, or those totally opposed to the Vedas. These are all, in fact and form, philosophical systems, and their elucidation falls directly within the proper sphere and aim of the present Treatise. We shall consider them in the order above stated.

SECTION I.

EXPOSITION OF THE GENERAL DOCTRINE OF THE VEDAS.

As preparatory to a distinct understanding of these systems, we would, first of all, direct attention to the general doctrine of the Vedas, from which all these systems, as we have already stated, are professedly derived. The best exposition which we have yet met with of this doctrine is contained in the following extract from a work entitled 'An Epitome of the History of Philosophy,' a work translated from the French by Professor C. S. Henry, D.D., and published by the Harpers in 1842. Our knowledge of the Hindu Philosophy has been derived primarily from this work, secondarily from special treatises on the Hindu religion and Philosophy, and lastly from intelligent missionaries who have spent many years in that country. As all the sources of information to which we have referred perfectly agree in regard to the Hindu systems of Philosophy, the reader may safely rely upon the correctness of the expositions which we shall give of these systems. Let us now attend to the exposition of the general doctrine of the Vedas.

'1. Brahm existed eternally—the first substance—infinite—the pure unity He existed in luminous shadows—shadows, because Brahm was a being indeterminate, in whom nothing distinct had yet appeared; but these shadows were luminous, because being in itself is light. Brahm is represented also as originally plunged in a divine slumber, because the creative energy, as yet inactive, was, as it were, asleep.

'2. When he came out of this slumber, Brahm, the indeterminate being of the neuter gender, became the creative power Brahma, of the masculine gender. Brahm became also the light, determinate intelligence, and pronounced the fruitful word ("I am") which preceded all creation.

'3. There came forth besides, from the bosom of Brahm, the Trimourti: Brahma, the creator; Vishnu, the preserver of forms; and Seeva, the destroyer of forms, who, by this very destruction, causes the return of beings to unity, and their re-entrance into Brahm. But the Trimourti does not develop itself in Brahm until he has produced another principle, Maya, of which it is now necessary to speak.

'4. In Brahm there was originally existent Swada, or the golden womb, the receptacle of all the types of things, when he produced Maya (*matter* or *illusion*), the source of all phenomena, and by means of which individual existences made their appearance. Maya existed at first as a liquid element, the primitive water, which in itself has no particular form. In Maya reside three qualities—goodness, impurity, obscurity.

EXPOSITION OF THE GENERAL DOCTRINE OF THE VEDAS.

'5. From the union of Brahm, which contained the types of all things, with Maya, the principle of individualization, and under the influence of the three qualities, resulted the whole creation. But the universe existed at first in two original productions, which were, so to say, the two great germs of it. These were: Marhabhouta, which is the condensation of all souls, all subtle elements; and Pradjapati, which is the condensation of all the gross elements.

'6. From Pradjapati, combined with Marhabhouta, sprang all the genii, and the human race in particular. Pradjabhouta was thus the primitive man, who, dividing himself into two, produced man and woman.

'7. Human souls are subject, as also the genii themselves, to the universal law of transmigration, which consists in passing successively into bodies more or less perfect, before being finally reunited to the great soul, Atma. The object of religion is to procure more favourable transmigrations, or to abridge the duration of them, or to secure even a complete exemption from them, provided one has followed with perfect fidelity the prescriptions of the Vedas. The reunion of the soul with Atma constitutes its final salvation.

'We observe here, once for all, that the doctrine of transmigration is common to all the philosophical schools of India, of which we are to give an exposition. Each school has for its object to furnish, by its teachings, means of deliverance from the necessity of transmigration.'

GENERAL REFLECTIONS ON THE HINDU DOCTRINE.

1. The reader will bear in mind that the Vedas are received by the Hindu people, not as original productions, but as a compilation of previously existing forms of belief, the name of the compiler being known. Four important questions here arise, to wit: Are these primordial beliefs correctly represented in these books? Were not those beliefs, on the other hand, corrupted by the compiler, and moulded anew in conformity with newly developed ideas? Again, have not the ancient books themselves been interpolated by the Brahmins? Finally, were not these books, as corrupted and interpolated, adopted in their revised forms, and in these forms imposed by the civil authorities upon the people? Caste, which universally prevails, and that as a part of the religion as well as the civil organization, was not a primordial, but wholly a new and forced state of society. Was not the Hindu faith itself similarly reorganized and forced upon the people? When we contemplate Hindu society as it existed prior to its being disorganized by foreign invasion, we find not only its religious, but domestic and civil organization all existing as parts of a perfectly systematized whole. Since the origin of the race, no state of society has been so completely organized throughout, in all departments

of domestic, social, civil, and religious life, as obtained among this one people; nor has any organization ever existed so unlike the primitive condition of mankind. Shall we not suppose that the same ideal, which thus transformed the state throughout, imparted a similar transformation to the pre-existing religious faith? No other hypothesis has the remotest form of probability in its favour.

Events which have recently transpired in India render this hypothesis nearly, or quite, demonstrably evident. There has arisen there a class of men of the highest learning and talents who, by an appeal to historic facts, are confounding the Brahmins, with proof adduced, that the Vedas in their present forms are not only corruptions of the original faith of the people, but of the same books as originally written. These men present the most weighty proof of the fact, that the original faith of this people was a pure Theism which wholly excluded the doctrine of Polytheism, a Theism which includes the idea of a personal God, a creation proper, in opposition to that of origination by emanation, of man as a personal moral agent destined to a retributive immortal existence after death. Such, these men also show, were the teachings of the Vedas, as they originally existed. This important fact we shall have occasion to recur to again, when we come to a consideration of the question, What was, IN FACT, the primitive religious faith of the race? The conclusion to which we have arrived upon this subject is further confirmed by what appears in the Hindu writings themselves. The 'Bhaghavat-Geeta,' one of the poems of Vyasa, the compiler of the Vedas, a poem of which a Latin translation was given by Schlegel, has, in the language of the authors of the epitome referred to above, 'developed the system (of Pantheism) in all its metaphysical strictness, and in its principal moral consequences. Having taken the ground that the Infinite is the sole existence, and consequently the only being that wills and acts, or, rather, seems to act, the author of the "Bhaghavat-Geeta" infers not only the uselessness of works, but their absolute indifference, or the nullity of all distinctions between virtue and vice.' Now, Pantheism is not a primitive form, but one of the latest forms, of human thought. We have no evidence, then, but positive proof to the contrary, that the Vedas contain a correct compilation of the pre-existing religious faith of the Hindu people.

2. In none of these writings is there an attempt to *prove* the existence, or attributes, of Brahm, except what is contained in the idea of Brahm as the sole existence. If there existed out of Brahm, say the Hindu philosophers, realities, manifold, limited, compounded, they must have been produced by Brahm. But the production of them would be impossible, except so far as Brahm possessed in himself the real principle of imperfection, limitation, multiplicity—things which are all repugnant to his very existence. The doctrine of Brahm is simply *assumed*, as a truth

self-affirmed, and with it the assumption that but one substance, or principle of all things, exists. A missionary, returned some time since from India, admitted himself to have been convinced, by means of his intercourse with those learned men, of the truth of the assumption last designated. The doctrine of Brahm, with that of but one substance or principle of all things, is assumed as a self-evident principle of science, and as such, is laid at the basis of the whole superstructure of the Hindu religion. Nothing is proven. All is begged by the fundamental assumptions under consideration.

3. In Hinduism we have a religion determined in all its parts, and systematized, by Philosophy. Hence, in the construction of that religion, there is system throughout. Philosophy not only determines the religion, but itself becomes a fundamental element of the same. It can hardly be said of the learned Hindu, that 'he worships he knows not what.' He not only knows what he worships, but the why also, and that for reasons, not only perfectly satisfactory to himself, but equally so to the people, reasons, also, which impart to the non-worshipper even the highest conceivable sacredness with the masses around him. The apprehension of his, the non-worshipper's, curse is a matter of greater dread than is that of any of the gods whom they worship. The gods, as well as men, are considered subject to his blighting curse, and, at will, he imprecates it upon whom he pleases. He never labours, and never asks a gift, nor expresses thanks for the gifts lavished upon him. When he seats himself in a public place, the people lavish upon him their choicest treasures for no other reason than to avoid his blighting curse.

Those who worship, on the other hand, who make pilgrimages, wash in the Ganges, or do any form of religious service, do it for specified reasons, not only escaping from evils, the averting the wrath or the securing of the favour of the gods, but above all, the procurement of favourable exemption from many transmigrations, that the soul, emancipated from the snares of illusion, may be re-absorbed in Atma.

Nor does the Hindu worship the images before which he bows, but genii imagined to be present in the images. When asked why he prays before the image, the learned Hindu replies by asking another question, to wit, 'Why do you pray into the air? You pray to God as present in the air. We pray to Him as present in the image. Where lies the difference?' We state these facts to indicate the character of the Hindu religion. It is, throughout, a systematized whole, and is fully understood by its learned expounders, the Brahmins. The important bearing of these facts will appear hereafter.

4. The language in which the doctrine of Brahm is set forth in these books, naturally gave rise to the various sects and schools in Philosophy—schools such as that of Pantheism, Pure Idealism, and Materialism, for

example—schools of which we are about to give an account. Brahm originally existed 'in luminous shadows,' a 'being indeterminate.' Is this language to be understood literally, or symbolically? As individuals interpret this language for themselves, such will be their theory of existence and its laws. Some would naturally suppose that the original, undeveloped, and mysterious state of Brahm as a pure spirit, or as pure thought, is symbolically represented by such language. This exposition would give rise to Idealism in its various forms. Such systems, conformed as they are more or less perfectly to the prevailing idea of Brahm as a spiritual essence, and also to the positive teaching of portions of the Vedas, would be regarded as orthodox, or semi-orthodox. Others, giving to this language a more literal construction, would deduce from the same what are designated as heterodox systems. We have here what will be regarded, as we judge, a satisfactory account of the origin of the various conflicting systems, all of which are professed expositions of the Philosophy taught in the writings under consideration.

Philosophers and Religionists of India.

Before proceeding to an elucidation of the Hindu systems of Philosophy, one other topic needs a still further elucidation than we have yet given it—the character and relations of the philosophers and religionists of that country. The common doctrine of all the sacred books of the people is this—man seeks, as the end and sole good of his being, for absolute repose, a state in which all thought, all feeling, all desire, and all activity of every kind for ever cease. This consummation can be reached but by one of two methods—science and religious observances. The former is the most direct, and by far the shortest, method, inasmuch as it brings the mind into immediate association with what is immutable, eternal, and the original source of being. This state of immediate vision, and contemplation, of what cannot change being attained, the mind waits but for death, which is freedom from the illusion of the flesh, when it is at once absorbed in Brahm, or enters into a state of non-being, perfect unconsciousness and inactivity being attained equally in both cases.

According to the universal Hindu faith, also, none but the few who have special powers of thought and insight have any capacity whatever for the method of science. But one method remains for the masses, that of religious observances. Religion does not, like science, free the soul from the necessity of transmigrations, but does diminish their number and continuance, and render present illusions more tolerable than they otherwise would be. The gods also, which these religionists worship, are not uncreated and eternal existences; but, like man, finite and temporary emanations from the sole real existence, Brahm; and though superior to man, yet, with him, subject to the necessity of transmigration. Nor is the worship of the Hindu prompted by the sentiment of love, or adoration, but wholly by that of fear of the curse of the higher genii, the gods on the one hand, and indefinite and protracted transmigrations on the other.

That which elevates, in the regard of the people, the scientist above the rest of the race, and even above the gods, is his supposed relation to the Infinite and Absolute, his consequent freedom from the necessity of transmigration—an evil common to men and the gods—and his nearness to the state of absorption in Brahm, or to non-being, the state which is to all the object of supreme desire. It is this imagined relation which imparts to this man, in popular regard, his fatal curse-power over gods and men.

The Hindu scientist, so intelligent missionaries have informed us, thus illustrates his imagined relations to Brahm, or to non-being: 'You see that vessel turned upside down. The air within is identical with that without the shell, but is confined where it is by that shell. Break the shell, or remove the vessel, and the confined air instantly intermingles with the encircling atmosphere. So I, who am a part of Brahm, or of the source of being, am now separated from Brahm, or non-being, but by one illusion, that of the body. At death this shell is broken, or this last illusion, which now confines me, is dissipated, and absorption, or non-being, instantly follows.' The way is now fully prepared for an elucidation of the varied systems of the Hindu Philosophy—systems which we shall present in the order already indicated.

We begin with the *orthodox systems, or those conformed to the Vedas.*

SECTION II.

THE MIMANSA AND VEDANTA SYSTEMS.

OF this class, two systems have the highest place in Hindu thought—the Mimansa and the Vedanta systems. The specific object of the former, which is attributed to an author of the name of Djaimini, is to give rules for the correct interpretation of the Vedas. This author but indirectly, and that very obscurely, indicates a system of doctrine. A presentation of the subject-matter of his work does not, consequently, fall in with the plan of this Treatise. A single extract from the 'Epitome of Philosophy' may, perhaps, interest the reader. 'In the Mimansa the breath of God is represented as the primary divine emanation, from whence proceed the sounds which produce letters. These sounds—these letters—are, as it were, an ethereal word, or writing, of which beings are the grosser forms. The Mimansa hence concludes that the relation of articulate sounds to ideas is not conventional, but original and necessary, human speech being itself a reproduction of the creative word. Hence the efficacy of invocation and of incantation.'

The Vedanta System.

Who the author of this system was is uncertain. Some have ascribed the work to Vyasa himself, but probably with no good reason. The real author, however, whoever he was, is to be regarded as no common world-thinker. To understand the system we must call to mind two fundamental characteristics of the Hindu faith—that 'the whole end of man' is to attain to a state of absolute quietude—a state in which all consciousness and mental activity for ever and wholly cease, and that the immutable condition of attaining this state *at death*, and thus escaping unhappy transmigrations, is, through pure science, a direct and immediate vision of the Absolute as the sole reality. When the soul has attained this vision, it is at once freed from all disturbing illusions of the outward senses, and of the inward consciousness, of all illusions but one—the bonds of the flesh or of the body. At death, this last illusion wholly disappears, and the emancipated spirit is reabsorbed in Brahm, the only real and absolute being.

This scientific insight, this direct vision of the absolute as the only reality, together with the knowledge that all else is illusion, cannot be attained through the senses, or through the reflective consciousness. Observation, inward reflection, and reasoning pertain only to what is mutable and relative, and can, consequently, never attain to an apprehension of the absolute. On the other hand, there must be a voluntary closing of the senses to all visible objects; a suspension, in every possible form, of all desire, of all reflection, reasoning, and mental activity. The mind must hold itself, on the other hand, in the absolute stillness of pious, unreflective meditation.

When this absolute stillness of unthinking thought has been fully attained, the soul then receives the absolute revelation of science, a revelation comprehended in this one apprehension, '*Brahm alone exists; all else is illusion.*'

The following, as described to us by learned missionaries, is the process by which the philosopher of India induces this inward mental stillness and non-thought, which he designates as 'pious meditation.' He first of all places himself in the condition of the greatest possible solitude, where he is encircled with the fewest possible external objects to attract and distract attention, and where the atmosphere is perfectly still around him. Here, having seated himself upon the ground, he closes his eyes, or fixes them directly upon the end of his nose, suspends all thought and reflection, desire, and inward voluntary activity. Then he closes one nostril, holds his breath as long as possible, and, when he must breathe, exhales and inhales the air with the least possible physical exertion. All within and without is now in a state of perfect stillness. One desire possesses the whole being, a vision of the absolute. Here, as above stated, the great revelation of absolute science opens with perfect distinctness upon the mental vision, to wit: 'Brahm is the sole existence; all beside him is illusion.' These periods of 'pious meditation,' or non-thought, are renewed from time to time, with sufficient frequency to render the great revelation omnipresently real, and of absolute validity to the mind.

According to the 'Bhaghavat-Geeta,' an older work than the 'Vedánta,' when the Yogee, or devotee, gives himself up to this pious, unreflective meditation, he should not absolutely *close* his eyes, but hold them fixed towards the end of his nose, so as to perceive no other object. The mystic of the Middle Ages fixed his eyes, not upon the end of his nose, but upon that of his navel. All the orthodox schools of India agree in this, that absolute suspension of thought and mental activity is the necessary condition of attaining to the revelation of science above designated. 'When the Yogee,' says the 'Geeta,' 'renounces all assistance from the understanding, and remains without the exercise of thought, he is identified with Brahm.'

This omnipresent apprehension of the Absolute is what these philosophers denominate the waking state of man. When he thinks of himself and visible objects around him as realities in themselves, realities distinct from the Absolute, man is then dreaming, and illusions become real to him. When, on the other hand, he apprehends Brahm as the sole reality, and all else as emanations from him, and advancing towards final reabsorption in him, and all individual things as illusory forms of being, then, and then only, is the mind really awake, and apprehends realities as they are.

In his subsequent experience the Yogee is not at all times wholly free from the illusions of sense and inward reflection. They are to him, however, as dream-visions are to man when awake. But he is free, however, from all ignorance and error, and becomes possessed of all knowledge, which consists in knowing Brahm to be the only real existence, and all else to be illusion. To know this is to know everything.

He is also free from all obligation and all possibility of sinning. The ideas of right and wrong are illusions, implying a distinction of kinds in action, whereas all distinctions of every kind disappear in Brahm.

In his direct apprehensions of Brahm as the sole existence, the absolute unity which excludes all distinctions and all change, he becomes perfectly free from all desire, all passion, and all activity. All actions and events, all relations in society, domestic, social, and civil, all good and ill, become absolutely indifferent to him. At death all illusions even disappear, and all thought and activity for ever cease. As the river is lost in the ocean, so is the Yogee lost in Brahm, and never returns to consciousness again.

The following extract from the 'Bhaghavat-Geeta,' one of the most sacred books of India, will fully evince the correctness of the exposition we have given of the Vedanta Philosophy. Two vast armies are about to engage, armies both of which are of the same country and kindred. Friends and countrymen are about to slaughter each other. Arjoon, a brave young warrior, is about engaging in such a conflict. 'Krishna,' so we read in the work referred to, contemplating him influenced by compunction, his eyes overflowing with tears and his breast oppressed with deep affliction, thus addressed him. We cite the passage as adduced in Cousin's introduction to the 'History of Philosophy': 'Truly, Arjoon, your pity is exceedingly ridiculous. Why do you speak of friends and of relations? Why of men? Relations, friends, men, beasts, or stones are all one. A perpetual and eternal energy has created all which you see, and renews it without cessation. What is to-day a man was yesterday a plant, and to-morrow may become a plant once more. The principle of everything is eternal; what value has aught else? Beyond this principle everything is illusion. The fundamental error is, to consider as true that which is only apparent. If you attach any value to appearances you deceive yourself; if you attach it to your actions, you deceive yourself again; for as all is illusion, action itself, when regarded as real, is illusion also. Nothing exists but the eternal principle; being in itself. It follows that it is the supreme of wisdom to let things pass; to do what we are compelled to do, but as if we did it not, and without concerning ourselves about the result, interiorly motionless, with our eyes fixed unceasingly upon the absolute principle which alone exists with a true existence.'

Specific Expositions of the Vedanta System.

1. It has been often and well said by those who have studied the Vedanta system, that in it we have the doctrine of Pantheism in its perfection of physical statement and development. Nothing of any essential importance has ever been added to the doctrine. Nor has any new method of development or deduction been introduced. Schelling, for example, can only be said to have given us a new but hardly a revised edition of the Vedanta. This statement will be fully verified when we come to compare the two systems, the ancient and the modern, together.

2. We referred, in the commencement of our statement of the doctrine of the Vedas, to the question whether the language employed to represent fundamental ideas pertaining to the nature and attributes of Brahm was

to be understood as a literal or symbolical representation. In the 'Geeta' and other sacred books, we have definite statements that this language is wholly symbolical. It is only in this sense that he is represented as a mass of clay of which particular beings and objects are the forms: 'The eternal spider which spins from its own bosom the tissue of creation; an immense fire from which creatures ray forth in myriads of sparks; the ocean of being, on whose surface appear and vanish the waves of existence, the foam of the waves, and the globules of the foam, which appear to be distinct from each other, but which are the ocean itself.'

3. In creation Brahm appears both as active and passive, active because he originates all phenomenal forms or illusions, and passive because he who transforms, and he who is transformed, is one and identical. These transformations become more and more distinct, dissimilar, and unlike one another and their common original, that is, more and more illusory, in exact proportion to their distance from Brahm. Hence the more clear our apprehensions of these forms, and the more perfect our discrimination between them, the more deep is our dream-life, and the more intense its illusions. When, for example, we have obtained a distinct apprehension of any object, when we come to regard it as a reality in itself, and as such distinct from Brahm, on the one hand, and other surrounding objects, on the other, and when we have designated this object by a particular name, then the dream state is perfect, and the illusion complete. When, on the other hand, the soul comes out of the dream and illusory into the waking state, that of pure science, then, in the language of the author from whom we have so frequently quoted, 'all forms, all names, all distinctions vanish, and we no longer perceive anything but substance without distinction, without name, without form, the pure unity where the knowing and the known are identical.'

4. In the Vedanta system, as we have seen, the validity of the doctrine of Brahm is *assumed*, not as a deductive truth, but as one which is *à priori* self-affirmed; that is, as self-evidently true, and thus true in two forms—that Brahm does exist in fact, and that his existence, on the ground of absolute incompatibility, implies, of necessity, the non-being of any finite realities. Here we have two naked, lawless assumptions which have, and can have, no place on *à priori* or *à posteriori* grounds as principles in science, the place which they do occupy in the system before us. Space and time are necessary realities. They are and must be real, whether any other object does, or does not, exist. But space and time do not, of themselves, imply any other reality. Nor have we any *à priori* grounds for affirming that any reality does, or does not, exist in space or time. We cannot look off into infinite space and duration and determine *à priori*, we repeat, what realities do, or do not, exist there. This is self-evident. If God exists, reason and revelation both affirm that His existence can

become known to us but 'by the things which are made.' Actual creation, and nothing else, implies a creator. Until we apprehend the universe as a creation proper, we have no ground for the *à priori* or *à posteriori* deduction that God, or Brahm, the creator of all things, does exist. Nor is the idea that the Infinite does exist in any sense or form incompatible with the idea that the Finite is real also. The idea that the Infinite and Finite exist, as distinct and separate entities, is no more self-contradictory than is the idea that they are one and identical. The question, What realities do exist in time and space? must be regarded simply as a question of fact, to be determined not *à priori*, but by evidence. If matter and finite spirit are consciously revealed as facts of existence, on the one hand, and that of the Infinite and Perfect, on the other, we must accept of all in common, as knowable and known realities, or compel ourselves to treat as illusion the clearest and most absolute principles and laws of inductive and deductive science.

5. As a further condition of fully comprehending the character and foundation of Hindu Pantheism, we need to explain the relations of the philosopher and the rest of his kind to real and assumed truths of science. The masses, in common with the philosophers, can understand a doctrine when stated as a fact, and as clearly understand the proximate and final deductions from that doctrine. The philosopher, on the other hand, comprehends the same doctrine in its systematized connections with its basis principles, fundamental facts, and proximate and final deductions. In these two forms, philosophers and the masses believe in the validity of the Copernican system.

Through the general concurrence of educated minds, deductions of true and false science often, for long periods, command the belief of our race. In these two forms, the Yogees and common people of India hold the doctrine of Pantheism, as expounded in the Vedanta and other schools. The faith of that people, as we have seen, as far as the induction of principles and facts is concerned, rests upon no scientific basis, but upon lawless assumptions.

What rational basis has that faith, as far as the consent of men of science is concerned? What if the people of Christendom, in this nineteenth century, should consent that a class of self-constituted philosophers should retire to places of perfect stillness and solitude, and then, when in a state of pure voluntary, unreflective non-thought, with their eyes closed, or fixed upon the ends of their noses, or the points of their navels, should give forth as truths of absolute science, the apprehensions which might then and there arise in their minds, in regard to metaphysics, the natural and physical sciences, and the mechanism of the universe? Our faith in regard to all such truths would, undeniably, have a basis just as rational as has that of the Hindu in regard to the higher doctrines pertaining to spirit, matter, time, space, God, duty, immortality, and retribution. We shall soon be able to determine whether the faith of the Pantheist, and with him that of the Subjective and Pure Idealist, the Materialist, and Sceptic, have, in fact and truth, any more scientific or rational basis.

6. The moral bearings of the doctrine of Pantheism are presented in their most rigid applications by the Vedanta and other like schools in India. Illusions, or emanations from Brahm, are of two kinds, material and mental, or illusory forms of matter and spirit. Both matter and spirit, as soul and body, are united in man. The former, as a direct emanation from Brahm, is in itself, but not as an emanation, eternal, incorruptible and incapable of sin. The body is the exclusive source and cause of seeming corruption. All its activities, being subject to the law of cause and effect, cannot but be what they are. Moral criminality, therefore, is impossible to man. Forms of phenomena, and acts of men, differ from one another, and one is in itself relatively more perfect than another. Men are divided into three classes: the Yogees, who, by science, know Brahm—those who worship and perform good works—and those whose activities are under the control of the bodily propensities. 'The knower of God becomes God.' Such is the express teaching of the Vedanta. The second class are perfect in a lower sense. 'Good works and ceremonies,' says the 'Geeta,' 'confine the soul, and do not liberate it.' 'The knowledge which realizes that everything is Brahm,' it says again, 'alone liberates the soul. It annuls the effect both of our virtues and vices.' The latter class are debased by ignorance and vice. The soul, however, which, in its essence is identical with Brahm, is, like Brahm, incapable of natural or moral corruption. The Yogee, when expostulated with by the missionary for the beastly vices and gross crimes which he often practises and perpetrates, replies that all these belong to the illusions of the flesh, and do not touch the soul.

Ancient and Modern Pantheism.

It has been said with perfect correctness, as we have before stated, that 'the Vedanta Philosophy is an exhibition of Pantheism in its greatest metaphysical strictness. It has given a complete formula of it. All the systems of Pantheism which have since been imagined have added nothing fundamental. The following considerations and facts will fully verify the above statements. We will consider modern Pantheism as presented and elucidated by its great modern expounder, Schelling. On the relations of the two systems we remark:

1. That the *formulas* in which the doctrine is set forth in the two systems are perfectly identical in meaning, and almost as perfectly so in in their forms. The Hindu formula we have already given—to wit,

'Brahm alone exists; everything else is illusion.' The following is the formula of modern Pantheism, as stated by Schelling :

'The self-existent One must be the only absolute reality; all else can be but a developing of the one original and eternal being.' Again, 'The Absolute, from the first, contains in itself, potentially, all that it afterwards becomes actually by means of its own self-development.' In the modern system, also, God is called, not only the Absolute, but 'the All-One;' the meaning being, that 'the universe is God, and God the universe; or that 'God, developing Himself in various forms, and according to necessary laws, is the only existence.'

Both systems speak of the phenomenal, or illusions, and in the same sense. Illusions, as real developments of, or emanations from Brahm, we are expressly taught in the Vedanta system, are realities. They are illusions when, and only when, they are regarded, not as emanations from Brahm, but as distinct and separate existences in themselves. The same identical distinctions are expressly made in the systems of modern Pantheism.

In both systems, also, Brahm, and 'the All-One,' is each expressly represented as being, prior to creation, undeveloped, and as being developed in creation. The same kind and form of activity and passivity are, in both systems, attributed to God, the developed and that which develops being represented as one and identical. According to the formula of the modern system, 'from the absolute subject, or *natura naturans*, is derived the absolute object, or *natura naturata*.' According to the ancient formula, as we have seen, 'he who transforms is, at the same time, he who is transformed.' The above facts and statements absolutely verify the identity of the ancient and modern systems. This identity is admitted by Coleridge, and is adduced by him as proof of the truth of each.

2. Our second general remark upon these systems is this. Both in common are not only based upon mere assumptions, but upon the same identical assumptions. In neither is the doctrine of Brahm, or 'the All-One,' as the sole real existence, presented as a *deductive* truth, but a first truth, or original and basis-principle in science, a self-evident principle, one whose validity is self-affirmed. The only proof which the Vedantists present of their doctrine is exclusively derived, as we have seen, from what is contained in 'the very idea of Brahm.' In all the axioms in all the sciences, we do not go outside of the axiom itself to find its absolute and necessary validity. From what is intrinsic in the axiom itself its validity is wholly self-affirmed. So the Vedantist begins and ends with the doctrine of Brahm as a self-evident truth, a first principle in science. In the 'Geeta' we find the following paragraph, which explains the method by which the truth of the doctrine of Brahma is discerned : 'One cannot

attain it through the word, through the mind, or through the eye. It is only reached by him who says, "It is! it is!" He perceives it in its essence. Its essence appears when one perceives it as it is.' In other words, this doctrine must be assumed to be true, or it can by no possibility be regarded as true.

The absolute identity of the ancient and modern systems, as far as relates to basis-principles, has already been shown by a passage in which Schelling affirms the immutable condition of entrance into and progress in the Speculative Philosophy is the assumption of the doctrine of 'the All-One' as a first, self-affirmed truth in science. For the sake of distinctness of comparison, we cite the paragraph again. We give it as it appears in Morrell's 'History of Modern Philosophy': 'Unless we can disenthral ourselves from our unreflective habits of thinking—unless we can look through the veil of surrounding phenomena—unless, by this spiritual vision, we can realize the presence of the Infinite as the only real and eternal existence, we have not the capacity,' said Schelling, 'to take the very first step into the region of Speculative Philosophy.' In other words, unless you can begin with the assumption 'It is! it is!' your *entrance* even into the Speculative Philosophy is for ever barred; indeed, capacity for philosophic thought, 'the intellectual intuition,' is wholly wanting in you.

By the express confession and showing of all Pantheists of ancient and modern schools, their system has no other basis whatever but a mere assumption, and stands revealed as nothing but a logical fiction, unless it can be shown that the doctrine of Brahm or 'the All-One,' as 'the only real and eternal existence,' has absolute self-evident validity. Who will pretend that this doctrine has this form of validity? Is it a truth self-evident that no real finite objects do exist? Have we not just as much ground for the assumption which is taken by the Materialist, on the one hand, and the Subjective Idealist, on the other, that the finite alone is real, as we have for the assumption that Brahm, or 'the All-One,' is the sole reality? Is it to be assumed, as a self-evident truth, that matter, finite, spirit, space, time, and God as the Infinite and Perfect, do not all exist together as each a reality in itself? Where is the *à priori* ground for the determination of the question, What realities do and do not exist in time and space? We affirm, without fear of rational contradiction, that no such grounds do exist, and that that is a fictitious Philosophy which has, as Pantheism in all its forms has, no other basis than *à priori* assumption.

3. Both systems, also, are developed throughout in absolute conformity to the same identical *method*. The method of construction and development strictly common to each is exclusively *à priori*. All induction of facts of external and internal perception is ignored and repudiated.

Thought is sent off into infinite space and eternal duration to determine, by exclusive *à priori* insight, what realities exist in the one, and what events are passing in the other.

The Yogee, as preparatory to the enjoyment of this divine insight, in the language of the 'Bhaghavat-Geeta,' 'renounces all assistance from the understanding, and remains without the exercise of thought'—'keeps his head, his neck, and body steady without motion, keeps his eyes fixed on the end of his nose, and looks at no other place around.' In this state of utter non-thought, as we have seen, the absolute revelation of science is received—the revelation in which the problem of universal being and its laws is fully solved.

Let us now compare the above with the method of the modern Transcendental Philosophy, and discern, if we can, the real difference between this and that above presented. Before the mind does, or can, according to the express teachings of Coleridge, enter the sphere of philosophic thought, it must, as we have seen, *voluntarily* repudiate as utterly illusive and invalid all previously existing forms of world-knowledge, and compel itself to treat that knowledge, though 'innate and connatural,' 'as nothing but a prejudice.' 'This purification of the mind,' he says, 'is effected by an absolute and scientific scepticism, to which the mind voluntarily determines itself for the specific purpose of future certainty.' Such is the avowed method of all philosophers of the Idealistic school in all the world. 'I put myself, when I begin to philosophize,' says Krug, one of the great expounders of the modern system, 'into a state of not knowing, since I am to produce in me for the first time a knowledge.' 'I accordingly regard all my previous knowledge as uncertain, and strive after a higher knowledge, that shall be certain, or be made so.' In this state of 'not knowing,' which is undeniably identical with the Yogee's non-thought, our modern philosopher receives his revelation of 'absolute science.' Whether the latter, like the former, does, while waiting for this revelation, remain in the same physical stillness, with 'his eyes fixed upon the end of his nose,' we are not informed. The *mental* state, however, and this only, is material, the mental state is in both cases absolutely the same, and the one as perfectly adapted to receive the revelation as the other.

It is a remarkable fact also that, according to the express teachings of the two systems, 'the absolute revelation of science' is received, after the voluntary non-thought conditions have been fulfilled, by and through the same 'faculty of intellectual intuition'—a faculty conferred by nature upon the philosopher, and denied to the rest of mankind. The sacred books to which we have referred assign this as the specific reason why the Yogee can, and the rest of the race cannot, attain the desired consummation by science—that the *faculty* through which he received that absolute revelation is possessed by none but him. So Coleridge and Schelling speak of the special 'philosophical talent,' and of the special 'faculty of intellectual intuition,' and speak of this faculty as possessed only by the philosopher. The forms of world-knowledge common to all the race, we are told, 'are to all but the philosopher the first principles of knowledge, and the final tests of truth.' The philosopher, and he only, has the faculty which pierces the veil of the phenomenal, and beholds 'the All-One' face to face. Hence his philosophy, because it pertains to the realities which transcend the powers of thought common to the race, is called 'the Transcendental Philosophy.'

4. An identity equally absolute pertains, not only to the necessary moral consequents of the two systems, but equally to the express moral *teachings* of the same. If Brahm, or the All-One, is the sole existence, and if the universe with all its facts, causes, and seeming acts of creatures, is but God in a state of development, as both systems absolutely affirm, to say that real moral evil exists is to affirm that the Infinite and Absolute is a sinner. This necessary consequence of the system, both the Hindu and the modern Pantheist clearly perceive, and consequently, in fact and form, deny the possibility of moral evil. This, as we have already shown, and might show by numberless other references, is expressly taught in the Hindu books to which we have referred. "Vice and crime,' we are expressly taught in the modern system, 'are normal states of human nature.' 'Holding as they do but one essence of all things, and that essence God,' says a leading modern pantheist, and none deny his statements, 'Pantheism must deny the existence of essential evil.' Again, 'Sin is not a wilful transgression of righteous moral law, but the difficulty and obstruction which Infinite meets with in entering into the finite.'

The above considerations and facts fully evince the absolute identity, in all fundamental particulars, of Hindu and modern Pantheism. The latter has in reality added nothing to, and taken nothing from, the former. The researches of more than twenty centuries have added nothing to the claims, or the evidence, of the validity of the system. 'All remain as they were from the beginning.'

THE FIXED METHOD OF PANTHEISM AS SEEN IN THE LIGHT OF THE IMMUTABLE PRINCIPLES OF TRUE SCIENCE.

A moment's reflection will convince every thinking mind that no process of induction and deduction can be at a farther remove from all the principles known to true science than is the fixed and immutable method of the Pantheistic and Transcendental Philosophy. True science begins universally with facts of real knowledge, with necessary principles implied by such facts, and then with rigid integrity deduces the conclusions necessarily yielded by such principles and facts. Suppose now that in all our universities, colleges, and schools, all the ordinary sciences, pure and mixed, were interpreted and taught throughout in conformity with such a method as this. The professor, or teacher, should first of all, in conformity with the method of the yogee, 'renounce all assistance from the understanding and remain without the exercise of thought,' or with the modern Rationalist, 'put himself into a state of not knowing,' 'and regard all previous knowledge as uncertain,' and then from pure *à priori* insight interpret for the pupil all problems in the mathematics, the natural sciences, physiology, and astronomy. Would not the world justly affirm that our institutions had run mad? Your child is sick with a perilous disease. The physician you call in seats himself by its side, and having 'voluntarily determined himself "to" an absolute scientific scepticism' in regard to all existing forms of medical knowledge, 'with his eyes fixed upon the end of his nose,' or directed nowhere, by 'pure intellectual intuition,' he determines the nature and state of the disease of his patient, and the remedy to be applied. If you are a man of the world, you will kick the fool out of your house. If you are a Christian, you will kindly, but firmly, tell him to take up his legs and walk home. Yet in avowed and exclusive conformity to this identical method, the Pantheist of all ages, and the Rationalist of all schools, interprets for us the problem of universal being and its laws; the great problems, we repeat, in regard to matter, spirit, time, space, God, duty, and immortality. Shall we 'compel ourselves to regard' and treat them as the 'lights of the world'?

'I had a vision in my sleep' some time since—a vision which impressively illustrates the state into which the Pantheist, at the beginning, voluntarily places himself relatively to the great being-problem which he attempts to solve. I had heard the sentiment quite frequently expressed that in eternity, as well as here, the soul would make its own heaven or hell. My thoughts upon the subject entered into my night vision, and took definite form there. My soul had left the body, and in company with an unknown spirit, was passing through empty space. We seemed to touch nothing, and were yet in motion. There was merely light sufficient to render emptiness visible. At length we stopped, when my companion said to me, 'Now, sir, you must, right here, make your own heaven,' and instantly passed from sight. Standing for a moment in this void, I sent forth a cry, 'Will not *some* being communicate with me here?' Not even an echo replying, the silence became more audible and emptiness more vacant than before. Again I cried, with the same result as before, 'Will not some being communicate with me here?' With a lamentable cry, I exclaimed a third time, 'Will not some being communicate with me here?' Finding that if I had a heaven at all, I must make it myself, and not finding 'things without me,' with which to construct anything, thought turned inward to discover what materials existed there. Here I found nothing but 'imaginary substrata.' I accordingly determined to try my hand at making poetry. Not having been born a poet, and never having apprenticed myself to the trade of verse-making, and having nothing but the poorest conceivable materials to work upon, I found my heaven taking on the rudest and most miserable form imaginable. In short, I found myself in the most ridiculous limbo that mind ever fell into, even in dreamland. When I awoke my mind returned with fresh interest to the old idea that 'God hath builded for them a city,' and that in that city 'the smile of the Lord is the feast of the soul.' I have ever since had the impression, also, that in that mental limbo I was in as favourable a state to make, for myself, my own proper heaven as the Pantheist, or Transcendental Philosopher, is after he has perfected his 'state of not-knowing when he begins to philosophize,' to rear up the superstructure of universal being and its laws. We appeal to the common-sense, and to the scientific insight, of the world, whether the cases are not perfectly parallel, and whether it would not be as wise for us to agree to accept, for our eternity, the heaven which the philosopher can construct out of absolute emptiness, as it would be for us to accept of his solutions, by such a method, of the great problems under consideration?

CONDITIONS ON WHICH THE RACE CAN ENJOY THE BENEFITS OF 'THE REVELATION OF ABSOLUTE SCIENCE.'

It is not, as we have seen, by induction and deduction that even the Yogee and Transcendental Philosopher receive and enjoy the benefits of 'the revelation of absolute science.' It is, as they affirm, exclusively through *à priori* insight, by means of the special 'faculty of intellectual intuition' which they do, and the world does not, possess. Neither they nor we can, by appeals to facts of world-knowledge, verify that revelation, nor can we, who want the special faculty, attain to said revelation by intuition. If we would enjoy the benefits of this revelation, we must renounce 'the light of the world,' and the apostles and prophets, and all the revelations of our own faculties, and receive as absolute truth the reported dicta of the special faculty of the Yogee and the Transcendental Philosopher. We must renounce all confidence in revelation and our own intelligence, and assume the scientific insight of the Yogee, and Schelling, and Spencer, and Emerson, to be absolutely infallible. We challenge the world to disprove the validity of these statements. We have dwelt thus long upon this one department of the Hindu Philosophy, on account of the fundamental bearings of our present remarks and deductions upon our future inquiries.

SECTION III.

THE SEMI-ORTHODOX SYSTEMS.

THE SANKHYA OF KAPILA.

THE object of this system, like all others of India, is to induce by science absolute mental quietude here, and real non-being hereafter. The Sankhya is divided into two parts, the metaphysical and logical. What we shall say upon the latter topic is reserved for a separate section in which we shall speak particularly of the Hindu Logic.

To understand the metaphysics of the Sankhya, we must recur to the teachings of the Vedanta system. According to its teachings, it will be recollected, Brahm, the only real existence, has being in two states, the undeveloped, or original, and the developed, which equals nature. Nature, as Brahm developed, is real, and is illusory but when regarded as constituted of real individual and separate existences. Brahm, as nature, appears in two distinct and opposite forms, matter and spirit. These, as apprehended by us, are wholly phenomenal forms; the reality existing behind all appearance and constituting its form and substance is Brahm.

Kapila, in the Sankhya, denies absolutely the being of Brahm as the sole existence and principle of all things. For the non-being of Brahm, as the author and principle of nature, Kapila presents the following affirmed demonstration: 'The act of creation implies a pre-existing desire to create. But desire implies want, or imperfection, which is incompatible with the idea of Brahm as infinite. Being infinite and perfect, he could not desire to create, and therefore could not do it. Having the desire, he could not, being thus finite and imperfect, create at all.'

Behind the phenomenal, Kapila, consequently, postulates two eternally existing, but wholly undefined and undeterminable entities, which constitute the sum of being, and the principle and cause of phenomena, to wit: Prakiti, as matter primordial and indeterminate, and Atma, as the ethereal spirit, which, as it is in itself, is unknowable and unknown. From the action and reaction of these two unknown and unknowable entities upon each other, the Prakiti being the active and the Atma the passive principle, results the phenomenal universe. Phenomena are real as emanations from the Prakiti and Atma. They are illusory when considered as manifestations of real, distinct, and separate existences. When the soul thinks of itself, as Prakiti and Atma developed, it thinks of itself as it is. When it thinks of itself as a distinct, separate, individual existence, and of nature around as constituted of real distinct forms of being, then all is illusion. The phenomenal universe is constituted of three orders of existences—that above, which is inhabited by beings superior to man, and among whom virtue prevails ; that below, which is inhabited by beings inferior to man, the world of obscurity and illusion ; and the human world, where passion predominates, and misery is the result. In man, as a phenomenal existence, distinct, opposite, and contradictory qualities exist in conflict, qualities eight in number, as virtue, knowledge, impassibility, power, which are of the nature of goodness ; and sin, error, incontinence, and weakness, which are of the nature of darkness. The intermingling of these qualities induces passion and misery, the present condition of man. What man desires is salvation, which is absolute quietude here and non-being hereafter. These two states the Yogee attains by science. The former is impossible to the mass of men here, and the latter but through indefinite transmigrations hereafter. Salvation is attained by the Yogee through the revelation of absolute science, the revelation in which he recognizes his own and all other seeming individual existences as illusions, illusions from which, at death, he is to be for ever freed, all thought, all consciousness, being then 'swallowed up and lost in the wide womb of uncreated night.'

The preliminary process preparatory to the reception of this revelation is the same with the disciple of Kapila as with the Vedantist, to wit : a voluntary suspension of all thought, desire, and activity, with the body in a sitting posture, the neck, the head, and all other members in a state of perfect stillness, and the eyes closed, or fixed upon the end of the nose. In this state the absolute enfranchisement of absolute science is received. The manner and form in which this enfranchisement is received is thus given in the work from which we have so frequently quoted before : 'Salvation is the being set free from the bonds in which nature has enveloped the soul.'

The soul becomes free from these bonds by recognizing that they are nothing but phenomena, or appearances.

Thus it begins by recognizing that the gross elements are something purely phenomenal. This done, it is freed from the illusions of the body; nevertheless, it is still enchained within the subtle (incorporeal) person through which its individuality is maintained.

But next it recognizes successively that the principles which enter into the composition of the incorporeal person are nothing but illusions.

In the first place, it perceives that the organs of sensation and of action, and the five subtile particles, that is to say, that which constitutes the organism of individuality, are nothing real.

But it is still implicated in self, in consciousness, which is the internal form of individuality. From this it is in like manner enfranchised.

There remains no longer anything but the root of individuality, the

Intelligence, which, as a particular form of matter or Prakiti, is still something determinate. But yet, inasmuch as it is still a form, it is also to be conceived as something phenomenal.

Disengaged thus at last from all which produced the subtile person, the soul is set free from all the bonds of nature. Thus, by the study of the principles of all things, science conducts to this definite, incontrovertible sole truth: *Neither do I exist, nor anything which pertains to myself. All individual existence is a dream.* Such is the enfranchisement of 'truth.'

When the Yogee has fully comprehended the fact that he is encompassed with nothing but illusions, and has nothing real to concern himself about, then a state of perfect quietude arises, a state of absolute indifference to whatever may seemingly, but not really occur, and waits for final absorption in the Prakiti.

The moral teachings of the 'Sankhya' are in perfect accordance with its essential principles, virtue being nothing but a development of the Intelligence, and all actions being alike void of moral character.

The Sankhya system, as we have seen, is a dualism, admitting of two principles, the material, Prakiti, and the spiritual, Atma, or the soul. As a dualism, this system differs in certain particulars from all other similar systems. In other systems the soul is active and matter passive; the soul a unity and matter the multiple. In other systems, also, there is a recognition of God in some form. The reverse of all this obtains in the teachings of this system. According to it, all emanations are from the material principle, which is one and not many. Souls, on the other hand, are many. In the final consummation, all emanations are absorbed in the Prakiti, and souls will form a universe of atoms where no original unity is found. In this system, also, the idea of God wholly disappears, and is not recognized even as a regulative principle.

The Sankhya and Vedanta Systems Compared.

While there is in the development of the former system more of the appearance of induction than in that of the latter, the method of both in common is, in all essential particulars, *à priori.* From what is intrinsic in the *idea* of Brahm, the latter system professedly demonstrates his existence as the sole principle and substance of all things. From what is intrinsic in the same idea, the former system argues, with affirmed self-evident truthfulness, the absolute non-being of Brahm as such principle and substance. While the latter system, without proof or argument, assumes Brahm to be the source of all emanations, the latter, in the same form, assumes the Prakiti to be that source. In a state of voluntary non-thought, and through exclusive *à priori* intuition, the Vedantist receives the enfranchising revelation of absolute science—to wit, 'Brahm alone exists; everything else is illusion.' In the same state, and by means of the same identical insight, the disciple of Kapila receives the equally absolute opposite revelation—to wit, 'Neither do I exist, nor anything which pertains to myself. All individual existence (even that of Brahm) is a dream.' Without proof or argument, the latter system assumes the existence of but one substance or principle of all things. In the former there is a similar assumption, that two substances or principles do exist. In justice to Kapila, we should state that he has a formal argument to prove the reality not of the human soul, but of the uncreated spiritual existence. All emanations from the Prakiti, he assumes, are manifestly for the use of some foreign being, who can be no other than a soul, a knowing principle. The soul, therefore, as distinct from phenomena on the one hand, and the material principle on the other, does exist. This argument rests upon the assumption, that the material principle, without intelligence or design, and from laws inhering in itself, acts in the production of emanation in absolute conformity to the wants of a foreign reality possessed of intelligence.

Hindu and Modern Dualism.

The doctrine of Dualism will demand attention from time to time during the progress of our investigations. As preparatory to a full appreciation of what will be presented upon the subject, it may be well for us to stop here for a few moments, and compare the Hindu with the modern system. We shall find, in all essential particulars, the same identity here that we did in respect to the doctrine of Pantheism. On the subject before us, we remark:

1. Both systems agree in the assumption, that two, and only two, substances, as principles of all things, do exist, substances denominated Prakiti and Atma in the Hindu, and noumena, as subject and object, in the modern system, and that these substances, which stand behind all phenomena, are, and ever must be, unknown. We need not cite any passages from the author of the Sankhya system, in addition to that cited above, to show that such are the teachings of that system upon this subject. What are the teachings of the modern system upon the same subject? 'We are not acquainted merely obscurely, but not at all,' says Kant, 'with the quality of things in themselves.' Again, 'It remains wholly unknown to us what may be the nature of objects in themselves.' 'We know nothing but our manner of perceiving them.' Such are the united teachings of all dualists, ancient and modern, upon this subject.

2. Both systems agree absolutely in teaching that all our world-knowledge, objective and subjective, is exclusively phenomenal or illusory. The formula of the Sankhya is this: 'Neither do I exist, nor anything which pertains to myself. All individual existence is a dream,' an illusion. The formula of modern Dualism is thus expressed by Kant: 'We have,

therefore, intended to say, that all our intuition is nothing but the representation of phenomenon—that the things which we envisage' (perceive and think about) 'are not that in themselves for which we take them; neither are their relationships so constituted as they appear to us.' 'We know nothing but our manner of perceiving them.' We believe in ourselves, and in objects around us, as realities in themselves, and as known as they are in themselves, as Kant affirms, 'because we have to do with unavoidable illusions.'

3. In the Sankhya system, the doctrine of God is formally denied. In modern Dualism, God, like time and space, appears but as 'a regulative idea,' a law of thought. When we think of God, as Kant affirms, 'it is only a being in idea that we think.' This idea, he tells us, is 'in many respects a very useful idea.' Modern Dualism, also, expressly identifies God with the laws of nature. In reference to the order and harmony of the universe, 'it must be the same thing to us,' he says, 'when we perceive this, to say that God has so wisely decreed, or that nature has wisely ordered it.' In respect to the doctrine of God, as the Author of nature, either by emanation or creation proper, both agree in absolutely denying His existence. In other words, both in common are absolutely atheistical in their principles and teachings.

4. Both systems also agree, not only in affirming the universe of perception, external and internal, to be nothing but phenomena, or illusions, but that such illusions are emanations from one or the other of the two original substances or principles of all things. Creation, as it appears to us, is, according to the Sankhya, a production of, or emanation from, the Prakiti, or material principle. Creation, according to the modern system, is a product of, or emanation from, the subjective or spiritual principle. According to the latter system, the material principle is passive but in the origination of sensation; according to the former, the immaterial principle is passive but in perceiving the emanations from the Prakiti. Both systems, we repeat, agree that creation is by emanation, and has no existence but in a development of its subject, or apart from the subject.

The place which the idea of God has in the two systems is determined, we remark here, by the peculiar assumptions in regard to the special source of emanations. If emanation proceed, as the Sankhya system affirms, from the material principle, there is no place for God in the system. If, on the other hand, emanations, as the modern system avers, proceed from the immaterial principle, then space, time, and God have place, not as realities in themselves, but as laws of thought, regulative ideas, the place which they do occupy. Both systems in common must deny His existence as Creator proper.

5. The two systems rest, not only upon an assumption, but upon one

which is absurd in itself. If all emanations, or illusions, the mind and body of man included, proceed from the Prakiti, or material principle, as affirmed by the Sankhya system, not even a conjectural place remains for the doctrine of souls. If, on the other hand, the same phenomena proceed from the immaterial principle, as affirmed by the modern system, the idea of the reality of the material principle has not even conjectural validity. That principle is not necessary to account for the fact of sensation, and its reality has never been assumed for any other purpose. The doctrine of the sole existence of two entities, as the exclusive principles of all things, is not self-evidently valid; nor do even Dualists pretend that that doctrine can be verified by induction. The doctrine undeniably rests upon no other basis than a mere lawless assumption—an assumption, as we have shown, infinitely absurd in itself.

6. Each of these systems, also, rests upon another common assumption more absurd, if possible, than the one just presented—to wit, that objects of whose reality we are directly and absolutely conscious are unreal, while those of which we know, and can know, nothing are realities in themselves. Such an assumption undeniably has, and can have, no self-evident validity. Is it, can it be, self-evident that the consciously real does not exist at all, and that the consciously unknown is a reality in itself? Equally evident is the fact that this assumption cannot be verified by valid proof. To accomplish this result some fact must be adduced—a fact of the reality of which we are, and must be, more certain than we are, or can be, of our own existence and of that of objects around us—a fact absolutely incompatible with the real being of the known self and not-self. Who does not absolutely know that no such fact can be discovered?

7. We remark once more that the *method* of induction and development, strictly common to each of these systems, is in all essential particulars, and that exclusively, *à priori*. The Yogee, on the one hand, and the modern Dualist, on the other, '*puts* himself, when he begins to philosophize, into a state of not knowing,' assuming all existing forms of knowledge to be uncertain and illusory. This is done on the affirmed authority of *à priori* insight. He then looks off into boundless space and infinite duration, and by the same assumed insight, determines what realities and facts exist and occur there. From the elements of knowledge thus obtained, he constructs his system relatively to universal being and its laws. No method of philosophizing can be more **absurd in itself and more certain to culminate in fundamental error.**

SECTION IV.

THE YOGA SHASTRA OF PATANDJALI.

The system above named differs, in certain particulars, from the Vedanta on the one hand, and from the Sankhya system on the other, and in particulars equally essential, agrees with both. For the sake merely of historical completeness, we present the essential features of this system.

1. In opposition to the latter system, and in conformity with the former, the Yoga Shastra recognizes the being and government of God. Nor is the sleep of Brahm as distinctly recognized in this, as in the Vedanta system. Patandjali announces the doctrine of God in this formula: 'God, Iswara, the Supreme Ruler, is a soul distinct from all other souls, inaccessible to the evils which afflict them; indifferent to actions good or bad, and to their consequences, and to the ephemeral thoughts of men, which are but as dreams.'

2. In common with the teachings of the Vedanta, and in opposition to those of the Sankhya, the Yoga Shastra teaches that final salvation consists in absorption in God.

3. In opposition to both the systems named, Patandjali teaches, that the final salvation, the common end of all systems, is to be attained, not by science, but exclusively through practices of devotion, practices which have for their object the subjugation of the mind and body. The subjugation of the mind is to be sought by voluntarily inducing states of non-thought, states in which the mind thinks of no particular object whatever. The subjugation of the body is secured by preventing the senses from disturbing the non-thought of the mind.

4. To induce this utter cessation of all mental and physical activity, the pupil of the Yoga Shastra resorts to the same identical means that the Vedantist and the disciple of Kapila do to obtain their specific revelations of absolute science. By a voluntary suspension of all thought, desire, and mental and physical activity, with the body in a fixed and moveless position, and the eyes centred upon the end of his nose, the Vedantist receives one, the disciple of Kapila another and contradictory revelation of absolute science, and the disciple of the Yoga Shastra receives no revelation at all. What is the reason of these opposite results from the same real cause? Why is it that things so apparently equal to the same things turn out to be so unequal to one another? The reason, which will be fully explained and elucidated hereafter, is, in short, undeniably this: Each enters into the state described for the specific purpose of obtaining the identical results which he, then and there, does obtain.

The results secured are all predetermined, and the Yogee 'puts himself into the state of not-knowing,' for the purpose of obtaining those predetermined specific results. If he was not sure of experiencing those specific results, he would never put himself into that state.

4. The method of induction and deduction, and the moral teachings of all the three systems under consideration, are identical. The method is exclusively *à priori*, and the moral teachings confound all distinctions between virtue and vice, and subvert utterly the foundation of moral obligation.

SECTION V.

THE VAIESCHIKA SYSTEM OF KANADA.

ACCORDING to the Vedanta and Yoga Shastra systems, God, as an infinite spirit, and God alone, exists. In the Sankhya system, the being of God, as such a spirit, is ignored or denied, and two eternally existing and self-acting finite principles, the material and spiritual, are substituted in their place. Kanada repudiates the doctrine of spiritual existence in all forms, and postulates the material principle as the only existing substance. Matter exists in two forms, as atoms and as aggregates. The former are eternal, the latter transient. Each atom has some qualities common to all others, and some peculiar to itself. On the ground of this unity and diversity in atoms, and the manner of their aggregation in specific cases, Kanada accounts for the varied phenomena of nature. Atoms whose natures are predominantly alike mutually attract each other and aggregate together. Those whose natures are predominantly opposite repel each other. Thus aggregates distinct and separate are formed, while, by means of the nature common to all, they are all aggregated together in the system of the universe. When atoms having very special and common peculiarities aggregate, they form bodies which manifest the phenomena of animal and vegetable vitality. When atoms within these bodies, atoms of special ethereal peculiarities, aggregate, we have the phenomena which are denominated mental life, the phenomena of thought, feeling, and willing. Salvation consists, not merely in the dissolution of the body, but of those special aggregates from which mental phenomena result. The Yogee secures this result by science. By 'putting himself into the state of not-knowing,' above described, he, then and there, receives the revelation of absolute science—to wit, that matter only is real; all else is illusion. This ensures salvation at death. Other individuals, by practices of devotion, and other austerities, obtain for themselves short and favourable transmigrations. Those, on the other hand, who neglect science and such devices, must pass through long and painful transmigrations before the end desired can be attained. Here we have another case in which the Yogee, in his state of not-knowing, obtains a predetermined result.

The method of science, and the moral teachings of the Vaieschika, correspond in all respects with those of the systems already elucidated.

The atomic theory of Kanada, in fundamental particulars, resembles, and differs from, the later-developed system of Epicurus. Both agree in the assumption that matter only is real, and exists in the form of atoms, or aggregates, and that atoms are eternal, and aggregates of transient duration. According to Epicurus, as we shall see hereafter, atoms are identical in nature, but diverse in form, and by laws of motion diverse forms combine and separate, and thus produce the phenomena of nature mental and physical. According to Kanada, atoms, aside from their common properties, are diverse from one another both in form and nature, and aggregate and separate, by reason of this identity and diversity. By no à priori insight can we determine, on the hypothesis that one of these theories must be true, and the other false, which is to be preferred.

On à priori grounds and arguments, also, the claims of all the systems which we have considered are absolutely balanced. We have just as much reason to assume mind to be the only existing substance, and the exclusive principle of all things, as we have to assume matter to be that substance and principle. The Materialist, on the other hand, has just as much ground for his exclusive assumption, as the Idealist has for his; and neither has any reason whatever to assume that matter or spirit is the only form of real being !

SECTION VI.

THE HINDU LOGIC.

The logic of a people hardly belongs to the history of Philosophy. Yet we need to refer to their logic as a means of clearly understanding their progress in mental culture. For this reason we shall make a few general observations upon the logic by which the learned Hindu receives his chief intellectual training. The special subject of our remarks will be the Nyaya system, of which Gotama was the author, and of which the Vaieschika Philosophy is considered as the complement. We remark, then:

1. To show how exhaustively the science of Logic is treated of in this system, we present the following enumeration of topics which are therein discussed and elucidated: '1. Proof; 2. The object or matter of proof; 3. Doubt; 4. Motive; 5. Example; 6. Truth demonstrated; 7. The

regular argument; 8. Reduction to the absurd; 9. Acquisition of certainty; 10. Debate; 11. Conference, or interlocution; 12. Controversy; 13. Fallacious assertion; 14. Fraud and unfair construction; 15. Futile reply; 16. Defect in argument.' It is no more than justice to Hindu thought to say that all these topics are ably discussed and elucidated in this logic.

2. The Hindu syllogism, though not so simple as that developed by Aristotle, and which we employ, yet presents a complete enumeration of the elements which, in fact, enter into almost every common argument, and is hardly less effective than ours when contemplated as a discipline of thought. The Hindu syllogism, or complete argument, is composed not of three, as ours is, but of five members: the proposition, the reason, the example in illustration, the application, and final conclusion. The following may be presented as a fair example of this syllogism:

> '1. The mountain is burning;
> 2. For it smokes;
> 3. That which smokes burns, as the kitchen fire;
> 4. Accordingly the mountain smokes;
> 5. Therefore it burns.'

3. Among no people is the principle of contradiction, the reduction to the absurd, fallacies of assertion, fraud and unfair construction, defects of argument, and logical consecutiveness of discourse, and other kindred topics, better understood than among the learned Hindus.

Hence it is that among no people on earth do we find better-trained and more skilful logicians or fairer reasoners in debate than here. In an argument with an opponent, the learned Hindu never quibbles about words, or takes advantage of a mere mistake of his antagonist. The first object is to have a fair and common understanding of the subject matter in dispute. Here the issue is joined wholly upon the *thought* itself, as all understand it.   discourse of one party has logical consecutiveness throughout, the opposite party will freely join with the audience in expressions of admiration of the fact. If the discourse of the missionary has these characteristics, such men, if present, will openly commend it to the audience. If they present any objections or difficulties in respect to what has been spoken, and receive a pertinent reply, one which even confounds the objector, he will say to the audience, 'That is admirably said.' If the missionary finds it difficult, from ignorance of the language in which he is speaking, to express his thoughts, the learned Hindu will help him to accomplish his object, and will lend that aid in such a manner as to evince that it is done with the most perfect integrity. If the discourse has logical consecutiveness, it will be openly commended to the audience. If, in the judgment of the learned Hindu, the discourse lacks these characteristics, very probably a conversation in this form will pass between him and the speaker:

Brahmin: Did you not, in such a part of your discourse, utter such a sentiment?

Missionary: I did, sir.

B. Did you not, in another part, utter such a sentiment?

M. I did.

B. Did you not, in still another part, utter such a sentiment?

M. I did.

B. There is a contradiction here, sir. Your discourse is not worthy of our regard.

In nine cases out of ten the missionary will stand confounded before the audience. Christian men deeply read in the things of God, and those profoundly read in science, and especially well-trained logicians, such men, and such only, are qualified to grapple with learned Hindu thought.

No class of trained thinkers so nearly resemble each other in fundamental particulars as the learned Hindus and the learned Germans. Both excel all other peoples in *systematizing* thought, and reasoning with perfect consecutiveness from admitted premises. If you start with them on any given track, you must, or convict yourself of logical infidelity, enter the final depôt with them. No class of world-thinkers, also, so uniformly construct their systems upon principles valid or invalid, principles formally laid down. On the other hand, no class of world-thinkers are so reckless as they in the induction of principles, and the substitution of mere lawless assumptions in the place of valid principles of science. If you would overthrow the system of a Hindu or German world-thinker, be very wary indeed about assailing his logic or final deductions. Always scrutinize with profound care the *principles* which lie at the foundation of the system. Here, if the system is false, is to be found the source of its false deductions, as well as its utter impotency.

Two fundamental vices very commonly characterize systems erected by Anglo-Saxon thought: the fact that, for the most part, they are not in reality or form based upon principles, and that they lack logical consecutiveness in the arrangement of their parts, the parts not unfrequently being incompatible with each other. Kant, the great systematizer of thought, and one of the most reckless thinkers that ever lived, in the induction of principles, gave form to German learned thinking. Locke, who repudiated axioms, or principles, as useless in science, gave form and direction to Anglo-Saxon scientific thought. Hence the want of reference to principles in the construction of systems, the want of consecutiveness in the putting of the parts together, and, finally, the so frequent occurrence of absurd contradictions. We have no training in logic proper.

Our logics, with very few exceptions, pertain but to classification, and teach us to reason but from general notions, and not from universal and necessary principles.

In India educated mind is now being directed to the *principles* on which their old and venerated systems are based, and the conviction is becoming widely extended that those principles are false, and, consequently, that they have been venerating logical fictions instead of creations of truth. This is the ground-swell which is now heaving up the Philosophy and Heathenism of that people, and will soon engulf both in a common destruction.

SECTION VII.

THE HETERODOX SYSTEMS.

The Djainas and Buddhists.

ALL the systems which we have thus far considered were professedly founded upon the Vedas, and on account of the peculiar language of these writings, may be justly regarded as conformed, in whole or in part, to their professed original. We now advance to a consideration of systems whose authors openly and avowedly rejected the Vedas. These heterodox systems bear a strong resemblance, in many respects, to those which we have considered. All oriental systems were developed in fixed conformity to one and the same method, and with few, if any exceptions, teach the doctrine of transmigration. In all essential particulars, also, they agree in respect to the doctrine of final salvation, as consisting in absorption in God, or in a final absolute sleep of the soul, a sleep which amounts to annihilation. They generally agree, also, that this salvation is to be attained by science, or good works. The real differences between these systems pertain almost exclusively to questions of ontology. Of the heterodox systems of India, two only claim our attention—that of the Djainas, and that of the Buddhists. These we shall consider in the order named.

I. The System of the Djainas.

The Greeks mention certain philosophers of India as Gymnosophists. In India, they are called Digamhoras, which means, *devoid of clothing*. As ontologists, the Djainas hold the doctrine of Materialism in its strictest form. In their exposition of this doctrine, they differ from Kanada, the author of the Vaieschika, and agree strictly with Epicurus. The universe, material and mental, they hold, is constituted wholly of identical or homogeneous *atoms*. Diversity of forms of existence arise wholly from diversity of combination of the original elements. Forms of existence are divided into two classes, the inanimate and animate, the latter being the *subjects*, and the former the *objects* of knowledge and happiness. Animated beings are constituted of four elements—earth, water, fire, and air, which are themselves aggregates of the primitive elements. According to Mr. Huxley, and scientists of his school, animated beings are constituted of 'carbonic acid, water, and ammonia.' No essential difference obtains between the ancient and modern schools, the form of the teachings of the latter being more nearly conformed to the nature and revelations of modern science. Animated beings are also eternal, but material and mental phenomena result wholly from 'molecular changes in the matter of life.' That material thing called the soul may exist, they hold, in either of three states—a state of *bondage* through its own activity, a state of *freedom* from the *necessity* of action, and a state of *perfection* in which all activity of every kind for ever ceases. Their teachings in respect to the *causes* which impede or facilitate the advance of the soul from a state of bondage, through freedom, to final perfection, differ in no essential particulars from those of the Hindu schools generally, and differ from them only so far as is required by diversity of ontological teachings. Nothing further need be added in respect to the system of this school.

II. The Buddhists.

The term Buddha means, to know, or, the 'Intelligent One.' The author of the Buddhist system was the son of a king, who reigned some six or seven centuries before Christ, in a country north of Central India, and is known by several names, as Siddortha the Buddha, Sakhya-mani the Buddha, and Gautama the Buddha—that is, the Knowing One. Having exhausted all the luxuries of life, in his twenty-ninth year, he abandoned his palace, his family, and all forms of sensual gratification, and having put on a shroud taken from the dead body of a female slave, he commenced the life first of an anchoret, then of a public teacher, and finally, of a dictator of professedly inspired utterances, which, as published by the Chinese Government in four languages, consists of some 800 volumes. Two-fifths of the race hold the doctrines of Gautama, the Knowing One. Disgusted with the mutabilities, miseries, and momentariness of life, oppressed with the conviction that conscious existence is a curse, he cried out, from the depth of his inner being, for what is real, stable, permanent. How could a revelation of this absolute good be obtained? Not by reasoning, or speculation, or reflective thought; but by direct, immediate, intuitive knowledge. The reality must be *seen* in order to be known. To prepare himself for the reception of this revelation of absolute truth was the object of all his fastings, self-inflictions, and non-thought meditations. After a whole week of deep meditation, after remaining seated under a tree, without motion, and with his face to the east, for a night and a day, he received the revelation which he was seeking. All illusions passed away; he became 'wide awake;' the reality was directly before him, and he became Buddha, the Knowing One. What is the absolute truth thus revealed to Gautamá? As taught by him, and as received by all Buddhists, this doctrine, in the language of Mr. J. F. Clarke, in his 'Ten Great Religions,' is all embraced in the four following propositions:

1. All existence is evil, because all existence is subject to change and decay.
2. The source of this evil is the desire for things which are to change and pass away.
3. This desire, and the evils which follow it, are not inevitable; for, if we choose, we can arrive at Nirvana, where both shall wholly cease.
4. There is a fixed and certain method to adopt, by pursuing which we attain this end, without possibility of failure.

These four truths are the basis of the system. They are—1st, the evil; 2nd, its cause; 3rd, its end; 4th, the way of reaching this end.
Then follow the eight steps of this way, namely:—

1. Right belief, or correct faith.
2. Right judgment, or wise application of that faith to life.
3. Right utterance, or perfect truth in all that we say or do.
4. Right motives, or proposing always a proper end and aim.
5. Right occupation, or an outward life not involving sin.
6. Right obedience, or faithful observance of duty.
7. Right memory, or a proper recollection of past conduct.
8. Right meditation, or keeping the mind fixed on permanent truth.

After this system of doctrine follow certain moral commands and prohibitions, namely, five which apply to all men, and five others which apply only to novices or monks. The first five commandments are—1st. Do not kill; 2nd. Do not steal; 3rd. Do not commit adultery; 4th. Do not lie; 5th. Do not become intoxicated. The other five are—1st. Take no solid food after noon; 2nd. Do not visit dances, singing, or theatrical representations; 3rd. Use no ornaments, as perfumery in dress; 4th. Use no luxurious beds; 5th. Accept neither gold nor silver.

The central doctrine of Buddhism is, that the fundamental condition of attaining Nirvana is *merit*. All things are governed by eternal and immutable laws; but these laws immutably determine human destiny in conformity with one idea, *merit*. If our conduct is good, or meritorious,

Nirvana, or non-being, is to us a necessary certainty. If our actions are unmeritorious, or wicked, the same laws as necessarily determine for us an eternal existence in hell. The merit of all actions, also, depends upon the *motive*, and the motive, to be right must be purely disinterested. Kindness done to any being is meritorious. But to do good to the vilest is more meritorious than it is to do the same thing to the best of men, the motive in such case being the more disinterested. For the same reason it is more meritorious to do good to a beast than to a man, and to the vilest of beasts than to the most useful. Hence it is that Buddhists show supreme kindness to such creatures as sharks, tigers, hawks, and venomous serpents. To merit Nirvana, a Buddhist gave his own body to be devoured by a famishing tigress. When a Buddhist, or other religionist in India, desires to violate a moral principle, he finds in the expositions of his sacred books definitions and elucidations which, like the traditions of the elders, make void every moral principle, and render it even meritorious to violate it. A lie, for example, is defined as that which *tends* to evil, and truth, as that which tends to good. If, then, perjury will secure a desired end—saving the life of a friend, for example—perjury is truth, and true testimony a lie. In all India the English judges have failed to find a man whose oath is reliable in any case wherein the individual has an interest which he can ensure by perjury. The same is true in the case of all moral principles in common. These religions are throughout irreligious, and their morality is immoral. In Buddhism in all its forms, God and a world of superior beings are either wholly ignored or denied. The only object of religious worship is Gautama, the Buddha. By attaining to absolute knowledge he has not only attained to Nirvana, or utter inactivity, but has made himself infinite. In the worship of such a being—a being who has by knowledge and desert attained to absolute nothingness—there is, they assume, infinite merit.

Our main concern, however, is not with Buddhism as a religion, but with its philosophical systems. The sacred writings of this sect, like those of the Hindus, have given rise to certain systems of philosophy to a consideration of which special attention is now invited. Before proceeding to the accomplishment of this object, permit us to state the following fact, the bearing of which upon our present inquiries will be at once apprehended. About forty years since Dr. Bradley, who had spent a long time as a missionary in Siam, revisited his native country, bringing with him his motherless children. Among these were two daughters, one eight and the other some ten or twelve years of age. While these daughters were at my house in Oberlin, I invited them, not for their profit, but amusement, to attend one of my lectures. The subject of the lecture was the German Philosophy. My object was to explain to the class the diverse systems of Kant, Fichte, Schelling, and Hegel.

I noticed with surprise that those children listened with the intensest interest to all I said. Meeting with Dr. Bradley a day or two afterwards, he told me that on his return to his lodgings he found his daughters engaged in a very earnest conversation about the lecture. He found, also, that they fully comprehended all they had heard. They then explained to him the four German systems referred to, and showed how perfectly they corresponded with that which they had heard him and others so often explain as being taught in Siam and Hindostan. 'You know,' said one of them to the other, 'the questions I put to you as we were entering the harbour at St. Helena. When you expressed such delight at the scenery around, I asked you how you knew that there was any such objects there as you seemed to perceive? "How do you know," I asked, "but that all these objects are nothing but ideas and feelings in your own mind?"' This conversation, of course, induced me to obtain from Dr. Bradley a full exposition of these Indian systems—systems which he had profoundly studied. When I have found the expositions of such missionaries fully confirmed by all that I have read in the ablest statements of the same systems as given in books, I feel assured that I am, in no essential respects, misleading the reader in my own expositions. Let us now consider those

Buddhist Systems of Philosophy.

Among these systems three only demand particular elucidation, and these we will present in the following order.

Pure Idealism.

One of the chief schools holds, in its strictest forms, the system of Pure Idealism—the system which denies the reality of all *substances* finite and infinite, and resolves all real existences into pure ideas. The language employed by this school induced early Orientalists to impute to it the doctrine of absolute Nihilism. Its philosophers speak of vacuum and non-being as representing their doctrine, forms of language not employed even by any sect who denies the reality of matter, but admits that of spiritual substances. Maturer inquiries have evinced that by such forms of speech, these philosophers intend to deny merely the reality of all forms of existence as *substances*, especially as material substances. While this school wholly denies the reality of matter in all its forms, it admits that of spiritual existences only as ideal forms of being. In this school Idealism has reached its full and final consummation. At the basis of all other systems we have real substances, material or mental, known or unknown. Pure Idealism, under the assumption that being and knowing must be one and identical, takes away all substances in common, and affirms ideas with their necessary laws to be alone real. Such is the final development of Idealism in India.

Subjective Idealism.

Idealism in another form presents itself among the Buddhist systems. Pantheism and Pure Idealism begin with the Infinite and Absolute, as substance or idea, and deduce from the same, as ideal existences, all finite forms of being. Subjective Idealism, on the other hand, begins with the individual finite self, as the eternal and sole reality, and deduces all phenomena, and even time, space, and God, as ideal existences, from this finite self. The former schools deduce the Finite from the Infinite. This school deduces the Infinite from the Finite. Subjective Idealism, in its most perfect forms, is taught in one of the leading Buddhist schools. To the teachings of that school Fichte and his successors have, in fact, added nothing. The method and ontological deductions of the ancient find their perfect counterparts in those of the modern system. Each school distinguishes between the real and the ideal self, the eternal substance which lies at the basis of all phenomena, and the *conscious self*. This last, in common with all apparent existences around, has only an *ideal* existence. This ideal self, the I of consciousness, becomes, according to the teachings of the Buddhist system, reabsorbed in the real self, and thus becomes wholly inactive, on the same condition on which unconscious non-being is obtained according to other systems.

The Buddhist Material Systems.

In opposition to both of the above systems, another school of Buddhist world-thinkers maintain, in its strictest and most exact forms, the doctrine of Materialism. According to the united teachings of all sections of this school, all our knowledge is through sensation and external perception. At this point the school, in accordance with the diverse and opposite teachings of modern Materialism, in its different forms, divides into two sections.

According to the first, our knowledge of matter, as far as its essential characteristics are concerned, is direct and immediate, and, therefore, valid for the reality and character of its objects. As perceived, matter exists as aggregates, or compounds. But aggregates imply the simple, or atoms. Each aggregate derives its properties, or qualities, from the nature of the atoms of which it is constituted. As aggregates or forms, matter has only a temporary existence. As original atoms, it is, with its necessary laws, eternal. Forms are phenomenal, and cease to exist when not perceived. Atoms, we repeat, are eternal, and are constantly entering into new forms.

The other section of this school teach that our knowledge of matter is indirect, and mediate, through sensation. From sensation as effect, in accordance with Caudilac and his associates in France, this section of Buddhist Materialism reason, by induction, to matter as the object and cause of sensation. Having, by opposite processes of deduction, come to common conclusions in respect to the doctrine of matter itself, as to its aggregate and atomic forms, both sections fully agree in their subsequent expositions of that doctrine. Both deny the being of God, excepting as a law of matter, and also of the soul, excepting as a phenomenon of atomic combination. The soul, as a material form, may be of temporary or eternal duration. By merit, sensation, and with it all mental phenomena, may for ever cease. By demerit the soul may entail upon itself an eternal existence in hell.

RELATIONS OF THE BUDDHIST AND HINDU SYSTEMS TO EACH OTHER.

The reader will readily apprehend the relations to each other of the Hindu and Buddhist systems. The orthodox systems of the former all agree in the doctrine of God as the only real existence. All those of the latter either wholly ignore or deny the doctrine of a Supreme Being. Final salvation, according to both, is absolute and eternal unconsciousness, or inaction of every kind, a state equivalent to annihilation. This state, according to the former system, is attainable at death by science, through shortened and favourable transmigrations after death, by good works, and after long and unhappy transmigrations, as a consequence of a wicked life. The only condition of attaining this state, according to the latter system, is merit, or the desert of annihilation. According to the former system, all ultimately are saved, that is, annihilated. According to the latter, none but the meritorious do, or can, attain this high consummation. According to the former system, the wicked are miserable only for an indefinite period. According to the latter, they are, or may be, all miserable to eternity. According to both systems, no being is worshipped from sentiments of real piety, but wholly from subjective considerations, ultimate unconsciousness or annihilation.

SECTION VIII.

GENERAL REMARKS UPON THE INDIAN PHILOSOPHY.

1. IN none of these systems is there the remotest recognition of the doctrine of a *personal* God, of God as possessed of moral perfections, or as exercising, in any proper sense, a moral government over a realm of moral agents. Nor is there, in any of these systems, any recognition of the doctrine of creation proper. The doctrine of God is either ignored, denied, or recognized but in the pantheistic sense. If God is recognized

at all, he is identified with Nature, and Nature with him. Creation, too, is ascribed to God in but one exclusive sense—*emanation*. Nor is God presented in any of these systems as, in any proper sense, an object of worship, worship from sentiments of gratitude, love, or adoration. All religious service, when performed at all, has exclusive reference to personal ends. The Yogee, having by science attained the end he seeks, does not worship at all. The religionist goes through his ceremonials for the same exclusive personal end for which the Yogee attains scientific intuition. Nor is there a solitary attribute ascribed to God, in any of these systems, which renders Him a proper object of love, praise, or worship. When the passage, 'Behold, what manner of love the Father hath bestowed upon us, that we should be called the sons of God,' was read to a learned Hindu, he wept like a child in the presence of the divine idea. The idea of God as a Father, and of mankind as His 'sons and daughters,' had never through his philosophy or religion approached his mind. Natural evil, as an object of fear, is the only motive for action in any form, a motive presented by any of these systems. Evil, and only evil, continually, evil in its natural form necessarily attaches to conscious being in all conditions, evil the only escape from which is non-being.

2. Nor has *morality*, in its true and Christian form, any place in any of these systems, morality in the form of love to God and goodwill and benevolent activity towards man. The Yogee who has attained to absolute perfection inspires his fellow-creatures around him with but one sentiment in regard to himself, dread of his curse. Religious perfection in its highest form is as compatible with the life of a Thug as with any other form of activity. In most of these systems moral obligation is not only ignored but denied. In all of them, when God is acknowledged, He is represented as indifferent to the character of all human activity in common. With the Hindu, the act of killing a cobra di-capella is far more dreaded than that of killing a man, and perjury is truth when contemplated as a means of attaining a desired end. With the Buddhist, whose system is professedly a moral one, merit is least when kindness is shown to the best, greater when shown to the worst, of men, still greater when shown to a brute, greater still when shown to the most venomous of all the animal creation, and reaches perfection when one gives his own body to be devoured by a famishing tigress and her cubs. Moral virtue, in its personal form, does not consist in total abstinence from what is hurtful and wrong in itself, and in the temperate, self-controlled, use of what God has 'created to be received with thanksgiving,' but in all possible forms of abstinence from the good and evil alike. Perfection consists not in self-controlled enjoying, doing, and enduring what infinite wisdom and love appoints us, but in absolute indifference to good and evil, in

all their forms alike, that is, not in the *right use*, but in the *non-use*, of our faculties.

3. In the different philosophical schools of India we have, Scepticism excepted, all forms of the anti-theistic philosophy that, in any age or nation, have been developed by human thought. We have these systems, also, in absolute perfection of development. Even modern thought has not added a single essential element to these systems of India. In the Hindu schools, for example, and in that of the Djainas and Buddhists, we have Materialism in every form known to the history of Philosophy. In the Dualism of Kapila we have, in perfection of development, that of Kant. The German thinker has been fully anticipated by his Hindu predecessor. In the Pantheism of the Vedanta, we have the substance of which the Pantheism of Schelling and of his successors is 'the exact image.' In the two idealistic schools of Buddhism, we have Subjective and Pure Idealism, in specific forms of development to which Fichte and Hegel, and their schools, have added little or nothing. Kapila and the Buddhist schools, by teaching that all our knowledge is, in fact and form, exclusively phenomenal, and that substances, as they exist in themselves, are and ever must be unknown, have given the fixed formula of Scepticism in all subsequent ages. Of the anti-theistic systems of these and subsequent ages it may be said with absolute truth: 'The thing that hath been, it *is that* which shall be; and that which is done *is* that which shall be done: and *there is* no new *thing* under the sun. Is there *any* thing whereof it may be said, See, this *is* new? it hath been already of old time, which was before us.' Nor is it possible to conceive of an anti-theistic system developed in a form diverse from any and all those developed by Indian thought. There is a sense in which Scepticism has no place in oriental thought. All its systems are positive. While it has, as shown, given the form of Scepticism, oriental thought never developed doubt in systematic form. Scepticism, as a *system*, was originated, as we shall see hereafter, by the Grecian mind.

SECTION IX.

THE CHINESE PHILOSOPHY.

CHINA has produced one, and only one, world-renowned philosopher, Lao-Tseu, and but one world-famous teacher of morals, Confucius. The latter avowedly confined himself to moral teachings. The sentiment which he continually repeated to his hearers was this: 'I teach you nothing which you might not learn for yourselves, if you would only make a proper use of the faculties of your own minds. Nothing is more natural, nothing more simple, than the principles of morality which I endeavour to inculcate in its salutary maxims.'

Lao-Tseu, on the other hand, was the founder of a system of philosophy, a system, however, borrowed from the same sources, and having the same essential characteristics, as those originated by his Indian neighbours. For Brahm, he substituted a sublime and indefinable being, whom he denominated Reason. This Reason, in the language of Lao-Tseu, is 'the principle of all things.' 'The (primordial) reason,' he says, 'can be subject to reason (as expressed by words); but it is a supernatural reason. Without a name it is the principle of heaven and earth; with a name, it is the mother of the universe. It is necessary to be without passions in order to contemplate its excellence; with passions we contemplate only its less perfect state. There are but two ways of designating a single unique source, which may be termed *impenetrable depth*. This abyss contains all the most perfect beings. Before chaos, which preceded the birth of heaven and earth, there existed but one sole being, infinite and silent, immutable, always acting, yet never changing. We may regard it as the mother of the universe. I know not its name, but I designate it by the word *reason*.' So in the Hindu system we read: 'Brahm existed eternally, the first substance—infinite—the pure unity.' Again, 'He is the one eternal, pure, rational, unlimited being.' So also, as evincing a similar identity of idea and representation, says modern Pantheism: 'Before the time when motion began, we may imagine that an infinite mind, an infinite essence, or an infinite thought (for here all these are one) filled the universe of space. This, then, as the sole-existent One, must be the only absolute reality; all else can be but a developing of this one original and eternal being.' The manner in which all things proceed from this absolute unity, 'this universal soul,' or 'mother of the universe,' differs only in form of statement from that taught by the Vedas. After this life, the good are reabsorbed in 'the universal soul,' the bad, never. Of the first doctrine, the destiny of the good, Lao-Tseu says, 'I teach in this only what I have been taught by others.' Of 'the destiny of violent and evil men' (that they will not be united to the universal soul), 'on this point,' he says, 'it is I myself who am the father of the doctrine.' Nothing further is required in elucidation of this system.

SECTION X.

THE PERSIAN SYSTEM.

THE Boundehesch, which means *that which has been created from the beginning*—that is, an account of the creation, contains the doctrine of Cosmogony as taught among the Persians and Chaldeans, the former especially. The work has, by many, been attributed to Zoroaster, and he may safely be assumed to have been its author.

ZOROASTER AS A TEACHER OF MORALS AND PHILOSOPHY.

Zoroaster, in common with Confucius, was a teacher of morals, and like Lao-Tseu, he was also an originator of a system of philosophy. In both relations he differed very essentially from all oriental moralists and philosophers. Gautama and Confucius ignored God and religion in their moral teachings. Zoroaster laid the idea of God and religion at the basis of all his moral teachings. In other oriental systems, God, if presented at all, is disrobed of all moral attributes. Moral perfection is the leading idea of God as He is presented in the system of Zoroaster. Hence piety, gratitude, praise, worship, and heart-service, have place in this system only. Thus he writes : ' I worship and adore the Creator of all things—full of light.' 'I desire by my prayer with uplifted hands this joy—the pure works of the Holy Spirit, Marsda . . . a disposition to perform good actions . . . and pure gifts for both worlds, the bodily and spiritual.' 'I have entrusted my soul to Heaven . . . and I will teach what is pure so long as I can.' ' We honour the good spirit, the good kingdom, the good law—all that is good.'

Prominent among his moral and religious teachings was the doctrine of *repentance* for sin. 'I repent of all sin. All wicked thoughts and works which I have meditated in the world, corporeal, spiritual, earthly, and heavenly, I repent of in your presence, ye believers. O Lord, pardon through the three words.'

In the system of the Boundehesch, also, we have the first appearance among Oriental teachings of the idea of *moral* good and *moral* evil in conflict in this world, and of human destiny as conditioned fundamentally upon *moral* character and conduct. We have, also, the doctrine of the immortality of the soul, the fall of our first parents, and the consequent ruin of the race by sin, the possibility of recovery by repentance and trust in God's mercy, a state of future, though not eternal, retribution, the resurrection of the dead, and the final purification of the universe from natural and moral evil by fire. Zoroaster, in common with such teachers as Socrates and Plato, taught the doctrine of the Coming One by whom the world shall be morally renovated. Among the successors of Zoroaster were 'the wise men' (Magi) 'from the east,' who worshipped the infant Jesus at Bethlehem.

THE COSMOLOGY OF THE 'BOUNDEHESCH.'

The idea of God as the principle of all things, or as the unconditioned cause of all conditional existences and facts, is represented in the Hindu system by the term Brahm, and in that of China by that of Reason. In the 'Boundehesch' the term Time illimitable, or Terava-Akerana, is employed to represent the same idea. In this system this Eternal or Absolute being is represented as the creator of all things in the sense that in the beginning he gave being to Ormuzd and Ahriman, the former supremely pure and good, and called the Light and the Creative Word, and the latter the Evil Being and the principle of darkness. Ormuzd organized the invisible and visible universe, filled the heavens with pure genii, and the earth with clean animals and wholesome plants, and then gave being to man, who, like all the creations of 'the word,' was originally pure and holy. Ahriman, whose supreme aim is to defeat the wise and benevolent purposes of Ormuzd, filled the heavens with evil genii, and the earth with unclean and venomous animals and noxious plants, and finally seduced man to evil. Hence in the world above and the world below good and evil are in perpetual conflict, light being opposed by darkness, natural good by natural evil, and moral good by moral evil. In this world man is the supreme centre on which this conflict turns, Ahriman, with all his wicked genii, struggling to perpetuate human subjection to natural and moral evil, and Ormuzd, with all good genii, struggling to redeem man back to the possession of natural and moral good.

Under the two-fold influence to which men are thus subjected, as free moral agents, they make their election between the evil and the good. Those who hearken to Ormuzd, and choose the good, will, at death, be united with him and the good genii in the world of light and blessedness. Those who follow Ahriman, and do evil, will dwell in misery with him and the evil genii, the Dews, in the abyss of darkness.

At the final consummation, when the Infinite and Eternal One shall purify the universe by fire, Ahriman himself and evil genii and wicked men will be subdued and purified, and the conflict of creation shall cease for ever. The doctrine of final optimism favours the idea of those who believe that the real doctrine of Zoroaster was that Ahriman and all evil beings were originally like man, pure and holy, and fell from the state in which they commenced moral agency. This doctrine, however, was lost among the followers of Zoroaster.

It is to this duality of creative good and evil that the Scriptures refer, Isa. xlv. 5—7, 'I *am* the Lord, and *there is* none else; *there is* no God besides me: I girded thee, though thou hast not known me: that they may know from the rising of the sun, and from the west, that *there is* none besides me. I *am* the Lord, and *there is* none else. I form the light, and create darkness: I make peace, and create evil: I, the Lord, do all these *things*.' God here denies creative power and agency of all beings but Himself, claims to be sole Creator of the universe and of all beings and objects in it, and the sole Governor and Lord of all, creating

THE PERSIAN SYSTEM.

light and darkness, and dispensing good and evil to creatures according to His will. Moral good and evil of creatures, that is, their voluntary acts of obedience and disobedience, were not represented even in Persian Mythology as objects of creative power.

As our object is to represent merely the essential features and elements of systems of Philosophy, we have not given in detail the Persian Mythology; nor have we named all the sacred books of that people, books from some of which we have made quotations. We shall have occasion to refer again very particularly to the teachings of the 'Boundehesch,' 'Vendavesta,' and other sacred books of this people, when we come to consider the original religion of the race, as indicated by facts, and the Scriptures of Oriental nations.

SECTION XI.

THE EGYPTIAN SYSTEM.

THE Egyptians had no sacred books or works on Philosophy which have come down to us. Their religion, also, had two distinct and opposite phases, exoteric and esoteric, that is, an exterior theology for the people, and an interior one for the priests and wise men. The former presents the popular Mythology, in which not merely gods without number who were superior to men, but four-footed beasts, fowls of the air, and creeping things, are presented as objects of worship. Animals with the Hindu are sacred, but not objects of worship. With the Egyptian animals, clean and unclean, were not only sacred, but objects of formal worship. Spirit is the object of Hindu worship; body and form that of Egypt. The Mythology of this people, however, is not the subject of our inquiries and elucidations.

It is to the esoteric teachings of the priests that we are to look for the Egyptian Cosmology, teachings which were carefully concealed from the people, and communicated only to the initiated. These esoteric teachers left us, as we have said, no treatises on any of the sciences; nor did the record of their sacred doctrines appear upon monuments, or on the swathing folds of mummies. We have no records of these sacred teachings but such as became known to learned men of Greece and other nations. Such authors as Diodorus Siculus, Herodotus, and the Alexandrian philosophers, Iamblicus and Porphyry, furnish us all the information we have upon the subject. The following is the substance of what learned men have derived from these and kindred sources:

1. As existing from eternity and before all created objects, in the place of Brahm, Reason, the Eternal, or Time without bounds, the Egyptian

Cosmology places God without a name as 'the primitive obscurity, the incomprehensible being, the hidden principle of everything that exists, the invisible source of all light and all life, who is above all intelligence.' The reader will perceive at once that the common Oriental idea of God is here given by exposition, though not designated by any term. The Egyptians sometimes employed the term 'Piromis' to represent their idea of the supreme divinity, a term which means man supereminently, to signify, as some suppose, that Piromis is supreme among the gods, as man is supreme among the animal creation.

2. At a definite, but to us unknown, period in the eternity past, the supreme divinity became a producer or generator. Whether by emanation or by a creative word is not very clearly stated. All representations of subsequent originations, however, indicate that primal creation was in the form first designated. According to Herodotus, the first creations, or emanations, were three orders of finite divinities, eight of the first, twelve of the second, and seven of the third, order. Bunson believes that he has succeeded in discovering and designating all these in their proper order from the monuments. From these divinities the visible universe was originated, or rather emanated, the purer and higher elements from the higher, and the grosser from the lower orders. Of the first order, for example, Kneph is 'the efficient reason of things, the creator, the demiurgus,' and Phta is 'the organizer of the world, the God of Fire, the vital principle.'

3. All emanations in common—and here we have a striking peculiarity of the Egyptian Cosmology—all emanations, we say, proceed in a kind of syzygy; that is, each emanation is attended with another which possesses inferior, and sometimes opposite, elements and characteristics. Hence the intermingling, everywhere in nature, of order and disorder, beauty and deformity, good and evil, life and death.

4. The evil principle is represented by the term 'Typhon,' and the good, perfection, or absolute beauty, by the word 'Niphthys.' From the marriage of these, visible forms proceed, and hence good and evil constitute the very essence of the world.

5. Souls are immortal, but subject to cycles of transmigration, each cycle occupying a space of three thousand years. During this period the soul dwells successively in the bodies of every variety of beasts and insects, and then reinhabits a human body. Thus human existence continues for ever. Here we have the doctrine of transmigration in an essentially different form from that affirmed in other Oriental nations. The soul, according to the Egyptian idea, does not leave the body until the latter has decayed; hence they embalmed the body, and thus shortened the cycle of transmigration for at least one thousand years.

The doctrine of transmigration, as taught in Egypt, differs in two fundamental respects from that taught in all other Oriental countries. With the latter, it was in all cases to be but of temporary continuance; with the former, it was to be in all cases eternal. With the latter, it might by science be wholly superseded by immediate absorption in God at death, and in all cases might be shortened and modified by religious observances; with the latter, the state of the soul during the period of transmigration could not be affected either by moral character or religious services; all that could be done was, to retain the soul for long periods in the body by embalming the latter. Evil, as presented in all these systems in common, the Persian excepted, is natural rather than moral, and necessary instead of voluntary. *Moral* responsibility, in its true and proper sense, is either ignored or denied in all these systems.

SECTION XII.

GENERAL REMARKS UPON THE ORIENTAL SYSTEMS.

WE have now completed our expositions of the various forms of the Oriental Philosophy. It remains to resurvey the ground we have gone over, and to gather up such reflections and general observations as may have an important bearing upon our subsequent inquiries. Among these observations and reflections, the following demand special attention:

I. THE CONNECTION OF THESE SYSTEMS WITH RELIGION.

In the common histories of Philosophy these systems have been represented as being wholly religious in their character, and, consequently, as not belonging properly to a history of this science. 'Where and when does Philosophy begin ?' asks Schwegler. 'Manifestly,' he answers, 'when a final philosophical principle, a final ground of being, is sought in a philosophical way; and hence, with the Grecian Philosophy, the Oriental—Chinese and Hindu (so-named philosophies, but which are rather theologies or mythologies)—and the mystic cosmologies of Greece in its earliest periods, are therefore excluded from our more definite problem. Like Aristotle, we begin the history of Philosophy with Thales. For similar reasons we exclude also the Philosophy of the Christian Middle Ages, or Scholasticism. This is not so much a philosophy as a philosophizing or reflecting within the already prescribed limits of positive religion. It is, therefore, essentially theology, and belongs to the science of the history of Christian doctrines.'

Here we have a fundamental mistake in regard to the proper sphere of the history of Philosophy itself, and also in respect to the relations of the systems referred to and religion. 'Philosophy,' says this author, and rightly too, 'examines every individual thing in reference to a final principle, and considers it as one link in the whole chain of knowledge'— 'follows it out to its ultimate grounds.' Every people, who have attained to any degree of civilization, have their ideas in regard to 'the final principle' and 'ultimate grounds' referred to, and in regard to the relations of individual things and particular facts to such principles and grounds. Here we have the Philosophy of such peoples. The religious ideas of all peoples also, in particulars perfectly fundamental, take form from their philosophy. All systems of Philosophy are religious or non-religious in their *ultimate* deductions. One of the fundamental aims of every true history of Philosophy is to show what are 'the final principles' and 'ultimate grounds' to which each people refer all individual things and facts, and how they explain the latter by the former, and, finally, how far their religious ideas were moulded and determined by their philosophy. Oriental and mediæval systems, therefore, have place within the sphere of the history of Philosophy, for the same reasons that those of Greece have.

In all Oriental systems, also, we have religion, in all its forms and applications, determined, in fact, by Philosophy. In all such countries religion is esoteric and exoteric: the former for the initiated (the Yogees), and the latter for the people. Religion, in its exterior or popular form, is wholly the creation of esoteric thought, and, as thus developed and perfected, was adopted and imposed upon the people by the sovereign authorities. The three orders of gods of Egypt, Brahm, Vishnu, Siva, and other gods of India, Yang and Yn of China, and Ormuzd and Ahriman of Persia, are creations of the Philosophy of those nations. Their religion being determined by their philosophy, we cannot understand the latter without reference to the former.

Compte, for example, gives us first the Positive Philosophy, and then a fully developed system of religion, the latter being determined through and by the former. Suppose that, when the two systems were completed, the Philosophy on the one hand, and the religion on the other, the Government, having the power to do it, had adopted both as the science and religion of the people, and had perforce imposed the latter upon the nation. We should have here a case perfectly parallel to what did obtain in all the Oriental nations. Would not the Philosophy of France, in that case, come as fully within the sphere of a history of Philosophy as that of Compte now does? For such reasons we have gone back, in our inquiries, to these Oriental systems.

RELATIONS OF ORIENTAL RELIGIONS TO THE PRIMITIVE RELIGION OF THE RACE.

A question of great importance here presents itself, namely, what are the relations of these Oriental religions to the *primitive* religion of mankind? All these religions, as we have seen, and as none will deny, are, in fact and form, creations of preformed and perfected systems of Philosophy, and consequently cannot be regarded as being themselves primitive religions. Philosophy is one of the latest, and indeed the latest of all, forms of human thought. A religion which arises after, and takes form from, Philosophy, must stand at a very wide remove from the primitive faith. If we would inquire, with any rational hope of success, for the characteristics and elements of this primordial religion, we must find them *in those elements which are common to all religions which have assumed definite and ultimate forms.* All derivative religions will contain, in their positive or negative forms, all the essential elements of the common religion from which they were derived. The validity of these statements, we are quite sure, no thoughtful minds of common integrity will deny. What, then, are the elements common to all these religions? They are, among others, the following:—

Monotheism, the Original Faith of the Race.

1. The doctrine of *one*, and only *one*, *eternally existing* and *supreme God* —God in this form, and in no other, is acknowledged, as a matter of fact, in all these religions without exception. In all antitheistic systems, also, the doctrine of one God, in this one exclusive form, is either ignored or denied. Between man and this supreme God, 'there are gods many and lords many.' All these intermediate divinities, however, are, without exception, regarded and worshipped, not as uncreated beings, but as being in common with man, and in the same sense that he is, creatures of God. In no nation under heaven did Polytheism ever obtain but in this one exclusive form. Nor were 'four-footed beasts, fowls of the air, or creeping things,' ever worshipped but as created objects—creatures of this one God. The lowest Feticists never worshipped stones and herbs, and beasts, and birds, and insects, as eternally existing, and uncreated verities, but as being, like themselves, creatures of God. Did Egypt worship the ox, or crocodile, as eternally existing and uncreated beings? We all know they did not. Nor have we the remotest evidence, but positive evidence to the contrary, that any people ever worshipped any such objects under the impression that they were uncreated beings. No people ever held the doctrine of more than one original, eternal, and uncreated divinity. What, then, must have been the original religious faith of the race? No people, as we have formerly shown, do exist, or ever have existed, with-

out religious ideas of some kind. The idea of creation and of a Creator is as old and as universal as human nature itself. Theistic ideas of some kind, mankind, from the immutable laws of our intellectual nature, must have. In all religions one idea is omnipresent, that of creation in some form, and also that of God as the Author of nature, either by emanation, or creation proper. What, then, we ask again, is the original divine idea? It was not, we answer, either Feticism or Polytheism. Gods in these forms are worshipped, not as uncreated but created beings, not as eternal existences, but as creatures of time, like man himself. Not a solitary exception to these statements can be found in the history of the race. Nor was this idea that of God as Creator by emanation. This idea of God is a dream of Philosophy. The human intelligence, in its natural, spontaneous, intuitive procedures, never identifies God with nature, or nature with God, but always cognizes Him, worships Him, and prays to Him, not only as the Author and Governor of nature, but as being separate from, over, and above 'the things that are made.' Philosophic thought must have long pondered the problem of universal being and its laws, and must have wandered to an infinite distance from its point of departure, before the idea could have approached the human mind that Brahm, reason, time illimitable, Reason, or the Infinite and Absolute, 'alone exists; everything else is illusion.' The divine idea, in its original form, can have been nothing else but this—that of one personal God, who, as a free self-conscious personality, is the Author of nature by creation proper.

What holds true of the Oriental religions holds equally, as we shall see hereafter, of those of Greece, Rome, and all other heathen nations. The Greeks had their Zeus, and the Romans their Deus, whom they regarded as the sole supreme God. Between this eternal being and man stood thousands of superior beings called gods; not one of these, however, was regarded by their most devoted worshippers as an eternal and uncreated existence, but as, in common with man, a created being, and as such a creature of time. Heathen Mythology records the birth and parentage of these inferior and finite deities—deities represented by their worshippers as not only finite, but imperfect, and even sinful creatures like men.

Feticism, also, wherever it exists, has being, like that of Egypt, as a socially *organized* religion—religion with a formal priesthood. In the original religions there are no priests as a separate class. The father of each family was the only priest, as well as ruler, known in the primitive state of mankind. As we descend historically, or by observation, towards this primitive state, the number of nominal gods diminishes until we come to 'the poor Indian,' whose only object of worship is 'the Great Spirit.' The rudest African known is not a Feticist. Nor is he, as mature investigations have demonstrated, void of religious ideas. On the other hand, he worships and prays to the great spirit—the supreme divinity whom he designates by a peculiar name.

A profound study of the immutable laws of mind renders it demonstrably evident that mankind cannot exist in any state without religious ideas and sentiments. On the perception of body, succession, and events, for example, reason necessarily apprehends space, time, and cause as the necessary condition of the existence and occurrence of substances and events. In the presence of facts of external and internal perception, the mind apprehends two orders of existence, namely, those represented by the terms matter and spirit. Thus four realities are, and must be, represented in human thought—to wit, space, time, spirit, and matter, the two former being given as absolutely infinite, and necessarily existing, realities. While all substances and events are necessarily cognized as existing and occurring in space and time, the mind cannot but apprehend itself, and all visible objects around it, as finite and dependent forms of being, and as a consequence, must apprehend an unconditioned and eternally existing power on which finite and dependent forms of being depend. From the necessary principles and laws of our intellectual and moral nature, such a power must suggest itself and become omnipresent in thought. Of the reality of such a power, the mind, in its original and intuitive procedures, can no more doubt than it can the fact of its own conscious being and that of realities around it. As in universal thought, the conditioned necessarily *implies* the unconditioned, and the finite as necessarily *suggests* the infinite, and the imperfect the perfect, and the dependent the independent, and all sustaining power, the mind would naturally, if not necessarily, apprehend the unconditioned cause as infinite and perfect, and would no more, in its original and intuitive thoughts and convictions, doubt the reality of that cause than it would the validity of the principle that every event must have a cause. Nor is there any law of thought by which this power would present itself to the mind as being, not one, but many. The Unconditioned we never think of as a multiple, but as a unity.

While the mind, also, intuitively distinguishes itself, as spirit, from all material existences around it, it can never, in its primary and intuitive procedures, apprehend this eternal verity, this unconditioned and universal cause of all conditioned forms of being, as an inhering law or property of matter, but as, like itself, a free, self-conscious spirit, and as such, unlike the finite self, an infinite and perfect mind. Unless mind itself is a lie, Monotheism must have been the primitive religion of the race. It is a shallow and unreflective and unobserving philosophy that represents the primitive race of mankind, a realm of rational personalities, as void of religious ideas and sentiments, and then as ascending from Feticism, through Polytheism, to Monotheism. There is not a known fact in the history of the race to justify such a deduction. Polytheism and Feticism, on the other hand, are degenerate forms of original Monotheism, the pure religion corrupted and 'spoiled by Philosophy,' or by 'science falsely so-called.' The cannibals of New Zealand, and of the islands of the South Pacific, are many of them, to say the least, Feticists, and they are in the lowest state in which humanity has ever been found. The question is, are they degenerates from a former higher state of civilization, or are they at this point in the scale of ascent from a still lower stage ? Many points of physical resemblance, as well as traditions and customs which obtain among them, absolutely evince the fact that they are degenerate descendants of a comparatively civilized people who formerly emigrated thither from Ceylon and Southern India. In India, for example, they have an annual festival in commemoration of the escape of Noah and his family in the Ark. The same custom obtains among these cannibals. They have not only a specific tradition of the Flood, but build vessels in imagined conformity to the ark in which Noah and his family escaped. The animals and reptiles which the people of India regard as sacred, these degenerate savages, in conformity with Egyptian custom, worship, not as supreme divinities, but as containing the spirits of finite but higher genii. No Egyptian or cannibal, we repeat, ever worshipped an animal under the impression that man is a creature of whom the animal is the creator—that man is ' a creature of yesterday, and the animal an eternal and uncreated being. The objects of fetich and idolatrous worship are all, without exception, worshipped as creatures standing between man and his creator. All known facts of observation and history render demonstrably evident the teachings of the class of learned men recently risen in India, the class to whom we have formerly referred—that the original religion of India and the race was Monotheism ; that all idolatrous religions are corruptions of the primitive faith of the race ; that Monotheism is the doctrine originally taught in the Vedas ; that these sacred books, in their present form, are corruptions of the original text, corruptions introduced by the priesthood—a fact evinced by many passages found in these writings in their present form.

2. *Relations of these Systems to the Doctrine of the Soul as Distinct from all Material Existences, and as Immortal.*

In all the Oriental systems we also find, either in its positive or negative form, the clearest recognition of the human soul as a form of being distinct and separate from all material existences. In every such system the idea of matter on the one hand, and of the soul on the other, is referred to in the identical form in which the idea of each is represented in universal thought. Oriental Materialism denies, indeed, the reality of spirit, and Idealism that of matter. In both alike, however, the *two ideas*, in the *universal forms* designated, are distinctly represented. In the same positive or negative form, the doctrine of the immortality of the soul is distinctly and definitely represented in all these systems. Now, ideas must have existed in the human mind prior to their distinct, affirmative, or negative embodiment in systems of Philosophy. What, then, must have been the pre-existing and original faith of the race on all these subjects? It must have embodied, with greater or less distinctness, not only the doctrine of creation 'by the word of God,' but of the universe as constituted of two distinct and separate orders of being, matter and spirit, and, finally, that of the immortality of the human soul. On no other hypothesis can the facts before us be accounted for.

3. *The Relations of these Systems to the Doctrine of Right and Wrong, of Moral Obligation, Moral Desert, and Retribution.*

One of the most noticeable features of all these systems is the *distinctness* and *definiteness* with which all the doctrines just named are recognized, generally in their negative forms, in them. Every one of these systems refers to the law of duty, to human obligation, to the desert of obedience and disobedience, to God's relations to moral action, and to the bearing of present character and conduct upon immortal destiny. With few exceptions, they in fact and form deny all moral distinctions, all moral desert in human character and conduct, all forms of future retribution, and represent God as wholly indifferent to human conduct as right and wrong. These very denials, however, imply absolutely the omnipresence in human thought of the doctrines denied. Even 'science, falsely so-called,' does not deny what nobody believes, and more especially that not previously represented in thought. What, then, must have been the pre-existing and primitive faith of the race in regard to all these doctrines? That faith, we answer, must have embodied, in their strictly positive forms, the doctrines of right and wrong, of obligation, of moral desert, and future retribution. A fundamental element of that faith, also, must have been the idea of God as the moral Governor of the universe.

4. *Relations of these Systems to the Doctrine of Human Sinfulness.*

In all these systems without exception, man is represented as in a *fallen* state, and as being miserable in consequence of his *lapsed* condition. The question definitely proposed, and professedly answered, in every one of them, pertains wholly to the *condition* and *means* of escape from present and impending evils. In all the systems but one, that of Zoroaster, man is affirmed not to be guilty for his sinfulness, and consequent misery. Yet the idea of the co-existence of these evils, and their necessary connection, is omnipresent in all these systems. Every system, we repeat, affirms the fact of sin, and of misery as its consequence, even while man's responsibility for both is denied. Such facts absolutely evince the omnipresent consciousness in the human mind of the fact of sin, and of misery as its necessary consequence, together with the immutable conviction of human responsibility for both.

5. *The Idea of Salvation from Sin, the Common Element of all these Religious Systems.*

One other element common to all these systems claims our special attention, the idea of *salvation from sin and its consequences*. The *evil* and the *remedy* are ideas omnipresent in all these systems. The forms of absolute truth, as apprehended by Gautama Buddha, embraced the following elements: the evil—the cause of the evil—the fact that salvation is possible, and the means of attaining this end. Yet Gautama utterly ignored, or denied, the doctrine of God. The same holds true of all these systems in all their forms. All affirm the doctrine of man as a fallen being, and of salvation on conditions with which man may comply. The *form* of the affirmed evil, and of the remedy, is one thing; the *fact* of both is quite another. This central fact is what is material in the present argument, as it discloses, as omnipresent in human thought, the great truth of salvation from sin as revealed to man immediately after the Fall—a truth which enters as a fundamental element into all the diverse religions of the race.

What, then, are the essential elements of the primitive religion of man, the religion of which Heathenism, Feticism, and Anti-theism, in all their forms, are corruptions? This primordial religion must have embraced, among others, the following elements, namely, the doctrine of the being and perfections of a free, self-conscious, and personal God— that of creation, not by emanation or natural law, but 'by the word of God'—creation constituted of matter and finite spirit—of the human soul, under moral law, and in a fallen state, and miserable on account of sin—of salvation on conditions with which man may comply—of duty, responsibility, immortality, and retribution. All these elements are, in fact and form, present, as specifically affirmed or denied, in all religions, and in all systems of Philosophy ancient and modern. The law of universal deduction, as announced by Kant, and which none will deny, is most strictly applicable here, namely, '*Facts strictly common to a great variety of diverse cases must have a common ground for their existence and occurrence.*' Here we have a class of doctrines, every one of which is specifically affirmed, or denied, in every religion, and in every system of Philosophy, which has ever been the object of human thought. This universal fact, we say, can be accounted for but upon one exclusive hypothesis, namely, that all these religions and systems are pure, or corrupted, streams from one common source—a primordial religion once co-extensive with the race, a religion in which all these doctrines were affirmed, as forms of absolute truth. The validity of this hypothesis will receive additional confirmation in all our subsequent investigations.

VI. The Idea of Human Existence and Salvation, as it Appears in the Light of all these Systems.

Gautama Buddha has expressed two ideas which, in their essential forms, are strictly common to all Oriental religions and systems of Philosophy, that of Zoroaster excepted—those of human existence as a curse and non-being, as the only possible salvation from that curse. All these systems agree absolutely in regard to the doctrine first named, and differ only in form in regard to the second. In all these systems *conscious* existence is represented as the curse, and annihilation, or utterly *unconscious* being, as salvation. These are now, and have been for the past 2,500 years, at least, the two fundamental and avowed articles of the religious and philosophical faith of three-fifths of the race. These two doctrines, in their essential forms, enter, as essential elements, into the systems of Materialism, Idealism, and Scepticism, of all ages. Materialism presents, as our hope of redemption from admitted existing evils, death as an eternal sleep. Idealism gives us the hope of redemption through reabsorption in the Absolute, or non-consciousness. Scepticism substitutes for an eternally conscious future an eternal blank. Yet men regard teachers who unfold eternal non-being, as the only hope of soul-salvation, as benefactors of their species.

Wherein lies the secret of the power which the idea of real annihilation has over the human mind? Wherein, for example, lies the secret of the world-wide and fascinating power of Byron, the poet-prophet of modern Buddhism? We judge that we have before us the true, and only true, answer to such inquiries. The Christian religion, while it admits, and affirms, the universally conscious *fact* of human sin, and misery in consequence of sin, takes away the effect by removing the cause, and opens upon the mind of all who, as Zoroaster did, will repent of sin, and accept of God's remedy from its death-inflicting power, the bright vision and assured hope of immortal purity, and consequent fellowship with the infinite and eternal mind. Ever since this star of hope rose upon the sin-darkened and terror-stricken vision of humanity, in Eden, all who have followed the guiding light of that star have sought, not non-being, or eternal unconsciousness through absorption in Brahm or the Absolute, but 'a country,' 'a better country, that is an heavenly,' 'a city which hath foundations,' a city into which sin and its death-curse enter not, and in which God is the soul's 'everlasting light, and the days of its mourning are ended.' To all such existence is an infinite good.

But what is the character of all these hopeless religions and godless Philosophies? They all in common leave the primal curse, conscious sin and its death-sting, unremoved and remediless. They give to the mind a godless universe, or a god without emotion, without love, at a prayerless remove from human suffering and human woe, and as coldly indifferent to human want, human destiny, and human desert, as is the heart of infinite space. Let mind, under the omnipresent pressure of conscious sin and ill-desert, from which it cannot escape, become oppressed with the idea of existence in such a dead universe as these religions and philosophies reveal to its vision, and what will be its necessary estimate of enduring the perpetually accumulating weight of oppressive thought, feeling, and action to eternity? What will be its necessary estimate of conscious existence itself? Just what Gautama found it in his revelation of absolute truth, to wit, 'All existence is evil.' Escape from conscious to unconscious being will be salvation, 'a consummation devoutly to be wished.' Let the doctrine of future non-being take form before the mind as a doctrine of science, a revelation of absolute truth, and to all who will not repent of sin and seek redemption from its curse-power, that doctrine will have attractions of infinite strength. Here, undeniably, lies the secret of the power of Buddhism, Brahmanism, Materialism, Idealism, and Scepticism, in the present and past ages.

VII. WHAT HAS THE RACE REASON TO EXPECT FROM THE ANTI-THEISTIC PHILOSOPHIES WHICH ARE BEING COMMENDED TO HUMAN REGARD?

Error, like truth, always approaches the mind with 'a promise of life,' and commends itself to human regard as an infallible remedy for all the infinite 'ills that flesh is heir to.' Never did Anti-Theistic Philosophies hold out to sin-burdened humanity such promises as now, and these Philosophies are swarming upon us in all the forms in which they have ever before appeared. Long and fully tested experience, and that in every conceivable human condition, is a chart which may be safely and wisely consulted by 'the men of this generation' in regard to these old lights which are now held out. Not a solitary new system is before us, nor any old system in any essentially new form. In the affirmed and uninterrupted light of these systems three-fifths of the race have been advancing or retrograding for more than two thousand years. The power of these systems for good or ill has been fully tested by the best thinkers of both hemispheres during all this period. The tendency of these systems to mar human advancement we can read in the rise and fall of Greece and Rome, in the state of that 'basest of kingdoms,' Egypt, and in the dead moral debasement and stolid mental immobility of India and China. We can read their tendency to remedy the ills of life in the undeniable fact that, during all these years, these systems have rendered, in the estimate of three-fifths of the race, conscious existence the curse of humanity, and the eternal escape from all thought, feeling, and activity, salvation. Yet we are assured that if we will take to our heart-embrace these old, dead, decayed, and death-imparting systems, we shall have life, and humanity will bloom with a deathless vigour. For these spectres of darkness, which are lifting their horrid and lifeless forms amid the tombs of all the great empires of the old world, and which have blighted the morals and the intelligence of three-fifths of the race for more than twenty centuries, for these soulless forms, we are called upon to look away from 'the face of Infinity unveiled' to our moral vision, to 'deny the Lord that bought us,' to close our eyes to the illuminations of the Eternal Spirit, to surrender our 'everlasting consolations and good hope through grace,' to give over our divine fellowships and immortal fruitions and assurances of an eternity in the kingdom of light, and all for what? For the sublime privilege of thinking with Messrs. Compte, Mill, Spencer, Huxley, and Emmerson, that nothing is real but thought, that matter alone is real, that spirit only has reality, and that 'it is certain that we can have no knowledge of the nature of either matter or spirit,' that we 'know this only, that we nothing know,' and, finally, that with these self-affirmed world-thinkers we are descending the rungs of a ladder that leads down into the abyss of the eternal sleep, 'perhaps to dream' there, and whether we shall or shall not dream, or 'what dreams may come' there, these men cannot assure us.

What reason have we to suppose that this hydra-headed 'New Philosophy,' which is, in fact, as old as the revelations of Gautama Buddha, will produce any better results in the present than it has in past ages? With what new and all-vitalizing principles has it been galvanized? What has this Philosophy done for France, whose Communists desecrated and burned the cathedrals and churches of Paris, as buildings 'owned by a Mr. Jehovah'? Under these old systems, which are being commended to the world as something 'new under the sun,' are we likely to have a millennium of pure morals and universal physical plenty? What is there intrinsic in these systems that gives promise of such results? When we come to think that a human soul may be developed out of 'mutton,' that thought, feeling, and willing are nothing but 'molecular changes in the matter of life,' that human progression is 'advancing from the definite homogeneous to the definite heterogeneous,' that 'matter and spirit are nothing but names for imaginary substrata of groups of natural phenomena,' that 'matter may be regarded as a form of thought,' and that 'thought may be regarded as a property of matter,' that we 'have no knowledge of the nature of either matter or spirit,' that knowledge is possible but in reference to 'things without us,' that knowledge is impossible but in reference to things within us, that 'being and knowing are one and identical,' that our great-great-great-grandmammas and papas were monkeys, that 'the inmates of our prisons and brothels are advancing towards eternal life,' and that 'death is our eternal sleep,' when physiology shall have for ever supplanted and superseded metaphysics, and 'the realm of matter and law is co-extensive with knowledge, with feeling, and with action,' and Materialism shall be repudiated 'as involving grave Philosophical error,' when there shall be a deep and dark and permanent eclipse of faith in the doctrine of God, duty, and immortality, and all religious inquiry shall be sneered at as 'lunal politics,' when this consummation shall have been reached, will not the vernal bloom of humanity be eternal? On the other hand, have we not already the clearest indications that, should the reign of the New Philosophy become universal, 'chaos would come again,' and that the idea of existence would be in the regard of *all* mankind what the same Philosophy has rendered it to three-fifths of the race for more than two thousand years? Have we not absolute proof that the New Philosophy has already rendered, in the judgment of its most enlightened advocates, even eternal existence an object not to be desired, and the loss of all hope of such an existence a matter of no regret? These men speak of the 'loss of this intellectual being' with the same trifling indifference that they do of the annihilation of the vitality of a mushroom or a monkey. Mr. Huxley, for example, compares 'the great lamentation which is arising' 'over the threatened extinction by matter' of the human soul to that 'which was heard over the death of Pan.' Under the death-chill which this Philosophy, from its very nature, brings over the mind, the idea of existence, and especially of eternal existence, ceases, of necessity, to have any attractions to the mind. An aged man of our acquaintance, a man of intelligence, wealth, and influence in community, this man, on being condoled with on the recent loss of the wife of his youth, and the mother of a large family of promising children, exclaimed: 'Tut, what do I care about that woman? I can get another as good as she in a week.' We drew this inference from this fact, that that pure and devoted wife and mother had ceased to be 'a thing of beauty' or wealth in the estimation of that husband. So, when we hear the advocates of this falsely so-called New Philosophy treating with contempt all regard for the soul's immortality and dread of the final loss of 'those thoughts that wander through eternity,' we do them no wrong when we infer that their Philosophy is doing in them what the same Philosophy did in the mind of Gautama Buddha more than two thousand years ago, and that here we have an undeniable revelation of the necessary 'death-doings' of that Philosophy. The validity of all these statements will be fully verified in subsequent inquiries.

PART II.

THE GRECIAN PHILOSOPHY.

INTRODUCTION.

SECTION I.

THE RELATIONS OF THE GREEKS TO THE ORIENTAL NATIONS.

GRECIAN civilization, religion, and Philosophy, as is well known, were all of later growth and development than those of Egypt and other leading Oriental nations. The former, also, though in certain important particulars peculiarized by the genius and institutions of the people, were all, in certain particulars equally important, determined by the latter.

The leading statesmen, literati, and philosophers of Greece, travelled extensively among Oriental nations, studied in their schools, acquainted themselves with their civilization, arts, literature, science, Philosophies, religion, and institutions, and, on their return to their native country, imparted to their countrymen the knowledge with which foreign travel and study had furnished them. Egypt and other Oriental nations were to Greece what Germany has for a long period been to the Anglo-Saxon race. The Anglo-Saxon who would perfect himself in any of the leading sciences very commonly finishes his education in some of the great universities of Germany. Grecian scholars, in like manner, finished their education in the schools of their Oriental neighbours.

The Greek scholar, however, was not, any more than the Anglo-Saxon, a mere copyist. Oriental thought, when subjected to the scrutiny of the Greek mind, took on, in many important respects, new forms and aspects. This was especially true of systems of Philosophy. When a given system passed over from an Oriental nation to Greece, that system most commonly stood connected, in the latter country, with problems unknown to Oriental thought, and disconnected from important elements with which it was originally associated.

In Greece, also, systems of Philosophy appear which have no place whatever in Oriental thought. In the study of the Greek Philosophy we shall meet with old systems connected with new problems and disconnected from certain old associations, and with new systems unknown to Oriental thought. The following facts and statements will present a sufficiently adequate view of the resemblances and differences which obtain between the Grecian and Oriental systems.

CORRESPONDENCES AND DIFFERENCES BETWEEN THE GRECIAN AND THE ORIENTAL SYSTEMS.

1. In the Oriental systems, that of Zoroaster excepted, the doctrine of God is either denied, as in the Materialistic, Dualistic, Subjective, and Pure Idealistic systems, or is affirmed but in the strictly Pantheistic sense, as in the Vedanta, Chinese, and Egyptian systems. In the Grecian systems we meet with not only all these forms of doctrine, but also with that of an infinite, perfect, and personal God, a God distinct from nature and exercising a providential and moral government over the universe. The doctrine of one supreme, personal God was, as we shall find hereafter, the popular doctrine of Greece.

2. In the Oriental systems, with the single exception referred to, we have the doctrine of creation in but two forms, that of natural law and by emanation. In the Grecian systems we find, in addition to these two forms of doctrine, that of creation proper, creation 'by the word of God.' This last form of doctrine was, as we shall find, the generally received doctrine of the people, and constituted the fundamental elements of systems taught by such thinkers as Thales, Anaxagoras, Empedocles, Socrates, Plato, and Aristotle.

3. The doctrine of transmigration, which constitutes an essential element of most of the Oriental systems, seldom has place, but in a modified form, among the Greeks. Plato, for example, held the doctrine of the pre-existence of the soul. The latter state, however, he held to be superior to the present, as the future will be. Transmigration, in the Oriental sense, was from human to brute conditions of existence. Plato desired death as the condition of restoration to pre-existing relations to the Infinite, the True, and the Good. The popular theology of Greece affirmed the doctrine of the immortality of the soul in its proper sense.

4. The *method* of philosophizing which obtained among the Orientals was almost, or quite, exclusively à *priori*. While this was adopted in many of the schools of Greece, in others the à *posteriori*, or inductive method, was adopted. In this country, indeed, the only true method was originated.

RELATION OF THE GREEKS TO THE ORIENTAL NATIONS.

5. While the *moral* teachings of the Materialistic and Idealistic schools of Greece perfectly accorded with those of the same schools in Oriental countries, in the proper Theistic schools of Greece, the doctrine of Right and Wrong, Duty, Moral Desert, and Retribution, received a distinctness of recognition and fulness of elucidation totally foreign to Oriental thought, the system of Zoroaster excepted. The moral teachings of such men as Socrates, Plato, and Aristotle, though in many respects imperfect, were preparatory to the introduction of Christianity.

In Greece we have all the Oriental systems fully represented with their special methods of philosophizing, and with their Theistic doctrines and moral teachings fully developed, the doctrine of transmigration and kindred appendages being finally omitted. In Greece, also, we have what we do not find in the product of Oriental thought, the introduction of a new method in Philosophy, a method which, in the sphere of metaphysics especially, thinkers have been slow to appreciate and adopt, a method which, when perfected and carried out to its ultimate deductions, will dissipate the baleful fog in which false science has bewildered the human mind, and lead it out into the clear sunlight of absolute truth.

SECTION II.

THE RELIGION OF THE GREEKS.

To understand the philosophy of any people, we must know their religion. To know their religion, also, we must understand their philosophy. To comprehend fully the genius and character of the people, we must know both their religion and their philosophy. Nor will the religion and philosophy of any people become fully developed and perfected until their religion assumes the form of real science, and their philosophy becomes, both in its spirit and ultimate deductions, really and truly religious. The philosophy of any people will either affirm or deny their religious ideas and principles, and in fundamental particulars their religious ideas and principles will take form from their philosophic teachings and deductions. Hence the importance of a distinct understanding of the religion of the Greeks, as preparatory to an elucidation of their systems of Philosophy.

Grecian Polytheism.

In common apprehension the religion of this people was exclusively idolatrous and polytheistic in its character. That they were idolaters and did 'worship and serve the creature more than the Creator,' and finally, 'that the things which they sacrificed, they sacrificed to devils and not to God,' are not only truths of inspired testimony, but undeniable facts of history. Not one of 'the gods many and lords many,' which were the common objects of popular worship, were, even in the regard of the worshipper, morally pure, or could be worshipped without morally debasing the worshipper. These facts were admitted and deplored by the best thinkers and writers of the nation. Nor were these multitudinous so-called divinities, in the regard of their worshippers, *uncreated* and *eternally existing* personalities. On the other hand, they were 'worshipped and served' as created beings, creatures of time, erring and sinful, like, and often more corrupt and morally debased than, their worshippers.

The worship of Venus, for example, was the worship of a surpassingly beautiful, but of an openly acknowledged prostitute. One of the Grecian moralists affirms that if he could approach her, he would thrust her through with his spear on account of her demoralizing influence upon the people.

'Could I but only seize Afrodite' (Venus), says Antisthenes, the friend of Socrates, 'I would pierce her through with a javelin, so many virtuous and excellent women has she seduced among us.'

Any one who will read Professor Tholuck 'On the Nature and Moral Influence of Heathenism' will be fully convinced that what Paul has affirmed in the first chapter of Romans and elsewhere upon the subject is but the shadow of the reality. The historians of the time, Petronius especially, give us such specific facts as the following: 'The temples were frequented, splendid sacrifices were made, altars were crowned, and prayers were offered to the gods in order that the gods might render nights of unnatural lust agreeable! that they might be favourable to acts of poisoning; that they might cause robberies of widows and orphans to prosper.' 'How great is now,' exclaims Seneca, 'the madness of men. They lisp the most abominable prayers in the ears of the gods; and if a man is found listening, they are silent. What a man ought not to hear, they do not blush to rehearse to God.' Yet Roman Polytheism was known to have been far less corrupting than the Grecian.

The Monotheism of Greece.

But were the Greeks simply Polytheists? Did they not, also, believe in one supreme God, the Creator of the universe? The gods of popular worship were, as we have seen, distinctly and definitely regarded as created and finite beings. Did they, also, recognize the being, perfection, creative energy, and supreme control of one eternal and uncreated divinity? The Scriptures affirm of the heathen that 'they know God, but do not glorify Him as God.' We have the most absolute historic proofs of the perfect and unqualified truthfulness of this testimony.

So universal and omnipresent among even the common people of

Greece and Rome was the idea of one supreme God, that under sudden and unexpected perils they never prayed to any one, or to all their minor gods, but always to the one only living and true God; and they never turned their faces in prayer toward their idol temples, but always upward toward God Himself. This impressive fact is stated both by Christian and heathen writers. 'The common people,' says Tertullian, 'in the deepest emotions of their minds never direct their exclamations to their false gods, but employ the words, *By God! As truly as God lives! God help me!* Moreover, they do not thereby have their view directed to the capitol, but to heaven.' Aulus Gellius says, 'The ancient Romans were not accustomed, during an earthquake, to pray to some one of the gods individually, but only to God in the general, as the Unknown.' Lactantius dwells more extensively upon this, and remarks that 'it was in misfortune and danger that they made use particularly of the appellation Deus. After the danger and fear were over,' he adds, 'they then resorted to their temples.'

The concurrence of the learned and the ignorant throughout the Pagan world in the doctrine of one supreme God is thus affirmed by Maximus Tyrius, a celebrated heathen philosopher: 'If there were a meeting called of all the several trades and professions .... and all were required to declare their sense concerning God, do you think that the painter would say one thing, the sculptor another, the poet another, the philosopher another? No; nor the Scythian neither, nor the Greek, nor the Hyperborean. In regard to other things we find men speaking discordantly one to another, all men, as it were, differing from all men. .... Nevertheless, on this subject you may find universally throughout the world one agreeing law and opinion, that there is one God, the King and Father of All, and many gods the sons of God, and co-reigners together with God.'

The tragic and comic poets of Greece were among the educators of the popular mind in religion, and at the same time most distinctly and specifically represent the popular belief in respect to the subject now under consideration. In their writings the doctrine of one, and only one, supreme, all-perfect, personal God, is most distinctly and absolutely affirmed.

Æschylus, one of the oldest and most influential authors of this class, applies to God such expressions as the following, expressions which, as Dr. Cocker well observes, 'approach very nearly to the Christian idea of God,' to wit, 'He is the Universal Father,' 'Father of gods and men,' 'the Universal Cause,' 'the All-seer and All-doer,' 'the All-wise and All-controlling,' 'the Just and the Executor of Justice,' 'true and incapable of falsehood,' 'holy,' 'merciful,' 'the God especially of the suppliant and the stranger,' 'the Most High,' 'Perfect One,' 'King of kings, of the happy most happy, of the perfect most perfect for ever, blessed Zeus.'

Sophocles, the most celebrated of all the tragic poets, thus sets forth the doctrine of but one supreme God: 'There is, in truth, one only God, who made heaven and earth, the sea, air, and winds.' Other stanzas from the same author are thus rendered by one of our own poets:

> 'Still in yon starry heaven supreme,
> Jove, all-beholding, all-directing, dwells,
> Spurning the power of age, enthroned in might,
> Thou dwellest mid heaven's broad light;
> This was, in ages past, Thy firm decree,
> Is now and shall for ever be.'

Philemon, the comedian, thus speaks: 'Believe in one God and revere Him.' 'Revere Him continually as being and as being nigh thee.' Two Greek poets have given utterance to the doctrine cited by Paul, 'We are all His offspring.' The stanza from Aratus of Cilicia, Paul's native city, is thus rendered, a stanza especially noticeable as expressing both the omnipresence and all-presiding providence and agency of God:

> 'Jove's presence fills all space, upholds this ball,
> All need His aid; His power sustains us all,
>   *For we His offspring are.*'

Cleanthus, who was both a poet and philosopher, thus speaks:

> 'Great and divine Father, whose names are many,
> But who art one and the same unchangeable, almighty power,
> O thou supreme Author of Nature !
> That governest by a single, unerring law !
>   Hail, King !
> For Thou art able to enforce obedience from all frail mortals,
> *Because we are all Thine offspring,*
> The image and the echo only of Thine eternal voice.'

The same doctrine we find avowed by the most eminent authors and philosophers of Greece. Longinus, for example, cites, not only as an example of the sublime, but with expressions of especial admiration, the first verse of the first chapter of Genesis, 'In the beginning, God created the heavens and the earth.'

Zenophon not only avows a belief in this doctrine, but defends at great length, and with much ability, the views of Socrates upon the same subject. In a letter to Æschines he says, 'For that divine things lie beyond our knowledge is clear to all; it is enough, therefore, to revere the power of God, which is above all things.'

Plutarch, in the following passage, not only avows his own, and the common belief among all nations, in the doctrine of one supreme God, but also the distinction between this supreme God and subordinate divinities. 'We do not believe that there are different gods among different nations of men, the Grecian and the foreign, the southern and the northern, but as the same sun and moon and heaven and earth and sea are common to all men, though differently denominated by different nations, so in diverse countries there are different kinds of worship and different appellations fixed by the laws, while one Intelligence orders all, and one Providence orders all, and subordinate powers are appointed over all.'

The leading Greek philosophers, while they admitted a plurality of inferior so-called gods, unitedly affirmed the doctrine of one, supreme, uncreated, all-perfect, and all-controlling, personal God. We refer, of course, to such individuals as Thales, the Father of Greek Philosophy, Xenophanes, Anaxagoras, Empedocles, Socrates, Plato, and Aristotle.

'God,' says Thales, 'is the oldest of all things, because He is unmade and ungenerated.' 'There is one God,' says Xenophanes, 'the greatest among gods and men.' 'All things that are upon the earth,' says Empedocles, 'may be truly called the works of God, who ruleth over the world, out of whom proceed all things, plants, men, beasts, and gods.' This supreme God, he tells us, 'is wholly and perfectly mind, ineffable, holy, with rapid, swift glancing thought pervading the whole world.'

'He who raised the whole universe,' says Socrates, 'and still upholds the mighty frame, Who perfected every part of it in beauty, and in goodness, suffering none of those parts to decay through age, but renewing them daily with unfading vigour—even He, the Supreme God, still holds Himself invisible, and it is only in His works that we are capable of admiring Him.'

The following quotation from the work of Dr. Cocker on 'Christianity and the Greek Philosophy' presents all that need be said in this connection, in regard to the views of Plato, on this subject:

'It were needless to attempt the proof that *Plato* believed in one Supreme God, and *only* one. This one being is with him "the first God;" "the greatest of the gods;" "the God over all;" "the sole principle of the universe." He is "the immutable," "the All-perfect," "the eternal Being." He is "the Architect of the world;" "the Maker of the universe;" "the Father of gods and men;" "the sovereign Mind which orders all things, and passes through all things;" "the sole Monarch and Ruler of the world."'

In the following passage Aristotle not only, as he does most absolutely elsewhere, avows his belief in one Supreme God, but also the great fact which we have so strongly maintained elsewhere, that the then-existing Polytheism was a corruption of the ancient Monotheism. 'The tradition has come down to us,' he says, 'from very ancient times, being left in a mythical garb to succeeding generations, that these' (the heavenly bodies) 'are gods, and that the Divinity encompasses the whole of nature. There have been made, however, to these certain fabulous additions for the purpose of winning the belief of the multitude, and thus securing their obedience to their vows, and their co-operation towards advancing the general welfare of the state. These additions have been to the effect that these gods were of the same form as men, and even that some of them were in appearance similar to certain others amongst the rest of the animal creation. The wise course, however, would be for the philosopher to disengage from these traditions the false element, and to embrace that which is true; and the truth lies in that portion of this ancient doctrine which regards the first and deepest grounds of all existence to be the *Divine*, and this we may regard as a divine utterance.

'In all probability every art, science, and philosophy has been over and over again discussed to the farthest extent possible, and then again lost; and we may conceive these opinions to have been preserved to us as a sort of fragment of these lost philosophies. We see, then, to some extent, the relation of the popular belief to these ancient opinions.'

The specific denials of this one doctrine, that of one, and only one, Supreme God, the denials which appear in all forms of the Atheistic and Sceptical systems of the Greek Philosophy, clearly evince the existence of that doctrine as an essential element of the popular faith among this people. Philosophers—we repeat what we have formerly stated—are not accustomed to deny what is not generally believed. Thus Protagoras, of Abdera, was, for his avowed Scepticism, banished from the city, and his books burned in a public assembly of the people.

We should here remark that the Supreme God of the *popular* faith of the Greeks was no impersonal essence like the God of Pantheism, but a free, self-conscious personality, the Creator proper of a created universe. Such was, also, the character of God as affirmed in the theistic and denied in the anti-theistic philosophies of that people. In one form the Greeks, with the Roman and surrounding nations, were idolaters and Polytheists. As far as the doctrine of one, and only one, supreme, eternally existing, all-creating, and all-controlling, personal God is concerned, they were, in the strictest sense, Monotheists. This great fact will be a central light in all our future inquiries and deductions.

SECTION III.

NATURE, CHARACTER, AND MUTUAL RELATIONS OF KNOWLEDGE A PRIORI AND À POSTERIORI. THESE FORMS OF KNOWLEDGE DISTINGUISHED AND DEFINED.

ALL philosophers of all schools of the present era of science, with very few exceptions, agree, that actual knowledge in these two forms does exist in the human mind. An agreement equally universal also obtains in respect to the general and distinguishing characteristics of these two kinds of knowledge. Whatever form of knowledge has the fixed characteristics of absolute universality and necessity takes rank as knowledge *à priori*. Forms of real knowledge, on the other hand, which want these characteristics, are denominated knowledge *à posteriori*.

Ideas whose objects are apprehended as real, with the absolute impossibility of conceiving them as not being real, or as being, in any respects, different from what we apprehend them to be, we call necessary ideas, and our knowledge of such objects is denominated knowledge *à priori*. Ideas, on the other hand, whose *objects* are *known* to be real, with the possibility of conceiving of their non-reality, or of their being different from what we apprehend them to be, are denominated contingent ideas, and the knowledge we have of such objects is denominated knowledge *à posteriori*.

Time and space, for example, are apprehended as real, with the absolute impossibility of conceiving them not to be realities, or as being, in any respect, different from what we apprehend them to be. We accordingly designate our ideas of these realities as necessary ideas, and affirm said realities to be the objects of *à priori* knowledge. Matter and spirit, on the other hand, we know to be realities in themselves; while we thus know them, we can *conceive* of their non-reality, or as being different realities from what we apprehend them to be. We therefore designate our ideas of these realities as contingent ideas, and regard said realities as the objects of knowledge *à posteriori*.

The same distinction obtains in regard to judgments. Those judgments which we know to be universally true, with the absolute impossibility of conceiving them as not being true, we denominate *necessary* judgments, or judgments *à priori*. Those judgments, on the other hand, which we know to be true, with the possibility of conceiving of them as not being true, are denominated contingent judgments, or judgments *à posteriori*.

Such judgments as the following, Body implies space, Succession implies time, Events imply a cause, Phenomena imply substance, and Things equal to the same thing are equal to one another, are necessary, or *à priori* judgments. The reason is obvious. We not only know such propositions to be true, but know equally that they *must* be true, their non-truth being absolutely inconceivable, and, consequently, impossible. Such propositions, on the other hand, as Mind exists, Body exists, are known with absolute certainty to be true. Yet we can conceive that they may not be true. Such judgments, therefore, we denominate contingent judgments, or judgments *à posteriori*. The judgment Things equal to the same things are not equal to one another, for example, is false not only in fact, but self-contradictory, and therefore absurd. The judgment Mind does not exist is false in fact, though not self-evidently so. It is an untrue, but not an absurd proposition.

A fundamental distinction between necessary ideas here demands special attention. Those of time and space have *absolute*, or *unconditional* necessity. Their objects must exist whether any other realities do, or do not, exist. The ideas represented by such terms as substance and cause are only *conditionally* necessary. In other words, events and phenomena being given as real, substances and causes must exist. If, on the other hand, phenomena and events are not given as real, substances and causes cannot be affirmed to exist. The ideas of substance and cause are, therefore, not regarded as unconditionally, but conditionally, necessary. We have, then, two, and only two unconditionally necessary ideas, to wit, those of time and space. Such ideas as those of substance, cause, and personal identity, are, in all their forms, conditionally necessary ideas.

Thus far we have gone over ground, for the most part, occupied in the general Introduction. Nor will the validity of the above expositions and elucidations be questioned by real thinkers of any school. The *relations* really existing between knowledge à *priori* and à *posteriori* have not yet been satisfactorily determined in any known school of Philosophy. Those relations must be fully determined, or we shall advance without clear insight in our future inquiries. What, then, are the fixed and immutable relations between the two forms of knowledge under consideration, to wit, knowledge à *priori* and à *posteriori?* They are among others the following:

Relations between Knowledge à priori and à posteriori.

1. As far as *certainty* is concerned, there is no real difference. Real knowledge, throughout its appropriate sphere, admits of no degrees as far as the element of *certainty* is concerned. I know myself, for example, as a personal being, exercising the functions of thought, feeling, and willing, just as certainly as I know time or space. Our knowledge of facts may be, and often is, just as real and certain as that of the necessary principles by which said facts are explained and elucidated.

Knowledge à *priori* and à *posteriori*, in all their real forms, differ as far as our modes of apprehension are concerned, but not in respect to the element of certainty. Apprehensions which have the elements of uncertainty in them are not forms of real knowledge. Our knowledge of the essential qualities of spirit, on the one hand, and of matter, on the other, is, in fact, just as real and certain, as is that of space and time. Great injury is done to the cause of truth when it is admitted that the characteristic of uncertainty inheres in our apprehensions of the essential qualities of these substances. It should be borne in mind, that all who impeach the validity of our knowledge of these substances do the same in respect to our knowledge of the objects of necessary ideas and principles. Those who affirm mere relativity of our knowledge of matter and spirit affirm the same thing of our knowledge of space and time, and of all necessary principles. There is no stopping short of the deduction, that knowledge, in all, or in none, of its real forms, has the element of uncertainty in it.

2. Knowledge *à priori*, in all its forms, is specifically given in the universal intelligence as directly and immediately *implied* by knowledge *à posteriori*. Hence, the principles and axioms: Body *implies* space, Succession *implies* time, Events *imply* a cause, and Phenomena *imply* substance. In all such judgments the subject represents the perceived or *à posteriori* element, and the predicate, the implied or *à priori* element.

We have here, as a careful analysis will absolutely evince, the fixed and immutable relations between these two forms of knowledge. The latter is always given through, and as implied by, the former. If we had no ideas of body and succession, we could have no apprehensions of space or time which are given in the universal intelligence only as the real or possible places of substances and succession. If we had no ideas of phenomena or events, we could have none of substances or causes. We know space, time, substance, and cause, but as implied by body, succession, phenomena, and events, and as the necessary condition of their existence and occurrence. If we had no ideas of events occurring in fixed order, we should have none of law. If we had no apprehensions of agents possessed of certain powers, and existing in certain relations to each other, we could have none of moral law, duty, desert, and retribution. Everywhere when the *à priori* form of knowledge appears, it is always manifested as implied by definite forms of *à posteriori* knowledge. In the latter we have the elements of *perceived*, and in the former that of *implied* knowledge. Unless the perceived or *à posteriori* elements were given, the implied or *à priori* elements could not be given. If no phenomena or events should appear, how could we know that substances or causes do exist? The same holds true universally. Without the perceived or *à posteriori* element, we could not have the implied or *à priori* element, and the latter is always given through, and in no other form but as implied by, the former.

3. In the order of actual *development* in the Intelligence, the *à posteriori* always precedes the *à priori* form of knowledge. In other words, body, succession, phenomena, and events must have been perceived before there could have been any apprehension of space, time, substance, and cause. This is absolutely evinced by the fact that the latter are, and can be, apprehended but as sustaining fixed relations to the former. If the *à priori* form of knowledge was developed in the mind prior to the *à posteriori*, the former could be apprehended without reference to the

latter. But this is impossible. We cannot define space and time but as the places of body and succession, or substance and cause but as realities of which phenomena are properties and by which events are produced. We can, on the other hand, define body, succession, phenomena, and events without reference to space, time, substance, or cause. Nothing can be more evident than the fact that in the order of actual origination, the *à posteriori* forms of knowledge always precede the *à priori* and occasion and imply the latter. There can be no more fundamental mistake in psychology than is made by the assumption that the *à priori* form of knowledge does, in any case, precede the *à posteriori*.

4. While, in the order of actual origination in the Intelligence, the *à posteriori* always precedes the *à priori* elements of knowledge, in the *logical* order, the latter, as universally, precedes the former. In other words, if space, time, substance, and cause did not exist, there could by no possibility be any such realities as body, succession, phenomena, or events. The reality of the object of the *à priori* is always given as the necessary condition of the possibility of the reality of the object of the *à posteriori* form of knowledge. Science is greatly indebted to Cousin for having developed and evinced the logical and chronological order of these two forms of knowledge.

5. A careful and correct analysis of the elements which constitute these two forms of knowledge will, as already indicated, absolutely evince the fact that the elements of the *à posteriori* are all given by perception external or internal, or by both combined; while those of the *à priori* are implied by, and given through, what is perceived. We perceive body, succession, phenomena, and events. On occasion of such perceptions and through the same, we apprehend space, time, substance, and cause, as implied by what we perceive.

Necessary Deductions from the Preceding Analysis.

We now advance to a consideration of certain necessary deductions from the preceding analysis. Among those which might be adduced, special attention is requested to the following:

1. All the original elements of knowledge *à posteriori* are given, as we have seen, through perception external and internal. This fact implies two faculties of perception, that which perceives internal or subjective, and that which perceives external or objective phenomena. The former we denominate Consciousness, or more properly, perhaps, Self-consciousness. The latter we denominate Sense. The faculty of implied or *à priori* knowledge, we designate by the term Reason. Consciousness, Sense, and Reason are the primary faculties of the Intelligence, and furnish the original elements of universal knowledge in all its forms. The secondary faculties—the understanding or conceptive faculty, the judgment or

logical faculty, the memory or associating principle, and the imagination or blending faculty—all do and must operate exclusively upon materials furnished by these three primary faculties.

2. The spheres and exclusive functions of these primary faculties are also, by the preceding analysis, perfectly fixed and determinable. The exclusive sphere of Self-consciousness is to give the mind itself in the actual exercise of its faculties. That of Sense is to give matter through its manifested properties. That of Reason is to give the realities implied by what is perceived through Sense and Consciousness, realities such as space, time, substance, and cause. Each faculty has absolute authority within its own sphere. Reason can merely give what is implied by objects perceived, and has no authority whatever in determining the validity or non-validity of perception. Nor has one perceptive faculty any authority in determining the validity of the dicta of the other. What, for example, has Sense to do in the determination of the reality or non-reality of facts of mind, or of the validity or non-validity of our knowledge of the same? Consciousness, also, can do no more than give the actual form of external perception, the fact that it is direct or indirect. With the validity of the perception, Consciousness has nothing to do.

How can the secondary faculties judge of the validity or non-validity of the affirmations of any or all of the primary ones? There can be no more absurd procedure in science than that in which an attempt is made to force one faculty into the proper and exclusive sphere of another, that the former may sit in judgment upon the validity of the determinations of the latter.

By some philosophers, Reason, the simple faculty of *implied* knowledge, has been actually deified as 'God in us.' Hence, all the other faculties have been arrayed at the bar of this divinity, and having been 'weighed in the balances' there, have, of course, 'been found wanting.' All our world-knowledge and necessary ideas have been found to be nothing but 'unavoidable illusion which inheres in Reason itself.'

Hence, this same Reason has been compelled, through its direct and immediate *à priori* insight, to determine what realities do, or do not, exist.

From the multitudinous self-contradictory and absurd responses, which have been wrung from her under such crucifixions, she could justly be convicted of intellectual aberration. At one time she has been made to affirm absolutely the existence of two unknown and unknowable 'noumena' as the exclusive principles of all things; at another that matter alone exists; then that 'the I myself I' only has being; again, that the Infinite and Absolute is the sole principle of all things; and, finally, that no substances of any kind exist, that thought only is real, and that time and space are nothing but special forms of thought. All these responses are given forth as veritable revelations of absolute truth. Nothing is, or can be, more utterly absurd and lawless than Reason, or any other faculty, when forced out of its proper sphere and compelled to act there. When we refuse, in the construction of our world-systems, to accept as veritable truths of science all the real elements furnished by all the faculties of original intuition, and with absolute integrity, to incorporate into our building the materials thus furnished, and *as* furnished, we shall, and must, lawlessly construct nothing but logical fictions which scientific scrutiny will not fail to break to pieces.

3. We are now fully prepared to designate all the forms of real knowledge which can have being and place in the human mind. All must consist of what is perceived, of what is implied by what is perceived, and finally of what is combined and logically deduced from what is perceived, and from what is implied by the perceived. Here, undeniably, is the exclusive sphere, the extent and limits, of true science. If any of the original intuitions, whether empirical or *à priori*, are omitted, or any elements introduced not given by such intuition, we shall, with inevitable certainty, rear up structures of false science.

4. We have now an infallible criterion by which we can, with absolute certainty, discriminate between real and unreal forms of affirmed *à priori* knowledge. The objects of *à priori* knowledge in all its forms lie wholly out of, and beyond, the sphere of perception and of knowledge *à posteriori*. An object, or reality, is affirmed to exist, a reality affirmed to be the object of knowledge *à priori*. If a valid knowledge in this form of that object does exist, we shall be able to designate some object of actual perception, an object the existence of which necessarily implies the existence of the reality referred to. If no such perceived object can be designated, we may know with absolute certainty that the form of affirmed *à priori* knowledge before us is an illusion.

À priori knowledge, when its validity is not necessarily implied by some known form of knowledge *à posteriori*, does not and cannot exist. An individual affirms the existence in time and space of a certain reality which is not an object of perception external or internal, and affirms that reality to be the object of *à priori* knowledge. If he can designate no object of perception whose existence necessarily implies that of the reality affirmed to exist, we may affirm with absolute assurance that a fiction of a bewildered brain is obtruded upon us as a necessary truth of science.

If, on the other hand, this individual does designate a known form of *à posteriori* knowledge, a form the validity of which necessarily implies that of the form of *à priori* knowledge presented, we violate all the principles of true science if we do not admit the existence of the reality under consideration. Any form of affirmed *à priori* knowledge, the validity of which is not implied by some known form of real knowledge *à posteriori*, is undeniably an illusion. The criterion under consideration has equal validity in determining the claims of all forms of judgment affirmed to possess *à priori* certainty. In all such judgments the reality of the *object* represented by the *subject* of such judgment implies of necessity that of the *object* represented by the *predicate* of the same judgment. In such judgments, for example, as Body implies space, Succession, time, and Events, a cause, the existence of the object represented by the subject, in every instance, implies absolutely that of the object represented by the predicate. Such judgments have *à priori* certainty, and may be rightfully employed as principles of science. But whenever such relations between the subject and predicate do not obtain, and yet the judgments presented are set forth as having *à priori*, or self-evident certainty, we may know absolutely that mere lawless assumptions are being imposed upon us as principles or axioms in science. An individual, for example, lays down the proposition, as a principle in science, that but one substance or principle of all things does exist. We ask him to verify his proposition by proof. He not only refuses compliance with our request, but denies our right to demand proof, claiming for his judgment self-evident, or *à priori*, validity. Where is the ground for such a claim? Where is the necessary connection between the subject and predicate in such judgment? If an individual should affirm that two or three such substances do exist, he would, undeniably, have just as clear a right to claim for his proposition *à priori* certainty, as the individual before us has for his. Philosophers should be held to the strictest account when they require our assent to judgments, or propositions, which they urge upon us as self-evident, or *à priori*, principles of science.

5. We are also furnished, in the above discriminations and expositions, with an absolutely valid criterion by which we can discriminate, with perfect certainty, between all forms of valid and invalid claims of *à priori insight*. An individual claims, for example, that in the presence of all perceived substances, he is able, by Reason, to apprehend the realities, not directly perceived, but necessarily implied by what is perceived. On the actual perception of body, succession, phenomena, and events, for example, he does apprehend, as real, space, time, substances, and causes, and affirms himself to be actually possessed of such a power of *à priori* insight. We should give the lie to all the fundamental facts of our own Consciousness, if we should deny to this individual the actual possession of *à priori* insight in the form claimed. An individual, on the other hand, affirms, that having 'put himself into a state of not-knowing,' after having 'assumed all existing forms of knowledge to be uncertain,' and ignoring wholly all facts and objects of external and internal perception, he can, through *à priori* insight, look off into infinite space and duration, and determine, with absolute certainty, what reality or realities

do, and do not exist, and then what are their relations, and from the elements of knowledge thus obtained, that he can construct a valid system of universal being and its laws. We should dementate ourselves, if we should give the remotest credit to the affirmed fact, or validity of such insight. The individual who claims to know through such insight what realities do and do not exist in infinite space and time does, in fact, claim the possession of absolute omniscience. None but absolute omniscience can determine, by such insight, what are their relations and laws.

We, as human beings, have our fixed conditions, and privileges of knowledge, and these, when rigidly adhered to, and rightly used, are abundantly adequate to all needful purposes of science and of life. When perverted and disregarded, 'the light that is in us becomes darkness,' and the Intelligence itself, under will-compulsion, lands us in the abyss of error. Each faculty of the Intelligence has a fixed and readily determinable sphere of activity. We can, if we will, determine the number of these faculties, the peculiar and special sphere of each, its authority within its own sphere, and the mutual relations and dependence of these faculties one in respect to each and all of the others. When scientific inquiry is conducted according to the fixed laws of the Intelligence, when each faculty, with the facts which it really furnishes, is duly respected, and no one faculty is forced out of its own proper sphere, our whole line of induction and deduction will be under the eternal sunlight of truth. But if we adopt assumptions instead of valid principles, and adduce 'imaginary substrata' instead of facts of real intuition, our inquiries will conduct us into the midnight of error.

6. We are also prepared, in view of our previous expositions, to determine fully, and with perfect certainty, the nature and spheres and mutual relations to each other of the *à priori*, or pure, and of the *à posteriori*, or mixed, sciences. The distinction under consideration lies here. All the real sciences are wholly constituted of principles and facts, and deductions from said principles and facts. In the *à priori*, or pure sciences, all the principles (axioms and postulates) and facts are furnished exclusively through *à priori* insight. In the *à posteriori*, or mixed sciences, the principles are *à priori*, or self-evident judgments, while the facts are objects of perception, that is, of knowledge *à posteriori*. In the former class of sciences, not only the principles, but equally the facts, are the objects of necessary knowledge. In other words, the principles and facts will, all alike, be given with the absolute knowledge, that they must be as we apprehend them to be. This we all know to be true of the principles in all such sciences, principles such as these, Things equal to the same thing are equal to one another, and The whole is greater than any one of its parts. In all such judgments, the subject implies the predicate.

The same holds equally of the facts in such sciences. Said facts are given by definition, which has in all cases *à priori*, or necessary, validity. Space implies the existence in itself of points and figures, such as straight lines, triangles, squares, circles, and ellipses. In the elucidation of the nature, properties, and relations of such points and figures, we have the science of numbers and quantity, as the mathematics. In these sciences, the principles, definitions, facts, and deductions, all in common, have *à priori*, or necessary validity. They are given as valid with the utter impossibility of conceiving of their invalidity. In the *à posteriori*, or mixed sciences, the principles, all in common, have *à priori*, or necessary validity, while the facts, we repeat, are the objects of knowledge *à posteriori*, objects known to be real, but with the possibility of our conceiving of their non-reality. The pure, or *à priori* sciences, pertain to number and quantity which exist as properties of space and time themselves. The *à posteriori*, or mixed sciences, pertain to phenomena, and events, and substances, and causes, existing in time and space. Nothing can be more clear and distinct, than what obtains relatively to the spheres and nature of these two classes of sciences.

ALL QUESTIONS PERTAINING TO ONTOLOGY BELONG EXCLUSIVELY TO THE À POSTERIORI, OR MIXED SCIENCES.

We can now determine with demonstrative certainty to what sphere, that of the *à posteriori*, or *à priori*, sciences, all questions of Ontology, of Being, its laws and relations, and of substances and causes, proximate and ultimate, exclusively belong. They pertain, we answer, wholly and exclusively, not to the *à priori*, or pure, but to the *à posteriori*, or mixed sciences. The reason is most obvious. Whatever is given as existing in time and space is, in fact, given exclusively as the object of contingent, or conditionally implied knowledge. We can conceive of space and time as occupied by, or as utterly void of, phenomena and events, substances and causes. As each state and relation is equally conceivable, and, therefore, possible in itself, we have no grounds whatever for an *à priori* determination of the question whether any, and much less what particular and specific causes, substances, phenomena, and events do exist and occur in time and space. One philosopher sets forth, as an *à priori* principle in science, the dogma that but one substance or principle of all things does exist. Another philosopher affirms, as a similar principle, the existence of two entities, *noumena*, as the principle of all things. How can we determine which is right, and which wrong, or whether both are not mistaken? As it is equally conceivable, and therefore possible in itself, that either one, as that the other, may be right and his antagonist wrong, or that both may be in error, we have, and can have no *à priori* grounds for the determination of any such question.

One philosopher affirms knowledge to be possible and actual but in its subjective form; another, that it is possible and actual but in its objective form; another still, that no valid knowledge, in either form, is possible; and a fourth, that it is both possible and actual in both forms. There is nothing self-contradictory in either hypothesis. Either therefore may be true, and all the others false. What ground have we, or can we have, then, for an *à priori* determination of the question which is, and which is not true? None whatever. The question, which is, and which is not true, is a simple question of fact—a question to be resolved exclusively, not by *à priori*, but by *à posteriori* insight, that is, by an appeal to facts of Consciousness. No truth can be more demonstrably evident than this, that all questions of Ontology, questions pertaining to Being and its laws, and substances, and causes, proximate and ultimate, come exclusively within the sphere, not of the *à priori*, or pure, but of the *à posteriori*, or mixed sciences. In all our inquiries throughout the wide domain of ontological science, we are absolutely confined to facts of actual intuition, to substances and causes implied by such facts, and to the logical deductions which such facts, substances, and causes yield.

8. We can, also, determine with equal absoluteness what is the true, and *only* true, method of induction and deduction in the domain of ontological science. Two, and only two, methods are known to science, the *à priori* and the *à posteriori* or inductive. In the pure sciences, the former, and in the mixed the latter, exclusively obtains. In the former all principles and facts are given as necessarily valid and real. In the latter we have our necessary principles, while our facts are given exclusively through perception or intuitive insight. Suppose now that the *à priori* method, the method which has place in the pure sciences only, is carried over into the universe of facts and objects of contingent ideas, and an attempt is made through such method to resolve all questions of facts pertaining to Being and its laws. As a matter of course and necessity, we shall substitute lawless assumptions in the place of valid *à priori* principles, and imaginary facts and substrata in the place of intuitively known realities and their attributes.

All our deductions, consequently, will have no more validity for real existences and their laws than the wildest fables possess for historic verities. The report of an individual of his personal knowledge in regard to the visibilities of London or Paris, an individual who has merely passed through its streets with his eyes and ears and senses so closed that he could see and hear and feel nothing, would be just as reliable as are the *à priori* visions of the greatest philosopher in regard to facts of universal being and its laws. Conceive such a philosopher located in empty space, with an absolute oblivion of mind and matter, time and space. Require him, under these conditions and circumstances, to determine wholly by *à priori* insight what reality or realities do, or do not, exist, and what are their nature, relations, and laws. This, undeniably, is a far more favourable condition for such insight than a location amid the 'unavoidable illusions' and 'prejudices' and deceptive appearances of perception. All such illusions and prejudices and appearances can do nothing but darken *à priori* insight of absolute truth, if the power of direct vision of such truth exists in the mind. The Yogee, with the Transcendental Philosopher, does all he can, 'when he begins to philosophize,' to put himself into the very state above described. 'He puts himself into a state of not-knowing,' and 'assumes all existing forms of knowledge to be uncertain,' and 'by an absolute and scientific scepticism to which he voluntarily determines himself for the purpose of future certainty,' 'compels himself to *treat* such knowledge as nothing but a prejudice.' It takes a world of trouble to effect such 'a purification of the mind' as this, and while by this higher *à priori* insight the vision of the Absolute is being received, these 'unavoidable illusions' will return and force themselves upon the attention, and thus disturb 'pious meditation' and cloud the desired vision of real being and its laws. But let this state of not-knowing 'be perfected by an absolute oblivion of these otherwise unavoidable illusions'—an utter oblivion of matter and spirit, time and space. Nothing would then be left to disturb 'pious meditation,' or cloud the vision of 'the faculty of intellectual intuition.' Here, if by any possibility the end can be accomplished by *à priori* insight, and the *à priori* method of philosophizing in the domain of Ontology, we should obtain an absolutely verified system of universal being and its laws.

We lay this down as a proposition which no candid thinker who has comprehended the above facts and arguments will question, that every system of Ontology—a system developed and constructed in conformity with the principles of the *à priori* method of philosophizing—stands revealed as a demonstrated fiction of false science. The era has arrived when, but in the sphere of pure science, the mathematics, the *à priori* method of philosophizing in the domain of real substances and causes, and of universal being and its laws, should be left and for ever remain among the 'fossilized precepts' or illusions of bygone eras.

We have but one exclusive method left us for the determination and solution of all questions and problems pertaining to substances and causes, Being and its relations and laws, the *à posteriori* or inductive method. In conducting our inquiries, there must be, in the light of undeniably valid criteria, a careful discrimination between real principles of science and assumptions, and between mere opinions, beliefs, and conjectures, and forms of valid knowledge, and from such principles and knowledges our system of Being and its laws must, with rigid integrity, be deduced.

Then, and then only, will such systems lay veritable claims to our regard as 'knowledge systematized.' Hitherto philosophic inquiry has for the most part been conducted without any proper determination of the distinctive characteristics and spheres of the *à priori* and inductive methods in science, without any proper determination of the question which method has exclusive place and authority in the domain of ontological inquiry, and without a scientific determination of the criteria by which principles in science are distinguished from assumptions, and forms of real valid knowledge from mere opinions, beliefs, and conjectures pertaining to facts and realities in the universe within and around us.

If the wisest philosophers of the age were required to give specific information on all these topics of fundamental interest, we venture the opinion that most of them would be at a loss to furnish it. If all philosophic inquiry into Being and its laws were suspended until all the questions and problems above suggested were fully solved, and if from that time onward all forms of ontological induction and deduction should be conducted in strict accordance with the method and principles thus developed and verified, the fog and miasma of false science would soon pass away, and humanity would move on in the bright sunlight of real science.

9. Enough has already been said, perhaps, in regard to the claims set up by certain philosophers, that they possess a faculty of special 'intellectual intuition,' or *à priori* insight, by which they are able, independently of facts of *à posteriori* knowledge, to furnish us with absolute information pertaining to universal being and its laws. As we shall hereafter, as we have so frequently met in the past, meet with this profession, and encounter imposing systems reared up under its affirmed guidance, we shall be pardoned for a special consideration of this profession in this connection. We are now able to demonstrate this profession, with all its *à priori* systems of ontology, to be nothing but the veriest and most absurd illusion that has ever appeared in the sphere of scientific thought. The well-known characteristics of *à priori* knowledge, in all its forms, are absolute *universality* and *necessity*. In other words, the objects of such knowledge are conceived of as existing with the utter impossibility of even conceiving of them as not existing. If these philosophers are really possessed of this *à priori* insight, the forms of knowledge furnished through it will have the two fixed characteristics under consideration. So of the systems of Ontology thus furnished. Such systems, in all their principles, facts, and deductions, will have all the forms and degrees of absolute and necessary certainty that the pure sciences have.

Now there is not a solitary form of cognition, a form which has ever been furnished by this insight, which has any such characteristics whatever. Not one principle, fact, or deduction thus furnished has even the appearance of universal and necessary certainty. On the other hand, all the multitudinous forms of Being thus affirmed, as objects of absolute knowledge, have, in themselves, the fixed characteristics of objects of contingent knowledge, and the existence of every such object is absolutely incompatible with that of every other. Take, as an example, this affirmed à *priori*, or necessary, principle of science, the principle affirmed to be such by Materialism and Idealism in all their forms, to wit, 'that but one substance or principle of all things does exist.' If this is, as it is affirmed to be, a real à *priori* principle, it would be just as absolutely impossible for us to conceive of its non-validity, as it is to conceive of the non-validity of the principle, 'Things equal to the same things are equal to one another.' Who does not perceive that the former has none of the essential characteristics of the latter? While we do, and cannot but know, that the latter is, and must be, true, without the possession of absolute omniscience, we cannot determine whether the former is, or is not, true, much less whether it *must* be true.

In the sphere of Materialism we have this absolute revelation of 'intellectual intuition,' or à *priori* insight, that matter is the only existing substance. In the sphere of Idealism we have, as the revelation of absolute truth, the dogma that spirit, or its operations alone, has being, a revelation given forth by this same 'faculty of intellectual intuition,' or à *priori* insight. In one of these cases, at least, this infallible organ of 'intellectual intuition,' or à *priori* knowledge, must have erred fundamentally. The faculty of real à *priori* insight, however, can, by no possibility, err in any case. All its revelations are absolute, and cannot even be conceived to be untrue.

If we take either of these propositions by itself, we shall find that it has not a single characteristic of intuitive, or necessary certainty. Nor, without the possession of omniscience, or a revelation from a being really and truly omniscient, could we know the proposition to be true, even were it true.

So we may take up, one by one, all the particular revelations of this faculty, and all the multitudinous, conflicting, and contradictory systems of universal being and its laws, systems constructed from elements furnished by this faculty, and demonstrate that not one of them presents a solitary element or form of intuition, or à *priori* knowledge. Not one of these philosophers can give us any more proof, or evidence, that he is, in truth, possessed of any such faculty, than he can that he is really and truly possessed of the attribute of absolute omniscience. A claim set up to the actual possession of such an attribute would be no more preposterous and absurd, than is the claim of an actual possession of such faculty. No human being can have any more real and valid à *priori* knowledge of the substances and causes, and forms and laws of Being, existing and acting in time and space, than he can, by mere à priori insight, determine the exact quantity of water which has fallen in any given shower of rain, or the exact dimensions and weight of the Earth, or of Jupiter. Whenever we shall meet, in our subsequent inquiries, with a philosopher claiming such insight, and with world-systems constructed by means of such affirmed insight, science absolutely demands that we shall regard the man as under a bewildering form of philosophic hallucination, and his system as constructed of materials as insubstantial as 'airy nothing.'

There are still other equally fundamental views which should be taken in regard to this claim of a power of à priori insight relatively to Being and its laws. By this insight a direct and immediate vision is had, it is affirmed, of the inner nature and principles of substances and causes. If this vision of the interior of such realities is had through the *attributes* of substances and causes, we have nothing but forms of ordinary vision, and no à priori knowledge at all. The character of the knowledge secured is wholly contingent, and not necessary, that is, à priori, in any sense. If these objects are perceived without, and not through, their attributes, then no knowledge of any kind, knowledge à priori or à posteriori, is obtained. To know realities without knowing their attributes is not to know anything about them.

By no possibility can the Knowledge affirmed be obtained of any such Substances or Causes.

There is a still greater absurdity and hallucination connected with this profession. By this insight certain philosophers profess to know, not only that certain perceived realities *do* exist, but that others not perceived do not exist. We have a direct perception, we will suppose, of some reality. That perception is valid for the existence of the object, and for nothing more. In regard to the question whether some other, and not incompatible object does, or does not exist, this perception has no validity whatever. This principle does, and must apply to à priori, as well as to every other form of insight. The insight can, say what we will, have validity but for what is actually seen. As against the existence of any other not incompatible reality, such vision can have no validity whatever. Now these philosophers profess to obtain, in all their à priori visions, not only a knowledge that what they see does exist, but that this is the sum of all existence, and that nothing else does, or can, have being. The disciples of Kanada and Compte, by à priori insight, perceive matter not only to be real, but to be the only existing reality. The disciples of Kapila and Kant, by the same insight, perceive and affirm the existence of two unknown entities, *noumena*, as the sole existences and principles of all things. The disciples of the Buddha and Transcendental Subjective

Idealistic school, perceive absolutely by the same insight, that the finite, 'I myself I,' and that alone has real being. Those of the Vedanta and Pantheistic schools of all ages perceive absolutely, and by means of the same identical insight, that Brahm, or the Absolute, alone exists, and exists as the exclusive principle of all things. Finally, the Pure Idealists of the Buddha and Transcendental schools perceive, if possible, with still greater absoluteness, that thought is, and that nothing else is real. Each school obtains an *à priori* revelation of absolute truth, that a specific form of being is real, and that nothing else does, or can exist. Who does not perceive, at once, that the validity of such insight is an utter nullity, and that the professed power of perceiving any object, as not only being a reality in itself, but as being the *only* form of real existence, is the grossest conceivable absurdity?

When we perceive any substance, or cause, or form of being to be real, unless we can perceive, at the same time, that it so occupies infinite space as to render the existence of any other object an absolute impossibility, our perception that said object is a reality presents not the remotest degree of even probable evidence that nothing else is real. The positive and negative form in which this affirmed *à priori* insight always acts renders demonstrably evident the fact, that the idea of the existence of such a faculty is one of the wildest conceivable forms of scientific hallucination.

Taking as valid the result of the testimony of all these schools in its only admissible, that is, in its positive forms, what do we obtain? We obtain, we reply, an absolute proof of the validity of the hypothesis which they all, in common, deny, to wit, the reality of matter and spirit, and of time and space. All these are absolutely affirmed realities in these several schools, one in one school, and another in another, and in all are thus affirmed by the same form of insight. In one school spirit, and in another matter, is given as the object of absolute knowledge, and no philosopher can show why the evidence presented is not just as valid in one case, as in the other. We are necessitated to affirm either that these philosophers have no such insight as they assume themselves possessed of, or that we have both an *à priori* and *à posteriori* knowledge of space and time, matter and spirit, as realities in themselves.

SECTION IV.

MYSTERY AND ABSURDITY DEFINED AND DISTINGUISHED.

In the science of Natural Theology, we have very carefully defined, and distinguished from each other, the ideas represented by these two terms. The fundamental bearing of these discriminations upon our future inquiries will be our apology for introducing the same subject in the present connection. What, then, do we mean by these terms, and wherein do they differ the one from the other?

An absurdity involves a *contradiction*, and appears in two forms— affirming that the same thing is, at the same time, true and not true of the same object, or affirming what is palpably contrary to, or incompatible with, an absolutely known truth. The nature of the absurd in the first form designated is so obvious, that but a single example in illustration is required. A philosopher affirms that in all cases of vision the object really perceived is not an external form, but an image on the retina. He then employs vision itself to prove the existence of the image in the assigned locality, the image which is now an exterior object. According to the theory, the image itself cannot be seen, but only an image of an image. There are two absurdities in this argument—proving by an image which, by hypothesis, is not seen, that nothing but an image is ever seen at all, and inferring from the assumed existence of the image that it, and not the object of conscious vision, is seen.

An individual is affirmed to be blameable for not having done what is admitted to have been impossible to him. We recognise ourselves at once as in the presence of an absurdity of the second class, the possible being absolutely known to be the only conceivable object of moral obligation. The same form of the absurd appears, when an argument or objection is held to be valid in disproof of a given hypothesis, when the same argument or objection holds in all its force against another hypothesis known or admitted to be true. A philosopher proposes to give us real science in the admitted and affirmed sphere of the unknown and unknowable, or 'to demonstrate' for us 'a single *physical* basis of life underlying all the diversities of vital existence,' or that 'a unity of power or faculty, a unity of form, and a unity of substantial composition, does pervade the whole living world,' and then gravely informs us that 'it is certain that we can have no knowledge of the nature of either matter or spirit.' In all such cases, the absurd has reached its consummation. A fact, we will suppose, is known to us as an event of actual occurrence. The reason or cause of its occurrence is, to us, unknown and unascertainable. The *event*, in such case, would rank as a fact of actual knowledge, while the cause would be a mystery. It is thus that the known and mysterious everywhere lie out side by side before us. If we will admit no fact to have occurred, and no object to be real, the occurrence and existence of which involve a mystery, we shall for ever remain, in the strictest sense of the words, 'know-nothings.' No fact or proposition, falling within the proper sphere of the self-contradictory, or absurd, can be an object of rational belief, because that, by no possibility, can such an event occur, or any such proposition be true. The element of Mystery, however deep, on the other hand, is no proof whatever that a given fact has not occurred, or that a given proposition is not true. Almost no discriminations can be of greater importance in science than those just made between the absurd and the mysterious. Any fact, the possible occurrence of which is conceivable, is a possible event, and its occurrence may, on adequate evidence, be an object of rational belief, and a denial of its occurrence may be most irrational. Any form of being, the existence of which is conceivably possible, is a possible form of existence; and a belief in it as real, the fact of its existence being affirmed by adequate evidence, is most rational, and disbelief under such circumstances is equally irrational. Positive belief in the absurd, and disbelief in the presence of valid evidence, and doubt in the presence of real proof, are intellectual states equally credulous and irrational, and moral states of the greatest criminality.

Existence involves a Mystery.

Of all forms of the mysterious none are, or can be, greater than that involved in the idea of existence, that is, when we ask the question, not *what* is real, but *why* a given form of being or substance is real instead of not real. 'We may know absolutely,' as we have said in another work, 'that a certain substance does as a matter of fact *exist*. But when we attempt to go beyond the mere fact and to determine the question *why* the substance does exist instead of *not* exist, we find that we can discover neither in the fact referred to, nor in the nature or relations of the substance revealed as existing, any light whatever in regard to such inquiries.' Any *conceivable*, we repeat, is a *possible* form of existence, and any one such form is just as possible as any other. Belief in the reality of any conceivable form of being, when affirmed as real by adequate evidence, is most rational, and disbelief most irrational. The questions what realities do exist, and *why* they exist, are questions totally distinct and separate the one from the other. The depth of the mystery involved in the *why* of existence is no reason whatever for disbelief in the *fact* of existence. The belief in the reality of one form of being is no reason whatever for disbelief in that of another and not incompatible form of existence. As the *why* of existence is, in all conceivable forms of being, alike and equally mysterious, and we are of necessity confined to the mere and exclusive question, *What* is real? one form of conceivable existence is in itself and on *à priori* grounds just as possible and probable as any other; nor can we on such grounds determine at all what substances and causes are and are not real.

The law of rational belief and disbelief, in respect to being and its laws, is absolute, and may be thus stated—to wit, *Whatever conceivable forms of being are manifested as real, and none others, must be admitted as actual*, that is, all forms of being directly and immediately *perceived* to be real, together with all implied by and logically deduced from what is thus perceived, all these, and nothing more, must be taken into account as real in the constitution of our theory of existence and its laws. The conscious conceivability of any form of existence demonstrates it as a possible form of being, and removes utterly and absolutely all antecedent probability against its reality. The fact of its consciously direct and immediate manifestation as a real form of being must be to the mind, on scientific grounds, perfect proof of its real existence.

Bearing of these Conclusions upon our former Deductions.

As we have formerly shown, and as admitted and affirmed in all schools of Philosophy, matter and spirit, and time and space are actually conceivable and conceived forms of existence. Nor, as all admit, is the idea of the existence of any one of them conceivably incompatible with that of any other. They all, then, stand demonstrably revealed as possible existences with no antecedent probability against their being, all in common and all together actual existences, their united existence being utterly undeniable on *à priori* grounds. The simple question for science, then, is this, Are we conscious of matter and spirit as objects of direct and immediate perception, and of time and space as necessary forms of being whose reality is implied by what is consciously perceived? Numberless, impenetrable, and unsolvable mysteries may hang about the *why* of their existence and manifestation. The *fact* of both may be objects of absolute knowledge, and therefore real. If we shall hereafter meet with philosophers who deny the fact that we are conscious of a direct and immediate perception of matter and spirit as distinct and separate and actual forms of being, and of knowing time and space as necessary forms of existence absolutely implied as real by what we consciously perceive, we shall deny the correctness of the psychology of such thinkers, and shall sustain that denial by an appeal to the already absolutely pronounced judgment of the universal consciousness. If these philosophers shall deny the validity of such conscious forms of absolute knowledge for the reality and character of their objects, we shall deny the correctness of the logic of these thinkers, and shall sustain that denial by an appeal to the already pronounced judgment of the same tribunal as before. The undeniable fact should fully satisfy every friend of true science that the validity of our knowledge of each of these realities, in common with every other, cannot be denied without an absolute impeachment of the integrity and validity of the universal intelligence itself as a faculty of knowledge.

The Existence of a Power of Knowledge involves a Mystery equally profound.

Knowledge, as shown in the General Introduction, implies a *power* and an *object* of knowledge, and these in such relations to each other that real knowledge arises by virtue of the nature and relations of the power and object referred to. If we inquire for the reasons *why* such power exists, *why* such conditions are necessary to its action, and *why* knowledge does arise when these conditions are fulfilled, all is an absolute mystery to us, excepting what is implied in the statement above given. We know, and cannot but know, that knowledge, in any and every form, does and must imply a power and object of knowledge, and that whenever knowledge does arise, it must exist in consequence of the relations and corelated nature of said power and object. If philosophers are not satisfied with the *why*, as revealed in the above necessary and self-evident principle, then this *why* must for ever remain to them and to us a profound and impenetrable mystery. We have no means of knowing why any conditions are necessary to the existence of real knowledge, and aside from the reason above given, why knowledge arises when these conditions are fulfilled. By absolute necessity our legitimate inquiries are wholly confined to the actual conditions, objects, and forms of knowledge which in fact do exist, and to what is implied by the same. *À priori* we can by no possibility determine whether any power, and much less what power of knowledge, does exist, what are its objects, and what are the necessary conditions of its action. The existence of a power of knowledge can be known but through the conscious fact of actual knowledge. The nature of that power can be determined but through conscious forms and objects of knowledge. The conditions of the possibility of human knowledge can be determined but through the conscious conditions in which actual knowledge does, in fact, arise. The extent and limits of our faculty of knowledge are determinable but through the actual facts, forms, and objects of human knowledge and what is implied by the same. The absolute validity of all the above statements is, undeniably, self-evident. If neither philosophers nor anybody else can conceive how and why knowledge in any given form is possible and therefore real, that is no reason whatever why we, in the presence of the conscious fact of such knowledge, should deny its actual existence, the how and the why in the sense now under consideration being in all cases of real knowledge equally and absolutely mysterious to us.

No forms of philosophizing can be more absurd than is the assumption of certain schools in Philosophy that they can determine *à priori* whether any and what real powers of knowledge do exist, what is the nature of the human intelligence, what objects does it and can it know, and what are the specific conditions, extent, and limits of human knowledge.

Any conceivable is undeniably a possible form of knowledge, and any one actually conceivable form is in itself just as possible and probable a form as any other. How, then, can anyone determine à priori that this form does exist, and that that cannot, and does not, exist? and that this or that is the immutable condition of valid knowledge in all cases? On the assumed authority of à priori insight, the Materialist affirms that the immutable condition of valid knowledge is that the subject and object of knowledge shall be exterior to each other. On the assumed authority of the same insight, Idealists of one school affirm that valid knowledge is conditioned on a 'synthesis of being and knowing;' and another, on 'the absolute identity of being and knowing.' Sceptics, on the same authority, affirm actual knowledge impossible on any of these conditions. Realists, on the other hand, on the undeniable authority of consciously conceivable, possible, and actual facts of actual knowledge, affirm knowledge to be possible and actual both in its exterior and interior forms. Now, we affirm that the Materialist, Idealist, and Sceptic have just as much and no more power to determine à priori the specific number, form, and dimensions of all objects on the other side of the moon, as they have to determine the specific nature of the human intelligence, its objects of valid knowledge, the conditions of its valid activity, and the extent and limits of its sphere. Some philosophers affirm that the *how* and the *why* of knowledge are to them conceivable but in one specific form; others, that to them this how and why are conceivable but in another and opposite form; while others affirm that the same how and why, but as above stated, are to them equally mysterious in all forms. What shall we do? This only can we do. We can determine, through conscious facts, *what* we know, and what is implied by actually existing forms of conscious knowledge. We can thus, and thus only, fully meet all the real demands of science upon this subject.

SECTION V.

IN WHAT SENSE AND FORM IS HUMAN KNOWLEDGE RELATIVE AND PHENOMENAL?

ALL our world-knowledge, we are taught in certain schools, is merely phenomenal, and in no case has anything more than a relative validity. In what sense and form are such statements valid? The primary meaning of the term 'phenomenon' is appearance. An object is manifested to us. The *form* of the manifestation is called a phenomenon of said object. All the forms of its manifestation are called its phenomena. The question, and the only question, for science in this connection is this: In phenomena, are realities manifested as they are, or as they are not? Is perception, external and internal, what the Transcendental Philosophy affirms it to be, 'an unavoidable illusion inhering in reason itself,' or is it a source of real, valid knowledge?

In Phenomena, Objects are Manifested as they are, and not as they are not.

Let us first contemplate perception in its consciously indirect and mediate form, through sensation. A sensation, we will suppose, is induced in the mind. As an object of direct and immediate consciousness, we undeniably know the *sensation* itself as it is, and not as it is not. So far the phenomenal and the real are identical. With the sensation, however, a form of necessary and absolute knowledge arises—to wit, that this sensation had, and must have had, a cause. Two forms, not of illusory, but of real knowledge, are obtained by sensation : a real knowledge of the subjective state itself, and of the fact that real causes do exist—causes adapted and adequate to produce said states. So far our knowledge is undeniably not illusory, but real; and this is all that is given as actually known in the case. For all practical purposes we are able to determine, with sufficient accuracy, in what specific objects these causes exist. What is given as absolutely known, however, is the fact and nature of the sensation itself, and the actual existence in the universe of real causes adequate and adapted to produce the sensation. It alters not the reality or validity of our knowledge to affirm that if our sensibility was differently constituted from what it now is, our sensations would be diverse from what they are. Suppose that this department of our nature was changed, and that in each change totally new sensations were induced. In such case our knowledge of the possibilities of our sensitive nature, and of the nature of existing causes, would be enlarged, but would not be less real and certain than it now is. So far, then, we repeat, the phenomenal and the real are identical.

The case holds, with the same absoluteness, in respect to all forms of consciously direct and immediate knowledge. In all such cases, in the language of Sir William Hamilton, 'the object is conceived as perceived,' and to affirm 'that we perceive the object to exist, and know it to exist, is to affirm the same thing.' In all such conscious forms of knowledge, to affirm that we do not know objects as they are, and that the phenomenal and the real are not one and identical, is, in the language of the same author, to affirm 'consciousness to be a liar from the beginning.' It is, undeniably, a hallucination of false science to affirm that phenomena, or illusory appearances, stand between the Intelligence and the conscious objects of direct and immediate knowledge.

The Dogma that all our World-Knowledge is mere Illusory Appearance.

Let us for a few moments contemplate the dogma that all forms of world, and we might add necessary, knowledge is mere illusory appearance. This is the common doctrine, as Mr. Herbert Spencer rightly affirms, of all anti-theistic philosophers of all ages. At the same time, all these philosophers agree and avow that the Intelligence is so constituted that it does and must originate these phenomena, and also believe in their validity. We need not repeat what is quoted in the General Introduction from such authors as Kant and Coleridge on this subject. To the same effect we now cite the authority of Mr. Spencer himself. 'It is impossible,' he says, 'to get rid of the consciousness of an actuality lying behind appearances ;' and 'from this impossibility,' he adds, 'the indestructible belief in that actuality.' The common doctrine of all these systems embraces the following essential items : 1. The Intelligence is so immutably constituted that, from its changeless nature and laws, it must originate these illusions. 2. For the same reasons, it must believe in the actuality of the objects of these appearances—that is, in illusions. 3. From its nature and laws, it finally discerns the unavoidable cheat which it necessarily perpetrates upon itself. 4. After the cheat has been discovered, the belief in the actuality of the objects of these known illusions remains as 'indestructible' as before. 5. To be philosophers, we must, ' by a scientific scepticism to which we voluntarily determine ourselves,' compel ourselves to treat these 'indestructible beliefs,' which 'cannot be removed by grounds or arguments,' 'as nothing but a prejudice.' Such, undeniably, is the real creed of these philosophers. This creed palpably embraces this dogma—that the Intelligence, from its changeless nature and laws, must believe in a lie, knowing and avowing it to be such.

On the supposition that the Intelligence is *divinely* constituted, we have here an infinite slander upon our Creator, to wit, that He has so constituted that faculty that it must originate a lie, then discover the falsehood, and finally believe in it after its character is known. It is undeniable that an infinite and perfect God might have constituted, in the stead of such a lying power, a faculty of real knowledge. What must be His character if, instead of a faculty of real integrity, He has originated such a monstrosity as these philosophers make the human intelligence to be ? If, on the other hand, this Intelligence was not divinely constituted, we have, in the dogma before us, a slander equally monstrous upon nature itself ; for we have here the doctrine that nature in her highest laws, those of the Intelligence, is throughout a blank lie, and nothing else. Such are the absurdities which we must embrace or admit and affirm the identity of the phenomenal and real.

The Real Relativity of Knowledge.

It is only to us as human beings, it is gravely affirmed, that our world-knowledge and necessary ideas have validity for realities as they are in themselves. To intelligences constituted intellectually, or even sensitively, different from us, there may be no such realities as matter and spirit, time and space, and no validity to the proposition $2 \times 2 = 4$, or to the axioms such as 'Things equal to the same things are equal to each other.' In reply we have only to say that if mankind alone can apprehend and comprehend such simple truths as these, human beings are the only rational beings that do exist. We meet with a human being who cannot be taught that $2 \times 2 = 4$, or that a circle is not a square. We justly regard and treat him as an idiot. So ought we to regard all beings who reveal similar forms of incapacity.

To affirm that there can be rational beings who can comprehend the axioms, numbers, and figures referred to, and not judge of them as we do, is one of the greatest conceivable absurdities. Knowledge is, undeniably, not relative in this sense, that it does not really and truly represent its objects.

The opposite dogma is certainly incapable of proof. No one will pretend that it has self-evident validity. Nor can any class of real intelligents be produced to whom matter and spirit and time and space are not realities, and with whom 2×2 does not equal 4, or things equal to the same things are not equal to one another. Nor can we form any conception of the nature of that kind of rationality to which $2 \times 2 = 10$, or things equal to the same things may be one of them twice as large as the other. In no such sense as that under consideration has our knowledge a mere relative validity. If the term relativity means that the extent of real knowledge with us is limited by the nature of our faculty of knowledge, that is, that we cannot know realities which we are not capacitated to know, we have before us a mere truism, a truism very needlessly uttered. 'A thing of which one has no knowledge,' as Professor Samuel Harris, D.D., has well said, 'is neither false nor true for him, but simply unknown. Philosophy would have been saved from a great deal of confusion on this point had it been kept in mind that false and true apply only to the knowable or the known.'

If the term relativity is assumed to mean that we can know, not substance itself, that is, substance without attributes, but only the attributes of being, we find ourselves in the presence of two essential errors, namely, that there may be substance or being without attributes, and that there may be attributes without substance. Pure being, that is, substance without attributes, is a non-entity, and the idea of attributes without a subject involves the same form of contradiction as that of an event without a cause. Substances and attributes are necessarily connected, and substances must be as their attributes. So far, therefore, as we know the attributes of being, we know being itself; and so far as we know the real attributes of being, we know being as it is. Our knowledge of being is limited because our knowledge of its attributes is limited. If we knew all the attributes of being, we should have a perfect knowledge of being itself. Limited knowledge, also, as far as it extends, is just as real and true of being as full or perfect knowledge. The idea that there may be something in what is called the ultimate essence of being which will invalidate our present knowledge of its attributes, or do away with these attributes, is a chimera of false science. We have quite as much reason to affirm that the ultimate essence is wholly embraced and revealed in its *known* as in its *unknown* attributes; and we have no reason whatever for either supposition. Ultimate essence is partially revealed by every known attribute, and, we repeat, it is fully revealed when all attributes are known.

Nor does the fact that only a part of the attributes of being are known invalidate the classification of substances in view of their known attributes. We may not know, for example, all the properties or relations of the circle or square. Notwithstanding this, we know absolutely, on account of their known properties and relations, that a circle is not and cannot be a square. We are also, no doubt, profoundly ignorant of many of the attributes both of matter and spirit. In view of their known attributes, however, we are as absolutely and rationally assured that matter is not spirit as we are that a circle is not a square.

Relativity of knowledge is, by some philosophers, affirmed to mean that we know merely the relations of qualities, and not the realities themselves. 'Every complete act of consciousness,' says Mr. Spencer, ' besides distinction and relation, also implies likeness. Before it can become an idea or constitute a piece of knowledge, a mental state must not only be known as separate in kind from certain foregoing states to which it is known as related by succession ; but it must further be known as of the same kind with certain other foregoing states.'

Here we have quite a number of fundamental errors of the gravest character. Among them we specify the following : 1. The Intelligence has the capacity to discern the relations of things without knowing at all what these things themselves are, that is, in absolute ignorance of the numbers 2 and 4, we can know absolutely that $2 \times 2 = 4$. Without fear of contradiction we affirm that a greater absurdity can hardly be imagined. 2. Until after classification, and not even then, it should have been said, can we have any conception whatever of the realities classified. ' Before the feelings produced by intercourse with the world have been put in order, there are no cognitions strictly so-called.' In other words, Field-

Marshal Maltke must have fully organized his armies before he could have known that a single soldier existed to be organized. The antecedent is here substituted for the consequent. Cognitions of individuals must exist before classification is possible. 3. According to this dogma, we have derivative cognitions without the primitive. The latter must in its original form have pertained to one single individual irrespective of every other. For the real cognition must have arisen, or the derived could not exist, unless the axiom, 'Ex nihilo, nihil fit,' is false. The idea that relations are discernible in utter ignorance of the things related is an absurdity than which none can be greater. In no such sense as this, then, can relativity be affirmed of human knowledge. When an object 'has absolutely no attribute in common with anything else,' Mr. Spencer assures us 'it must be absolutely beyond the bounds of knowledge.' Such an object, we reply, can be both known and classified. By intuition we could perceive and conceive its real attributes. On reflection we could, in view of the principle of unlikeness, separate it from all other known objects. According to Mr. Spencer, knowledge, in any new form, is impossible, such knowledge being unlike all existing forms. How, then, is progression possible? that is, in the language of our author, 'advancing from the definite homogeneous to the definite heterogeneous'?

SECTION VI.

PHYSIOLOGY AND METAPHYSICS.

PHYSIOLOGY and other physical sciences among the Greeks, that is, in certain schools of Greece, did supplant metaphysics. The disciples of the New Philosophy in modern times affirm that 'as sure as every future grows out of the past and present, so will the physiology of the future gradually extend the realm of matter and law, until it is coextensive with knowledge, with feeling, and with action.' Thus we are informed that the halcyon day is near when the scalpel and microscope will supersede consciousness and reflection in the development of the science of mind. The time is come when the fundamental distinction between metaphysics and all other sciences should be distinctly understood.

Our hypothesis on this subject is this, that mental science proper is just as distinct, separate from, and independent of, physiology, as it is of the mathematics, astronomy, natural philosophy, or geology. The telescope of the astronomer, and the hammer of the geologist, have just as much, and no more, to do in the sphere of metaphysics, as the crucible of the chemist, and the microscope and scalpel of the physiologist. What are the real, and only real phenomena of the mind? They are, undeniably, all comprehended in these three classes—thought, feeling, and willing. If we will take into consideration any mental state or act, and ask ourselves the question, What is the nature of this state? we shall find that from no physiological fact, and from no state of the brain or nervous system, can we gain the remotest conception of this mental state. There are, for example, physiological conditions of sensation. But when we ask the question what sensation, as a sensitive state, is, we can gain no more light upon this subject from the action of our physical system, than we can from that of a steam-engine. What if a physiologist should assure us that by a careful analysis, under a strong microscope, of the nerve of the tooth, together with the connection of that nerve with the other portions of the body, he had discovered the exact nature of that peculiar form of sensation denominated toothache? We should hardly hesitate to affirm, that the proper place for 'our new philosopher' is the Lunatic Asylum. Geology and rail-splitting throw just as much light upon the nature of all our sensitive and emotive states as physiology does.

The same holds true of all our intellectual states. External perception, for example, is always preceded by certain physiological conditions. In the analysis and study of these conditions, however, we can no more determine what perception is in itself, or what are its objects, extent, and limits, than we can in the study of chaos. Does the physiology of the eye reveal the nature and objects of vision? The conditions of vision are one thing. Vision itself is quite another. What resemblance is there between the brain and thought? The nature of the action of the faculty of Self-consciousness is no more revealed through the physiology of the human brain than it is through that of the trunk of an elephant. There is not a single state or movement of the body that reveals, in any form, the nature of any sensitive, emotive, or intellectual state.

The same remarks are equally and especially applicable to all mental states denominated will. Two individuals affirm themselves able to explain, and fully elucidate, the nature and laws of all the phenomena of this mysterious faculty denominated the human will. One of these men has gotten all his knowledge upon this subject in the profound study of the mechanism and workings of a windmill, and the other in a similar study of 'the house we live in'—the human body. We have just as much reason to expect real light from one of these individuals, as we have from the other. In metaphysics we have but one faculty for the determination of facts—Self-consciousness. All questions resolvable throughout the entire sphere of this science are to be resolved in the light of facts, not of external, but exclusively of internal perception. Metaphysics is wholly an internal science, and all its valid deductions have but one basis, facts of internal perception. Physiology is wholly an external science, and has its exclusive basis in facts of external perception. Physiology is as really and truly an external science as is geology or astronomy. We might as properly base our deductions in mental science upon geological or astronomical, as upon physiological facts. We might as properly determine the nature of thought, feeling, and willing, and consequently the faculties and laws of mind, in view of the properties and relations of a triangle, a circle, or square, as by means of an analysis of the brain, or the nervous system. The immutable laws of induction and deduction in the science of mind, laws as stated by Cousin, have absolute and universal authority, namely, Omit no conscious facts, and suppose none not given by Consciousness. The facts thus given are not to be moulded to meet the exigence of desired hypotheses, but are to be interpreted with absolute integrity. If metaphysicians would accept of the real facts of the universal consciousness just as they find them, if they would abjure all 'acts of scientific scepticism to which they voluntarily determine themselves,' if they would repudiate all assumptions, and honestly discriminate between facts of real and assumed knowledge, and with all integrity seek to know mind as God made it, and not as they would have it, the time is not distant when there will be as little difference of opinion in metaphysics as in natural philosophy.

SECTION VII.

FORMS OF PROGRESSION COMMON TO ANTI-THEISTIC SYSTEMS OF PHILOSOPHY.

ANTI-THEISTIC systems of Philosophy always take their points of departure and their specific forms from negations of particular kinds. In all ages and among all schools in which the reality of matter and spirit, and time and space, and the validity of our knowledge of the same, have been admitted, the being and perfections of a personal God have been affirmed. A denial of this doctrine has always been based upon a denial of the validity of our knowledge of matter, on the one hand, or of spirit, on the other, or of both in common. Idealism takes rise and form from the first form of denial, Materialism from the second, and Scepticism from the last. These systems have generally followed each other in the order above named. Anti-theism has never, for any considerable time, taken on any specific and fixed form, a denial of the doctrine of a personal God excepted, but has embodied itself in each system of unbelief as it and while it was an object of the popular faith. As God stands prominently revealed in the popular mind as the Creator of the visible universe, a denial of His being and perfections is most commonly in its first form, based upon a denial of the validity of our knowledge of said universe. Hence the rise of Anti-theism in the form of Idealism, which in succession takes on the form, first of Ideal Dualism, then of Subjective Idealism, then of Pantheism, and finally of Pure Idealism. For no considerable period can the mind in any age continue long within the circle of either of these systems, but passes successively from the first, through the intermediate forms, to the last, 'the driest place,' which 'the unclean spirit' of unbelief ever traverses. Finding less rest and assurance here than in any previous forms of anti-theistic thought, and pressed with the reality of the external universe, another class of thinkers arise—thinkers who affirm the validity of our knowledge of matter, and deny its validity of spirit. Materialism, and with it Atheism now takes on the form of popular belief. After reposing for a period amid the naked forms of a godless universe, the mind becomes oppressed with a sense of inward desolation and want, and also with the immutable conviction that it has precisely the same reasons for denying the validity of matter that it can have for impeaching our knowledge of spirit. Another class of thinkers now arise, denying the validity of knowledge both in its subjective and objective forms, and confounding the advocates of these antagonistic systems with the arguments which they have been employing against each other. As both parties are perfectly powerless against this new form of attack, Scepticism in its turn becomes ascendant, and commands the popular faith. During the freshness of its early espousal, universal doubt appears to the general mind as an angel of light. Absolute vacancy, universal doubt, and hopeless nescience, each and all are states so unnatural and repulsive to our necessary and irrepressible desires for real knowledge, that Scepticism never can, for long periods, hold the human mind under its barren control. Humanity, from its nature and laws, will believe in 'chimeras dire,' rather than in the impossibility of knowing anything.

Under such circumstances, the mind will accept of the doctrine of a personal God, or reaccept some of the forms of Idealism, the first most likely. Then the mind will recommence the circle of successive beliefs above described, and return finally to the sceptical form of thought. Ever since the commencement of the anti-theistic philosophy, as far as the mind has been subjected to its influence, Anti-theism has been moving in this one fixed circle, successively embracing and repudiating the same identical systems. Anglo-Saxon unbelief is now under the control of the oldest form of Scepticism known in the history of Philosophy—a form miscalled 'The New Philosophy.' We shall see hereafter that this affirmed new system is, in fact and form, as old as Protagoras and other Greek sceptics, now known as the ancient Sophists. The next great movement of philosophic thought will be in the direction of the doctrine of a personal God, and of creation 'by the word of God,' or a recommencement of the old cycles which have been so often repeated in the history of past ages, and which we are hereafter to elucidate. We state the above facts as preparatory to a distinct apprehension of the systems which we are to examine. In Greece we shall find the old Oriental systems, with the exception of Theism proper and Scepticism, repeated in fact and form. In modern forms of philosophical thought we shall find the Grecian repeated, the theistic and sceptical included.

SECTION VIII.

THE SCHOOLS OF PHILOSOPHY IN GREECE.

PRIOR to the Socratic period three leading schools in philosophy arose in Greece, that of Ionia, the Italic, and the Eleatic schools, the two last named being located in what was denominated Græcia Major. As the result of the teachings particularly of the two schools last named, there arose in different parts of Greece a class of sceptics known under the title of Sophists.

After Socrates Athens became the great centre of literature and philosophic thought in Greece. Here various schools arose, such as were generally known as the Cynic, the Sceptical, the Platonic, Aristotelic, Epicurean, and Stoic schools. The general doctrine of members of these schools was identical, while each school was peculiarized by special moral teachings from which it received its special designation. After what is generally denominated the Socratic period had passed, the era of what is called the decline of the Greek philosophy commenced—the era in which the doctrines of previous schools, especially those of the Platonic, took on in important particulars new forms.

We shall accordingly comprehend our examination of the Greek philosophy in three general divisions—the *Pre-Socratic*, the *Socratic*, and the *Post-Socratic* periods or schools.

With equal propriety the Greek philosophy as a whole might, as has been done in some important works, be divided into two principal evolutions, the first extending from Thales to Socrates, the second from Socrates to Sextus Empiricus. For the sake of special distinctness, we have taken into account the three general evolutions above designated, and shall divide our examination of this philosophy into a corresponding number of chapters. The following extract from the epitome of the History of Philosophy will enable the reader to appreciate what will be found in these chapters:

'The Greek colonies of Asia Minor and of Italy connected by position, the former with Phœnicia and Chaldea, the latter with Egypt, were the double cradle of Hellenic philosophy. In this respect they were in advance of Greece proper. We might say that before throwing itself into the country which was destined to become the theatre of its great conflicts, Philosophy took its position around it and made as it were preparatory attempts at conquest. But the two tendencies begun in the former period were reproduced in this. The Italic school continued under the new forms the theological and the metaphysical speculations of the East. The Ionic school separated Philosophy much more from traditional science preserved in the sanctuaries. As the several schools of Philosophy—schools originally formed in Asia Minor—and the Greek portions of Italy were transferred to Athens, they brought with them, we would add, their special peculiarities of doctrine and methods of philosophizing, and thus imparted, by the collisions and interminglings of opposite principles and methods, a peculiar character and movement to philosophic thought throughout the Socratic and Post-Socratic periods.' Without a distinct apprehension of the facts above stated, it would be much more difficult to comprehend the diverse and opposite phases and methods of the Greek philosophy. The reader who has fully comprehended the statements and discussions of the present introduction, together with what has gone before, will readily understand and appreciate what is to follow.

CHAPTER I.

THE PRE-SOCRATIC EVOLUTION IN PHILOSOPHY.

SECTION I.

THE IONIC SCHOOL—THALES OF MILETUS.

THALES of Miletus, born about six centuries before the Christian era, and founder of the celebrated school of Ionia, is, by general consent, regarded as the father of the Greek philosophy. With him, unquestionably, commenced the first marked evolution of Philosophy among this people. In such regard was he held by his countrymen that he takes rank as one among the seven wise men of Greece. As a scholar he was not only acquainted with the literature and philosophy of the Eastern nations, but was 'learned in all the wisdom of the Egyptians,' having frequently visited Egypt for purposes of observation and study. With him originated also the maxim which has justly immortalized his name—to wit, 'Know thyself.'

Exposition of the Doctrines of Thales.

We shall with great care exhibit the ascertained views of this philosopher, because we shall thus obtain a central light which will guide us safely in subsequent and darker inquiries. All agree that he taught the reality of matter and of an organized material universe. All agree, also, that he held and taught a definite hypothesis in regard to the nature and state of the material elements prior to their organization as we now find them. Nor do any doubt that he held and taught definite views in regard to the ultimate and unconditioned cause of the change of the condition of these material elements from their primal chaotic state to one of which order is the 'first law' and all-controlling principle. At this point a difference of opinion arises. Some affirm that under Thales the Ionic school was materialistic, and consequently atheistic in its teachings and influence, while others maintain that he held and taught the doctrine of one supreme God as the Creator proper of the universe. Holding, as all admit and affirm that he did, to the real existence of matter and to its original existence in a chaotic state, he must have held and taught that the material elements were brought into a state of universal organization by a law of order existing and acting potentially in matter itself, or by a divine force or cause *ab extra*. As the writings of this author have not come down to us, we are necessitated to depend upon the records of his utterances and doctrines handed down by others living at subsequent periods. Such sources of information, as we shall find, are perfectly satisfactory. We will first consider the cosmological and then the theistic doctrine and teachings of this world-renowned thinker.

THE COSMOLOGICAL DOCTRINE AND TEACHINGS OF THALES.

The common idea of all world-thinkers who hold the doctrine of material existence is that the primal state of matter is properly represented by the term chaos. Whether this chaos was in a fluid, nebulous, igneous, or aeriform state, here a difference of opinion obtains. What were the teachings of Thales on this subject? All authors, ancient and modern, agree that, according to this thinker, the primal state of matter is represented by the term fluidity—in other words that the material universe was developed out of water. Earth he held to be water condensed, air to be water rarefied, and fire to be rarefied air.

Hippo, of Samos or Regium, a philosopher who lived about two centuries after Thales, maintained the same doctrine, affirming moisture, or water, as embracing the constituent elements of the material universe. Aristotle suggests that 'Thales was impressed with the idea that water contains the constituent elements of all material forms, by observing the fact that all things appear to be nourished by this element, and that it is present in all.' We very probably have here one real cause of the idea under consideration. We suggest another equally probable co-operating cause, to which we shall subsequently refer. Thales, in his multitudinous travels and researches for information, could hardly have remained ignorant of such an author as Moses, from whose account of the creation Longinus subsequently cites. Had Thales not read or heard that, according to Moses, the material universe rose from chaos, because 'the Spirit of the Lord moved upon the face of the waters'? As we are now treating of probabilities, no material error can arise from either of the suggestions before us.

The Theistic Doctrine and Teachings of Thales.

We now advance to the consideration of a question about which a difference of opinion does obtain among modern writers on the history of Philosophy. We refer to the Theistic doctrines and teachings of Thales.

The issue before us is this—Did this philosopher teach that the material universe took form from a law of order acting potentially in matter itself, or from the all-formative agency of God? To affirm that he taught the doctrine of creation by natural law is to charge him, without proof, to have held and taught a palpable absurdity. A law of order existing and acting potentially in matter, and thus existing and acting through no exterior cause, must, by hypothesis, have existed and acted there from eternity, and from eternity matter must have existed in an organized, and not in a disorganized, state. A primal chaos could by no possibility have produced order. This principle, as we shall find hereafter, early suggested itself to the Grecian mind, and gave peculiar and special forms to the doctrine of Materialism. The absurdity of the doctrine of organization from chaos by an eternally existing and acting natural law or cause is, we admit, no absolute proof that Thales did not hold and teach it; because, as it has been well said, no great absurdity can be named which has not for ages been a leading dogma of some leading sect in Philosophy. What we do argue is this—that without positive proof (and no such proof exists), no such absurdity should be charged upon this great philosopher.

While a difference of opinion does exist among *modern* historians about his views on the subject before us, no known ancient author, as we shall see, charged him with being a mere Naturalist. This is a very important fact to be taken into account in the formation of our judgment on this question. But what positive proof have we that he was, in the strictest sense of the word, a Theist? On this subject we invite a careful examination of the following facts and considerations:

1. From the known circumstances of his birth and life, and the recorded facts pertaining to his travels, studies, and habits of thought, the deduction is undeniable that he must have been fully informed of the nature and character of Theistic ideas and doctrines, and must have maintained definite views in respect to the doctrine of ultimate causation. We have no evidence at all, but positive proof to the contrary, that the doctrine of one Supreme God, the Creator and Governor of the universe, was ever absent from Greek thought. We have proof equally positive, as we have shown, that this was the common doctrine of all surrounding nations, barbarian and civilized. In his travels and studies in Egypt and other countries he must have become familiar with the doctrine of God as expounded by learned men among the Egyptians, Phœnicians, Chaldeans, and Persians. Nor could he have been ignorant of the doctrine of his near neighbours the Jews pertaining to the being and government of God. The fame of Solomon and the prophets, and especially of Daniel, his contemporary, must have reached Ionia, and have been known to Thales. The captivity and dispersion of the Jews by the Assyrians and Chaldeans, events which transpired prior to and during the age of

this individual, spread the knowledge of the writings and doctrines of that people over all Asia Minor and the Eastern nations. To affirm Thales to have been ignorant of the doctrine of God, is to affirm him to have been one of the most stupid, unobservant, and ignorant men that Greece ever produced—and all this without evidence not merely, but in the face of positive proof to the contrary—and to affirm it from no other reason than to sustain a false and absurd modern theory pertaining to the origin of Theistic ideas. We have, in the above undeniable facts, a full refutation of the argument of such authors as Hegel and Lewes, that Thales could not have held and taught the doctrine of God, because the idea of God had, in his age, no place in the Grecian mind.

2. The testimony of Aristotle—testimony a part of which has been so often cited to the contrary—the testimony of Aristotle taken all together, we say, is perfectly conclusive that Thales was, in the proper sense of the term, a Theist. The statement of Aristotle so often cited to prove Thales to have been a mere Naturalist, proves, in fact, no such thing. The passage is this: 'Of those who first philosophized, the majority assumed only material principles as elements—Thales, the originator of this philosophy, taking water for his principle.' Had Aristotle said no more, there might be found in this passage conjectural, though not conclusive, ground for the inference that Thales, among others, was a mere Materialist.

Let us now contemplate the positive testimony of Aristotle bearing in the opposite direction. Thales 'is reported,' says Aristotle, 'to have said that the loadstone possessed a soul because it could move iron.' Here, then, we have a distinct statement of the fact that Thales held the old doctrine, avowed even by Newton, of the *vis inertia* of matter. So strongly did he hold to this doctrine, that he attributed the attracting power of the loadstone, not to a principle inhering and acting potentially in matter itself, but to the moving power of a spirit acting in that material object. We perceive, also, how clearly the ideas of matter on the one hand, and of spirit on the other, were distinguished and separated in the mind of this philosopher. If this philosopher, as he undeniably did, held the doctrine of the inertia of matter in such an absolute form, that he would not admit the possibility of the attractive power of the loadstone, but through the moving agency of mind, much less could he have held the doctrine of the formation of the material universe from water through the exclusive influence of a law of material order existing and acting potentially in such a dull and inert thing as he held matter to be. If he attributed even the attractive power of the loadstone to the moving agency of spirit, much more must he have held the doctrine of the organization, by mind, of the universe from chaos to perfect order.

'Some think,' says Aristotle once more, 'that *soul* and *life* is mingled with the whole universe, and thence perhaps was that [opinion] of Thales that all things are full of gods.'

This 'perhaps' pertains merely to the *origin* of the belief of the universality of the divine agency in the universe. If we had no testimony but that of Aristotle, we should be bound to regard Thales as a real Theist.

3. But the direct and positive testimony which has been handed down to us from other ancient authors fully vindicates for Thales a place among the great Theistic thinkers of the world. 'Thales of Miletus,' says Cicero, 'the first who engaged in these inquiries, says that water is the original of all things, and that God is that Intelligence who from water formed all things.' Again, as recorded by another ancient author, Thales said, 'God is the most ancient of all things, because he is unmade and ungenerated.' Diogenes Laertius, after attributing to him the same sentiment that Aristotle does, 'that the world is animated and full of gods,' records another of the utterances of Thales in this form, 'God is the most ancient of all things, for he has no birth; the world is the most beautiful of all things, for it is the workmanship of God.' The author of 'De Placitis Philosophorum,' as cited by Cudworth, affirms, that in common with Pythagoras and Plato, 'Thales held the soul to be an incorporeal, self-acting, and intelligent substance.' No one who is guided by evidence, and no pre-formed hypothesis in respect to the origin of Theistic ideas, will doubt for a moment the fact that Thales held and taught the doctrine of the real existence of matter and spirit as distinct and separate entities, and of a supreme personal God, the Creator proper of the universe.

Anaximander and Anaximenes.

Thales had presented, for all who admitted the existence of matter and of a material universe, the definite problem, what was the primeval state of the material elements, the state which preceded organization. The ancients almost, or quite, universally divide the material elements into four classes, earth, air, fire, and water. Hypotheses pertaining to the primeval state of the material elements would naturally take form from one or the other of these classes. As no one would suppose, that the primeval state was that of solidity, but four hypotheses would naturally present themselves, to wit, the fluid, the aëriform, the igneus, or the indefinite. Thales had adopted the first: Anaximander, who is generally reported to be the immediate successor of the founder of the school, adopted the last; Anaximenes adopted the second.

Anaximander assumed, that the primeval state of matter must have been a formless one. This state, he argues, could not have been a fluid one, because fluidity implies form. For the definite, he consequently assumed the indefinite, as representing the primeval state after which we are inquiring. Repudiating, also, the doctrine of God as needful to

12—2

account for the organization of the universe, he affirmed that 'the Infinite is the origin of all things.' How this philosopher deduced the finite from the infinite, not enough is known of his system to enable us to decide. All that we know is, that through this thinker a kind of indefinite form of Pantheism, and that in an indefinite material form, was early introduced into the sphere of Grecian thought.

Anaximenes assumed a position intermediate between the undefined Infinite of Anaximander and the definite hypothesis of fluidity adopted by Thales. For the indefinite, on the one hand, and the more solid element of water, on the other, Anaximenes substituted air, as constituting the original substance. Air was without him and within, and was everywhere more widely diffused than water. All things visible, then, were developed out of this element. Generally, if not universally, among modern historians, but for what definite reasons, as Dr. Cocker has well observed, none can inform us, this thinker has been supposed to agree with Anaximander, in denying the agency of God in creation. If Anaximenes, in common with the founder of his school, was a Theist, the former would argue the question at issue between him and his predecessor, just as he has done, and the record, or accounts of this discussion, and not their points of agreement, might come down to us in their present form. We can perceive no good grounds, therefore, for charging him with Atheism, or for affirming that he was a Theist. When nothing positive is known, wisdom and integrity prohibit the expression of positive opinions.

Anaxagoras.

The inquisitiveness of the Greek mind would not be long in apprehending the difficulty, or impossibility, of deducing by natural law the perfectly determinate from the absolute indeterminate, or universal order from utter chaos, whatever the form of the latter. It was in this state that Anaxagoras of Clausamenæ, in Asia Minor (500—428 B.C.), took up the question of the origin of the universe. In early life he became so enamoured with Philosophy that his great estate which he had inherited was neglected and ran to waste. When reduced to beggary he exclaimed, 'To Philosophy I owe my worldly ruin, and my soul's prosperity.' Leaving his own country, he came to Athens and commenced teaching, having for his pupils such scholars as Pericles, Euripides, and the young Socrates. His great popularity and success soon begat him enemies, through whose influence he was tried and condemned to death, as his pupil Socrates afterwards was. The death-sentence of the former, however, was exchanged for banishment. In his banishment he remarked: 'It is not I who have lost the Athenians; it is the Athenians who have lost me.'

The philosophy of Anaxagoras stands at an equal remove from Materialism, on the one hand, and from Idealism on the other. No philosopher of any age has more clearly marked the distinction between matter and spirit and the material and mental universe, or more distinctly affirmed God as its author, than he. The primal chaos of the material elements he represented as an infinite or indefinite number of material particles diffused through infinite space. The power which organized these particles into the universe which now is, is the infinite and eternal mind. On all these subjects the teachings of this philosopher are perfectly explicit. Matter, as substance, he held to be eternal; as organized, to be an event of time. 'Wrongly do the Greeks,' he says, 'suppose that aught begins or ceases to be; for nothing comes into being or ceases to be; but all is an aggregation or accretion of pre-existent things; so that all becoming might more correctly be called becoming mixed, and all corruption becoming separate.'

His idea of God is thus expressed in a passage from him preserved by Simplicius: 'Intelligence' (Νοῦς. or God) 'is infinite and autocratic; it is mixed up with nothing, but exists alone in and for itself. Were it otherwise, were it mixed up with anything, it would participate in the nature of all things; for in all there is a part of all, and so that which was mixed with intelligence would prevent it from exercising power over all things.' In another portion of the passage preserved by Simplicius, Anaxagoras says: 'Intelligence is, of all things, subtlest and purest, and has entire knowledge of all. Everything which has a soul, whether great or small, is governed by the Intelligence. Intelligence knows all things, both those that are mixed and those that are separate, and the things which ought to be, and the things which were, and those things which now are, and those things which will be; all are arranged by Intelligence.' The original term here rendered Intelligence is unquestionably employed by this philosopher to represent the idea of the Supreme God, and God is here represented not only as the all-formative and all-controlling power, but as the all-knowing Intelligence.

'The Νοῦς (God) of Anaxagoras,' says Simplicius, 'as cited by Aristotle, is a principle, infinite, independent, omnipresent, the subtlest and purest of things, and incapable of mixture with aught besides; it is also omniscient and unchangeable.' God, according to the teachings of Anaxagoras, is neither identified with nature, nor nature with him. No modern Theist can more distinctly and clearly set forth the doctrine of matter and spirit, of creation and a Creator, and of God as distinct and separate from the universe which He created and controls, than is done by this ancient philosopher.

The criticism of Aristotle upon the doctrine of Anaxagoras, while it confirms the fact that the latter did teach as above stated, is a just cause of the deepest reproach to the critic. 'Anaxagoras,' says Aristotle, 'uses Intelligence as a machine in respect to the formation of the world; so that when he is embarrassed how to explain the cause of this or that, he introduces Intelligence; but in all other things it is any cause but Intelligence which produces things.' Anaxagoras, in common with all men, spoke of two classes of causes, the proximate and the ultimate. When speaking of the former he did not, and when speaking of the latter he did, refer to Intelligence. The same distinction, as Mr. Lewes observes, Aristotle himself makes.

We cite one other passage from Anaxagoras, a passage preserved by Diogenes: 'Formerly all things were a confused mass; afterwards, Intelligence coming, arranged them into worlds.' Did not this philosopher receive his ideas of the creation, and of God as the Author of that creation, from the first chapter of Genesis?

To Anaxagoras belongs the honour of presenting the only possible solution of the problems raised by the Ionic School on the one hand, and the Italic or Pantheistic School on the other. The problem raised by the former school is this—how to deduce universal order from chaos, or unity from 'the many.' That raised by the latter school, which taught that but one absolute unity exists, as the sole substance or principle of all things—the problem raised by this school is this: how to deduce, from absolute unity, 'the many.' Materialism falls to pieces upon the first problem, and Idealism upon the second. Anaxagoras accepted of the doctrine of matter, as affirmed by the former school; and of one infinite and eternal spirit, as affirmed by the latter. Through the all-creative and controlling agency of the infinite and eternal Spirit upon matter or 'the many,' the latter becomes, from 'a confused mass' or indefinite and disorganized 'many,' an absolutely organized unity.

As the merits of Anaxagoras in developing the true answer to the great question of the origin and certainty of human knowledge cannot be more correctly or better expressed than has been done by Dr. Cocker in the work to which we have before referred, we most gladly avail ourselves of the following paragraph from said work on the subject before us: 'On the question as to the origin and certainty of human knowledge, Anaxagoras differed from the Ionians and the Eleatics. Neither the sense alone, nor the reason alone, were for him a ground of certitude. He held that reason ($\lambda o\gamma o\upsilon$) was the regulative faculty of the mind, as the $No\upsilon\varsigma$ or Supreme Intelligence, was the regulative power of the universe. And he admitted that the senses were veracious in their reports, but that they reported only in regard to phenomena. The senses, then, perceive phenomena, but it is the reason alone which recognises *noumena;* that is, reason perceives being in and through phenomena, substance in and through qualities—an anticipation of the fundamental principle of modern psychology, "*that every power or substance in existence is knowable to us so far only as we know its phenomena.*" Thus, again, does he bridge the chasm that separates between the Sensationalist and the Idealist.'

Mr. Lewes corrected.

We stop here for a moment to notice the attempt of Mr. Lewes to prove that Anaxagoras held the modern Idealistic distinction between phenomena and noumena, and confined our knowledge to the former. '*Noumena*,' says Mr. Lewes, 'is the antithesis to *phenomena*, which means *appearance*. Noumena means the *substratum*, or, to use a scholastic word, the *substance*. Thus, as matter is recognized by us only in its manifestations (phenomena), we may logically distinguish these manifestations from the thing manifested (noumenon). And the former will be the *materia circa quam;* the latter, the *materia in qua*. Noumenon is, therefore, equivalent to the essence; phenomena to the manifestation.' Now, in ' manifestation' or 'phenomenon,' 'noumenon' or 'substance' must be perceived as it is, or as it is not. In the former case, phenomenon, as far as it extends, and noumenon, or substance, are one and identical, and our knowledge of substance has perfect validity. In the latter case, we have no manifestation of substance at all—that is, we have a manifestation which is no manifestation; substance, not revealed as it is, is not manifested at all. Further, in external perception, the percipient subject and the thing perceived (phenomenon) are perfectly distinct and separate the one from the other, or, in the language of Sir William Hamilton, 'consciousness is a liar from the beginning.' If phenomenon is distinct and separate from the exterior substance, as it is from the percipient subject, then we have three forms of being, all equally real—the perceiving mind, the phenomenon perceived, and the substance not perceived at all. In other words, we have existing without us real appearances which are realities in themselves, and which are the attributes of no substances, and real substances existing, it may be, without attributes. The doctrine of appearance in which nothing appears, of manifestation in which nothing is manifested, and of phenomenon without substance, is, in the language of Mr. Lewes, 'the greatest discovery of modern psychology,' and one of the greatest absurdities, we add, that ever danced in the brain of a crazy philosophy. Anaxagoras neither clearly, nor 'dimly and confusedly,' approached such a discovery. On the other hand, he affirmed, according to Sextus Empiricus, that 'phenomena are the criteria of things beyond sense.' Anaxagoras undeniably believed in matter and spirit as distinct, and separate, and known entities, and in the infinite and eternal Intelligence as the Author and Governor of the universe, and as 'clearly seen, being understood, by the things that are made.'

OBSERVATIONS UPON THE TEACHINGS AND DOCTRINES OF THE IONIC SCHOOL.

We here close our lengthened examination of the teachings and doctrines of this celebrated school in Philosophy. Other philosophers of eminence belonged to this school. As their doctrines are, in all essential particulars, represented through the systems above examined, no further examples are required. Diogenes of Apollonia (520—490 B.C.) might not improperly be ranked as belonging to this school. He agreed with Anaximenes in making air the principle of all things, and differed from him in regarding this element as endowed, not only with vitality, but even with conscious intelligence. He agreed with Thales and Anaxagoras in maintaining that order can result but from intelligence. 'Without reason,' he says, 'it would be impossible for all to be arranged duly and proportionately, and whatever object we consider will be found to be arranged and ordered in the best and most beautiful manner.' The philosophy of Diogenes, like that of his master, Anaximenes, seems to have been a kind of material Pantheism. The following observations upon the doctrines and teachings of the great masters of this school, deserve special attention.

1. The *method* of this school was for the most part inductive. It was this method which preserved the elements of truth within the circle of Grecian speculation, and rendered the Grecian Philosophy so influential as introductory to Christianity.

2. The most renowned of all the philosophers of Greece, so far as their teachings ran upon the track of truth, were indebted to this school for their method of thought and leading deductions. To the teachings of Anaxagoras in Athens, Socrates, and through him, Plato and Aristotle, were more indebted than to any other sources of philosophic thought.

3. We have, in the final deductions of this school, an example of one great central fact in the history of Philosophy, or better, perhaps, of two fundamental facts. They are the following: 1. Whenever and wherever the distinction between matter and spirit has been recognized, and these have been regarded as separate and known realities, the doctrine of one infinite and perfect personal God—the Creator and Governor of the universe—has been distinctly admitted and affirmed. The absolute validity of this statement is fully verified by all the known facts developed in the history of philosophic and Theistic thought, and nowhere in the present or past can a single exception to it be found. 2. In no age of the world, and in no system of so-called Philosophy, has that doctrine been denied but upon one exclusive basis—an impeachment, in fact and form, of the *validity of our knowledge* of one or the other of these substances, or of both in common. We do not affirm that all who

have denied the validity of our knowledge, in either form, have denied the doctrine of a personal God. What we do say, we repeat, is that this doctrine has never, in any single case, been denied but upon the express ground of the impeachment designated. Admitting the reality of matter and spirit, and the validity of our knowledge of the same, and the truth of the doctrine of a personal God is so absolutely obvious that no thinker of any school would for a moment deny it. Hence the fixed persistency, in the present and in all past ages, of Anti-theism in all its forms, in its assaults upon the validity of the Intelligence as a faculty of knowledge.

4. In this age Theists should be distinctly aware of the only real and fundamental issue between Theism and Anti-theism. All is, in reality and visibly, involved in the one single question before us, *the validity of the Intelligence as a faculty of knowledge.* As long as the Theist will grant to his opponent that the Intelligence, either in respect to facts without or facts within us, is a lie, the argument will be with the latter. The dogma that we can advance through 'the palpable obscure' of an unknown and unknowable nature to a known God, is too obviously absurd to command the respect of scientific thought.

SECTION II.

THE ITALIC SCHOOL.

PYTHAGORAS.

IN writing a Critical History of Philosophy, that, of course, cannot be a proper object of criticism which cannot be understood. These remarks have a special application to the system of Pythagoras (540—500) and of the Italic School, which he founded in Magna Grecia. If the founder of the school, or his disciples, understood what he or they taught, it is more than their ancient or modern readers and commentators have done. We have positive testimony that they did employ such language as the following: 'Number is the essence of things—everything is Number.' When the question is asked whether such language is to be understood in a literal or symbolical sense, here the highest authorities are at issue. Aristotle is perfectly positive in favour of the former construction. 'They maintained,' he says, 'that Number was the beginning (principle) of things, the cause of their material existence, and of their modifications and different states. The elements of Number are odd and even. The odd is finite, the even infinite. Unity, the one, partakes of both these, and is both odd and even. All Number is derived from the one. The heavens, as we said before, are composed of numbers.' Again, 'The finite, the infinite, and the one, they maintained to be not separate existences, such as are fire, water, etc.; but the abstract infinite and the abstract one are respectively the substance of the things of which they are predicated, and hence, too, Number is the substance of all things.' Among the ancient authorities we look in vain for any specific statement of the Pythagorean system—a statement which is incompatible, in any essential particulars, with that given at length by Aristotle.

Among modern authorities of the highest eminence, some, with Mr. Lewes, affirm the correctness of Aristotle's statement; others, such as Ritter and Cocker, take the opposite ground, and affirm that the term Number, as employed by Pythagoreans, is to be understood in a symbolical sense. The reason for this construction is thus stated by Dr. Cocker. 'On a careful review of all the arguments, we are constrained to regard the conclusion of Ritter as most reasonable. The hypothesis "that numbers are real entities," does violence to every principle of common sense.' We do not perceive the force of this argument, for the reason that in this doctrine, as expounded by Aristotle, we can perceive no greater absurdity than is involved in the system of Pure Idealism as avowed by modern thinkers of the greatest eminence—to wit, that pure thought—thought without subject or object, is the sole existing reality and the principle of all things. We can perceive no greater difficulty in combining and consolidating a granite boulder from elements extracted from number, than from those extracted from mere thought.

Nor do we believe in the validity of the following fundamental canon in 'interpreting the philosophical opinions of the ancients': 'The human mind has, under the necessary operations of its own laws, been compelled to entertain the same fundamental ideas, and the human heart to cherish the same feelings, in all ages.' If we should take this canon as our guide, we should never admit that in Philosophy such systems as Materialism, Idealism in its hydraheaded forms, and Scepticism, had ever been developed, and that in religion 'four-footed beasts, fowls of the air, creeping things,' and even 'devils,' had been objects of worship, and that in morals all moral distinctions had been denied, in short, that 'professing themselves to be wise, men had become fools.' The true canon is, to take systems as we find them, and determine the depth of possible human absurdity by the actual absurdities which men have avowed. Nor are philosophers to be exempted from a rigid application of this canon. Undeniable facts of the past render it à *priori* probable that of all human absurdities the greatest will be found in systems of false science.

Nor have any who have contended for the symbolical explanation of the language under consideration been able to tell us what the real system is which such forms of utterance do symbolize. The doctrines of the Pythagerian school are, by such construction, merely transferred from the palpable absurd to 'the palpable obscure.' If we were to hazard a definite opinion about the real system of the Pythagoreans, we should designate it as Pure Idealism. This is the identical sphere in the firmament of Grecian thought to which, after careful reading and reflection, we have assigned this school. Number is itself a form of thought. To affirm that Number is the substance and principle of all things is but another form of utterance in which pure thought under the laws of Number is the substance and principle of all things. As Anaxagoras selected the term, Intelligence, to represent his idea of God, so we judge that Pythagoras selected the term, Number, to represent the idea of pure thought, thought under the law of absolute order and harmony. In this conclusion, Dr. Cocker really harmonizes. 'Thus we have, in Pythagoras,' he says, 'the dawn of an Idealistic school.' For the validity of this deduction we have also the highest French authority. In the 'Epitome of the History of Philosophy,' from which we formerly made important citations, 'the work adopted by the University of France,' we find the following statements :

'Pythagoras took a point of departure opposite to that of the school of Thales, and followed a method the reverse of the empirical process of the Ionians. The latter set out from facts, and endeavoured by generalization to arrive at their principles. Their logical process was that of induction. Pythagoras set out with the most general ideas and proceeded by the method of deduction. The principle of things with him is absolute unity, which comprehends everything. He designates this by the name of Monad, synonymous with the originating being of God. The Monad includes spirit and matter, but without separation and without division. They are confounded together in an absolute unity of substance. From unity proceeds multiplicity, and this multiplicity is the universe, wherein that which exists in God in the state of unity is produced in the state of separation and multiplicity.'

Specific doctrines of Pythagoras, as well as peculiar terms employed by him, evince the fact that his Philosophy is of Oriental origin. Such terms as Monad and Dyad, the doctrine of transmigration, and of salvation by absorption into God, all indicate his Egyptian and Oriental scholarship. Nor was he the first to employ the term Number, to represent the principle and substance of all things. 'Reason,' says Lao Tseu, the Chinese philosopher, 'has produced one; one has produced two; three has produced all things.'

To us it is quite evident that while the Idealism of Pythagoras is really identical with that of Hegel, the method of developing the system adopted by the former has merit equal, if not superior, to that adopted by the latter. When thought, the only real existence, becomes self-conscious, it is, according to Hegel, powerless for self-development, until it apprebends, in idea, something and nothing, together with the relation of absolute incompatibility between them. From the perpetual recurrence of the idea of this relation of incompatibility, the universe, a mere ideal creation, rises up before us, as a reality in itself. When thought becomes self-conscious it apprehends itself as one, with an idea of its incompatible opposite, the many. From the perpetual recurrence of the idea of the relations of the one and the many, the universe, a mere ideal creation, rises before us as a real existence. We leave it to 'Chaos and Old Night' to determine which system has the highest merit in its form and principle of development.

SECTION III.

THE ELEATIC SCHOOL.

Two schools in philosophy originated in Elea, a city in Grecia Major. The one first originated was denominated the metaphysical, and the other the physical school. The doctrines of the former were, in common with those of the Pythagoreans, Idealistic. The latter developed, in full perfection, the system of Materialism. We shall consider the teachings of these schools in the order designated.

The Eleatic Metaphysical School.

The principal representatives of this school were three, Xenophanes, Parmenides, and Zeno The views of each seem to have been, in certain particulars, peculiar to himself, each of the two latter being in advance of his predecessors in the direction of Pure Idealism.

Xenophanes, the founder of the school, was born in Colophon, in Ionia (569 B.C., according to Ueberweg, and forty or more years earlier according to other authorities). About the period 549 he left his native country, and after wandering for years as a rhapsodist, finally settled at Elea, dying at about 100 years of age. His doctrines have come down to us in fragments of his poems, which have been preserved to us by ancient authors, and in authentic statements of his utterances and doctrines, handed down through the same authorities. We have conclusive proof, we judge, that with Thales and Anaxagoras, he believed in the reality of an external, material universe, on the one hand, and in the doctrine of one supreme and personal God on the other, while he differed from both, and other great thinkers of Greece, and surrounding nations, in denying and repudiating utterly the Polytheism of all ages. Xenophanes was, in the strictest sense of the word, a Monotheist. A mature examination of the subject has removed all doubt from our mind in regard to the above statement, which we will now proceed to verify.

He affirmed that earth and water are the elements of all created things. 'All things were made from earth and water.' He also taught that the earth extends to an unlimited distance downward, and the air upward, a dogma disputed by Empedocles as being held by Xenophanes. Ueberweg has dispelled all doubt in respect to the fact, that Xenophanes held to the doctrine of the real existence of the physical universe.

The following stanzas evince with equal absoluteness his belief in the doctrines of one Supreme God:

> 'There is one God, of all beings, divine and human, the greatest,
> Neither in body alike unto mortals, neither in mind.'
>
> 'All sight, all ear, all intelligence;
> Wholly exempt from toil, he sways all things by thought and will.'

Take the following, as an example of his opposition to the Polytheism of his own and of surrounding nations:

> 'But men foolishly think that Gods are born like as men are,
> And have, too, a dress like their own, and their voice and their figure;
> But if oxen and lions had hands like ours and figures,
> Then would horses like unto horses, and oxen to oxen,
> Paint and fashion their god-forms, and give to them bodies
> Of like shapes to their own, as they themselves, too, are fashioned.'

Of the doctrines of Homer and Hesiod, he thus speaks:

> 'Such things of the Gods are related by Homer and Hesiod
> As would be a shame and abiding disgrace to any of mankind,
> Promises broken, and thefts, and the one deceiving the other.'

It could hardly be said that Paul, or any Christian, or Theistic author has given forth utterances more true, or appropriate than the above. Xenophanes was not a Pantheist, as Mr. Lewes affirms, nor a Polytheist, as other Grecian philosophers generally were, but a Monotheist, who believed in the reality of matter and spirit, and in God as the creator and governor of the universe, 'by *thought* and *will*.' If Pantheism represents such an idea of the universe and God as this, ' our heart's desire, and prayer to God' would be, that all men were Pantheists.

Parmenides (B.C. 536, according to Lewes and Cocker, and 569, according to Ueberweg) succeeded Xenophanes, as the leader of the Eleatic School, and was the first among the Greeks to give form and system to the doctrines of Idealism. He set out with a fundamental distinction between '*truth*,' real knowledge, and '*opinion*.' The faculty which gives the former is reason, that which gives the latter is sense. He took no account of consciousness, a fundamental error in Philosophy. Reason, by direct and immediate insight, gives absolute truth, or being, that which is real, necessary, immutable and eternal. The objects of sense, on the other hand, depending as its insight does upon the ever varying organism of the individual, and varying as that organism varies, the objects of sense, therefore, are the mere '*seeming*,' and not realities in themselves. The invalidity òf sense-perception, he thus argues : An object either does, or does not, exist. 'The non-existent is the unreal. Between the existent and non-existent, there is no intermediate form of being. To say, that a thing is "becoming," and is not, is absurd.' So far, our philosopher was undeniably right. To say, as philosophers, whose doctrines we are hereafter to consider, did teach, that there may be a becoming which never becomes, is, undeniably, one of the greatest conceivable absurdities. All objects of sense-perception, Parmenides affirmed, were of this fixed character, ever varying and variable, always seemingly, and never really becoming. Such objects have a mere illusory, and no real existence. Thus, the reality of the universe of matter and finite spirit was denied. Nothing is left as real, but the immutable, the necessary and eternal, which is the object of reason.

In such reasoning, we hardly need to add, we have the vicious error of deducing the universal from the particular. Knowledge, through sense and consciousness, is in certain respects variable and changeable, and in others, as we have formerly shown, absolutely fixed and immutable. Our apprehensions of the particular *states* of these substances do vary, because such states vary. Our apprehensions of the *essential* characteristics of each, on the other hand, are, as we have said, as fixed and immutable as they are of a circle or a square. In these respects, therefore, we have the same grounds for affirming the validity of knowledge by sense and consciousness as by reason.

In developing his system of being, he has anticipated Schelling and Hegel in announcing the fundamental principle of Pantheism, on the one hand, and of Pure Idealism, on the other. The form in which this principle or assumption is announced in the German schools is, '*Being and knowing are one and identical.*' As announced by Parmenides, it stands thus, '*To be and to know is identical,*' or '*Thought and being are identical.*' The final deduction from this principle, as affirmed in the ancient and modern school, is one and the same—namely, that 'The All is One,' or that but one substance, or principle of all things, does exist. When this deduction is stated in one form, we have the doctrine of Pantheism ; and when in another, we have that of Pure Idealism. In one or the other of these categories Parmenides must be located—that is, he must be regarded as 'a spiritualistic or idealistic Pantheist.' Substituting that of the Hindoo Brahm for 'the One' of our philosopher, and we have the Oriental formula in the precise form announced in the Vedanta system—to wit, 'Brahm alone exists ; everything else is illusion.' Substituting for 'the

One' 'the Absolute,' or 'the All-One,' and we have the precise formula of modern Pantheism—namely, 'The self-existent One must be the only absolute reality; all else can be but a developing of the one original and eternal being,' or 'The absolute exists as the only substance and principle of all things.' If the words, 'Being and knowing are identical,' be understood in the Pure Idealistic sense, then the systems of Parmenides and Hegel stand revealed as being identical in fact and form, and neither thinker has any advantage over the other, with the difference that for ages the former anticipated the latter, while both were anticipated by systems developed by Oriental thinkers.

THE ELEATIC ZENO, the scholar and successor of Parmenides, was born about the year 500 B.C. With him originated a logic of dialectics, a form of argument much used subsequently by Socrates and Plato—a logic which develops the art of establishing truth by a refutation of error by the *reductio ad absurdum*. Throughout his whole public career he was a fierce polemic. Up to his time various and contradictory systems had been developed, with little collision between them. Now one system was to be verified, and all others refuted. The system to be verified was that of Parmenides; those to be refuted were the Materialistic, on the one hand, and the Theistic, on the other. The claims of the last two systems rested wholly, as the subject was then understood, and as it is now beginning to be understood, upon the question of the validity of the perceptive faculties, Materialism affirming the validity of perception in its exterior, and denying it in its interior, form, and Theism affirming its validity in both forms. The position assumed was, that all our world-conceptions of every kind are, and must be, utterly void of validity, for the reason that they are all in common self-contradictory, and therefore absurd. He thus, professedly, proved the doctrine of his predecessor of the real existence of ' the One.' The form of his proof of the former, and disproof of the latter doctrine, is thus given by Mr. Lewes: ' There is but one being existing, necessarily indivisible, and infinite. To suppose that the One is divisible, is to suppose it finite. If divisible, it must be infinitely divisible.'

There cannot, for example, be a straight line in space one inch long, because such a line is divisible, and infinitely so. Who would infer from such an argument that there can by no possibility be such a line? Yet we have here a fair example of the most important contradictions which Zeno or Kant ever found in any of our essential world-conceptions. 'But, suppose,' says Zeno, 'two things to exist, then there must necessarily be an interval between those two—something separating and limiting them. What is that something? It is some *other* thing. But then, if not 'the *same* thing, it also must be separated and limited, and so *ad infinitum.*

Thus only one thing can exist as the *substratum* for all manifold appearances.'

By the same argument we will prove, with the same identical absoluteness, that there can be but one and the same *appearance*, and that appearance must be 'necessarily indivisible and infinite.' If the appearance is finite, it must be divisible, and infinitely so. But suppose two appearances to exist, then there must necessarily be an interval between the two—something separating and limiting. What is this something? It must be some *other* appearance. But then, if not the *same* appearance, *it also* must be separated and limited, and so on *ad infinitum*. Thus only one appearance can exist as the *substratum* for all manifold appearances. Is not the reader now convinced that there can by no possibility be but 'one being existing,' and but one and the same appearance, and that both must be in themselves, and both must *appear* to be, 'necessarily indivisible and infinite'?

If the first argument is to be regarded as valid, we may safely challenge the world to prove the invalidity of the second. Are not appearances, to say the least, manifold and finite? Why, then, may there not be just as many manifold and diverse and finite realities, as there actually are manifold and diverse finite appearances? Two finite objects, we will suppose, exist in space at a distance of ten miles from each other. What reality must exist between them? Space *must* be, and nothing else need be there. Separation does not imply that anything but empty space does exist between the objects separated. Where is there even the appearance of contradiction and absurdity here? Nowhere but in the brain of a bewildered and self-sophisticated philosopher.

Zeno and our modern Idealists would have us believe that real motion is an absolute impossibility, that is, that a body at one point can by no possibility be made to move to any other point in space. There may be *apparent*, but not *real* motion. The same argument which would disprove the latter would have equal validity in disproof of the former. Take also Zeno's argument on this point, as stated by Mr. Lewes, 'Motion is impossible, because before that which is in motion can reach the end, it must reach the middle point; but this middle point then becomes the end, and the same objection applies to it, since, to reach it, the object in motion must traverse a middle point, and so on *ad infinitum*, seeing that matter is infinitely divisible.' If this argument is valid, must not the following have a validity equally absolute?

Apparent motion is impossible, because before that which appears to move can appear to reach the end, it must appear to reach the apparent middle point; but this apparent middle point then becomes the apparent end, and the same objection applies to it, since to appear to reach it the appearance in motion must appear to traverse an apparent middle point;

and so on *ad infinitum*, since that appearance is infinitely divisible. From this time forward let no apparent human being who appears to himself to be sitting upon an apparent railroad, and appears to see an appearance of a seeming train of cars appearing to be moving with great rapidity towards him, have any fear. That apparent thing can never, even in appearance, touch that apparent man; for that apparent object can never appear to traverse the infinity of apparent points between the self-apparent man and the apparent approaching object. Let no one affirm that there is, or ever has been or can be, an apparent universe, or apparent men, or apparent accidents to apparent men, in the same. For the same identical contradictions undeniably exist in all our ideas of appearances that can be found in those of realities. All the contradictions and antinomies of pure reason, of Zeno, and Spencer, and Kant, absolutely disprove the non-being of what they all admit to be real, to wit, appearances, or they have no validity whatever anywhere.

Mr. Lewes' Vindication of Zeno's Argument.

'Plato,' says Mr. Lewes, 'has succinctly characterized the difference between Parmenides and Zeno by saying that the master established the existence of "the One," and the disciple proved the non-existence of the many.'

When he (Zeno) argued that there was but one thing really existing, all others being only modifications or appearances of that One, he did not deny that there were *many appearances;* he only denied that those appearances were real existences. So, in like manner, he denied motion, but not the appearance of motion. Diogenes, the cynic, who, to refute his argument against motion, rose and walked, entirely mistook the argument; his walking was no more a refutation of Zeno than Dr. Johnson's kicking a stone was a refutation of Berkeley's denial of matter. Zeno would have answered: 'Very true, you walk; according to Opinion you are in motion; but according to Reason you are at rest.'

As a question of fundamental importance in Philosophy here presents itself, we shall be indulged in a full consideration of said question. Appearances (phenomena) are many, and they are real. 'The many' are not and cannot be real, because the idea of 'the many' is self-contradictory. By the same identical argument we will prove, and have proven already, that there are not and cannot be 'many appearances.' The reason is obvious and undeniable. The same identical affirmed contractions which have place in our ideas of 'the many' realities, as we have shown, appear with the same obviousness in our ideas of 'the many appearances.' But appearances, these seeming contradictions, to the contrary, notwithstanding, are real. This is admitted and affirmed by Zeno, Lewes, Kant, Coleridge, Spencer, Mill, Emerson, and Transcendentalists of all schools, and denied by none. 'The many,' therefore, notwithstanding the same identical seeming contradictions, are, or may be, real. This we must admit, or affirm that things equal to the same things are not equal to one another. It is, undeniably, no more self-contradictory to affirm that behind appearances which all admit and affirm to be real, diverse, and manifold, there may exist a corresponding number of distinct and separate realities, than there is in the idea that these diverse, distinct, separate, and manifold appearances are the diverse and manifold manifestations of one and the same reality. If the seeming contradictions, or antinomies, we repeat, demand that we deny the existence of manifold realities, they demand with the same absoluteness that we deny the reality of manifold appearances. When we shall come to consider Kant's 'Antinomies of Pure Reason,' and Spencer's 'Contradictions,' we shall render it demonstrably evident that if these 'Antinomies' and 'Contradictions' have any validity whatever in disproof of the validity of our essential apprehensions of mind and matter (noumena), they have the same identical validity in disproof of the validity of our knowledge of appearances, or phenomena. The undeniable consequence will be that we must deny absolutely that these seeming 'Antinomies' and 'Contradictions' have any validity whatever in disproof of anything; or we must affirm not only that mind and matter are non-realities, but that neither they nor anything else even *appear* to be real, and that there has never been any conception of them, as existing or not existing. We must deny the reality of even thought itself, and the reality of that denial. There can be 'no thought, no being, none,' or these 'Antinomies' and 'Contradictions' are mere sophistical puzzles which are a disgrace to Philosophy in any age, and especially to the philosophic thought of the nineteenth century.

THE METHOD OF THIS SCHOOL.

The exclusive method, both of the Eleatic and Pythagorean school, is the Oriental or à priori one. Both, in common, recognized but two primary intellectual faculties—Sense and Reason. The validity of the former, for facts, was wholly denied. Reason only remained as the exclusive organ of Philosophy, Reason, through which, in imagination, they obtained a direct, immediate, and absolute à *priori* insight, or knowledge, of real being and its laws. Nothing real was revealed through perception. All its revelations were appearances, or illusions. Reason, looking off into infinite space, and away from all phenomena, or manifestations of existence, directly and immediately perceived the Absolute, and affirmed the real, the necessary, and exclusive existence of 'the One.' As long as this idea of the sphere of Reason is admitted to be valid, Philosophy will, of necessity, be a chaos. The forms of the Absolute, or 'the One,' thus apprehended, will be almost as diverse, and manifold, and contradictory, as the appearances of 'the One' are now, even by Idealists, admitted to be.

The Physical School of Elea.

The metaphysical speculations of Parmenides and Zeno were not long in producing their natural results in the same locality. When metaphysicians, dwelling in the sphere of pure thought, deny the validity of Sense, and through affirmed insight of Reason, resolve all being into spirit, thinkers whose speculations refer mainly 'to things without us' will naturally distrust the validity of subjective knowledge, and especially of that affirmed to have been obtained through the insight of a faculty of the existence of which no one is conscious, and whose revelations exist nowhere but in the brains of certain wild and lawless speculators. Denying the validity of Reason, and an affirmation of that of Sense, was a short, and easy, and not unnatural passage from 'the One' to 'the Many,' that is, from the ultimate deduction of Idealism to that of Materialism. This passage may also be made on purely *à priori* grounds. To Reason itself, assuming the existence of such a faculty, there is as valid ground for the assumption that matter only is real as there is, or can be, for the assumption that spirit alone exists, and that spirit 'the One.' Appearances which are multitudinous, and of an infinite diversity of forms, may on *à priori* grounds be as reasonably assumed to be manifestations of 'the Many,' as of 'the One.' This passage from 'the One' to 'the Many,' or from the ultimate deduction of Idealism to that of Materialism, was made by two physicians of Elea, Leucippus (500-400 B.C.), whose birthplace is uncertain, and by his disciple Democritus of Abdera (460-357 B.C.). The latter is said to have visited Egypt, Ethiopia, Persia, and to have communicated with the Djainas of India. The accordance of the teachings of these philosophers with that of their Indian predecessors referred to render it altogether probable that their system had an Oriental derivation. As these philosophers fully agreed in the doctrine, we shall speak of their system as their joint production. As they, first of Grecian thinkers, gave being and form to the system of Materialism afterwards perfected by Epicurus, and which with slight modifications has passed down through all subsequent ages to the present time, we shall be at special pains, not only to present the system as it came from these authors, but in some of its important relations to other systems of the same class, systems previously and subsequently developed.

Exposition of the System of these Philosophers.

For 'the one' of Parmenides and Zeno they substituted 'the many,' and for the one spiritualistic or idealistic form of being affirmed by the former, they affirmed an infinite number of material atoms. Their formula of being may, in their own words, be thus stated: 'Atoms and space alone exist,' or 'Atoms and vacuum (space) were the beginnings of all things.' The cause of organization and all attending phenomena is motion, which is represented by the word necessity. Speaking of Democritus, Diogenes Lactantius says: 'Motion, which is the cause of the production of everything, he calls necessity. Atoms they hold to be not only infinite in number, but to be possessed of an equal diversity of forms. Here they agree with Kanada, and differ from the Djainas and other materialistic schools of India, as well as from the materialistic doctrine of Anaxagoras. Atoms differed, they taught, as Aristotle informs us, 'in the three particulars of shape, order, and position,' and these differences, they held, are sufficient to explain all diversities of phenomena. Atoms also differ in size and weight, their weight being as their size. Originally all atoms existed separately in infinite space. If there was no space between, motion and, consequently, organization would be impossible.

Such being the original state of all material substances, the question arises—to wit, how shall all the changes and movements which we witness be accounted for? Why do atoms enter into their endlessly diversified combinations and bring forth the organic and inorganic forms which the world and universe present? The following is the account which Leucippus gives of the origin and cause of these wonders: 'Many bodies of various kinds and shape are borne by amputation from the infinite' (atoms being infinite in number and then in a chaotic state) 'into a vast vacuum' (how thus borne we are not informed), 'and then they, being collected together' (how collected is left unexplained), 'produce a vortex, according to which they, dashing against each other and whirling about in every direction, are separated in such a way that like attaches itself to like; bodies are thus, without ceasing, united according to the impulse given by the vortex, and in this way the earth was formed.'

Democritus affirmed, not only that atoms eternally exist, but also eternally and necessarily in a state of motion. This motion was in straight lines downward (just as if there is any down or up in infinite space). In their descent the motion of the larger and more heavy bodies being more rapid than the rest, collisions occurred, and the smaller bodies secured a lateral and upward motion. Thus a rotary motion was generated, and as this extended farther and farther the vortex was produced, which occasioned, in accordance with the principle of Leucippus, the formation of worlds. When the earth, which was at first in motion, came to a state of rest (the Copernican system was then unknown) by spontaneous generation, organized beings arose from the moist earth, and thus our world became filled with vitalized forms of existence.

Man has a material body and a material soul, the former being composed of the grosser, and the latter of the finer, the round, smooth, and fiery atoms. The psychology of these philosophers has certain noticeable peculiarities. To sensation or perception, they added not reason, but the faculty of reflection. This last-named faculty has a sphere, according to these philosophers, analogous to, if not identical with, that assigned to reason in the metaphysical school. Atoms are not perceived but apprehended by reflection, as implied by the aggregates which are perceived.

Neither do we have any direct and immediate perception or knowledge of any forms of existence around us. Hence Democritus has been understood by some as denying wholly the validity of our world-knowledge. All that he can be shown to have meant is that our knowledge, being not direct and immediate, was therefore, though real, not full and perfect. Perception he thus accounts for. From all organized forms of being there are constantly sent off images—ideas he sometimes calls them—of said forms. Thus images which can but imperfectly represent the forms from which the former proceed enter the body through the eye and other senses, and become present to the soul as objects of perception. Here we have the origin of the doctrine of exclusively representative knowledge of nature—a doctrine which has had a most controlling influence in the sphere of philosophic thought, from the era of Democritus to the present time. The moral teachings of these philosophers accord with their material principles. As there is nothing but perception in man, and nothing but atoms in the universe, there can be no place for an absolute law of right and wrong or duty. All must be a simple calculation, through the faculty of reflection, of prudence.

The highest good is happiness, and this is attained by avoiding extremes, and keeping within limits fixed by nature. Such is the system of Materialism, as first developed within the sphere of Grecian thought. We close our notice of these two philosophers with a few general reflections upon their system.

General Reflections upon this System.

1. We have in our examination of this, and of systems before, noticed a striking illustration and example of what may be denominated the element of perfection which characterizes Grecian thought. The actual forms of Grecian architecture, statuary, and painting, have remained fixed ideals for all future generations. The same holds equally of their philosophical system. The system may be false or true. But each of its kind takes from the first a nearly, or quite, perfected form. The Theism of Anaxagoras, the Pure Idealism of Pythagoras, the Ideal Pantheism of Parmenides and Zeno, and the Materialism of Leucippus and Democritus, are the ideals from which systems of the same kind have

since, in all essential particulars, taken form. It is only in non-essential details that the modern or any intermediate atomic theory differs from that which we have first considered. 'The modern atomic theory,' says Mr. Lewes, 'is the law of definite proportions; the ancient theory is merely the affirmation of indefinite combinations.' Here is an essential error in regard to both theories. Each theory in common holds the doctrine of definite combinations. The first holds to combinations in accordance with 'the law of definite proportion,' and the latter in accordance with a law acting from necessity, and which, by necessary consequence, must act in accordance with 'the law of definite proportions.' Thus we have a mere difference of statements, and not, as Mr. Lewes would have us understand, of essential principles.

2. We notice, also, a fundamental difficulty which the doctrine of Materialism encountered as soon as it was subjected to the searching scrutiny of Grecian thought. The fundamental principles and starting-point of the system in all its forms was a primal chaos of material forms or atoms, atoms eternally existing under an immutable law of order and universal organization as an *event of time*.

Both these conditions were distinctly present, and that from the first, to Grecian thought. The problem presented was this: How can organization, as an event of time, be deduced from a primal chaos of eternally existing atoms under the control of an eternally acting law of order? It was at once perceived, that if, in this primal chaos, these atoms were at rest, the beginning of motion could not be accounted for. Motion was, therefore, assumed as an eternal and necessary condition of all material elements, and as the cause of law and order, and universal organization. Thus was Descartes anticipated in his memorable utterance, 'Give me matter and motion, and I will organize the universe,' that is, explain the fact of its organization. Grecian thinkers assumed both as eternally existing facts. Motion being given as the law and cause of organization, what must be its eternal form to account for organization as an event of time? This was the problem. The first assumption was the idea of an infinity of atoms eternally moving in parallel lines. To this, it was soon replied that in such case the atoms would never meet, and organization could never occur. To avoid this difficulty, Democritus assumed the eternally downward movement of atoms in such lines, and also that in consequence of the more rapid movement of the larger and heavier bodies, a final collision would occur, and hence organization. To this, it was replied that as this more rapid movement was from eternity, the collision of atoms and consequent organization must have been from eternity, and not an event of time. In this desperate state of the problem, Epicurus took it up. He assumed the eternal existence of an infinity of homogeneous atoms, eternally moving in converging lines. To this it was replied that in such case, the concussion of atoms, and consequent organization, must have been from eternity, and could not have occurred in time. To avoid this fatal rock, the Epicurean physists, as we shall see hereafter, assumed the original motion of matter in straight lines, and their subsequent diversion and concussion by a *spontaneous* activity of the particles. Here the question arose, How can particles, moving under a necessary law of motion, spontaneously change the direction of motion in opposition to that law ? Such, however, was the assumption, an assumption in which Mr. Huxley finds himself anticipated by a Grecian thinker who lived several centuries prior to the Christian era. Mr. Huxley finding that the theory of Mr. Darwin could not be defended at all, if the validity of the axiom affirmed as true by Mr. Darwin himself be admitted, namely, that 'nature does nothing *persaltum*,' denies the principle, affirming that nature does sometimes act by 'fits and starts.' In one of these periods of convulsion, a monkey begat a man. The Greek mind—whether from greater or less respect for science than appears among certain modern scientists, we will not now say—the Greek mind, we say, regarded the idea that the organization of the universe was occasioned by a spontaneous change from the line on which atoms had, under a necessary law, been moving for a whole past eternity, as equivalent to an event without a cause. Such an hypothesis was accordingly rejected, and Materialism found itself once more stranded upon a fatal rock.

As a last resort, the doctrine of free-will was affirmed, as a universal property of matter itself. Man is a material agent, and yet he is consciously free. The power to change its movements from one direction to another, and this from the action of no cause *ab extra*, *inheres*, as a fixed property in all atoms. By a volutionary deflection from straight lines 'the atoms strike against each other, and by the concussion new movements arise.' Thus was occasioned the organization of the universe. We shall make larger extracts to the same point when we come to a direct examination of the system of Epicurus. The great problem forced upon Materialists by the exigences of their system, the problem which must be fully solved, or the system itself suffer a hopeless shipwreck, was left unsolved by Grecian and mediæval thought, and in that state has been handed down to modern advocates of the system. The problem is this, matter being given in a state of perfect chaos, and acted upon by no cause but its own eternally inhering laws, to deduce exclusively from such premises the universe as it is, and the origination of that universe as an event of time. Modern materialists have, in their manner of treating the subject, admitted their own necessary problem to be absolutely insolvable, as it undeniably is. They argue as boldly and fiercely for Materialism as Kanada, Democritus, or Epicurus ever did. But when pressed with their own necessary problem, they all in common dodge the issue by affirming an absolute ignorance of the subject matter about which they are arguing. 'It is certain,' they unitedly affirm, 'that we can have no knowledge of the nature of either matter or spirit.' Why, then, press upon us your Materialism? Here is the hopeless limbo into which this bald system has now fallen.

3. We now perceive the fundamental advantage which Materialism has in its controversy with Idealism. Take away Reason as defined by Idealists of all schools, ancient or modern, and their system is absolutely baseless. As they themselves have defined the term, Reason is represented as a faculty which acts independently of all others, and perceives no reality whatever *through* phenomena, but having affirmed all forms of perception to be illusory, looks off into infinite space, and by direct *à priori* insight, apprehends absolute and eternal truth. Now, no man living or dead ever did adduce, or can adduce, the remotest evidence that any such faculty exists. No man is consciously possessed of such a faculty. The multitudinous and contradictory forms of absolute truth, forms obtained through this affirmed insight, render demonstrably evident the fact that this boasted faculty is nothing but a fiction of false science. Besides, the affirmed *à priori* visions of the Materialists have all the marks of credibility that those of Idealists do or can possess. We undeniably have just as good ground for affirming the reality of 'the Many' as we have for affirming that of 'the One.'

On the other hand, the Materialist bases the claims of his system upon the revelations of a faculty, sense-perception, of the existence of which all men are absolutely conscious, and in whose validity they as absolutely confide. When the election, then, is between Materialism and Idealism, with good reason the former will command popular favour.

4. We have, in our examination of these Grecian systems of Materialism and Idealism, another illustration of the validity of a statement formerly made, to wit, that all these systems are built, not only upon mere assumptions, but upon assumptions all of which have the vicious characteristic of begging the question at issue. Had Democritus or Epicurus, for example, been asked for the reasons why they affirmed the existence of atoms of homogeneous or heterogeneous character, why they affirmed them to be identical or diverse in size, weight, and form, why they attribute to them such contradictory kinds of motion, and why, at one time, they affirmed them to be under the law of necessity, and at another as possessed of free-will, but one answer could be given, to wit, their assumptions were always determined, not by facts, but by the exigencies of their system. This holds true of the method of all the advocates of all such systems, in all ages and in all forms. We look in vain into such systems for anything in the form of induction proper. Whenever an

exigency arises, a new form of absolute truth is presented, not because it is demanded by facts, but by the exigencies of an hypothesis. All issues are begged, and nothing proven.

SECTION IV.

THE INTERMEDIATE SCHOOL.

Heraclitus and Empedocles.

We notice these two individuals together, and rank them as belonging to a common school, not because they fully agree in their teachings, or taught in the same place, but because they were each of them, in important senses, eclectics, taking their positions intermediately between opposing systems, and attempting to reconcile or to develop the truth out of their differences. Of the system of Heraclitus, who was born at Ephesus, and flourished about the years 500—420 B.C., little that is intelligible can be said, because his contemporaries could not fully understand his writings, he being called 'the obscure,' and but a few fragments of these have come down to us. Of the book of this thinker Socrates said that 'what he understood of it was excellent, and he had no doubt that what he did not understand was equally good; but the book requires an expert swimmer.' We shall, therefore, attempt nothing more than to present a few obvious features of his system, if he had any fully developed system, features which may be of interest to the inquirer after truth.

In one of his utterances he gave a criterion of valid knowledge—a criterion by which, with absolute certainty, all forms of such knowledge may be distinguished and separated from all mere assumptions, opinions, and beliefs which are of no certain validity. In this particular he takes just rank as a foremost thinker of the race, no one before him having attempted to give such a criterion. 'Universal and divine reason,' he says, 'is the criterion of truth. That which is universally believed is certain, for it is borrowed from that common reason which is universal and divine; and, on the contrary, every individual opinion is destitute of certainty, this common reason being nothing but the picture of the universe. Whenever we derive anything from it, we possess the truth; and when we interrogate only our own individual understanding, we fall into error.' Had mankind accepted of this criterion and strictly adhered to it, the chaos of ages would long since have passed away, and order and harmony and unity would be as absolute in the sphere of philosophic thought and inquiry as they are in the system of external nature. As is too commonly the case, however, the thinker who first announced the principle was among the first to depart from it.

In his physics fire, not as flame, but a boundless ether, is assumed to be the substance and principle of all things. 'The world,' he says, 'was neither made by the gods nor men, and it was and is and ever shall be an *ever-living fire,* in due proportion self-enkindled, and in due measure self-extinguished.' Here, undeniably, we have what is not 'universally believed;' and have consequently, by our philosopher's own 'criterion of truth,' 'a picture of the order of the universe,' which is not true. The same holds in respect to his doctrine of 'becoming' a peculiar doctrine, first announced, we believe, by Heraclitus, and which subsequently had not a little influence with leading thinkers. Permenides had affirmed that there is and can be no intermediate form of being between existence and non-existence, 'the ens and the non-ens.' Heraclitus held to 'a becoming' in which 'things are and also are not.' The ethereal fire was in a continual flux, an eternal flow in which there was a perpetual formation and transformation, and continuance was not real, but only an appearance. 'Into this same stream,' he says, 'we descend, and at the same time we do not descend; we are, and also we are not.' 'Unite,' he says again, 'the whole and the not-whole, the coalescing and the not-coalescing, the harmonious and the discordant, and thus we have the one becoming from the all, and the all from the one.' Ever since the days of Heraclitus, philosophers of certain schools have been engaged in a vain endeavour to catch this no-thing which stands intermediate between the real and the not-real, and to represent this becoming which never becomes as the real universe. Either the absolute 'criterion of truth' before us is false, however, or this doctrine of, at the same time, being and not being, is an error.

This fiery ether, according to Heraclitus, has spiritual attraction, of which intelligence is one. 'Inhaling,' he says, 'through the breath of the universal ether, which is divine reason, we become conscious.' Heraclitus therefore, like Anaximander, must be regarded as a kind of Materialistic Pantheist, both thinkers having apparently engaged in the vain attempt, as intermediators between Materialism and Idealism, to materialize spirit on the one hand, and to spiritualize matter on the other. It was against this doctrine of a becoming which never becomes that Anaxagoras arrayed himself in his teachings in Athens.

Empedocles, of Agrigentum, in Sicily, and who was born about fifty years later than Heraclitus, held but few principles in common with, and strongly combatted others of his predecessor. Empedocles, as we have shown, and that unlike his predecessor, held the doctrine of one supreme God, who is distinct from nature, and 'ruleth all things by reason and will.' 'All things that are upon the earth and in the air and water may,' he says, 'be truly called the works of God.' We might make other citations to the same effect, but these are fully sufficient to verify for their author a right to a place among true Theists. When contemplating his doctrine of cosmology, we must bear in mind that he never refers to organization by mere natural laws, but as occurring under divine control. While Aristotle censures Anaxagoras for not referring to his first cause, Intelligence, but upon emergencies, he says, that 'Empedocles employs this more abundantly, though not sufficiently.' This shows that God was ever present to his mind as the first and all-controlling cause, to whom frequent and specific reference was had, as facts rendered such reference necessary. In opposition to Heraclitus, and in accordance with the principles of Parmenides and Anaxagoras, he denied the doctrine of 'becoming,' and affirmed with the latter that existing elements may be mixed and separated, but never destroyed.

The Ionian philosophers had reckoned but three original material elements, earth, air, and water. To these Empedocles added a fourth, fire. By the ancients he is regarded as the author of the doctrine of the four named primal material elements.

SECTION V.

THE SOPHISTS.

In their attempts to explain everything, the various schools of Greece had left almost everything unexplained. The system which one school had set up another had demolished, while that of the latter had fallen to pieces under the heavy blows of its antagonists. Nothing appeared of which any man could say, 'See, this is true.' Hence a general or widely diffused sentiment obtained in the popular mind that real knowledge on any subject was impossible. Hence, also, a new class of thinkers arose, a class essentially diverse from any which before had entered the sphere of scientific thought. Oriental thinkers, and Grecian, too, up to that time, had all been positivists. In all schools in Philosophy, absolute truth, in some form, had been professedly obtained. Now, nothing seemed to have a real scientific basis but universal *doubt*, a sentiment thus announced by Metrodorus, of Chios, a disciple of Democritus, to wit, 'I do not even know that I know nothing.' The advocates of this doctrine of universal and absolute nescience assumed the favoured cognomen of Sophists, or wise men. So we have been informed by a modern thinker of the same school that himself and fellow-thinkers have attained to a knowledge of the fact that it is impossible for us to 'have any knowledge of the nature of matter or spirit,' and that all inquiries pertaining to religion and God, and the soul's eternity, are as foreign to the proper sphere of human thought and inquiry, as 'lunar politics,' that to all this utter and hopeless nescience himself and associates have attained 'by their wisdom.'

Common Doctrine of the Sophists.

The doctrine common to Sophists of all classes was the absolute impossibility of a real knowledge of any form of existence, if any reality does exist. Hence, all in common, while they denied the validity of positive system in all their forms, refrained from propounding any such system as their own.

> 'The first and wisest of them all professed
> To know this only, that he nothing knew.'

The manner in which this doctrine of absolute and necessary nescience of all truths was assaulted by certain thoughtful Greeks presents a striking illustration of the subtlety of the Grecian mind. You affirm, was the substance of their reply to the Sophist, that a knowledge of truth in any form is impossible to man. You either do, or do not, know your own doctrine to be true, that is, you know, or do not know, that you doubt the possibility of knowing truth in any form. If you know that you thus doubt all things, something is known as it is in itself, and your doctrine is false. If you do not thus doubt, you have no ground whatever for affirming your doctrine to be true. In either case, we are bound to discredit your teachings. This argument has confronted Scepticism from that time to the present, and has never yet, even in pretence, been replied to. Yet that argument must be fully met, or we subject ourselves to the just charge of infinite folly and presumption if, for a moment, we accept the doctrine of universal nescience as true. The only reply to the argument ever attempted was that of Metrodorus recorded above. He fancied that he had placed the elements of doubt so far back, that nothing positive could be detected in it. The positive affirmation, to wit, 'I don't know,' appeared as before. It is absolutely impossible for the mind to take the first step in the direction of sceptical thought without perpetrating a palpable self-contradiction. The simple fact, which cannot be denied, that we can know one reality as it is in itself, to wit, our own doubt, implies the fact that we may know other realities as they are in themselves. The fact that doubt is known to be real, and is known as it is in itself, implies that the Intelligence is relatively to this fact a power, and that it is to the Intelligence an object of valid knowledge. On the same conditions, other realities may be to this same Intelligence objects of real valid knowledge. The question whether doubt, or any other reality, is to the Intelligence such an object, is a pure question of self-consciousness. We know that we know doubt, because we are conscious of knowing it. If we have a consciousness of similar absoluteness of any other form of knowledge, whatever its object may be, we must admit the strict validity of such knowledge, or displace ourselves from the sphere of valid science

The Method of the Sophist.

In their general method of induction and deduction, there was an agreement strictly universal among the Sophists. Materialism had professedly demonstrated the absolute invalidity of all affirmed knowledge of spirit, whether through Consciousness or Reason. Idealism had professedly done the same thing in respect to all professed knowledge of material substances. The Sophist accepted the validity of this impeachment of the Intelligence as a faculty of knowledge in respect to matter and spirit both. To the Materialist on the one hand, and the Idealist on the other, they replied, You are both right, and both wrong. You are, each of you, right in the form in which you have impeached the Intelligence as a faculty of knowledge. Each of you have demonstrated his antagonist to be wrong in respect to the forms of valid knowledge of which each of you affirms himself possessed. The Sophist presented no form of proof or disproof of his own theory. He simply, through the mutually destructive arguments of positivists, each against the system of his antagonist, rendered it demonstrably evident, the validity of said arguments being admitted that no positive system can have any claim to be regarded as true.

Here the Sophist found himself within a citadel of impregnable strength, a citadel from whence he was able to hurl weapons of annihilating power against all positive systems around. When, however, he was assaulted, not from without but from within his own fortress, when required to turn from outward positions, and to defend by valid grounds and arguments the truth of his own dogma of universal doubt, here he found himself the weakest of men. Here, as we shall see hereafter, lay the secret of the power of Socrates in his assaults upon the Scepticism around him. When modern Scepticism is thus assailed, as it will be when thinkers have well considered the subject, their folly will be seen, as 'an unclean spirit gone out of man,' and 'wandering through dry places seeking rest, and finding none,' with no mind 'empty, swept, and garnished' to receive it again.

The Sources of the wide-spread Influence of the Sophists.

Two facts then existing gave an extensive influence to the Sophists over the Grecian mind—the chaos into which positive systems generally, in their destructive assaults one upon the other, had been reduced, and the fact that the Sophists, in public estimation, excelled all other thinkers in the presentation of forms of real knowledge which were most needful to the people. The Sophists excelled in general learning, and were the instructors of the people in whatever was generally deemed of public utility. 'Protagoras,' in the language of Schweghler, 'was known as a teacher of virtue, Gorgias as a rhetorician and politician, Prodicus as a grammarian and teacher of synonyms, Heppias as a man of various attainments, who, besides astronomical and mathematical studies, busied himself with a theory of mnemonics; others took for their problem education, and others still the explanation of the old poets; the brothers Enthydemus and Dionysidorus gave instruction in the bearing of arms and military tactics. Many among them, as Gorgias, Brodicus, and Hippias, were entrusted with embassies; in short, the Sophists, each one according to his individual tendency, took upon themselves every variety of callings and entered into every sphere of science; their method is the only thing common to all.' Scepticism was never boldly presented to the people, but was cunningly blended with what was really useful, and presented as if it was a necessary element of the same. The same thing is being repeated in our own age. The system 'has no root in itself,' but is everywhere visibly, like the mistletoe, attached to some other vital form of science, and appearing as if it was a branch or shoot of the same.

General Reflections suggested by the preceding Analysis of the Pre-Socialistic Systems of Philosophy.

1. We notice, in the first place, the circumstances and influences under which diverse systems of Philosophy arise and take form in the human mind. They are among others such as the following: (1) In all ages and under all circumstances, wherever the integrity of the Intelligence is respected and each faculty is held as having within its own proper sphere, and in respect to its proper objects, absolute authority for the truth, there arises a fixed and immutable faith in the reality of matter and spirit, time and space, a personal God, duty, immortality, and retribution. We find, also, that the distinctness and absoluteness of faith in these verities is always in exact accordance with the fulness and distinctness of the recognition and respect under consideration. If any faculty is overlooked or its integrity is in the remotest degree questioned, there will be so far a cloud between the mind and these verities. We may refer to Thales, Anaxagoras, Zenophanes, and Empedocles as examples exemplifying and verifying the above statements. (2) If the integrity and validity of the faculty of Sense, or external perception, is impeached and denied, and those of internal perception, or of Reason as the faculty of *à priori* insight relating to being and its laws, are affirmed, then there arises a faith in the deductions of Idealism in some of their forms, and with that faith a denial of the doctrine of a personal God and other kindred doctrines. The Pythagorians and Metaphysicians of the Eleatic school are veritable examples of the validity of these statements. In no

age or nation did the doctrines of Idealism, in any of their forms, ever arise but upon the one condition above stated. Why did Pythagoras and Parmenides and Zeno, for example, assert the doctrine of 'the One'? Because, and for the express reason that they denied the integrity of the faculty of external perception for the reality of 'the many.' (3) Whenever the validity of the faculty of internal perception, relatively to mental facts, and of Reason, relating to being and its laws, is impeached and denied, and that of Sense affirmed, the system of Materialism commands the individual and popular faith, as in the examples of Anaxamander, Leucippus, and Domocritus. (4) When the integrity of all the faculties, as organs of truth, is impeached, then, as in the case of the Sophists, Scepticism has the place and dominion in popular thought. The history of Philosophy presents no exceptions to the above statements. We thus have an historical verification of the account given in the General Introduction of the 'Origin and Genesis of Various Systems of Philosophy.' There have been a few individuals in the history of the past who have denied the integrity of sense-perception and affirmed the validity of a so-called *à priori* insight of Reason, who have yet been real Theists. The reason is plain. When an individual imagines himself possessed of this power or faculty, he will obtain, through its affirmed insight, just those, and no other, forms of supposed 'absolute truth' which he previously regarded as such. Those who are in heart Theists may affirm the doctrines of God, and those who do not 'like to retain God in their knowledge' may deny His existence for mere imaginary reasons. What we maintain is that Materialism, Idealism, and Scepticism never, as a matter of fact, have place in human thought but for the reasons above assigned.

2. We notice, also, in our preceding criticisms of particular systems, a practical illustration of the fundamental fallacy involved in the doctrine of affirmed *à priori* insight in all its forms, to wit, its assumed positive and negative revelations. The Oriental Yogee of the Vedanta school, for example, in one and the same act of insight, not only, as he affirms, perceives that Brahm exists, but that nothing else does exist. The modern Transcendentalist, in one and the same act of 'intellectual intuition,' not only perceives that the Absolute does, but that nothing else can exist. The Idealist of Greece, by direct and immediate insight of reason, perceives not only that 'the one,' the I, exists, but that 'the many' do not exist. By the same form of insight the ancient and modern dualists obtain a revelation of absolute truth in an exclusively negative form. The modern formula is thus given by Kant: 'The things which envisage are not that in themselves for what we take them; neither are their relationships in themselves so constituted as they appear to us.' The ancient formula, as given by Kapila, is this: 'Neither do I exist,

nor anything which pertains to myself,' the ancient and modern formula being really identical in meaning. Now, a greater and more absurd hallucination in science could not be conceived of, than we actually have in all the above cases. Direct and immediate insight has, and can have, nothing negative in it. Perception, empirical and *à priori*, gives its object as a real existence, and can do nothing more. With my face turned towards the south, I clearly and distinctly perceive a train of cars in motion. In the same identical act I affirm myself to perceive that no other train on earth is or can be at the same time in motion. The world would very properly regard me as demented. Yet this is a case of hallucination no more palpable and real than is true of all the forms of insight above adduced. The Materialists, for example, has a direct and immediate perception of 'the many' as actually existing. Such perception, granting it to be real, is valid for the reality of said object, and for all realities necessarily implied by the same, to wit, time and space. Nothing is, or can be, given in the act of perception itself but 'the many.' In the same perceptive act, however, our scientist professes to perceive that nothing but matter does exist, a palpable hallucination of false science. The Yogee, the Transcendentalist, and the Grecian Pantheist, affirm that by direct and immediate *à priori* insight they perceive Brahm, 'the Absolute,' or 'the One,' to exist. That perception, supposing it real, is valid for the existence of its object, and in itself is, and can be, valid for the existence or non-existence of no other reality. But these individuals affirm that in one and the same act they not only perceive Brahm, 'the Absolute,' or 'the One,' to be real, but that nothing else does exist. If the same form of hallucination was manifested in any other sphere of thought but that of philosophy, the subject would justly be sent to a lunatic asylum. Perceptive insight, we repeat, is valid for the reality of its object, and, in itself, is valid for nothing else. If the existence of the reality perceived necessarily implies the being, or non-being, of some other object, its being or non-being may be affirmed, not as *perceived*, but as *implied* by what is perceived. In the affirmed *à priori* insight of the Yogee, the Trancendentalist, and Grecian Pantheist, Brahm, 'the Absolute,' or 'the One,' is affirmed to be perceived, not only as real, but as the only reality. Unless we can begin with the intuitive perception, that the Absolute exists, as the sole and exclusive reality, that is, that the Absolute, and that nothing else, does exist, we cannot, Schelling affirms, 'take the first step in the speculative philosophy.' In other words, unless we can at the outset perpetrate the greatest absurdity that ever danced in the brain of a crazy philosophy, we cannot even cross the threshold into the high sphere of speculative thought.

The fact that matter is real does not, in itself, imply the non-being of spirit. The fact, then, that we perceive 'the many' to exist has, in itself, nothing to do with the question whether 'the One' does or does not exist. Nor is the idea that 'the One' exists, in any sense or form incompatible with the idea that 'the Many' exist also. Nothing can be more undeniably evident than the fact that Materialism and Idealism, in all their forms and deductions, are based wholly upon the grossest and most palpable forms of scientific hallucination ever conceived of, an hallucination only equalled by the sceptical formula, that we don't know that we don't know anything.

3. We have also, in our preceding elucidations, a practical illustration of the absolute impossibility of vindicating for any form of Materialism, Idealism, or Scepticism, even an apparent scientific basis. Such basis, to be really and truly scientific, must, undeniably, be either a judgment self-evident, or one whose validity has been strictly demonstrated to be true. We have already carefully examined every principle on which every such system rests, and have found every such principle to be utterly void of self-evident or demonstrated validity, while their fixed characteristics as mere assumptions have been absolutely evinced.

Each of the two systems first named has its positive and negative side. The positive side is this: one substance, or form of existence, is real. The negative side is this: no other substance, or form of existence, is real. Now, the validity of this negative side is neither self-evident, nor can it, by any possibility, be verified for science. That this principle has self-evident validity, no one will affirm. We have before us two absolutely incompatible judgments: to wit, that spirit is, and matter is not, and that matter is, and spirit is not, real. Have each of these judgments self-evident validity? Each or neither must be thus evident. Both cannot, and, therefore, neither can be self-evident.

Equally impossible is it to *prove* the one to be true and the other false, the positive evidence in favour of each, and against the other, being absolutely balanced. The identical form of evidence which can be adduced in favour of the existence of one of these substances, can be adduced in favour of that of the other; and every form of disproof which can be adduced against the reality of one, may be adduced, with equal force, against that of the other.

Neither of these systems, then, can, on its negative side, at least, have any scientific basis at all, and both together must fall to pieces.

Scepticism, also, in all its forms, has its positive and negative sides. It admits and affirms the absolute validity of human knowledge in one form at least. It admits and affirms that we doubt, and know that we doubt. 'It is *certain*,' we are told, 'that we can know nothing of the nature of either matter or spirit.' Relatively to two fundamental facts, then, *doubt* and *nescience*, the Intelligence is a faculty, and they are to it objects of real knowledge. This is the positive side of the system.

'Now, here,' we say, in looking at the negative side, 'is a strange thing,' that the Intelligence should be capacitated to know its own doubts and ignorances just as they are, and should be incapacitated to know any other facts or realities, as they are in themselves. That 'we know this only, that we nothing know,' is surely not a self-evident truth. How can the Sceptic prove his doctrine? The least, as we have shown already, that can be required of him is, that he adduce facts and arguments of the reality and validity of which we can and must be more absolutely assured than we actually are of our own existence, and of that of material forms around us, facts and arguments which necessarily imply the utter invalidity of our knowledge of mind and matter. The Sceptic knows, and all mankind know, that no such facts and arguments can be adduced. No scientific basis, therefore, can be adduced for any one of these systems.

For the doctrine of spirit, matter, time, space, God, duty, and immortality, on the other hand, such a basis can be most readily verified. All the facts and principles which lie at the basis of our faith in all these verities, are affirmed as real and valid by the direct, immediate, and absolute testimony of the universal Consciousness. No grounds or arguments against this faith, can, by any possibility, be adduced of the validity of which we are, or can be, so absolutely and rationally assured, as we are and must be of the reality and validity of these facts and principles. When the Sceptic shall adduce against our faith in these verities, 'grounds and arguments' of the validity of which we are and ought to be more assured than we are of our own personal existence, and of the reality of material forms around us, then, and not until then, will we, or ought we, to admit that the faith under consideration has no scientific basis. The basis on which this faith rests is the conscious integrity of the universal Intelligence. If this is not a scientific basis, no science has such a basis.

Much is said in certain schools of the progress of our race, and very much may veritably be said upon the subject. There is a fundamental difference, however, between progress in government, civilization, the arts, and sciences in general, and real progress in ontological systems. In the particulars first named, progress has been visible and marked. In respect to those last named, Theism excepted, there has been no real progress whatever for the last twenty-five centuries. There is method, even in madness. So there is in error. When the mind diverges from the track of truth, it must diverge, as we have shown, from certain fixed points, and move from thence on certain determinable lines. If it shall construct certain systems of false science, it must construct them after one or another fixed form. There is but one system of truth, and there can be but a certain number of systems of false science. When that number is completed, error must conform to one or the other of these fixed forms, and thus, as ages roll on, repeat itself. In the General Introduction, we determined the number and forms of all conceivable and possible systems of Ontology. In our examination of the Oriental and Grecian systems, we have found every system we then designated, and in the exact form there represented. Hereafter we shall search in vain for Anti-Theism in any new, or more perfected form than we have already considered. Kant, Fichte, Schelling, Hegel, Condilac, and Comte, for example, we shall find to be nothing more than unimproved copyists of Vyasa, Kapila, Kanada, Gautama Buddha, Pythagoras, Parmenides, Zeno of Elea, and Democritus. Messrs. Emerson, Mill, Spencer, and Huxley, will be found to be mere repetitions of Gorgias, Protagoras, Prodicus, Polus, and Metrodorus. Even Mr. Darwin will be found to be but a very imperfect edition of Anaximander. How our ancestors were nursed by their monkey parents, and how these ancestors afterwards lost their hairy covering and long tails, Mr. Darwin tells us very imperfectly. According to the Grecian sage, those ancestors, without any such covering, or tails, were begotten as veritable men and women in the bellies of fishes, and having been kindly nursed there until they were able to care for themselves, were spewed out upon the dry land, and sent forth to seek their fortunes. If compelled to make our election between the two theories, we should unhesitatingly prefer the latter. To us, there is more of dignity, and quite as near an approach to rationality, in the whale, as in the monkey. If nature can make a leap from the irrational to the rational, why not from a whale to a man? We must regard the Anglo-Saxon theory as a degenerate spawn from the Grecian.

CHAPTER II.

THE SOCRATIC EVOLUTION IN PHILOSOPHY.

INTRODUCTION.

PSYCHOLOGY AND PHILOSOPHY.

THE OBJECT OF PHILOSOPHY.

THE object of Philosophy, as we have formerly stated, is not the science of mere facts, or of mere existences, but of the *reason*, the *ultimate* reason especially, why the facts of the universe are as they are, and not otherwise, and why real existences are related to one another as they are, and not otherwise. 'Philosophy,' says Schwegler, and rightly so, 'is never satisfied with receiving that which is given simply as it is given, but rather follows it out to its ultimate grounds; it examines every individual thing in reference to a final principle, and considers it as one link in the whole chain of knowledge.' Of all the sciences, Philosophy, as we have also formerly said, is the ultimate. The entire sphere of the admitted unknowable and unknown, Philosophy recognizes as such, and never attempts the elucidation of facts, or relations of existences, lying within that sphere. In the presence of real facts, the specific reasons for the occurrence of which are unascertained, or unascertainable, Philosophy recognizes the known on the one hand, and the mysterious on the other, and locates such facts within the sphere of the present, at least, inexplicable. In the presence of self-contradictory judgments, Philosophy recognizes the absurd, and locates the objects of such judgments within the sphere of the impossible. Explicable facts of real knowledge, and explicable relations of known existences, these, and these exclusively, fall within the sphere of Philosophy. Whenever we find ourselves in the presence of such facts and relations, and the question arises, why are said facts and relations as they are, and not otherwise, the great problem which it is the exclusive province of Philosophy to solve rises before us.

The Immutable Characteristics of all Explicable Facts and Relations.

A question of fundamental interest here arises, namely, what are the *fixed and immutable characteristics of all explicable facts and relations ?* A known fact, or class of admitted facts, are before us. A specific reason for their existence and occurrence is asked for. If these facts are of such a character as to be fully explicable on some one specific hypothesis, and upon no other, we find ourselves in the presence of explicable facts. If these facts suggest no specific hypothesis of any kind, they belong to the sphere of the mysterious. If they suggest a certain number of hypotheses, one of which must be true, and all the others false, while they are equally compatible with, and explicable by each, such facts are not fully explicable, but sceptical in their character. Explicable facts are always of such a character as to imply necessarily the specific cause or law of their existence and occurrence. When we inquire for such a cause or law, it is not sufficient to prove that the facts are merely *consistent* with a given hypothesis. When we have gone thus far, we have only proven that said hypothesis may be, and not that it is, true, much less that it *must* be true. Facts are really explained when, and only when, an hypothesis is found which is absolutely perceived to be not only compatible with said facts, but as necessarily implied by the same. In other words, it must be seen, in the light of said facts, not only that said hypothesis *may* be, but that it *must* be, true, and all other and opposite ones, consequently, must be false. The facts of the universe, material and mental, for example, are before the mind. The question to be answered is, what is the ultimate reason, or cause, why the facts before us are as they are, and not otherwise ? Two, and only two, hypotheses present themselves. One of them, consequently, must be true, and the other false. That reason, or cause, as all admit, must be an inhering law of nature itself, or the agency of a personal God, acting upon nature from without. If the facts before us are of such a nature as necessarily to imply that one of these hypotheses must be true, and the other false, then, relatively to such cause or law, the facts under consideration are explicable. If, on the other hand, these facts are found to be equally compatible with each hypothesis, then they are not explicable, but inexplicable, or sceptical in their character. Explicable facts, we repeat, always themselves imply the hypothesis by which they are explained and elucidated, and not only imply but always reveal the hypothesis under consideration. In other words, real causes and laws, when ascertainable, are both revealed and implied by the facts which the former produce and determine. There can be no greater and more obvious hallucination in science, than is involved in the idea that causes and laws may be discerned, not through facts by which such laws and causes are implied, but by direct and immediate *à priori* insight. Suppose that in utter ignorance of facts the mind should have, were the thing possible, a direct vision of a cause or law, that is, a vision of such objects *in se*. What would such objects be to the mind? Nothing, we answer, but meaningless entities, and no real causes or laws at all. By no possibility can causes, substances, or laws, be known to the human mind, but *through* the phenomena, or facts, by which the former are implied, and known as thus implied.

THE GREAT PROBLEM OF PHILOSOPHY.

We are now prepared to state definitely the great and exclusive problem, the solution of which devolves upon Philosophy. With existences *in se*, that is, with substances, causes, and laws, and relations of existence, not implied by, and known through, phenomena, and facts known to be real, Philosophy has no more to do, than it has in determining the specific size, weight, and form of objects on the further side of the moon. The real problem under consideration is this: 1. In the light of valid criteria, to distinguish and separate forms and facts of valid knowledge from all mere assumptions, opinions, beliefs, and conjectures which may, or may not, be true. 2. To deduce the substances, causes, and laws and relations of existence implied by the real facts which are the objects of valid knowledge. Through the known, Philosophy is burdened with the single problem, to determine the existences, and laws and relations of existences, implied by the facts which are known.

Remove the phenomena and facts, and no problem whatever remains for Philosophy to solve. Assume that 'the things which we envisage are not that in themselves for which we take them,' and that 'neither are their relationships in themselves so constituted as they appear to us,' and we are left in the same condition as before, with no basis to stand upon, and no real substances and causes to inquire for. All problems are located in the sphere of the unknown and unknowable. If we should assume that appearances or illusions may be known as they are in themselves, we are in the same limbo as before. The same Intelligence which 'envisages' realities, not as they are, but as they are not in themselves, will 'envisage' appearances, not as they are, but as they are not in themselves, and so on for ever. We can never find a valid basis from which to reason about anything. If while we admit the validity of our knowledge of certain facts, we ignore, or deny a part of such facts, or include others which are not thus known, Philosophy is then deflected from the line of truth, and is started in the fixed direction of fundamental error, and is certain to land us there. The first problem for Philosophy, we repeat, is this—to wit, What are the facts known to be real, and what are the principles known to possess universal and necessary validity? The second is like the first, namely this, What are the substances, causes, and laws and relations of existence, necessarily implied by said facts and principles? Any departure from these fixed laws of induction and deduction, or any other method of philosophizing, is, and must be, 'vain wisdom all, and false philosophy.'

THE RELATIONS OF PSYCHOLOGY TO PHILOSOPHY.

The real relations of Psychology to Philosophy involve questions of fundamental importance in science, questions, however, which philosophers have seldom pondered at all, or wrongly resolved when inquired into. The end and aim of Philosophy, in its analysis of the human intelligence, is to determine the number of the intellectual faculties, primary and secondary, the exclusive sphere and objects of each faculty, their mutual relationships to one another, and their individual and combined relationships to science. If any one of these faculties is ignored, falsely explained, or displaced from its appropriate and exclusive sphere, Science will be made to rest upon a false basis, or will substitute vain imaginings for truth.

Intellectual Faculties, Primary and Secondary.

Facts or phenomena, as we have formerly shown, are exclusively known by perception, external and internal, and imply two such faculties—Self-consciousness, which apprehends mind in its operations, and Sense, which apprehends matter in its phenomena or manifestations. All the material and mental facts which lie at the basis of all deductions in the science of Ontology are given exclusively through the intuitions of these two faculties. Take away the facts thus given, or deny the validity of our knowledge of the same, and nothing whatever is left for Philosophy to elucidate or inquire about. Deny the validity of our knowledge of subjective or objective facts, and affirm it of one class exclusively, and Philosophy, with one eye put out, is sent off in the direction of Materialism or Idealism, as the case may be. Take these facts just as, by the Intelligence, they are handed over to Philosophy, let them be carefully separated from all elements introduced by the action of will and sensibility, let all realities be accepted which are necessarily implied by facts perceived, and all principles which arise from the necessary relations between said facts and realities; and finally, let all deductions necessarily arising from said facts and principles be given, and then we shall have a veritable and scientifically evinced Philosophy or system of universal being and its laws.

The original elements of all our knowledge, in all its forms, are constituted of facts perceived and realities, such as space, time, substance, and cause, directly and immediately implied by said facts. The faculty which gives these implied realities we have denominated Reason. The primary faculties of the Intelligence, then, are three—Self-consciousness, the organ of subjective; Sense, the organ of objective; and Reason, the organ of original implied knowledge. The sphere of Reason, then, is just as fixed and definite as is that of either of the perceptive faculties. Consciousness and Sense give us facts or phenomena, mental and physical. Reason apprehends the realities implied directly, immediately, or intuitively by the facts or phenomena which are perceived. The action of Reason is always conditioned on the prior action of the other faculties, and the nature and character of its apprehensions are determined by those of the other faculties. Reason cannot apprehend substances, causes, and laws but through facts or phenomena previously perceived, and the nature of the substances, causes, and laws, which it apprehends, is always and of necessity as is that of the facts referred to. If facts are not perceived, no substances, or causes, or laws are manifested, and none can be apprehended. Nothing can be more manifest. Reason, we repeat, apprehends substances, causes, and laws through facts or phenomena, and as implied by the same. The real and relative sphere of the three primary faculties is, therefore, perfectly fixed and determined. Reason can do no more nor less than apprehend the realities implied by facts of external and internal perception, realities such as time, space, substance, cause, etc.

Of the *secondary faculties*, the first which claims attention is the *Understanding* or conceptive faculty—the faculty which combines the elements given by these three primary ones into conceptions or notions, particular and general. When we analyze correctly any conception or notion which we have of any object of perception, external or internal, we shall find said conception to be constituted of two classes of elements—the perceived and the implied, or the contingent and the necessary. Our idea of body, for example, is constituted of two classes of elements—qualities perceived, and substance implied by what is perceived. Perception gives the former, Reason the latter. The same, undeniably, holds equally in regard to all our conceptions of all perceived objects of every kind, whether mental or material. Such palpable facts absolutely identify Reason as a primary intellectual faculty, and also as the organ of intuitively implied knowledge. The same facts as absolutely determine and evince the exclusive sphere of the Understanding, namely, to combine into conceptions the elements of original intuition—elements furnished by the three primary faculties designated.

The *Judgment* now intervenes and affirms the *relations* existing between conceptions, or the objects of the same. Judgments are of two classes, intuitive and deduced. In every judgment in which the subject implies the predicate, we have not only an intuitive but necessary judgment.

The judgments, body implies space; succession, time; events, a cause; phenomena, substance : and things equal to the same things are equal to one another, are of this character When, in any judgment, the subject does not imply the predicate, but the relation between them is directly and immediately perceived, we have an intuitive but contingent judgment. When this relation is discerned, not immediately, but through other judgments, then we obtain a derivative or inferred judgment. The judgment is the *logical* faculty.

We need merely to refer to the two other secondary faculties—the associating principles, as Memory and Recollection, and the Imagination, the faculty which blends the elements of thought, given by all the other faculties, into conceptions corresponding, not to realities as they are in themselves, but to ideas of the beautiful, the grand, the sublime, etc.

The primary faculties, then, are three in number—Consciousness, or the faculty of subjective knowledge; Sense, the faculty of objective knowledge; and Reason, the faculty of intuitively implied knowledge.

There are, on the other hand, just four, no more and no less, secondary faculties—Understanding, or the notion-forming or conceptive faculty; the Judgment, or the faculty which apprehends and affirms the relations existing between conceptions or their objects; the associating principle, including Memory and Recollection, and the Imagination, or blending faculty. A correct Psychology will not fail to recognize all these faculties, will never ignore or omit any one of them, will add none to them, and will never confound any one of them with any other, so marked and distinguished from every other is each by readily discernible phenomena, and so definitely fixed and determinable is the sphere of each.

Relations of these Faculties to Science.

All the above-named faculties, primary and secondary, the Imagination excepted, have their fixed and definitely assignable sphere and authority, in every valid scientific procedure All the original elements which enter into every such procedure are furnished by the three primary faculties. The first step in true science is a full separation of all elements of original intuition from all foreign admixtures, and the adoption of the former as the exclusive basis of all scientific deduction Every procedure into which none but such elements enter, and from which none thus given are excluded, has, so far, an absolutely valid basis, or we have and can have no such basis whatever.

Apprehensions represent two classes of phenomena, conceptions, and ideas. The former represent our apprehensions of objects of external and internal perception, our apprehensions of matter and spirit, for example; the latter represent our apprehensions of objects of intuitively implied knowledge, such as space, time, substance, cause, and personal identity. Ideas, in the sense under consideration, of course, have universal and absolute validity. Understanding-conceptions have such validity when, and only when, they embrace nothing whatever but the elements of original intuition, elements perceived and implied. If such conceptions exclude any elements really thus given, or include any not thus given, we shall, of course, arrange, classify, and elucidate objects, as they are not, and not as they are.

When, in the sphere of the Judgment or logical faculty—the province of the associating principles, as Memory and Recollection, being too obvious to require particular specification in this connection—when in the sphere of the logical faculty, we say, none but conceptions, and ideas which, in the sense defined, are really valid, have place, when all judgments pertaining to the relations to one another of conceptions and ideas, or their objects, have absolute intuitive or deductive validity, all mere assumptions, opinions, beliefs, and conjectures, which may or may not be true, being excluded, then, and only then, we have true science. When we depart in any direction, from the line of induction and deduction above laid down, we are moving on the track of false science.

COMPARATIVE VALIDITY AND AUTHORITY OF THESE FACULTIES.

The above analysis of the intellectual faculties fully evinces the fact, that each one of them has a particular, distinct, exclusive, and readily definable sphere. While each acts in perfect harmony with all, and all with each, the functions of each are exclusive, and peculiar to itself, and furnish us forms and elements of knowledge impossible to every other. The faculty of external perception, for example, has a function and sphere which no other faculty can perform or occupy. We are necessitated to accept as valid for science the intuitions of this faculty, or to repudiate them altogether, such intuitions having absolute validity, or none at all. The same undeniably holds true of every other faculty. Its authority, within its proper sphere, must be regarded as absolute, or utterly repudiated. Its functions no other faculty can discharge, and hence, in all scientific procedures, it must be accepted as a valid organ of truth, or repudiated as 'a liar from the beginning.'

True science, consequently, will permit the validity of no faculty, within its proper sphere, to be questioned at all without the weightiest conceivable reasons. Suppose, that the validity of any one faculty is impeached. To what faculty or faculties shall the appeal be made to test the validity of such impeachment ? No faculty can go out of its own and enter the sphere of another, and there sit in judgment upon the procedures of the latter. No faculty has, or can have, valid insight but within its own proper and exclusive sphere. No faculty, therefore, can authoritatively adjudicate upon the validity of the procedures of any other. Before any faculty can be impeached and its authority set aside, we repeat what we have often said before, a form of knowledge must be adduced of the validity of which we are, and must be, more absolutely assured than we are, or can be, of the validity of that furnished by the faculty under consideration, and the forms of knowledge presented must be absolutely incompatible with one another. Until, as we have often said before, the Idealist, Materialist, or Sceptic, shall adduce 'ground and arguments' of the validity of which we cannot but be more assured than we are of the fact of our personal existence, and that of material objects around us, 'grounds and arguments' which necessarily imply the invalidity of our convictions of the reality of the self and of the not-self, we should act most irrationally and absurdly if we should, for a moment, doubt the validity of these convictions.

SECTION L.

SOCRATES.

THE name of Socrates is a household word among all who know anything of Greece, and to all such the memory of Socrates is 'as ointment poured forth.' As the Catholic is taught 'that there is no salvation out of the Catholic Church,' so we, from childhood up, had been taught that outside of the circle of revealed truth, no one ever had attained to the real possession of moral virtue or eternal life. When in our classical studies, however, we, through the writings of Xenophon and Plato, came to know the man as he was, when his life, his character, and doctrines lifted their divine forms before our mind, the conviction forced itself upon us that Greece, in the midst of her crimes and vices and errors, had known at least one wise and good man—one whose home is now 'the bosom of God.' This fixed conviction we did not disclose even to our classmates; for why, when no good could be attained thereby, should we consent to suffer the imputation of heresy? Thus that conviction remained until, in the Theological Seminary, we came under the instruction of the venerable Moses Stuart. When speaking to us of 'the wise men from the East,' as we recollect, he turned aside to give us his impressions of Socrates. Up to a few years previous, he informed us, he had entertained the fixed conviction that no one, not favoured with the light of inspiration, had become morally virtuous or had been saved. Being aware that Socrates was one of the most perfect characters ever originated amid heathen darkness, he read all that remains on record of this man's life and teachings, and did this for the express purpose of being able to discover and designate the fundamental moral and religious defects in his character. Instead of finding what he anticipated, he was forced to confess to himself that Socrates was both a wise and good man, and that he is now, as he hoped to be when he was dying, 'among the blessed.' From that time onward we have not hesitated to avow the opinion which we here record.

The Socratic evolution in Philosophy produced three great central lights—Socrates, Plato, and Aristotle. In a moral point of view, Plato, in our judgment, ranks with Socrates. Of Aristotle we cannot thus speak. Yet our heart is moved with melting hope towards him when we consider his dying exclamation—to wit, 'I was born in sin; I have lived unhappily, and I die in perturbation. Cause of causes, pity me.' Would that modern scientists, who have far less profoundly studied the problem of being and its laws than Aristotle, had his humility, wisdom, and integrity. When, from the moral standpoint, we contemplate the two men, Plato and Aristotle—while we are constrained to admit that the latter was far more correct in his method of induction and deduction, and taught, perhaps, quite as many truths and fewer errors than the former, we would rather err with Plato than hold the truth with Aristotle.

Socrates was born in Athens about the year 470, and died about 400 B.C. At the time when he assumed the functions of a public teacher, Scepticism was the prevailing belief of the people, of the most intelligent especially, and Philosophy, degraded by the flippant puns of the Sophists, had ceased to be a grave and serious matter of thought and inquiry. Scepticism, the fundamental principle or assumption of which is that the basis of all Philosophy is absolute nescience, and that the elements of the entire superstructure are wholly extracted from 'air nothing,' becomes and can become, in every department of thought and inquiry, nothing but a flippant trifler, and can do nothing for mankind but induce them to laugh at the infinite vacuity in which 'proud science' has located them. Years ago there appeared a series of fictions denominated 'Hogg's Tales.' The tales ran in circles. The reader would be started off in a certain direction, and that with appearances which would excite expectation that wonderful disclosures were just ahead. After being carried round a wide circuit with this expectation constantly increasing, he finds himself set down at his point of departure without really having been shown anything at all. He would then be started off again under the same expectation, and after going a similar round, would find himself at his point of departure precisely as before. The final result was a reaction which induced a hearty laugh. The same holds true of sceptical thinkers of all ages, and never more so than with the self-styled Scientists of this age. They do now, as they did in Greece, present themselves to the world as alone possessed of 'the key of knowledge,' and as being 'the knowing ones' of the race. After laying down, as the basis of all valid scientific deduction, the proposition that we 'don't know that we don't know anything,' or 'that all our knowledge is mere appearance,' and 'that the reality existing behind all appearance is and ever must be unknown,' we are assured that now the problem of universal being and its laws shall receive a final solution, that the era for demonstrative certainty has arrived, that 'as surely as every future grows out of the past and present, so will the physiology of the future gradually extend the realm of matter and of law until it is co-extensive with knowledge, with feeling, and with action,' that 'matter and law will devour spirit and spontaneity,' and that 'thought is the expression of molecular changes in the matter of life.' After being carried round such a circle with expectation on tip-toe of attaining 'the revelation of absolute truth,' we are at length set down exactly at our point of departure, being assured that 'it is certain that we can have no knowledge of the nature of either matter or spirit.' The result is an almost irrepressible disposition to laugh at 'the trick played upon reason' in our sight. Just what existed in Athens at the time when Socrates appeared upon the stage, and existed as the result of the sceptical teachings of the Sophists, we are now witnessing, as the result of the influence of 'the New Philosophy,' in the prevailing flippant dogmatism, want of respect for truth and moral worth, the readiness with which the shallowest sophistry, if it bears against the doctrines of God, duty, and immutability, determines the popular faith, and the consequent appalling revelation of an utter want of trustworthiness in almost every department of life. The admonition of Socrates to his countrymen, relative to the Sophists of that age, has place relatively to the Sophists of our own, Sophists who commend themselves to our regard as the disciples and expounders of the 'New Philosophy.'

'Is not, O Hippocrates, a Sophist, a seller or vendor of the articles on which the soul is fed? He seems to me to be something of that kind.'

'What, Socrates, is the soul fed? Pray, on what?'

'On the lessons of teachers, and we must take care that the Sophist does not cheat us in selling his wares, as the sellers of food for the body often do. For they, without knowing what is good for the body, praise all their wares alike, and the buyer knows just as little, except he be a physician or a training-master. And just so these vendors of lessons, who carry their wares about from city to city, and sell them to every one whom they can persuade to buy, praise all the articles which they sell; but very likely some of these, too, know very little what is good for the soul and what is not; and the buyers know just as little, except any of them be soul-physicians. If, then, you are a judge of what is good in this way, and what is not, you may safely buy lessons of Protagoras or of any one else. But if not, take care, my good friend, that you do not run a dreadful risk in a vital concern; for there is far more danger in buying lessons than in buying victuals.'

It was in the midst of the trifling flippancy of a sceptical age, and just as a reaction against the influence of the Sophists had commenced, that Socrates appeared as a teacher of truth. The central peculiarity of his character was an absolute respect for truth, and a corresponding assurance that the human Intelligence is a faculty of valid knowledge. With him 'life was real, life was earnest,' and the questions, what am I?—where am I?—what ought I to do, and to become?—and what is my eternal destiny? were all solvable questions. Mind is not encircled with illusions, but realities, realities known and knowable, and through a known creation man may find God, as the known Creator and Governor of the universe. Socrates was not, as some represent, like Confucius, a mere teacher of morals, but of truth in all its forms, and of morality as the great central truth of all science. Up to that time Philosophy had concerned itself mainly with exterior problems, the maxim of true knowledge, 'Know thyself,' having been disregarded. Socrates recalled Philosophy to a consideration of the interior and weightier problems which the central facts of mind, those of its moral nature, especially, present. True Philosophy has its moral and religious sides, as well as its physical, and the former excel the latter, as the infinite excels the finite. So Socrates regarded and treated these two classes of problems.

COMMON-SENSE.

Socrates was to his age what Reid, Beattie, Stewart, and Jouffroy are to our own, the veritable philosopher of Common-sense. This term or phrase, which for the first time appears in this Treatise, we will permit the individual last named to define for us. 'The history of Philosophy presents a singular spectacle: a certain number of problems are reproduced at every epoch; each of these problems suggests a certain number of solutions, always the same; philosophers are divided, discussion is set on foot, every opinion is attacked and defended, with equal appearance of truth. Humanity listens in silence, adopts the opinion of no one, but preserves its own, which is what is called *common-sense*.' 'Everybody understands by common-sense a certain number of principles and notions, evident, of themselves, from which all men derive the grounds of their judgments, and the rules of their conduct. But it is not sufficiently known that these principles are merely positive solutions of all the great problems which Philosophy agitates.' 'Common-sense, therefore, is nothing but a collection of solutions, to those questions which philosophers agitate. It is another Philosophy, prior to Philosophy properly so called, since it is found spontaneously at the bottom of every consciousness, independently of all scientific research. There are, accordingly, two votes on the questions which interest humanity, namely, that of the mass and that of the philosophers; the spontaneous vote and the scientific vote, common-sense and the systems.' 'If we compare the solution given by common-sense to any problem whatever with the different solutions which have been proposed by philosophers, we shall always find that the solution proposed by common-sense is more comprehensive than the philosophical solutions. This may be proved by examples. Zeno defined good, that which is in accordance with reason; Epicurus, an agreeable sensation; Kant, that which is obligatory. Common-sense adopts all these opinions, and for that reason cannot be confined to any of them. The exclusive Spiritualists affirm the existence of spirit; the exclusive Materialists, that of matter; but the former end with denying matter, and the second with denying spirit. Common-sense equally admits both matter and spirit, and places itself in contradiction to each of these systems. The empirics recognised no authentic sources of knowledge but the eyes and the hands; Descartes admits none but consciousness; Plato and Kant make reason and conception predominate over that which can be attained by the sense or consciousness; common-sense acknowledges the authority of consciousness, of the senses, and of reason, at the same time. If we pursue the parallel in regard to other questions, we shall always find the same result. We hence obtain this important consequence, that if common-sense does not adopt the systems of philosophers, it is not because those systems say one thing and common-sense another, but because these systems say less, while common-sense says more.'

Now, as long as Philosophy shall continue to place itself in open antagonism to the common-sense of the race, that is, to the spontaneous and necessary intuitions of the universal Intelligence; in other words still, so long as a voluntarily determined partialism shall control her induction of facts, so long will her proud creations be nothing but an endless and monotonous succession of dissolving views, chaos returning in orderly intervals, through the lawless and wildly destructive influence of the Sceptical Philosophy. Philosophic thought will stand revealed, as employed in the toilsome and senseless labour of successively, without improvement or modification, rearing up, and toppling over, the old and rotten systems of Vyasa, Kapila, Kanada, the Buddhists, Pythagoras, Zeno of Elea, Democritus, and Protagoras. Partialism, if it creates anything, must recreate and then destroy these identical systems. When, on the other hand, Philosophy shall accept the entire facts handed over to her by the intuitions of the universal Intelligence, and shall accept of these facts as given, when she shall repudiate nothing thus given, and assume nothing not thus given, when she shall find the principles implied by these, and separate from the same, all assumptions of every kind, and when, finally, the entire deductions necessarily resulting from these facts and principles shall be presented to the world as verities of science, then we shall have a philosophy of being and its laws which will stand the test of ages, a system of such transcendent beauty and perfection, that even the infinite and eternal Mind shall have no occasion to be ashamed of it. Within the circle of the intuitions under consideration lies the rock of eternal truth. Every man-constructed system that 'shall fall upon that rock will be broken, and upon whatsoever systems it shall fall it will grind them to powder.'

THE ERA OF THE PUBLIC TEACHING OF SOCRATES.

It was, we repeat, amidst the decay and disappearance of grave philosophic thought among the Greeks, and when the reaction against the teachings of the Sophists had commenced, that Socrates appeared as the expounder and advocate of truth, the philosopher of Common-sense, the interpreter of interior as well as of exterior facts and principles. His first object was a refutation of the principles and reasonings of the Sophists, or Sceptics, and thus to destroy their influence with the people. Here we have what may be called his disproof, or the negative side of his system. *Something*, even the Sophists, in common with all Sceptics, admitted, may be known. In other words, the Intelligence, relative to *some* realities, to say the least, the fact of nescience, for example, is a faculty, and they are to it objects of real knowledge. This is the common postulate of all systems, the point from which they all in common take their departure. You, yourself, admit, Socrates would say to the Sophist, that something, your doubts, at least, are knowable and known verities. Why do you affirm these to be objects of valid knowledge? But one answer could be given, to wit, I am conscious of doubting. If you admit the fact of doubt to be real, because you are conscious of doubting, then, Socrates would add, you must admit the reality of any other fact or form of being, which is to you an object of the same conscious knowledge. In short, you must admit the fact of your own personal existence, as exercising the functions of thought, feeling, and willing. Nor can you stop here. You have the same absolute consciousness of knowing your own body and the universe around you, as veritable objects of actual knowledge. 'Man,' says the Sophist, 'is the criterion of that which exists.' Granted, replied Socrates. Look, then, into mind, and read its thoughts, feelings, and activities, especially the facts of its moral nature, and thus learn what the soul is. Read the forms of knowledge of which it is consciously possessed. Thus he not only silenced Scepticism, but brought back public thought to self-reflection, and to a proper consideration of the soul. Of all the philosophers, Socrates was the first who made the soul, its relations, duties, and destiny, one of the central problems in Philosophy. Socrates, in the beautiful and impressive language of Cicero, ' brought Philosophy down from heaven to earth, and introduced it into the cities and houses of men, compelling men to inquire concerning life and morals, and things good and evil.'

THE METHOD OF SOCRATES.

Socrates, also, first of all philosophers, popularized the inductive method of inquiry and deduction, the method of reasoning from facts to principles, from phenomena to substance, from events to causes, and from the conditioned to the unconditioned. In his argument for the being and government of God, for example, he has fully anticipated Paley, with the addition that Socrates did what Paley forgot to do: adduced the central facts of mind, as having a fundamental bearing upon the problem. We will here present an example of the reasoning of Socrates upon this subject, an example recorded by Xenophon, and thus translated by Mr. Lewes. Before giving the extract, we would direct special attention to a demonstrably evident postulate strictly common, and distinctly recognized in all the philosophical schools of Greece, those of Idealism not excepted. All recognized the fact of the origin of the present universe *as an event of time.* To this statement, as we shall see, Aristotle is an exception. The primal state of the universe was an undeveloped form of spiritual essence, or a chaos of material elements. This, we also observe, is the common postulate of all hypotheses ever presented by human thought, of the origin and genesis of the universe as it now is. All start with the idea of a beginning in time. The following is the statement of this postulate as given in the Timæus: 'Let this universe be called *heaven,* or the world, or by any other name that it usually receives; and let us, in the first place, consider respecting it, what ought to be investigated at the very outset of our proposed inquiry about the universe—whether it always existed, having no beginning, or was generated, beginning from some commencement. It is generated.' Anti-theism, in our age, may and must take one of two positions—that the universe has existed from eternity, or took form and order, as an event of time. The first position is confronted by the intuitive convictions of the race, and all the palpable facts of the universe. The second presents, as we have formerly shown, for Anti-theism, this great problem. Given the primal elements of nature, whatever they may be, in an undeveloped state, or in that of universal chaos, to explain from laws eternally existing in said elements, the universe organized as it now is. Universal order and development from such a cause is no more conceivable, or explicable, than is an event without a cause.

The argument of Socrates is this: creation from a primal chaos, or as an event of time, is explicable but upon one exclusive hypothesis—the creative agency of a personal God. Here, aside from the fact stated above, we notice the perfection which characterizes the argument of

Socrates, and the fundamental defect in that of Paley, and all who follow him. Paley argues from mere facts of order, without basing his argument fundamentally upon the undeniable fact of the origin of order as an event of time. Socrates, in fact and form, argues from a universe organized in time to a creative power out of and above nature. We now present the extract referred to:

'I will now,' says Xenophon, 'relate the manner in which I once heard Socrates discussing with Aristodemus' (a Sophist or Sceptic) 'concerning the Deity; for, observing that he never prayed nor sacrificed to the gods, but, on the contrary, ridiculed those who did it, he said to him:

'"Tell me, Aristodemus, is there any man you admire on account of his merits?"

'Aristodemus having answered, "Many"—

'"Name some of them," said Socrates.

'"I admire," said Aristodemus, "Homer for his epic poetry, Melanippides for his dithyrambics, Sophocles for his tragedy, Polycletus for his statuary, and Zeuxes for his painting."

'"But which seemed to you most worthy of admiration, Aristodemus, the artist who forms images void of motion and intelligence, or one who has skill to produce animals that are endowed, not only with activity, but understanding?"

'"The latter, there can be no doubt," replied Aristodemus, "provided the production was not the effect of chance, but of wisdom and contrivance."

'"But since there are many things, some of which we can easily see the use of, while we cannot say of others to what purpose they are produced, which of these, Aristodemus, do you suppose the work of wisdom?"

'"It would seem the most reasonable to affirm it of those whose fitness and utility are so evidently apparent," answered Aristodemus.

'"But it is evidently apparent that he who at the beginning made man, endowed him with senses because they were good for him; eyes to behold what is visible, and ears to hear what was heard, for say, Aristodemus, to what purpose should odour be prepared, if the sense of smelling had been denied? or why the distinction of bitter or sweet, of savoury or unsavoury, unless a palate had been likewise given, conveniently placed to arbitrate between them and proclaim the difference? Is not Providence, Aristodemus, in a most eminent manner conspicuous, which, because the eye of man is so delicate in its contexture, hath therefore prepared eyelids like doors whereby to secure it, which expand of themselves whenever it is needful, and again close when sleep approaches? Are not these eyelids provided, as it were, with a fence on the edge of them to keep off the wind and guard the eye? Even the eyebrow itself is not without its office, but, as a pent-house, is prepared to turn off the sweat, which, falling from the forehead, might enter and annoy that no less tender than astonishing part of us. Is it not to be admitted that the ears should take in sounds of every sort, and yet not be too much filled with them? That the fore-teeth of animals should be formed in such a manner as is evidently best for cutting, and those on the sides for grinding it to pieces? That the mouth through which this food is conveyed should be placed so near the nose and eyes as to prevent the passing unnoticed whatever is unfit for nourishment, while Nature, on the contrary, hath set at a distance and concealed from them all that might disgust or any way offend them? And canst thou still doubt, Aristodemus, whether a disposition of parts like this should be the work of chance or of wisdom and contrivance?"

'"I have no longer any doubt," replied Aristodemus; "and, indeed, the more I consider it, the more evident it appears to me that man must be the masterpiece of some great artificer, carrying along with it infinite marks of the love and favour of Him who formed it."

'"But further (unless thou desirest to ask me questions), seeing, Aristodemus, thou thyself art conscious of reason and intelligence, supposest thou there is no intelligence elsewhere? Thou knowest thy body to be a small part of that wide-extended earth thou everywhere beholdest; the moisture contained in it thou also knowest to be a portion of that mighty mass of waters whereof seas themselves are but a part, while the rest of the elements contribute out of their abundance to the formation. It is the soul, then, alone, that intellectual part of us, which is come to thee by some lucky chance, from I know not where. If so there is no intelligence elsewhere, and we must be forced to confess that this stupendous universe, with all the various bodies contained therein, equally amazing, whether we consider their magnitude or number, all have been produced by chance, not by intelligence."

'"It is with difficulty that I can suppose otherwise," returned Aristodemus, "for I behold not the gods whom you speak of as framing and governing the world; whereas I see the artists when at their work here among us."

'"Neither yet seest thou thy soul, Aristodemus, which, however, most assuredly governs the body; although it may well seem, by thy manner of talking, that it is chance and not reason which governs this."

'"I do not despise the gods," said Aristodemus; "on the contrary, I conceive so highly of their excellency as to suppose they stand in no need of me or of my services."

'"Thou mistakest the matter, Aristodemus; the greater magnificence they have shown in their care of thee, so much the more honour and service thou owest them."

"'Be assured,' said Aristodemus, 'if I once could persuade myself the gods take care of man, I should want no monitor to remind me of my duty.'

"'And canst thou doubt, Aristodemus, if the gods take care of man? Hath not the glorious privilege of walking upright been alone bestowed on him, whereby he may with the better advantage survey what is around him, contemplate with more ease these splendid objects which are above, and avoid the numerous ills and inconveniences which would otherwise befall him? But it is not with respect to the body alone that the gods have shown themselves bountiful to man. Their most excellent gift is that of a soul which they have infused into him, which so far surpasses what is elsewhere to be found; for by what animal except man is even the existence of the gods discovered, who have produced and still uphold in such regular order this beautiful and stupendous frame of the universe? What other creation is to be formed that can serve and adore them? In this, Aristodemus, has been joined to a wonderful soul a body no less wonderful; and sayest thou, after this, the gods take no thought of me? What wouldst thou, then, more to convince of their care?'

"'I would they should send and inform me,' said Aristodemus, 'what things I ought or ought not to do, in like manner, as thou sayest, they frequently do to thee.'

"'And what then, Aristodemus? Supposest thou, that when the gods give out some oracle to all the Athenians they mean it not for thee? Consider, my Aristodemus, that the soul which resides in thy body can govern it at pleasure; why may not the soul of the universe, which pervades and animates every part of it, govern it in like manner? If thine eye hath power to take in many objects, and these placed at no small distance from it, marvel not if the eye of the Deity can, at one glance, comprehend the whole. And as thou perceivest it not beyond thy ability to extend thy care, at the same time, to the concerns of Athens, Egypt, Sicily, why thinkest thou, my Aristodemus, that the providence of God may not easily extend itself through the whole universe?

"'As, therefore, amongst men we make best trial of the affection and gratitude of our neighbour by showing him kindness, and make discovery of his wisdom by consulting him in our distress, do thou, in like manner, behave toward the gods; and if thou wouldst experience what their wisdom and their love, render thyself deserving of some of those divine secrets which may not be penetrated by man, and are imparted to those alone who consult, who adore, and who obey the Deity. *Then shalt thou, my Aristodemus, understand there is a Being whose eye passes through all nature, and whose ear is open to every sound; extends to all places, extending through all time; and whose bounty and care can know no other bounds than those fixed by his own creation.*'"

According to Aristotle, Socrates introduced the method of induction and definition, which, as stated by Ueberweg, 'sets out from the individual and ends in the definition of the general notion.' Had Plato and Aristotle strictly adhered to this method, the history of Philosophy would never have had occasion to treat of the decline of Grecian Philosophy.

Special Doctrines Taught by Socrates.

Inasmuch as this renowned world-thinker first gave, to say the least, a distinct development and prominence to the method of induction among the Greeks, and stands before us more distinctly than any other ancient philosopher, as the great representative of the doctrine, or philosophy, of Common-sense, it becomes a matter of no little interest to determine clearly the most important doctrines which he did teach. To this inquiry we would, therefore, direct very special attention. In regard to this inquiry we remark:

1. We need not go beyond the extracts above given to evince absolutely that he clearly and definitely distinguished between *matter* and *spirit*, and regarded them as real, distinct, and separate entities. No writer, for example, more clearly and definitely distinguished between the soul and the body, and between the former and all visible existences and forms of material organization in the universe around us; equally manifest is the fact, that Socrates also held the doctrine of time and space, as realities in themselves. Our knowledge of the four verities he adduces as having absolute validity, and as the basis for scientific deductions pertaining to the distinct and opposite nature and destiny of the soul and body, and also in regard to the being, perfections, and government of God. Socrates, in short, in the strictest sense of the term, and in the sense in which we have defined the same, was a Realist.

2. With equal absoluteness, Socrates held and taught the doctrine of the being of one supreme, infinite and perfect, personal God. It would be entirely superfluous to verify these statements by any additional citations, citations which could be readily multiplied to any extent desired. We have here another very important example in verification of a fundamental fact formerly asserted, to wit: that, in all ages in which the validity of our knowledge of Matter and Spirit, and Time and Space, is admitted, the doctrine of a personal God is also affirmed.

3. No thinker, in ancient or modern times, has more clearly recognized the absolute distinction between moral right and wrong, the sacredness of duty, and ill desert of sin, than did Socrates. So prominent were his teachings on these fundamental subjects, that, by not a few writers on the history of Philosophy, he is regarded rather as a teacher of morals than of Philosophy. It would be more proper to affirm that, in his

regard, moral virtue was not the only science, but the science of sciences. 'The name for the result of a right constitution of the body,' says Socrates, 'seems to me to be *healthfulness*, from which arise health and other bodily excellences. And, in like manner, the result of a right constitution of the soul is lawfulness (that is, law-regardingness) and law: and by this men are law-regarding and orderly: and this is justice and self-control.' 'I say, then, that if a soul which is temperate is good, a soul which is intemperate is bad. And a temperate soul, a soul under due control, will do what is right towards the gods, and towards men. It would not be under due control if it did not. Now what is right towards man is justice; what is right towards the gods is piety: and he who does such things is *just* and *pious*.' 'The good and the pleasant are not identical,' as Callicles argued. 'Is the good to be sought for the sake of the pleasant, or the pleasant for the sake of the good? The pleasant for the sake of the good.' 'Taking the two things, wrong-doing and wrong-suffering, we have to say that wrong-doing is the greater evil of the two.'

4. Between virtue and happiness, and sin and misery, there is, even in this life, Socrates held, an inseparable connection, and hence taught that it is better to suffer death itself, rather than perpetrate the least form of wrong-doing. His doctrine on this point is thus stated by himself: 'A good and virtuous man or woman, I say, is happy, and an unjust and wicked one, I say, is miserable.' 'He who does well must be happy; and the bad man who does ill must be wretched.' Hence his prudential maxim, that it is better, more for our real happiness, 'to suffer wrong than to do wrong.' The wicked may be visibly prosperous in and through their crimes, and untold visible evils, even death, may come upon the virtuous on account of their virtues. Yet the former are miserable, and the latter happy, even in this life. The great object of the Dialogue entitled 'Gorgias,' is to enforce this doctrine: 'For a good man no event can be evil, whether he lives or dies, seeing his concerns are never disregarded by the gods.'

5. Another fundamental doctrine of Socrates was the immortality of the soul. This was a leading theme of all his discourses. When asked in what way his friends should bury him, he replied, 'Even as you will, if you catch me, and I do not give you the slip.' 'I cannot persuade Crito, my friends, that it is I who am now talking with you, and determining what to say. He thinks that I am that dead body which he will soon see here, and asks how he shall bury me.' 'When I have drunk the poison, I shall be with you no longer, but shall depart hence to the happiness of the blessed.'

6. Socrates not only held and taught the doctrines of the immortality of the soul, but that of future retribution. 'Those who have lived in

eminent holiness are taken from this region as from a prison and placed in that pure upper region of the earth.' 'If I did not expect that I should go to the realms of the wise and good gods, and to the company of men better than those who are here, I should be wrong not to grieve at death. But be well assured that I do expect this—that I shall be among good, though this I do not feel so confident about, but that I shall go to gods who are good governors—be assured that if there be anything of this kind about which I am confident, I am confident of this. And hence it is that I do not feel sorrow, but am full of hope, that those who have left this life are still in being, and the good in a better condition than the bad.' On another occasion he said, 'I make it my aim that I may appear before my judge with my soul sound and healthy. I put aside the honours and objects of men in general. I aim at truth alone. I try to live, and I shall try to die, when the time arrives, as virtuous as I can.' 'But if the soul depart from the body polluted and impure, as having always been mixed with the body, and having served it, and delighted in it; and having allowed itself to be bewitched by it, and its desires and pleasures; so that nothing appeared to be real which was not corporeal, something that could be touched, and seen, and eaten, and drunk, and used for enjoyment; and having always hated, and feared, and shunned that which is invisible to the bodily eyes, the intellectual objects of which Philosophy aims, do you conceive that such a soul can be pure in itself, or fitted for a region of purity?'

THE DÆMON OF SOCRATES.

Of the Dæmon of Socrates much has been written, and few seem to have attained to settled convictions in regard to his views upon the subject. The following is his own account of the matter: 'I have a divine Monitor of which Meletus in his indictment makes a charge in so extravagant a manner. This Monitor I have had from childhood—a voice which warns me, which constrains me constantly from what I am about to do, but never urges me on to do. This was what stood in the way of my undertaking public affairs.' Because he was not warned against it, Socrates, as he himself affirmed, adhered to the plan which he had adopted, relatively to his defence in the trial in which he was condemned to die, and to his course after that event. We perceive no evidence whatever that he regarded his divine Monitor as a familiar spirit. As one, also, who never had any form of experience such as Socrates professedly had, we would say that we see nothing superstitious or improbable in the above account.

SECTION II.

PLATO.

PLATO, the central figure in the realm of Grecian world-thought, and that figure 'a thing of beauty'—Plato, who, without having himself given any determinable system of Philosophy, has imparted a more powerful impulse to philosophic thought than any other ancient thinker, was born in Athens or Ægina 428, and died in the city first named 347 or 348 B.C. Up to the time of the death of Socrates, one of his most devoted pupils and disciples was Plato. After the death of his illustrious teacher (399 or 400 B.C.), Plato, with the teachers of Philosophy, fled from Athens to escape persecution and probable death, spent some time with Euclid of Magara, then visited various countries, as Grecia Major, Cyrene, Egypt, and Asia Minor, and when about forty years of age returned to Athens, where he remained, with short intervals of travel, until the time of his death. During this last interval his time was devoted to teaching and to the preparation of his world-renowned dialogues. The place where he taught was called the Academy—the 'Grove of Academus'—a gymnasium outside of the city, where was a garden which he had inherited from his father. From the Academy women were most rigorously excluded, unless stealthily intruded in the dress of men.

PLATO AS CONTRASTED WITH SOCRATES, ARISTOTLE, AND ANAXAGORAS.

In all respects Plato, as a teacher, was diverse from Socrates. The latter spoke openly before the people, and 'in secret said nothing.' The former never, as a teacher, appeared in public, but imparted his doctrines to a select few, who by previous intellectual training were prepared to receive them. The teachings of the latter all could readily understand. Those of the former the best thinkers of the world have been studying for more than two thousand years without being able to agree upon their real meaning in particulars most essential. Socrates invited the aged and the young, the learned and the ignorant, all in common to listen to his wise discourse. All who approached the gate to the Academy saw over that gate a hand-writing prohibiting admission to all but those who, by prior mental training, were prepared to understand and appreciate the esoteric doctrines of Philosophy. Hence, as the philosopher of Common-sense, the doctrines of Socrates, in all essential particulars, remain as truths for all ages; while the doctrines of Plato, as the results of partial induction, were, in particulars equally essential, repudiated by not a few of his immediate disciples, and in their original forms were rejected in a subsequent age by the New Academy.

In particulars equally essential Plato differed from his early pupil and subsequent opponent, Aristotle. The method of the latter was, in fact and form, essentially inductive. That of the former was as essentially, to say the least, à priori. Aristotle deduced the general from the individual, and found all the elements of the latter in the former. Plato, as far as science is concerned, began and ended with the universal, or deduced the ideal individual from the ideal universal. Aristotle vindicated the validity of our knowledge of mind and the visible universe, and from facts of consciousness and external perception, argued the being and immortality of the soul, the sacredness of the law of Deity, and the existence of God. With Plato the universe of perception is a mere becoming which never becomes, or 'really is' a something intermediate between 'being and non-being, and which cannot be said either to be or not to be,' real existence in all its forms, as matter, the soul, and God as 'existences *in se*,' being the exclusive objects of reason or à priori insight. With Aristotle nothing really exists but individual forms of being. With Plato the necessary and universal are the real, while the individual is that which is always 'becoming but never is.' 'Raphael in his school of Athens,' as Ueberweg states, 'represents Plato as pointing towards heaven, while Aristotle turns his regard upon the earth.' We are indebted to Ueberweg, also, for the following impressive representation by Goethe of the characteristics of Plato. 'Plato's relation to the world is that of a superior spirit, whose good pleasure is to dwell in it for a time. It is not so much his concern to become acquainted with it—for the world and its nature are things which he presupposes—as kindly to communicate to it that which he brings with him, and of which it stands in so much need. He penetrates into its depths more that he may replenish them from the fulness of his own nature than that he may fathom their mysteries. He scales its heights as one yearning after renewed participation in the source of his own being. All that he utters has reference to something eternally complete, good, true, beautiful, whose furtherance he strives to promote in every bosom. Whatever of earthly knowledge he appropriates here and there, evaporates in his method and in his discourse.'

In the 'Phædo,' we have Plato's reasons given through Socrates idealized, why the former repudiated the teachings of Anaxagoras. 'When I heard that Anaxagoras was teaching that it is Intelligence that sets in order and is the cause of all things, I was delighted with this cause, and it appeared to me in a manner to be well that Intelligence should be the cause of all things, and I considered with myself, if this be so, then the regulating Intelligence orders all things, and disposes each in such a way as is best for it. If any one, then, should desire to discover the cause of everything, in what it is produced, or perishes, or exists, he must discover this respecting it, in what way it is best for it either to exist, or to suffer, or to do anything else.' 'I thought that, in assigning the cause of each of them and to all in common' (the form of the earth, 'the sun and moon, and other stars, with respect to their velocities in reference to each other, and their revolutions and other conditions'), 'he would explain that which is best for each, and the common good of all. Great was my hope, and equally great my disappointment.' Anaxagoras inferred from the fact of creation as an event of time, and from facts of universal order everywhere apparent in it, that the universe is the result of contrivance and design, and is, consequently, the handiwork of a personal God, and then, as a Theistic Materialist, attempted to explain, not how such a being should create and order all things, but how, as a matter of fact, he did do it. Here was the cause of Plato's dissatisfaction with the teachings of his renowned predecessor.

Plato's Method.

We will now give Plato's method of induction and deduction, and do it in his own words. 'I was afraid lest I should be hindered in my soul through beholding things with the eyes, and endeavouring to grasp them by means of the several senses. It seemed to me, therefore, that I ought to have recourse to *reasons,* and to consider in *them* the truth in things. Perhaps, however, this similitude of mine may in some respects be incorrect; for I do not altogether admit that he who considers things in their reasons considers them in their images, more than he does who views them in their effects. However, I proceeded thus, and on each occasion laying down the *reason,* which I deem to be the strongest, whatever things appear to me to accord with this I regard as true, both with respect to the cause and everything else, but such as do not accord I regard as not true.'

Here we have a distinct and specific statement of the method of this philosopher as an interpreter of the facts of the universe, and in the solution of the great problem of being and its laws. In the interior of his own mind, irrespective of conscious and visible facts, he, first of all, determined *how* all things should be ordered, and then considered whatever things appeared to accord with this, 'both with respect to the cause of everything else, as true, but such as did not accord, as not true.' In fixed accordance, as we shall show, with this fixed and avowed method, Plato did attempt a solution of this problem. No one who does not explain Plato from this, his own definitely avowed standpoint, will explain him as he was.

That we may not appear to have deduced our idea of the method of

Plato from a single passage, we present another citation, the meaning of which cannot be misunderstood. 'But what with respect to the acquisition of wisdom is the body an impediment or not, if anyone takes it with him in the search? What I mean is this: Do sight and hearing convey any truth to men, or are they such as the poets constantly sing, who say that we neither hear nor see anything with accuracy? If, however, *these* bodily senses are neither accurate nor clear, much less can the others be so, for they are all inferior to these. Do they not seem so to you?'—'Certainly,' he replied.—'When then,' said he, 'does the soul light on truth? for when it attempts to consider anything in conjunction with the body, it is plain that it is then led astray by it.'—'You say truly.'—'Must it not then be by reasoning, if at all, that any of the things that really *are* (any form of real existence) becomes known to it?'—'Yes.'—'And surely the soul then reasons best when none of these things disturb it, neither hearing, nor sight, nor pain, nor pleasure of any kind, but it retires as much as possible within itself, taking leave of the body, and, as far as it can, not communicating or being in contact with it, it aims at the discovery of that which is?'—'Such is the case.'—'Does not the soul of the philosopher, in these cases, despise the body and flee from it, and seek to retire within itself?'—'It appears so.'

'Would not he, then, do this with the utmost purity?' (discover what does and does not exist) 'who should in the highest degree approach each subject by means of the mere mental faculties, neither employing sight in conjunction with the reflective faculty, nor introducing any other sense together with reasoning, but who, using pure reflection by itself, should attempt to search out each essence by itself, freed as much as possible from the eyes and ears, and, in a word, from the whole body as disturbing the soul, and not suffering it to acquire truth and wisdom when it is in communion with it? Is not he the person, if any one can, who will arrive at the knowledge of that which is?' To this question a most absolute and emphatic affirmative answer is returned.

It is undeniable that Plato borrowed his method of philosophizing from the Orientalists, and that modern Transcendentalists borrowed theirs from Plato. We are now prepared to consider the solution which Plato has given us of the great problem under consideration, that of universal being and its laws.

GENERAL CHARACTERISTICS OF PLATO AS A THINKER.

If we should form our judgment of Plato as a thinker and writer from the multitudinous expositions which have been given of his teachings, we should regard him as one of the most self-contradictory and least understood authors that ever existed. One class represent him as the 'great Idealist,' another as the great expounder of Theism, and kindred doctrines, while others still regard him as a mystic, and the author of 'a poetical philosophy.' In regard to doctrines which were, with Plato himself, of fundamental interest, and which he has most extensively discussed, authors of the greatest eminence give perfectly distinct and opposite expositions of his views. With one class of writers, for example, Plato's *Ideas* are archetypes in the divine mind, archetypes after which God organized the universe; with others the same 'Ideas are not the thought of God, but objects of his thought.' Some represent these Ideas, as in the judgment of Plato created archetypes, while others affirm that he regarded them as eternal and immutable. We shall not stop here to explain the reason for this diversity of exposition. It may be that Plato did in different dialogues unconsciously contradict himself. It may be, also, that at one period of his life he held one view, and an opposite one at a later period, and that in his successive dialogues we have a record of these successive changes in his own apprehensions. It may be, also, that in attempting, as an eclectic, to extract from existing systems the elements of truth which he supposed to dwell in each, he failed, as eclectics generally do, to construct a harmonious system of his own. 'The Socratic doctrine,' says Dr. Döllinger, 'of the absolute good and beautiful, and of Deity revealing himself to man as a kind Providence, formed the basis on which he started, as channels for the Heraclitic doctrine of the perpetual coming into being and flux of all things, together with the Eleatic of the eternal immutability of the one and only Being. The dogma of Anaxagoras of a world-ruling spirit was serviceable to him, and with it he had the skill to connect the Pythagorean view of the universe, as an animated intelligent whole, in a spiritualized form.' No wonder that an individual who undertook to construct a harmonious system out of such incongruous materials, should contradict himself, and should, as Dr. Hodge has well observed, 'speak at one time as a Theist and at another as a Pantheist.' While authors thus differ in regard to the real teachings of Plato on certain subjects, there are others of equal importance about which no such diversity obtains. We propose, in our own expositions, to begin with what is admitted to be plain and explicable, and from these to advance to a consideration of what appears to be obscure and of doubtful significance. Among the doctrines of the former class we specify the following:

DOCTRINES, WHICH, AS ALL AUTHORITIES ADMIT, PLATO DID HOLD AND TEACH.

1. Plato held and taught the doctrine of the real existence of spirit and matter, as distinct and opposite substances. God and matter he held to be eternally existing and separate forms of being. Matter, to be sure, as Plato defines it, is almost without properties, 'an invisible species and

formless universal receiver,' or a mere receptacle of forms. Being 'itself imperishable, it furnishes a seat to all that is produced,' and must be 'somewhere, and occupy a certain space.' The existence of such a substratum is a condition necessary, according to Plato, to the organization of the visible universe. That Plato also believed in the soul, as a real existence, need not be confirmed by more than a single citation. The doctrine of the human soul as an immaterial and spiritual principle, distinct from the body and all material forms, is the leading theme of all his teachings. 'The Deity himself,' says Plato, 'formed the divine, and he delivered over to his celestial offspring the task of forming the mortal. These subordinate deities, copying the example of their parent, and receiving from his hands the immortal principle of the human soul, fashioned subsequently to this the mortal body,' which they consigned to the soul as a vehicle, and in which they placed another kind of soul, mortal, the seat of violent and fatal affections.' The rational soul, he held to be, not only possessed of intelligence, but of the power of self-moved or free activity. 'Self-activity,' he says, 'is the very essence and true motion of the soul.'

2. Plato also held and taught the doctrine of the being and universal providence of an infinite, and perfect, personal God. The organization of the universe, he held, as we have before shown, to be an event which occurred in time, and implies creation through the agency of a supreme Intelligence. Having stated, that originally the elements of universal nature existed 'irrationally and without measure,' that is, in a state of total chaos, he adds: 'And let us above all things hold, and ever hold, that the Deity made them as far as possible the most beautiful and the best, when before they were in a totally different condition.' Plato was no Pantheist, though he sometimes speaks as if he were one. The doctrines of the eternal co-existence of spirit and matter, of the organization, by the power of God, of the universe from a primal chaos, and that as an event of time, and of a divine providential government over the realm of matter, on the one hand, and a moral government over a realm of free moral and spiritual agents, on the other. These, and other kindred doctrines, locate Plato and the Pantheist at an infinite remove from one another.

Nor was Plato, in any proper sense of the term, an Idealist. Idealism denies wholly the reality of a material creation, and resolves all existences into spirit, or its operations. While Plato fully believed in the ideality of the world of perception, he held, that behind the phenomenal there existed a realm of spiritual existences, and also a material creation, a creation not perceived through the senses, but knowable and known through Reason. We may dispute his psychology, but cannot justly deny that he was a Realist.

That Plato held not only to the personality of God, but also to His infinity and perfection, is perfectly manifest from the passage cited relatively to his theistic teachings, in the article on 'the Religions of the Greeks.' Nothing further need to be added upon this subject in this connection.

3. While Plato held that no man is 'willingly evil,' that is, chooses evil for its own sake, no ancient thinker ever taught with more distinctness and force than he did, the absolute distinction between the right and the wrong, the sacredness of the law of duty, the desert of virtue, and the demerit of sin. While he regarded mercy as an attribute of God, one of the problems which he was avowedly unable to solve, is the compatibility of the forgiveness of sin with the attribute of justice in God. In God every form of moral virtue exists in absolute perfection. Moral virtue in man consists in moral resemblance to God. 'This flight,' he says, 'consists in resembling God, and this resemblance is the becoming just and holy with wisdom.'

Sin, on the other hand, consists in the enslavement of the will to the lower propensities, a state in which 'pleasures and pains are unduly magnified; the democracy of the passions prevail, and the ascendency of reason is cast down.' This doctrine of Plato, that moral evil is never chosen for its own sake, that the conscience is immutably on the side of the right and against the wrong, and that in their moral nature all men approve the right when they refuse obedience to the law of duty, and hate the wrong while they perpetrate it, is a doctrine most common, even among the heathen. Lactantius represents the heathen as saying, 'I prefer, indeed, not to sin, but I am overcome; for I am possessed of a fragile nature. I am, therefore, led on as one uncertain,' that is, blinded by passion, 'and I sin not because I prefer it, but because I am impelled (by passion). 'I knew,' says one, 'that it was becoming, but me, miserable! I could not do it.'

'I know,' says Euripides, 'that such things as I am about to do are evil, but my mind is better than my inclinations.' 'I perceive and approve the right,' says another, 'but follow the wrong.'

The leading aim of life, as Plato affirms, should be the purification of the soul from the dominion of evil principles and propensities, and the recovery of its lost likeness to God. 'If the soul is immortal,' he says, 'it requires our care not only for the present time, which we call life, but for all time; and the danger would now appear to be dreadful if one should neglect it. For if death were a deliverer from everything, it would be a great gain for the wicked, when they die, to be delivered at the same time from the body and from their vices together with the soul; but now, since it appears to be immortal, it can have no other refuge from evils nor safety except by becoming as good and wise as possible.'

4. A leading doctrine and theme of Plato, as all admit, is the immortality of the soul. While the main basis of his argument to prove the doctrine none now regard as valid, the doctrine itself is set forth in his writings with most impressive distinctness.

5. With the doctrine of a future life for the soul, Plato connected that of retribution according to moral desert. 'But when, on the other hand, the soul shall remain, having an intercourse with divine virtue, it becomes divine pre-eminently; and pre-eminently, after having been conveyed to a place entirely holy, it is changed for the better; but when it acts in a contrary manner, it has under contrary circumstances placed its existence in some unholy spot. This is the judgment of the gods who hold Olympus. 'O thou young man' (know) 'that the person who has become more wicked, departs to the more wicked souls; but he who has become better, to the better both in life and in all deaths, to do and suffer what is fitting the like.' The doctrines of immortality and retribution according to moral desert, everywhere stand out with great prominence and impressiveness in the writings of this author. So far, the teachings of Plato are so plain that very little, if any, difference of opinion obtains among historians and commentators about their meaning.

The Psychology of Plato.

It is almost exclusively of the intellect that Plato gives any analysis of the mental powers. The idea of a mental faculty he has thus defined. To know any power, he tells us, and very correctly, 'I must look at the power itself, and see what it is and what it does. In that way I discern the power of each thing, and that is the same power which produces the same effect, and that is a different power which produces a different effect.' The question which now arises is this, What kind of intellectual faculties is the mind, according to Plato, possessed of? We shall, for the most part, answer this question in the language of Plato himself. 'He that knows anything,' asks Plato, 'does he know something that is or is not? Of course something that is; that which is not cannot be an object of knowledge. That which is universally may be known universally; that which is not anywhere must be universally unknown. But if there be things which are both to be and not to be, they must lie between that which is absolutely and that which is nowhere. And knowledge belongs to that which is; ignorance to that which is not; to that which is between belongs something between knowledge and ignorance, that is, opinion. And thus knowledge and opinion have different objects.' As the nature of a faculty is determined by that of the objects perceived, we have, according to Plato, two faculties of original perception—Reason, the faculty which perceives and apprehends realities in themselves, and Opinion, sensation, or sense-perception, which perceives and apprehends that which 'is and is not.' 'Knowledge is concerned with that which really is, and knows it as it is.' 'Opinion,' sense-perception, 'deals neither with that which is nor that which is not,' but with that 'which is of such a nature that it is and is not.'

Intermediate between Reason and Sensation we have, according to this philosopher, a third faculty, the Judgment, the faculty of conceptions, the faculty through which we obtain a knowledge of the mathematics and kindred sciences. 'Conceptions' are mental apprehensions, not of visible objects, but such as 'geometrical conceptions of figures.' Conceptions, we repeat, as the term is employed by Plato, represent 'the definitions and postulates' of the sciences, our conceptions of a circle, triangle, and square, for example. The objects of these conceptions are '*one* kind of intelligible things.' These sciences, according to Plato, have for their basis 'assumptions' for which 'no reason is given,' and reasoning from these assumptions, 'as evident to all,' we 'have the propositions which we have in view.' 'In dealing with these the mind depends upon assumptions, and does not ascend to first principles.' The knowledge obtained by means of these sciences has, consequently, as he affirms, a less degree of certainty than that obtained by Reason. Reason, on the other hand, regards the 'assumptions of the sciences as' (what they are) 'assumptions only, and uses them as occasions and starting points, that from these it may ascend to the *Absolute*, which does not depend upon assumption—the *origin* of scientific truth. The reason takes hold of this *first principle* of truth, and availing itself of all the connections and relations of this principle, it proceeds to the conclusion, using no sensible image in doing this, but contemplates the idea alone, and with these ideas the process begins, goes on, and terminates.'

'I apprehend,' said Glaucus, 'but not very clearly, for the matter is somewhat abstruse. You wish to prove that the knowledge which by reason, in an intuitive manner, we acquire of real existence and intelligible things, is of a higher degree of certainty than the knowledge which belongs to what are commonly called the sciences; such sciences, you say, have certain assumptions for their bases, and these assumptions are by the student of such sciences apprehended not by sense, but by a mental operation, by conception.

'But inasmuch as such students ascend no higher than assumptions, and do not go to the first principles of truth, they do not seem to have true knowledge, intellectual insight, intuitive reason on the subjects of their reasonings, though the subjects are intelligible things. And you call this habit and practice of the geometers and others by the name of *Judgment*, not reason, or insight, or intuition, taking judgment to be something between **opinion on one side and intuitive reason on the other.**'

'You have explained it well,' Plato replies. 'And now consider these four kinds of things of which we have spoken as corresponding to four affections (faculties) of the mind. Intuitive Reason, the highest; Judgment, the next; the third, Belief; the fourth, Conjecture or Guesses; and arrange them in order so that they may be held to have more or less of certainty, as their objects have more or less of truth.' To understand fully and clearly the psychology of Plato, we must obtain full and definite apprehension of the nature and objects of each of these faculties, as he understood and presented them. We begin with—

Reason and Judgment.

Reason, according to this philosopher, is the exclusive faculty of real or absolute knowledge, the only faculty which perceives and apprehends that which really exists. Even the real truths to which 'the assumptions,' as he calls them, of the pure sciences actually pertain, are apprehended not by the Judgment but by Reason. Knowledge by Reason, then, has greater certainty than that obtained through these sciences by means of the Judgment. Knowledge through the latter is indirect and mediate, through assumptions and conceptions of the same. Knowledge through Reason, on the other hand, is direct and immediate or intuitive.

Yet Reason in man, in his present state, has no direct and immediate knowledge of realities, or of absolute truth. In a former state, 'the soul, in journeyings with Deity,' had an insight of *being in se*, or of existences as they are in themselves. The knowledge which it now has of such realities 'is a recollection of those things which our soul formerly saw when journeying with Deity.' Souls which took no such journeyings, and never thus saw existences as they are, or who have perhaps lost all such visions, Plato absolutely affirms, can have no such knowledge. The apprehensions of all such are necessarily limited to the dark sphere of sense, and can but 'opine that which is of such a nature that it is and is not.'

While the minor faculties are common to all men, Reason—'the faculty divine,' according to Plato, has place as a faculty in but a very small number of human minds. 'Of true opinion,' he says, 'every man has a share; but of Reason only the gods and some small portion of mankind.' Those who do possess this divine faculty are, as our philosopher expressly affirms, 'inspired men,' and ought to rule the race. Those thinkers fundamentally err who cite Plato as authority for ranking Reason as a faculty of the human mind in its present state. The psychology of this philosopher is expressly, not the psychology of the human mind, but of that of gods and philosophers. The mass of men in their former state never 'journeyed with the Deity' at all, and never had any visions of existence *in se*, or have so absolutely lost those reminiscences that they cannot by any possibility be, in this life, recalled.

Sensation or Sense-Perception.

As we have already shown, Plato held and taught the eternal existence of matter as a reality distinct from God. In its primal state this substance was 'formless and figureless, but recipient of all forms. And as constituting all bodies this matter was divisible and of the nature of the manifold.' This originally formless and figurativeless 'substance God organized into a material universe which now exists in that form.' This really existing universe, however, is one thing—that which we seem to cognize through Sensation, sense-perception, is quite another. The latter is but the shadow of the former. It is the world of perception, and not the actually existing universe of matter, that Plato affirms to be 'of the nature of that which is and is not.' The opinions which we obtain through Sensation, according to the Platonic hypothesis, Plato is at great pains to elucidate and explain in Book VII. chapters i. and ii. of the Republic. We give what is essential to an apprehension of his meaning in his own words.

' " Behold men, as it were, in an underground cave-like dwelling, having its entrance open towards the light and extending through the whole cave, and within it persons, who from childhood upwards have had chains on their legs and their necks, so as, while abiding there, to have the power of looking forward only, but not to turn round their heads by reason of their chains, their light coming from a fire that burns above and far off and behind them ; and between the fire and those in chains is a road above, along which one may see a little wall was built along."—" I see," said he.—" Behold, then, by the side of this little wall, men carrying all sorts of machines rising above the wall, and statues of men and other animals wrought in stone, and other materials, some of the bearers probably speaking, and others proceeding in silence."—" You are proposing," said he, " a most absurd comparison, and absurd captives also."—" Such as resemble ourselves," said I ; " for think you that such as these would have seen anything of themselves or one another except the shadows which fall from the fire on the opposite side of the cave ?"—" How can they," said he, " if they be through life compelled to keep their heads unmoved ?"—" But what respecting the things carried by them—is not this the same ?"—" Of course."—" If they had been able to talk with each other, do you not suppose they would think it right to give names to what they saw before them ?"—" Of course they would."—" But if the prison had an echo on its opposite side, when any person present were to speak, think you they would imagine anything else addressed to" (that is addressing) " them, except the shadow before them ?"—" No, by ——, not I," said he.—" At all events, then," said I, "such persons would deem truth to be nothing but the shadows of exhibitions."—" Of course they would."'

Such, Plato held and taught, are our relations to the material universe which really exists. Of it, or any realities in it, we have no real knowledge whatever. What we do perceive is but a shadow—a dimly reflected image of what really exists. Yet all but philosophers deem these shadows, which they do see the only world which does exist. Ourselves and the men which we think we see and converse with, are mere shadows—images of men, and not real men. So in all other cases. The only approach, as we shall see hereafter, that we can make, either by Reason or otherwise, to a knowledge of real material forms as they are in themselves, is to abstract from classes of individuals, whom we seem to perceive, the elements strictly common to all, and combine these common elements into a general conception. While individual conceptions most remotely, these general notions more nearly, resemble actually existing realities. The knowledge, however, which we obtain of these realities through these general notions, the only form of such knowledge now possible to us, is nothing but 'a bastard form of knowledge.' Three classes of realities exist—ideas, of which we are to speak in another connection, material forms, and the shadows which are produced by the two former. 'Thus the universe is constituted of Idea, Matter, and Sensible Objects, the offspring of the other two.' 'And these things, being three, are known in three ways—the idea, by Intellect, as science; matter, by a bastard kind of reasoning, for we cannot yet attain to discern it directly, but by analogy; and the product of these' [things which are and are not] 'by Sensation and opinion.'

According to Plato the entire race, a few philosophers excepted, are in a very pitiable condition relatively to all forms of real knowledge. Of ideas, those 'ungenerated and unchanged and permanent' verities, they can know nothing whatever, excepting through 'the reminiscences' or *à priori* insight of philosophers, whose revelations are as contradictory as those of 'Chaos and Old Night.' What they can glean through the Judgment has no other basis but mere assumptions; while, in their confinement within the low cell of Sensation, they are compelled to regard, as alone real existences mere shadows 'which are of the nature of that which is and is not.'

GENERAL REMARKS UPON THIS PSYCHOLOGY.

In regard to the psychology of this philosopher, we would remark in general, that there never was a system proposed more fundamentally defective, on the one hand, or erroneous, on the other. While essential faculties are omitted, not one that is given is located in its proper sphere, or has assigned to it its proper functions. There are no facts of mind that can be explained by this psychology just as they are given in the universal consciousness. These statements we will now proceed to verify. We remark, then:

1. The idea that there is, or can be, a something intermediate between real existence and non-existence, a something 'which is of the nature of that which is and is not' is one of the most palpable absurdities that ever approached human thought. As rendered demonstrable before Plato began to write by Parmenides, the Idealist, on the one hand, and Anaxagoras, the Realist, on the other, we are necessitated by an immutable law of thought to regard every object as a real existence, or as not existing at all. To affirm, that there may be a something 'which is of the nature of that which is and is not,' a something which is always becoming and never becomes, is, undeniably, perfectly identical with the absurdity that the same thing may at the same moment exist and not exist. No philosopher can show the difference between this dogma of Plato and the absurdity before us. Plato's theory of sense-perception, therefore, cannot be true.

2. Facts and objects of sense-perception are not consciously perceived, as Plato affirms them to be. Every object perceived, on the other hand, stands before the mind as a real and palpable existence, and in no sense or form as a something which is always becoming but never becomes. Plato *thought*, or attempted to *think*, of these objects in that light; but they were never thus present to him, nor are they thus present to anybody else, as objects of perception. Nor, as perceived, are these objects in appearance the fleeting, and ever-changing shadows which he affirms them to be. The *substances* which constitute all visible material forms are universally thought as permanent entities. These entities may from time to time enter into new combinations, but they themselves never change. Nor are the *forms* of material combination the ever-changing shadows which Plato imagines. In every visible combination the essential qualities of matter, extension, and form, are always present. Then, as Aristotle has truly said, there are objects, such as the stars of heaven, whose forms never change. The globe on which we dwell is, to the universal mind, and to philosophers as well as others, an enduring entity. On it are 'the everlasting mountains,' and 'the perpetual hills,' and the ocean, whose enduring permanence renders it the proper and impressive symbol of eternity. Everything about us, as perceived, is not a becoming which never becomes, but a definite existence. The honoured Presidents of Yale, Harvard, and our State University, for example, are philosophers possessed of Sensation and Reason. Permit us to ask them, in serious earnestness, whether they are to themselves, and their associate Professors are to them, not real men, but what Plato affirms all men to be, 'the

shadows that fall from the fire on the opposite side of the cave? Plato affirms that 'a proof that lacks anything, however little, of completeness, and is a proof *in some measure merely*, is not satisfactory. Defect is not the measure of anything.' Plato's exposition of sensation, or sense-perception, is not only defective, and therefore not the measure of the conscious reality, but, what is still worse, is false in fact.

3. Equally defective and erroneous is Plato's exposition of the sphere and the validity of the action of the faculty of Judgment. Mathematics and other kindred sciences instead of being based, as he affirms them to be, on mere assumptions, are, in fact and form, based upon universal, necessary, and intuitive truths, or principles. Every one of their axioms and postulates have both necessary and intuitive certainty. Are the axioms, 'Things equal to the same things are equal to one another,' and 'A straight line cannot enclose a space,' and, 'It is impossible for the same thing, at the same time, to exist and not to exist,' mere assumptions? Is it not perfectly evident that Plato never thought of the distinction between assumptions and real principles of science? Nor can we be more certain of any truths than we are, and must be, of the validity of the principles and deductions of all the real sciences. No greater mistake can be made in science than appears in the doctrine, 'that the knowledge which, by Reason, in an intuitive manner, we may acquire of real existence and intelligible things, is of a *higher degree of certainty* than the knowledge which belongs to what are commonly called the sciences.' Will some philosopher designate some truth of which we are, or can be, more certain, than we are of the truth of the axioms above designated, or of the demonstrated truth, that the square of the hypothenuse of a right-angled triangle is equal to the sum of the squares of its two sides? Can there be a higher degree of certainty than necessary certainty? When Plato, therefore, placed the pure sciences, and that on the score of *certainty*, as 'something between opinion, on the one side, and intuitive reason on the other,' he fell into a fundamental error in science.

4. One of the greatest and most dangerous of all the errors of Plato, is the doctrine that Reason in philosophers and finite gods, or in anybody else, is a faculty which has, not through facts consciously perceived, but by direct, intuitive, and independent insight, a perception of 'real existence and intelligible things.' Plato's method of philosophizing, we have already fully explained. Facts of perception are, by him, not only ignored, but repudiated as clogs in the matter of intuitive insight through Reason. All the works of Plato are constructed in perfect accordance with this exclusive method. If our previous discussions have established anything, they have demonstrated the fact that the mind has no such faculty as that which this thinker professedly used when philosophizing. Whether any substances or causes, and what substances and causes, do exist in

time and space, we can know but through facts and qualities perceived to be real. A correct analysis of all our conceptions and judgments, also, renders it demonstrably evident that all our ideas of substances and causes were thus derived. Our conception of body, for example, is constituted exclusively of qualities perceived and substance implied by what is perceived. All our conceptions of the self and not-self, are of this exclusive character. Every cause which we regard as existing and acting in time and space is given and known, and that exclusively as implied by events and facts perceived to have occurred. There is not a necessary idea in the mind which is not given in the universal consciousness as implied by facts and objects of perception, and known exclusively as thus implied. The ideas of space, time, substance, cause, duty, and God, for example, are given as implied by body, succession, phenomena, events, and conscious facts, which we perceive to exist. When we analyze our judgments which possess necessary and universal intuitive certainty, we find this relation to exist between the subject and predicate, that the former, as the contingent, or perceived, implies the latter as the necessary, element or object. Of this character are all such judgments as, Body implies space; Succession, time; Phenomena, substance; and Events, a cause. Such facts absolutely evince that the object or implied idea, is apprehended through that of the contingent conception. Space, time, substance, and cause, and all other objects of universal and necessary ideas, are not perceived directly and immediately, but through body, succession, phenomena, and events, and other objects of perception, and the former class of realities are always apprehended as implied by that of the latter, and as known through the same.

In no other sense than as implied by phenomena and events, are the ideas of substance and cause, in any form in which they appear, necessary ideas at all. Suppose that any substance or cause was directly perceived by Reason, or any other faculty; the idea of such object would, in that case, be a contingent, and not a necessary one. Why do we say that our conception of body is a contingent idea? Because we can conceive of its object as existing or not existing. If we should perceive, directly and immediately, any substance or cause to exist, we could conceive such object also to exist or not to exist, and we should derive from it a contingent and not a necessary idea. The conception, also, would be one of an individual object, an object which would have no element of universality about it. When we perceive 'existence *in se*,' we always do, and from the necessity of the case must perceive, not forms of universal, but individual being. It is only when we apprehend substance and cause through phenomena and events, and as implied by the same, that the element of universality does, or can, attach to our ideas of the former. To affirm that Reason, or any other faculty, directly and immediately perceives existence *in se*, or universal and necessary truths, is an undeniable absurdity. The object of perception, whether through Reason or any other faculty, must, we repeat, be an individual object, and can be nothing else. Universal *relations* do exist, but a universal thing, or object, or substance, cannot exist. The cause of all conditioned forms of being, and events, may be and is, one and the same. The cause itself, however, as an existence, must in itself be an individual existence. It is only when apprehended as sustaining universal and necessary relations, that the characteristics of universality and necessity do, or can, attach to it. Suppose it should be said, that by Reason, we perceive directly and immediately universal relations. But relations can be perceived only through the objects related.

It is one of the greatest absurdities conceivable, also, that perception through one faculty has higher certainty than through another, when perception, in both cases, is consciously direct and immediate. The mind, with all its faculties, is confined within the body. We are conscious of a direct and immediate knowledge, through external and internal perceptions, of the qualities of matter and spirit. Suppose, now, that we do have, through Reason, a conscious vision of 'existence *in se*.' On what authority, we ask, can it be affirmed that vision, in this last form, is, and is not in either of the others, valid for the reality and character of its objects ?' If perception consciously direct and immediate is, in one form, valid for the reality and character of its objects, and not in another, then things equal to the same things are not equal to one another. From whatever stand-point we consider the subject, we must conclude that the faculty of Reason is totally mislocated by Plato, and that the faculty, as he has defined it, has no being at all. The dogma that mind, while in the body, cannot know itself or objects immediately around it, but can look off into infinite space and eternal duration, and discern absolutely what realities and events exist and are passing there, is an absurdity which ought never to have had place in philosophic thought, and never especially in that of the nineteenth century.

5. But mislocation and erroneous exposition of the intellectual faculties are not the only or the greatest errors in Plato's psychology. Omission of fundamental faculties is another error quite as obvious and important as any which we have designated. In this psychology the faculties of Self-consciousness and Understanding have no place. Yet without these, facts of mind as they actually exist, together with the processes of true science, cannot be correctly explained nor elucidated.

6. While existing mental phenomena and the entire process of real science are wholly inexplicable through the psychology of Plato, all are perfectly and readily explicable through that which we have given. The elements of universal knowledge, in all its forms and developments, can be

demonstrated to have been furnished by the three primary faculties which we have designated, to wit: Sense, Consciousness, and Reason, and through these faculties acting in the identical spheres and relations to which we have assigned them. The most critical analysis of all our conceptions, ideas, judgments, memories, and creations of the Imagination, will demonstrably evince, that not a single element can be discovered in any one of these, an element not originally furnished by one of the primary faculties which we have designated. All the elements of thought, in all its forms, were furnished by perception, external or internal, or by Reason as implied by what is perceived.

Through the elements thus furnished we can account for the entire action of the Understanding in combining these elements into notions or conceptions, just as they exist in the mind. In an analysis of such conceptions, the individual elements furnished by each faculty can be specifically designated, and no elements can be found which cannot be thus referred and accounted for.

Then, through the proper action of the Judgment, we can explain the process by which, first of all, these conceptions are analyzed and resolved into their original elements, and how from these, individual, specifical, generical, and abstract conceptions, together with ideas of Reason in their universal forms, are obtained. Having thus explained and elucidated the origin and genesis of the phenomena designated, a ready explanation can be furnished of the entire process of classification and generalization.

An explanation, equally and obviously scientific, can then be given of the origin and genesis of all judgments, contingent and necessary, intuitive and deductive, together with the entire process of valid induction and deduction. The facts, principles, laws, and nature of all the sciences, pure and mixed, can be demonstrated to be perfectly explicable through the faculties presented by this psychology. Not a single element of thought, not a conception, idea, principle, or deduction, can be found in any procedure of any of the valid sciences, which will not be found to be perfectly explicable through these faculties.

Through this psychology we are also furnished with explanations absolute of the entire procedure of false science. We can readily explain the points from which error always takes its departure from the track of truth, the lines on which it must move, and the forms which it does, and must, assume. Absolute criteria can be furnished by which original intuitions, valid conceptions, ideas, facts, principles, and deductions, may be distinguished and separated from all assumptions, opinions, beliefs and conjectures, which may or may not be true, and from all inductions and deductions which have place in systems of false science. In short, true and false science, in all their characteristics and procedures, can be demonstrated to be perfectly explicable through the faculties furnished by this psychology. All the above statements we pledge ourselves to verify most fully at the close of this treatise. Our present object is to indicate with sufficient distinctness the reasons for which we reject wholly the psychology of Plato and others and adopt the one presented.

Plato's Doctrine of Ideas.

All who have at all studied Plato are agreed in the fact that all his teachings revolve about his doctrine of Ideas. When we ask the question, what this doctrine really is, here the highest authorities are divided, and irreconcilably so. These diversities, however, take on two, and only two, general forms. Ideas, as expounded by Plato, are, according to one school, 'the eternal thoughts of the Divine Intellect,' 'the types, models, patterns, ideals according to which the universe was fashioned,' and 'we attain truth when our thoughts conform with His' (God's), 'when our general notions are in conformity with the Ideas.'

According to another school, Platonic Ideas are not 'eternal thoughts of the Divine Intellect,' but objects which have 'real existence, colourless, figureless, and intangible Existence, which is visible only to mind.' 'Socrates,' says Aristotle, 'gave neither to general terms nor definitions, that is, to the objects represented by such terms and definitions, any distinct existence. Those who succeeded him gave to those general terms a separate existence, and called them Ideas.' In our discussion of the subject we will first consider what Plato has himself said upon it, then endeavour to show which of the above constructions is correct; and, lastly, present the consequences which necessarily follow from each construction.

In what Language and Form Plato has stated his own Doctrine.

The idea is a very singular one, that such a thinker as Plato should make a doctrine perfectly fundamental in all his teachings, should present it in every conceivable diversity of form, and should take, to appearance, all possible pains to render his meaning intelligible, and yet should leave his real views unascertainable. In the *Phædrus* we have this description of Ideas: 'The region above heaven no poet has ever sung of, nor ever will sing of as it deserves. It is, however, as follows, for surely I may venture to speak the truth, especially as my subject is truth: for essence, that which really exists, colourless, formless, and intangible, is visible only to Intelligence which guides the soul, and around it the family of true science have this for their abode.' During its circuit above heaven, the soul 'beholds justice herself, it beholds temperance, it beholds science, in that which really is. And in like manner, having beheld all other things which really are, and having feasted on them, it again enters into the interior of heaven, and returns home.' 'There are many beautiful things, many good things.' 'But essential beauty, and essential goodness, and the like, which appear in these things, we regard as each a single Idea' [of which these things partake]; 'and referring things to this Idea, we call them by their qualities. And we hold that the things can be seen, but not conceived; the Ideas are conceived, but not seen.' 'There are two causes of all things: Mind, the cause of things which are made according to reason; Necessity, the cause of things which happen by force according to the power of bodies. And of the former the cause is of the nature of good, and is called God, and is the principle of what is Best, but the consequences and co-operating causes are referred to necessity. And thus the Universe is constituted of Ideas (things made according to reason), Matter, and Sensible Objects, the offspring of the two.' 'The former, the Idea, is ungenerated and unchanged, permanent, of the nature of the Identical; intelligible, and the paradigm of things created, which are in constant change. But matter is the impressible material, the mother and nurse, and is the source of generation of the third kind of being. For receiving the likeness (of the Idea) into itself, and as it were being moulded on them, it produces all created things. And this matter was eternal, but not unchangeable; and itself formless and figureless, but the recipient of all form. And as constituting bodies, this matter was divisible, and of the nature of the manifold.' 'And things, being three, are known in three ways; the Idea, by Reason, as science; Matter, by a bastard reasoning, for we cannot yet attain to discern it directly, but by analogy; and the products of these by Sensation and opinion.' 'If those ideas really exist' ('Rightness, Goodness, and the rest'), 'our souls must have existed before we were born.' 'The Ideas which we spoke of a little while ago; the realities to which we refer in our discussions, absolute Equality, absolute Goodness, absolute Beauty, and the like, these are always the same, and do not suffer the smallest alteration.' The next passage to which we refer is of great importance in its bearing upon the question which we are now to argue. In a passage cited above Plato affirms 'Ideas to be ungenerated, and, consequently, eternally existing verities.' In the passage now to be cited these same Ideas are affirmed to be derived, that is, created entities. 'We may say, therefore, as to the things cognizable by the Reason' (Ideas), 'that they became cognizable not only from *the good* by which they are known, but likewise that their being and essence are thence derived, while *the Good* itself is not essence, but beyond essence, and superior to both in dignity and power.' In the Republic, Plato refers expressly to the 'creation of Ideas,' and in the Timæus as expressly to the 'eternity and uncreated nature of Ideas.' In the tenth book of the Republic we have a specific statement of the distinction between Ideas and visible objects, and of God's relation to the former especially. In respect to classes of objects which are 'embraced under one general Idea,' Plato thus illustrates his own conception of the relation between the former and the latter. 'Take anything you like. For instance, there is a multiplicity of beds and tables,' and the 'two kinds are comprised, one under the Idea of a bed, and the other under the Idea of a table.' 'The carpenter,' he says, 'makes one of these, and the artist paints another.' Neither, however, 'makes the Idea itself.' Each, in what he does, looks to the Idea and imitates that. Both are alike imitators, and produce nothing real. The painter 'makes an apparent table; not a real table.' So of the carpenter. 'He does not make the thing that *is*, but only something that is like it. If any one says that the thing produced by any handy-craftsman has a real existence, he will be in error.' 'There are three kinds of tables; the first, the essential, the ideal one, which God himself makes; and then the one which the carpenter makes; and then the one which the painter makes.' 'The one which God makes is single, unique; there are not, and will not be, more than one. There cannot be two or more,' and 'this would be the real Idea of table. And thus God is the real author of the real table.' All universals, as genera, are, with Plato, real existences, and are by him represented by the term Ideas. These are real '*existences per se.*' Individuals are existences so far only as they participate of Ideas. That such is the language of Plato none will deny. Equally universal is the admission of all thinkers who study Plato, that Ideas, according to him, are the archetypes after which all generated objects are formed. But what is the nature of these Ideas? Are they the eternal thoughts of the Divine Intellect, 'or are they real existences distinct from God, in the same sense that 'things that are made' are distinct? On this subject the following considerations demand special attention.

Plato's Real Doctrine of Ideas.

1. In favour of the validity of the latter construction, we have the positive testimony of Aristotle, together with the fact of the origination by him of a school in Philosophy openly opposed to Plato relatively to his affirmed teaching on this point. We here adduce the passage from Aristotle, cited above: 'Socrates gave neither to general terms nor to definitions distinct existence.' 'Those who followed him gave to these general terms a separate existence, and called them Ideas.' None doubt that here a special reference is had to Plato. Again says Aristotle: 'Intelligible essences he (Plato) called Ideas, adding that sensible objects were different from Ideas, and received from them their names; for it is in consequence of their *participation* in Ideas, that all objects of the same genus receive the name of Ideas.' The testimony of Aristotle, as we perceive, is perfectly positive on this subject. Nor does anyone doubt

that Aristotle separated from his former instructor, and set up a school in opposition to him, on the ground that the latter did teach that the objects represented by general terms are real and separate existences. That Aristotle misunderstood Plato, none will affirm. A misunderstanding between them in the relations which they sustained to each other, was undeniably impossible. If the former misrepresented the latter, he did it deliberately, and founded his school upon a conscious falsehood, and palpable and slanderous misrepresentation. Can anyone assign, real character out of the question, any rational motive for such a misrepresentation, and for an attempt on the part of such a man as Aristotle, to found a school upon it, and to do this in Athens, in the very vicinity of the Academy? Above all, can anyone account for Aristotle's success in founding such a school under such circumstances? He must have been fully aware that the truth or falsehood of his representations would be 'known and read of all men.' The case was too palpable to admit of any doubt on the subject. Nor could disciples have been drawn off from Plato and gathered around him, were there no real and fundamental difference between the two, in regard to the doctrine of Ideas. Both believed in God, and taught that He created the universe in conformity to ideas pre-existing in the divine mind. If this was really and truly, and of course avowedly, Plato's doctrine of Ideas, two opposite schools could never have been formed under these philosophers, schools professedly divided in respect to a doctrine about which all avowedly agreed.

2. Neither Plato, nor any of his followers, nor any other ancient writer, charges Aristotle with the misrepresentation under consideration. Plato and his school accepted the issue presented by Aristotle and his school, in respect to the doctrine before us, and argued it accordingly. The silence of all ancient authorities, as far as any charge of misrepresentation on the part of Aristotle is concerned, presents the strongest conceivable proof that no ground for such a charge did exist. Modern authorities, who adduce this charge, support it by no citations from the ancients.

3. The origin and continuance for so many centuries of two distinct and opposite sects in Philosophy—the one having its basis in the teachings of Plato, and the other in those of Aristotle, sects the exclusive issue between whom pertained to the doctrine under consideration—the origin and continuance of these sects, we say, are explicable but upon one exclusive hypothesis, the correctness of Aristotle's exposition of Plato's real doctrine of Ideas. We refer, of course, to the sects known as Realists, and Nominalists. The former sect, as the world very well knows, originated with Plato, and the latter with Aristotle. What were the doctrines of these sects? 'The Realists,' in the language of Mr. Lewes, 'maintain that every General Term (or Abstract Idea), such as Man, Virtue, etc., has a real and independent existence, quite irrespective of any concrete indi-

vidual determination, such as Smith, Benevolence, etc. The Nominalists, on the contrary, maintain that all General Terms are but the creations of the mind, designating no distinct entities, being merely used as *marks of aggregate conceptions.*' Did Plato and Aristotle divide philosophic thought against itself, and that in respect to a doctrine about which the former agreed with the latter? The world, we reply, has not thus misunderstood these men in regard to a single doctrine about which an issue was slanderously originated by one of them against the other, when no real difference of opinion existed between them in respect to it.

4. Our next argument is based upon the fact that language employed by Plato himself, to represent his own doctrine, admits of no other construction but that which Aristotle put upon it. Ideas, as thoughts in the mind, may be, and are, archetypes; but are they 'essences'? The universe is constituted after a model in the mind of God. But do they, with matter, *constitute* the universe? Do Ideas, as thoughts in the mind of God, exist by themselves, in a region above the heavens, and become visible there to the Reason, as the mind moves round in a circle? Do God's Ideas, or thoughts, exist there as '*essence*, that which really exists, colourless, formless, and intangible'? A 'colourless' thought! It is a slander upon Plato, even worse than that which some moderns attribute to Aristotle, to affirm that he thus expressed himself. Aristotle did not misunderstand, or misrepresent his former instructor. If he did, Plato alone was in fault in the matter. Let anyone carefully read over the passages which we have cited from Plato, and multitudes of others of the same character might be adduced, and then determine for himself what such language means.

CONSEQUENCES WHICH FOLLOW FROM EACH EXPOSITION WHICH HAS BEEN GIVEN OF PLATO'S DOCTRINE OF IDEAS.

Two, and only two, expositions have been given of Plato's doctrine of Ideas—that of Aristotle—and the modern one which affirms these Ideas, as understood by him, to be 'the eternal thoughts of the Divine Intellect.' Important consequences follow from each of these constructions, consequences to each of which special attention is now invited. We will first consider the construction last designated. Among the consequences necessarily following from this construction, we adduce the following:

Consequences resulting from the Exposition which affirms Plato's Ideas to be 'the Eternal Thoughts of the Divine Intellect.'

1. According to this construction, while we have no faculty by which we can know at all 'the things which are made,' or can apprehend matter itself but by 'a bastard kind of knowledge,' we have a faculty

which, 'in an intuitive manner,' looks off, not only into infinite space and perceives real existences as they are, but also looks directly into the infinite and eternal mind, and perceives 'the Divine thoughts' eternally dwelling there, the thought-archetypes in conformity to which God created the universe, yes, even the thought-models after which craftsmen and artists of all ages shape their productions. Further, the knowledge which 'Reason,' not by revelation, or through the Divine works, but 'in an intuitive manner' obtains of these thought-archetypes and thought-models in the mind of God, 'has a higher degree of certainty' than is, or can be, obtained of any forms of truth, by means of demonstrative sciences. Did Plato teach such a doctrine as that? and if he did, who will endorse it? If we know anything, we know this, that no one Intelligent can, 'in an intuitive manner,' know the thoughts which exist in the mind of another, and especially know these with 'a higher degree of certainty' than we can obtain of any truth in the pure sciences. We can know God's thought-archetypes and thought-models, not 'in an intuitive manner,' but by direct revelation from Him, or through His works.

2. The doctrine of the *certainty* of knowledge, in all its actual forms, by Reason, does, and must, according to this construction, rest upon mere assumption. Reason, as the organ of necessarily and intuitively implied knowledge, was unknown to Plato and his adherents. Knowledge through perception is repudiated, as having no validity; while knowledge through Reason is affirmed to have absolute certainty. Suppose that we do have a consciously direct, immediate, and intuitive vision of the thought-archetypes and thought-models, in the mind of God, or of any form of real existence in space. We have, undeniably, and absolutely, and just as consciously, direct, immediate, and intuitive, vision of the self and not-self. On what 'grounds and arguments' is the validity of knowledge in the first form affirmed, and that in the last denied? We undeniably, in such a case, make a distinction without a difference. We lay down this proposition as having self-evident, or demonstrative, validity, that if the validity of knowledge, by Perception, is denied, that of knowledge, by Reason, cannot be vindicated.

3. According to this construction, thoughts, and not substances nor causes, have real being. Ideas, according to Plato, not only exist, but constitute existence, 'the things which really are.' Now, thought, undeniably, is neither essence, nor substance, nor being, but a *state* of mind. To represent a mere mental state as an 'essence,' as 'existence *per se*,' as the sum and substance of what 'really exists,' is a most palpable absurdity, an absurdity which never had place in the mind of such a thinker as Plato. This construction of Plato's doctrine of Ideas, which makes such Ideas 'Divine thoughts,' cannot be vindicated. But the opposite con-

struction of this doctrine involves consequences which render it demonstratively evident that that doctrine in neither form can be true. Among these consequences, we simply designate the following:

Consequences Resulting from the Doctrine that Plato's Ideas are Real Separate Existences.

1. The universe is not only constructed in accordance with archetypes which have an eternal and separate existence, but is, in part, *constituted* of these archetypes. 'The universe,' says Plato, 'is constituted of Idea, Matter, and Sensible Objects, the offspring of the two.' The archetype must be one thing, and the creation, formed in conformity to the archetype, must be another. Plato makes the two, in part, at least, one and identical.

2. According to this doctrine, the real doctrine of Plato, objects possessed of colour, form, and tangibility, were constructed, not after thought-archetypes, or thought-models, but after real and separately existing archetypes and models, which are utterly 'colourless, formless, and intangible.' What if an individual should tell us that he had seen a *visible* model for a building, a real house, a model which had neither colour, form, nor tangibility? Plato was, undeniably, right in affirming it to be impossible for God himself to make more than one such model table, or bed. We sincerely doubt whether he ever did make any such.

3. We deem it important to notice but one additional consequence of this affirmed, and what we regard as the real, doctrine of Plato. It is this: Of objects utterly void of colour, form, and tangibility, and existing apart by themselves, away off above the heavens, we can have, by Reason, 'in an intuitive manner,' a more certain knowledge, than we can of demonstrative truth, while of palpable realities within and immediately around us, we can have, at best, but 'a bastard kind of knowledge.' This Reason, while utterly blind to things immediately before it, and with but a very obscure insight in the sphere of the demonstrative sciences, has real omniscience in respect to colourless, shapeless, and intangible entities existing somewhere in infinite space above 'High Olympus.' In every form and aspect in which this world-renowned doctrine of Ideas is rightly contemplated, it stands revealed as characterized by the greatest conceivable absurdities.

General Remarks upon Plato as a World-thinker.

As our object is a criticism of the *system* of Plato, and not of his entire teachings, we omit all notice of that portion of his writings which does not strictly fall within our specific line of thought and inquiry. There are certain general reflections, however, pertaining to him, as a world-thinker, to which we deem it important to refer.

Plato, when in the Sphere of Socratic Thought, and when Philosophizing.

There were two distinct spheres of thought in which the mind of Plato, from time to time, moved—that of Common-sense, or the Socratic sphere, and that in which, under the affirmed insight of Reason, he considered himself as philosophizing. Nor does Plato himself appear to be aware, at all times, in which sphere his thoughts are moving. When in the former sphere, few men, if any, not under the light of inspiration, ever uttered more of truth, or clothed his utterances in better form, than did this wonderful man. Here we listen with the deepest interest and conscious profit to his teachings in regard to the soul, God, duty, immortality, and retribution.

When, however, he closes his intellect to all facts of perception, and, with the Oriental Yogee, and modern Transcendentalist, as 'he begins to philosophize,' 'puts himself into a state of not-knowing,' now he is one of the most unsafe and lawless thinkers the world ever knew. Take the following, as one example of his gravest utterances in *The Laws:* 'We say, then, that we ought not to search after the greatest good, and the whole order of the world, nor to be busy in explaining the cause (of things), for it is not holy. It seems, indeed, that if the contrary took place, it would take place correctly.'

In the *Timæus* the Creator of the universe is, in reality, identified with Brahm of the Hindoos. First of all, each world is organized as an animal animated by a soul, and thus the earth, the sun, moon, planets, and stars became gods. Then were originated the various gods of Greece. Deity now delivers a formal speech to the various generated divinities, committing to them the government of the universe, and devolving upon them the responsibility of completing the work of creation and governing all things after that consummation should be reached. 'Three classes of mortals,' the generated gods are told, 'yet remain to be created. Unless these be created, then, the universe will be imperfect; for it will not contain within it every kind of animal, though it ought, in order to be quite perfect.' These Deity did not himself create, because in that case they would 'become equal to the gods.' Man accordingly, with the inferior animals, was left for the gods to create. We now come to the passage in which the Supreme Divinity is identified with Brahm. 'The Creator, after arranging all these particulars, then retired to his accustomed repose.' In the same dialogue there is fully set forth the doctrine of transmigration, and that, with very slight deviations, in a strictly Oriental form. The *Timæus*, which contains these doctrines, is one of the latest and most strictly expository of all the productions of Plato. We have here, consequently, his most deliberate and material teachings.

No writer ever was a more intense polytheist than he, and his theology, when he is philosophizing, is as strictly Oriental in fact and form.

Plato, as furnishing another example of the validity of à priori insight and of the à priori method of Philosophizing.

No philosopher was ever more avowedly and strictly *à priori* in his entire method of philosophizing than Plato. All facts of perception are expressly located by him within the circle of 'opinion,' and are as expressly repudiated as data for scientific deduction. 'The knowledge which by Reason, in an intuitive manner, we acquire of real existence and intelligible things,' of such truths only, he affirms, we have absolute certainty, and of truths thus acquired, we have, he also affirms, 'a higher degree of certainty than the knowledge which belongs to what are commonly called the sciences.' Among the sciences, Geometry is expressly specified by Plato. For forty years, at least, this philosopher was employed in developing and perfecting 'the knowledge which by Reason, in an intuitive manner, we may acquire of real existence and intelligible things,' and the results of his discoveries in this high sphere of affirmed absolute knowledge we have in his multitudinous writings. Æneas affirmed that if Troy could have been 'defended, it would have been by his right hand.' The same Plato might have affirmed in respect to Reason, as the infallible organ of absolute truth. If such validity can be vindicated for it, this end would have really and practicably been accomplished by 'the divine philosopher.' We are now in circumstances most favourable to test, through Plato, the validity of this faculty as such an organ. We may in the first place test its validity by referring to the character of its actual revelations through him. We may then compare these revelations with those obtained by other world-renowned philosophers who have sought for absolute truth by the same method, and in the affirmed use of the same faculty.

For 'knowledge obtained through Reason, in an intuitive manner, of real existence and intelligible things,' Plato expressly claims, 'a higher degree of certainty than the knowledge which belongs to what are commonly called the sciences,' to Geometry, for example, a science to which he refers as illustrating his meaning. A peculiarity of demonstrated truth is this: when the demonstration has once been understood, that truth is never, and never can be, doubted in any subsequent age, but absolutely commands conviction for all future time. Now if Plato, or any other thinker, has given us real 'knowledge by Reason, in an intuitive manner, of real existence and intelligible things,' as he affirms himself to have done, it will be even more impossible for the mind to doubt the validity of the forms of knowledge which he has furnished, than it is to doubt that of any demonstrated mathematical truth. What are the facts of the case? Take Plato's definition of 'opinion,' and compare with it his affirmed revelations of absolute truth obtained 'in an intuitive manner' and 'by Reason,' and we shall find that they all belong to the sphere of mere opinion, and never approach that of absolute knowledge. Of these opinions, mistaken for absolute truths of Reason, we shall also find that at least nine tenths of them failed to obtain credence in that age, have never since been accepted as true, and are now known to be false. Who now, for example, believes that the earth, the moon, the sun, and all the planets and stars, are real animals with souls, and consequently gods? Who believes that the earth is the fixed centre of the universe, and that the inclination of the ecliptic 'is the result of the inferior perfection of the spheres underneath the spheres of the fixed stars'? Who believes in the doctrine of the transmigration of souls, that after the work of creation had been advanced to a certain extent, the Supreme God 'returned to his accustomed repose,' and left his imperfect works to be finished by finite, erring, and rival divinities? Who believes that there is, or can be, a form of existence intermediate between being and non-being—a something 'which is and is not,' which is 'always becoming and never is'? Who believes that the beds and tables which we see and sleep and eat on have not 'a real existence,' but that somewhere above the heavens a table and a bed, one of each, exist which have real being? These and kindred absurdities, which nobody now believes, are the most of them, to say the least, absolute truths of Reason, according to Plato. Plato's own teachings of affirmed absolute truth, render it demonstrably evident that the idea, that Reason in him and philosophers, to say nothing of the gods—Reason, as he has defined it—is, or ever was, an organ of absolute truth, is one of the wildest hallucinations that ever approached human thought.

If we compare together the results of the action of this Reason in Plato and other world-renowned philosophers, the same conclusion will force itself upon us. Reason, through the same identical method of philosophizing, Reason through the Oriental Yogees, Idealists, and Materialists of all ages, gives, as the revelation of absolute truth, Brahm, the Absolute, the All-One, Pure Ideas, two Unknown and Unknowable Entities, and Matter, each one in particular as the sole existence. Through this same Reason in Plato we have as another revelation of *absolute truth*, God as the creator of all things, and a creation distinct from Him; a creation constituted of 'Idea, Matter, and Sensible Objects, the product of the two,' things which always are and are not. When we can affirm of systems of universal being and its laws, systems absolutely contradictory to one another, that they can all in common be at the same time true and not true, then we can, as rationally as we in such mental states can hold anything, regard Reason, as defined by these philosophers, as the organ of absolute truth. Until we have ascended into the high sphere of thought in which we can KNOW that the same thing may, at the same time, exist and not exist, we must, if we think rationally, affirm that Reason, as thus defined, has no existence at all as a faculty of the human mind.

The Faculty, or Faculties, actually employed by Plato and other Philosophers who adopt the à priori method when Philosophizing.

Every reflective mind must infer, we judge, from our previous discussions, that Reason, as defined by Plato and all philosophers who employ the *à priori* method in philosophizing, does not exist at all as a faculty of the human mind, and that Reason properly defined is not the faculty which they use when thus employed. A single consideration will render the validity of these statements undeniably manifest. Truths of Reason, when distinctly developed and apprehended, as in the pure sciences, command the assent of the race. Now no philosopher, or school in Philosophy, that employs this method, has ever yet reached thereby a single deduction which has thus commanded the assent of mankind, or even that of a majority, or a considerable minority, of philosophers. *À priori* thinkers are everywhere and in all ages divided into schools, and each school, in all its principles and deductions, is in deadly antagonism with every other. What agreement, but in their method, obtained, for example, between the schools of the Vedanta, of Kapila, Kanada, and the Buddhist schools of Subjective and Pure Idealism in India? What agreement had Zeno of Elea with Democritus, or either with Plato? What agreement have the schools of Kant, Fichte, Schelling, and Hegel, with one another, or either with that of Condilac or Comte? Every deduction of each school is repudiated, not only by the mass of mankind, but by four-fifths of philosophers. How absurd is the idea and pretence that these philosophers are employing Reason, as they define it, or as it should be defined.

What faculty or faculties, then, do they employ? It is, we answer, the Judgment, not acting in conjunction with the Understanding and primary faculties, the only faculties, together with Memory, with which it does or can act in real science, but the Judgment under the lead of the Imagination and Will. The Materialist imagines Matter to be the only form of real existence, and then compels his Judgment to construct a system of universal being and its laws from the data thus furnished. The Idealist imagines two unknown and unknowable entities, or spirit, or pure thought, to exist as the sole principle of all things, and then compels his Judgment to originate a system from which all material elements are utterly excluded. The Sceptic imagines this, that we 'don't know that we don't know anything,' and then compels his Judgment to construct a system from 'imaginary substrata.' Plato imagined the being of God as the Creator of a universe distinct from himself, then imagined that universe as 'constituted of Idea, Matter, and Sensible Objects, the product of the two,' and finally compelled his Judgment to give forth a system constructed from the materials thus furnished. In all cases, the Imagination and Will furnish the *material* and *form* of the building, while the Judgment constructs it accordingly. On no other hypothesis can the existence and form of these antagonistic systems be accounted for. The 'Divine Commedia' is no more a creation of the Imagination than are the systems of Vyasa, Kapila, Kanada, Gautama Buddha, Zeno, Democritus, Plato, Kant, Fichte, Schelling, Hegel, Condilac, Comte, and Spencer. The validity of these statements will become more and more manifest as we advance in our criticism.

Plato as a Logician.

One or two examples must suffice, as illustrative of the character of Plato as a logician. 'The universe,' he affirms, is constituted of Idea, Matter, and Sensible Things, the product of the two.' 'Idea and Matter' are with Plato actually existing entities, eternal verities. 'Sensible Things' are a something 'intermediate between existence and non-existence.' Can any philosopher tell us how, or by what possibility, the resultant of the union of two such entities can be a *tertium quid*, which 'is of the nature of that which is and is not'?

The painter and craftsman originate productions which are mere copies, for example, of a single model chair and table which exists somewhere above the heavens. The models are really existing objects; the copies, because they are copies, have no real existence at all. 'If, then, he' (the craftsman) 'does not make the idea of the bed' (the real bed), 'he makes nothing real, but only something which represents that which really exists. And if anyone maintain that the carpenter's work has real existence, he will be in error.' That, then, which is constructed after no model at all, really exists; but that which is constructed after a model has no real existence. The universe, then, does not exist; for it, according to Plato, and according to truth, was constructed after a Divine model. There is, undeniably, no incompatibility between the idea of the real existence of a model, and of a bed, table, or building, constructed after a model.

'Plato's proof of the world being an animal,' says Mr. Lewes, 'is too curious a specimen of analogical reasoning to be passed over.' There is warmth in a human being; there is warmth also in the world. The human being is composed of various elements, and is therefore called a body; the world is also composed of various elements, and is, therefore, a body; and, as our bodies have souls, the body of the world must have a soul.'

The Doctrine of Innate Ideas.

The doctrine of Plato on this subject is very correctly stated by Dr. Cocker, to wit, '*There are ideas in the mind which have not been derived from without,* and which therefore the mind brought into the present state of being.' According to Dr. Hodge, 'The knowledge of God is innate.' Such knowledge, he defines as 'opposed to knowledge founded on experience.' 'All that is meant is, that the mind is so constituted that it perceives certain things to be true without proof and without instruction.' 'The word innate simply indicates the source of the knowledge.' According to this definition, all our knowledge through perception in both its forms, external and internal, must be innate. 'We are so constituted that we perceive certain things' (all facts of perception) 'to be true without proof and without instruction.' Nor is a knowledge of these facts 'acquired by a process of research or reasoning.' Ideas of all kinds must constitute a faculty of the soul, or exist, if they exist at all, as actual forms of thought. If ideas constitute a faculty of the soul, perceptions, conceptions, memories, judgments, and imaginings, are not forms of thought, but constitute so many different faculties, and these last are just as innate as is that one constituted by ideas. No thinker, we are quite sure, will perpetrate the absurdity of confounding ideas of any kind with any original faculty of the soul. Nor will anyone affirm that ideas, as forms of thought, existed in the mind before it began to think at all. Equally absurd would it be to affirm that ideas of Reason, in distinction from other forms of thought, necessarily, on account of the nature of the faculty of Reason, arise in the mind whenever the proper conditions are fulfilled, this being equally true of all forms of thought acquired through any other faculty. To affirm, then, innateness of ideas of Reason in distinction from other forms of thought, is to use words without meaning, or to involve ourselves in error. Either *no* forms of thought are innate, or *all* forms are equally so.

What is the truth in this case? Prior to the commencement of thought in any and every mind, the soul exists, and the world, time, space, and God exist, the soul, as a faculty, and all the realities designated, as objects of knowledge. All these realities in common, however, are to the soul, as objects of knowledge, as if they did not exist at all. The action of each intellectual faculty depends upon the fulfilment of the proper conditions. When these conditions are fulfilled, said faculty must act, and the *form* of knowledge thus furnished will be as is the nature and character of the *objects* of cognition. The question, what are these conditions, involves inquiries of fundamental importance in Philosophy. The condition of the action of consciousness, for example, is the pre-existence in the mind of some positive mental state, some thought, feeling, or act of will. When such state is induced, consciousness directly and immediately apprehends such state, and the mind in the same, as they really are. The condition of the action of Sense-perception is the immediate presentation to the mind of some external material substance, a substance to which the mind is correlated as a *faculty*, and it to the mind as an *object* of knowledge. When this condition is fulfilled, then a perception, or knowledge of that object as it is, necessarily arises. The condition of the action of Reason is the actual perception, through Sense or Consciousness, of some fact, or reality, the existence, or occurrence, of which necessarily implies the existence of some reality not perceived. When such perception occurs, Reason necessarily apprehends the reality whose existence is implied by what is perceived. When nothing is perceived, Reason cannot act at all. When any fact is perceived, Reason must apprehend the unseen reality whose existence is necessarily implied by the fact which is perceived. Through external and internal perception, we, as we have said elsewhere, apprehend body, succession, phenomena, events, and conditioned facts. Through Reason, on the occurrence of such perceptions, and as implied by the facts perceived, we apprehend Space, Time, Substance, Cause, and God, as the unconditioned Cause of all that conditionally exists. Thus, between the perceived and implied forms of knowledge, and, consequently, between Reason and the other primary intuitive faculties, relations perfectly fixed and determinable exist. Reason can no more act, but upon the condition of the prior action of those faculties, than there can be an event without a cause. Nor can it, by any possibility, give any more, nor less, nor any other forms of knowledge than those implied by facts and objects of actual perception.

Here we have absolute criteria by which we can distinguish all real from assumed forms of knowledge by Reason. The validity of the former can always be verified, as necessarily implied by facts of actual knowledge, as perception. The latter can be as absolutely shown to pertain to mere 'imaginary substrata' assumed to be objects of intuitions of Reason. There is not a solitary reality known through Reason, which cannot be demonstrated to be known as implied by facts and objects of perception. Reason has no independent insight of 'being *per se*,' or of 'being *in se*,' or of any other realities. Take away facts of perception, and Reason is as absolutely blind and unseeing as are Sense and Consciousness in the total absence of all objects to be perceived, and Reason, we repeat, can apprehend nothing more, and nothing less, of 'being *per se*,' or of 'being *in se*,' but forms of the unseen whose existence is necessarily implied by facts which are perceived. Ideas of Reason are innate in the same sense, and in no other, than knowledge through the other intuitive faculties is. Take any idea of Reason you please, and all the evidence that can be adduced to prove it innate, can be adduced in all its strength in favour of the claims of any other form of intuitive knowledge to the possession of the same characteristic.

As we are now upon the subject, we will merely allude to the conditions on which the Secondary Intellectual Faculties do, and must, act. When the elements of thought given by the Primary Faculties are present in the mind, the Understanding does and must take the initiative, and combine these elements into conceptions or notions. In the absence of such elements, this faculty cannot act at all. When they are present, it must act.

The condition of the actions of the judgment is the prior origination in the Consciousness of conceptions. When these are absent it cannot, and when they are present it must, act. The conditions of the activity of Memory and the Imagination are too obvious, and too universally acknowledged, to require specification or elucidation.

These are the real and the only real faculties of the human Intelligence, and these, also, are the immutable conditions of their action. These faculties, too, are possessed, though some of them in different degrees, by all mankind in common, philosophers among the rest. When philosophers claim, for themselves, the possession of any faculty or faculties not strictly common to the race, while 'some may think them wondrous wise,' the world ought to 'believe them mad.'

THE IDEA OF REASON AS A FACULTY POSSESSED ONLY BY PHILOSOPHERS.

The ancient Yogees and modern Transcendentalists, in common with Plato, claim for themselves a special faculty denominated Reason, or intellectual intuition, a special faculty denied to the rest of mankind. We have already shown that this faculty, as these thinkers have defined it, has no existence in any mind. One great central fact in respect to Reason, as properly defined, we deem it important here to state. Reason is a faculty not only possessed by all mankind not demented or deranged, but equally by all. Other faculties are possessed by different individuals in different degrees. Reason, on the other hand, in all minds in which it exists at all, exists in equal degrees. Hence it is, that all mankind have common and equally absolute apprehensions and convictions in regard to time, space, substance, cause, personal identity, God, duty, immortality, and retribution. Truths of Reason are absolute truths, and when known at all, they are not known in different degrees, but absolutely known. All men know as absolutely as do philosophers, that every object exists somewhere and in some time, that every event has a cause, that phenomena imply substance, and that things equal to the same things are equal to one another. The same holds true in all other cases. When Plato proved, that in the mind of Meno's slave there existed the ideas of time, space, substance, cause, etc., proof was presented, not that the soul had existed in a prior state of being, nor that it brought these ideas with it, when it came into the world, or that it has any innate ideas of any kind, but that the faculty of Reason exists alike in all rational minds, and equally in all.

Three great Central Truths, for the first Scientific Enunciation of which the world is indebted to Plato.

The individual who first announces a great central truth, may justly be regarded as a leading benefactor to his species. Plato's psychology, his doctrine of Ideas, and his method of philosophizing, remain but as recorded errors of the past. There are three great truths, however, which, in a scientific form, he was the first to announce—truths which will ever remain as central lights in the firmament of science—truths, also, the enunciation of which distinguish him as one of the greatest thinkers of the race. Plato, as we have stated, is the first thinker who formally propounded the doctrine of *creation as an event of time*. This, as we have also stated, is the great central fact about which the whole argument for the being, creative agency, and providence of God must revolve, if that argument shall take on the real characteristic of scientific validity. Paley infers, from marks of design in a watch, that it was the production of a watchmaker. We will assume that the watch has existed from eternity, that is, that it was not made at all. How can we argue, from any facts in it, to the existence and agency, in its production, of a watchmaker? So, if we assume that the universe has existed from eternity, that is, that it was not made at all, whatever appearances of design may be found in it, no ground remains for our 'faith that the worlds were *made* by the Word of God.' If the world was not *made*, that is, if creation was not an event of time, there is no world-maker to be inquired about. The undeniable and demonstrably evincible fact of creation, as an event of time, absolutely evinces the doctrine of God as the Creator of the universe. Plato has the high honour of having first, in a scientific form, furnished to Theism this great central fact.

In his Tenth Book of the *Laws*, in an argument against Atheists, he first of all distinguishes two conceivable classes, among others, of objects capable of motion—those which are incapable of motion but from an impelling power from without, and can communicate to others motion but through the momentum thus received—and those capable of self-originated motion, in the first place, and then of communicating motion to other objects. Matter is a power of the class first designated. It cannot originate motion at all, and it cannot communicate motion but through the momentum which it has passively received. It becomes demonstrably evident that the originating cause of creation, which was an event of time, cannot have been a material one, it being undeniable that that cause must have possessed the power of self-motion, and through this self-originated motion of imparting motion to matter, and thus bringing order out of chaos. That cause, on the other hand, must have been spiritual. Mind only is conceivably capable of self-originated action in any form. He therefore, by whom 'the worlds were made,' must have been a mind, a free, self-conscious personality. Such is the sum of the argument presented in full detail in the work to which we have referred. In this argument, together with the great central fact above adduced, the argument for the being, creative agency, and providence of a personal God, attains, in its strictest and most scientific form, demonstrative certainty. To us it has long been a matter of surprise and deep regret that Theists have, almost universally, ignored the forms of the argument for the doctrine of God, in which Plato has presented it. As long as this form of the argument is ignored, the doctrine under consideration will fail to possess the appearance even of a truth of science.

The third great central truth, which Plato was first to announce in a scientific form, we have before stated. It is that of the *human* soul as capable of free, self-determined, and, therefore, of morally responsible activity. If man can act but through, and in the direction of momentum received from without, and can act upon others but by the momentum thus received, he is no more responsible for his own activity, or its results, than is a cannon ball for its motions and their results. If, on the other hand, the soul, God, and the universe are, as they actually are, what Plato, in his argument, affirms them to be, then God stands demonstrably revealed, not only as the Creator of a universe worthy of Infinity and Perfection, but as an all-wise and righteous moral Governor over a countless realm of moral agents, each and all 'created after his own image and likeness.' *We* honour Plato, not for his avowed method of philosophizing, for his psychology, or his doctrine of Ideas, 'things which can be shaken,' but for the great central truths of the science of sciences, 'things which cannot be shaken'—truths which he was the first to announce, and which will ever shine in the high firmament of scientific thought as fixed stars of the first magnitude.

SECTION III.

ARISTOTLE.

ARISTOTLE, who originated a system which, in all its essential principles and deductions, was the opposite of that of Plato, was born at Stagira, in Thrace, 384, and died at Chalcis, 322 B.C. In his eighteenth year he became a pupil of Plato, and remained such for twenty years. After the death of Plato (347 B.C.) he spent several years in various countries; seven at the court of Philip of Macedon, and three as the tutor of Alexander the Great. He then returned to Athens, and founded, in the Lyceum, a school over which he presided for twelve years.

It is hardly conceivable that two such minds as Plato and Aristotle, in the age and circumstances in which they lived, should agree in the construction of a system of universal being and its laws. The temperament of Plato was imaginative, idealistic, and mystical. That of Aristotle was prosaic, dry, and practical. Plato naturally first of all fixed upon the general and universal, and hardly condescended to descend to the individual. Aristotle as naturally started with the individual, and by careful induction ascended to the general. The method natural to Plato was the *à priori*. The only leading method possible to Aristotle was the *à posteriori*. Each had powers of thought and industry which could not fail to render him a central light in the sphere in which he should choose to move.

ARISTOTLE'S CLASSIFICATION OF THE SCIENCES.

At the time when Aristotle assumed his place at the head of the Lyceum, even leading thinkers had very confused ideas of any proper classification of the sciences, or of the exclusive sphere and real principles and method of each. Such separation and classification, with a consequent determination of the true and exclusive method of each science, was the first aim of this great philosopher, and here we find, if not the chief, one of his chief merits as a teacher and expounder of Philosophy. Hence the origin of his world-renowned Organon. In this one work Aristotle did more for science than in all his other productions combined. Of the science of Philosophy he made a three-fold division, namely, theoretic, practical, poetic. The object of the first is Ontology, the science of existence. That of the second is Morality, or rules for moral conduct, and naturally divides itself into two departments —ethics, or individual, politics, or social duties. The third, the Poetic, refers to the proper shaping of materials, or to 'the technically correct and artistic creation of works of art.' In another connection, he divides theoretical Philosophy into Mathematics, Physics, and the 'First Philosophy,' or Metaphysics. Whatever may be thought of the above classification, the merit of having first presented and developed the idea of classification itself belongs to Aristotle, and in that idea he stands revealed as a world-benefactor.

QUESTIONS AT ISSUE BETWEEN ARISTOTLE AND PLATO.

Where two systems stand over against each other as essential opposites, each will be best understood by a distinct presentation of all specific issues between them. There were five central doctrines in respect to which Aristotle took open issue with Plato—the doctrine of Ideas; the validity of knowledge through Sensation or Sense-perception; the Summum Bonum, or the Greatest Good; the doctrine of pre-existing state of the soul, and of creation as an event of time. We propose, as a basis of our elucidation of the system of Aristotle, to contrast the teachings of each of these authors in respect to each of these doctrines, and that in the order above stated. Nothing can be more delicate or appropriate than is the manner in which Aristotle introduces the questions at issue between himself and his former venerated instructor.

'But perhaps,' says Aristotle, 'it would be better to examine the theory of universal good, and to inquire what is meant by it, although such an inquiry involves difficulties, because men who are our friends have introduced the doctrine of *Ideas*. But perhaps it would be better, and even necessary, at least for the preservation of truth, that we should do away with private feelings, especially as we are philosophers, for both being dear to us, it is a sacred duty to prefer truth.'

The Doctrine of Individual Existence as Opposed to that of Ideas.

Plato, as we have seen, attributed to generals, or universals, a real existence, and called them Ideas. Aristotle, on the other hand, not only denied this doctrine, but placed himself on the opposite extreme, affirming that nothing really exists but individual forms of being. Plato not only affirmed this doctrine of Ideas, but denied all reality to individuals excepting so far as they participated of the universal. Aristotle denied wholly real existence of universals, excepting so far as they were immanent in individuals. Even Plato's universals, as defined by himself, Aristotle affirmed were nothing but individual forms of being. Of the universal or general forms of being, for example, represented by the terms bed and table, Plato affirmed that there could by no possibility be but *one* of each, that is, his universal bed was nothing but a single or individual bed. Plato's doctrine of Ideas, therefore, if it could be true, implied merely an increase of the number of individual existences. General ideas, therefore, represent no separate existences, but only the common qualities immanent in each individual of the class which each general idea represents.

In favour of his own doctrine, and against that of Plato, the argument of Aristotle has, undeniably, absolute validity. Whatever objects exist must exist as *this* or *that* particular reality. Nothing is or can be real but individual forms of being and their *relations* to one another. Relations may be universal, general, or particular. Individuals alone can possess real existence. No idea can be more absurd than that of a universal man, horse, or cow, excepting that which affirms that the individual has real existence but by participating in the universal. Suppose that a something did exist represented by the true man, how can John and

George become participants of this one universal man, and not equally so with one another? This one universal man is, undeniably, just as distinct from John as the latter is from George. In every point of light in which Plato's doctrine of Ideas is contemplated, it becomes more and more manifested as an hallucination of false science; while that of Aristotle, by the same means, becomes more and more distinctly revealed as an essential truth of real science.

The Validity of Sensation, or Sense-perception.

Sensation, as the term was employed by the Greeks, represented not only the sensitive state now exclusively represented by the term Sensation, but also the exercise of the faculty of external perception, which we designate by the term Sense. According to Plato, the world of perception, that is, all objects of Sense-perception, have only an ideal existence. What we actually perceive are nothing but shadowy reflections of things really existing without us. Matter, and an organized material universe, really exist. Of these various forms of existences, we have no real knowledge, and of the material universe which exists behind the phenomenal, we have, and can have, but 'a boasted kind of knowledge.' Aristotle, not only affirmed the real existence of an organized material universe, but also affirmed and verified the validity of our knowledge of the same. 'Experience,' he says, in other words, facts, or phenomena, perceived, 'furnishes the principles of every science,'—and 'phenomena are more to be trusted than the conclusion of Reason.' Aristotle is here contrasting his own, with the doctrine of Plato. Plato asserted, as we have seen, that through Reason-intuitions, we have absolute knowledge of real being and its laws, and that through Sensation, we have no real knowledge at all. In opposition to this doctrine, Aristotle affirms, that through Sense-perceptions, 'phenomena,' we obtain more certain knowledge than can be obtained through reason, as defined and affirmed by Plato. In the following memorable passage, Aristotle thus sets forth his own doctrine:

'Experience furnishes the principles of every science. Thus Astronomy is grounded on observation; for if we were properly to observe the celestial phenomena, we might demonstrate the laws which regulate them. The same applies to other sciences. If we omit nothing that observation can afford us respecting phenomena, we could easily furnish demonstration of all that admits of being demonstrated, and illustrate that which is not susceptible of being demonstrated.' When phenomena or facts fail us, he bids us wait for their appearance before deducing our conclusions. 'We must wait,' he says, 'for further phenomena, since phenomena are more to be trusted than the conclusion of Reason,' that is, than any deductions not based upon known facts. Sounder and more fundamental principles of induction and deduction were never before or since introduced into the sphere of science. Here, at a distance of about two thousand years, Aristotle anticipated Bacon.

The arguments by which Aristotle vindicated for the mind a valid knowledge of nature, we have stated in our remarks upon the opposite doctrine of Plato. These arguments, we would remark, have never yet been answered, and we are quite sure they never will be: 'They that depreciate sensible objects as perpetually changing, unstable, and unknowable, make the mistake,' he says, 'of confining their attention to the sublunary interior of the Cosmos, where indeed generation and destruction largely prevail. But this is only a small portion of the entire Cosmos. In the largest portion—the visible, celestial, super-lunary regions—there is no generation or destruction at all, nothing but permanence and uniformity. In appreciating the sensible world, philosophers ought to pardon the short-comings of the smaller portion on account of the excellencies of the larger; and not condemn both together on account of the smaller.' When philosophers shall cease their attempts to demonstrate to the Intelligence, by the Intelligence, that this same Intelligence is a faculty of nescience, and not of knowledge, philosophy, will be saved from its 'many blunders and foolish notions.'

The Summum Bonum.

There is one great central doctrine about which philosophers are yet in doubt, and have been ever since human thought was directed to it—the doctrine of the 'Greatest Good.' One class, under the lead of Plato, place this in moral virtue, moral resemblance to God, as this philosopher states it. The other class, under the lead of Aristotle, find this good in happiness. In determining this problem, Plato looks simply at the question, what ought we to be and to become? His consequent answer is, moral virtue. Plato does not overlook the necessary connection between virtue and happiness. 'Our object in founding the states is,' he says, 'that not a class, but that all may be made as happy as possible.' 'Happiness,' he says again, 'depends on culture and justice, or on the possession of moral beauty and goodness.' If by the doctrine, that 'the possession of moral beauty and goodness' should be the end of all our aims, Plato means, that absolute conformity to the law of duty should be the supreme and all controlling intent of all our moral activity, who would dispute with him? If he meant, as he obviously did not, that nothing but the possession of moral virtue should be regarded as a good in itself, none surely ought to agree with him.

The explanation which Aristotle gives of this doctrine is based upon an answer to the single question, 'What do all men desire?' To this question, he answers, with undeniable correctness, 'happiness.' Happiness, he hence concludes, is the 'summum bonum,' and affirms, as his final deduction, that the question what is right and wrong in itself, must be determined exclusively from a consideration of the connection of the act referred to with happiness. If the meaning of Aristotle is, that happiness is a good in itself, and should, for its own sake, be thus regarded by us, and that it is our duty to will, and as far as able, to promote the happiness of all beings capable of it, he would find none to dispute his doctrine. If, on the other hand, he meant that the ultimate reason for duty, not in some, or many, but in *all* its forms, is found in a simple consideration of happiness as a good in itself, many would dispute his doctrine. If the question be asked, which theory, that of Plato or Aristotle, should be adopted, if we must adopt one to the exclusion of the other, as our exclusive standpoint from which to determine questions of moral obligations, and from which view does duty become most sacred in human regard, we should unhesitatingly decide in favour of the former and against the latter. If the question be also asked, from which standpoint is a *system* of moral duty most readily and safely determinable, we should still agree with Plato, as against Aristotle. If, as a final inquiry, the question should be asked, which theory shall be adopted to the exclusion of the other, we should unhesitatingly answer, neither. Duty in *all* its forms, is explicable from neither standpoint. There are, undeniably, for example, two classes of duties which we owe to God—the one class finding its ultimate reason in his moral perfections—and the other in his susceptibilities for happiness. The same holds true of our duties to all other moral agents. Willing happiness as a good in itself is virtue, but not all virtue. We please God just as fully when we esteem and respect Him for no other reason than His moral perfections, as we do when we will His happiness from respect to his susceptibilities.

A president of one of our leading colleges, who was himself the author of an important work on Moral Philosophy, gave some years since in one of the religious papers, a very lucid statement of the various conflicting theories pertaining to the foundation of moral obligation. After stating the one above indicated, his own being different from that, he remarked, 'This is the hypothesis of President Mahan, and the mass of mankind agree with him.' Had he asked for the reason of this agreement, he would have found it identical with that for which the deductions of Common sense differ from the systems of philosophers, the former including more real facts, and consequently being more true than the latter. When a philosopher affirms that duty, in certain specific forms, finds its ultimate reasons in character, we yield our full assent to his doctrine. When another philosopher affirms that happiness is good in itself, and should be willed for its own sake, we assent as before. But when each claims for his hypothesis exclusive validity, we dissent from both, and the common-sense of the race is, of course, with us. So will it be in all cases in which systems are based upon a partial induction of real facts.

Doctrine of Reminiscence.

All thinkers now agree with Aristotle, in rejecting Plato's doctrine of pre-existence, and especially in repudiating his hypothesis of Reminiscence. No facts of consciousness exist the explanation of which demands the admission of any such hypothesis. When we take into the account the entire facts of perception, together with the realities necessarily implied by said facts, the origin and genesis of all knowledge, in all its actual forms, receives a full and ready explanation. Had Aristotle and Plato both recognized the existence and character of contingent and necessary forms of thought, together with the manifest relations between the two, neither of them would have erred in Philosophy as he has done.

The Universe as an External Existence, and as Organized in Time.

Plato, as we have seen, taught the doctrine of creation as an event of time. Aristotle, on the other hand, affirmed the eternity of the present order of things. What is very remarkable here is, the fact that Plato, who was so exclusively *à priori* in his method of philosophizing, based his deductions in this case wholly upon facts of induction, while Aristotle, who is avowedly inductive in all his reasonings, based his conclusion exclusively upon *à priori* grounds. In such a case, as a matter of course, the former was right, and the latter wrong. The argument of Plato, we have before presented. Aristotle argues the eternity of the universe from the fundamental idea of God as a necessary activity. Hence, he draws the following deductions from that idea: 'Not at any time did God shape the orderly world; He conditions and determines the order of the world eternally, in that He exists as the most perfect being, and all things else, seek to become like Him. The world as an articulate whole has always existed, and will never perish.' In creation, also, God is not active, but passive, and 'acts by virtue of attraction which the loved exerts upon the loving.' We have here another form of 'absolute truth' obtained through *à priori* insight, a form irreconcilably contradictory to all other revelations ever obtained by the same infallible form of vision.

Such were the essential issues between Plato and Aristotle—issues from which the distinct and opposite systems of each took its specific form. We will now turn our attention to the diverse assumed forms of systematized truth which Aristotle based upon the principles above elucidated.

Aristotle's Logic.

Of all his productions, the Logic is the most complete in itself, and has had the widest and most controlling influence. For about two thousand years the logical thought of Christendom has taken form from this single production. Yet when contemplated in the light of the laws of thought in general, or of reasoning in its universal forms, none of the productions of this author were less perfect or complete. In this work we have the logic of classification and generalization simply, and not of reasoning in its universal forms. His celebrated dictum, when scientifically examined, is found to be applicable to but a single class of propositions—those in which the subject and predicate are related as *inferior* and *superior* conceptions, as in the judgment, All men are mortal. To such judgments the dictum, 'Whatever may be affirmed or denied of any term distributed, may, in a similar manner, be predicated of every individual who comes under that term;' to all such judgments, we say, this dictum is applicable. In converting universal affirmative judgment of this class, we have to change the quantity of the judgment from a universal to a particular—Some mortal beings are men. Hence the universal law of distribution, as given in all Aristotelean Logics of all ages, that 'All negative and no affirmative judgments distribute the predicate.' Now, with the single exception of that one class of judgments, in which the predicate represents a superior and the subject an inferior conception, all universal affirmative judgments distribute both terms. We may safely challenge the world to find an exception to this statement. Is not the converse, as well as the exposita, in the judgment, Things equal to the same thing are equal to one another—a universal proposition? The same, undeniably, holds true of all universal affirmative judgments throughout the entire range of mathematics, and in respect to all such judgments but those of the single class above designated. In the single sphere of classification into species and genera, Aristotle's principle of distribution and conversion holds true. Outside of this sphere, where a vast majority of all our judgments are found, his principle utterly misleads the student.

The same holds true of his laws of the Syllogism. In the first figure, we are informed, affirmative and negative conclusions, in all their forms, may be obtained, while in the second figure we can obtain only negative, and in the third only particular conclusions. This law has validity but in the single sphere of classification, when the conceptions, in each judgment, stand related as inferior and superior conceptions, that is, as species and genera. In all other cases we obtain the same kind of conclusions, affirmative and negative, universal and particular, in all the figures in common. We will give a single example in which we obtain affirmative conclusions of the same class in each of the figures.

I.	II.	III.
$M = X$,	$X = M$,	$M = X$,
$Z = M$,	$Z = M$,	$M = Z$,
$Z = X$.	$Z = X$.	$Z = X$.

If the terms in these syllogisms represented inferior and superior conceptions, the conclusion would be valid but in the first figure. Representing, as they do, *compared* quantities, the conclusions have the same validity in all the figures. In the single sphere of classification, the Logic of Aristotle is 'perfect and complete, wanting nothing.' As a science of the Laws of Thought, and of reasoning in all its forms, it has misled Christendom for nearly twenty centuries.

The reason is obvious. 'Real existences,' according to Aristotle, and according to truth, are exclusively individual forms of being. General conceptions, therefore, can represent nothing but the qualities common to all the individuals which such conceptions represent. The question which here arises is this, How do we advance from the individual to the general? Plato's answer to this question has already been given. In a former state, he affirmed, the general, as a distinct form of being, was an object of mental vision; and in the present state, there is a reminiscence of those general forms which were there perceived. Aristotle denied wholly the reality of such separate forms of existence, together with the whole doctrine of reminiscence. To obtain the general at all, then, it must be deduced by induction from particulars. Induction he designates as the pathway from the particulars to generals, and denominates this process as an art. 'Art commences,' he says, 'when, from a great number of experiences, one general conception is formed which will embrace all similar cases.' 'Thus,' he adds, 'if you know that a certain remedy has cured Collias of a certain disease, and that the same remedy has produced the same effect on Socrates and on several other persons, that is Experience; but to know that a certain remedy will cure all persons attacked with that disease is Art; for Experience is the knowledge of individual things; Art is that of Universals.'

So far Aristotle was unquestionably correct. Wherein, and, why did he err? In the assumption, we answer, that *all* universals are obtained by means of this form of experience, that is, finding in many particulars their common qualities or characteristics, and then combining said qualities into general notions, and finally from these deducing our general judgments; as, All men are mortal, and, All men are animals. Not one of our universal ideas, such as that of time, space, cause, substance, personal identity, the soul, God, duty, immortality, and retribution, represent qualities common to individual existences, or were combined from qualities thus abstracted. The elements constituting these ideas were not given *in* perception, but represent realities implied *by* what is perceived. We do not, for example, find space in body, which we perceive, and do not abstract it from body, but apprehend it, as a separate existence whose reality is implied by what we perceive. The same holds true of all our necessary ideas. Nor were these ideas originated in the mind by the induction of any number of particular facts. The first time we perceived body we through Reason, apprehended space as the place of body, and as implied by the same. If the first facts of succession, phenomena, and events, did not induce, through Reason, the apprehension of time, substance, and cause, no multiplied perceptions of the same kind could do it. To obtain a general conception, a number of particulars more or less numerous must be perceived. To develop a necessary idea but a single fact need be given. If one single event does not imply a cause, an infinite number would not do it. If each phenomenon does not imply substance, all phenomena together do not do it. If each particular body and fact of succession do not imply space and time, the universe itself, with all events, does not do it. In connection with the first fact given, Reason must apprehend the reality implied by the fact, or it can never apprehend that reality.

At the basis of all the sciences, also, we find the axioms and postulates which, from the perceived relations between their subjects and predicates, have intuitively, absolutely universal and necessary certainty, a certainty, also, which can neither be increased nor diminished by the induction of any number of particular facts. An individual with a yard stick in his hand, for example, is present in a room with a philosopher, an uneducated man, and a child who has never before witnessed any such event as that which we are about to relate, but can perceive and apprehend the simple facts of the case. The individual holding the yard-stick applies it to a table there, and finds that they exactly agree in length. He then takes his company into an adjacent room, and applying the yard-stick to a table standing here, finds the same perfect correspondence as before. What, without a word being spoken, will be the inference of each of these four individuals from the facts under consideration? All will affirm, and affirm with the same absoluteness, the equality of the two tables, as far as the quality of length is concerned. The reason is, that every one does and must, in the presence of such facts, though perceived for the first time, apprehend, in the concrete, what the philosopher alone knows in the abstract form, the principle which lies at the basis of every such conclusion, namely, that things which are equal to the same thing are equal to one another. So the first time the idea of an event enters the mind of a child, he knows as absolutely as the philosopher does, that it occurred somewhere, in some time, and from some cause. Neither universal ideas, as those of space, time, substance, and cause, nor intuitively universal and necessary judgments were derived from the observation of many facts, but are, all in common, given in each particular fact by which their validity is implied.

Here, then, we have a full explanation of the essential imperfection of Aristotle's Logic. Beginning with the idea of individuals as the only realities, he sought to deduce from what was immanent in them, all our general and universal conceptions and ideas. When he had thus found the general, that is, the generic conception, he assumed, that he had found all universal ideas. From individual, specifical, and generical conceptions, none but judgments whose subjects and predicates are constituted of inferior and superior conceptions can be obtained. With these, consequently, Aristotle constructed his Logic, and gave us, of course, the principles and laws of classification, and not of judging and reasoning in their universal forms. Classification is only preparatory to science proper, and all the sciences are based, as we have seen, upon principles, or judgments, fundamentally unlike those obtained in the sphere of classification, judgments not of mere experience, but having intuitively, universal and necessary validity. In judgments of this latter class, we have the relations intuitively perceived to exist between forms of perceived and implied knowledge, and hence we obtain intuitive judgments which have universal and necessary validity.

Aristotle, pressed by an apprehension of the want of universality in his system, did attempt to remedy the defect, by setting forth two universal principles—that of contradiction, and excluded middle. He gave these, not because they were implied by his principle of deducting his general from particular conceptions, but because he did have in his mind, what all other men have in theirs, ideas of Reason, and consequently could not but apprehend, in some of their forms, the necessary relations between perceived and implied forms of knowledge, and must have apprehended some, at least, of the basis principles of the sciences. The two given by Aristotle, however, constitute but a small portion of the axioms and postulates of the various sciences, and these, as we have said, he obtained in contradiction to his avowed principles of deducing the universal from the particular.

Fundamental Error of Mr. Mill in his Logic.

The Logic of Mr. Mill is, in reality, only a new edition or reproduction of that of Aristotle—an attempt to restrict the science even farther than the latter did—to wit, within the sphere of mere classification. Mr. Mill has, in fact and form, endeavoured to invalidate the principle of contradiction, and the apprehended necessary connection between the subject and predicate in a given judgment as a test of truth. 'It must be granted,' he says, 'that in every syllogism, considered as an argument to prove the conclusion, there is a *petitio principii*. All inference,' he adds, 'is from particulars to particulars; general propositions are merely registers of such inferences already made and short formula for making more. The major premise of a syllogism, consequently, is of this description; and the conclusion is not an inference drawn *from* the formula, but an inference drawn *according to* the formula—the real logical antecedent, or premise, being the particular facts from which the general proposition was collected by induction.'

We are, then, to understand Mr. Mill to affirm that all his deductions, in his extensive criticisms on the doctrines of Sir William Hamilton, are simply and exclusively begged, and have no other basis than mere sophistry. We must also draw the same conclusion, in regard to his doctrine, that 'all inference is from particulars to particulars,' and affirm that what we have here is only another flagrant example of *petitio principii* —'a short formula for making more' baseless deductions of the same kind. We breathe quite freely when we take up a work of formidable dimensions, and which seems to lead only in the direction of fundamental error, to know that in the judgment of the author himself, in every inference deduced in it, 'there is a *petitio principii*,' one of the most vicious forms of sophistry known to the science of Logic.

In the interests of a certain hypothesis, pertaining to universal being and its laws, Mr. Mill has endeavoured to reduce all the self-evident, universal, and necessary principles which lie at the basis of all the sciences in common to mere general contingent judgments obtained by abstracting the elements common to certain particular facts in accordance with the example pertaining to medicine given by Aristotle. We believe, for example, that things equal to the same things are equal to one another, not because we perceive any necessary connection between the subject and predicate in such propositions, but because that, in many particular instances, we have first compared a given object—a yard stick, for example, with two others, and finding it equal to each, we have then brought the objects (tables in this case) together and found them to be equal to one another. We repeat such experiments for a given number of times, and always with the same result. We register these results in our thoughts as 'short formulas for making more,' that is, to guide us in judging in regard to what *may* be true in other cases. If we reason from the formula, things equal to the same things are equal to one another, as a valid principle in science, we reason falsely, involving ourselves in the vicious sophistry of *petitio principii*, or begging the question. So of all the axioms and postulates in all the sciences. As convenient formulas, having no other basis than connections which we have found to exist in particular cases of observation, they have their use. When regarded as valid principles in science, they are utterly fallacious, and deflect the mind from the track of truth. Now Mr. Mill, and all the race who know anything at all, can but know that he has here given an utterly false exposition of the necessary procedures of the Intelligence. Take, as an example, the case which we stated, and let it be presented in logical form. Things equal to the same thing are equal to one another. The two tables designated are each in length equal to that of the same yardstick. Therefore 'these tables are, in length, equal to one another. Mr. Mill and all the universe of intelligent beings know, and cannot but know, that every such inference has absolute scientific validity, that it is, in fact and form, 'drawn *from* the formula,' and not '*according to* the formula.' The same holds true of all inferences in all valid sciences. They all have their ultimate basis in self-evident principles which do, and must, have universal and absolute validity. All such principles, we repeat what we have often said before, represent, not what appears intrinsically in mere facts, but necessary relations intuitively perceived to exist between real facts and realities implied by said facts.

The exigencies of Mr. Mill's hypothesis of being and its laws require us to admit facts to be *real*, but to affirm that they imply nothing, and, consequently, that nothing but mere facts do exist. Now we know not only that facts are real, but that they do and must imply the existence of other realities also. We know body, succession, events, and phenomena to be real, and we know, with the same absoluteness, that these verities do and must imply the reality of space, time, cause, and substance. As a necessary consequence we know that the principles, Body implies space; Succession, time; Events, cause; Phenomena, substance; Things equal to the same things are equal to one another, and, It is impossible for the same thing at the same time to exist and not exist, etc., have absolute validity for truth, and do constitute a valid basis for real scientific deduction. We know, also, that when 'inferences are drawn *from* such formulas,' we have no *petitio principii.*

ARISTOTLE'S FORMULA PERTAINING TO THE ORIGIN, SOURCE, AND CONSEQUENT ELEMENTS, OF ALL OUR KNOWLEDGE.

Aristotle is affirmed by many to have furnished for all ages the fixed formula of the doctrine of Materialism, a formula which we have never found but in its Latin form, to wit, 'Nihil in intellectu non prior in sensu.' When combating the doctrine of Plato, that all knowledge having absolute validity is through Reason, Aristotle might very naturally have affirmed the opposite doctrine, that all real knowledge is through Sensation, and that the elements of all ideas in the Intelligence were originally derived from this one source. If he did give utterance to such a formula, it is undeniable that he held it only as a general, and not universal truth; for he himself admitted the distinction between contingent and necessary ideas, and affirmed the reality of forms of being which are not objects of sense-perception, the soul and God, for example. Whether he was, or was not, the author of this formula, we shall not undertake to decide. As we here meet with it for the first time, and as it has constituted, in fact and form, the basis and principle of

Materialism in all subsequent ages, we shall give it a fundamental examination.

The argument of Materialism based upon this formula, as set forth by Condilac, and all other Materialists, is this. The origin and source of all our knowledge is Sensation. The object and cause of Sensation must be matter. Matter, therefore, and it only, really exists. No philosopher ever set forth the Materialistic argument in any other essential, or stronger form than this. Let us give this argument a full and careful examination.

We grant the reality of Sensation, and of its object and cause as having real extension and form, and, consequently, the real existence of matter. Here, however, the argument, in this direction, comes to a final determination. Matter is real. This is undeniable, and this is all the deduction that the fact of Sensation does or can yield us. We have, as yet, found no basis whatever for the deduction, that nothing but matter exists, and here we meet with the infinite logical leap of Materialism. Matter does exist; therefore, nothing but matter has being. Can any philosopher show us the connection between premise and conclusion in this case? John does exist. Therefore, Thomas does not exist. The Materialist is welcome to hang his system upon such Logic as this, and he can find nothing else upon which to hang his deduction.

But the Materialist replies, we *know* that matter does exist, and do not know that anything else is real. We must, therefore, exclude from our theory of existence, all but the known, and, therefore, assume matter to be the only reality. Let us consider the argument from this standpoint. Sensation exists—that is granted on all sides. Now, Sensation implies a *subject*, as well as *object and cause*, and the nature of this *subject* must be as that of its phenomenon, Sensation. Sensation, as a perception, or sensitive state, has, undeniably, neither length, breadth, weight, nor colour, and does not permit us to affirm either of its subject. Feeling has no likeness whatever to extension and form. We have before us, then, two distinct and separate entities—the subject of Sensation—and its object and cause. The one entity is as undeniably real as the other, and between the two, not a single common quality can be found. Science, therefore, absolutely prohibits our attributing to them a common nature.

The argument, however, does not stop here. Sensation not only exists, but exists as a *known* fact. Were it not so, we could not reason about sensation as a fact, or about a subject, or its object and cause. Sensation, and the knowledge of the same, undeniably pertain to the one and the same subject, and imply in that subject a power of valid self-knowledge on the one hand, and a susceptibility of feeling, on the other. Thus, at a still greater, and more unapproachable remove from each other, do the subject of Sensation and its object and cause appear.

But this is not all. As this knowing subject reflects upon the self and the not-self, new forms of thought appear upon the theatre of consciousness, and these thoughts induce new feelings unlike Sensation. Thus, there is revealed in this subject new capacities for knowledge, and a great deep of emotive sensibilities in its inner being. In the midst of these new thoughts and emotions, other and still more mysterious phenomena present themselves—those of free activity; and mind, at length, stands revealed to itself as a self-conscious personality endowed with the powers of thought, feeling, and voluntary determination, a personality existing, not only amid material forms, but other verities infinite and eternal. Now, these phenomena of thought, emotion, and free-determination, are just as real as Sensation itself, and the powers which they imply are just as real as are the object and cause of Sensation. When we compare the phenomena of the object and cause of Sensation with those of its subject, we find nothing whatever in common between them, nothing by which we can identify them as having a common nature, but everything to distinguish and separate them the one from the other. We must fundamentally violate all the known and conceivable laws of scientific induction and deduction, before we can identify mind and matter. That is, undeniably, a one-eyed Philosophy, and a blear-eyed Philosophy at that, which, in the presence of Sensation, inquires only for its object and cause, and having found that, affirms dead matter to be the only reality. For the same reason, that, also, is a one-eyed and a blear-eyed Philosophy, which in the presence of the same phenomenon, Sensation, looks only in the direction of the subject, and finding that to be spiritual, affirms that nothing is real but mind, or its operation.

Aristotle's Ethics.

In the department of Ethics the world owes very little to Aristotle. When all forms of activity are judged of from the single standpoint of their perceived adaptation to promote the most perfect happiness, we need the power of omniscience to determine specifically for ourselves what we ought to be and what we ought to do. When, therefore, he affirms that moral virtue consists 'in a perfect practical activity in a perfect life,' we are, in fact, no more morally instructed than we were before. Equally in the dark are we, as far as all morally practical purposes are concerned, when he tells us that the good 'is the end towards which nature tends.' Moral virtue, according to Socrates and Plato, is a science, revealing a standard of duty and rules for moral conduct which can be understood and defined. Moral virtue with Aristotle is an art, 'the habit of deliberately choosing, existing as a mean which refers to us, and is defined by Reason, and, as a prudent man would define it, is a mean between two evils, the one consisting in excess, the other in defect; and further, it is a mean in that one of these falls short of, and the other exceeds, what is right both in passion and actions; and that virtue both finds and chooses the mean.' It is an interesting fact, and one to be deeply pondered, that those who teach that actions are right and wrong in themselves, and that duty is to be respected for its own sake, give us more intelligible, safer, and more perfect rules of moral character and conduct than those who contemplate the subject from the Aristotelian standpoint. While we differ totally from Kant in the sphere of Philosophy, we are compelled to regard him as a far more correct and safer expounder of moral principles than Paley.

'THE FIRST PHILOSOPHY,' OR METAPHYSICS OF ARISTOTLE.

Aristotle believed in and taught the doctrine of the real existence of matter, the human soul, and God. In these general doctrines he agreed with Socrates and Plato. Matter, unorganized, exists merely as a passive susceptibility of being organized into forms. Of the human soul, as an Intelligence, and capable of virtue and vice, he speaks with perfect definiteness. Of the doctrine of the immortality of the soul he says but little, and teaches nothing with special definiteness, though he never denies the doctrine, but seems to accept it as a well-known truth. In respect to the doctrine of future retribution, we are able to discover nothing upon the subject in any of his recorded teachings. His avowed perturbation and prayer for mercy, however, as he approached eternity, clearly evince his intuitive belief in all these doctrines. So far, therefore, he may be safely affirmed to have substantially agreed with the two individuals above named.

In theology Aristotle in one respect differed in the direction of truth from Plato. The latter, as we have seen, was an intense Polytheist. While Aristotle does but incidentally recognize a plurality of Gods, the manifest tendency of his leading doctrines was the overthrow of Polytheism. It was probably for this, as one of the reasons, that he fled from Athens, after having presided with such wondrous success over the Lyceum for the space of twelve years.

In his teachings pertaining to the doctrine of the Supreme God, Aristotle, and that in the direction of fundamental error, differed not only from Plato, but from all other thinkers who believe in the existence of a material universe as a creation of God. In Himself Plato held that the Most High is a free activity, capable of self-originated action. The organization of the universe, as an event of time, was the result of the free act, creative fiat of God. According to Aristotle, God eternally exists as infinite, and all-perfect, and necessary, inactivity, 'the motionless cause of motion,' a being absolutely perfect, and happy, and yet utterly void of moral attributes. 'All moral virtues,' he says, 'are utterly unworthy of being ascribed to God.' Aristotle divides existences into three classes, that which is perpetually moved, that which moves and is moved, and that which moves all things and remains itself unmoved.' This unmoved and 'motionless cause of motion' is God. 'God,' he says, 'is absolutely spirit, which thinks itself, and whose thought is therefore the thought of thought. His agency as the cause of motion is not active and formative, but passive, for it remains itself unmoved.'

Aristotle's Proof of the Divine Existence.

Aristotle presents the argument for the being of God in what he regards as the scientific, on the one hand, and the popular form on the other. To him, in presenting the argument in the first form, the world is indebted for such proof in three distinct forms, the Ontological, Cosmological, and Teleological forms, kinds of proof which yet have place in Theistic teachings, as the only grounds of valid proof, although Kant has absolutely demonstrated them, each in succession as possessing by itself no scientific validity. From the nature of the case there can be but one form of valid proof in regard to causes, proximate or ultimate. We must first find a principle, or principles, which, of necessity, imply the being of God as the creator of the universe provided the facts of nature, material and mental, take rank under said principle, or principles. Here we have our major premise, or premises, in this argument. It must then be demonstrated, as the minor premise, that said facts do come under said principle or principles. The Theistic deduction then takes rank as a demonstrated truth of science. In this one form alone can the deduction have validity with logical thinkers. As long as the argument is presented in the Aristotelian form, it will not only fail to convince sceptical minds, but will be regarded as resting upon a basis, the invalidity of which has been fully evinced.

For the argument of Aristotle in the popular form, the argument as translated into our language, we are indebted to the translator of Ueberweg's 'History of Philosophy': 'Imagine men who have always dwelt beneath the earth in good and well-illuminated habitations, habitations adorned with statues and paintings, and well-furnished with everything which is usually at the command of those who are deemed fortunate. Suppose these never to have come up to the surface of the earth, but to have gathered from an obscure legend that a Deity and divine powers exist. If the earth were once to be opened for these men, so that they could ascend out of their concealed abodes to regions inhabited by us, and if they were to step forth and readily see before them the earth, and the sea, and skies, and perceive the movements of the clouds and the violence of the winds; and if then they were to look up at the sun and become cognizant of its magnitude and of its workings, that he is the author of day, in that he sheds his light over the entire universe; and if afterwards, when night had overshadowed the earth, they were to see the whole sky beset and adorned with stars, and should contemplate the changing light of the moon in its increase and decrease, the rising and setting of all the heavenly bodies, and their course to all eternity invariable and unalterable; truly, they would then believe that gods really exist, and that these mighty works originate with them.'

In his scientific argument, Aristotle refers only to the one Supreme God. In his popular argument, no doubt in accommodation to public opinion, he employed the term God in the plural form. The theology of Aristotle, as well as his moral teachings, are strictly non-religious. God is represented as an infinite and perfect passivity. 'A necessary being,' and, by virtue of such necessity, 'the all-perfect being,' who creates and governs by a necessary law of his eternal and immutable nature. Being all-sufficient in himself, and dwelling eternally alone within the circle of his own 'thought of thought,' he is above all moral action, and without moral attributes, and unmoved by human weal or woe. Even inferior gods, if they exist at all, are without moral attributes. 'What moral actions,' he asks, 'can we attribute to them?' In his Ethics, consequently, no reference is had to piety as a moral virtue. As God has no care of man, man owes no worship or service to God. Nor is moral virtue any very serious concern with Aristotle; the happiness which arises from it, he tells us, 'occupies the second place in regard to happiness.' 'Moral virtue,' he adds, 'even seems, in some points, to be the consequence of our corporeal nature, and in many to be intimately connected with the passions.' 'Happiness, in its highest form, results from the exercise of pure thought. In giving ourselves up to thought, we are not only most happy, but most pleasing to the gods, if, indeed, they have any regard for man.' Such are the express teachings of this philosopher in Book x., ch. 8, of his Ethics.

As he consciously neared eternity, however, his philosophy failed him, and the acts of a sinful life, and the facts of his moral consciousness, became realities to his mind, and now he prayed. It is no uncommon event for philosophers to be godless in their philosophy, but like other men when the moral acts of their lives, and the facts of their moral consciousness, force themselves upon their minds.

EVIDENCE OF THE BEING, PERFECTIONS, AND PROVIDENCE OF A PERSONAL GOD, AS DEDUCIBLE FROM THE PLATONIC, ARISTOTELIAN, AND THE ONLY OTHER CONCEIVABLE STANDPOINT.

Plato held and taught the doctrine of creation proper, that is, the organization of the universe as an event of time. Aristotle, on the other hand, affirmed the eternity of the present order of things. There remains but one other conceivable hypothesis, that of an eternal succession of dissolutions and reorganizations, the present organization being the last of the infinite series. Whichever of these hypotheses may be true, the ultimate cause of the series of past and present events must, undeniably, be an inhering law of nature itself or a cause *ab extra*—the agency of a personal God—there being no third conceivable hypothesis of ultimate causation. We propose to present the evidence of the being of God, first, from a general view of the facts of nature, without reference to the question which of the three hypothesis above designated is true, and second, as deducible from each of these hypotheses.

Argument in the most general form.

Contemplating the subject in its most general aspects, without reference to the question which of the three hypotheses above designated is true, the following considerations present themselves as having a fundamental bearing upon our present inquiries.

1. The doctrine of ultimate causation, through inhering, or Natural, Law, can on no conditions, actual or conceivable, be *proven true*. No one will claim for this doctrine self-evident validity, nor can a single fact be adduced which is not just as obviously and undeniably explicable upon the Theistic hypothesis as upon the one under consideration. If we cannot prove 'that the worlds were made by the Word of God,' no man can prove that they were originated by Natural Law. If order or facts of any kind are explicable by Natural Law, they are, undeniably, equally explicable on the opposite hypothesis.

2. For the reasons already stated, no form or degree of *positive* evidence can be adduced in favour of the doctrine of ultimate causation by Natural Law. All facts of every kind being just as explicable on the opposite hypothesis as upon this, the possibility of any positive evidence being adduced in favour of the latter hypothesis, as against the other, is absolutely excluded.

3. Nor can there be shown to exist any degree of *antecedent probability* in favour of this doctrine of Natural Law as opposed to the opposite hypothesis. To claim nothing more in this connection, it is just as antecedently probable that universal order is the result of intelligent foresight and design, as of blind and unconscious Natural Law.

4. The deduction is undeniable that the hypothesis of Natural Law, when held or asserted as a positive truth, has no other basis than mere naked assumption not self-evidently true, which is wholly unsusceptible of being proved true, and in favour of which no form or degree of positive evidence or antecedent probability can be adduced, an assumption which cannot be held as such a truth without a palpable violation of

the immutable demands of science. In no other respect is the demand of science more absolute than it is in requiring for all positive opinions a strictly positive basis. We have here demonstrative evidence that Antitheism, in none of its forms, has any other basis than lawless assumption.

5. In favour of the Theistic Hypothesis, on the other hand, we have, first of all, the intuitive convictions of the race. The truth of this statement has been fully evinced in our former discussions. Here is positive evidence which demands the implicit faith of the race. Anti-theism impeached this intuitive conviction or faith of the race, and must verify that impeachment by absolute proof, which, as we have shown, is impossible, or itself stand convicted of holding positive opinion without evidence, on the one hand, and of fundamental error on the other.

6. This universal and intuitive faith is also verified by proof of the most absolute kind. The formula of La Place cannot be disproved or reasonably doubted, that in view of the nature of the order which pervades the universe, the probability stands as infinity to unity in favour of the hypothesis of Theism as opposed to that of Natural Law. This order accords throughout with laws and principles of Pure Intelligence. The order in nature, also, is throughout a wisely adjusted system of means and ends, the wants of rational mind being the end, and all other adjustments sustaining the visible relation of a means. Nor can anyone wisely study the mechanism of the universe without perceiving that one of the chief ends of universal order is the *scientific education* of rational mind. When, also, we profoundly study the principles, laws, and instinctive wants of the higher departments of our rational and moral nature, it becomes demonstrably evident that rational mind is immutably constituted as the fixed correlate to one exclusive idea of Ultimate Causation, that of an infinite and perfect personal God. When we worship, pray to, seek the fellowship of, and order all our activity with reference to, the will of such a Being, we act in as absolute conscious harmony with the immutable demands of our rational, moral, and spiritual nature, just as we accord with the laws of our physical nature in seeking food and raiment. Throughout all departments of nature, also, this principle holds universally, that for every want of sentient existence there is a corresponding provision, and for every essential adaptation a corresponding sphere of activity. Now, rational mind is no more the fixed correlate to the social principle than it is to the ideas of God, duty, immortality, and retribution. Universal nature, the universe, and rational mind especially, are a lie, or order—the order visible before us—is the result of the creative and controlling agency of a personal God. Such is the necessary deduction from the most general standpoint from which the subject before us may be contemplated. We have before us two utterly incompatible

hypotheses, one of which *must* be true, and the other false. In favour of one, no form or degree of proof, positive evidence, or antecedent probability, can be adduced. In favour of the other, we have all the forms of proof, positive evidence, and antecedent and deductive probability which any question of causation, proximate or ultimate, admits of.

The Argument as Deducible from the Platonic Standpoint.

The doctrine of Plato, as we have before stated, is that of creation as an event occurring in time. If we grant the validity of this hypothesis, the Theistic argument assumes a character in the strictest sense demonstrative. Ultimate causation by Natural Law, implies, of necessity, either the eternity of the present order of things, or an eternal succession of organizations and dissolutions. A cause acting from necessity, must act as soon as the conditions of its activity are fulfilled. The conditions of ultimate causation must have been fulfilled from eternity, or that which fulfilled these conditions, and not the cause referred to, would be ultimate. A necessary cause, with the conditions of its activity fulfilled from eternity, must have acted from eternity. Creation through Natural Law, and such creation as an event of time, is inconceivable and impossible. In other words, creation as an event of time, implies, as its ultimate cause, a free, self-conscious Intelligence. No deduction can have more demonstrative certainty than this.

Such is the obvious character of the Theistic argument as deduced from the Platonic standpoint. If we should inquire for the validity of the doctrine of creation as an event of time, we should find that doctrine verified by evidence of the most conclusive character. Not a solitary fact of nature can be adduced in disproof of this doctrine, or which renders its validity doubtful. The validity of that doctrine, on the other hand, is affirmed by the intuitive convictions of the race, and by all the known facts and valid deductions of all the sciences bearing upon the subject. The statement of Locke that 'we have demonstrative proof of the being of God,' is capable of the fullest possible verification.

ARGUMENT FROM THE ARISTOTELIAN STANDPOINT.

The strict eternity of the present order of things was, as is well known, the fixed doctrine of Aristotle. Yet he also maintained that God is the eternal Author of this order which, as he affirmed, had no beginning, and will have no end. If we grant the validity of this hypothesis, no positive basis, as we have shown above, is thereby obtained for the doctrine of ultimate causation by Natural Law. For aught that appears in the facts, an eternal order may be the result of the agency of a personal God, as well as of any law, inhering, and acting potentially, in nature. In favour of the latter, and against the former hypothesis, not the remotest degree of valid proof, positive evidence, or even of antecedent probability, can by any possibility be adduced. In favour of the former hypothesis, on the other hand, we have all the positive evidence deducible from the intuitive convictions of the Universal Intelligence, the peculiar and special nature of the order to be accounted for, and from all the higher and most fundamental facts of the universe, the laws, principles, and fixed adaptations of the rational, moral, and spiritual nature of universal mind. In the presence of such evidence, no evidence at all, in any form, existing on the opposite side, the best that can be said of Anti-Theism, in any of its forms is, that it presents a palpable example of science run mad.

When we inquire for the evidence of the validity of this hypothesis of the eternity of the present order of things, we find not only no evidence at all, in any form, in its favour, but such palpable proof of an opposite character, that no respectable thinkers of any school now advocate said hypothesis. The universally admitted deduction of all the sciences bearing upon the subject is the non-eternity of the universe as now constituted. So far, the Theistic argument has the strictest demonstrative validity.

The Argument as Deducible from the only remaining Standpoint, no other Hypothesis being Conceivable.

It is undeniable, either that creation must have been an event of time or that the present order of things must have been eternal, or that the progress of nature must have been an eternal succession of organizations and dissolutions, universal order and absolute chaos being the two ultimates towards which all things have been eternally tending. Under this last and only remaining hypothesis, the Theistic argument becomes even more absolute in its validity, than when deduced from the Aristotelian standpoint. In both cases, the argument takes on the same identical form and force, with this difference, that, in the former case, the same argument is affirmed and re-affirmed, an infinite number of times. In both cases, we have the same absence of all proof, positive evidence, and antecedent probability, against the Theistic hypothesis, and in favour of that of Natural Law, and the same universal intuitive convictions and adamantine facts, material and mental, against the latter hypothesis, and in favour of the former.

In addition to all this, we have the same want of evidence on the one hand, and, on the other, the same form of proof repeated in each successive organization of the universe from eternity to the present time. Having no facts to reason from but those of the present order of things, and having no evidence to the contrary, we must suppose that each of these eternally successive organizations, supposing them to have occurred, must, in all essential particulars, have accorded with the present. We must, therefore, postulate an infinite number of universes, each in succession originated from a pre-existing chaos—each organized in strict accordance throughout with ideas and principles of pure science as they exist in self-conscious Intelligence—each organized exclusively as a system of means and ends, the wants of rational mind being the final end, and all else a means to that end—each organized in palpable conformity to one idea, the intellectual, moral, and spiritual education of rational mind—each peopled by an indefinite number of rational beings, all in common intuitively affirming a personal God, as the ultimate cause of this order, and all, in the higher intellectual, moral and spiritual departments of their nature, being immutably constituted as the exclusive correlates of the Theistic idea of ultimate causation—a universe, finally, in which there is, undeniably, for every essential want of sentient existence a corresponding provision, and for every essential adaptation of such creatures a corresponding sphere of action. Conceive of an infinite number of successive creations of this character, each originated from a pre-existing chaos, and the Theistic argument, with no evidence whatever in opposition to its claims, attains to a weight strictly infinite. To whichever of these three, the only conceivable standpoints, Anti-Theism turns itself, it is encountered with evidence absolutely destructive. Its condition is well represented by that of 'the man who fled from a lion and a bear met him, who went into the house and leaned his hand upon the wall, and a serpent bit him.' If we inquire for the proof of the validity of this last hypothesis, we find the total absence of all forms and degrees of evidence in its favour on the one hand, and the presence of the most absolute forms of disproof on the other. What is there, what can there be, in the idea of universal chaos, to justify the assumption of its origination from a previous state of universal order? Universal order, and universal chaos, are two distinct opposite and incompatible ultimates which have, and can have, no adaptation to produce, and reproduce, in eternal succession, one another. The hypothesis under consideration stands revealed, as a naked and lawless assumption, which is based upon no evidence of any kind.

On the other hand, this hypothesis is encountered by forms of disproof of the most absolute character. Nothing can be more slanderous upon the infinite and eternal Mind than the idea that He has been eternally employed as an organizer and disorganizer. The idea of such successive organizations and disorganizations by Natural Law, involves, undeniably, an infinite absurdity. It implies that Nature, acting eternally under the principle of necessity, fundamentally changes and reverses from time to time her own necessary laws. In a state of utter chaos, Nature, from necessity, acts under the law of universal order, and continues thus to act until order is 'the first law' of all things. Then she reverses this law, and acts under the law of universal disorganization, and so on from eternity to eternity. Further, when the worlds have been originated, and brought into a state adapted to sustain vital organizations, Nature now, by necessary laws, acts wholly as an *originator*, producing from the crude elements of matter the needful organizations. When this work of origination has proceeded to a needful extent, she reverses this law, and adopts that of *propagation* from pre-existing organizations. Finally, when, through propagation under the fixed law of *natural* and *sexual selection*, fishes have produced reptiles, reptiles mammals, monkeys men, she reverses this law also, and adopts, as her immutable principle, that in which vegetables, fishes, reptiles, monkeys, and men, all vital organizations in common, immutably produce their own kind. Such, undeniably, are the necessary procedures of Nature, according to the hypothesis of an eternal succession of creations and dissolutions by Natural Law. There is no sounding the depths of credulity and absurdity to which mind descends in the adoption of such an hypothesis as this. We oppose this and the Aristotelian hypothesis simply because they are false in fact, and not because they render the doctrine of Theism indefensible. From whatever standpoint it is argued that doctrine stands evinced, as an eternal verity 'which cannot be shaken.'

SECTION IV.

THE EPICUREANS.

EPICURUS (341—270 B.C.), a pupil of Nausiphanes, a Democritean, after having taught Philosophy in Mitylene and Lampsacus, finally, when about thirty-five years of age, founded in Athens a school over which he presided until his death. Under his teaching Materialism, and with it Atheism, was so fully systematized and perfected in form and development, that in subsequent ages Epicureanism became a representative term designating Materialism, both in its ontological and moral deductions. Having assumed matter to be the only existing substance, he rigidly adhered to and systematized the deductions which necessarily follow from that assumption. He not only repudiated the Polytheism of his age, but denied the existence of a Supreme God, and all forms of the supernatural in Nature. The term 'pleasure' represents the entire morality of Epicureanism, the only moral problem which the system presented for solution being the single question, What form of activity will ensure for the individual in this life the greatest amount of sensitive enjoyment?—in other words, the greatest amount of pleasurable sensations. In our remarks upon the system of Leucippus and Democritus, we have anticipated most that need to be said as expository of that of Epicurus.

We shall, therefore, confine our remarks in explaining the latter system to a few of its special features—the explanation of which may conduce to the end we are seeking, a full understanding of the true and proper principles of philosophic induction and deduction.

Perceived and Implied Forms of Knowledge.

Epicurus seems to have been the first ancient thinker who clearly apprehended the distinction and relations between perceived and implied forms of knowledge, and, in fact and form, applied the principle in the sphere of the science of Ontology. His first principle was, that body implies space. If what we call vacuum, or space, did not exist, he argued, 'there would be nothing in which bodies could exist and move.' Bodies do, in fact, exist and move. There *must*, consequently, be space. The idea of space, also, is always connected in thought, and necessarily so, with the apprehension that it is, and must be, infinite. Body, which is finite, does imply space, but not infinite space. In its own nature, however, space is, and must be, infinite, and is necessarily thus represented in thought.

The second form in which Epicurus presented the principle of the necessary relations of perceived and implied knowledge, is this—the compound implies the simple. Body, as perceived, is an aggregate, a compound. If the simple was not real, the aggregate, or compound, could not exist. The aggregate, which is perceived, is real. The simple, or atoms, which are not perceived, must therefore exist. Thus reasoned this acute thinker, and so far his reasoning has absolute validity. If he had rigidly adhered to his own principle of reasoning from the perceived to the realities implied by what is perceived, he would now stand before the world, not as the representative of fundamental error both in morals and Ontology, but as a central light in the firmament of true science. He would have perceived not only that body implied space, and the compound the simple, but that phenomena imply substance, and perception a subject as well as an object; and that the phenomena of the subject and object, being fundamentally unlike one another, imply the actual existence of two distinct and dissimilar substances, matter and spirit. He would thus have apprehended as actually existing four instead of two realities. He would have recognized as real, not merely atoms and space, but spirit and matter, and time and space, and the facts of the universe as necessarily implying, as their ultimate cause, the agency of an infinite and perfect personal God. With matter as atoms and with space, however, Epicurus stopped, and, consequently, with other errorists, built up his theory of existence and its laws upon a partial induction of actual facts.

Test of Valid Knowledge.

One of the fundamental aims of Epicurus was to vindicate for perception an absolute validity for the reality and character of its object, matter. His argument on this point was based upon the undeniable principle that the burden of proof lies with those who impeach the validity of our knowledge of 'things without us,' and that this knowledge must be held as valid until its invalidity has been fully demonstrated. Science knows no sounder principle than this. The validity of our knowledge, he argued, cannot be disproved. Perception can be proved false but by other perceptions or by Reason. To suppose that perception can invalidate itself is self-contradictory. To suppose that this can be done by Reason, is to suppose that forms of implied knowledge can contradict and invalidate that by which they are implied, and from which they borrow all their authority. Such, in fact and form, is the substance of the reasoning of Epicurus on this point. 'No perception,' he says, 'can be proved false whether by other perceptions (whose authority cannot be greater than that of the perception in question), or by Reason, which is simply an outgrowth of perceptions.' We may safely challenge the world to produce sounder arguments on any subject than this. We commend this argument to the serious consideration of Mr. Spencer and others who impeach the validity of Sense-perception. How, permit us to ask these gentlemen, can you sustain your impeachment? Undeniably, you cannot do this through perception itself. If this faculty is 'a liar from the beginning,' you cannot torture it into a confession of the fact. Nor will it furnish you data for its own conviction. If you appeal to consciousness, it, as we have shown, will simply give the facts of perception as they are in themselves, and then leave them to speak for themselves. If you apply to Reason, it will simply present you with the realities implied by the facts of perception, and will and can do nothing more. If you turn to the secondary faculties, they can and will do nothing more nor less than combine into conceptions and judgments, just as given, the elements furnished by the primary faculties, and leave these conceptions and judgments to speak, also, for themselves. Do what you will, you will find it absolutely impossible to bribe, even, any of the intellectual faculties to give a solitary utterance against the perfect integrity and validity of Sense-perception. If, as a last resort, you should affirm, that our conceptions of material forms are all self-contradictory, and therefore invalid, you would be at once confronted and contradicted by the most palpable facts. All our conceptions of material objects pertain, without exception, to said objects, as compounds constituted of simples, or aggregates constituted of atoms. No philosopher, however 'minute,' can discover, as we have demonstrated elsewhere, even the appearance of contradiction here. All the affirmed contradictions which Zeno and Kant, and Spencer and others, profess to find, exist, as we have also shown, in fictions of their own formation, and not at all in our world-conceptions, as they actually exist in the Universal Intelligence. To *prove* perception false is, therefore, an absolute impossibility. The deduction, that it is, or can be, false, can have place in the human mind, but as a sentiment of will, that is, through 'an act of (assumed) scientific scepticism, to which the mind voluntarily determines itself,' and thus 'compels itself to *treat* as nothing but a prejudice, innate indeed and connatural, yet nothing but a prejudice,' 'the intuitive, unavoidable and irradicable faith,' of the race in 'the reality of things without us.' Here, however, we meet with mere assumption, and proof in no form. The validity of the deduction is absolute that the faculty of Sense-perception cannot be proven false, or shown to be self-evidently so, and that all impeachments of its validity have, and can have, no other basis than mere lawless assumptions.

Epicurus undeniably started upon the track of truth, and demonstrated the fact that he did so. Had he continued true to his own method of induction and deduction, he would have been of the most renowned world-thinkers the race has ever known. Failing to do this, his name is, as we have said, synonymous with error in its worst form, and even the name of the garden in which his celebrated school was held, the garden then called a sty, now represents the filthiest spot known on earth. 'A lie that is half a truth is often the blackest of lies.' So, the most 'disastrous twilight' known to human thought is 'shed over' the mind by those forms of error in which half-truths are imposed upon the world as the sum and substance of all that is real.

The General Psychology of Epicurus.

Epicurus clearly recognized in the human mind three distinct general faculties: Intellect—Sensibility—and Will. In respect to the nature of the faculty last named, his school differed fundamentally from all other Materialistic schools, ancient and modern. To the Will he distinctly attributed the power of free, in opposition to necessitated, choice and activity, and as definitely based moral obligation upon such power of choice. 'Virtue,' he taught (we quote from Mr. Lewes), 'rests upon Free Will and Reason, which are inseparable; since, without Free Will our Reason would be passive, and without Reason our Free Will would be blind. Everything, therefore, in human actions which is virtuous or vicious depends on man's *knowing and willing*. Philosophical education consists in accustoming the mind to judge accurately, and the Will to choose manfully.' The doctrine of Epicurus, as expressed by himself, and attributed to him by Cicero and Diogenes Laertius, is thus summarily stated by Ueberweg: 'There is no fate in the world. That which depends on us is not subject to the influence of any external power, and it is our power of free self-determination which makes us proper subjects of praise and blame.'

So far, also, we find our philosopher moving upon the track of truth, and revealing himself as a very profound analyzer of the facts of Consciousness. In his doctrine of the *nature* of the soul, however, the central error of his whole system makes its appearance. The soul, he taught, is distinct from the body, but yet material, and constituted of a combination of atoms, 'exceedingly diminutive, smooth, and round, and connected with or diffused through the veins, viscera, and nerves.' The combination of such particles, he admits, is ' not adequate to generate sensible motions (sensations), such as evolve any thoughts in the mind.' A certain fourth nature or substance must, therefore, necessarily be added to these that is wholly without a name; 'it is a substance, however, than which nothing exists more active or more subtle, nor is anything more essentially composed of small and smooth elementary particles, and it is this substance which first distributes sensible motions through the members.' If our philosopher had been asked the question how he knew that this 'fourth nature or substance,' 'that is wholly without a name,' is material at all, he would have at once found himself in the same 'paradise of fools' in which all Materialists find themselves when confronted with similar inquiries. We must admit the mind to be possessed of the powers of Thought, Feeling, and Free Will, or impeach the integrity and validity of the Universal Consciousness; and no man but a very great philosopher can conceive and digest in his own mind, and then seriously propound to the faith of mankind, such a monstrous absurdity as is involved in the dogma that thought, feeling, and Free Will can exist as properties of such a thing as matter. Why a material aggregate, constituted of 'round, small, and smooth particles,' and it alone, must possess the powers of thought, feeling, and Free Will, Epicurus has failed to inform us, just as our modern Materialists—the advocates of the New Philosophy—fail to explain to us *how* and *why* matter, in any form, exercises all mental functions, and *how* and *why* the existence of a monkey accounts for the origin of man. Nothing but will-power can solve such problems.

Epicurean Doctrine of Creation.

Two, and only two realities, according to Epicurus, namely, matter and space, exist. With this assumption he connected the doctrine that no new form of being can be originated, nor any existing substance be annihilated. The first principle he designates in two forms—to wit, 'Nothing which once was not can ever of itself come into being,' and 'nothing is ever *divinely* generated from nothing.' The second principle he thus announces: 'The universal whole was always such as it now is, and always will be such.' The term 'universal whole,' here refers, not to the universe as now organized, but to the original elements of which it is constituted.

The primal state of matter was a chaos—an infinite number of atoms diffused through infinite space. The only qualities possessed by atoms are form, magnitude, and density, of which qualities each one is possessed in degrees diverse from all others. The world-problem presented was this. Matter, as a chaos of atoms, and infinite space being given, to account from such data for the organization of the universe, as we now find it. Undeniably, the cause of this organization cannot be found in space, that being mere vacuum, and no cause in any sense. Nor can this cause be any power exterior to matter—matter by hypothesis being the only existing substance. From 'the faultiness' which he perceived to exist in the universe, he affirmed that 'it cannot be the work of a divine power.' The cause, then, of the organization of the universe must be found in the nature and relations of the atoms themselves. The following is the Epicurean exposition of the great fact before us.

If atoms infinite in number were diffused through infinite space, and in a state of rest, no one particle touching any other, organization would be impossible. If the contact of the atoms was eternal, the consequent organization of the universe would be from eternity, and not an event of time, as palpable facts affirm it to have been. These atoms must have been, from eternity, in a state of motion, and their contact, one with another, an event of time. If motion were from eternity, and the atoms moved in converging lines, or the motion of certain particles was more rapid than others, and thus their contact, as affirmed by Democritus and others, was occasioned, such contact and the consequent organization must have been from eternity. Every such hypothesis, therefore, must be abandoned. So reasoned Epicureans. How, then, can motion be eternal, and the consequent organization be an event of time? The following are, as we showed in another connection, the Epicurean solutions of this problem. All atoms, by virtue of their own weight, had, from eternity, a downward motion, and all moved with the same rapidity and in parallel lines. At an unknown period of the past, there was a spontaneous deflection of certain atoms from the lines on which they had been moving from eternity. Thus one particle impinged against others, and thus were produced 'movements from high to low, from low to high, and horizontal movements to and fro, in virtue of this reciprocal percussion.' Thus the universe was organized, and finally peopled, as we now find it.

A fundamental difficulty in this exposition soon suggested itself to Grecian thought. How could atoms, moving under a necessary law of motion, and having moved so from eternity, spontaneously, and of their own accord, change the direction of that motion? To avoid this difficulty, a power of free activity, which undeniably belongs to the human mind, which was assumed to be material, was attributed to all matter. The deflection, and consequent collision of particles referred to, was occasioned by voluntary acts on the part of certain atoms. 'The system of Nature,' says Lucretius, 'immediately appears as a free agent, released from tyrant masters, to do everything of itself spontaneously, without the help of the Gods.' If the reasoning from man to matter in all its forms, the form of reasoning adopted by Epicurus and his followers, has validity as far as the power of free activity is concerned, then all matter must be possessed, not only of Free Will, but also of Intelligence and Sensibility. We do not see how this conclusion can be avoided. We thus, as in all 'the twistings and turnings' of error, find ourselves freed from one difficulty by being shoved into another infinitely greater. Thus the materialistic world-problem, unsolved, and to all appearance of impossible solution, is handed over for solution to the advocates of 'the New Philosophy.' The problem handed down to them is plainly this: Matter and space, and duration, if you please, being given as being alone real, to demonstrate the validity of the doctrine of the absolute eternity of the present order of things, or to account for the organization of the universe as an event of time. We honestly believe that not one of them will even attempt the solution of this problem in either of these forms; that its solution in any form from the materialistic standpoint is impossible. On the other hand, when pressed with the difficulties of their system, and confronted with their own problem, they will, unquestionably, as we have formerly stated, after boldly asserting matter to be the only real substance, and affirming themselves able to demonstrate for life, and thought, and activity in all its forms, an exclusively 'physical basis,' they will finally dodge all real issues by affirming that 'it is certain that we can have no knowledge of the nature of matter and spirit.' What will they do, we ask, when it shall become demonstrably evident that, while the Sceptical hypothesis cannot be defended, the facts of the universe, as actually given by the Universal Intelligence, are equally inexplicable both from the Materialistic and Idealistic standpoint? They will, no doubt, continue, first of all, to dogmatize, as knowing all things, and, finally, 'when sorely pressed,' will dodge all issues by affirming an absolute and hopeless ignorance of all realities about which they have been so proudly dogmatizing, and that in the name of absolute science.

SECTION V.

THE STOICS.

ZENO (about 350—248 B.C.), born at Citium, a city of Cyprus, founded in the Stoa, or Porch, at Athens, a school over which he presided for quite half a century. This school took its name, Stoic, from the place where it was founded. The Stoics classed themselves among the followers of Socrates, though they differed from him in fundamental particulars. This school numbers among its teachers and disciples not a few thinkers of eminence, such as Zeno, its founder, Cleanthes and Chrysippus among the Greeks, and Seneca and Marcus Aurelius among the Romans.

Philosophy with the Stoics culminates in, and is ancillary to, morality. To understand their morality, however, we must know their Physics or Ontology. Here a difference of exposition obtains among those who have studied the teachings of the Stoics. That their doctrines were essentially Pantheistic all agree. But whether their Pantheism was in its nature Materialistic or Idealistic, here the highest authorities are at issue. Perhaps clear light will be shed upon this question as we proceed in our expositions.

CRITERIA OF TRUTH ACCORDING TO THE STOICS.

The Stoics and Epicureans were the thinkers who first made the question, by what criteria shall truth be distinguished from error, a fundamental problem in science. In the former school this problem had a wider place than in the latter. The question, what is the test of truth, Aristotle treated with contempt. With the Stoics and Epicureans, the former especially, and the Post-Aristotelians, this question was regarded as of fundamental interest. The Sceptics denied the validity of the intellectual faculties entirely. That error, in some form, had place in the human mind, all had to admit. The question, then, by what criteria shall we distinguish truth from error, became one of fundamental interest.

The test proposed by the Stoics was really identical with that set forth by Sir W. Hamilton, and that to which we have so often referred, to wit, Knowledge consciously direct and immediate, must be accepted as valid for the reality and character of its object. They designated this form of Knowledge by such phrases as 'certain and incontestable apprehension,' an apprehension by which the soul 'grasps the object of representation,' a representation 'impressed and sealed on the mind, and incapable of existing without the existence of the object.' 'In our perceptions of external objects, and also of internal states,' says Chrysippus, 'the originally vacant soul is filled with images, and as if with written characters.' In modern scientific language this criterion of valid knowledge may be thus expressed : *Knowledge, consciously direct and immediate, with all that it intuitively and deductively implies, must be accepted as having absolute validity for the existence and character of its objects.* The validity of this criterion, which the Stoics undeniably intended to express, has the same claims to scientific recognition that any other axiom has. Had the Stoics stated the criterion in this form, its validity could never have been doubted. In the light of this criterion we distinguish between our knowledge of the primary and secondary qualities of matter. Our knowledge of the latter qualities being consciously indirect and mediate, has only a relative, while that of the former, being consciously direct and immediate, has absolute validity for the reality and character of its objects. So far we find science in its most important form among the Stoics.

THE PHYSICS OF THE STOICS.

The doctrine of Physics, as taught by the Stoics, included both Cosmology and Theology. The criterion of truth which they have set forth implies, undeniably, their belief in the real existence of matter. Were they, in the strict and proper sense of the word, Materialists? As neither Zeno, nor his immediate successors, left any treatises of their own which have come down to us, we are necessitated to rely upon the fragmentary testimony of ancient authors who did know what were the real doctrines of this school. Schwegler, among the moderns, gives the following account of the doctrines of the Stoics : 'Matter is the passive ground of all things, the original substratum for the Divine activity. God is the active and formative energy of matter dwelling within it, and essentially united to it ; the world is the body of God, and God is the soul of the world. The Stoics, therefore, considered God and matter as one identical substance ; on the side of its passive changeable capacity they call it matter, and on the side of its active and changeless energy, God.' 'The Stoics,' says Ueberweg, the latest modern authority, 'teach that whatever is real is material. Matter and force are the two ultimate principles. Matter is, *per se*, motionless and unformed, though capable of receiving all motions and all forms. Force is the active, moving, and moulding principle. It is inseparably joined with matter. The working force in the universe is God.' While the justness of such representations of the views of the Stoics is questioned by other modern authorities of the highest order, by Dr. Cocker, for example, we have been wholly unable to obtain from them, or from any other source, any intelligible account of any system which the Stoics may be supposed to have held differing from that presented by the authors above referred to. The Stoics held, according to Cicero, as cited by Dr. Cocker to disprove the exposition of Schwegler, that all things are 'contained by one *Divine Spirit*,' that reason in man is 'nothing else but part of the *Divine Spirit* merged in a human body.' 'They say,' says Diogenes, as cited for the same purpose by the same author, 'that principles and elements differ from each other. Principles have no generation or beginning, and will have no end; but elements may be destroyed. Also, that elements have bodies, and have forms, but principles have no bodies and no forms.' To perceive the bearings of this passage, we must determine the meaning of the term 'Principles' as here employed. Principles may be conceived to exist independent of matter, and to act upon it as an exterior cause, or as inhering in it, and acting potentially as such an inhering cause. That the latter is the true meaning of this term in the passage before us seems quite plain from the following passage, cited also from Diogenes. 'God is a being of a certain quality, having for His peculiar manifestation universal substance. He is a being imperishable, and who never had any generation, being the Maker of the arrangement and order that we see; and who at certain periods of time absorbs all substance in Himself, and then reproduces it from Himself.' Matter, then, and God, as 'a being of certain quality,' must be one and identical. 'The Stoics,' says the same author in another place, 'defined the passive principle as unqualified substance, or matter, and the active principle as the reason immanent in matter, or Deity.' 'Chrysippus teaches,' says Plutarch, 'that at certain periods the whole world is resolved into fire, which fire is identical with the soul of the world, the governing principle, or Zeus; but at other times a part of this fire, a germ, as it were, detached from the whole mass, becomes changed into denser substance, and so leads to the existence of concrete objects distinct from Zeus.' Again, 'That part of Deity which goes forth from him for the formation of the world is called the *seminal reason* of the world, and is resolved into a plurality of *seminal reasons.*' We are compelled, therefore, to regard the Stoics as Pantheists of the Materialistic School, fire, and spirit, and principle being, with them, synonymous in their meaning. That they should speak of this omnipresent, all-formative, and all-controlling fire as having intelligence and other analogous attributes, accords with common usage among the ancients.

Some of the Special Doctrines of the Stoics.

Among the special doctrines of the Stoics we notice the following. The human soul they held to be an emanation from God, and destined to final absorption in Him. All souls, according to Cleanthes, exist until the general conflagration. Chrysippus affirmed that all but the wise perish, or are absorbed, at death. Others denied the future existence of all souls in common. The universe, they regarded as limited in extent, and Space and Time as infinite; in accordance with the modern exposition. All moral actions they held to be, of necessity, of an unmixed character. Every man, for the time being, is either perfectly virtuous or vicious. In this doctrine they agreed with Aristotle. Zeno divided men absolutely into two classes—the good, and the bad. The sage differed from Zeus but in non-essentials. Chrysippus, according to Plutarch, affirmed that 'Zeus is not superior to Dio in virtue, and both Zeus and Dio, in so far as they are wise, are equally profited the one by the other.' In opposition to the Epicureans, the Stoics affirmed the doctrine of universal fate. Evil actions were by some, as by Cleanthes, in his hymn to Jupiter, excepted in a certain undefined form from the law of absolute necessity, 'but that which is evil,' he adds, 'is overruled by thee for good, and is made to harmonize with the plan of the world.' Absolute fatalism, as controlling all events, and all actions human and divine, is the avowed doctrine of the school of Stoicism.

The Ethics of the Stoics.

The Summum Bonum, with the Aristotelians, is happiness; with the Epicureans, pleasure; and with the Stoics, virtue. In this doctrine the Stoics and Platonists agreed. They differed fundamentally, however, in respect to the doctrine of Free Will, and the consequent moral desert of human action. With the latter, the doctrine of moral obligation, moral desert and retribution, was prominent in all their teachings. While in the teachings of the former virtue has supreme prominence, obligation, desert, and retribution, have almost no place.

Moral virtue, as taught by the Stoics, took form from their ideas of the fatal necessity which absolutely controlled all events. All things *must* be as they are, and cannot in future but occur as predetermined by necessary law. The absolute consent of Will that all things shall be as they cannot but be, *that* is moral virtue, that is the absolute perfection of the sage. 'Endure,' 'endure,' 'this is the whole duty of man.' The universal formula of moral duty, Diogenes Laertius expresses in this form : 'Live conformably to Nature—that is, to Reason, or the will of the Universal Manager and Governor of all things.' 'Dare to lift thine eye to God, and say,' says Epictetus, '"Use me hereafter to whatever Thou pleasest, I agree, and am of the same mind with Thee, indifferent to all things."' To place all good in virtue, that is, in being stolidly 'indifferent to all things,' to regard pleasure and happiness as not real good, and pain as no evil—this is living according to nature. External objects were classed as things to be preferred, and things not to be preferred. 'As life belongs to things indifferent, suicide was permissible, as a rational means of terminating life.'

Among the teachings of the Stoics, a few utterances of such men as Marcus Aurelius excepted, we search in vain for any features or elements of moral virtue which correspond with the true or Christian idea. Indifference to what *may*, because it *must* occur, acquiescence in the Divine will, as a decree of 'fate which neither divinity nor humanity can change,' is one thing; and loving God with all our power, because He is love and first loved us, placing an infinite value upon our own and our neighbour's good, and for that reason loving him as ourselves, regarding pain as real evil, and seeking to remove all the remedial 'ills that flesh is heir to,' acquiescing in Providence because infallible Wisdom and perfect Love has determined our state—here are forms of real virtue to which Stoicism is an utter stranger, and which it has no tendency to induce. It is no matter of wonder that a long-continued attempt to conform, by a proud and self-reliant dint of will, to such a cold and soul-desolating ideal as Stoicism presented, rendered such minds as Zeno, Cleanthes, Cato and Seneca so intolerably weary of life, that they escaped from it by acts of suicide.

CHAPTER III.

THE DECLINE OF THE GRECIAN PHILOSOPHY.

INTRODUCTION.

SECTION I.
CAUSES OF THIS DECLINE.

WITH Plato, Aristotle, Epicurus, Zeno, the Stoics, and their immediate successors, Grecian Philosophy reached its consummation. With the disappearance of this constellation of great thinkers, the decline, or better, perhaps, the eclipse of this Philosophy, commenced—an eclipse which continuously grew more dim and deep until 'darkness all, and ever-during night,' seemed to surround the human mind. We know of but one expression which properly represents the state of philosophic thought, both in Greece and Rome, at the time when 'the Sun of Righteousness rose upon the earth with healing in His wings'—to wit, 'chaos has come again.' Under the teachings of false science Greece had lost her liberty, her forms of sober thought, and her morals. Under the same influence, associated with the pride of conquest and superabundant luxuries, Rome had descended to a state in which, in the impressive language of Tacitus, 'she could neither endure her vices, nor the remedy.'

If we should inquire for the cause of this decline, we should find it in the state in which the great problem of universal being and its laws was handed over by these thinkers to their successors. In the Academy, the Lyceum, the Garden, and the Porch, in each school, the problem under consideration was presented to the world as fully solved. Yet the solution presented by each was, in essential particulars, perfectly antagonistic to that presented by every other. The phase in which each school contemplated this problem, together with its method of induction and deduction, was, in important respects, special and peculiar. At the same time no generally recognized criteria were then known — criteria by which truth could be distinguished from error. Each school had its own exclusive method of induction and deduction, and its own peculiar and special tests of truth and error. Yet there seemed to be a necessary connection between the method and criteria of each school and its final deductions. In the then existing state of science the best thinkers found it very difficult, or impossible, to determine why the method or deductions of any one school should be regarded as less valid than those of any other. But one alternative seemed left for those who were seeking truth—an unqualified adoption of the exclusive system of one of those schools, and a repudiation of those of all the others—a procedure for which no even *apparently* good reasons could be offered—or a repudiation of all systems in common, and that by a general impeachment of the Intelligence itself as a faculty of knowledge—an impeachment seemingly sustained by many apparently valid reasons, as presented in these various schools. The Platonists, while they affirmed absolute validity for *à priori* insight through reason, utterly repudiated the validity of Sense-perception, and affirmed a mere 'bastard kind of knowledge' of matter. Aristotle, while he impeached, and for undeniably valid reasons, the validity of knowledge through Reason, as far as Platonic Ideas are concerned, affirmed that knowledge, in no form, is more certain than that obtained through Sense-perception. The Epicureans and Stoics, while they verified by criteria of undeniable validity the absolute truthfulness of knowledge through Sense-perception, denied utterly the validity of knowledge in all other forms. The same diversity and antagonism obtained relative to the teachings of these schools in respect to fundamental morality and the doctrine of the Summum Bonum. The Platonists and Stoics affirmed a necessary and immutable distinction between the right and the wrong, and, for morality, an immovable basis in the nature of things. The Aristotelians and Epicureans affirmed, for the right and the wrong, no other distinction, and for morals no other foundation, than what is found in a perceived tendency to insure happiness or misery, pleasure or pain. All these antagonistic hypotheses had advocates of the highest eminence, and were sustained by reasons of equally apparent validity. The only seeming alternative, we repeat, which remained for thinkers, was either to repudiate all hypotheses in common, and that by a denial of the possibility of valid knowledge, in any form, or to adopt some one exclusive system which was verified by no reasons of higher apparent validity than was each of the others. The Greek mind would not long remain in such a dilemma. Nor in human thought, in that era, did the idea obtain a place that all these schools were essentially right on the positive sides of their systems. Plato and Aristotle, for example, unitedly taught the fundamental distinction between spirit and matter, and the real existence of each form of being. The Epicureans and Stoics both verified, by undeniable criteria, the validity of Sense-perception for the reality of 'things without us.' Here we have the positive teachings of all these schools, and so far we find essential truth. Had these positive teachings been accepted, and with them the validity of the distinction between matter and spirit, and of our knowledge of the same, Philosophy would, from that time onward, not only have moved upon the track of truth, but would have permanently commanded the faith of mankind. Greek thought, however, naturally took the direction of Scepticism as its prevailing movement. Hence, in Greek and Roman thought, doubt became the prevailing faith of the schools especially. In addition to the above, which may be regarded as the chief causes of the decline of the Grecian Philosophy, other and incidental causes acted with great power to induce the same results. Among these incidental causes we would specify the following:

INCIDENTAL CAUSES OF THE DECLINE OF THE GRECIAN PHILOSOPHY.

1. One of the main causes which incidentally led to this decline, was the almost boundless sphere professedly occupied by Grecian philosophic thought in its different schools. In Grecian thought, in its positive forms, as we have before stated, there was no place for the mysterious. Universal being and its laws were, throughout all departments of real existence, knowable, and all its facts were equally explicable. The philosopher affirmed himself, and that before the world, possessed of universal knowledge in all these forms.

Plato, for example, professed to *know* that all forms of Sense-perception are illusory, and that all the realities thus apprehended are 'of the nature of that which is and is not,' and that matter, which he affirmed to be real, is the object of a mere 'bastard kind of knowledge.' At the same time, 'through Reason in an intuitive manner,' he professed himself possessed of a universal and absolute knowledge of 'being *per se*,' that is, of all that really exists, together with all its relations. In his multitudinous productions, he professedly unfolds to us 'all mysteries and all knowledge,' on all subjects pertaining to 'being *per se*,' its relations and laws. He, accordingly, gives us, first of all, what is the nature of matter, its primal state, and its absolute subjection to *Necessity*. He then informs us how that God, wishing to make the universe as perfect as possible, 'persuaded Necessity to become stable, harmonious, and fashioned according to Excellence.' Then we have a minute and detailed account of the entire process of creation, the form and location of the earth, and its relations to all other planets, and the principle which determined the distances of the earth and planets from one another, how far the Most High did himself carry forward the work of creation, the identical speech which he delivered to the inferior gods when he committed to them the completing of the work commenced, and the perfecting and final control of the same, and how he then fell back into his usual repose. This is only a mere example of Plato's absolute and universal revelations pertaining to 'being *per se*.' Now when an individual attempts to fill out such a boundless sphere as this, he will of necessity, to say nothing of his method, set forth numberless forms of readily detected error and absurdity, the exposure of which will throw serious doubts, to say the least, over the validity of all his teachings. No system excited such antagonisms as that of Plato, and none ever presented so many sides where it could be successfully assailed. Hence no system sooner fell under the shock of criticism. In a very short time the Old Academy was wholly supplanted by the New, in the latter of which the teachings of Plato received fundamental modifications, and finally were utterly subverted.

Remarks perfectly similar apply to the teachings of Aristotle. In method he professedly differed in fundamental respects from Plato. While the latter took positions in the sphere of 'existence *in se*,' the former located his standpoint within the circle of facts of perception. In this sphere, however, Aristotle really attempted an exposition of universal science in all its forms. Hence, he 'made nothing perfect,' and so intermingled important truth with manifest fundamental error, as to induce a general doubt of the possibility of science in any form.

Similar remarks are almost equally applicable to the productions of other schools. One of the most multitudinous of all the ancient writers was Epicurus. Yet no author was more obviously inconclusive than he in his endlessly diversified deductions. When the undeniable errors of such pre-eminent thinkers become known and read of all men, the popular mind was, almost of course, thrown under the power of Scepticism.

2. The character of *absoluteness*, which was attached in all these schools to their varied deductions, was another very efficient cause which operated to induce the general Scepticism of the succeeding era. The deductions of each school were in open antagonism with those of every other, and many of these deductions were manifestly false. Yet each deduction, however grossly absurd, and manifestly false, and however contradictory to others coming from authorities of equally apparent validity, was given forth as absolute truth. Nothing but an almost resistless reaction against the idea of the possibility of science itself is to be expected under such circumstances. When Plato, for example, affirmed that 'the knowledge which by Reason, in an intuitive manner, we may acquire of real existence and intelligible things, is of a higher degree of certainty than the knowledge which belongs to what are commonly called the sciences,' of which mathematics are specified in illustration; and when, through this affirmed insight of Reason, he gave forth, as forms of absolute truth, enunciations

which, in other schools, were demonstrated to be nothing but absurdities and errors of the grossest character, it is no matter of wonder that mankind, at length, doubted and denied the validity of Reason-insight in all its forms.

3 The high personal pretensions of philosophers in all the schools, pretensions which stood out visibly associated with demonstrated forms of gross absurdity and error, were another cause which powerfully operated to induce a general distrust of the possibility of valid knowledge in any form, and to render doubt the prevailing faith of the race. Plato, for example, claimed for philosophers, not only inspiration, but the possession of a faculty of absolute insight pertaining to 'real existence and intelligible things,' a faculty possessed only by the gods and a very small portion of mankind, and claimed, finally, that none but these philosophers were qualified to rule the human race. In all schools in common, philosophers unblushingly claimed, that 'they were the men, and that wisdom would die with them.' They only were Philosophers (lovers of wisdom, and possessed of the same), Sophists (wise men), Sages (men of gravity and universal knowledge). They held 'the key of knowledge,' and were alone possessed of power to teach the truth. Now, when men of such high pretensions will convict each other before the world of the grossest errors and absurdities, will agree in nothing among themselves, and never unite but to dispute, their combined influence tends in but one direction—universal Scepticism.

4. We refer to but one other incidental cause of the decline of the Grecian Philosophy—the absence of any generally admitted criteria of valid knowledge. Aristotle, as we have seen, ridiculed the idea that such criteria exist. Plato makes no allusion to the subject. Heraclitus, the Epicureans, and Stoics, recognized and affirmed the importance and necessity of such criteria, and did set forth, as we have seen, criteria which, when clearly defined, must be admitted to have absolute validity. Outside the individual schools themselves, the validity of these tests was denied. In their endless disputations neither party could present any criteria by which truth could be distinguished from error—criteria the validity of which the opposite party admitted. Such disputations, consequently, could settle nothing. The final result of such disputations could hardly be anything else than general doubt of the possibility of knowledge in any form.

SECTION II.

THE SCEPTICAL PHILOSOPHY.

WE have, perhaps, on former occasions said all that need be said in refutation of the Sceptical Philosophy. As we have now approached the era of its full and perfect development, the era in which it commanded a wider assent from the race than ever before, or since, and as we have before us all that modern thought has developed in connection with this system; further, as we have in Mr. Lewes' statement of the doctrine the exact issue between Scepticism and Realism, the issue as presented in ancient and modern times, we shall in this connection give to the subject a special consideration, craving indulgence for a necessary repetition of some forms of thought formerly presented. We will present the issue as stated by Mr. Lewes himself.

THE ISSUE AS STATED BY MR. LEWES.

'*What Criterion is there of the truth of our knowledge?*'
The Criterion must reside in Reason, in Conception, or in Sensation. It cannot reside in Reason, because Reason itself is not *independent* of the other two: it operates upon materials furnished by them, and is dependent upon them. Our knowledge is derived from the senses, and every object presented to the mind must consequently have been originally presented to the senses. On their accuracy the mind must depend.

Reason cannot therefore contain within itself the desired Criterion Nor can Conception, for the same argument applies to it. Nor can the Criterion reside in Sense; because, as all admit, the Senses are deceptive, and there is no perception which cannot be false. For what is Perception? Our Senses only inform us of the presence of an object in so far as they are affected by it. But what is this? Is it not *we* who are affected, *we* who are modified? Yes, and this modification reveals both itself and the object which causes it. Like light, which, in showing itself, shows also the objects upon which it is thrown; like light also, it shows objects in *its own colours*. Perception is a peculiar *modification of the soul*. The whole problem now to solve is this: '*Does every modification of the soul exactly correspond with the external object which causes that modification?*' We give the above passage as we find it, italics and all. Now, there are in the above passage more errors of even a fundamental character than we shall have space to notice. Among the most important of these we specify the following:

ERRONEOUS STATEMENTS AND EXPOSITIONS OF MR. LEWES.

1. There is no such 'problem now to solve' as he has presented. No thinker now affirms, or ever did affirm, that 'every modification of the soul exactly corresponds with the external object which causes that modification.' All admit and affirm that *Sensation*, as a *sensitive* 'modification of the soul,' does not, in any sense, correspond with 'the external object which causes that modification,' that is, the Sensation. All admit and affirm that the *secondary* qualities of matter are the unknown causes of known, or conscious, states of the *Sensibility*, namely, of Sensations.

On the other hand, it is affirmed that the *primary* qualities of this substance are the *known objects* of consciously known states, or acts, of the *Intelligence*, Sense-perception. Sensation, as a *sensitive* 'modification of the soul,' is one thing. Perception, consciously direct and immediate, perception as an *intellectual* act, state, or 'modification of the soul,' is quite another. 'The whole problem now to solve' is this: Not whether 'every modification of the soul exactly corresponds with the external object which causes that modification,' but, Does knowledge consciously direct and immediate, or intuitive, what all admit to be true of our perceptions of the primary qualities of matter, does knowledge *in this absolutely conscious form*, represent its object as it is, or as it is not? In other words, is knowledge consciously direct and immediate, or presentative, to be regarded as valid or invalid, veritable or false, truthful or deceptive? No philosopher, 'from Protagoras to Kant,' or from Kant to Mr. Lewes, Spencer, or Huxley, will deny that our knowledge of the secondary qualities of matter is consciously indirect and mediate, through Sensation, or representative; and that our knowledge of the primary qualities of the same substance, extension and form, for example, is as consciously direct and immediate, or presentative. 'The whole problem now to solve,' we repeat, is this: Not whether knowledge consciously indirect and mediate, or representative, but whether knowledge, consciously direct and immediate, intuitive, or presentative, is true or false, veritable or deceptive.

2. 'As all admit,' says Mr. Lewes, ' the senses are deceptive, and there is no perception which cannot be false.' Now all deny what he here affirms that 'all admit.' All mankind do believe, and ever have believed, in the validity of external perception. Nor is Protagoras, or Kant, or Mr. Lewes himself, an exception to this statement. Philosophers may call 'this universal faith in the reality of things without us,' 'illusory,' or 'nothing but a prejudice.' Yet they must admit, with Kant and Coleridge, and Plato, and all other philosophers, that this faith is universal with the race, 'innate indeed and connatural,' 'unavoidable and irradicable,' and as a principle 'inheres in reason' itself.

It would be nearer the truth to affirm that the senses never deceive us than to affirm them to be always deceptive. As we have formerly stated, we are conscious of Sensation as a fact. Here the object, the Sensation, is known as it is in itself. The Sensation, as an object of consciousness, is never deceptive, but is known as it is. The object and cause of the Sensation is consciously given as real, but unknown, and here the senses do not deceive us. If the secondary qualities of matter were given as the known objects of conscious states of the Intelligence, instead of the unknown causes of conscious states of the Sensibility, we should be deceived.

In external perception, also, as far as what is really perceived is concerned, there is no deception. The objects of direct and immediate knowledge really exist, and the qualities actually perceived are real. In our judgments, assumptions, and guesses, in regard to objects perceived, here, and here exclusively, all our mistakes, deceptions, 'blunders and foolish notions,' are formed. The confounding of facts of real perception, that is, what is actually perceived, with the judgments, opinions, conjectures, and guesses, which are connected with and based upon such facts, has occasioned all the errors of philosophers in respect to the validity of Sense-perception. Instead of there being 'no perception which cannot be false,' there can, in fact, be no real perception which is not true, perception being a pure and intuitive intellectual state, and being necessarily conformed to its object. That is undeniably 'science falsely so-called' which affirms the Intelligence itself, in its necessary and intuitive procedures, to be a faculty of deceptive error.

3. In the following statement of Mr. Lewes, also, we detect error of a perfectly fundamental character: 'Our knowledge is derived from our senses, and every object presented to the mind must consequently have been originally presented to the senses, and on their accuracy the mind must depend.' Space and time, we know to be realities, or we know and can know nothing, and each of these realities is known to be infinite. Have infinite space and eternal duration ever 'been presented to the senses?' Have the principles, Every event must have a cause, Body implies space, Succession implies time, and Things equal to the same thing are equal to one another, ever been 'presented to the senses?' What fact of mind was ever 'presented to the senses'? Sensation itself, as a subjective state, is real, and is known as such, and was never yet 'presented to the senses.' In addition to the faculty of Sense-perception, we have two other faculties of original intuition, faculties of which thinkers of the school of Mr. Lewes take no account, namely, Self-consciousness, and Reason the organ of intuitively implied knowledge.

4. The gravest of all the errors of Mr. Lewes, however, is his statement and location of the Criterion of truth. 'The Criterion,' he says, 'must reside either in Reason, in Conception, or in Sensation.' Unless some faculty can be found, we are here informed, which can be demonstrated to possess sovereign authority to sit in judgment over the validity of its own dicta, and those of all the other faculties, we have, and can have, no such Criterion whatever; 'vain wisdom all, and false philosophy.' Let us, in illustration, apply the principle here given to a single case. On a post-mortem examination, a substance supposed to be arsenic is found in the stomach of the deceased. The case is brought into court, and the usual Criteria are being applied to determine the nature of the substance under consideration. The attorney on one side rises, and objects to the whole procedure, as utterly invalid. 'The Criterion,' he affirms, if it exists at all, 'must be found in Reason, in Conception, or

in Sensation. It cannot reside in Reason, because Reason itself is not *independent* of the other two; it operates upon materials furnished by them, and is dependent on them.' 'Nor can Conception, for the same reason apply to it. Nor can the Criterion reside in Sense, because, as all admit, the Senses are deceptive, and there is no perception which cannot be false.' Mr. Lewes, perhaps, and philosophers of his school, would expect and demand a prompt dismissal of the case, the court having been demonstrated to be possessed of no 'Criterion' by which arsenic can be distinguished from mud. The judge would reply, however, that no one human faculty was in court at all, as containing the Criterion of truth. There were certain known facts, or characteristics, which distinguish arsenic from all other substances, and it was in the light of such Criteria, that they were about to decide the question before them. So we would inform Mr. Lewes, and all other philosophers who have erred as he has done, that he is right in arguing, that no one faculty of the Intelligence can sit in judgment upon the dicta of any other faculty; but that he fundamentally errs in assuming that unless such an all-authoritative faculty does exist, we have no Criterion of truth whatever. All admit, Sceptics among the rest, that there do exist in the human mind forms of real knowledge, forms of knowledge intermingled with assumptions, opinions, beliefs, and conjectures, some of which may be true and others false. Now there must be some fixed characteristics which distinguish and separate forms of knowledge proper from apprehensions which are, or may be, false. These Criteria exist, not in any one mental faculty, but in the apprehensions themselves. When we have determined what these characteristics are we have the Criteria after which we are inquiring. To admit, as we must, that such Criteria do exist, but that we cannot discover them, is an impeachment of the Intelligence which even Scepticism will be slow to make. Real knowledge in some form does undeniably have place in the human mind, and is possessed there of characteristics which we can discern, and thus distinguish and separate the real from the unreal. In former parts of this treatise we have designated and verified such Criteria. For the full accomplishment of the purpose we now have in view, we will restate, in this connection, some of these Criteria.

Criteria of Valid Knowledge.

1. Forms of *intuitive* knowledge strictly common to all the race, and that in all ages and under all circumstances of conscious existence, must be held as having absolute validity for the reality and character of their objects. We must admit the strict validity of this Criterion, or assume, and that for no reasons whatever, the Universal Intelligence itself to be a lie. The question now before us is not whether such forms of knowledge

do exist, but whether, supposing them real, they are, or are not, to be recognized as valid for truth. No thinker who has any respect for his character as such a person, will question the validity of this Criterion.

2. Forms of original intuition, apprehended by universal mind as *necessarily* true, must also be accepted as valid for truth. We must admit the strict validity of this Criterion, or deny absolutely the distinction between the possible and the impossible.

3. All forms of knowledge consciously *direct* and *immediate*, that is, *intuitive* and *presentative*, must be held as valid for truth. We have here, what even the Sceptic will not deny, an ultimate Criterion of truth—a Criterion of absolute validity. The Sceptic may deny the existence of such forms of knowledge. He will not, however, deny their validity, supposing them real.

4. Absolute fixedness and immutability is another Criterion of undeniable validity. Real knowledge, just as far as it extends, can be subject to no change or modification. To suppose it changeable would imply that it is not knowledge. Here lies the fundamental distinction between real knowledge on the one hand, and assumptions, opinions, beliefs, conjectures, and guesses on the other. The latter are continuously subject to change, modification, and displacement from human thought and regard. The former can never be changed, modified, or displaced from the mind.

5. The *universal consciousness of absolute certainty* is another Criterion of fundamental importance. All men regard certain apprehensions as false, others as possibly or probably true, and others as having undoubted certainty; while others exist as conscious forms of *absolute* knowledge. In all the cases first named we are conscious of the possibility of error. In reference to the cases last designated, we *know* that misapprehension is impossible. Now, when we meet with forms of knowledge strictly common to all minds in all circumstances of conscious existence, forms which are always characterized by this absolutely conscious certainty, we must recognize ourselves as in the presence of forms of absolute truth, or violate all the principles and laws of inductive science.

6. All forms of knowledge, we remark finally, whose validity is necessarily *implied* by forms of real knowledge, must be accepted as having absolute validity. The intuitively and necessarily implied has, undeniably, the same validity as that by which the former is implied.

If any thinker shall admit the validity of these Criteria, or that of any of them, he must, or convict himself of wanting logical integrity, admit the absolute validity of all forms of knowledge undeniably possessing these characteristics. If he should deny the validity of these Criteria, he will stand revealed as being as obviously convicted of fundamental error as these Criteria are obviously true. A man may in words deny the validity of the axiom, Things equal to the same thing are equal to one another. In that denial, however, he is as obviously wrong as that axiom is obviously true. Now no axiom is, or can be, more obviously true than are the above Criteria. If the Sceptic shall choose to confront, with a denial, such self-evident truths, the world may very wisely and properly 'leave him alone in his glory.'

NECESSARY DEDUCTION FROM A RIGID APPLICATION OF THESE CRITERIA.

The necessary deduction from the most careful and rigid application of these Criteria, is the absolute validity of our knowledge of Matter and Spirit, Time and Space. Let us now carefully apply to the forms of knowledge under consideration the Criteria above stated.

1. The knowledge which we have of each of these realities exists in universal mind as a form of *intuitive knowledge strictly common to all the race*, and that at all times, and in all ages, and under all circumstances of conscious existence. Not a tribe of men, as we have said, can be found who have not, and ever have not had, distinct apprehensions of Matter and Spirit, Time and Space, who have not distinct and separate terms to represent all these realities, and who confound any one of them with any other. Mind cannot and never did and never could think at all without definitely distinguishing and separating between the self and the not-self, the me and the not-me, and without apprehending these realities, not only as being distinct and separate from one another, but each as existing in time and space. Nor in the interior of the mind is there, or ever was there or can there be, a shadow of doubt about the distinct and separate existence of all these realities. All this, as we have shown on former occasions in the progress of this work, philosophers of all schools, Sceptics among the rest, fully admit and affirm. Nor can they, as they themselves admit, 'treat this faith,' in the construction of their system, 'as nothing but a prejudice,' but by a compulsory assumption of will. While they consent to be guided by their own and the Universal Intelligence, they do and they must, as they themselves acknowledge, absolutely believe in the validity of our knowledge of all these realities. We must, then, admit the validity of our knowledge of all these realities, or affirm, and that for no reason but will assumption, that intuitive knowledge, strictly common to all the race, and that under all circumstances of conscious existence, is a blank illusion.

2. These forms of universal intuitive knowledge which we have of all these realities, are apprehended by universal mind as *necessarily* true. Time and space we not only know to be realities in themselves, but also know that they *must* thus exist. In other words, we know absolutely that the knowledge we have of these realities, not only is, but must be valid.

So, also, we necessarily recognize matter and spirit as realities whose distinct and separate existence is as necessarily *implied* by their attributes which we do, and must know to be real. The axioms, Events imply a cause, and Phenomena substance, are false, or our knowledge of matter and spirit, as distinct and separate entities, must be valid. All admit that we do really *know* the phenomena, or attributes, of each of these substances. Now, phenomena do not imply substance, and substances, consequently, are not as their essential phenomena, or we do have a valid knowledge of matter and spirit, as realities in themselves, and as distinct and separate entities. If the Sceptic denies the validity of this deduction, he is just as obviously and undeniably wrong, as the axioms, Body implies space, Succession implies time, Events imply a cause, Phenomena imply substance, and, Things equal to the same thing are equal to one another, are obviously and undeniably true.

3. These realities are ever present to the mind as the objects of consciously *direct* and *immediate* knowledge, or as realities whose existence is, by direct and immediate intuition, implied by what is thus known. Mind is ever present to itself as the direct, immediate, and absolutely consciously *subject* of thought, feeling, and voluntary determination. Matter, in its *secondary* qualities, is ever present to universal mind, as the *unknown cause* of known, or conscious, states of Sensibility, Sensations; while in its primary qualities, as extension and form, it is equally present as the consciously, and directly, and immediately *known object* of conscious states of the Intelligence, Sense-perception. Time and space, on the other hand, are present as realities which *must* exist, realities, also, whose existence is necessarily implied by that of objects of consciously direct and immediate knowledge. No philosopher who makes any pretensions to integrity will deny the perfect correctness of the above statements. ' The problem now to be solved is this '—*Is the fact of knowledge consciously direct and immediate to be regarded as a valid Criterion of truth?* The Sceptic may deny this, if he chooses.

4. The knowledge we have of all these realities has, in universal mind, and that in all circumstances and relations of conscious existence, the characteristics of *absolute fixedness and immutability*. Every individual of the race, who thinks at all, as we have often said, apprehends the self, the mind, as a self-conscious personal existence endowed with the attributes of thought, feeling, and willing; and matter, as an exterior object existing in and occupying space, and consequently, as possessed of the fixed qualities of extension and form, and time and space as the places of substances and events. While assumptions, opinions, beliefs, conjectures, and guesses, appear and disappear in the sphere of human thought, while they change their forms there, and take on the appearance of endlessly 'dissolving views,' the apprehensions under consideration, in the forms designated, remain in universal mind as fixed and immutable, as

are any of our ideas of any mathematical figures whatever. All this is just as true with the Sceptic, and with philosophers of all schools, as with the rest of mankind. While the Sceptic says to himself, in the language of the Oriental Yogee, 'Neither do I exist, nor anything which pertains to myself; all individual existence is a dream,' an illusion; phenomena only are real; while our philosopher is saying all this, the 'I,' and the 'not I'—that is, matter and spirit, time and space, are just as real to him, and just the same as they were before he began, in the language of Kant, to 'play tricks upon Reason.' When the Pure Idealist is endeavouring to demonstrate to himself, and to all the world, that nothing but thought is real, he is ever present to himself, not as a form of thought, but as a great and substantial thinker, and the inquiry is perpetually before his mind, What will *real* thinkers think of this ? Without a violation of all the principles and laws of scientific classification and induction, we cannot confound these fundamental apprehensions with changeable assumptions, opinions, beliefs, and conjectures, nor locate them anywhere else but within the sphere of real knowledge.

5. The apprehensions which we have of the realities under consideration exist in all minds, under all circumstances of conscious existence, as conscious forms of *real*, and absolutely *certain* knowledge. We do not opine, imagine, conjecture, or guess, that we exist. We *know* it. In the same form, we consciously *know* that matter is before us, as an exterior object, having real extension and form. We also *know* space and time, as necessarily existing realities. There is not on earth a mind possessed of Reason in which the apprehensions under consideration do not exist in this one exclusive form. This conscious *certainty*, also, is just as absolute in the mind of philosophers of all schools, as in that of any other individual. They may, if they choose, 'compel themselves to *treat* this faith as nothing but a prejudice.' Yet they can, by no possibility, force into the sphere of real thought the appearance even of real doubt of the *certainty* of our knowledge of 'the me and the not-me,' or of time and space. We have, by a forced assumption of will, to 'put ourselves into a state of *not knowing*, when we begin to philosophize,' or we cannot even *treat* as illusions our knowledge of these realities. Knowledge, then, is not knowledge, or our knowledge of the essential nature and attributes of matter and spirit, time and space, has absolutely certain validity.

6. Matter and spirit, time and space, we remark finally, stand revealed in the Universal Intelligence as realities whose existence is necessarily implied by fundamental facts of absolutely conscious knowledge. Phenomena, as conscious facts of external perception, all men, and philosophers of all schools, admit and affirm to be real. If the axioms, Body implies space, Succession implies time, Events imply a cause, Phenomena imply substance, and Things equal to the same thing are equal to one another,

are true, then our knowledge of mind and matter, time and space, have undeniable validity. The Sceptic can deny this deduction but by denying the reality of conscious facts which all admit on the one hand, or the validity of the above axioms on the other. In the one case, he is just as obviously and undeniably wrong as universally admitted conscious facts are real. In the other case, he is just as obviously and undeniably in fundamental error as the above self-evident axioms and principles of all science are of obvious and undeniable validity. In the light, therefore, of six undeniably valid Criteria of real knowledge, the deduction takes on the form of demonstrated certainty, that we have a scientifically ascertained valid knowledge of these four realities. The Sceptical Philosophy can, by no possibility, be true, unless all the above designated Criteria, together with all the axioms in all the sciences, are false.

The Sceptical Doctrine Self-contradictory.

Mr. Lewes presents a formal argument to *prove* the doctrine that we have no Criterion of truth. In this he follows the example of all who belong to his school. What is the principle which lies at the basis of his whole argument? It is undeniably this. Doctrines of a certain character, the absence of all valid Criteria of truth, for example, may be absolutely verified by argument. In other words, we can know, and can know that we do know, certain propositions to be true. How can this be so, in the utter absence of all Criteria by which we can distinguish between valid and invalid arguments, and between what judgments are true and what false? Why do Mr. Lewes and his school regard his argument as valid for truth? For this reason exclusively. It induces in their minds a certain form of conviction represented by the term *conscious certitude.* When an argument induces in all minds an absolute certitude of its validity, they hold that argument as valid for the truth of the deduction reached. Universal and absolute conscious certitude, then, is, with them even, as it should be, a valid Criterion of truth. Were this not so, it would be absurd for them to attempt to verify their own doctrine. The proof they offer is proof absolute that they themselves do not believe their own doctrine. If universal and absolute conscious certitude is a test of truth, and it is so, or the attempt to prove anything is absurd, then, as above demonstrated, we have an absolute valid knowledge of spirit, matter, time, and space.

THE SCEPTICAL DISTINCTION BETWEEN PHENOMENA AND NOUMENA.

Sceptics of all ages make a fundamental distinction between phenomena and *noumena.* The former they define as 'the appearance of things,' or 'modifications of the soul.' *Noumena,* on the other hand, are the realities themselves, existences *in se.* It is very important that we clearly and fully understand the Sceptical doctrine in regard to the relations of phenomena to noumena, and those of our Intelligence to each class of objects. The following are the essential elements and features of this doctrine, to wit: 1. We do know phenomena, but can know nothing whatever of noumena. 'Our knowledge,' says Mr. Lewes, 'is the knowledge of phenomena, and not at all of noumena, because we only know things as they *appear* to us, and not as they really are; all attempts to penetrate the mystery of Existence must be vain, for the attempt can only be made on appearances.' After defining phenomena as mere 'appearances of things,' 'modifications of the soul,' Mr. Spencer sets forth this formula, as embodying not only his own, but the doctrine of all philosophers of his school, 'from Protagoras to Kant,' namely, 'the reality existing behind all appearances is, and ever must be, unknown.' 2. While there can be no real knowledge of realities, *noumena*, there may be a real science of phenomena. 'Although *absolute* truth is not attainable by man, although there cannot be a science of Being, there can be a science of appearances. Phenomena, they' (sceptics) 'admit, are true as phenomena. What we have to do is, therefore, to observe and classify phenomena.' In the above presentation Mr. Lewes has most accurately, as all will admit, stated the doctrine of Scepticism as avowed by its advocates in all ages. 3. While we cannot have any science of real Being, we can not only know and classify phenomena, but determine their mutual relationships and laws, their co-existences and sequences. 'What we have to do,' says Mr. Lewes, 'is therefore to observe and classify phenomena; to trace in them the resemblances of co-existence and succession; to trace the connection of cause and effect; and, having done this, we shall have founded a science of Appearances adequate to our wants.' 'Fact' (phenomena) 'I know,' says Mr. Huxley, 'and Law I know.' 4. The reason why we can have no science of Being, *noumena*, is the fact that we have no Criterion of truth. 'The stronghold of Scepticism,' says Mr. Lewes, 'is impregnable. It is this: There is no *Criterion* of truth.' This is, and ever has been, the fundamental deduction of Scepticism. 'Phenomena are the appearances of things. But where exists the Criterion of the truth of these appearances?' Such are the positive teachings of Scepticism in regard to the relations of phenomena and *noumena* as real Being. To the following observations upon these dogmas we would invite very special attention.

OBSERVATIONS UPON THE SCEPTICAL DOCTRINE ON THESE SUBJECTS.

1. According to the fundamental doctrine and principles of Scepticism, we have no more real knowledge, and can have no more real science of phenomena than of noumena, or real Being. We cannot have knowledge, or science, of substances or causes, says the Sceptic, 'because we have no

Criterion of truth.' On the authority of what Criterion, then, do you affirm that 'you know Phenomena ?' 'The Criterion,' you say, 'must reside either in Reason, in Conception, or in Sensation,' and you have demonstrated that this Criterion cannot be found in either of these faculties, and have hence inferred that we have *no* Criterion whatever of truth in any form. You are absolutely necessitated, therefore, by your own principle, to affirm, with the Pyrrhonists, that you do not know that you know, not merely Being *in se*, but Phenomena also. You are bound, by all the principles of logical integrity, to affirm that there can be no more real knowledge or science of Phenomena than there can be of *Noumena*, and that in the same sense in which knowledge and science in one form is impossible, it is equally so in the other.

The universal boast of Sceptics is that they can, and do know Phenomena, and can, and do know Law; but that they do not, and cannot know Substances and Causes. Now Law is just as invisible, and in the same identical sense invisible, as are Substances and Causes. Phenomena *imply* Substances and Causes in the same sense in which they imply Law. In the same identical sense in which we perceive Law, we perceive also Substances and Causes in Phenomena. In the same sense and form in which we perceive or know Phenomena, we perceive and know Substances and Causes in and through Phenomena. By the same identical Criteria by which we know that we have a valid knowledge of Phenomena, we know also that we have an equally valid knowledge of Law, Substances, and Causes. Necessarily implied knowledge has, undeniably, the same validity as that by which the former is implied.

2. In the Sceptical Philosophy we have a fundamentally false idea and definition of Phenomena. They are affirmed to be 'modifications of the soul.' Modifications of the soul are Phenomena of the soul and of no other substance. Phenomena of matter, on the other hand, are qualities or properties of this substance; qualities or properties *perceived* by the soul, or the Intelligence. So the term Phenomena is regarded by the universal Intelligence, and defined by all standard authorities. Nowhere but amid the illusions of false science are the Phenomena of one substance defined as modifications of another substance. The secondary qualities of matter are not modifications of the soul, Sensations, but *causes* of such modifications, that is, qualities of the exterior, material, substance. The primary qualities are never conceived, or defined, as in any sense 'modifications of the soul,' but as qualities or properties of matter, qualities or properties directly and immediately perceived by the mind. The only proper definition of Phenomena is the properties, or qualities, of substances perceived by the mind. Qualities in themselves constitute the real nature of substances. Qualities, when perceived, are called the Phenomena of said substances.

3. Hence, we remark in the next place, that there is no such distinction as the Sceptical Philosophy affirms to exist between Phenomena and *Noumena*. Phenomena, we repeat, are the real qualities, or properties, of substances, qualities or properties perceived by the mind. Phenomena and Noumena, God and Nature, and the Universal Intelligence, have immutably 'joined together,' and false science can, by no possibility, 'put them asunder.' The idea of appearance in which nothing appears, that is, Phenomena in which no substances are revealed, is admitted by Kant to involve an absolute absurdity. If in Phenomena substances are represented as they are not, and not as they are, they are not manifested at all, and we have appearance in which nothing appears. Appearance in which no reality appears, this is the sum and substance of the Sceptical Philosophy.

4. The Sceptical Philosophy, we remark again, involves a fundamental psychological error. Phenomena, even of matter, are, according to its teachings, consciously given as 'modifications of the soul.' On no other hypothesis can they be affirmed to be such modifications. Here we have one of the most obvious errors in psychology, errors known to science. No rational being but a bewildered philosopher ever imagined Phenomena to be anything else than perceived qualities of some definite substance.

5. The last, and one of the greatest absurdities that we shall notice as connected with these dogmas of Scepticism, is found in its admission of the reality of Phenomena, and of our knowledge of the same, and a denial of the validity of forms of knowledge whose validity is absolutely implied by what Sceptics themselves admit and affirm that we do know. Phenomena are real, says the Sceptic in common with all the race, and we have a valid knowledge of Phenomena. Let him admit every form of truth which admitted Phenomena imply, and neither himself nor any other rational being can be a Sceptic. We cannot be more certain of the reality of Phenomena than we are, and must be, of the absolute validity of the principle, that Phenomena imply substance, or real being, and that substances must be in themselves *as* their essential Phenomena. We cannot be more assured of the fact that events are real, than we are of the validity of the principle that events imply a cause. We cannot be more assured of the fact that we know Phenomena and events, than we are and must be, that through these we do know substances and causes. We cannot be more assured that we really *know* Phenomena and events, substances and causes, than we are, and must be, that we *know* their implied realities, time and space. There can be no more fundamental form of error than is involved in the idea, that we can, and do know Phenomena and events, and do not and cannot know the substances, causes, and realities, the existence and character of which are absolutely

and necessarily implied by what it is admitted and affirmed we can, and do know.

Positive Sides of the Sceptical Philosophy.

While Scepticism has to appearance none but merely negative sides, it is, when carefully considered, as manifestly as any other a *positive* system, and has as many positive sides as any other hypothesis. It bases all its deductions, for example, upon the absolutely affirmed facts, that we have, and can have, no Criterion of truth; that while we do, and can have no knowledge whatever of real substances and causes, we can, and do have valid knowledge of Phenomena and Law; that the Phenomena which we do know are not qualities, or properties, of objects perceived by the mind, but 'modifications of the soul;' that these modifications validly represent no realities whatever, and that while we can, and do have a valid knowledge of these modifications, that is, of Phenomena, we can have no real knowledge of the substances, causes, and other realities, whose existence and character are given in the Universal Intelligence, as necessarily implied by Phenomena of which even Scepticism itself admits and affirms that we do have a valid knowledge. These, among others, constitute the positive sides of this Philosophy, and all these principles must be true, or Scepticism must be a system of fundamental error. Let us now consider some of the necessary deductions which arise from these, the known basis principles of this system.

Necessary Deductions from Fundamental Principles of this System.

1. All these principles in common are, in fact, nothing but bald *assumptions*, which have no self-evident validity, which have no antecedent or deductive probability in their favour, and can by no possibility be verified by proof. Is it self-evident, for example, that we have no Criterion of truth—that the Phenomena which we consciously perceive as qualities of a not-self, are mere modifications of the self—that realities are not what we consciously perceive them to be, and that we can know Phenomena and Law, and cannot know the substances, causes, and realities whose existence and character are given in the Universal Intelligence as necessarily implied by Phenomena which we undeniably do know? By what process of induction, or deduction, can it be shown that these Sceptical principles have any antecedent probability in their favour? It is, undeniably, just as antecedently probable, and infinitely more so, that realities are, as that they are not, what we directly and immediately perceive them to be. Nor, by any actual or conceivable process of induction, can the Sceptical hypothesis be proven true, and its opposite false. By what process of reasoning can the Sceptic render us more absolutely

or rationally *assured* that we do not, than we are that we do, exist as personal beings exercising the functions of thought, feeling, and free determination? How can he render us more absolutely and rationally *certain* that matter is not, than we actually are that it is directly and immediately before us as possessed of the real qualities of extension and form? How can he render us more rationally and assuredly *certain* that such axioms as the following are false, than we are that they are and must be true, namely, that Body implies space; Succession implies time; Phenomena imply substance; Events imply a cause, and that Substances must be as their essential Phenomena? Unless the Sceptic shall demonstrate all the above propositions, his hypothesis, undeniably, stands before us as a mere bald and lawless assumption—what he can no more accomplish than he can prove to us that $2 + 2 = 6$.

2. The Sceptical Philosophy is not only based upon a mere assumption, but upon an assumption which is most palpably *self-contradictory and absurd*. On the assumption that we have no *Criterion* of truth, the deduction is based that we cannot have valid knowledge of truth in any form. Notwithstanding the want of such Criterion, and in the face of the universal deduction based upon that want, we are absolutely assured that we do have a valid knowledge of Phenomena and even of Law. Now if, in the absence of such Criterion, we do and can have rationally self-assured knowledge of Phenomena and Law, we may, notwithstanding the want of such test, have an equally absolute and rationally self-assured knowledge of the substances and causes, the existence and character of which are necessarily implied by Phenomena which we do know. If the want of Criteria proves the fact that we can have no valid knowledge of substances, this want is equal proof of the invalidity of our knowledge of Phenomena and Law.

3. Scepticism in its fundamental principles and deductions involves the absurdity of making a discrimination where, undeniably, no difference exists. 'I know Fact, and I know Law,' says the Sceptic. Real knowledge then, in some form, does exist. This all Sceptics admit. If they doubt everything else, they do not and cannot doubt that they doubt. Now there is nothing of which we can be more certain than we are of our own personal existence, of the reality of matter as possessed of extension and form, and of the existence of time and space. Scepticism assumes one form of knowledge to be really valid, and then affirms that another form which has, undeniably, the same kind and degree of certainty, to be utterly illusory, thus making a fundamental discrimination, where, most obviously, no difference whatever does exist. If we admit, as all Sceptics do, that one form of consciously certain knowledge is valid, we convict ourselves of the grossest logical insincerity if we deny the validity of any other form of knowledge undeniably possessed of the

same kind and degree of certainty. We cannot be more certain that we know Fact and Law, that we know Phenomena, and that we have doubts, than we are that we know 'the self and the not-self,' and time and space, as realities in themselves. To affirm that we do know Fact and Law, and that we do not know 'the me and the not me,' is simply to convict ourselves of the most palpable self-contradiction and absurdity.

4. This hypothesis has its basis not only in the error of making a discrimination where no difference exists, but in other equally fundamental forms, that of *confounding* things that essentially differ from one another. Knowledge through Sense-perception, it is argued, cannot be valid, because 'the Senses are deceptive, and there is no perception which cannot be false.' In two fundamental respects, the Sceptical deduction is based upon the error of confounding things which fundamentally differ—confounding Sensation considered as a sensitive state, and Sense-perception considered as an intellectual state, on the one hand; and confounding the real fact of Sense-perception with the assumptions, opinions, beliefs, conjectures, and guesses which are based upon such facts.

In all the writings of Sceptics upon the subject we search in vain for any proper discrimination between the primary and secondary qualities of matter, and between the forms of knowledge which we obtain of this substance *indirectly* through the consciousness of sensations, and *directly* through consciously presentative perception. To know a substance as it consciously affects our sensitivity, is one thing; to know its essential qualities, as extension and form, by perception consciously direct and immediate, is quite another. Scepticism universally confounds these fundamentally diverse forms of knowledge with each other, and bases its deduction upon the assumed identity of things which essentially differ from one another, and thus finally convicts itself of fundamental error.

Again, it is argued that 'the senses are deceptive,' because men differ and contradict each other about the same things. Facts, it should be borne in mind, are one thing; while assumptions, opinions, and conjectures based upon such facts are quite another. As far as facts of actual perception, external and internal, and the intuitive convictions directly, immediately, and necessarily, connected with such facts are concerned, men do not differ at all. All are conscious of themselves as exercising the functions of thought, feeling, and willing, of matter as an exterior substance having extension and form, and of time and space as realities, whose existence is necessarily implied by conscious facts, and all in common intuitively believe in the reality of matter, and spirit, time and space. So far all men agree, and here we have facts of actual perception, and intuitive convictions directly, immediately, and necessarily connected with such facts. Here, also, we have all that the Senses and other primary faculties give us, and here we are never deceived at all.

Outside of these perceptions and convictions in respect to which all men do, and must, agree, and in respect to which we are not, and cannot, be deceived—outside of these intuitive perceptions and convictions, and based upon the same, we say, we meet with conflicting and contradictory assumptions, beliefs, opinions, conjectures, and guesses, in which there is a 'confusion worse confounded,' of error and truth. The reason is, that in this last-named sphere we have convictions of the Intelligence intermingled with sentiments of Will and of the Sensitivity. Now Sceptics confound these assumptions and opinions, etc., with actual facts of real perception, and with the intuitive convictions immediately and necessarily connected with these facts and convictions, and hence conclude that the 'Senses are deceptive,' a fundamental error in science. In actual perception, we repeat, and in the intuitive convictions directly and necessarily connected with the facts thus given, error is impossible, and here men do not, and cannot, differ. The confounding of forms of knowledge, consciously indirect and mediate, with those as consciously direct and immediate on the one hand, and facts of real perception and truths of actual intuition which must be true, with assumptions, opinions, beliefs, conjectures, and guesses which may or may not be true—here we meet with the fundamental errors of the Sceptical Philosophy.

4. While we remark, finally, the Sceptical Philosophy is not self-evidently true, while it has no antecedent probability in its favour, and cannot be verified as really, or even probably, true, it may be demonstrated to be a system of fundamental error. This hypothesis is just as obviously and undeniably false as the fundamental axioms in all the valid sciences are obviously and undeniably true. No axiom in any science can be more self-evidently and necessarily true than are those to which we have so often referred—to wit, Body implies space, Succession implies time, Phenomena imply substance, Events imply a cause, and Substances are, in themselves, as their essential Phenomena. Take the Phenomena which Sceptics admit to be validly known, take these Phenomena just as given in the universal consciousness, and no deduction in any science can be rendered more demonstrably evident than may that of the validity of our knowledge of spirit and matter, and time and space. Scepticism is just as undeniably and obviously false, as these principles are self-evidently and necessarily true. We either do not know Phenomena as given in the universal consciousness, or we do know matter and spirit, and time and space, as realities in themselves. We must either admit and affirm, that known facts imply nothing, or admit and affirm that the facts which we do know imply the existence of all the realities under consideration. If thought, for example, implies a thinker, we exist as thinkers. If you deny this principle, you are as obviously and necessarily wrong, as this principle is obviously and necessarily true. You must deny, that we

think and feel, and will, at all, or admit that we exist as self-conscious personalities possessed of the powers of thought, feeling, and willing. If the qualities of extension and form imply the existence of a material substance, then matter exists as such a substance. If you deny the validity of the principle, you are as obviously and necessarily wrong as this principle is obviously and necessarily true. If you deny the existence of such qualities, you are as obviously and absolutely wrong, as knowledge consciously distinct, direct, and immediate, is obviously and absolutely true. Scepticism cannot be true unless all the axioms in all the sciences are false, and the universal consciousness is 'a liar from the beginning.' We are now fully prepared to enter upon the consideration of the system which arose during the period denominated 'the Decline of the Grecian Philosophy.'

DECLINE OF THE GRECIAN PHILOSOPHY.

SECTION I.
THE PYRRHONISTS.

PYRRHO of Elis (about 360—270 B.C.) was the founder of the Sceptical school in Philosophy which bore his name. As the founder of this school left no writings which have descended to us, and as we have to do with systems rather than with men, we shall set forth the doctrines of this school as interpreted by its leading advocates, such as Timon of Philus, and Sextus Empiricus. The fundamental doctrine of the school was universal and absolute doubt. We assert nothing, was their avowed maxim, not even that we do not assert anything. 'Nothing is certain of itself, as is proved by the discrepancy of opinions concerning all that is perceptible or thinkable; and therefore nothing can be made certain by proof, since the latter derives no certainty from itself, and if based on other proof leads us either to a *regressus in infinitum*, or to a circle in demonstration.' The following is their argument in refutation of the principle that every event must have a cause. 'A cause is a *relativum*, for it is not to be conceived without that which it causes; but the relative has no existence except in thought. Further, in each case cause and effect must be either synchronous, or the former must precede or follow the latter. They cannot be synchronous, for then cause and effect would as such be undistinguishable, and each could with equal reason be claimed as the cause of the other. Nor can the cause precede the effect, since a cause is no cause until that exists of which it is the cause. Lastly, the supposition that a cause follows its effect is without sense, and may be abandoned to those fools who habitually invert the order of things.' 'Every syllogism,' says Sextus Empiricus, 'moves in a circle, since the major premise, on which the proof of the conclusion depends, depends for its own certainty on a complete induction, in which the conclusion must have been contrived.'* On the above dogmas and reasoning we remark:

1. We have here a most palpable example of the self-contradictory and absurd. Absolute proof is professedly presented that proof in all forms, actual and conceivable, is utterly impossible; just as if we can demonstrate the absolute impossibility of demonstration in any and in every form. Mr. Mill here finds himself anticipated in his famous argument in which, according to his own reasoning, he *begs* the deduction that all deduction involves the vicious error of *petitio principii*. How can the doctrine that all proof in every form is impossible be proven? If we cannot attain to certain knowledge on any subject, how can we know that all, or any, opinions are deceptive?

2. We have also in the above expositions and deductions the vicious error of drawing universal conclusions from a partial induction of facts. 'Opinions,' we are told, 'concerning *all* that is perceptible, or thinkable,' are discrepant. In regard to what is most essential concerning 'things perceptible and thinkable,' all mankind, as we have absolutely evinced, perfectly agree. All have common and identical ideas and convictions in regard to matter and spirit, time and space. These ideas and convictions, even sceptics admit, are 'innate and connatural,' 'unavoidable and irradicable,' and 'remain proof against all attempts to remove them by grounds and arguments.' Nor do the points of real disagreement among mankind, assumptions excepted, have any bearings whatever in the sphere of the Science of Being. Leaving out all assumptions, we have only to adduce those necessary ideas and intuitive convictions, strictly common to the race, to verify absolutely the validity of our knowledge of Matter, Spirit, Time, Space, God, Duty, Immortality, and Retribution. All denial of any one, or all, of these doctrines has been, in fact and form, based upon an impeachment of the validity of these necessary ideas and universal intuitions. We may safely challenge philosophers of all schools to furnish a single exception to the above statement.

3. We have also, in the above expositions and dogmas, the necessary consequence of ignorance of the doctrine of the validity of intuitively *implied* knowledge. The principle of Causality, the necessary idea, or axiom, that every event implies a cause, cannot by argument be proved or disproved; and that for the obvious reason, that as a principle, a principle having self-evident and necessary validity, it lies with other principles of the same class, at the basis of all proof. The occurrence of an event implies, of necessity, the prior existence of a power adapted and adequate, when the proper conditions are fulfilled, to produce such events,

* Ueberweg, pp. 216, 217.

and the action of that power, as a cause, in the production of this one event. If an individual demands proof of the validity of self-evident and necessary principles which lie at the basis of all proof, his demand may, in the impressive language of Sextus Empiricus, 'be abandoned to those fools who habitually invert the natural order of things.' If he attempts to demonstrate the invalidity of such principles, this attempt also may very properly 'be abandoned to those fools' just designated.

The modern argument, as stated by Mr. Hume, against the validity of the principle under consideration demands special notice. 'The *origin* of the notion,' Mr. Hume argues, 'cannot so be accounted for as to justify our relying upon it as a form of cognition.' This argument, if valid at all, we remark, in the first place, would condemn reliance upon any of the axioms in any of the sciences, and would render science in any form impossible. We can, undeniably, as readily account for the origin of this as of any other self-evident principle that can be named. Let Mr. Hume, or any other individual, account for the *origin* of the principles, Body implies space; Succession, time; or Things equal to the same thing are equal to one another, and we will, on the same principle, account for the origin of the axiom, Every event implies a cause.

But suppose we could not account for the *origin* of this or any other self-evident principle: must we for that reason deny its validity, notwithstanding we know, and cannot but know, that it is and must be true? The origin, in thought, of an idea is one thing—the validity of that idea is quite another. In absolute ignorance of its origin we may have absolute knowledge of its validity. We might as properly deny the existence of the Aurora Borealis because we cannot account for its origin, as deny the validity of a self-evident principle because we cannot explain *its* origin.

In the case before us, however, we are at no loss for the explanation demanded. We have a faculty of knowledge, Reason—a faculty which, in the presence of perceived facts, apprehends the realities necessarily and intuitively implied by said facts. Hence, on the perception of body, succession, phenomena, and events, Reason gives us, as implied by such facts, space, time, substance, and cause. We have another faculty, the Judgment, which, in the presence of the perceived and implied, affirms the intuitive, self-evident, and necessary relations between what we perceive and their implied realities. Hence we have a ready and scientific exposition and explanation of the *origin* of all self-evident truths, such as, Body implies space; Succession implies time; Phenomena imply substance; Events imply a cause, and Things equal to the same thing are equal to one another. None but 'those fools who habitually invert the natural order of things,' will question the validity of any of these principles.

The Peculiar Form of the Pyrrhonic Scepticism.

Professedly, Scepticism is a system of universal nescience, as far at least as realities are concerned. The difficulty with its advocates has ever been to find a formula which will express that doctrine—a formula which shall not be palpably self-contradictory. If we affirm that nothing can be known with certainty, or that real knowledge is impossible, in the very affirmation we profess certain knowledge in one form at least, and thus contradict ourselves. We also take away all grounds for a denial of the possibility and actuality of real knowledge in all other conceivable forms. If the Intelligence is a faculty of knowledge relatively to the extent and limits of its own nescience, it may also be relatively to the self and not-self, and time and space. If we affirm that we can, and do know phenomena, but cannot, and do not know *noumena*, we find ourselves involved in difficulties no less inexplicable than before. Some of these essential and admitted phenomena are given in the universal consciousness, not as 'modifications of the soul,' but as the directly and immediately and absolutely perceived, or known, qualities of external substances, the qualities of extension and form, for example. As modifications imply the real existence of the subject modified, so the external qualities referred to imply the real existence of an extended or material substance. There is, and can be, no landing place between the doctrine of universal and absolute nescience and that of a valid knowledge, not only of phenomena, but of all realities which phenomena, as actually given in the universal consciousness, imply. In other words, the era has arrived when thinkers of all schools in common will find themselves necessitated to make their election between the doctrine of absolute and universal nescience, on the one hand, and Realism on the other. On the authority of any Criterion on which any thinker will prove the validity of our knowledge in any form whatever, we will demonstrate the fact that we have a valid knowledge, not only of phenomena, but of matter and spirit, time and space. But the doctrine of nescience cannot be represented in thought or embodied in any formula actual or conceivable without involving the absurdity of palpable self-contradiction. To think is to affirm, and every scientific formula involves the affirmation of real knowledge. To affirm that we don't know, that we don't know anything, is to affirm that we do know our own nescience, and thus to contradict ourselves. The same holds equally when ancient and modern sceptics, such as Pyrrho, Timon, and Mill, professedly prove that proof, in all its forms, is impossible, that is, involves the vicious error of *petitio principii*.

We have already indicated the formula of the Pyrrhonists—to wit, 'I assert nothing, not even that I assert nothing; for I do not know that

I do not know anything.' The Pyrrhonists were accustomed to contrast their doctrine with that of the Scepticism of the New Academy in this form. The latter affirmed that they did know one thing—to wit, that nothing is knowable, whereas the former denied the possibility of knowledge even in this one form, vainly supposing that in this denial they escaped the palpable contradiction which a profession to know that nothing is knowable undeniably involves. Such is the absurdity and self-contradiction of false science.

THE CONSUMMATION SOUGHT BY THE PYRRHONISTS THROUGH THEIR PHILOSOPHY.

When men philosophize they have an end in view, just as they have when engaged in any other occupation. The end which the Pyrrhonists professedly sought through Philosophy was *ataraxy*, or absolute quietude and imperturbableness of mind. The immutable condition of attaining this state, they affirmed, was an utter suspension of all judgments in respect to all realities in common. Hence they denied all knowledge of all objects, even of our ignorance of the same, all distinctions between right and wrong, beauty and deformity, great and small, pleasure and pain, and even life and death. The Yogee of the school of Kapila affirmed that when he had attained to a distinct recognition of the absolute validity of the formula, 'neither do I exist, nor anything which pertains to myself; all individual existence is a dream,' an enfranchisement resulted in which the mind had absolute quietude in regard to all objects and events. So the Pyrrhonists, borrowing the idea no doubt from their Oriental predecessors, affirmed that when there is a distinct recognition of the formula, that nothing is knowable, that to the Intelligence all objects and events are absolutely alike, and that even between life and death there is no recognizable difference, there then resulted a state of absolute and unchangeable ataraxy—an indisturbable mental immovableness, which is the *Summum Bonum*—a state attainable by the science of absolute nescience.

All this, supposing absolute immobility and indifferentism to be the *Summum Bonum*, would be a very direct and almost instantaneous method of attaining this state, provided the Intelligence could be brought really thus to regard all objects and events, and provided also that our Sensitivity is affected by no causes but the states of the Intelligence. Neither of these conditions, however, is possible. Gout and rheumatism and the toothache are none of them intellectual states, and yet they terribly affect us. We may affirm that there is no difference between these so-called pains and the sensations induced by the sweetest music ear ever heard. Yet even the Pyrrhonist would infinitely prefer the latter to the former. If all objects are in themselves alike, they *seem* different, and as causes of states of the Sensitivity, they are 'what their seeming shows.'

Wherein lies the real difference between life and death, according to the teachings of modern any more than ancient Scepticism, to us it is impossible to determine. All correct definitions enable us to distinguish the things defined from all other objects. The common definition of a square, for example, enables us at once to distinguish all such figures from a circle or a triangle. The following, after many discriminations, is the definition of life given by Mr. Spencer, the central light of modern Scepticism. 'Life,' he says, 'is the definite combination of heterogeneous changes both simultaneous and successive, together with external co-existences and sequences.' Two forms are before us, the one living, and the other dead. The problem to be solved is—the real difference between them, and that in the light of this definition. Undeniably there are, in each alike, 'changes both simultaneous and successive, together with external co-existences and sequences.' So far, life and death are absolutely identical. The only remaining question is in which of these forms is there, and in which is there not, a '*definite* combination of *heterogeneous* changes,' and these identical changes 'both simultaneous and successive?' We may defy the world to show in the light of this definition the real difference between these two forms, that is, between life and death. Thus it is that the ancient Yogee and Pyrrhonist, together with the modern Sceptic, after carrying us round, after the method of Hogg's Tales, a vast circle, promising all the while to 'show us great and wondrous things that we knew not of,' set us down at last at our point of departure, just as we were when we started, with this difference, that during our false progress a fatal disregard has been induced with respect to the greatest of all concerns, those involved in our vital relations to God, duty, immortality, and retribution.

SECTION II.

THE OLD, MIDDLE, AND NEW ACADEMY.

THE epoch in which the doctrines of Plato were adhered to by his successors is called the Old, that in which important, but not fundamental, changes were made in his doctrines, is designated as the Middle, and that in which his teachings were totally subverted, or abandoned, is named the New Academy. The following extract from the 'Epitome of the History of Philosophy,' presents, perhaps, a better account of the progress of philosophic thought in the Platonic School than is given in any other work.

'Of all the Greek schools, Platonism had the most elevated pretensions. Its theory of ideas involved the complete and absolute knowledge of things in themselves. Platonism, in this point of view, represented, so to say, the high aristocracy of the intellect, and must needs have been, accordingly, the particular object of attack by the other schools, among whom a common jealousy united against it. But the more attractive this science was, which was to dissipate all darkness from the human mind, the more difficult it was to hold firmly to it in the midst of the incessant objections opposed to it on all hands by its adversaries. As the Platonists held in contempt all the theories of knowledge maintained in the other schools, they would naturally, when once they admitted a doubt as to their own theory, begin to despair of the human intelligence itself. This explains the apparently singular phenomenon, namely, that Platonism, which exalted the human mind to the greatest height, was the first to descend towards the opposite extreme—the first to establish a mitigated Scepticism. In the period which we are surveying, it no longer attributed to the human Intelligence the power of knowing things in themselves and with certainty; it allowed to Reason no other *Criterion* than probable appearances.' We accordingly find that at the opening of the Christian Era, while Peripatetics, Stoics, Epicureans, and Sceptics were numerous throughout the Roman Empire, or the then civilized world, those who maintained, in fact and form, the doctrines of Plato, were found nowhere, not even in Greece itself. As long as Plato lived, his character and reputation saved his doctrines from disrespect. When he left the scene, and his successors attempted to defend his doctrines from the common assaults of all the other schools, they found the task too great for them. They could neither disprove the doctrines of their opponents, nor defend their own. Plato denied the validity of sense-perception, yet affirmed the absolute validity of perception the same in kind in a former state. Of present perception we are immediately conscious. Of perception in a former state, but 'a small portion of men' have only that form of knowledge which results through *reminiscence*. Where is there, or can there be, any ground whatever for denying wholly the validity of conscious perception, and affirming the absolute infallibility of mere reminiscence? No system thus proudly pretentious, thus foundationless in its principles, and thus open to attack, could long sustain the shock of criticism.

THE PROBABLE SUBSTITUTED FOR THE ABSOLUTE.

The first modification which occurred in the Platonic doctrine was made in what was called the Middle Academy, and consisted in the substitution of *probable* for absolute forms of knowledge. We know not, and cannot know, it was affirmed, realities as they are in themselves. All that we can know of them is through appearances, *images* which come to us from objects around us. Whether these images do, or do not, correspond with their objects, we cannot know with certainty, because we cannot compare the former with the latter. That there is such conformity, however, more or less exact, is altogether probable, and this probability was increased by such circumstances as the following: the liveliness of the impression; the agreement of one appearance with others; and an examination of the same appearance under different aspects. If, under diverse aspects, the appearance always remains the same in all essential particulars, it would demand, in connection with other Criteria, a form of assurance which rationally excludes all doubt. The difference between this doctrine and the Scepticism of the Pyrrhonists is thus shown by Sextus Empiricus. 'Many persons,' he says, 'confound the Philosophy of the Academy with that of the Sceptics. But although the disciples of the New Academy declare that all things are incomprehensible, yet they are distinguished from the Pyrrhonists in this very dogmatism: they affirm that all things are incomprehensible; the Sceptics do not affirm that. Moreover, the Sceptics consider all perceptions perfectly equal as to the faithfulness of their testimony; the Academicians distinguish between probable and improbable perceptions; the first they class under various heads. There are some, they say, which are merely probable, others which are confirmed by reflection, others which are subject to no doubt. Assent is of two kinds: simple assent, which the mind yields without repugnance as without desire, such as that of a child following its master: and the assent which follows upon conviction and reflection. The Sceptics admitted the former kind; the Academicians the latter.'

If we were necessitated to abandon the doctrine of *certain* knowledge, which we are not, and then to make our election between that of Probability and absolute Scepticism, we should select the former as being infinitely the more reasonable and the more safe. Scepticism has no form, nor degree, not only of positive proof or evidence, but even of antecedent probability in its favour. On the other hand, the probabilities are as infinity to unity in favour as against the doctrine of the soul, of matter, time, space, God, duty, immortality, and retribution. *Action* with us must in most cases, even in the most important concerns of life, have no other basis than probability. In concerns of infinite moment, as in the case of a care, or non-care of the soul, of worship or non-worship, and of Infinity and Perfection, where no form of proof, positive evidence, or even antecedent probability exists in favour of the Sceptical hypothesis, and the case, as La Place affirms, stands 'as infinity to unity' in favour of the Theistic doctrine, we should morally and intellectually dementate ourselves, if we should make the Sceptical sentiment the guide of our life.

Among the Greeks, Arcesilaus (316—241 B.C.), and Carneades (214—129 B.C.) are the most celebrated representatives of this new doctrine. In their disputes with the Stoics they took the ground of extreme Scepticism, denying absolutely that we have any Criterion of truth. In their controversy with the Sceptics they opposed to absolute and universal Doubt the doctrine of Probability. Of the doctrine last named, Cicero was one of the most able and illustrious defenders. 'It is more reasonable and safe,' he argued, 'to care for the soul than to disregard its possible immortal interests. If we care for such interests, and the soul dies with the body, the Sceptic will not be with us in eternity to laugh at us for our superstition. If, on the other hand, the soul is immortal, the Sceptic may forever regret his temerity in disregarding its immortal interests.' This is the substance of Cicero's argument upon this subject. His famous argument for the doctrine of God is familiar to our readers, and annihilates forever all excuse for a Godless life.

In the New Academy the doctrine of Scepticism became more and more intense, until in the school which he had established nothing of Plato remained but his name. In his first lecture in Rome, for example, Carneades delighted even the Stoic Cato with his able and eloquent exposition of the doctrine of Justice. The next day, however, he astonished the same audience by a professed demonstration of equal brilliancy, that knowledge on all subjects in common is utterly void of certainty, and by an affirmed refutation of all the arguments which he had the day preceding presented in favour of the doctrine of Justice. Cato, in view of such subverting intellectual jugglery, persuaded the Senate to banish such philosophers from Rome. We have here 'the oppositions' (antitheses, antinomies) 'of science falsely so-called' to which Paul refers, 'Antitheses of Science,' and 'Antinomies of Pure Reason' which lie at the basis of ancient and modern Scepticism. In all such processes, there is this fundamental sophism, that by proof the invalidity of all proof may be demonstrated, and that by processes of reasoning the invalidity of all facts and principles, which lie at the basis of all reasoning, may be established. If all argument, with its basis, facts, and principles, is invalid, such invalidity cannot be verified by argument. What is the wisdom or use of begging, as Mr. Mill and all Sceptics do, that *all* deduction is begged? Can any argument have validity the conclusion of which *is*, that *all* argument is invalid, and that the same is true of all facts and principles that lie at the basis of all argument? Such juggling in logic as this can have place but in the brain of false science. Besides, as we have formerly stated, the conclusion deduced from these affirmed antitheses must undeniably have greater certainty and validity than is possessed by the intuitive and necessary convictions which are thereby impeached. Can we be as certain of the validity of the Sceptic's argument as we are of the fact of our own existence, and of that of material forms around us?

SECTION III.

CONTINUATION OF THE ARISTOTELIAN SCHOOLS.

In the theology of Aristotle God had place but as the *passive* cause of the organization of the universe, and of the events of universal providence. In the teachings of his successors, the Divine Idea gradually faded out, and was at last supplanted by Absolute Naturalism. Theophrastus (373—287 B.C.), who was selected by Aristotle as his successor, while he in general remained true to the doctrines of his predecessor, gave great prominence to the idea of motion as a primal cause in nature, and even represented thought as a species of motion. Virtue he taught to be worthy of being sought on its own account; yet affirmed that slight deviations from rules of morality were permissible when great good could be secured, or great evils averted thereby. External good he held to be essential as a means of cultivating virtue. The Stoics attributed to him the maxim, that fortune, and not wisdom, or virtue, is the rule of life.

Strabo of Lampsicus, the successor of Theophrastus, reduced the doctrines of Aristotle to a Pure Naturalism. Perception and thought, he held, were identical, and denied that mind has any existence separate from the body. Other Peripatetics, as stated by Ueberweg on the authority of Cicero, while they agreed with Aristotle in the general doctrine of the soul, taught that 'There exist no individual substantial souls, but only in its stead, one universal, vital, and sensitive force, which is diffused through all existing organisms, and is transiently individualized in different bodies.' We thus perceive the consequences of a fundamental error introduced into a system otherwise true. Out of Aristotle's doctrine of the absolute passivity of God in creation and providence, there resulted, among his early successors in his own school, the doctrine of Pure Materialism on the one hand, and Immaterial Pantheism on the other.

The writings of Aristotle, however, continued to be generally read and studied, and were the subjects of many commentaries in the schools, not only of Greece, but of Egypt and Rome. Thus the way was prepared for the perpetuity of his influence for ages after the commencement of the Christian era. In the school of Aristotle, the doctrine of Nominalism, and in that of Plato, that which, for ages, was designated as Realism, were fully developed, and were handed down to posterity for elucidation.

4. The fundamental question agitated in all the schools of Greece was in substance this: What is the *Summum Bonum*? In other words, On what conditions can human misery be terminated, and perfect happiness be secured? All men were visibly and consciously evil and unhappy, and all as consciously desired to find a remedy for the evil and its consequent misery, and to attain rest. While all these schools agitated these great problems, all as visibly failed in their solution. Yet the agitation kept the problems distinctly and impressively before the popular mind, and induced a universal yearning for a discovery of the secret which should 'end the heartache, and all the ills that flesh is heir to,' and thus prepared the way for a ready reception of the sovereign remedy which Christianity did reveal.

SECTION IV.

NEO-PLATONISM.

In its attempts to solve the problem of universal being and its laws, Grecian thought was, even to itself, a demonstrated failure, and had settled down into the general formula of Scepticism, 'that we do not know that we do not know anything.' Such was the general sentiment of the leading Grecian Schools. At this era Greece ceased to be the home of Philosophy. Grecian thinkers no longer respected at home travelled, and carried their doctrines into other countries, particularly into Rome and Egypt. Roman thought took form from the Grecian, but originated nothing even apparently new. At Alexandria in Egypt, however, a famous school of thinkers arose, who attempted to create a new system out of the blended forms of Oriental and Grecian Positivisms. The mind can never long rest in the blind negations of Scepticism. The dominion of Sceptical thought has, consequently, always been superseded by Positive systems of some kind. Hence thinkers of Alexandria, such as Philo the Jew, Ammonius Saccas, and Plotinus, were all Positivists. In Grecian thought, as has been well said, 'Theology was much less developed than Cosmology, and Cosmology than Anthropology. In Oriental thought, on the other hand, Theology has the first place, Cosmology the second, and Anthropology almost no place at all. In the schools of Alexandria Theology became the leading object of thought and inquiry.

In the system of Philo, who was born a few years prior to the Christian Era, we meet with the doctrine of a personal God, 'the object of immediate subjective certainty,' and also inferrible from creation, an inference based upon the axiom, 'No work of skill makes itself.' So far we have essentially the doctrine of the Old Testament. In creation, however, God acts through delegated powers originally created by Him, particularly through the highest of all the divine forces, the *Logos* (the

Word). This Logos is styled by Philo, 'the Son, the Paraclete, the Mediator between God and man.' Virtue consists in likeness to God. Man is strong and wise, instead of weak and foolish, when his 'soul becomes the dwelling place of God,' and the soul's 'highest blessedness is to abide in God.' The central Christian idea, that 'the Word became flesh and dwelt among us,' has no place in the teachings of this thinker. His doctrine of the Logos, leaving out the idea of incarnation, is Arian, on the one hand, and Platonic on the other. For a full statement of the doctrines of this author, we would refer especially to Ueberweg's 'History of Philosophy.' In Plotinus (204—269 A.D.) a disciple of Ammonius Saccas, of whom we shall speak more at large in another connection, Neo-Platonism reached its consummation, and with him the history of Grecian Philosophy properly terminates. In the system of Plotinus, we have a reproduction, in fact and form, of the ancient, Oriental, prior Grecian, and an anticipation of modern Pantheism, and this doctrine was by him presented in opposition to Christian Theism. From Plato he borrowed the doctrine that all science must be of universals. Individuals are nothing but phenomena which have no real existence. Universals alone, as ideas, have real existence. Ideas as Noumena are but manifestations of one common Noumenon, the sensible world being the phenomenon of the Ideal world, and the Ideal world the mode of the divine existence. The condition of real knowledge is the absolute identity of the subject and object of knowledge, or of thought and the thing thought of. The faculty by which the mind knows the Infinite, as the only real existence, is called *Ecstasy*.

'If,' says Plotinus, as cited by Mr. Lewes, 'knowledge is the same as the thing known, the Finite, as Finite, never can know the Infinite, because *it* cannot be Infinite. To attempt, therefore, to know the Infinite by Reason is futile; it (the Infinite) can only be known in immediate presence. The Faculty by which the mind divests itself of its personality is Ecstasy. In this Ecstasy the soul becomes loosened from its material prison, separated from individual consciousness, and becomes absorbed in the Infinite Intelligence from which it emanated. In this Ecstasy it contemplates real existence—it identifies itself with that which it contemplates.'

Various terms are employed by Plotinus to represent the primal essence or thought of which all appearances are emanations, such as 'the First,' 'the One,' 'the Good,' and 'that which stands above being.' When he attempted to find terms by which to represent any definite idea of this primal essence, he found himself at an utter loss, not having any definite views himself upon the subject. On the negative side, he denies of this essence, 'all thinking and willing,' 'all energy,' 'life' and 'essence.' On the positive side, he affirmed that this essence 'needs nothing and can desire nothing,' that it is 'above energy,' and can 'neither be expressed nor thought.' Yet it is the producer of all things—the producer, not by a voluntary creative fiat, but by necessary emanation. From excess of energy, that which has no energy nor being, but is above both, radiates images of itself, just as the sun emits rays of itself. These images involuntarily turn towards their original in order to behold it, and thus become mind. In this mind ideas are immanent as essential parts of itself. In becoming conscious of these immanent ideas, mind apprehends the self and the not-self, that is, the universe of matter and spirit, and God as the Author of all things. In Ecstasy, mind apprehends the self, the world, and God, as one and identical. Perhaps Mr. Lewes, in the following expressive sentence, has represented as clearly as can be done the real idea of this last of the Greek philosophers. 'God therefore in His absolute state—in His first and highest Hypostasis—is neither Existence nor Thought, neither moved nor mutable; He is the simple Unity, or, as Hegel would say, the Absolute Nothing, the Immanent Negative.'

In his system Plotinus professedly embodied the ultimate deductions of all the forms of Oriental and Grecian Idealism. Had his ecstatic visions given him a knowledge of the future, he might have said with equal truth that he had fully anticipated, in all essential particulars, the systems of modern Pantheism and Pure Idealism. The following facts will fully verify all the above statements.

1. The faculty of Ecstasy is undeniably identical with that of Intuition or Reason affirmed by the Oriental Yogee, the Nous or Reason of the Grecian Idealist, and 'the Special Faculty of Intellectual Intuition' of the Modern Transcendentalist. In all these schools the same identical offices or functions are performed by the faculty represented by these different terms.

2. The method of induction and deduction is also one and identical. In no case is there, in any form, an induction of facts of external or internal perception. On the other hand, ' by an act of (so-called) scientific Scepticism to which the mind voluntarily determines itself,' such facts are *treated* as nothing but a prejudice. In all systems in common, the subject 'puts himself into a state of not knowing, when he begins to philosophize,' and then, by direct, immediate, à *priori* intuition, apprehends 'Brahm,' 'Pironis,' 'the One,' 'the Absolute,' or 'the Immanent Nothing,' as the only real existence.

3. All philosophers of all these schools also agree in this, that with none of them are these visions of the primal essence *habitual*. In all the ordinary circumstances of life, they think, and feel, and act; eat, drink, sleep, and believe, just as all the rest of us poor mortals do. But when they all in common 'put themselves into a state of not-knowing and begin

to philosophize,' a part of them sitting in a moveless posture, with 'their eyes fixed upon the end of their noses,' 'they become wide awake,' have visions of 'existence *in se*,' and behold face to face 'the primal essence,' which is 'neither Existence nor Thought,' 'Brahm,' 'the One,' 'the All One,' 'the Immanent Nothing,' and behold this 'Simple Unity' as the only real existence, all seeming realities being only reflections of their original and identical with it. It is only occasionally, we say, that any of these philosophers, as they themselves admit, enjoy 'these visions of the Absolute.' 'Only rarely,' says Plotinus, 'does the direct vision of the Supreme God fall to the lot of the best of men, the virtuous and wise, the God-like and blessed.' Porphyry informs us that it was only *four times* during the six years which he spent with Plotinus, that the latter attained to those 'Ecstatic visions,' 'this unification with God.'

4. All these philosophers also agree in calling these occasional visions *science*, and in enthroning them as of supreme authority above all intuitions of the Universal Intelligence, and all deductions from the same. All admit that if we rely upon intuition and deduction from intuition, we cannot be Idealists. Absolute faith in *à priori* visions of the Absolute, call this faculty by what name you will, is, as these philosophers all teach, the immutable condition of 'taking the first step in the Speculative Philosophy.' If we ask the question, *Why* shall we accept of these 'Ecstatic visions' and *à priori* insights, and reject universal intuition, and all deductions from the same, as truths of science, these philosophers are silent. 'The German philosophers,' says Mr. Lewes, 'proceed with peaceable dogmatism to tell you that God is this or that; to explain how Nothing *becomes* the existing world, to explain many other inexplicable things; and if you stop them with the simple, How do you know this—what is your ground of certitude? they will allude blandly to their *Verunst*, and continue their exposition.' It is high time for all thinkers who would not be fatally misled in respect to questions of eternally vital concern, to 'become wide-awake' to one immutable conviction, that where so-called systems of science, however logically self-consistent, and by whatever names commended to our regard—that wherever and whenever such systems ignore, deny, and nullify all our universal and intuitive convictions of truth, we should question the validity of such systems, and require, before admitting their deductions at all, evidence of a higher and more absolute kind than we have of our own personal existence, and that of the universe around us. The time is coming, and quite near, we believe, when 'the absurdities of genius,' the extravagances of philosophers, and 'the contradictions of science falsely so-called,' will stand forth as the eighth wonder of the world, while the ninth and greatest wonder of all will be the fact, that under the lead of such monstrously absurd teachings any thinking portion of the race accepted of such extravagances as truths of

science, and repudiated universal and absolute intuition as illusion. Suppose that Mr. Schelling, or any other Transcendentalist, were required to give us specific reasons for the absolute authority claimed for this faculty of Intellectual Intuition (intellectuelle Anschauung), he would be put to silence in a moment. Every reflecting thinker, Mr. Schelling among the rest, cannot but be aware that no such grounds of certitude exist. If any thinker would seriously ask himself the question, Have I as real and as rational grounds for an assurance of the validity of the revelations of this 'Faculty of Intellectual Intuition,' or 'Ecstasy,' or of '*à priori* Insight,' as I have for my own conscious personal existence, and of that of the universe around me—he would perceive at once that while universal Intuition has the most absolutely rational basis, the revelations of this 'Intellectuelle Anschauung,' a faculty supposed to be possessed only by a very few of the race, rest upon the most shadowy grounds conceivable.

General Reflections on the Grecian Evolution in Philosophy.

We have now completed our criticisms of the Grecian Evolution in Philosophy. What remains is comprised in a few general reflections on the character and results of this Evolution.

Verification of our Statement in Regard to the Number and Character of all Possible and Actual Systems of Philosophy.

We have another fundamental verification of a statement made in the General Introduction, namely, that there never has been, and never can be, but a certain specific number of systems of Ontology, and that they all take form and character from certain definite postulates, pertaining to the relations of the human Intelligence to four realities, to wit, spirit and matter, and time and space. In our examination, first of the Oriental and then of the Grecian systems, we have found that each system took specific form from a definite hypothesis of this kind. Materialism in all ages and schools has, in fact and form, one exclusive basis—an affirmed validity of our knowledge of matter, and a denial of that of spirit. Idealism, as Ideal Dualism, Subjective Idealism, Pantheism, and Pure Idealism, has a basis equally specific—a denial of the validity of our knowledge of 'things without us,' and an affirmation of the validity of our knowledge of facts of mind. Scepticism has, and ever has had, one formal basis, an impeachment of our knowledge of both spirit and matter. All thinkers, on the other hand, who have admitted the validity of our knowledge of matter and spirit, and of time and space, have, without exception, been Theists, and with Theism have affirmed the doctrine of duty and immortality. These are all the systems that ever have arisen, and they have all, Theism excepted, ever since mind began to philosophize taken on the same essential forms, and been developed in fixed accordance with the same identical methods. When we have comprehended the Materialism of Kanada, of the Djainas, and of the Buddhists, we have discovered all that we can find in the systems of Democritus, Epicurus, Compte, and Condillac. The Ideal systems of Kant, Fichte, Schelling, and Hegel are mere repetitions, without any essential improvements whatever, of those of Plotinus, Parmenides, Pythagoras, Vayasa, Kapila, and those of the two Idealistic schools of the Buddhists. Nor have modern Sceptics changed or in any essential forms improved the systems of Protagoras, Pyrrho, and Carneades. The problems, methods, and solutions common to any one of these schools in any one age, are equally common to them in all ages. From the nature of the case such must be the results. In Theism there has been progression, because evidence and arguments in new forms have been constantly presenting themselves.

THE SYSTEMS PRESENT OR WANTING IN THE GRECIAN, AND COMMON OR PECULIAR TO ORIENTAL AND MODERN SCHOOLS.

In comparing the Grecian and the Oriental Schools with the Modern Evolution we obtain the following results. We find, as we have formerly stated, two systems, Theism and Scepticism, which are not found in the Oriental, present in the Modern Evolution. We find also two systems, Ideal Dualism and Subjective Idealism, wanting in the Greek, and common to the other two Evolutions. Subjective Idealism is naturally so remote from the sphere of spontaneous and reflective thought, and was originally developed at such a distance from Greece, that as a system, we have no evidence that it was ever, either historically or reflectively, present in the mind of any Grecian thinker.

In the presence of the same identical postulate, on the authority of which Ideal Dualism took form in Oriental and Modern Anti-theistic thought, Scepticism was originated and took form in Grecian thought. The fundamental postulate of the former system is this, 'that the things which we envisage are not that in themselves for which we take them, neither are their relationships so constituted as they appear to us, in other words, that we have no valid knowledge of mind or matter, time or space. In the presence of this postulate, Oriental and German thought dogmatized, and in their dogmatism constructed a positive system of Ontology, namely, that there exist *two* unknown and unknowable entities—Noumena, as the substances and principles of all things. Grecian thought was too discriminating to fall into such an absurdity as that. If, as Ideal Dualism affirms, we 'know nothing of realities but our manner of perceiving them,' if ours is a mode of perception 'peculiar to us, and need not be the same in any other class of beings,' and if it is only with this peculiar and special 'mode of perceiving we have to do,' the only formula which can have authority with us is the old sceptical one—to wit, 'I assert nothing, and deny nothing, not even that I deny anything.' For philosophers to lay down the principle that all our knowledge of realities is mere appearance, and 'that the reality existing behind all appearance is, and ever must be, unknown,' and then to set forth, as having claim to validity, a system of Ontology, is simply to convict themselves before the world, not only of the grossest scientific absurdity, but also of an absolute disbelief in the validity of their own fundamental principle.

On the score of scientific self-consistency, Grecian stands in most impressive contrast with Modern Scepticism. The former system has one obvious merit—the absence of Dogmatism; while no system ever was, or can be, more repulsively and imperiously dogmatic than the latter. The former had but one form of dogmatism in common with the latter, the professed power to *prove* that no form of proof is possible. In all other respects Grecian Scepticism is logically self-consistent. Modern Scepticism, on the other hand, seems to regard absolute and universal nescience of all forms and modes of real existence as the condition and starting point for the solution of the problem of universal being and its laws. We suppose it safe to affirm that no man is a more absolute Sceptic in theory than Mr. Emerson; and it is equally safe to affirm that no man living or dead is, or was, a more sovereign dogmatist; his dogmatic utterances, also, having chief reference to truth as it exists 'behind all appearance.' The same remarks have an undeniable application to the productions of such authors as J. S. Mill, Spencer, Huxley, and all other advocates of the New Philosophy—a system avowedly based upon the formula that 'it is certain that we can have no knowledge of the nature of mind or matter either.' On what authority, then, does Mr. Mill dogmatically affirm that matter is nothing but a *permanent susceptibility of sensation*'? If, as he affirms that he does, he knows nothing but phenomena, how does he know that there does, or does not, exist any susceptibility at all? After affirming, as the basis of all his deductions, that 'the reality existing behind all appearance is, and ever must be, unknown,' Mr. Spencer gravely informs us of the identical 'stuff that life is made of,' and of the specific elements which constitute progression, and that there can 'exist behind all appearance' no such power as Free Will. If he knows nothing about what realities exist behind all appearance, how can he know, or reasonably affirm, that a Free Will does not exist there? To induce Theists to surrender the doctrine of an infinite and perfect personal God, Mr. Spencer dogmatizes thus—'the choice is not between personality and something lower than personality, whereas the choice is between personality and something higher.' Here is absolute dogmatism about what the author affirms absolute ignorance. 'Is it not,' he adds, 'just as possible that there is a mode of being as much transcending Intelligence and Will, as these transcend mechanical motion?' For ourselves, we have no idea that Mr. Spencer himself seriously thinks that there can possibly be a mode of being as far above an infinite and perfect personal God as He is above mere mechanical motion. Our serious judgment is that he deliberately intended to test the question, by actual experiment, how far credulity among Theists would descend with him into the abyss of absurdity. Mr. Spencer is too much of a thinker to imagine even that there can possibly be a mode of being infinitely above that of infinite and perfect Intelligence and Will. Our object, however, is to illustrate by examples, the dogmatism of Modern Scepticism.

Let us for a moment contemplate a few other examples of the same character. Mr. Huxley, having assured us that 'it is certain that we can have no knowledge of the nature of either matter or spirit,' 'proposes to *demonstrate* to us that a unity of power or faculty, a unity of form, and a unity of substantial composition does pervade the whole living world.' Here we are, in fact and form, promised absolute demonstration in the sphere of affirmed and admitted absolute ignorance. Yes, our author promises to demonstrate the existence of 'a unity of substantial composition' in bodies, while he himself, in the same address, affirms 'that it is also, in strictness, true that we know nothing about the composition of any body whatever as it is.' While he affirms an absolute ignorance of the nature of matter and spirit, he affirms, as dogmatically, that matter, and not spirit, thinks and feels and wills. 'Thoughts are the expression of molecular changes in that matter of life which is the source of our other vital phenomena.' Again, 'as surely as every future grows out of past and present, so will the physiology of the future gradually extend the realm of matter and law until it is co-extensive with knowledge, with feeling, and with action.' Here dogmatism, resting upon admitted absolute ignorance of the subject matter to which that dogmatism pertains, has undeniably reached its consummation.

In Taine 'On Intelligence'—a work of another zealous advocate of the New Philosophy which, as we have said, affirms as its basis and starting point absolute nescience of matter and spirit—we have 'a general and abstract psychology' in which all facts of mind are dogmatically explained on the Molecular Theory. If we 'can know nothing of the nature of either spirit or matter,' how can we know, we ask again, that it is matter and not spirit which knows and feels and acts? How can we know that 'molecular changes in this *matter* of life' constitute any single element of mental phenomena? Yet in affirmed ignorance of the nature and relations of matter and spirit, these self-styled Scientists, or Knowing Ones, not only affirm that matter does think and feel and will, but dogmatically tell just how and why and where it performs these functions. 'Memory,' we are told by a central light in the high firmament of the New Philosophy, 'is fossil precepts.' 'I hold,' says another of these scientists of equal eminence, 'emotion to mean the special sensibility of the vesicular neurine to ideas.' 'The highest functions of the nervous system, those to which the hemispherical ganglia minister,' says the same authority, 'are the functions of intelligence, of emotion, and of will.' After giving forth a multitude of such lucid utterances, our author, in common with all advocates of this New Philosophy, affirms an absolute ignorance of the nature of the substances about which he thus imperiously dogmatizes.

Now Grecian Scepticism, with the exception above designated, cannot be charged with such gross and palpable forms of self-contradiction and absurdity. It never asserted an absolute ignorance of 'realities which exist behind all appearance,' and then imperiously affirmed, 'I *know* facts, and I *know* law,' law which, undeniably, exists 'behind all appearances,' and determines their character. Of all systems that ever appeared, Modern Scepticism, or the New Philosophy, is the most pretentious, imperious, and absolute in its dogmatisms, and the most shallow and sophistical in its 'grounds and arguments.' It has made a great stir and agitation in the sphere of Anglo-Saxon thought. Yet when the true state of the case comes to light, it is found that we have had nothing 'but a tempest in a mud-puddle.'

In What Sense and Form was Grecian Philosophy Introductory to Christianity?

The question has often been presented, whether Grecian Philosophy in its results was, or was not, introductory to Christianity? We should leave this treatise in an incomplete state did we not speak specifically upon this subject. We propose, then, to present the mature deductions bearing upon this inquiry, deductions to which real facts of history have conducted us.

In one fundamental respect the Grecian Evolution was a great impediment rather than an introduction to Christianity. In the sphere of scientific and popular thought that Evolution had determined no one doctrine or principle of Theism. It had failed utterly in popular regard to establish upon a scientific basis the doctrine of the existence of a Supreme God, or of the immortality of the soul. In all the popular philosophies which had place in scientific thought at the commencement of the Christian era, these doctrines were specifically denied. Never was philosophic thought in a more chaotic state than it was at the time when 'the Sun of Righteousness rose upon the world with healing in His wings.' Nor did the existing direction of scientific thought promise anything better for the future. Christianity in its early development, on the other hand, stood out before the world in open antagonism to the then received philosophies.

Yet Grecian Philosophy, while it had fully demonstrated in popular regard its own utter impotence to solve the problem of being and its laws, did exert an influence auxiliary to the Christian religion. We will now proceed to designate what we regard as some of the forms of this influence.

1. One of the most important of these propædeutic forms of influence arose from the fact that the conflicting schools of Greece held, in their discussions, affirmations, and denials, the doctrines of God, duty, well-being, immortality, and retribution, distinctly and constantly before the educated and popular classes. On all these subjects Christianity propounded no *new* themes, and solved no *new* problems. Former and existing discussions and failures had induced a general desire for reliable solutions of all such questions. When Christianity presented such solutions, the popular mind had, in the discussions referred to, been prepared to receive them. Though Grecian thought had not sown the truth, it had prepared the soil to receive the seed where sown upon it.

2. One great advantage which the early learned defenders of Christian doctrines of God, duty, and immortality, possessed, lay in the fact that their teachings on these high themes were confirmed, not only by the intuitive convictions of the race, but by the highest authorities in the sphere of Grecian thought, the authority and arguments of such minds as Thales, Anaxagoras, Empedocles, Xenophanes, Socrates, Plato, and Aristotle. Of such authority learned advocates of Christian doctrine made great use, and justly so, in their presentations of truth to the educated and popular classes. Here is the source of the most efficient influences of Grecian thought as auxiliary to Christianity.

3. In most of the Schools of Greece fundamental criteria of truth had been developed, criteria in the light of which the great central doctrines of Christianity stood revealed as demonstrated verities of science. Almost nothing else had greater influence in the hands of learned Christian teachers than the application of these criteria. In their light these teachers were able to demonstrate the fact that the essential doctrines and principles of Christianity must be true, or the Intelligence itself must be affirmed to be a lie. Thus, while Grecian Philosophy was not itself 'the light of the world,' it became a hindrance on the one hand, and an auxiliary on the other, to that light.

PART III.

BOOK I.

THE CHRISTIAN EVOLUTION IN PHILOSOPHY.

AMONG thinkers the impression very commonly obtains, and we often meet with statements to the same effect, particularly in treatises on the History of Philosophy, that the writers of the Old and New Testaments held and taught no system of Philosophy—that they simply taught doctrines, or facts, without any specific reference to questions of Ontology, or Ultimate Causation. In certain respects such statements are true, and in others, of equal importance, they are far from being true. In the multitudinous writings of Plato we find no systematic statement of truth. The careful readers of these writings, however, find everywhere underlying the same certain great principles which may readily be aggregated into a system. The same holds true of the Scriptures. Underlying all their teachings we find all the ultimate truths and principles which can be reached by science. Here we find a distinct hypothesis of Ultimate Causation—an equally well-defined doctrine of Cosmology—all the principles of fundamental morality—and a doctrine equally well defined of the eternal future of mind. We propose to notice and set forth the specific teachings of the Bible on these varied themes.

SECTION I.

DOCTRINE, OR HYPOTHESIS, OF ULTIMATE CAUSATION.

THIS hypothesis is distinctly stated by the Apostle (Heb. xi. 3), 'Through faith we understand that the worlds were made by the word of God, so that things which are seen were not made of things which do appear.' Here the Theistic hypothesis of Ultimate Causation is distinctly set forth both in its *positive* and *negative* forms. Positively, it is affirmed that the universe as now revealed to us took its existing form as the result of THE WORD, act of will, or creative fiat, of God. This is but a restatement in another form of the doctrine set forth in Gen. i. 1, 'In the beginning, God created the heavens and the earth.' In other words, when the universe was originated 'the heavens and the earth,' that is the entire universe, became an orderly and organized whole as the result of the creative agency of God. Then the sacred writer descends to particulars, and ascribes the organization of 'the heavens and the earth,' the world on which we live, together with the sun, the moon, and the stars, and the existence of all vitalized forms of being around us, to *the will* of God. 'He spake, and it was done: He commanded, and it stood fast,' that is, *He willed* that things should be thus, and so, and they took form accordingly. The doctrine of creation in its entireness as the exclusive result of the agency of the *will* of a personal God, is the specific hypothesis of Ultimate Causation set forth in the sacred Scriptures.

In its negative form the doctrine of creation through the will of a personal God is set forth in direct and specific opposition to the dogmas of heathen and Anti-theistic philosophies. The united teaching of all systems then taught was organization by natural law, or the development, or evolution, of 'things seen from things which appear,' that is, from pre-existing natural conditions. The whole passage is thus literally rendered by Conybeare and Howson: 'By faith we understand that the universe was framed by the word of God, so that the world which we behold springs not from things which can be seen.' 'The doctrine negatived,' they correctly say, 'is that which teaches that each successive condition of the universe is generated from a preceding condition (as the plant from the seed) by a mere natural development, which had no beginning in the will of God.' If we will carefully study the teachings of the Scriptures in respect to the doctrine of creation, we shall find that not only is the organization of the universe ascribed to the direct and immediate agency of God, but also the origination of every species of animals and plants. Moses, who was 'learned in all the wisdom of the Egyptians,' understood fully all the Oriental Philosophies. The common doctrine of all these systems was creation by emanation, or the development of all particular species from preceding ones of a lower type. Creation by natural law, by emanation, development, or evolution, was the common doctrine of all these philosophies in all their forms. In opposition to such philosophies we are informed that 'in the beginning,' not *natural law*, but 'God created the heavens and the earth.' The sacred writer then descends to particulars, and affirms that in the origin of animals and plants the agency of God was just as direct and immediate as it was in the creation of the universe, that all orders of vitalized existence were so organized at the beginning that each species should immutably propagate its kind, and not evolve itself into something higher, or diverse from its own kind, 'the fruit-tree yielding fruit *after his kind*, whose seed is in itself.' 'And God made the beast after his kind, and cattle after their kind, and every thing that creepeth upon the earth after his kind.' Nothing can be more evident than is the deduction, that at the beginning, species were originated, and not embryotic forms which should evolve themselves into species endlessly diversified. Then, as if to anticipate the modern monkey hypothesis, man is affirmed to have been created, and located at his creation in a definite region of the earth where monkeys have never existed. Taking into our reckoning not particular words merely, but the whole account of the organization of the Universe given in the first chapter of Genesis, and the deduction is absolute, that the fixed intention of its author was to present the revealed doctrine of creation throughout, in direct and open opposition to the teachings of the ungodly religions and godless philosophies of all prior ages, and this, not in their principles merely, but also in all their details. The conclusion is undeniable that Darwin or Moses has fundamentally erred. No explanation can be given of the peculiar phrases 'after his kind,' and 'whose seed is in itself,' but upon the hypothesis that the specific intent of the sacred writer was to deny the doctrines of emanation and development, or evolution, which were the fundamental characteristics of all the great systems of religion and philosophy then existing.

THE DOCTRINE OF PROVIDENCE.

Equally specific is the Doctrine of Providence taught in the Scriptures. God as here revealed is not only 'the former of all things,' but exercises a direct and immediate providential control over 'the things that are made,' the will of God being the *supreme* law of the universe, the wants of mind the end for which all material objects exist and are controlled. God is also distinctly revealed as present amid passing events around us, so that He is to His rational offspring, relative to their moral and physical necessities, a hearer of prayer. Every intelligent reader of the Scriptures is aware that the above statements perfectly accord with the plainest and most express teachings of the Sacred Word. All the facts of order which everywhere appear, all the movements of the sun, moon, and stars, sunshine and darkness, and all events of all the seasons, are revealed as determined by the will of God. In express reference to sickness and health, rain and sunshine, and all our daily concernments, prayer is affirmed to be of great avail.

Relations of the above Doctrines to Science.

Such, undeniably, are the Theistic teachings of Scripture on the subjects before us. What are the relations of these doctrines to science? To this question we answer:

1. All events which are, or may be known to science, are fully explicable on this hypothesis. The doctrine of a free, intelligent, personal God,

infinite and perfect in all His attributes, fully explains the organization of the existing universe, with all the facts and events which it presents. If the facts of geology, for example, facts which are supposed to favour the doctrine of Evolution, can be explained in accordance with that hypothesis, they cannot be shown to contradict the doctrine of the origination of species by the direct and immediate agency of God. The facts, to say the least, are just as explicable on the latter as on the former hypothesis. The same holds true of all facts and events known to science throughout the wide domain of universal nature. All such facts and event are undeniably explicable through the doctrine of a personal God. If visible and conscious facts do not affirm, they do not contradict the doctrine of Providence and of the efficacy of prayer. All that the Bible teaches in respect to creation, providence, prayer, miracles, and we may add, redemption, also appears as possible and fully explicable facts and events through the cause which it assigns for all these facts. In Natural Theism, and in that of the Scriptures, we have, we repeat, an hypothesis, in accordance with which all events known to science as possible in the nature of things may be fully explained and elucidated. There is no denying this deduction.

2. This fact, we remark in the next place, renders absolutely impossible all disproof of, and positive evidence, or even antecedent probability, against this hypothesis, on the one hand, and all forms of proof, evidence, or even probability in favour of any contradictory hypothesis on the other. All that can be done in any conceivable case in favour of the hypothesis of Natural Law, Emanation, Development, or Evolution, would be to prove, not that such hypothesis is in fact true, but that it *may* be true, that is, that in accordance with it existing facts are explicable. As long as the same facts remain equally explicable on a different and opposite hypothesis, all disproof of the latter, and proof, positive evidence, or even antecedent probability, in favour of the former, remain strictly impossible. The reader should bear in mind that while modern Scientists talk so loftily of the *science* of Emanation, Development, and Evolution, they are dogmatizing in respect to hypotheses which by no possibility can attain to the prerogative of science, hypotheses in favour of which no possible form of real proof, positive evidence, or antecedent probability, can be adduced. Granting all the facts adduced by Mr. Darwin and other Evolutionists, for example, said facts do not prove this hypothesis even probably true. The reason is obvious and undeniable. Said facts are all, to say the least, equally explicable on the hypothesis of the origination of species by the direct and immediate agency of God. The same holds true in all other cases. The hypothesis of ultimate and universal causation affirmed by Natural and Revealed Theism accounts fully for all facts and events in the universe. No form of disproof, positive evidence, or

antecedent probability can by any possibility, we repeat, be adduced against this, and in favour of any opposing hypothesis.

3. While it ever must remain true that upon no conditions, actual or conceivable, can the doctrine of natural and revealed Theism be disproved, or any real proof, evidence, or antecedent probability be adduced in favour of any opposite hypothesis, the common deduction of all the sciences bearing at all upon the subject, render the former hypothesis a demonstrated truth, and the latter, in all its forms, a demonstrated error. There is not a science that has the remotest bearing upon the doctrine of ultimate causation, a science which does not culminate in the deduction of the organization of the universe as an event of time. There is no doctrine in which the final deductions of all such sciences, and the admissions of all eminent scientists of all schools, more absolutely agree, than they do in the hypothesis of the non-eternity of the present order of things. Universal order from universal chaos is demonstrably explicable by no hypothesis of natural law. Universal order from any law of nature, or any necessary cause, order as an event of time, can no more be accounted for than the existence of an event without a cause. A necessary cause, whatever its nature, must act as soon as the conditions of its activity are fulfilled. The conditions of the activity of the ultimate cause of these facts must have been fulfilled from eternity, or said cause would not be the *ultimate*. That cause, on the other hand, which fulfilled these conditions would be said cause. Creation as an event of time; creation through any natural law, or necessary cause of any kind, is a palpable contradiction. A free cause, on the other hand, may or may not act in any given direction when the conditions of its activity are fulfilled. Hence creation from such a cause, creation as an event of time, is both possible and explicable. Either the final deduction of universal science is utterly false, or the Theistic and Christian hypothesis of ultimate causation is true.

4. This common deduction of all the sciences, viz., creation as an event of time, not only demonstrates the validity of the Theistic hypothesis, but utterly annihilates all objections to the doctrine of supernatural events as recorded in Scripture, and to the revealed doctrine of Providence, and of God in nature as a hearer of prayer. Either science, itself, is a lie, or creation is a supernatural event, and the occurrence of such events in nature is both possible and probable. Nothing is, or can be, at a greater remove from the domain of true science than the boasted Naturalism of the present and all past ages. These scientists never have adduced, and never can adduce, a single fact which presents the remotest degree of real proof, positive evidence, or antecedent probability, in favour of any one of their godless hypotheses. The fundamental fallacy in the reasoning of all these scientists is this, that *a given hypothesis may be proven true by facts which*

are equally explicable on a different and opposite hypothesis. Take any fact, or class of facts, ever adduced by any of these scientists to prove any one of his godless hypotheses, and place that fact, or class of facts, in the clear light of scientific induction and deduction, and the conclusion becomes at once demonstrably evident, that said fact, or class of facts, is just as compatible with, and explicable by, the hypothesis which he denies, as with and by that which he affirms. True science does and must affirm his proofs to be no proofs, his evidence to be no evidence at all, and his probabilities to be nothing but improbabilities. The real facts of the case can by no possibility, from the nature of the case, be otherwise.

SECTION II.
ONTOLOGY OF THE BIBLE.

IN the Scriptures also we have a distinct recognition of the doctrine of Ontology as developed in this Treatise, that of the real existence of four distinct and separate realities, namely, Matter, Spirit, Time, and Space. The terms everlasting, or eternity, and immensity represent the last two realities; while the terms earth, or dust, and spirit represent the two first designated.

Nothing can be more distinct, definite, and specific than is the distinction made in the Scriptures between matter and spirit, and the soul and the body. 'Then,' says the sacred writer, 'shall the dust return to the earth as it was, and the spirit shall return unto God who gave it.' Here the body is clearly affirmed to be material, and the spirit to be immaterial. The exact meaning of the passage may be thus expressed: 'Then shall the dust' (that part of man which is material) 'return unto the earth as it was, and the spirit' (that part of man which is not matter) 'will return to God who gave it.' The same distinction is most fully presented in the New Testament. 'Man,' we are informed, 'may kill the body, but cannot kill the soul.' The body is represented as a house, tabernacle, or tent, and the spirit as the occupant. The Scriptures make the same distinction between spirit and matter, the body and the soul, that all mankind do between a house and its occupants. The spirit of the believer, 'while at home in the body,' is affirmed to be 'absent from the Lord,' and when 'absent from the body,' to be 'present with the Lord.' During life the soul is affirmed to 'abide in the flesh,' or the body, and at death, not to die with, but to 'depart' from the body. Nothing can be more manifest than is the distinction made in the Scriptures between matter and spirit, and the recognition of both as distinct and separate entities.

With the same distinctness is the doctrine of the immortality of the soul presented in the Scriptures. 'We know that if our earthly house of this tabernacle were dissolved, we have a building of God, an house not made with hands, ETERNAL in the heavens.' 'Then shall we be FOREVER with the Lord.' 'Neither shall they die any more.' No intelligent reader of the Bible doubts that according to its express revelations the future being of the soul is coeval with 'the eternal years of God.'

With similar distinctness, also, is the future of the soul revealed as a state of retribution. 'It is appointed unto men once to die, but after this the judgment.' 'We shall all stand before the judgment-seat of Christ.' 'For we must all appear before the judgment-seat of Christ; that every one may receive the things done in his body, according to that he hath done, whether it be good or bad.' 'These shall go away into everlasting punishment, but the righteous into life eternal.' 'He hath appointed a day in which He will judge the world in righteousness.' In the opening revelation of the soul's eternity, God is revealed as 'the Judge of all.' The united consent of the ages fully verifies the correctness of the interpretation which we have given of the teachings of the Scriptures in respect to the doctrines now under consideration. The exceptions are too few to weaken at all this verification.

Relations of Science to the Doctrine of Scriptural Ontology.

No candid reader of the Bible will deny that we have correctly stated its doctrine of Ontology. The question which now arises pertains to the relations of the deductions of science to this doctrine. On this subject we remark:

1. All facts known to science, and all relations of such facts, are absolutely compatible with, and explicable by, this doctrine. If we postulate the actual existence of the four realities under consideration—to wit, Matter and Spirit, Time and Space, there is not a fact or event in the wide domain of nature—a fact or event which is not scientifically explicable through this postulate. No fact or event can be conceived of which is not perfectly explicable as an attribute or relation of matter or spirit, and as occurring in time or space. No one who holds as actually existing these four realities, finds any occasion to go outside of the same, or to postulate any other or different form of being, to account for any event known to science, or representable in thought. Take the ideas of Matter and Spirit, Time and Space, just as they exist in the Universal Intelligence, and in their light we can give a scientific explanation of the origin and character of all the sciences pure and mixed, and of all facts and events represented in human thought. No candid thinker will deny the validity of these statements. In the light of these same ideas, and of the principles and laws of thought which said ideas necessarily imply, we can, as we have demonstrated in former portions of this Treatise, explain the origin and character of all the assumptions and deductions of false science. In short, all forms of thought existing in mind, all the

sciences true and false, and all facts and events known to science, are most fully explicable in the light of the ideas and principles under consideration.

2. Such being the undeniable facts of the case, disproof of the ontological doctrine of Scripture is an absolute impossibility. Equally impossible is it, and must it be, to adduce any form of valid proof or positive or even probable evidence in favour of any doctrine of an opposite nature. To accomplish any such result, we must, as formerly shown, adduce some fact of the reality of which we are, and must be, more certain than we are of the existence of each of the four realities under consideration—a fact incompatible with the existence of such reality. Every fact representable in human thought must be a property, quality, or relation of Matter, Spirit, Time, or Space. As the existence of any one of these realities does not imply the non-being of any other, no perceived or apprehended property of any one of them can imply the non-being of its subject, or of any other reality or any of its attributes or relations. How, then, can the non-reality of Matter, Spirit, Time, Space, or the non-validity of our necessary apprehensions of the same, be an object of valid proof? All attempts to prove the doctrines of Materialism, Idealism, or Scepticism, in any of their forms, involve the senseless endeavour to realize the demonstrated impossible. If the advocates of any one of these dogmas could show that all facts and events known to science are explicable on their hypothesis, this would merely prove said hypothesis to be a *possible* truth. As long as the same facts are equally explicable on another and opposite hypothesis, the former can never take rank as a truth of science. To talk of the science of Naturalism in any of its forms, in other words, to speak of the science of Materialism, Idealism, Scepticism, Development, Evolution, or of any of the deductions of the New Philosophy, is simply to betray a fundamental ignorance of the nature of real science itself. No hypothesis which cannot be scientifically verified, no one, especially, in favour of which any positive or probable evidence can be adduced, can have a place within the sphere of true science.

Apply the principles under consideration to the doctrine of the Immortality of the Soul. By no possibility can the *materiality* of the soul be proved, no fact of consciousness or external perception verifying it as such a substance. The fact of its immateriality is, to say the least, just as evident and probable in itself as that of its materiality. The fact of its conscious existence as exercising the functions of thought, feeling, and voluntary determination, removes absolutely all grounds and arguments against its future existence. We *began* to think here. Why may we not *continue* to think hereafter? The beginning of thought, feeling, and voluntary determination is just as mysterious as is their future continuance. If the soul is now in the body, and not of it, it may continue to think, feel, and, act when out of the body. To prove, or render even probable, the mortality of the soul, its materiality must be absolutely verified. This can no more be done than can proof be found that scarlet colour is identical with the sound of a trumpet. All the known facts of the soul are, undeniably, just as compatible with its immateriality and immortality as with its materiality and mortality. Hence all disproofs of the former, and proofs of the latter, doctrines are absolute impossibilities. The same holds true of the Ontology of the Bible in all its forms.

3. While disproof of this Ontology is wholly impossible, its truth as fully accords with the immutable intuitions and convictions of the Universal Intelligence. 'Mankind generally,' says Alexander of Aphrodisias, 'do not greatly err.' 'In any matter whatever,' says Cicero, 'the consent of all nations is to be reckoned a law of nature.' That which accords with the universal and necessary intuitions and convictions of the race must be an immutable law of nature, that is, of universal mind, or we have no means of determining what a law of nature is. Now there is not a mind on earth—a mind in whom any ideas at all are developed—a mind in whom the same identical distinction is not made between the body and the soul, that is made in the Scriptures—in whom the body is not regarded as constituted of 'dust,' and the soul as an ethereal unity which is distinct and separate from 'dust.' There is not, consequently, on earth a mind void of the ideas of matter, spirit, time, and space, and of an immutable conviction of the actual existence of all these realities. Mind cannot exist and think at all without becoming possessed of these ideas and convictions; and in all their essential characteristics they are the same in all minds. All that 'know fact and law' know absolutely that here are fundamental facts and an immutable law of nature. The same remarks are equally applicable to the revealed doctrines of Duty, Immortality, and Retribution. By an immutable law of the Intelligence, universal mind apprehends and affirms the validity of these doctrines. Each member of the human family does, and must stand revealed to himself as a free moral agent, and as a child, not of time, but of eternity. We must cease to be conscious at all before we can cease to be conscious of our subjection to the law of duty, and accountable to a higher power for our moral conduct. Nor can we cease to be conscious of our spirits as naturally endowed with an immortal vigour, and as acting as probationers for a future state. Hence it is, that when these great central doctrines of inspiration are distinctly presented to universal mind, they 'commend themselves to every man's conscience in the sight of God.' When universal science shall reach its consummation, Natural and Revealed Theism, and the system of Rational and Revealed Ontology, will have a prominent

place within the sphere of scientific truth. The disciples of the New Philosophy have much to say about 'fact and law,' and about their absolute authority in science. In all this they are right. In obedience to conscious 'fact and law,' we believe in Matter, Spirit, Time, and Space, God, the Soul, Duty, Immortality, and Retribution. In disregard of conscious 'fact and law,' they disbelieve in these eternal verities. With them, it is science to believe in 'fact and law,' as far as matter is concerned, and un-science to believe in conscious 'fact and law,' as far as spirit is concerned. With us, it is science to believe in 'fact and law' in both particulars, and 'science falsely so called,' to disregard 'fact and law' in any sphere of thought whatever. Here lies the real difference between Theists and Anti-theists in all ages. The latter disbelieve in 'fact and law,' but in one exclusive sphere of scientific thought. The former believe in 'fact and law' throughout the entire domain of such thought.

SECTION III.
THE MORALITY OF THE SCRIPTURES.

THE questions, What ought we to be and to become, and, How ought we to act, enter, as problems of fundamental interest, into all systems of Philosophy. Modern Unbelief is now devoting its highest energies to prove that the morality of the Bible is in no essential particulars superior to, or diverse from, that taught in other systems of religion, and in the Philosophies of the world ancient and modern. The object of the present section is to develop the fundamental difference between the moral systems under consideration. On this topic, we designate the following particulars in which the moral teachings of the Bible are peculiarized from those of all the other systems referred to.

1. Moral virtue in all its forms, according to the Bible, has its spring and source in the inner man, the heart, and consists in supreme respect for the will and character of God on the one hand, and in impartial and universal goodwill to man on the other. Revealed Morality, consequently, assumes two forms—piety, or loving God with all our powers—and universal and impartial philanthropy, or 'loving our neighbour as ourselves.' In the exercise and practice of Christian virtue, man becomes, in the absolute sense, morally pure ; in other words, he becomes pure not only in the visible, but also in the inner life. We shall search in vain among all heathen religions or philosophies, for any such ideas of moral virtue. With very few, if any, exceptions, moral virtue pertains rather to the outer than the inner life, and is therefore fundamentally imperfect. A system of morality which does not include piety and philanthropy both, and has not a fundamental reference to the inner life, cannot induce real moral purity in those who perfectly conform to said system. An indi-

vidual, for example, may 'keep the whole law' as announced by the Brahminical and Buddhist religions and philosophies, and have no inner respect for moral virtue at all. An individual cannot be moral at all in the Christian sense, without being pure in the outer and inner life in common.

2. When we descend to a consideration of particular precepts of a fundamental character, the perfection of the Christian, in distinction from all other systems, becomes still more manifest. The only parallel ever adduced to the universal rule or maxim of our Saviour—to wit, 'Whatsoever ye would that men should do unto you, do ye also unto them,' is the negative principle of Confucius, namely, 'Whatsoever ye would that others should not do to you, refrain from doing unto them.' The real difference between these two precepts is world-wide. The latter requires no positive well-doing in any form, and is perfectly fulfilled when we refrain from positive acts. The former requires not merely refraining from wrong acts, but positive and unselfish well-doing in all its forms. When we contemplate such precepts as the following, however—to wit, 'Love your enemies,' 'When your enemy hungers, feed him,' 'Avenge not yourselves,' and 'Be not overcome of evil, but overcome evil with good,' we then find ourselves in the presence of a system of morals which stands in open contrast with that taught in all other religion, and in all the godless philosophies of ancient and modern times. Yet, without these peculiar and special principles and precepts, all moral systems are fundamentally imperfect and defective. In all particulars in which Christian morality becomes absolutely perfect, all other systems are fundamentally wanting.

3. Completeness and universality constitute another peculiarity which distinguishes the Christian from every other code of morals. In the Christian system no conceivable principle necessary to its absolute completeness and perfection is wanting. No such principle has ever been reached by human thought, a principle which has not a distinct and specific place in this system. On the score of completeness and perfection, all other systems are manifestly, and in fundamental particulars, defective; while they announce some excellent principles, they fail to present others equally important. Hence they have no adaptations whatever to take rank as universal systems.

4. While the Christian system is thus complete and perfect, it embraces no *false* principles. There is nothing in it which mars its beauty or perfection. While all other systems lack completeness and perfection, they also embrace principles fundamentally false, and subversive of all morality. While Confucius, for example, taught many excellent principles, he taught others which sanctify the absolute despotism of China, and shut out freedom of thought and action from one-third of the human

race. How perfect in certain particulars are the moral teachings of Plato. Yet in his Republic he in fact and form abolishes marriage, annihilates the family, makes the individual a mere commodity of the State, and sanctifies human servitude. Similar principles of false morality mar all the systems under consideration.

5. Hence it is that while the system of Christian morals has absolute adaptation as the guide of universal human life and conduct in all ages and all conditions of human existence, every one of the other systems under consideration failed almost utterly in their adaptation to the age and the people in which and among whom it was originated. In whatever light Christian morality is contemplated, it, like the Bible amid all other books, stands alone in the world, and stands revealed to us as not only having come down to us 'from God and heaven,' but as having originally proceeded from the heart of Infinity and Perfection.

SECTION IV.

SPECIAL AND PECULIAR DOCTRINES OF CHRISTIANITY.

EVERY religion has certain special doctrines and principles which peculiarize and separate it from every other religion. Such is the case with Christianity. Its *revealed* doctrines peculiarize and separate it to an infinite remove from all other religions. Among these doctrines we shall refer to but the following: The Tri-Unity of the Godhead, Incarnation and Atonement, and The relations of God to believers as a hearer of prayer. We shall refer to these doctrines in the order above designated.

THE TRI-UNITY OF THE GODHEAD.

Every individual who is at all acquainted with the Scriptures in their original languages, is aware of the fact that the first time in which the term 'God' appears therein, that term has not the singular, but the plural form. 'In the beginning God (Elohim) created the heavens and the earth.' Nor at that era of the world's history were any plural forms of words employed, as 'We, the king,' to represent any single personage. Immediately after this opening revelation the idea of a mysterious form of plurality in the Godhead is expressed in words utterly incompatible with the idea of absolute unity. 'And the Lord God said, Behold, the man is become as one of us.' By no usage in any age has any such form of words ever been applied to any single individual. There is, then, a plurality in some form in the Godhead. Nor is the doctrine of the divine unity ever affirmed in the Scriptures in the absolute sense, but always and specifically in opposition to the plurality of heathenism. 'For though there be that are called gods, whether in heaven or in earth (as there be gods many and lords many); but to us there is but one God, the Father, of whom are all things, and we in Him; and one Lord Jesus Christ, by whom are all things, and we by him.' In opposition to the plurality of heathenism, so the Scriptures teach, 'there is one God,' or Godhead. In opposition to an absolute unity there is a form of plurality in the Godhead. In the New Tastament this plurality assumes a definite form, and is represented by the terms, Father, Son, and Holy Ghost. The *fact* of this unity and plurality is clearly revealed. The *ground*, or *nature*, of this unity on the one hand, and plurality on the other, are not revealed at all. The *fact*, as coming within the sphere of revealed truth, 'belongs to us, and to our children.' The *ground*, or *nature*, referred to is among 'the secret things which belong to God,' and is consequently wholly excluded from the sphere of Theology and Speculative Thought.

As the immutable condition of a rational admission of any doctrine pertaining to God as true, science justly requires that said doctrine shall not be self-contradictory on the one hand, nor undeniably incompatible with our essential idea of infinity and perfection on the other. Neither of these objections, in any sense or form, holds against the doctrine under consideration. No one pretends that there is anything in the doctrine incompatible with our essential idea of infinity and perfection. Equally free is the doctrine from even the appearance of self-contradiction, neither the nature of the divine unity on the one hand, or plurality on the other, being even professedly defined in the Scriptures. The only appearance of contradiction ever found in the doctrine has arisen, not from the doctrine as revealed, but from the presumptuous attempts of theologians to define 'secret things which belong to God.' As a revealed fact, the nature and ground of which God has left a profound and inexplicable mystery, we rationally hold the docrine of the Tri-Unity of the Godhead, the issue between the Trinitarian and Unitarian believer in the Scriptures being left as a simple and exclusive question of Biblical interpretation.

Revealed Relations of these Tri-Personalities to one Another.

While the nature of the divine unity, on the one hand, and plurality, on the other, is not revealed, these Tri-Personalities do sustain certain revealed and consequently definable relations to one another. Whatever, for example, is represented by such words as *original, ultimate, and absolute authority; supremacy, and paternity*, is expressly in the Scriptures ascribed to the Father. The Son and Spirit in all they do act in absolute subordination to the Father, and exercise no form of power or authority but what is delegated to them by Him. As the Creator of the universe, the Son exercised a delegated power; 'the Father creating all things by Jesus Christ.' As the sovereign and judge of all, Christ thus acts because 'the government has been *laid* upon His shoulders,' because 'all power is *given* unto Him in heaven and in earth,' and 'the Father hath *committed* all judgment to the Son.' 'Christ came into the world, not to do His own will, but the will of Him that sent Him.' The same holds equally true of the Spirit. Like the Son, 'He speaks not of Himself, but what He hears, that He speaks,' and by the Father the Spirit was sent into the world, as Christ was sent into the world.

The Son, on the other hand, represents the Godhead in what may be denominated supreme *executive power, authority, and majesty*, the Son being the supreme authoritative executor of the Father's will. The agency of the Father is not directly exerted in creation and providence. The Father, on the other hand, 'created all things by Jesus Christ.' To the Son, the Father thus speaks: 'And Thou, Lord, in the beginning hast laid the foundations of the earth; and the heavens are the works of Thy hands.' By the same delegated power, 'Christ upholds all things,' and 'by Him all things consist'—are sustained and controlled. All the revelations of the Godhead are made through Christ, He being to the universe 'the brightness of the Father's glory, and the express image of His substance.'

The Holy Spirit, we remark, lastly, in this connection, represents the Godhead as that *invisible divine energy*, which everywhere acts potentially in nature, and directly and immediately brings to pass those results which God wills. 'And the Spirit of God moved upon the face of the waters.' Had we witnessed the results here referred to, nothing would have been visible to us but the simple agitation of the watery elements. Were we infidels, we should have attributed all to the exclusive action of natural law. The same holds true of the results produced by the agency of the Spirit everywhere, in the universe of matter and spirit. The *results* are manifest. The *cause* is invisible, and events appear as they would, were they the exclusive results of the internal powers of nature itself. All the miracles of Christ, we are told, were directly and immediately performed through the invisible agency of 'the Spirit of God.' Christ, for example, said to the winds and waves on the Sea of Galilee, 'Peace, be still.' The Spirit invisibly 'moved upon the face of the waters,' and energized in the atmosphere around, and thus induced the subsidence of the waves and the stillness of the atmosphere which immediately ensued. So in all other instances. As our object is simply to indicate the relations under consideration, we do not enlarge.

Between these Tri-Personalities, we remark once more, there is the revealed action of the *social principle*—relations analogous to those which result from the intercommunion and fellowship of mind with mind. Finite minds have 'fellowship (intercommunion) one with another,' while all the pure in heart have 'fellowship with the Father, and with His Son Jesus Christ,' the Finite with the Infinite. In the Godhead we have the revealed intercommunion and fellowship of the Infinite with the Infinite. The love, for example, which the Father exercises towards believers is affirmed to be the same in kind as that which He exercises towards the Son. 'That the world may know that Thou hast sent Me, and hast loved them AS Thou hast loved Me.' 'That the love wherewith Thou hast loved Me may be in them, and I in them.' The love also which Christ exercises towards the faithful believer, is affirmed to be the same in kind, and secured on the same conditions as that which the Father exercises towards the Son. 'As the Father hath loved Me, so have I loved you: continue ye in My love. If ye keep My commandments, ye shall abide in My love; even as I have kept My Father's commandments, and abide in His love.' The union and fellowship existing between true believers is also affirmed to be the same in kind as that which exists between the Father and the Son. 'That they may be one, even as we are one'—'That they all may be one: as Thou, Father, art in Me, and I in Thee, that they also may be one in us.' Nothing can be more plain than is the revealed fact, that between the Tri-Personalities of the Godhead, there is a form of the action of the social principle analogous to the actual intercommunion and fellowship of mind with mind—that of the Infinite with the Infinite.

Considerations which commend this Doctrine to our Reason and Judgment.

While there is nothing whatever in the doctrine under consideration against which science can object, there are considerations connected with this doctrine which commend it to our highest regard. Through this doctrine, for example, the Godhead is revealed to us in absolute accordance with our conscious necessities as creatures, and more especially as sinners. We consciously need a 'Father in heaven,' whom sinners may approach through a more than human—through a really and truly *divine* Mediator. We as consciously need an indwelling *divine* and 'eternal Spirit,' through whose infallible teachings and illuminations we can see ourselves as God sees us, can know ourselves, not only as sinners, but as 'the sons of God,' can 'behold with open face the glory of the Lord,' and thus become God-like and Christ-like in character and blessedness. Nothing can be more reasonable than a form of divine revelation which thus accords with the conscious necessities of universal human nature.

This doctrine, also, has in its favour the analogy of universal nature in all departments of sentient existence. How universal, in all departments of such existence, is the action of the *social principle*. If the same principle obtains in the Godhead, we have an explanation of the facts of sentient nature otherwise inconceivable, and the analogy between God and His works is perfect.

This doctrine and this exclusively, we remark once more, renders conceivable to us the *infinite blessedness* of God. The action of the social principle seems to be the immutable condition of real happiness on the part of all sentient, and more especially of all rational, finite natures. Nor could the action of this principle between the Finite and the Infinite meet the wants of the latter. A mind dwelling apart and alone in infinite and eternal solitariness, how can we conceive of the full and perfect blessedness of such mind, though it is infinite and perfect in itself? If there is, on the other hand, in the Godhead the actual intercommunion and fellowship of the Infinite with the Infinite, the result must be infinite and eternal blessedness. Hence it is, that whenever the idea of a divine unity which excludes wholly all plurality obtains, the idea of God as void of emotion prevails, and any thought of His blessedness has a very obscure and unimpressive place. Whenever, on the other hand, the doctrine of the Tri-Unity of the Godhead is held, then we find a distinct and vivid impression of the infinite blessedness of God. The reason is obvious. The idea of infinite blessedness, and that of infinite and eternal solitariness, seem to be incompatible ideas, while the former idea naturally arises when that of the intercommunion and fellowship of the Infinite with the Infinite has place. Reasons of infinite weight, therefore, commend this doctrine, as a revealed truth, to our highest regard.

The Doctrine of Incarnation and Atonement.

In the Old Testament God is affirmed to have made direct and audible communications with men. These communications were commonly made through some visible form of divine manifestation, as in the 'burning bush,' the pillar of cloud and of fire, the thunder cloud and thick darkness, or angelic or human forms. The term, 'Angel of the Lord,' was appropriated, as all careful readers of the Scriptures are aware, to represent the idea of Jehovah, not as He exists by Himself, but as thus manifested. Thus we read, at one time, that God, and at another that 'the Angel of the Lord,' spoke to Moses in the bush, and went before the hosts of Israel in a pillar of cloud by day, and of fire by night, the two terms being everywhere employed interchangeably in the Scriptures. In Mal. iii. 1, this visibly manifested Jehovah, this 'Angel of the Lord,' by whom the covenants, and all divine manifestations, were made, is identified with the promised Messiah, that is, with Christ. 'Behold, I will send My messenger, and He shall prepare the way before Me: and the Lord, whom ye seek, shall suddenly come to His temple, even the Messenger of the Covenant, whom ye delight in: behold, He shall come, saith the LORD of hosts.'

In the New Testament, this 'Angel of the Lord,' this 'Messenger of the Covenant,' 'the Lord,' who was not only 'the delight' of the Jews, but 'the desire of all nations,' 'the Word who was in the beginning with God, and was God,' the Word by whom 'all things were made, and without whom was nothing made that was made,' is affirmed to have 'become flesh, and dwelt among us.' Here we find ourselves in the open presence of the mystery of the Incarnation—'God,' not visibly manifested in transient, vanishing forms, but 'manifest in the flesh,' and '*dwelling among us.*' What has reason and science to say of such a doctrine? We answer:

Relations of the Doctrine of Incarnation to Reason and Science.

1. There is no element, or feature, or characteristic of this doctrine which has even the appearance of a *natural impossibility*. If a personal God exists, and there is no fact, truth, or principle known to science which contradicts this doctrine, it is undeniable that as a self-conscious personality God may, when He chooses, make communications to His rational offspring, and may do this through any visible forms he may select.

2. Nor is there anything in this doctrine which has the appearance of *incredibility*. If creatures need divine communications, and we all know that they do need them, it is not reason, but unreason, to suppose that such revelations will not be made. The making of such revelations through visible forms, renders God's personality, personal presence, and love and care for us, more distinct and impressive than is otherwise possible. Such considerations undeniably remove wholly every shade of incredibility from every form of divine manifestation recorded in the Bible. Grant the being of a personal God, and the conscious needs of universal mind, and the only mystery about the matter is that such manifestations have not been of far more frequent occurrence than the revealed record indicates.

3. The crowning glory of all such manifestations is 'God manifest in the flesh.' That God, in a human form and condition, should descend to us in our sin, ruin, and misery, should become our example, teacher, and guide, should reveal to us, not only our sin, but the conditions of escape from its bondage and curse-power, and should 'bring life and immortality to light' in the midst of our darkness and gloom—this great fact will fill eternity, and to eternity will constitute the central theme of thought and study with the great intelligences of the universe. The scoff of Unbelief at such a doctrine is nothing but a revelation of debasing ignorance, consummate folly, and reckless presumption. What does the unbeliever know of what is, and is not, possible with God? On what authority does he dogmatize in respect to God's thoughts and ways? With an

effrontery at which 'devils tremble,' the unbeliever advances boldly to the eternal throne, and questions God in respect to His judgments, thoughts, ways, dispensations, and forms of manifestation. God, while He responds not to such impious questionings, holds in reserve retributions according to deeds.

ATONEMENT.

The main revealed purpose of the Incarnation is Atonement, which embraces two chief elements—Substitution and Satisfaction. 'Christ died for our sins, the just for (in the place of) the unjust.' There is substitution. His sufferings and death, as 'a sacrifice for sin,' renders it 'just' in God to 'justify,' pardon, treat as just, or as if he had never sinned, 'him who believeth in Jesus.' There is satisfaction. Angels and redeemed sinners are together in heaven, and God and the rational universe are equally satisfied to have them together there. The former are there on the ground of personal desert, they having never sinned at all. The latter are there because Christ 'was slain, and redeemed them unto God by His blood,' that is, made atonement for them. The reason in both cases is equally satisfactory. Such is atonement. What are the relations of this doctrine to reason and science? We answer:

Relations of this Doctrine to Reason and Science.

1. While neither reason nor science can affirm Atonement to be impossible with God, for aught we do or can know, there may be in the Divine mind reasons of infinite weight why it should be known to the rational universe, that without an atonement sin will never be forgiven. The revelation of such provision may also be to the universe what revelation affirms it to be, the crowning glory of all the divine works, government, and manifestations. Through no conceivable form of manifestation can such love to creatures, such regard for their well-being, and such wisdom in making provision for their immortal interests, be shown. While atonement is above reason and science, they can appreciate the grace and glory manifested in it.

2. The fact that this is God's *revealed* method of 'making an end of sin, and bringing in everlasting righteousness,' should for ever silence all objections on the part of creatures against it. Salvation from sin is undeniably the great conscious necessity of universal humanity. If God has revealed a method for the accomplishment of this result, a method satisfactory to Himself and to the Intelligence of heaven, how impious in man to object against it!

3. This doctrine, instead of being opposed to reason, does in fact accord with the intuitive convictions of the race. The conciousness of sin and the consequent need of pardon is co-extensive with the human

consciousness itself. In all minds, in all ages, the idea of pardon has been immutably associated with that of some sacrifice as atonement for sin. The natural cry of conscious sin as the creature approaches his God is: 'Wherewith shall I come before the Lord?'—'Shall I give my firstborn for my transgression, the fruit of my body for the sin of my soul?' The atonement of Christ is but the antitype foreshadowed by the sentiment which thus lies upon the soul of universal humanity.

4. The pardon of sin, we remark once more, through a divinely originated atonement, is far more honourable to God, and more safe, as a method of Divine administration than any other conceivable condition. Pardon, under a purely legal administration, is one of the most perilous principles known under any form of government, inducing, as it does, in all minds the hope of impunity in crime. Pardon through atonement is not only most honourable to God, but renders perfectly safe all interests concerned, the law 'being magnified and made honourable,' while its penalty is remitted. While the doctrine of Incarnation and Atonement is above reason, it has, as a revealed truth, the most absolute sanction of the highest reason.

Relations of God to Believers as a Hearer of Prayer.

'Give us this day our daily bread.' 'The prayer of faith shall save the sick.' 'Is any man afflicted, let him pray.' 'The effectual fervent prayer of a righteous man availeth much. Elias was a man subject to like passions as we are, and he prayed earnestly that it might not rain; and it rained not on the earth by the space of three years and six months. And he prayed again, and the heaven gave rain, and the earth brought forth her fruit.' 'How much more shall your heavenly Father GIVE good things to them that ask Him.' 'And He spake this parable unto them, that men ought always to pray and not to faint.' 'Whatsoever ye shall ask the Father in My name, He shall give it you.' 'Ask, and ye shall receive, that your joy may be full—casting all your care upon Him, for He careth for you.' We give the above as examples of the teaching of inspiration on this subject. If we may credit 'what is written,' prayer has 'much avail,' not merely in the sphere of our spiritual interests, but equally in reference to all our temporal cares and concernments, and has power to secure changes which would not otherwise occur, not only in the wide realm of our moral and spiritual relations, but equally in respect to physical events in the world around us. Unbelief affirms that here, as elsewhere, Scripture and science are in conflict. What are the real facts of the case? On this subject we remark:

Relations of this Doctrine to the Teachings of Science.

1. No fact known to science affirms, or renders it even antecedently

probable, that the Spirit of God, as a self-conscious personal agent, is not omnipresent in nature, that every law of nature is not the expression of His will, and that every event in nature is not under His direct and immediate control. This fact has been rendered undeniably evident in our former discussions.

2. The dogma that all events in the world of matter are under the inexorable control of mere physical law, is perpetually contradicted by visible and conscious facts. Changes in nature—changes which would not otherwise occur—are perpetually visible all around us as the exclusive results of the action of free-will in man. The action of free-will in nature, and the contingency of physical events upon its action, is a fact just as manifest as is the occurrence of any events through physical law. The doctrine, that all physical events, not to speak of moral and spiritual, are under the same rule of physical law, is undeniably false in fact.

3. There is not a fact known to science, or within the range of human observation and thought, a fact which, in the remotest sense, contradicts, or renders improbable the doctrine that changes in the current of events in nature around us are produced by the action of the free-will of God, in a manner analogous or similar to that in which similar changes are being produced by that of the free-will of man. What, if the facts revealed through the telescope, the microscope, in the laboratory of the chemist, and the dissecting-room of the anatomist, were adduced to prove that no changes in nature do, or can, occur through the free action of the human will? Such reasoning would be no more illogical than is the inference from the same and similar facts, or from any facts known to man, that no such changes are ever induced through the free-will of God.

4. For aught that man does or can know upon the subject, the perpetuation of the universal order and harmony of nature through the exclusive action of mere necessary physical law, may be a natural impossibility. The preservation of the universal order we witness, the balance of worlds in empty space, and the harmony of events around us, may, for aught we do or can know, be necessarily contingent on changes produced by the direct action of the free-will of God. Of one fact we are absolutely sure, that our own ignorance on this subject is absolute. Equally assured are we that the ignorance of all scientists on the same subject is, and must be, as absolute as ours. Nothing can surpass the impiety and presumption of men who boldly and dogmatically assert, 'that they know fact, and that they know law,' and that all events are under the exclusive control of mere physical law, and that the free-will of God, equally with that of man, is not active in nature.

5. According to the infidel hypothesis, the free-will of God is less free, and more confined and limited in its action in Nature than is that of

man. The free-will of man undeniably can, and does, produce constant changes in the current of events around us, and this with no violation of any material law. What dogma can be more absurd than is the idea, that the free-will of the Author of Nature is limited in the Nature which he constituted to the exclusive control of blind, unconscious and bald, natural and necessary law? No more absurd conception ever danced in the brain of a crazy philosophy. The Christian hypothesis, as an object of thought, is infinitely superior to the godless dogma under consideration. The idea of a universe under the immediate direction and control of an infinite and perfect mind is as much superior to that of a godless universe under the domain of necessary physical law, as mind is superior to matter; while the most debasing and absurd of all possible conceptions is that of an infinite and perfect free Spirit in Nature, and that Spirit chained down and limited there to the iron control of blind material law. Nothing can be more senseless and absurd than is what Mr. Beecher rightly calls 'the perpetual twaddle of infidelity' about the universal and iron rule of necessary law in Nature.

6. Hence we remark finally, that no truth of nature or inspiration can be more reasonable in itself, more accordant with conscious facts of the human Will, more correlative to the conscious needs of human nature, and more in harmony with all proper ideas of God, and of His relations to His own works, than is the Doctrine of Prayer as set forth in the Scriptures. There is not a fact of nature known to mind that is in conflict with that doctrine. There is not a want of mind, or a known attribute of God, which is not in full harmony with this doctrine, and does not affirm its validity. Receiving as deductions of science this 'twaddle of infidelity' about the reign of universal and necessary law in nature, and the consequent limitations of our ideas of the proper sphere and efficacy of prayer, has been most manifestly a chief cause of that eclipse of the faith of the Church in God, and of His revealed truth. When our unbelief has closed the ear of God to our prayers relative to our sicknesses and daily cares and concernments, as well as to passing events in the world around us, we shall find our God nowhere. We may still chatter the words, 'Our Father, which art in heaven,' 'Give us this day our daily bread.' Our words, however, will be not only void of real meaning, but as powerless to stir the spirit of devotion, thanksgiving, faith, or hope, in our hearts, as if they were addressed to Juggernaut, or an iceberg. We stand before God as 'mockers,' when we ask of Him favours which we say in our hearts He will not give. Those who would take lessons about prayer from such men as Protagoras, Tyndall, Spencer, and Huxley, would do well to hold the admonition of Socrates about such teachers. The following passage we have quoted once before. It will well bear a second reading.

'Is not, O Hippocrates, a Sophist, a seller or vendor of articles on which the soul is fed? He seems to me to be something of that kind.'

'What, Socrates! is the soul fed? On what, I pray?'

'On the lessons of teachers, and we must take care that the Sophists do not cheat us in selling their wares, as the sellers of food for the body often do. For they, without knowing what is really good for the body, praise all their wares alike, and the buyer knows just as little, unless he be a physician or a training-master. And just so these vendors of lessons, who carry their wares about from city to city, and sell them to everyone whom they can persuade to buy, praise all the articles which they sell; but very likely some of these, too, know very little what is good for the soul, and what is not; and the buyer knows just as little, except any of them be soul-physicians. If, then, you are a judge of what is good in this way, and what is not, you may safely buy lessons of Protagoras, or anyone else. But if not, take care, my good friend, that you do not run a dreadful risk in a vital concern; for there is far more danger in buying lessons than in buying victuals.'

For myself, I would as soon purchase henbane as food for the body, as buy lessons from these men on so vital a subject as prayer.

The most senseless and perilous of all ideas pertaining to prayer for temporal good is, that its design is, not to secure help from God, but to quicken our own efforts in the use of means. Prayer, prompted by such a sentiment, will be as powerless to quicken our activities as it will be to move the heart of God. Prayer has the power which inspiration ascribes to it, or it is a senseless mockery of God.

BOOK II.

PHILOSOPHY OF THE EARLY CHRISTIAN ERA.

THROUGHOUT the entire sphere of philosophic thought which we have thus far traversed, one idea has everywhere, and in all systems in common, lifted its divine form before our minds—that of a personal God. In every system which the human mind has ever originated, this one idea has been omnipresent, either in its affirmative or negative form. In all systems alike the doctrine of God has been, in fact and form, specifically affirmed or denied, thus evincing the absolute omnipresence of the doctrine in human thought. Nor did Philosophy ever present or discuss this doctrine as an idea which scientific thought had of itself originated, but as an object of the pre-existing faith of the race. Philosophy never originates its own problems, but attempts the solution of those which the primitive thought of the race has previously originated. Had not the idea of Ultimate Causation, of the Organization of the Universe as an event of time, and consequently that 'the worlds were framed by the word of God,' previously presented itself to human thought, and become an article of the primitive faith of the race, Philosophy would never have originated the idea, or concerned itself with inquiries in respect to its validity or invalidity. Mind cannot exist and think at all without being confronted with the ideas of matter and spirit, time and space, of an organized universe, of proximate and ultimate Causation, and consequently, with those of God, Duty, Immortality, and Retribution. The central problem which Philosophy has ever concerned itself with is, Ultimate Causation by Natural Law, or by the Word of a personal God. This problem Philosophy cannot ignore if it would, and it should not do it if it could. Human thought will never rest until the doctrine of Ultimate Causation shall be finally settled, and that upon a strictly scientific basis.

Since the introduction of the Christian Era, the problem under consideration has assumed, in fundamental respects, aspects entirely new. In former ages Theism and Anti-theism confronted each other. Now the main issue, as presented in all philosophical systems, lies not merely between Theism and Anti-theism, but between the latter and *Christian*

Theism. The old issue is not ignored. Yet the main interest turns upon the real relations actually existing between science and the Christian religion. Wherever any contact occurs between the latter and any of the sciences, there a special issue is raised, not so much with Theism as with the idea of God as developed in the Christian Scriptures. Facts of Geology, for example, facts bearing also upon the antiquity of the human race, and the doctrines of Evolution and Development, are seldom or never adduced to disprove the doctrine of Theism by itself, but Theism as developed in these writings. With few and honourable exceptions, all who deny the divinity of Christianity impeach Theism itself. The leaders of the Broad Church openly avow a deeper sympathy with the Rationalism, Atheism, and Scepticism of the age than with Christianity. Such being the obvious state of facts, certain fundamental inquiries here arise, inquiries each of which demands a specific answer as preparatory to our future elucidations.

SECTION I.

RELATIONS BETWEEN THEISM PROPER AND CHRISTIAN THEISM.

WERE we to provide an illustration of our idea of the relations of Theism proper to Christian Theism, we should present the natural eye, in the first case, and then the same organ as aided by the microscope, on the one hand, and the telescope on the other. The real difference in the forms of vision in the two cases lies here. Vision in respect to all objects is far more distinct and impressive, and infinitely more enlarged in the latter case than in the former. In no respects is there a conflict between the two forms of Theism under consideration. As far as their revelations and deductions pertain to the same verities, a perfect harmony obtains between them. Yet, like that which obtains between the revelations of the natural eye and those of the microscope and telescope, an essential difference in important respects obtains between the revelations of natural and of Christian Theism.

Christian Theism renders infinitely more distinct and impressive the real verities apprehended through Natural Theism.

As we have stated, where the teachings of the two systems relate to the same verities, a perfect unity obtains between them. Yet even here an essential difference obtains, as far as the elements of *distinctness* and *impressiveness* are concerned, a difference like that which obtains in our vision of objects when seen under the dimness of star-light and the cloudless illumination of the noonday sun. The facts of nature, for example, facts material and mental, have rendered omnipresent in all minds in common the idea of a personal God, 'the Former of all things,' and rendered equally omnipresent the conviction of His being, perfection, and universal dominion. Nor are unbelievers of any school real exceptions to these statements. Notwithstanding all their affirmations to the contrary, in the interior of their own minds they as really believe in the actual existence of matter, spirit, time, space, and God as the universal Creator and Governor, as do the rest of mankind. When an individual, for example, enters into an earnest argument with me, to prove to himself and me that neither himself nor myself really exists, I am necessarily reminded of an ancient utterance, 'professing themselves to be wise, they become fools.' I know, in short, that he does not believe in the validity of his own theory or argument. If he truly believes that neither himself, myself, nor anybody else really exists, where is the ground for his solicitude to convince these nobodies that nobody exists? While no one does or can sincerely doubt his own or the existence of other beings, and of the universe around him, he must of necessity as really believe in the being of God. Yet God, as apprehended in the light of these mere facts, is to the mind one reality. As apprehended through the superadded light of inspiration He is the same, and yet quite another reality, the Supreme and all-overshadowing Presence. In the former state we believe in God. In the latter we need not only believe in, but *know* God, 'beholding with open face the glory of the Lord.'

The consciousness of sin and of ill desert on account of sin, is co-extensive with the action of human consciousness itself. Yet sin and its desert, as apprehended in the twilight of the natural conscience on the one hand, and in the light of inspiration, and especially of the convicting power of the Eternal Spirit on the other, hardly appear as the same thing. The same holds true of all verities of Nature, when apprehended under the sun-light of Revealed Religion. In the latter state they have a distinctness and impressiveness which do not and cannot belong to them in the former, 'Life and immortality are brought to light' (not originated, but brought out of obscurity and set in distinct and all-impressive visibility), 'through the Gospel.'

Christian Theism extends our vision of truth beyond the possible reach of Natural Theism.

Revealed religion not only illuminates what was previously known, but extends our vision of truth to spheres and relations of existence which lie wholly beyond the reach of our faculties when under the exclusive light of nature. Man is consciously a sinner, and is burdened with a conscious forfeiture of the Divine favour, and a corresponding desert of the Divine displeasure. If any destiny awaits us but that demanded by pure justice and our ill-desert, and especially if God has chosen to make special provisions for our deliverance from the curse-penalty of sin, and the power of evil principles and tendencies—in short, if we are under a dispensation of grace and not of justice, and if God is consequently in other than purely legal relations to us on all such subjects, all our knowledge must be a matter of pure and special revelation. We are in the midst of verities of infinite and eternal moment to us, verities, however, which lie wholly beyond the possible reach of our unaided faculties. All our light here must undeniably come directly and exclusively from God Himself.

To these inner and higher and most momentous of all verities, revelation professedly introduces us. Natural Theology reveals God to us in His original relations to the universe, and to us as mere *rational* beings. Inspired Theology reveals God to us in His new, self-moved, self-determined, and divinely adapted relations to our actual conditions and necessities, not merely as rationals, but as *sinners* in the, to us, remediless ruin of sin. What these new relations are, supposing them to exist, on what conditions the promises of 'life eternal' may become available to us, and what new light the revelation of these new relations may throw upon the Divine perfections and glory, and what, for the want of better terms, we may denominate the *modes* of the Divine existence and activity—all must be to us blank midnight but as we are directly and immediately, instrumentally it may be, 'taught of God.' The same holds equally true of our special duties and destiny in these new relations. As the Author of this new life and the revealer of God in these new relations, Christ affirms Himself to be 'the Light of the world.'

Christian Theism confirms and reaffirms the validity of the Doctrine of God as taught by Natural Theology.

We now notice one other relation of Christian Theism to the teachings of Natural Theology, a relation, in our judgment, singularly overlooked by Christian Theists. Christian Theism furnishes an *independent proof of the being and government of God*, a form of proof which would, upon purely scientific grounds, have absolute validity did none other exist. The occurrence of a single supernatural fact in nature, a fact which cannot be accounted for by reference to any inhering law of nature, absolutely evinces the existence in and over nature of a corresponding supernatural power. The great central facts recorded in Scripture, admitting their actual occurrence, furnish the same proof of the doctrine of God, that the known facts of astronomy do of the truth of the Copernican System. Nor does true science require any more valid proof of the reality of supernatural, than it does of that of astronomical facts. All that real science requires in any case is evidence having the known characteristics of absolute validity. All are aware that there are forms of evidence which often prove deceptive, and that there are other forms that never do, and never can, deceive. Nor is it difficult to furnish the criteria which distinguish the former kind from the latter. Were it fully ascertained that the evidence on which the deduction is based, that the sun is the centre of the solar system, is of the class first designated, that one fact would wholly invalidate the claims of the Copernican System to our regard. We believe in that system because the facts adduced, supposing them real, absolutely imply the truth of the system—and because the reality of the facts is evinced by evidence of no doubtful character, evidence which never does, and never can, deceive. Suppose now that the occurrence of facts of an undeniably supernatural character is affirmed by evidence, the same in kind and degree, evidence which never does deceive, and the invalidity of which is absolutely inexplicable. We should subvert utterly the foundation of all the physical sciences if we should then deny the occurrence of these facts, or refuse to admit the validity of all the deductions which they necessarily yield. Mr. Hume, with the entire school of unbelief, in his famous argument against the reality of miracles, an argument based upon the deceptive character of human testimony, forgot that there are two kinds of testimony—one which often deceives—and another which never does mislead. Let the evidence of miracles furnished by testimony be wholly of this latter kind, and let that evidence be confirmed by circumstances which never encircle a falsehood, and affirm its truth—in such a case we displace ourselves from the sphere of true science if we deny the reality of the facts, or the validity of the deductions which said facts yield.

We have, then, the same right to argue from the supernatural facts recorded in Scripture to the existence and agency in and over nature of a personal God, that we can have to argue from the known facts of astronomy to the truth of the Copernican System. In both cases in common the same inquiries are to be raised in respect to the reality of the facts adduced, and the same identical criteria are to be applied in determining the validity of the evidence presented of their occurrence.

We do not argue, it should be borne in mind, the validity of the claims of Theism from the testimony of the Scriptures to their truthfulness. Nor do we, in this connection, argue their Divine origin and authority from these events. All such questions are reserved for another department of our inquiries. What we do argue in this connection is this—that the facts recorded in Scripture, granting their occurrence, do furnish as valid a scientific basis for the claims of Theism, as those of astronomy do for the truth of the Copernican System, or as any facts can furnish for any deduction whatever in any of the physical or metaphysical sciences; and, as we shall hereafter show, we have evidence, the same in kind and degree, of the reality of the facts in the former case as we have in any of the latter cases. Such are the undeniable relations of Christian Theism to Natural Theology.

SECTION II.

THE RELATIONS OF CHRISTIAN THEISM TO THE SCIENCE OF COSMOLOGY.

To have a valid Ontology, that is, a true science of Being and its Laws, all actual facts must be taken into our reckoning, and be fully accounted for. If any real fact, or class of facts, is ignored, or repudiated as unreal, we should of necessity rear up a structure not of true, but of false science. We should assume forms of non-being as realities, and class realities among 'things that are not.' Facts are adamantine realities 'which cannot be shaken,' and every real fact will have its proper place and influence, and be fully accounted for in every scientifically constructed system of Cosmology. In the construction of most systems, facts are manufactured or ignored, assumed or repudiated, as existing exigencies require.

The actual occurrence of a single supernatural fact absolutely implies, as we have before said, the real existence, in and over nature, of a supernatural power. When the occurrence of such an event has been verified by valid evidence, the existence of the implied power must constitute an essential element and feature of our cosmological system. Otherwise the system which we shall construct will be a lie. In the presence of such a verified power, every true philosopher will be very modest in his affirmations about the extent to which passing events around us are under the control of mere naked physical law, or are determined, without violating any such law, by the action of this existing supernatural power. He will perceive nothing incredible in the idea that natural law itself may be so far under the control of the supernatural, that God, without violating any mental or physical law, may determine the current of events in specific accordance with the wants of mind, and be continuously manifested to the pure in heart as a hearer of prayer. The pedant Scientist, on the other hand, will imperiously dogmatize as if he were truly omniscient, just where his ignorance is and must, undeniably, be absolute. Listen, for a moment, to the dogmatic dicta of our embryo scientist. 'Fact I know, and Law I know.' My dear sir, should you ever become older and wiser than you now are, if 'wisdom shall enter into thine heart, and knowledge become pleasant unto thy soul,' you will blush with shame at the remembrance of such a presumptuous and absurd utterance as that. You are omniscient neither in respect to facts nor the ultimate law which determines their occurrence. Your ignorance is absolute in regard to the extent to which the natural may be determined by the supernatural in the current of facts which are moving by you. As a consequence, you stand convicted of imperiously and senselessly dogmatizing in respect to both universal 'Fact' and 'Law,' of which 'One part—one little part—you dimly scan.'

The Question of the Reality of these Facts, to be determined, first of all, wholly irrespective of their bearing upon the Claims of the Christian Religion.

The great central facts under consideration do have, as we have shown, their actual occurrence being admitted, a fundamental bearing in determining a valid system of Cosmology. The same facts, on the same admission, may have, and as we shall see hereafter, do have, a similar bearing upon the claims of the Christian religion. In determining the question whether those affirmed facts did, or did not occur, all inquiry in respect to their *bearings* in any direction is to be left wholly, for the time being, out of the account. If the facts did occur, and did occur as specific attestations of the truth of a particular religion, they do, undeniably, verify the existence of a supernatural and Divine power in and over nature, on the one hand, and the Divine origin and authority of that religion on the other. The question of the *actuality* of these facts, however, is to be determined by itself, and that by a rigid application of the laws of historic evidence. For aught we know to the contrary, God may in times past have interposed, and may interpose in the future, in forms undeniably supernatural, and that without revealing the specific reasons for such interpositions, His object being, it may be, simply to remind His rational offspring of His presence and agency in nature. It may be, on the other hand, that in connection with such interpositions the specific reason for their occurrence has been also revealed. All this, however, has nothing to do with the question, did or did not these events occur.

SECTION III.

RELATIONS OF SUPERNATURAL EVENTS, AND THE ACTION OF A SUPERNATURAL POWER IN NATURE, TO THE SO-CALLED LAWS OF NATURE.

IF a supernatural power actually exists in and over nature, the WILL of that power must be the *supreme* law of nature itself, and the ultimate and all-determining cause of the current of events around us, and each specific order of events must be an expression of the Will of that sovereign power. If the being in whom this power resides should choose that the order of events shall be, for the most part, in the fixed direction of uniform antecedence and consequence, but that as occasion requires there shall be special departures from this principle, there would be in such an arrangement an absolute conformity to the *supreme* law of nature, and no more violation of any specific law in one case than in the other. It is an immutable law of each physical substance in nature, that its motion shall ever be in the fixed direction of the strongest force acting upon it at each successive moment. It is, as we say, a fixed law of water and kindred fluids to run down an inclined plane. Suppose that by some attracting cause far stronger than that to which they are now subject, they should be drawn in the opposite direction. Their flow up, instead of down, the plane referred to, would in that case be just as natural, and as accordant with all existing laws of nature, as in their present direction. Any change whatever produced in nature by the action of a cause more powerful than those now determining the current of events, is as natural and accordant with all existing laws, as any other event can be. A *supernatural*, supposing it actual, is no *un*natural event, and its occurrence implies the violation of no existing law, but absolute accordance with every such law.

SECTION IV.

SUPERNATURAL, OR MIRACULOUS EVENTS DEFINED — THEIR POSSIBILITY, AND PROBABILITY — THEIR BEARING UPON THE CLAIMS OF CHRISTIAN RELIGION, ETC.

Such Events Defined.

WHAT then is a supernatural, or miraculous event, as distinguished from facts of ordinary occurrence? The real distinction, we reply, lies here. Whenever events occur in the fixed order of antecedence and consequence the *immediate* cause is not manifested. Their occurrence equally accords with two distinct and opposite hypotheses, and therefore implies the truth of neither in opposition to the other—the hypothesis of Divine Causation —and that of natural law. When, on the other hand, an event occurs in such relations and circumstances, as necessarily imply its production through the immediate agency of a supernatural cause, such event, to distinguish it from those of ordinary occurrence, is denominated supernatural, or miraculous. It is not thus designated because its occurrence was, in itself, less natural or more contradictory to any natural law, than is any other event, but because the former does, and the latter does not imply, and thus reveal, its *immediate* cause. *A supernatural, or miraculous event, then, is one whose occurrence cannot be accounted for through natural law—an event, therefore, which implies the existence and action in nature of a supernatural cause, and the presence and action of that cause in the production of said event.* A supernatural event, or a miracle, implies the violation or suspension of no existing law, but as perfectly as any other event accords with the ultimate and supreme law to which all facts are subordinate, and with the nature of all existing substances. It does, however, imply such a change in the common and visible order of events, as absolutely to imply the presence and immediate action of a supernatural power. If God should, as He often may do, produce invisibly to His creatures changes in the ordinary course of events, such changes, though in themselves as really supernatural as any others, would be no miracle to us. To be to *us* really supernatural, they must be events of which we can take such cognizance, that we can know that their immediate cause must be supernatural.

Conditions of the Possibility, or Probability of the Occurrence of Supernatural Events.

If a supernatural power does exist in and over nature, then undeniably the actual occurrence of supernatural, or miraculous events, is in itself just as possible as that of any other event, actual or conceivable. The occurrence of such events, granting the existence of the power under consideration, is just as probable as is the probability that exigencies may arise demanding such interpositions, and is absolutely certain whenever such exigencies do arise. The *impossibility* of the occurrence of supernatural events can be affirmed but upon one exclusive condition—an absolute denial of the existence of a supernatural power. Their *improbability* can be affirmed but upon a denial of the probability of the existence, in the past or future, of exigencies requiring their occurrence. The *certainty* of their non-occurrence can be affirmed, the existence of the power referred to being admitted, but upon an absolute denial of the occurrence, during the eternity past and the eternity to come, of any exigency demanding such interposition. We hold that no propositions can have greater intuitive and demonstrative certainty than those above presented. Omniscience is necessary for a valid denial of all past and of all future miracles.

The Knowledge which all who affirm the Impossibility, Improbability, or Non-actuality of Supernatural Events, do, in reality, assume the possession of.

We have already rendered it demonstrably evident, that the being of a personal God, or the existence of a supernatural power in and over nature, cannot by any possibility be disproved, and that against the doctrine no form or degree of positive evidence can be adduced. There is, undeniably, but two conceivable, and therefore possible hypotheses of ultimate causation—the Theistic, and that of Natural Law—and one of these must be true, and the other false. No form of valid proof, or positive evidence, can be adduced in favour of the latter hypothesis and against the former, because that all facts deducible in favour of the latter, are equally explicable on the former hypothesis. Nor can any antecedent probability be adduced against the Theistic hypothesis, and in favour of that of Natural Law. Against the possibility of miracles, therefore, no form of proof, positive evidence, or antecedent probability can be adduced. The same holds equally in respect to the idea of their probability, and actuality. To know that such occurrences are impossible and unreal, we must know that a supernatural power in and over nature does not exist. To know this, we must, undeniably, be possessed of absolute omniscience. We must have an absolute knowledge of all events, past, present, and to come, and of all substances and causes existing and acting in nature, and in infinite space. If there is any event of which we have not an absolute knowledge, that event may be, or may have been, produced by a supernatural cause. If there is any cause existing and acting in nature, or in infinite space, a cause of which we have not a similar knowledge, that cause, undeniably, may be a supernatural one. All scientists who affirm the impossibility of supernatural events do, in fact, arrogate to themselves the possession of absolute omniscience. They really and truly profess an absolute knowledge of all events of the eternity past, and of the eternity to come, and of all causes acting in infinite space, and eternal duration. On no other condition than the actual possession of such knowledge, can they, without infinite criminality and presumption, deny the possibility, probability, or actuality, of supernatural events in nature. When they make such denials, they positively assume to themselves, we repeat, the actual possession of an absolute omniscience of all events of the past and future, and of all causes existing and acting in infinite space and eternal duration. Well may every sober thinker, in view of the infinite impiety, folly, presumption, and arrogance of such men, exclaim, 'O my soul, come not thou into their secret; and into their assembly, mine honour, be not thou united.' Thinkers cannot be innocent who arrogate to themselves the actual possession of a perfect knowledge of all events of the past and future, of all exigencies which have arisen during the eternity past, or which may arise during the eternity to come, and of all causes which do exist and act in infinite space and eternal duration. We affirm, without fear of contradiction, that these men are not possessed of the knowledge of a single fact which, in the remotest degree, indicates the real impossibility, improbability, or non-actuality of supernatural events.

CONDITIONS ON WHICH WE ARE ABSOLUTELY BOUND TO ADMIT THE ACTUAL OCCURRENCE OF SUPERNATURAL EVENTS.

Against the possibility and actuality of supernatural events, as we have seen, no form or degree of real proof, positive evidence, or even antecedent probability can be adduced. On what condition, then, should we hold ourselves bound to admit the actual occurrence of such events in

SUPERNATURAL, OR MIRACULOUS EVENTS DEFINED. 373

any given case? On this one exclusive condition, we answer: *the actual presentation of that form and degree of evidence known to be valid in all other cases.* Just this and nothing more nor less have we a right to require, and just this we are bound to require in all such cases. Whenever the occurrence of an event, undeniably supernatural, has been fully verified by such evidence, we violate all the laws and principles of scientific induction and deduction, should we withhold a full and prompt assent to the actuality of the event itself, and to all the consequences which the fact implies. Against the occurrence of the fact, no form or degree of real proof, positive evidence, or antecedent probability can be adduced. In its verification, we have just that form and degree of positive evidence which never in any other case misleads, and which everywhere distinguishes the real from the unreal. No higher, or more abundant, evidence can rationally be required for miracles than for any other events in respect to which *certainty* is demanded. No more valid evidence have we a right to require, as the basis of religious belief, than is properly demanded as the basis of implicit belief in the science of Astronomy or any other of the *à posteriori* sciences. When the existence of Jesus Christ and the reality of the 'mighty works' ascribed to Him, have been verified to us by a rigid application of all the known laws and principles of historic verity, we justly forfeit the eternal life which He came to procure for and reveal to us, if we refuse to believe in Him. The sentiment so often repeated, that higher evidence is demanded to establish the occurrence of a supernatural event, than is required to verify, with perfect certainty, other classes of facts, is false in fact, and of most dangerous tendency. If higher degrees of evidence are to be demanded in the former than in cases of the latter kind, who can tell us what the form and degree of this higher evidence is? If evidence, known to be perfectly valid for certainty in all other cases, is not to be received as valid in the case of supernatural events, no one can inform us when and where assent becomes a duty, and dissent a sin. When evidence, known to have full validity in all other cases, is presented in verification of the occurrence of a supernatural event, obligation for assent becomes absolute and the criminality of dissent infinite.

Conditions on which we may Properly withhold Assent to the Actuality of Supernatural Events affirmed to have occurred.

The conditions on which we may rationally and virtuously withhold assent to a statement, that a miraculous event has occurred in any given case, now become obvious. They are the following:

1. The event may be in itself not of a supernatural character, but of naturally impossible occurrence. We meet with a statement, for example, not that an event has occurred in such relations and circumstances as

imply the presence and action of a supernatural cause, but that God had actually caused the same thing, at the same moment, to exist, and not to exist. We should dementate ourselves, if we should seriously inquire whether such an event had, or had not, occurred. Those who confound events which no power can produce, with those which a supernatural power, supposing it to exist, may produce, are without excuse.

2. There may be, in certain cases, a reasonable doubt about the *character* of the event, supposing it to be real. An event may occur, an event inexplicable through any causes known to us. Yet its character may be such as not necessarily to imply the presence and action, in its production, of a supernatural cause. In all such cases assent to the event as supernatural is not demanded. We may, on the other hand, properly wait for additional light. Our assent is demanded when, and only when, the character of the event as supernatural cannot be a matter of reasonable doubt, and when its occurrence is verified by evidence known to be valid in all other cases.

3. The obvious absence of evidence which is required in all cases where strict *certainty* is demanded is the only other proper ground of dissent in reference to cases under consideration. If our assent to a miracle is demanded on the basis of evidence, known to be deceptive in other cases, duty demands our dissent. Faith, as Christian virtue, is *absolute fidelity to valid evidence* or rational conviction. Unbelief, as sin, and affirmed as such in the Scriptures, is *infidelity to valid evidence* or rational conviction. 'He that doeth evil hateth the light, and will not come to the light.' The grounds of our revealed obligation to credit as real the supernatural events recorded as such in the Scriptures, are—that they are not, in themselves, events of impossible occurrence—that, granting their actuality, their supernatural character cannot be denied—and that they are affirmed as real by evidence, which, in all other cases in which strict certainty is required, has absolute validity.

Relations of these Events to the Christian Religion.

For aught that we know, or can know to the contrary, God may, as we have said before, change the visible order of events in forms which imply the presence and action in their occurrence of a supernatural power, and this without any revealed reasons for such interpositions. This, however, is not true of the supernatural events revealed in the Christian Scriptures. These events all stand before us as specific attestations of the truth of this religion. The actuality of these events being granted, no one will deny that Christianity lifts its divine form before us as the supernaturally revealed and attested religion of God.

Nor will any sober thinker question the *supernatural character* of these events, their actual occurrence being granted. We must absolutely deny their occurrence, or as absolutely affirm, with the magicians of old, 'This is the finger of God.' But one question remains for scientific determination—to wit, Did these events actually occur? This question of fact, as we have shown, is to be determined by a rigid application of the laws of historic verity. If in the light of the acknowledged Criteria which, in all other cases, distinguish the true from the false, and the strictly certain from the uncertain, they take rank among the true and the certain, they stand before us as absolutely verified facts of actual occurrence.

Admitting the actuality of these events, we must also admit the *divinity* of the Christian Religion, or affirm that God has actually attested the truth of a lie. These same remarks apply equally to all the *particular truths* of this religion. These supernatural attestations sustain the same relations to each specific truth that they do to Christianity itself. Everywhere they lift their heaven-illumined summits amid the great revelations of this religion, divinely attesting the truth of each and all in common.

Relations of these Events to the Christian Scriptures.

The Christian Religion, with all its specific teachings, exists as a revelation from God nowhere but in the Christian Scriptures. The supernatural events therein recorded, have the identical relations to these writings that the same events have to the religion of which said writings are a record. To deny the proper inspiration of the record, and to affirm that the religion which they record is a divinely attested religion, involves a gross and palpable contradiction. Let us suppose that in recording these events, together with the principles and doctrines contained in the same record, these writers were under no, to us, divinely attested supernatural guidance; that, on the other hand, they merely wrote out, as others might have done, facts as they saw them, and doctrines as they actually held them. We should, on that hypothesis, be bound to regard the facts recorded as supernatural events which divinely attest no religion whatever. Had Josephus, or Tacitus, after the appearance of the Four Gospels, compiled the same into a single treatise, and interspersed through the same his own honest views of doctrine and duty, the facts recorded would have the same identical relations to the doctrinal and moral teachings of the Gospel according to Tacitus or Josephus, that the same facts do have, on the present hypothesis, to the Gospel of Matthew or John. A denial of the Divine authority of the Christian Records, involves a corresponding denial of the Divine authority of the religion which they professedly record, and Christianity stands before us as a religion no more Divinely attested than is that of Brahm or of Buddha. We should on this hypothesis, we repeat, be bound to regard the Scripture facts as supernatural, but as having occurred for no revealed reasons whatever.

The events under consideration do, in fact and form, stand before us not only as Divine attestations of the Christian Religion, but equally so of the Divine authority of the writings which record that religion. The supernatural events recorded in Scripture everywhere present themselves as specific attestations, not only of the truth of a given religion, but equally so, of Moses and the Prophets, of Christ and His Apostles, as the divinely commissioned revelators of the specific truths of that religion. The miracles performed through Moses before Pharaoh and the Israelites, for example, were performed for two specifically revealed reasons—to verify his particular utterances, and verify *him*, as 'God's Mouth' to those to whom those utterances were addressed. The fire that descended on Carmel in answer to the prayer of Elijah, descended to verify two specific revelations—that Jehovah is the only true God, and that Elijah was His Prophet. 'The mighty works' performed by Christ, as he specifically informs us, divinely attested both the truth of his particular utterances, and verified *Him* as a 'Teacher sent from God.' Christ, also, gave absolute authority to His Apostles as revelators and teachers of truth. 'Whatsoever ye shall bind on earth shall be bound in heaven, and whatsoever ye shall loose on earth shall be loosed in heaven.' Christ not only taught the divinity of certain truths revealed in the Scriptures, but equally the absolute authority of the writings themselves. 'It is written'—'The Scriptures must be fulfilled.' 'The Scriptures cannot be broken.' 'Thus it is written, and thus it behoved Christ to suffer.' 'Think not, that I am come to destroy the law or the prophets : I am not come to destroy, but to fulfil.' The Apostles, also, as divinely commissioned teachers of truth give the same testimony to the Divine origin and authority of the Scripture records. 'Holy men of God spake as they were moved by the Holy Ghost.' 'All scripture is given by inspiration of God.' The supernatural events under consideration do not stand before us as meaningless interpositions of Divine power; nor as attestations of a religion nowhere divinely attested ; but as diverse attestations of the absolute authority of specified 'teachers sent from God,' and, consequently, of the Divine authority of specific records of a religion divinely attested to us through such teachers. To deny that the Scriptures are to us of Divine authority in matters of belief and conduct is to affirm that the supernatural events which they record were produced for no assignable reasons whatever. To prove the reality of these supernatural events implies a corresponding proof, not only of the divinity of Christianity itself, but also of the Divine origin and authority of the Scriptures which embody the truths of this religion.

There can be no more fundamental form of error than is embraced in the dogma, that Christianity itself is from God, and is contained somewhere in the Scriptures; but that these Scriptures are themselves of human origin and authority. It is, in fact, to assure us that the needle is somewhere in the hay-mow, and then to tell us to find it if we can. Suppose that God did reveal a religion, and then left the matter to individuals who might choose to attempt to record it to express their own apprehensions of that religion. Who would vouch for the correctness of such apprehensions, in the first case, and in the next for the correctness with which these uninspired men have expressed their own views upon the subject? Who can determine how much, and what form of error, may be intermingled with the truth in their apprehensions and representations? To us, error and truth, as intermingled in these writings, if they are intermingled at all, are alike divinely attested, or Christianity itself is in no form thus attested.

The idea which some appear to entertain, that the *vocal*, but not *written* utterances of the Prophets and Apostles were of Divine authority, is one of the most absurd forms of error that ever appeared. The terms 'whatsoever' and 'whosesoever,' in the commission to 'bind and loose,' 'remit and retain,' must have a special reference and application, if anywhere, to their written, that is to their permanently recorded, utterances. If their written utterances do not bind, nothing they ever said could have bound anybody. Will anyone put this construction upon our Saviour's words? 'Whatsoever (except when you write) ye shall bind on earth, shall be bound in heaven.'

SECTION V.

REVELATION AND INSPIRATION.

Terms Defined.

THE terms revelation and inspiration represent two distinct and separate ideas. The former represents the act of God in *making known* his truth to creatures. The latter represents a DIVINE GUIDANCE imparted to individuals in communicating to others truths which God has revealed to the mediums of Divine communication. God, for example, revealed certain forms of truth to Moses. This was Divine revelation. God then, by his own Spirit, guided Moses in communicating that truth to the people. This was inspiration. Revelation may pertain to truths previously known, or to such as have not before been apprehended. Truths of the former class, when divinely represented to the mind, or communicated to the world by inspiration, possess a sacredness and impressiveness which did not previously attach to them. The Ten Commandments, for example, contain few forms of duty of which the race was previously wholly ignorant. They now, however, possess a distinctness, sacredness, and impressiveness which could not otherwise belong to them. Revelation also presents to human apprehension truths which lie wholly beyond the reach of human thought.

Revelation, as it comes from God, must present to the mind pure truth and nothing else. To suppose the opposite would imply that God intentionally deceives His creatures. No one who has any respect for his Creator will impute to Him any such monstrous deceptions as this.

Divine inspiration, in all forms which bind the faith and obedience of those who receive its communications, must present the exclusive and pure truth previously revealed. The opposite idea implies the same kind of intentional deception on the part of God that deceptive revelations would. It is undeniable that God may so guide men whom He inspires to communicate His revealed truth that they shall present that truth in its purity and nothing else; or He may so influence their minds that in the same communications they shall intermingle and confound God's revelations with their own imaginings. The dogma that God, whenever He has inspired individuals to communicate His own truth, has chosen the latter in preference to the former method, when both were equally practicable, is, to say the least, a great absurdity.

But which of these is, in fact, the *inspired method revealed in the Scriptures?* On this subject we have the most clear and positive information in both the Old and the New Testament. In Exod. xx. 21, the people request that God would thereafter communicate with them, not directly, but through Moses. 'Speak thou with us, and we will hear, but let not God speak with us, lest we die.' In Deut. xviii. 15-19, we have a reference to the same subject, with a distinct revelation of the real relations of all future inspired Prophets to God on the one hand, and to men on the other. For the sake of distinctness we present the entire passage. 'The Lord thy God will raise up unto thee a Prophet from the midst of thee, of thy brethren, like unto me; unto him ye shall hearken. According to all that thou desirest of the Lord thy God in Horeb in the day of the assembly, saying, Let me not hear again the voice of the Lord my God, neither let me see this great fire any more, that I die not. And the Lord said unto me, They have well spoken that which they have spoken. I will raise them up a Prophet from among their brethren, like unto thee, and will put My words in his mouth; and he shall speak unto them all that I shall command him. And it shall come to pass, that whosoever will not hearken unto My words which he shall speak in My name, I will require it of him.'

This passage undeniably refers to every inspired Prophet that God has since raised up, and not exclusively to Christ, as some have supposed. Nor does Peter (Acts iii. 22-25) cite the passage as having an *exclusive* reference to Christ, but to Him as, among others, a Prophet. Peter also applies the passage to other Prophets in the sáme sense as to Christ. The Apostle reminds the people of their obligation to receive the words of Christ as if directly addressed to them by God Himself, for the reason that Christ was to them a divinely attested Prophet, 'a Prophet raised up from the midst of them,' according to Divine promise, His words also being confirmed by the voice of all the Prophets from Samuel onward.

In the passage from Exodus now under consideration, God Himself distinctly reveals the following truths. 1. From that time onward He would uniformly make revelations to men, not directly, but through Prophets whom He should 'raise up from among the people.' 2. To these Prophets He would first make His revelations of truth. 'I will put My words in his mouth.' 3. God would so guide the utterances of His Prophets that they should communicate just what He had communicated to them. 'He shall speak unto them all that I shall command him.' Here God promises that *inspired* truth, as communicated by the Prophets, shall be identical in all respects with *revealed* truth, as communicated by Him to the Prophets. 4. The utterances of the Prophets, when given forth 'in the name of God,' shall bind our faith and obedience in the same sense and manner that they would if directly uttered by God Himself. 'And it shall come to pass that whosoever will not hearken unto My words which he shall speak in My name, I will require it of him.' The great truth manifestly set before us in this whole passage is this: God is in the same sense responsible for the truth of all utterances of divinely attested Prophets, utterances given forth by them 'in His name,' as He would be, were these utterances directly addressed to us by God Himself; and these utterances as absolutely bind our faith and obedience in the one case as they would in the other.

The same great truth is repeated in the commission which Jeremiah received as a divine Prophet, 'Thou shalt be as My mouth.' Now, all the Prophets of the Old Testament do stand before us, as divinely attested Prophets of God, and all their communications do come to us 'in the name of the Lord.' We must, therefore, brand them as 'lying Prophets,' or accept their utterances as to us 'the voice of God.'

In the same light did Christ and His Apostles regard the utterances of these Prophets. It was no part of His mission, as He Himself informs us, to annul any of the teachings of the Old Testament, but to confirm them all. 'What is written,' He presents as having absolute authority over even Himself in His relations as a man. The Scriptures, He tells us, 'cannot be broken,' but 'must be fulfilled.' 'He became obedient unto death, even the death of the cross,' for this reason, that otherwise 'the Scriptures could not be fulfilled.' 'And He said to them, These are the words which I spoke to you, while I was yet with you, that all things must be fulfilled which were written in the law of Moses, and in the Prophets, and in the psalms, concerning me. Then he opened their understanding, that they might understand the Scriptures, and said to them, Thus it is written, and thus it behoves Christ to suffer, and to rise from the dead the third day.' Where is the *mustness* about fulfilling all that is written in the law of Moses, and in the prophets, and in the psalms, 'concerning Him,' if these writings are not of Divine authority? Christ did not, or these writings do, speak the words of God.'

To the same effect are the express teachings of the Apostles. 'God,' we are told (Hebrews i. 1) 'spake unto our fathers by the Prophets.' Another Apostle affirms (2 Peter i. 16-21) that none of the utterances found in these writings were of human origin. This is the obvious meaning of the words 'private interpretation.' That which is written, we are told, is not what men thought out, and willed to write, but what God thought, and willed to have written. 'What is written,' he affirms, has even higher authority than a mere report of what is seen, and heard 'from God out of heaven.' Let us read the whole passage. ' For we have not followed cunningly devised fables, when we made known unto you the power and coming of our Lord Jesus Christ, but were eye-witnesses of His majesty. For He received from God the Father honour and glory, when there came such a voice to Him from the excellent glory, "This is My beloved Son, in whom I am well pleased." And this voice which came from heaven we heard, when we were with Him in the holy mount. We have also a more sure word of prophecy; whereunto ye do well that ye take heed, as unto a light that shineth in a dark place, until the day dawn, and the daystar arise in your hearts: knowing this first, that no prophecy of the Scripture is of any private interpretation. For the prophecy came not in old time by the will of man: but holy men of God spake as they were moved by the Holy Ghost.' Nothing can be more plain than is the fact, that according to apostolic teaching, the *thoughts* which the Prophets uttered were not their own, but God's, and that the words through which those thoughts are expressed, are the words of God.

But did the Apostles, in this authoritative form, occupy the position of Prophets? They did, we answer, and that in the most important form ever occupied before. To this our Saviour refers (Luke vii. 28), 'For I say unto you, Among those that are born of women there is not a greater Prophet than John the Baptist: but he that is least in the kingdom of God is greater than he.' The term 'greater' evidently refers, not to mental powers, but to *position*. So after the term 'least' that of Prophet is to be understood, the laws of language requiring this. The meaning of the whole verse may be thus expressed: 'Among those that are born of women,' no Prophet of the past has ever yet occupied a position of greater dignity and importance than John the Baptist occupied; nevertheless, he that shall discharge the office of a Prophet in the lowest form in the New Dispensation, will occupy a sphere of greater dignity and importance than that occupied by John. The manifest object of the Saviour was to impress the Apostles with a consciousness of the dignity, importance, and responsibility of the prophetic office to which they were about to be introduced. In this passage, these Apostles, with Paul afterwards divinely associated with them, stand before us as divinely designated Prophets of God, Prophets in higher and more responsible relations than any Prophets had ever before been in. If the utterances of Prophets of the Old were, much more must those of the New Dispensation be to us, 'the voice of God,' and must, in the most absolute form, bind our faith and obedience.

On this matter we have also the most specific and absolute instruction from Christ himself. The following (Matt. xvi. 19) is the authority expressly conferred upon Peter, as an inspired revelator of Divine truth: 'And I will give unto thee the keys of the kingdom of heaven: and whatsoever thou shalt bind on earth shall be bound in heaven: and whatsoever thou shalt loose on earth shall be loosed in heaven.' The same absolute authority, as teachers of truth and duty, is, afterwards, as expressly conferred upon *all* the Apostles (Matt. xviii. 18). 'Verily I say unto you, Whatsoever ye shall bind on earth shall be bound in heaven: and whatsoever ye shall loose shall be loosed in heaven.' The words 'bind and loose' represent authority in the realm of inspired truth in its most absolute forms. The same absolute authority is reconferred upon all these Apostles in the following words (John xx. 23): 'Whosesoever sins ye remit, they are remitted unto them; and whosesoever sins ye retain, they are retained.' The sense in which the Apostles did 'remit and retain sins' was *declarative*, that is, they, as 'teachers sent from God,' declared, or revealed, the *conditions* on which men should receive, or fail to receive, the pardon of sin. Nothing can be more evident than is the fact, that Moses and the Prophets, Christ and the Apostles, stand revealed in the Scriptures as divinely attested Prophets of God, Prophets who 'speak by authority,' the authority of God, and whose words and writings are to us, when understood, God's laws of faith and conduct.

SECTION VI.

NEEDFUL EXPLANATIONS.

IF the doctrine of inspiration, as we have explained it, is true, it follows as a necessary consequence that when we have ascertained the *real meaning* of any passage of the sacred writings, we have found a divinely attested truth of God. Here we have the sense in which these writings differ from all others. When we have ascertained the real meaning of writings of mere human origin, another question then arises—to wit, Are the author's teachings in accordance with truth? When, on the other hand, we have ascertained the true meaning of any passage of Scripture, that meaning binds our faith and conduct. We make God a liar when we question the truth of 'what is written.' To teach that the Scriptures were given by inspiration of God, and yet to affirm that their ascertained meaning is not of absolute authority, is equivalent to the absurdity, that the Scriptures were, and were not, 'given by inspiration of God.'

Here also lies the real distinction between the believer and the infidel. The former does, and the latter does not, regard himself as bound in matters of faith and conduct by the ascertained meaning of the Scriptures. If an individual denies the proper inspiration, and with it the absolute Divine authority of the Scriptures, he is bound by the immutable laws of integrity to avow himself an infidel. This is the meaning of the term infidel, according to our standard lexicography. He who denies the proper inspiration and Divine authority of the Scriptures, and yet calls himself a Christian, not only 'denies the faith,' but is 'worse than an infidel,' that is, an infidel who admits himself to be such. We should be misunderstood here without a few words of special explanation.

Special Explanations.

1. When the Scriptures affirm, as a mere historic fact, that certain individuals did, on certain occasions, perform certain acts, inspiration is responsible for the real occurrence of the facts stated, and not at all for their *moral* character, unless such characteristics are revealed as approved or disapproved. It accords with revealed truth, that good men *may*, under temptation, do wrong, and even perpetrate crimes. The recorded acts of such men, when stated as mere historic facts, are to be judged as the doings of other individuals are.

2. The same principle applies to the *recorded utterances* of individuals. If such utterances are given as the real sayings of inspired Prophets or Apostles, inspiration is responsible both for the *fact* and the *truth* of such utterances. If the speaker, on the other hand, is not affirmed to have been, at the time, under the guidance of the Spirit of God, inspiration is responsible merely for the fact stated. The sayings of Job, and of his three friends, for example, are not recorded as *inspired* utterances, but as having been actually given forth by them on the occasion designated. Inspiration, therefore, is responsible for the *correctness of the record*, and not for the *truth* of what was uttered. This principle holds true in respect to all similar utterances recorded in Scripture. The

fact, that the sayings of an individual are recorded merely *as his* sayings, is no proof at all, that such utterances are of inspired authority.

3. To understand still more fully the bearings of the doctrine of inspiration upon the writings of the New Testament, we must also keep in mind the two distinct and separate relations which the Apostles sustained to what they uttered and wrote, as *witnesses* of facts of which they had a personal knowledge, and as inspired prophets. In the latter relation they speak with all authority, 'binding and loosing,' 'remitting and retaining,' as the spirit of inspiration dictated. In the former relation they could speak nothing but what they had 'seen and heard,' and *as* they 'had seen and heard.' Amid the melting and overwhelming agitations of their minds during the evening of 'the Lord's Supper,' for example, it would not be strange at all if, when Christ said directly to Peter, 'Before the cock shall crow twice, thou shalt deny Me thrice,' if the word 'twice' was heard and remembered only by Peter. When Matthew and John wrote *as witnesses*, and Luke as he received the facts from ear witnesses, they could state no more than was actually heard by themselves. Nor would the Spirit bring to remembrance anything but what they did hear and as they heard. Mark, on the other hand, who wrote under the direction of Peter, would give *all* that our Saviour did say. There is no discrepancy here any more than between any whole and its parts. In regard to the particular hours of the day, when the different scenes of the trial and crucifixion occurred, each would have his general impressions, some of them more, and some less specific, and none of them accurate as to the moment. Hence, when one tells us that 'it was the preparation of the passover, and about the sixth hour, and others give more specific and detailed statements in regard to the times when particular scenes occurred, there is not, when the subject is rightly viewed, even the appearance of contradiction. The Spirit of inspiration directed each writer to give, as a witness, his own impressions in respect to time and other circumstances, just as they existed in his mind. On no other conditions could the Apostles be to us *witnesses* of what they 'saw and heard.' Almost all the difficulties encountered in reconciling, with one another, the different statements of the Evangelists disappear at once when the distinction under consideration is kept in mind, while their credibility as witnesses is thereby absolutely verified.

4. A full and complete understanding of this great subject requires, we remark finally, a clear discrimination between 'the gift of the Spirit,' as promised to all believers and as confined to the Prophetic, under the Old, and to the Apostolic office under the New Dispensation. 'The promise of the Spirit' pertains to all believers in common, and as an illuminating and sanctifying power He is present in all who embrace the promise by faith. As a miracle-working power, He was, even in Apostolic times,

given to but few. Under the Old Dispensation none but divinely attested prophets had any authority at all in matters of faith and practice. Under the New Dispensation, while we have positive proof, as has been shown, that absolute authority, as revelators of truth and duty, was conferred upon the Apostles, we have no evidence whatever that such authority was conferred upon any but them. This fact was, from the first, clearly understood in the Primitive Church. No writings but the ascertained Apostolic, that is, such as were composed by Apostles, or under their dictation, were regarded as of Divine authority.

The distinction between 'the gifts of the Spirit' conferred upon the Apostles and all other believers, are specifically designated in the New Testament. This whole subject is at full length clearly set before us in the twelfth chapter of First Corinthians. We cite verses 28-30. After being informed that 'there are diversities of gifts, but the same Spirit,' and 'differences of administrations, but the same Lord,' we have the following fundamental statement in the verses referred to. 'And God hath set some in the Church, first apostles, secondarily prophets, thirdly teachers, after that miracles, then gifts of healings, helps, governments, diversities of tongues. *Are* all apostles? *are* all prophets? *are* all teachers? *are* all workers of miracles? have all the gifts of healing? do all speak with tongues? do all interpret?' The term *prophet* has a different meaning under the New, from what it had under the Old Dispensation. Under the latter, it designated a class of persons divinely attested as mediums of authoritative divine communication. Under the former, it designates a class who speak in the churches, not by authority, but under special Divine influence, and who consequently 'speak unto men to edification, and exhortation, and comfort.' The Apostles alone spake by authority. They, consequently, received the gift of inspiration proper, a gift differing from all others conferred by the Spirit, just as the 'gift of healing' differed from that of 'speaking with tongues.' It is hardly possible to announce a more dangerous error than that which is involved in confounding the gift of inspiration proper with the ordinary gifts promised to all believers in common, and representing the latter as differing, not in kind, but merely in degree, from the former.

This is the insinuating, but utterly subverting, form of error which is being urged upon the churches at the present time. In one or two articles recently published in that leading religious quarterly, *The New Englander*, articles containing a translation and abridgment of 'Rothe on Revelation and Inspiration,' we have the following:—'We must conclude,' says this author, 'from these data that the possession of the Spirit is not, according to the New Testament doctrine, confined to the Apostles, but extends to all true believers, without any specific difference.' Again, 'It is an idea foreign to the New Testament writings that the Apostles, in the composition of their writings, were under the influence of the Holy Spirit in a way specifically different from His usual indwelling in them.' Granting this, the deduction is absolute, that every believer, when 'filled with the Spirit,' as promised to all Christians in common, does in fact and form hold in his hands 'the keys of the kingdom of heaven,' and has all power to 'bind and loose,' 'remit and retain,' the same identical authority in kind and degree, the same authority which Christ conferred upon His Apostles. We must conclude, also, that all that we are told in the New Testament about 'the diversity of gifts,' the diverse kinds of gifts conferred upon the Apostles in distinction from others, a diversity which rendered the former, in distinction from the latter, *Apostles*, is essential error. Who are these men who are thus 'wise above what is written'?

SECTION VII.
OBJECTIONS ANSWERED.

THREE, and only three, hypotheses present themselves in regard to the inspiration of the Scriptures—that of Infidelity, which affirms, that they neither contain a revelation from God, nor 'were given by inspiration of God'—the Semi-Infidel, which affirms that Christianity itself was given by revelation, of which we have a human and fallible record in the Scriptures—and the Christian proper, which affirms that the Scriptures are an inspired record of an actual revelation, a record for the verity of which God holds Himself responsible. The infidel hypothesis is discussed in another connection. Our *present* concern is with the two last designated. We make no appeal to prejudice when we employ the term Semi-Infidel. We employ the term for the sake of convenience, and because no other term so correctly represents the hypothesis itself. The Christian hypothesis we regard as already established. Against the other it has also the highest probability in its favour. Christianity itself, *as a revelation from God*, none will deny, presents nothing but pure truth unmingled with error. If God had chosen, He could, as we have shown, have given to the world a record of this revelation just as free from error as the original communication was. Did He choose, after giving forth a revelation of pure truth to leave it to men to record, or not to record, what was revealed just as they should choose; and when they should attempt to give such record, to leave them so to intermingle their own imaginings with His own truth, that we can have no valid criteria by which we can distinguish the former from the latter? Did Christ, also, deliver to certain men 'the keys of the kingdom of heaven,' with absolute authority to 'bind and loose,' 'remit and retain,' and pledge His word that what they should require and prohibit, affirm and deny, should be verified in heaven—did Christ deliver all this to men upon whom He conferred no higher wisdom or authority than is possessed by all believers in whom the common 'promise of the Spirit' is fulfilled? What a senseless farce He acted before the world if this is the case!

Let us now turn our thoughts to the arguments adduced to sustain this Semi-Infidel hypothesis. One of the old and standing objections is the *style* of these writings. Our citations will be from the article to which we have referred, an article which embodies the argument in favour of this hypothesis in its fullest and strongest form. In regard to the style of the Bible our author thus writes: 'They wrote as they spake, out of their individual peculiarities. The one fact, that the later and less original ones made use of the earlier, is enough to disprove the theory'— that of the proper inspiration of the Prophets. 'The case is the same with the New Testament.' 'Moreover, these writers have each his own peculiar characteristic style of writing, and in the most of them we find a certain awkwardness in the use of language, and a ruggedness and stiffness of the forms of speech, as is natural and usual with writers who have not had much of the training of the schools, and are not accustomed to express their thoughts in writing. These things do not impair the value of the books for the purposes intended, but how can they be attributed to the Holy Spirit?' 'Would any recognise these books as writings in whose productiveness the authors are in a passive condition, labouring mechanically, mere slate pencils? The exact opposite strikes every reader.'

Here we have, in the first place, an utter and inexcusable misrepresentation of the doctrine of inspiration as held by Evangelical Christians of all schools. Until we met the misrepresentation in this article, we never before heard of the idea that inspiration proper implies 'the mechanical passivity,' or 'the slate-pencil state' of inspired men, when speaking or writing. The mind, when under the control of the Spirit of Inspiration so absolutely as to express just what God intends and dictates, and nothing more or less, does, or may, in fact, act as freely and naturally as in any other state. Misrepresentation is one thing; refutation is quite another.

Let us consider directly this argument deduced from such an idea of style. Lord Bolingbroke, we think it was, who was very much enamoured with the sublime in writing, presents this as an unanswerable argument against the inspiration of the Scriptures. If God were the author of these writings, every sentence found in them, he affirmed, would be characterized by infinite sublimity. Our author 'has been to school,' and he consequently thinks that if these were inspired writings, their style would savour of the University. This argument, we judge, is just as conclusive, and no more so, in one view as in the other. Permit us to ask this writer, and all others who reason like him, such questions as the following: Do you know, gentlemen, what the proper and exclusive Theodic style is? Do you know that it is not so, that when God employs the tongues or pens of individuals, to express to human beings His own thoughts, such thoughts will not be clothed in the words common to such individuals when not inspired? Do you know that if God should, for example, choose to communicate His own truth, and that infallibly, through a child, as in the case of little Samuel, that God's thought would not be expressed in the language and style of the child? Do you know that this is not the real and proper Theodic style, the style which it is wisest and best for God to adopt, whenever He makes individuals the mediums of Divine communication? Do you not, then, in impugning the inspiration of the Scriptures, for such reasons as you have employed in this case, stand convicted of 'speaking evil of that which you understand not'?

The above arguments, and all others based upon the style of the sacred writings, do not present the least form of positive, or probable, evidence against the *verbal* inspiration of these writings. Much less do such arguments have the remotest bearing against the doctrine, that the Scriptures, when rightly understood, are an infallible, and absolutely authoritative rule of faith and conduct. While we do not profess to know, of ourselves, what kind of a universe God should make, we can discern wisdom Divine in the universe He has made. So of God's higher creation, the Scriptures of truth. While we have no means of knowing but from the Bible what the real Theodic style is, we can perceive a Divine wisdom in the style which God has adopted. Among such indications of wisdom, we refer to the following:

1. Truth thus communicated is rendered more easy of *apprehension*, and is more *impressive* than it could be by any other method of which we can form a conception. By this method, truth is rendered impressive not merely by words, but by or through its actually illuminating and sanctifying power upon the heart. In other words, we apprehend the truth just as it lies in the heart, moves and purifies the affections, and moulds and perfects the moral character. It consequently comes to us with a distinctness of apprehension and a melting and transforming power otherwise impossible. In the Scriptures, we are not only in constant contact with Divine truth, but with that truth as a life-imparting power in the actual experience of the soul of man. We have no wish to be possessed of that form of wisdom which would impugn such a method of communication as this. Truth affects us most deeply when it comes to us warm from the heart of the individual through whom it is communicated, and in language and style most natural to him.

2. The method of inspired communication of revealed truth through *human* language renders the Bible capable of being *interpreted* by human beings. If the Scriptures were written in a superhuman or Theodic style, how could human beings interpret them? For their interpretation we should need a Theodic lexicon and commentary, and to understand these, a lexicon and commentary in human language and style would be finally demanded. Nor would the Scriptures be translatable into any language under heaven. As it is, they are subject to the laws of interpretation common to other writings, and can therefore be understood by human beings; and are translatable into all human languages, and can consequently be given to all men. 'Who hath known the mind of the Lord, or being His counsellor, hath taught Him?'

3. This method of inspiration also furnishes us with scientific *criteria* by which we can determine the eras in which various portions of the Scriptures were written, criteria to which a Theodic superhuman style would be inapplicable. Rationalistic criticism has created three great maelstroms, into which they cast different portions of Scripture, when the questions of their origin are discussed. The first is represented by the words, 'About the time of Ezra.' If we ask them at what era were the writings of Moses produced and completed—'About the time of Ezra,' is the reply. When was the book of Job written? 'About the time of Ezra.' When were all the historic portions of the Old Testament written? 'About the time of Ezra.' When were the portions of Scripture under consideration, together with the Psalms and works of Solomon, compiled? 'About the time of Ezra' is the monotonous reply. When, we again ask, were the leading prophetic writings of the Old Testament composed? At a period (the second maelstrom) not long prior to the Christian Era, after the leading events designated had occurred, is the reply. But when were the several books of the New Testament written? About (the third maelstrom) the close of the second or third centuries of the Christian Era.

Suppose, now, that the Scriptures were written in a superhuman or Theodic style. By no possibility could we determine from their language and style the era in which any portion of the sacred books were written. *Now* we have criteria of the most decisive character. We can say to our rationalistic critics that the book of Job, for example, could by no possibility have been composed 'About the time of Ezra.' The reason is obvious. The language of this book is wholly Hebraistic of the purest kind. The written and spoken language of the Jews 'About the time of Ezra' was not pure, but Chaldaic Hebrew. This book must also have been written by a learned Hebrew well versed in facts pertaining to Egypt and Arabia, and wholly ignorant of the Jews in Canaan and under Mosaic institutions and usages. On no other hypothesis can we account for the frequent allusion to facts of the former class, and the total absence of all reference to those of the latter.

The pure Hebrew of Moses, of the historic portion of the Old Testament, and of the leading Prophets prior to Daniel, render it certain that they could, none of them, have been written 'About the time of Ezra,' but long prior to that period; and that none of them could consequently have been written after the predictions of these Prophets were fulfilled. The Hebraistic Greek of the entire New Testament renders it perfectly evident that none of these books could have been written after the close of the Apostolic Era, their peculiarities of style having no existence in any language subsequent to that period. There are no more important sources of historic criticism than are found in the humanness of the language and style of the sacred writings.

4. The evidence of the actual inspiration of the Scriptures is, we remark finally, rendered demonstrative by the very style which is objected against. The language and style is human. The truths which they represent are wholly superhuman. No power but inspiration itself can by any possibility embody such truth in such human words and style. In the Scriptures the human and the Divine, the finite and the infinite, meet and blend in harmonious unity. The idea of the human origin of the Scriptures is, to a mind which has any adequate comprehension of the subject, as absurd as is that of the human origin of the solar system. The humanity of the style, in contrast with the divinity of the truth, which the former embodies, induces in every reflecting mind the immutable conviction that here is the handwriting of God.

In the midst of these great revelations, which lift their heaven-illumined summits above and around us, as we walk up and down among these sacred books, we find no forms of error of any kind intermingled with the Divine truths commended to our faith. In all human writings, which do embody important forms of truth, we find error, the same in kind, intermingled with what is true. Not so with the Scriptures. Their doctrines and moral teachings are not only true, but are wholly unmarred with error. This undeniable fact places the Bible, with its admittedly human language and style, at an infinite remove from all productions not really and truly 'given by inspiration of God.'

But while no forms of error are professedly found in the doctrinal and moral teachings of the Scriptures, the only material issue that could be raised, as an argument against the proper inspiration of the New Testament especially, is drawn from essential errors imputed to the writers of the same, in their Old Testament citations and references.

Thus, the writer to whom we have referred remarks: 'The New Testament writers often quoted the Old Testament from memory, and here and there with such changes in wording as materially alter the sense.' . . .

'These writers, too, quote from the Septuagint, for the most part, even when it misrepresents the original.' . . . 'Many of the proof-texts taken from the Old Testament by the writers of the New, are not proof-texts at all.'

It may be edifying to our readers to know that the errors and faults which this writer and others of his school impute to the Apostles, are by the same writers also imputed to Christ Himself. 'Christ,' we are told, 'did in common with the Jews treat the Old Testament revelation as of Divine authority. Undoubtedly, too, he treated the *letter* of the Old Testament as of Divine authority.' The New Testament writers, also, we are further told, 'Considered the Old Testament as the immediate Word of God, and our Lord left their conceptions undisturbed.' Unless Christ Himself, therefore, can be convicted of error, the Old Testament Scriptures, in their letter and spirit, are 'the Word of God,' and of absolute authority. Such writers as those under consideration do not blink the issue at all thus presented, but boldly impugn the Divine authority of Christ Himself. 'They are in error,' we are assured, 'who think of the Saviour as having a complete exegetical knowledge of the Old Testament.' 'The Saviour never professed to be an infallible and complete expositor of the Old Testament.' We judge that when our Saviour affirmed that He 'came not to destroy, but to fulfil the law and the Prophets,' and that 'not one jot or tittle should pass from the law until *all* shall be fulfilled,' that He did possess, and did affirm Himself to possess, a full knowledge of the subject matter to which He referred, that is, of the Old Testament Scriptures. We believe, also, that attributing *fallibility* to Christ is an eclipse of faith, as complete as would result to the earth from the total extinguishment of 'the light of the world.' The only form of evidence presented of His fallibility is His sacred respect for the Scriptures of the Old Testament as 'the Word of God.' We judge that He came forth from God as well informed on this subject as the semi-infidels of modern times.

We have, in the article under consideration, multitudinous references to passages in the New Testament to sustain the charge of error on the part of its writers in their citations from the Old Testament. No passages but one or two, however, are cited. Had the writer given citations instead of mere references, his own bald ignorance of the Scriptures and that of his school would have become manifest to every reader. We have been careful to search out all these references, and to compare each passage referred to with the known laws and principles of Biblical interpretation. As the result, we feel quite safe in affirming that in carelessness, not to say recklessness, in the interpretation of Scripture, this article, which, as we have said, embodies all that modern semi-infidelity has developed on this subject, can hardly be paralleled. Not a single passage referred to has, when rigidly interpreted in the light of correct exegesis, even an apparent bearing in favour of the author's position. Thus he affirms that 'Paul explains the same passage, Gen. xiii. 15, in two different ways, Rom. iv. 16, and Gal. iii. 16.' In Gal. iii. 16 Paul undeniably refers, not to Gen. xiii. 15 at all, but to Gen. xxii. 18, and he has given the true interpretation of the latter passage. When God said, 'In thy seed shall all the nations of the earth be blessed,' He unquestionably must have referred, as Paul says He did, not to Abraham's posterity in general, but specifically to Christ. What must we think of a Biblical interpreter who should affirm that Paul, in Gal. iii. 16, referred to Gen. xiii. 15, which thus reads, 'For all this land which thou seest, to thee will I give it, and to thy seed for ever.' So Paul, in Rom. iv. 16, simply asserts, and asserts correctly, without reference to any one particular passage, that God's promises to Abraham and his seed were, in fact, conditioned on faith.

Take another example. 'In Heb. x. 5 an argument is drawn from the words of the text, Ps. xl. 7, "A body hast Thou prepared me," which are a mistranslation of the original, and were in all probability introduced into the Septuagint through a blunder of the copyist.' Paul here quoted a whole passage from the Septuagint, which, with the exception of this phrase, accords with the ordinary Hebrew. The Arabic version agrees with the Septuagint. We have then, as the highest authorities suggest, three explanations of this difficulty:

1. An error in transcribing afterwards crept into the Hebrew, a change which, as Kennicot shows, requires but a slight change of the letters. If we could not otherwise defend the Apostle, we should take this position.

2. As the Septuagint and Arabic versions contain nothing contrary to the real sense of the Hebrew as it now stands, and as the slight discrepancy did not alter at all the actual bearing of the whole passage upon the Apostle's argument, and as his readers were acquainted with the Septuagint and not with the Hebrew text, the Apostle was fully justified, as Professor Stuart and other learned commentators have shown, in making the use he did of the passage, and the fact of such use is no argument against the inspiration of his writings.

3. There is, we remark finally, no certain evidence that the words 'A body Thou hast prepared me,' are given as a quotation from the Old Testament at all, but rather from Christ Himself. By a gift of the Father to men, and through the creative agency of the Spirit, 'a body was prepared for Christ,' and He was given as 'the sacrifice for the sins of the whole world.' To this fact Christ responds, 'A body hast Thou prepared for Me;' and then, in the language of prophecy, yields Himself to the Father's will, 'Lo, I come,' etc. Such being the obvious facts of the case, nothing

can be farther from the truth than is involved in a denial of the proper inspiration of the Apostle on account of the employment of these words.

We give another example. 'The words quoted, Heb. i. 6, "Let the angels of God worship Him," do not occur in the Hebrew at all, but are an addition to the Alexandrian version in Deut. xxxii. 43.' In reply, we would remark that we have no evidence whatever, but quite conclusive evidence to the contrary, that these words are quoted from any version of the Old Testament. They are cited expressly as uttered, not when Christ was given to the world in prophecy, but when He was 'brought into the world,' that is, at His birth or introduction to the world. Reference is unquestionably, as Professor Stuart has shown, made not to Deut. xxxii. 43, or to Ps. xcvii. 7, but to facts stated in Luke ii. 8. Here we have the fact recorded that the angelic host did pay homage to Christ. Paul, under inspired wisdom, informs us that this was done in accordance with a special command of God given at the time. If Paul employed, to represent this command, words found in the Old Testament, he did not employ them as having had an original reference to Christ.

We have given above the very strongest passages ever cited to sustain this semi-infidel impeachment of the inspiration of the New Testament writings. We would here add, that after all the clear light that has been thrown by modern criticism upon the manner in which the New Testament writers refer to the Old Testament Scriptures, it is an insult to the exegetical knowledge of this century to base upon such use an argument against the proper inspiration of the New Testament Scriptures. When we are told, as another argument against the inspiration of these writings, that the writers do not appear to have had any idea of the *use* that should be made of their writings, a fact is stated which, if admitted, has nothing to do with the subject. No Prophet, or Apostle, when he spake or wrote 'in the name of the Lord,' and as sent by Him, had, it may be, any idea of what use God, in His Providence, would make of his utterances. What has that to do with the question of the inspiration or authority of what was spoken or written? With the speakers and writers, as far as their vision extended, the end arrived at may have been a temporary and local one. With God the ultimate aim may have been, and was, 'the instruction and admonition' of mankind in all future time.

SECTION VIII.

THE PHILOSOPHY OF THE EARLY CHRISTIAN CHURCH.

THE doctrines of Matter, Spirit, Time, Space, the Soul, God, Duty, Immortality, and Retribution, either in their positive or negative forms, enter, as fundamental elements, into all the philosophical systems which we have investigated, and must be omnipresent in all systems. Indeed, the scientific solution of these doctrines, in all the forms suggested, constitute the central problem of Philosophy. The problem of Philosophy is, *being and its laws,* and the ultimate *cause,* or *reason* of the facts, and relations of the facts, of universal nature. Each system of Philosophy presents its systematized solution of this problem, in all the forms indicated. We cannot advance a step in the solution of this problem without touching the solution which Religion in general, and Christianity in particular, present of the same problem. As soon, for example, as our modern sceptical scientists had perfected their classification of the phenomena of nature, and their solution of the relations, or laws, of these phenomena, '*the physical value of prayer*' became, as they affirm, 'the bone of contention' between them and Christian students of science. The same holds true in all cases. The doctrine of Ultimate Causation, which Materialism, on the one hand, and Idealism, in all its forms, on the other, present, directly and openly confronts the doctrine of a Personal God, which Natural Theology and Christian Theism reveal and affirm. Every system of Philosophy has its specific ontology, and its specific deductions pertaining to the soul, its duties or non-duties, and its destiny; and these deductions either affirm or deny the deductions of Natural and Christian Theism in respect to the same subjects. Christian Theism, when its essential doctrines are fully developed and systematized, does neither more nor less than this: it presents specific and affirmed divinely attested solutions of the great problems pertaining to Ultimate Causation, to Being and its Laws—problems which Philosophy, in all ages, has endeavoured to solve. Christian Theism, if true, is, when its doctrines are thus developed and systematized, not merely a system of religious doctrines, but, also, a Divine Philosophy of Ultimate Causation, and of Universal Being and its Laws.

In this light, Moses and the Prophets, Christ and His Apostles, and the primitive teachers of Christianity, regarded and presented the subject. Everywhere they found themselves surrounded with *Systems* of Philosophy and of Religion. Everywhere they presented, in opposition to these Godless philosophies and irreligious religions, a supernaturally attested Divine Philosophy and Religion, and these as one and the same system. In opposition to the doctrine of Creation by Emanation, or Natural Law, for example, they taught, as we have before shown, as a deduction of Natural and Revealed Religion, 'that the worlds were made by the Word of God.' In opposition to the doctrine of Evolution, the idea that all visible animal life and vegetable forms of vitalized existence were developed by Natural Law from diverse pre-existing primordial forms, which were themselves the results of 'Spontaneous Generation,' they affirmed, 'that things which are seen (visible species) were not made (developed, evolved) out of things which do appear,' that is, from pre-existing visible forms; that God originally created and constituted each species, so that its offspring should be 'after its kind;' that 'God gives to each seed its own body'—a body like that from which it proceeded. In opposition to the solutions of the problems of Being and its Laws, solutions presented by these Godless philosophies, they presented opposite solutions, and verified the same by appeals to visible and conscious facts of nature, as in the case of Paul at Athens, before Felix, and in all his Epistles; and to supernatural facts undeniably real, as in the case of all these teachers. All men understood that in accepting the solutions of these teachers, they renounced those presented by all the Godless philosophies and opposite religions around them. They greatly err who represent these men as mere teachers of an unsystematized religion. They taught, on the other hand, a well-understood system of doctrines, and taught that system, as not only embodying a Divine Religion, but also a Divine Philosophy. We will give a single example of the philosophic teachings of the doctors of the Primitive Church.

An Example of the Philosophic Teachings of the Leading Doctors of the Primitive Church.

The common doctrine of the then existing Godless Philosophies was that of Fate, or Necessity. Against this doctrine these doctors specifically and unanimously protested. 'Every one,' says Mosheim, 'knows that the peculiar doctrines' (of which that of Necessity was one) 'to which the victory was assigned by the Synod (of Dort), were absolutely unknown in the first ages of the Church.' 'The Church teachers' (of the first three centuries), says Neander, 'agreed unanimously in maintaining the free will of man as a necessary condition of the existence of morality.' 'These Fathers,' says Whitby, 'unanimously declare that God hath left it in the power of man to turn to virtue or vice.' In full accordance with these statements, is the testimony of Calvin, and of all authorities of all schools.

The specific statements of these Fathers fully confirm the above opinions of these high authorities. 'If it happen by fate,' says Justyn Martyr, of the second century, 'that men are either good or wicked, the good were not good, nor should the wicked be wicked.' Again, 'Unless we suppose man has the power to choose the good and refuse the evil, no one can be accountable for any action whatever.' Again, 'God has not made men like trees and brutes, without the power of election.' 'Man can do nothing praiseworthy, if he had not the power of turning either way.'

'No reward,' says Tertullian, of the same century, 'can justly be bestowed, no punishment can justly be inflicted, upon him who is good or bad by necessity, and not by his own choice.' 'Man,' he says again, 'being appointed for God's judgment, it was necessary to the justice of God's sentence that man should be judged according to the desert of his free will.'

Irenæus, Bishop of Lyons, and of the same century, says, 'Man, a reasonable being, and in that respect like God, is made free in his will, and having power over himself, is the cause that sometimes he becomes wheat, and sometimes chaff.' In the following statement we have, not only an avowal, but a most perfect presentment of the doctrine of Free Will. 'They who do good shall obtain honour and glory, because they have done good when they could forbear doing it. And they who shall do it not shall receive just judgment of our God; because they have not done good, when they could have done it.'

'What is forced,' says the learned Basil, 'is not pleasing to God, but what comes from a truly virtuous motive; and virtue comes from the Will, not from Necessity.' 'The Will,' he says again, 'depends on what is within us, and within us is free will.'

'Forasmuch as God has put good and evil in our power,' says Chrysostom, 'He has given us a free power to choose the one or the other; and as He does not retain us against our will, so He embraces us when we are willing.' Again, 'After a wicked man, if he will, is changed into a good man; and a good man, through sloth, falls away and becomes wicked; because God hath endowed us with free agency; nor does He make us do things necessarily, but He places proper remedies before us, and suffers all to be done according to the will of the patient.'

'God,' says Jerome, 'hath endowed us with free will. We are not necessarily drawn either to virtue or vice. For when necessity prevails, there is no room left for damnation or the crown. 'Our will,' he says again, 'is left free to turn either way, that God may dispense His rewards and punishments, not according to His own pre-judgment, but according to the merits of every one.' 'Let the man who condemns free will be himself condemned.'

'The soul,' says Origen, 'does not incline to either part out of Necessity, for then neither vice nor virtue could be ascribed to it; nor would its choice of virtue deserve reward; nor its declination to vice, punishment.' 'How could God require that of man which he' [man] 'had not power to offer Him?'

'Neither promises nor reprehensions, rewards or punishments, are just,' says Clement of Alexandria, 'if the soul has not the power of choosing or abstaining.'

'The doctrine of Fate or Necessity,' Eusebius affirms, 'absolves sinners, as doing nothing of their own accord, which was evil; and would cast all the blame of all wickedness in the world upon God, and upon his providence.'

Didymus, of the fourth century, says of the doctrine of Free Will, 'this is not only ours, but the opinion of all who speak orthodoxly.'

Nor did even Augustine hold the doctrine of Necessity in the common form. 'They that come to Christ,' he says, 'ought not to impute it to themselves, because they came, being called; and they that would not come, ought not to impute it to another, but only to themselves, because, when they were called, it was in the power of their free will to come.' We perceive clearly that these doctors were not merely Christian theologians. They were also well-informed Christian philosophers. The Philosophy and Theology of the Church were thus identical, and the latter, in all proper forms, as the perfected system, determined the former.

As the systems of Aristotle and Plato, in opposition to those of the Epicureans, Stoics, Sceptics, and Idealists such as Plotinus, taught the doctrines of Matter, Spirit, Time, Space, the Soul, and God, these Doctors accepted the systems first designated as, in all essential particulars, true, and referred to the teachings of such thinkers as Thales, Anaxagoras, Socrates, Plato, and Aristotle, in confirmation of the fundamental doctrines of Christianity. In opposition to doctrines of Materialism on the one hand, and of Idealism on the other, they affirm the real existence of two distinct and separate principles, Matter, which they designated by such terms as *corpus* (σῶμα), and Mind, which they called *anima, spiritus, mens*. In opposition to the teachings of Plato and Aristotle, they generally denied the eternal existence of Matter, at the same time affirming that the idea of origination from nothing 'contains a radically inevitable and insolvable mystery.' Against the doctrine of creation by emanation or evolution, they urged such arguments as the following:—1. According to this system all beings are fractions or portions of God, and thus the Divine unity is broken up. 2. Evil infirmities and crimes attach to the Divine essence as parts of the same. 3. The Divine essence must be indivisible and incorruptible. Near the close of the fifth century, Boethius, a learned and Christian Roman senator, born 470 A.D., as an ancient philosopher on the one hand, and a Christian theologian on the other, developed in the West a system of Philosophy in professed conformity with both science and the Christian Religion. His works were held in high regard in subsequent centuries. Near the close of the sixth century, John Philaformus performed a similar work for the Churches in the East. Other great thinkers about the same time, thinkers such as Bede, Egbert, and John of Damascus, in Italy, Gaul, Spain, England, and the East, 'sent out rays of light upon the poor pale schools that glimmer remotely through the shades of barbarism.' As long, however, as the identity between science and the real doctrines of Christianity was maintained, and the latter, in the proper form, determined the former, Christianity maintained its ascendency as an all-conquering power. When, on the other hand, false science gave form to Christian doctrine, then the Sun of Righteousness went into a deep eclipse, and the midnight of the Dark Ages gradually overspread Christendom.

SECTION IX.
ANTI-CHRISTIAN SPECULATIONS.

DURING the first centuries of the Christian Era there arose, particularly at Alexandria in Egypt, certain schools in Philosophy, whose systems were utterly subversive of Christianity, but were presented to the world as perfected systems of Christian doctrine. These schools were divided into two general classes—Oriental, in which an attempt was made to blend Christianity with the systems of India and Egypt; and the Græco-Oriental, represented by the Alexandrian Electicism. These systems deserve our attention merely as furnishing the ground for an explanation of the origin and character of certain doctrines and usages which obtained in the early centuries of the Christian era, and marred the purity of Christian doctrine. We shall refer to these systems in the order above indicated.

ORIENTAL DOCTRINES.

These doctrines are represented by the General term Gnosticism, and present nothing but the Pantheism of India and Egypt, with Christianity blended as a common ingredient with said system. For the Brahm of India, and Pinoris of Egypt, the Gnostics (self-styled knowing ones) substituted the Abyss, who is the ground and substance of all being. Creation is wholly by *emanation*, and consists of emissions and manifestations of what is contained in the bosom and substance of the Abyss. The first emanations, proceeding as they do directly and immediately from the Abyss, are the most perfect, and constitute a universe of superior beings, the Plaroma, and are called Eons. The last of these emanations is the Demiurgus, a being constituted of light and ignorance, force and feebleness. From this imperfect being emanates the visible universe, material and mental, a universe in which consequently good and evil are intermingled, the latter greatly prevailing. Christ is the last and most perfect emanation from the Abyss, and as the leading Eon, His mission is to destroy the works of the Demiurgus. The source of all evil is the hylic or material principle, of which matter Ulé is the substance. Redemption consists in the emancipation of the soul from the hylic principle and rising to the *pneumatic*, or spiritual, state. The Jews worship the Demiurgus, or Jehovah, and were consequently psychical; the Pagans were subjected to the inferior world, and were hylic; while true

Christians are pneumatic. All who remain under the hylic principle will be annihilated; those who seek union with the Demiurgus will have a semi-happy existence with him, while the pneumatic will return to the bosom of the Abyss.

In the early part of the third century, Manes, born in Persia, developed a system known as Manichæism, a system in which Persian Dualism is combined with the doctrines of Christianity. According to Manes there are two principles from which all things proceed—the one a most pure and subtle matter, denominated light—the other a gross and corrupt substance, called darkness. Each of these is presided over by a being who existed from eternity. The being who presides over light is called God, and is supremely good and happy. He who rules over darkness is called Hyle, or Demon, and is evil and unhappy. Each of these beings originally produced an immense number of creatures resembling themselves, and distributed them through their respective provinces.

For a long period the Prince of Darkness remained ignorant of the Kingdom of Light. When, by means of a war in his own dominions, he became aware of a universe of pure and happy beings, he arrayed all his forces against them, and succeeded in seizing a large portion of the celestial elements of light, and intermingled them with masses of corrupt matter. The pure particles of the celestial matter, the Ruler of Light was not able wholly to rescue from the power of the Prince of Darkness. From the elements thus retained under his control, the Prince of Darkness created the human race, who were constituted of bodies organized out of corrupt matter and of souls possessed of a sensitive and lustful nature, on the one hand, and of a rational and immortal nature on the other, the latter being constituted of particles of the Divine light which he had carried away. God now created the earth as the abode of the human race, His object being the ultimate deliverance of the captive souls from their corporeal prisons, and to extract the celestial elements from the gross substance in which they were involved. To accomplish the work of human redemption, God produced from His own substance two beings of a Divine dignity—Christ and the Holy Ghost. In the progress of ages, Christ appeared among men as dwelling in a human body, taught them how to disengage the rational soul from the corrupt and the violent passions engendered by *malignant matter*, demonstrated the divinity of His mission by stupendous miracles, and was at last put to death by the Jews on an ignominious cross. All this was in appearance only, since spirit cannot be really united with matter without being corrupted by it.

Before leaving the earth, Christ promised His disciples to send them the Holy Ghost, the Paraclete, or Comforter, who should perfect for believers the revelation of truth. This Comforter is Manes, who reveals to mortals all truth needful to their final salvation, which consists in total purification from the contagion of matter. By renouncing the God of the Jews, who is the Prince of Darkness, by carefully obeying the laws revealed by Christ, and enlarged and illustrated by the Comforter, a purification will be partially effected in this life, and perfected in the next.

Souls, on the other hand, who neglect this work of self-purification pass after death through many and painful transmigrations until they have fully expiated their guilt. In the final consummation the universe will be purified by fire, after which the Prince of Darkness, with his own creatures, will be for ever excluded from the Kingdom of Light. To perpetuate the influence of his own teachings, Manes arbitrarily rejected all those portions of the sacred writings which were supposed to conflict with his own system.

The rules of life prescribed by Manes were most rigorous, requiring the mortification and maceration of the body as intrinsically corrupt and vicious, and a total denial and mortification of all the natural passions and instincts. His disciples were divided into two classes—the *elect*, and hearers. The former were required to abstain totally from flesh, milk, eggs, wine, and wedlock, and to partake of mere vegetables and bread sufficient to keep alive their emaciated bodies. The *hearers* were allowed, under severe restrictions, to possess houses and lands, to eat flesh, and enter into wedlock. Throughout Egypt and surrounding countries vast multitudes embraced the Gnostic and Manichæan doctrines. Hence, deserts and mountain solitudes were peopled with vast swarms of devotees, who fled from the habitations of men to escape the deadly contagion of the flesh.

The Græco-Oriental Philosophy.

In our exposition of the Grecian Evolution in Philosophy, we have superseded the necessity of enlarging upon the subject stated above. Near the close of the second century, Ammonius Saccas, an apostate from the Christian faith, opened in Alexandria an Eclectic school, in which he professedly blended into one harmonized system the essential elements of the Oriental, Grecian, and Christian doctrines. The teachings of this philosopher were enlarged, and more completely systematized, by such thinkers as Plotinus, Porphyry, and Proclus. In accordance with the teachings of Oriental and Grecian Pantheism, they taught the existence of one absolute unity as the principle and substance of all things, and of the universe as an emanation from this unity, all sensible objects beings the images and external representations of intellectual objects, or of ideas, which alone are real. With the doctrine of emanation they connected a certain form of the doctrine of the Trinity, of a

Mediator, and other forms of Christian truth, all moulded and transformed so as to harmonize with the essentials of Pantheism. The common attempt of all schools to harmonize Christian doctrine with their systems clearly evinces the fact that a conviction of the truth of that doctrine had become the common faith of the Roman Empire.

SECTION IX.

CHRISTIAN DOCTRINE AS CORRUPTED BY 'SCIENCE FALSELY SO-CALLED.'

WHILE the Doctors of the Christian Church, during all the centuries we are now considering, openly rejected and opposed the systems of the Gnostics, Manichæans, Alexandrian Eclectics, and other Anti-Theistic schools, there were certain principles maintained by these schools which were received by many of these Fathers, and thus corrupted Christian doctrine. The idea that matter, as a real or ideal substance, is the source and cause of human sin and misery, and that salvation is conditioned, not on a full regulation of the propensities, but upon an extinction of natural desires, constitutes, as we have seen, the common element of almost all the systems of false science in all ages. The validity of this idea, in its essential forms, had an early place in the teachings of leading fathers of the Christian Church, and gave rise to the Monastic institutions, usages, and doctrines of subsequent ages. During the progress of the second century, the moral teachings of the New Testament were divided into two classes—*precepts* and *counsels*. The former were absolutely binding upon all, and those who obeyed them fully were morally perfect. The latter were advisory, and not absolutely binding upon any. All who fully conformed to the *precepts*, and added thereto conformity to counsels, were not only morally perfect, but did more than their duty, and thereby attained to angelic perfection. Of this class were such as, from religious motives, voluntarily abstained from wedlock, denied themselves all luxuries, and practised the greatest austerities. Such teachers as Chrysostom and Athanasius affirmed that such individuals became possessed of forms of virtue which 'are above law.' Speaking of this class, Athanasius says, that 'the Son of God hath, besides His other gifts, granted unto us to have upon earth the image of the sanctity of angels.' Here we have the germ of the doctrine of Supererogation, on which was based that of Indulgences.

BOOK III.

THE MEDIÆVAL EVOLUTION IN PHILOSOPHY.

The period from the sixth to the ninth century constitutes the era of transition from the ancient and early Christian to what is denominated the Mediæval Evolution in Philosophy, and would, were it our object to present a mere history of opinions, constitute a distinct chapter. As the change was very gradual from the Patristic to the Mediæval period, little need be added, however, to what we have indicated in respect to this transition period. The leading thinkers of this period we have already designated. Of the specific forms of their teachings, we know but little, the fact excepted, that with them, science and religion were one and identical, or more correctly perhaps, that science is the handmaid (*ancilla*) of religion.

In Arabia there arose in connection with the rise of Mohammedanism systems which took form from Mohammedan and Christian doctrines on the one hand, and from Oriental dogmas on the other. The common doctrine of all these systems was that of absolute fate as taught by Mahomet. At the beginning these systems were purely Idealistic and Pantheistic; then Materialistic; and finally, of course, Sceptical, in fact and form. In the Secret Societies of Syria and Egypt, these were the most essential of the dogmas taught to the Initiated—to wit, 'There is no other God but Material Nature; no other religion but pleasure; and no other right than that of the strongest.' Scepticism took on two forms—a denial of all valid knowledge but through the Koran; and a denial of the possibility of real knowledge in any form.

The Rise of Scholasticism.

After the ninth and tenth centuries, when the Papacy was fully established, the authority of the Church became supreme in Religion, in Politics, and also in Philosophy; and Education in all its forms came under her direct and exclusive control. In science within certain limits liberty of thought and free discussion were fully tolerated, but not in contravention of any of the positive dogmas of the Church in any sphere of research whatever. Philosophy became nominally Christian, and assumed the general name of Scholasticism. We are not to suppose that this term represents a doctrine which always retained one and the same form. In its germ it existed in preceding ages, but at a much later period took on its final form. We propose to consider this evolution in these two forms.

Scholasticism in its Primal Form.

The Scholastic doctrine, in its primal form, was first distinctly announced by Anselm, Archbishop of Canterbury, who was born 1033. Christians, he affirmed, should advance to science through faith, and not to faith through science. This dogma, he announced through the following formula: 'Credo ut intelligam,' 'I believe that I may know.' According to the early Fathers, science and Christian doctrine were to be developed side by side, each on independent grounds, and each in harmony with the other. It was an early doctrine of these Fathers, that when any deduction arrived at in the scientific procedure contradicted any clearly ascertained truth of Inspiration, that deduction should be assumed to be false, and that the ground of the error should be searched out. They also held that the highest degree of certitude, that is, knowledge in its most absolute forms, in respect to the great problems of Philosophy, problems pertaining to Being and its laws, to Ultimate Causation, to God, the Soul, and Immortality, is not obtained through Philosophy unaided by revelation, but through revelation with Philosophy as the handmaid, and not the authoritative guide, of religion. 'The world, by wisdom' (Philosophy), they were taught and believed, 'had not known God,' and had not found truth; while the humblest believer had found both. Inspiration had affirmed a fact of the truth of which they were absolutely conscious—to wit, 'That no man can know the things of a man, save the spirit of man which is in him.' In other words, man can know himself but through internal facts of which he is himself conscious. Hence, it becomes a truth of absolute intuition and science, as well as of inspiration, 'that no man knoweth the things of God, but the Spirit of God,' and that we only do, or can, truly *know* God, but through Divine revelation and illumination. In this sense, these Fathers did, and most rationally too, hold the doctrine, 'Credo ut intelligam.' By this they did not understand that prior to faith in inspiration *nothing* is, or can be, known. Through conscious facts the soul has some knowledge of itself; through 'the things that are made,' 'the invisible things of God' (his essential attributes) 'are clearly seen;' and through supernatural attestations, Christianity is known to us as a Divine religion. All this must precede faith in this religion. When thus enlightened, however, we must now believe, or never attain to a consciously assured knowledge of even those forms of truth to which science aims to conduct us. If we turn away from this higher light, the light that was before within us becomes darkness, and in our self-affirmed wisdom, we 'become fools.' Such, undeniably, is the doctrine of the Bible; such was the belief of these Fathers; and such is the truth as verified by the history of philosophic thought from the beginning to the present hour. Let us consider a few facts in verification of these statements.

This Doctrine Verified.

Outside of the sphere of Theistic and Christian thought, and antagonistic to the same, there have been numberless schools in Philosophy, schools in all of which the ultimate problems of Being and its laws, and of final causation, have been professedly solved and absolute truth found. The leaders of these schools, not the world, have glorified themselves by manufacturing and exclusively appropriating to themselves as the self-inaugurated intellectual autocrats of the race such cognomens as Yogee, Buddha, Magi, Philosopher, Savan, Sophist, Gnostic, Illuminati, Scientist, Physicist, and Ists in such numbers as to exhaust the vocabulary of self-glorification. Not one of these terms, it should be borne in mind, was manufactured by the world, and conferred upon these men as a mark of world-respect. All, and for purposes of self-glorification, were self-manufactured, and self-appropriated. The common meaning of all these self-appropriated terms, it should also be remembered, is, Lover of Wisdom, the Wise Man, the Knowing One. Nor is this all. These men have, for the most part, claimed for themselves faculties of knowledge and powers of insight of which the rest of mankind are wholly destitute. What have they done to vindicate for themselves their high and self-appropriated claims? To such inquiries adequate answers have already been given, and will be given in future expositions. Nothing need be added upon the subject in this connection.

Let us now consider the real meaning of the doctrine, that faith must precede, not knowledge, but science. Faith, as defined in the Bible, and understood by the Fathers of the Church, is *fixed fidelity of will to valid evidence, or rational conviction.* Unbelief, on the other hand, is specifically set forth as *infidelity of will to such evidence and conviction.* 'This is the condemnation, that light is come into the world, and men loved darkness rather than light, because their deeds were evil.' Christ affirms, that the men of His age, who rejected or disbelieved in Him, would have been guiltless, had he not 'done among them the works which no other man had done,' that is, demonstrated before them the divinity of His mission. The heathen are affirmed to be without excuse, because 'they hold the truth in unrighteousness,' that is, know the truth, but do not obey it, and because they 'know God,' and 'do not glorify Him as God.' Voluntary infidelity to rational conviction is unbelief as defined in Scripture, and as understood by these Fathers.

Faith, on the other hand, is defined as 'the substance of things hoped for, the evidence of things not seen,' that is, in respect to 'things hoped for,' the object of faith is 'substance,' that which is real and true; and as far as it pertains to things unseen, it has for its basis 'evidence,' valid proof, or rational conviction. Faith, then, as defined in Scripture, is fidelity of will to valid evidence or proof, that is to rational conviction.

Now nothing can be more evident than is the fact that every peculiar deduction to be met with in the systems of Idealism, Materialism, and Scepticism, is utterly void of intuitive, or deductive validity, and can have no place in the human mind as rational conviction; but takes exclusive form there as a mere assumption that stands in open antagonism to the intuitive convictions of the Universal Intelligence. This fact has already been fully verified. Such deductions, therefore, have place in the mind as the exclusive result of infidelity of will to 'evidence,' or rational conviction.

Faith in its relations to science is absolute fidelity of will to valid evidence, or to the real dicta of the Intelligence, that is, to rational conviction. Whatever the Intelligence in its original and necessary intuitive procedures presents to the mind as real, faith accepts as a known verity; and whatever facts, whether natural or supernatural, are verified by the known laws of valid evidence, are accepted as actual. Nothing is assumed as real or actual but what the Intelligence, in its consciously valid procedures, verifies as such; and all, and nothing else that is thus verified, is accepted as the exclusive basis of all deductions in science. The first step in science is, consequently, based upon the postulate that Matter, Spirit, Time, and Space, are known realities, and known as distinct and separate, the one from each of the others. All these are postulated as such realities, because in its original, necessary, and intuitive procedures, the Universal Intelligence presents them as such verities. All the axioms in all the sciences are postulated as valid for truth, because to the Universal Intelligence they are *necessarily* true. All the great facts which enter as constituent elements into such sciences, together with the supernatural events which stand around the Christian religion and affirm its Divine origin, are accepted as actual, for the reason that to the Intelligence they are verified as such by valid evidence. In respect to 'the things of God,' reliance is reposed upon the revelations and illuminations of the Spirit of God, because in a validly verified revelation from God, all who seek it have the absolute promise of Divine teaching. When science moves upon the track here indicated, all its procedures will, and must be, within the sphere, and under the illumination, of the clear light of the Intelligence, and deductions logically reached will have the fixed characteristics of conscious certitude. In our systems of

Ontology, Cosmology, and Ultimate Causation, doubt will have no place, because nothing but what is to the Intelligence consciously known has place there; all forms of mere assumption, opinion, belief, and conjecture, being excluded. Nothing is, or can be, more evident than is the fact, that faith as above defined is the immutable condition and propædeutic of true science, and rational certitude in all scientific procedures. These primitive Fathers were undeniably right in their doctrine that faith precedes science, and in the maxim, as originally held, *Credo ut intelligam.* Voluntary integrity to the Intelligence, or absolute faith in its real dicta, is the immutable condition of conscious scientific certitude.

Nor can there be any departure from the track of scientific deduction above indicated, but through most palpable infidelity of will to the absolute dicta of the Intelligence; in other words, to rational conviction. Within the proper sphere of the Intelligence, there can be no form of doubt of the reality of Spirit, Matter, Time, or Space, or of either as an object of valid knowledge. We cannot deny the validity of our knowledge of either of these realities, but in the language of Coleridge, 'by an act of' (miscalled) 'scientific scepticism to which the mind *voluntarily* determines itself.' In other words, all the denials of Materialism, Idealism, and Scepticism, have their exclusive basis, not in data furnished by the Intelligence, but in mere assumption, voluntary determination, a sentiment of will—will data—which stand in open antagonism to original, universal, and necessary intellectual intuition.

SCHOLASTICISM IN ITS FINAL FORM.

'The effort of Scholasticism,' says Schwegler, 'was to mediate between the dogma of religion and the reflecting self-consciousness; to reconcile faith and knowledge.' Scotus Erigina, of the ninth century, in his attempt to produce this reconciliation identified the two. 'There are not two studies,' he said, 'one of Philosophy and one of religion; true Philosophy is true religion and true religion is true Philosophy.' This identity can be rationally established but by developing each system upon its own independent ground, rightly interpreting the Word on the one hand, and taking into account on the other all validly known facts; and finally, by comparison demonstrating the harmony between them. Others, as we have seen, attempted to evince this harmony, by advancing to religion through science, and determining from the deductions of the latter, not only religious doctrines, but the meaning of the Word of God. It was, in fact, by this method that Scotus Erigina made the two one and identical. He was avowedly a Pantheist, and developed not the doctrine of nature, but the entire system of Christian doctrine from the Pantheistic standpoint. God, he taught, is 'the substance of all things,' the substance 'in which all things end, and to which all things finally return.' As multiform developments of the Divine unity, he gave us not Oriental Polytheism, but the Trinity, Incarnation, and the whole system of Christian doctrine. The principle of determining the Word of God by the deductions, whether true or false, of science, has a place in modern theological thought. Whenever any of our Scientists set forth some special hypothesis, however crude and unverified, not a few of our theologians hasten to prove that the teachings of the Bible may be made to affirm the validity of that hypothesis. Thus the same passage has been explained in harmony with an endless diversity of conflicting hypotheses. By such procedure the Bible is not vindicated, but exposed to public contempt.

Others have attempted to harmonize 'faith and knowledge,' by advancing to Philosophy through religion. Holding as we do, as Christians, that nature and the Bible proceed from the same Author, we must hold that a Divine harmony does exist between the real teachings of the two. We must hold, for example, that the doctrines of Cosmology, Anthropology and Ultimate Causation, revealed in Scripture, are in absolute conformity with the same doctrines as far as they are revealed 'by the things which are made.' Yet the teachings of the Bible and the facts of nature are to be explained independently of each other.

The form which Scholasticism finally took on was, that 'the faith of the Churches is absolute truth,' and that it is exclusively through her dicta that we are to interpret both science and the Bible. Anselm, Archbishop of Canterbury, born, as we have stated, in 1033 A.D., first developed the doctrine in this form. This was the meaning of the famous maxim, '*Credo ut intelligam*.' No discussion, he taught, was to be held with men who denied the absolute authority of the Church both in matters of faith and of science. Discussion and examination were not to be repudiated, but were to pertain exclusively to an understanding and elucidation of what, on the authority of the Church, had been previously accepted as true: 'As the right order,' he says, 'demands that we first receive into ourselves believingly the mysteries of Christianity, before subjecting them to speculative examination, so it seems to me the part of negligence if, after having been confirmed in the faith, we do not endeavour to understand what we have believed.' Scholasticism in this form became soon after the immutable doctrine of the Papacy, and was enforced upon the people by the civil as well as the ecclesiastical authorities. Opposition to this doctrine, which was at length developed within the bosom of the Church, laid the foundation for the Reformation.

The Nominalism and Realism of the Middle Ages.

Philosophy, as accepted and taught by the leaders of the Primitive Church, took form chiefly from two sources—the original teachings of

Plato on the one hand, and of Aristotle on the other. Hence it was that during the entire Scholastic era a fierce antagonism existed between Realism as derived from the former, and Nominalism as received from the latter. The Realists held that ideas as universals, species and genera, have a real existence, and that the universal exists prior to the individual (*universalia anterum*). The Nominalists on the other hand, maintained that the individual alone has real being, and that universals are mere names (*flatus vocis*), without content and without reality. In favour of each of these hypotheses, the highest talent the world then knew, and we should very little fear the truth if we should add, as high as any since known, was arrayed. It was universally assumed that one of these hypotheses was right and the other wrong, none suspecting that both were in error. As each party had an erroneous position to assault, on the one hand, and to defend on the other, each was omnipotent in its assaults, and the perfection of weakness in self-defence. If the universal, the term man, for example, is a mere word, representing no valid idea in, and no reality out of the mind, then the proposition, 'John is a man,' is void of meaning. It does have real meaning however. The dogma of Nominalism, therefore, cannot be true. To this argument the Nominalist could make no reply. If the universal, man, for example, does represent an idea within and a reality without the mind, a reality distinct from the individual, then, as before, replies the Nominalist, the proposition, 'John is a man' is untrue or void of meaning, the proposition being equivalent to the affirmation that the individual and the universal, which are distinct from each other, are one and identical; nor would there be any difference between individuals. To this argument that truly great thinker, Duns Scotus, who died in 1308, made this reply: 'The individual and the universal, though distinct from each other, are always united in the same person. Individuals differ, not as containing the universal, but through the distinct qualities which constitute their individuality. The individuality of Peter, for example, consists, not in his humanity, but in his Peterity, or Peterness. Hence, Peter is both an individual and a man. John is a man and an individual also, but not Peter, because in the former not Peterness, but Johnity, is added to humanity.' To this argument Nominalists gave a reply which has never been answered: if the universal, as all admit, man, for example, is one and not many, how can humanity be at the same time present in John at Ephesus, and in Peter at Rome or Babylon? Thus each school utterly demolished the hypothesis of the other, and that because both were in error. In like manner, Materialism and Idealism, because both systems are false, have each omnipotent power in assaulting the position of its antagonist, and is utterly powerless when assaulted in return. When Scepticism also has annihilated the claims of both systems it, in turn, falls dead under the crushing blows of Realism. How often is it the case that when two fundamental errors stand opposed to each other, even thinkers assume that one of these errors must be true. A more dangerous mistake can hardly be made. The fact that Materialism and Idealism are incompatible and antagonistic systems, and that Scepticism is opposed to both, does not imply that either is true. Notwithstanding this deadly antagonism all these systems may be constituted of nothing but fatal error. Whenever two or more false and conflicting theories confront each other, there is always another hypothesis which includes all that is true, and excludes all that is false in each of these forms of error, an hypothesis consequently which must be true. Idealism, for example, affirms that we have a valid knowledge of spirit and its operations, but denies that we do or can have any such knowledge of Matter and its qualities. Materialism affirms that we do have a valid knowledge of Matter, but denies that we do or can have any such knowledge of Spirit. Scepticism affirms that we do have a valid knowledge of Phenomena, but denies that we do or can have any knowledge of Substance, or real being in any form, of realities such as Matter, Spirit, Time, and Space. Realism admits all that each of these theories affirms, and affirms all that they deny. They consequently are 'science falsely so-called,' while it embraces 'the truth, the whole truth, and nothing but the truth.'

The above elucidations have a direct application to Realism, Nominalism, and to a third hypothesis unknown to the ancients, namely, Conceptualism. All these hypotheses admit and affirm that *universally* the term man, for example, is applicable to each individual of the class which comes under such term, and hence that Socrates, Peter, John, etc., were each of them really and truly a man. The Realist affirmed that the term man represents a form of being which existed prior to all individuals of the race. Nominalists denied the existence of such anterior form of being, affirmed that nothing is real but particular or individual existence, and that general or universal terms are mere names, which represent no ideas in the mind, and no realities exterior to it. In their points of agreement that John is a man, for example, both are right. In their contradictions of each other, both rested upon fundamental error. All general terms do, as all men know, represent ideas in the mind and qualities exterior to it, but not the forms of being which the Realists affirmed. The term man, for example, represents the qualities common to all men, which did not exist prior to individuals of the race on the one hand, and a conception of those qualities in the mind on the other. In view of their individual peculiarities, we say, Peter is not John, and in view of their common qualities, we call each a man. Thus we have the hypothesis of Conceptionalism, which has now supplanted both of the ancient theories. The term Realism, as now employed, stands opposed, not to Nominalism, but to Materialism, Idealism, and Scepticism.

The Mysticism of the Middle Ages.

Ever since the second century of the Christian Era, a class of professed believers have existed in the Church, who have been denominated Mystics, and sometimes Quietists. They have received this designation, not exclusively, or primarily, on account of their doctrines, but because of their peculiar method of affirmed spiritual insight. Among the Mystics, while their method of insight was essentially one and the same, an endless diversity of form of belief obtained. What is now required of us is a distinct exposition of this method, together with an exposition of the reasons of the diverse and even contradictory forms of belief and sentiment evolved through one and the same method.

To accomplish our object, we would observe that, as is well known, there are two classes of sciences—the pure, or *à priori*, and the mixed, or *à posteriori*. In the former all principles and facts are given exclusively through *à priori* insight, the principles, facts, and deductions, all in common having universal and necessary, or apodictic, certainty. In the latter, while the principles are given through *à priori*, the facts are all and exclusively derived through *à posteriori* insight. There are, consequently, two distinct and separate methods of scientific deduction—the *à priori*, which has place only within the exclusive sphere of the pure, and the inductive, or *à posteriori*, which has exclusive place within the sphere of the mixed sciences.

The science of Ontology, Cosmology, Ultimate Causation, and of all problems pertaining to being and its laws, belong, as we have demonstrably evinced, to the exclusive sphere of the mixed sciences. In these sciences all valid deductions must be based upon facts of actual perception, and upon facts implied by what we perceive. In these sciences there are but two conceivable methods of reasoning, namely, the *à priori* and the inductive. In accordance with the latter method, we first of all determine the forms of valid perceived and implied knowledge, and then construct our systems accordingly, such systems being true when all forms of valid intuition, and none others, are included, and the validity of all our deductions are necessarily implied by our valid principles and real facts; and our conclusions will be false, if any real forms of knowledge are excluded, or any not valid are included as the basis of our deductions.

In the *à priori* method all the elements of thought given by perception external and internal are ignored, and all exercise of the faculties of Conception, Judgment, Association, and Imagination are suspended, and the whole being is held in waiting expectation for a direct, immediate, *à priori* insight, or vision of being *in se*, or of necessary, eternal, and absolute truth. Philosophers generally refer this vision of the Absolute to a special faculty called Reason or Ecstacy, while others identify this same faculty with God. The Christian Mystic refers such visions to direct and immediate illumination of the Spirit of God. All agree in this, that these visions are most full and perfect when the perceptive, and other kindred faculties referred to, are the most completely suspended, and all cognitions through them are the most fully ignored. The methods by which this common state of non-thought is induced are various. The Yogee and Buddhist having, by an act of will, suspended the exercise of the other faculties, seats himself in an immovable position with his eyes steadily fixed upon the end of his nose, or as fixedly directed towards the east, there and then awaiting the vision of absolute truth. The Grecian and Transcendental philosopher, 'when he begins to philosophize' without any such mere physical acts, 'puts himself into a state of not-knowing,' or, as Coleridge expresses it, ' by an act of scientific scepticism to which the mind *voluntarily* determines itself,' he 'assumes all previous knowledge to be uncertain,' and then and there awaits the 'vision Divine' of 'the Absolute.' Arabian philosophers of about the twelfth century recommended the following method of inducing this state of perfect non-thought. Setting out with the principle that the senses and other cognate faculties give us nothing but the transitory and perishable, they conclude from hence that reason should separate itself from all notions and conceptions, and even extinguish the imagination. 'The philosopher,' they say, 'who wishes to rise to the intuition of truth, should imitate the circular motions of the stars, in order to bring on a giddiness that may efface from the mind every trace—every recollection of the world of phenomena. In this state of isolation the intelligence of man, freed from all material obstacles, finds itself in direct communication with God. Everything visible has vanished away; Being only—the Absolute Being—appears in his essence, and the mind then comprehends that nothing exists—that nothing can exist out of that essence which is the sole reality.'

Christian Mystics had various methods of 'effacing from the mind every trace—every recollection of the world of phenomena.' Some, after voluntarily suspending the operation of the perceptive, conceptive, reflective, and reasoning faculties, seated themselves upon the ground with their eyes turned not to the east, nor fixed upon the ends of their noses, but upon the ends of their navels; others stood upon the tops of high posts with their eyes closed or turned upwards, while others still shut themselves up in cloisters, or 'wandered in deserts and in mountains and in dens and caves of the earth.' Everyone must perceive that the method of the *à priori* philosopher and Christian Mystic is really identical, and that the object of each is the same, the vision of absolute truth. The one expects this vision through insight of reason, the other through

Divine illumination. Both alike, according to all correct definition and classification, are Mystics—the one class in the mixed sciences, and the other in religion. The Christian Mystic holds that without the aid of the senses, of the reasoning faculties, or even of the Written Word, we attain, through direct and immediate illumination of the Spirit of God, to a knowledge of Divine truth. The Mystic in Philosophy expects, when he has 'put himself into a state of not-knowing,' by whatever method this state may be induced, a direct and immediate vision, through insight of reason, of absolute truth. Mysticism in Philosophy is the *à priori* method of scientific induction and deduction, the method which has place but in the pure sciences, forced, as the all authoritative method, into the sphere of the inductive or *à posteriori* sciences. Religious Mysticism, we repeat, is the same method of induction and deduction in the sphere of religious thought.

One inquiry of great interest and importance here arises—an inquiry which has been, in part, answered in other connections, namely, how is it that by strict adherence to the same method, and in the exclusive use of the same faculty and form of insight, there is obtained such a multitude of utterly contradictory visions of affirmed absolute truth? The importance of the subject will be our justification, we now being in the presence of all forms of development which Mysticism has ever taken on, should we repeat some ideas before expressed. As examples of these multitudinous conflicting 'visions of the faculty Divine,' permit us to request a careful consideration of the following statements, whose validity none will deny.

The Oriental Yogee of a certain class, the Grecian and Mediæval Idealist, and the modern Transcendentalist of a certain school, all in common, when they have ' put themselves into a state of not-knowing,' have or had direct visions, as a form of absolute truth, this formula: 'Brahm,' 'the All-One,' 'God as pure Being, or the Absolute,' 'alone exists; everything else is illusion.' Creation is exclusively by emanation. So far an absolute unity of vision obtains. So far as the *character* of these Divine emanations is concerned, the visions of 'this faculty Divine' are quite contradictory. The Hindoo Yogees reveal, first a Trinity of gods, and then numberless orders of inferior deities, all of whom seem to be evil, and are represented to the mind through monstrous images. The higher Grecian emanations are of a great variety of orders, and though not morally perfect, are presented with few exceptions through forms of beauty and power. The Pantheistic seers, who were educated in the presence of Christian ideas, apprehended forms of the Trinity, Incarnation, and various orders of superior beings, such as are designated in the Scriptures, but all revealed in harmony with the Pantheistic doctrine of *being in se*. The highest developments of the Absolute, and all Intelligence attributed to Him, by the Modern Pantheist, are represented in humanity and in human consciousness. The Christian Mystic had, for the most part, visions and revelations which accord with the evangelical faith, and of all the developments of the highest forms of the Christian life.

The disciples of Kapila and Kant, in the same 'state of not-knowing,' and through the same form of *à priori* insight, obtained this formula of absolute truth; 'Neither do I exist, nor anything which pertains to myself,' all our knowledge is merely phenomenal, and God exists but as a law of thought. Two unknown entities exist, as the substance and principle of all things.

Other Yogees, ancient and modern, in the same state of non-thought, and through the same identical form of insight, have a direct vision of matter as the only reality. With them Atheism is the form of absolute truth, and matter, with its laws, is the principle of all things.

Others still of the Buddhist, Pythagorean, Neo-Platonistic, and the Pure Idealistic school of modern times, have, as a similarly attained revelation of absolute truth, the formula that being and knowing are one and identical, and thought only exists as the principle of all things.

Plato and his school, after repudiating all knowledge through perception and understanding, and affirming that knowledge through the sciences has merely a subjective validity, obtained through direct and immediate insight of reason, and 'in an intuitive manner,' an absolute knowledge of Matter, Spirit, Time, and Space, as realities in themselves, of the eternal co-existence of matter and God—of God, as having organized the universe, after having persuaded Necessity to relinquish to Him the control of the material element; of His having committed for completion and final governmental control, His half-finished works, to a class of Gods whom He had created for the purpose, and then 'falling back into his usual slumber.'

We give the above as mere examples of the endlessly diversified and contradictory visions of 'absolute truth,' all of which are obtained through the same identical method, and by means of the same identical faculty of intuitive insight.

In what light, then, does impartial scientific integrity require us to regard the authority of this so-called 'faculty Divine;' this reason, and this method of induction and deduction, when carried over into the sphere of the mixed sciences, and their authority in the solution of the problem of being and its laws? If facts of the most palpable character constitute a basis for any deductions whatever, we are bound to regard this faculty and method as the most unreliable source of knowledge conceivable. External and internal perception, in the same circumstances, and when the same conditions are fulfilled, always, in the same individual, and in all men, give the same identical facts. This 'faculty divine,' this reason, this organ of intuitive insight, of '*being in se*,' and of universal, necessary, and eternal truth, and this method of science by which we attain a knowledge of absolute truth, when the same identical conditions are fulfilled, and in the same identical circumstances, give visions of the Absolute so endlessly diversified and contradictory as fully to realize the idea of 'confusion worse confounded.'

In the presence of these contradictory visions, we are also left without any criterion by which we can form even a probable conjecture as to which is true and which is false. We have, undeniably, the same identical *à priori* reasons for the assumption that matter alone is real, as we have that spirit alone exists, and we as undeniably have no such reasons for either affirmation. The *à posteriori* evidence is, also, equally balanced. From whatever standpoint the subject is contemplated, no grounds of discrimination exist, by which we can determine if any of these 'visions of the Absolute' are true, which are, and which are not, valid; while each form of vision is given forth as of absolute authority.

The very form in which these 'visions of the Absolute,' are set before us involve the grossest absurdities conceivable. Suppose an individual has a direct and immediate vision of matter as a reality in itself. Such perception is valid for the reality and character of its object. But suppose that our Yogee, or Scientist, affirms that in the same act of vision he perceives that nothing else but matter does exist, that is, that in infinite space no form of being but the material form does exist. Here we find ourselves in the presence of one of the grossest conceivable absurdities. Perception is always positive, and pertains exclusively to its object, and is valid for the reality of that specific object, and for nothing else. Unless the existence of matter necessarily implies, in itself, that nothing else does or can have being in infinite space, a perception of this substance as real, presents no grounds whatever for the deduction, or conjecture that any other conceivable form of being is, or is not, real. The same does, and must, hold true in all other cases. Knowledge direct and immediate of spirit finite or infinite, or of thought, feeling, or willing, is valid in itself for the reality and character of its object, and for nothing else, whose being is not necessarily incompatible with that of the object known to exist. Mr. Fichte, we will suppose, has had an actual knowledge, a reason-vision, of a real subject, 'a me,' which, from principles and laws inhering in its inner being, makes real to itself just such a universe as now lies out before us, with God as its author; the 'me' being the originator of all that appears as real to said 'me.' Mr. Schelling, on the other hand, has an equally valid vision of an 'absolute and infinite existence.' How the finite mind can have such a vision of 'being *in se*,' and that being infinite and absolute, is more than we can comprehend. We will suppose, however, that our philosopher has had 'through reason, in an intuitive manner,' a direct and immediate knowledge of such a being—a being possessed of the identical potences ascribed to it—one potence, that of reflection, in which this infinite substance 'embodies its own infinite attributes in the Finite,' and thus sees itself objectified in the forms and productions of the material world, that is, sees itself as being, in all respects, the opposite of what it really is; and another potence in which there is 'a regress of the Finite into Infinite,' and 'nature makes itself absolute,' and 'assumes the form of the Eternal.' Mr. Hegel, we will suppose finally, these examples being sufficient as illustrations, Mr. Hegel has had an actual vision, 'through reason, in an intuitive manner,' of 'a thought,' or 'idea,' which actually subjecticizes and objecticizes itself, as matter and spirit, as finite and infinite, and makes real to itself an organized material and mental universe, as existing in time and space, and under the control of an infinite and perfect mind; all this being generated by this thought wholly from itself, by itself, and for itself If these men have had such an absolute knowledge, of such a 'me,' such 'an absolute and infinite substance,' and such a 'thought,' we must admit the actual existence of just such realities. But when these philosophers assure us, that through the same absolute insight of reason, and in the same perceptive act, they had an absolute knowledge, the one of the ' me,' the other of ' an infinite substance,' and the third, of 'thought,' as the only existing reality, and as 'the substance and principle of all things;' here we find ourselves in the presence, not merely of absolute contradictions, but of the infinitely absurd. Absolute knowledge cannot contradict itself. and intuition simply, and exclusively, gives its object as real, and neither affirms, or can affirm, the reality, or non-reality, of any other object If thought can exist, and be perceived to exist, without a thinker, such a fact has no bearing whatever upon the question whether thought, in other cases, does, or does not, exist, as an act of a real subject who thinks; and the question whether such thinkers do exist, rests upon its own independent evidence. When an individual affirms that he has a direct and immediate knowledge of a certain form of being as real, we may, without violating reason, credit his affirmation. But when he affirms that, in the same intuitive act, he perceives that this object does, and that nothing else, does or can exist, we dementate ourselves, if we do not repudiate his pretension as perfectly absurd.

Now this is the exclusive character of all the professed visions of absolute truth under consideration. In the same intuitive act, our Yogee, Seer, Scientist, Philosopher, Transcendentalist, by whatever name we designate him, professes to perceive that one specific form of being exists as the sole reality, the substance and principle of all things; in other words, that this one object, and nothing else, does have being. A more absurd idea never had place in Bedlam.

The real character of the forms of absolute truth professedly found by these philosophers is also in palpable contradiction to their own formal definition of reason as an intuitive faculty. They all unite in defining this faculty, as the faculty which by direct and immediate intuitive insight, gives universal, necessary, and eternal truth. Not one of the forms of truth which they profess to find, through this faculty, has any such characteristic whatever. The peculiar characteristic of a necessary truth, is the absolute impossibility of even conceiving of the opposite as being true. Space, for example, we conceive to be real, with the absolute impossibility of even conceiving of its non-reality. Not so with any one form of affirmed absolute truth which these thinkers professedly find through insight of Reason. To every formula embodying such affirmed form of truth, another contradictory one stands opposed, and one is just as conceivably true as the other. To the proposition, God exists as the substance and principle of all things, for example, two others, whose validity is equally conceivable with this, stand opposed, namely, matter, exists as such a principle ; and matter, finite spirit, time, space, and a personal God are all realities in themselves. The doctrines of Materialism, Pantheism ; Ideal Dualism, Subjective, or Pure Idealism, are none of them forms of necessary truth, and cannot, therefore, have been given through *à priori* insight, as they are affirmed to have been.

The principles, we remark finally, which lie at the basis of all the systems constructed through this method and insight, are, as we have shown in other connections, mere assumptions which have not the remotest claims to validity. We refer to the assumption, that but one substance or principle of all things exists, and that knowledge but in its objective, or subjective form is possible, and is actual in one exclusive form. Take away either of these assumptions, and Materialism and Idealism, in all their forms, ' vanish into naught.' Now, as we have formerly demonstrated, no truth is, or can be, more evident than this, that neither of these assumptions is self-evidently true, and neither can be verified, as a deductive truth. In the absence of absolute omniscience, we cannot affirm what substances do, and do not exist, in infinite space. The avowal of such principles evinces infinite presumption in those who put them forward as principles in science.

What real claims, then, have this affirmed *à priori* insight of Reason in respect to ' being *in se*,' and to necessary and eternal truth, and this method of *à priori* induction and deduction in *à posteriori* sciences, what real claims, we ask, have this affirmed insight, and this boasted method, to our regard, as a means of attaining to a knowledge of truth in any form ? On purely scientific grounds, the results of such insight, and the deductions reached through such a method, have no more claims to our regard, as forms of real, and more than all, of absolute truth, than have the wildest visions and deductions of lunacy. The idea that men of a certain class, after 'putting themselves into a state of not-knowing,' after 'assuming all existing forms of knowledge to be uncertain,' after ignoring all facts of external and internal perception, and all deductions reached through the natural action of all the conceptive, associative, and reasoning faculties, can then look off into infinite space and eternal duration, and by *à priori* insight of Reason, know absolutely what substances and causes do, and do not, exist and act there—such an idea has nothing whatever but its presumptuous 'impudence,' and infinite absurdity, to commend it to our regard. Yet, when you deny the validity of such insight, you throw all the claims of Materialism and Idealism, in all their forms, into a midnight eclipse. The Christian mystic has open before him two books of God—that of Nature, and that of Inspiration. To each of these, he utterly closes his mind, and then in a state of blank non-thought, expects infallible Divine illumination. Can any expectation be more preposterous?

The Teachings of Thomas Aquinas.

Thomas Aquinas, sometimes called the Universal, and at others, the Angelic, Doctor (1225—1274), did more than any other individual to impart system to the scientific and theological thought of the Middle Ages. To give a full view of his varied teachings pertains to those whose object is a mere history of doctrine, and not to a fundamental criticism of systems of Philosophy. The following are among the most important of his teachings which possess a permanent interest for the race:

1. The object of science is the perfection of man, and each particular science has a specific relation to this one end. As individual men constitute a society organized for the end referred to, so the varied sciences; and that science is of all others the most regulative, which is most universal in its principles and deductions. This high and all regulative sphere is occupied by the science of Metaphysics, inasmuch as it treats of universal Being and its laws, and of causes, and especially of the great doctrine of Ultimate Causation. The origination of such a conception verifies its author as one of the truest and most profound of World-Thinkers. When the true doctrine of Metaphysics shall have been fully developed, this science will occupy the precise place at the head of all the sciences to which Aquinas has assigned it, and all the deductions of Anti-Theism, in all its forms, will disappear for ever from the sphere of scientific thought.

2. This great thinker, also, anticipated Dr. Reid in the solution of the problem which for ages had been agitated between the disciples of Nominalism and of Realism. He agreed with Aristotle in affirming that

individuals alone exist, and in denying the Platonic doctrine of the real existence of Universal Ideas. He differed equally from the Nominalists in respect to the dogma, that universals are mere words which represent no ideas in the mind or objects external to it. Ideas, as the archetypes after which all things were created, had an eternal existence in the Divine mind. General terms, also, as representing the qualities common to all individuals of a given class, and the conception of said qualities in the mind, do have a real, subjective, and objective existence. Here we have the real doctrine of Conceptualism, which is now universally admitted to be the true doctrine, and which Aquinas was the first to announce in a scientific form.

3. To Thomas Aquinas, we remark again, the world is indebted for the statement, in scientific form, of the only valid method of proving the existence of God. In the order of existence, he taught, causes precede their effects. In the order of human knowledge, however, causes are known but through their effects. God, for example, is known to mind, as 'the Creator of the heavens and the earth,' 'the Former of all things.' We do not know the universe through *à priori* knowledge of God, but God through or 'by the things that are made.' The truth of this doctrine is evinced by inspiration on the one hand, by Reason-intuition, on the other. The idea of God renders the universe conceivably possible, and its facts correspondingly explicable; but does not, in itself, imply the reality, either of a creation, or of a Creator. A doer can be known but by what he does. The doctrine of creation and a Creator does, and must, come under the same principle. The argument of Aquinas upon this subject is thus very clearly and succinctly stated in the 'Epitome of the History of Philosophy.' 'The philosopher can therefore arrive at a demonstration of God only by following an order relative to the human mind, by taking effects as the principle of the demonstration, in order to ascend to the cause as a logical consequence.' The *à priori* argument of Anselm, our author, as a consequence, rightly rejects as invalid.

In his presentation of the Theistic Argument, Aquinas fails in one essential particular. He rightly makes the fact of creation as an event occurring in time an essential principle and element in the argument; but wrongly bases the evidence of this fact, not upon deductions of the universal science of nature, but upon the affirmed natural, and self-evident impossibility of an infinite series of successive events. Thus, for ages, was a wrong direction given to Theistic thought, and a wrong basis furnished for the Theistic Argument.

4. The highest claims which this great Doctor has to our regard, are based, perhaps, upon the relation which he has most clearly and truly set forth between the doctrines of Natural and Revealed Religion. The former, he taught, such as those of God as 'the Former of all things,' the

soul, and duty, are common to revelation and to science both, and can be verified on rational grounds. The latter, such as the Trinity, Incarnation, and Atonement, are not contrary to, but above Reason. In the sphere of science, they may be vindicated, on account of their conscious accordance with the known condition and wants of man, as being probably true, and as not being self-contradictory, or opposed to absolutely known truths, and therefore absurd. In all other respects they are above science, and rest as objects of faith upon Divine revelation. No thinker has set forth these fundamental distinctions with greater clearness and force than has this 'Universal Doctor,' and here his teachings have claims of infinite weight upon theologians and philosophers of all ages. Their common duty is to vindicate for all truths of Natural and Revealed Religion a scientific basis, and for all doctrines which belong exclusively to Revealed Religion a full accordance with Reason in the sense above indicated. All who object to these doctrines must be held most strictly to these forms of disproof—a demonstration of their want of accordance with the conscious facts and wants of humanity—of their being self-contradictory—or of being, in fact and form, incompatible with absolutely known truths. No other forms of disproof or objection must be admitted as having any bearing whatever against any such doctrine, and these must lie against such doctrines, not as stated by certain individuals or sects, but as they are actually set forth in the Scriptures.

Decline and Fall of Scholasticism.

Scholasticism in its early developments, as represented in the maxim 'Credo ut intelligam,' met with strong opposition within the circle of leading teachers in the Church. Abelard, for example (1079—1142), laid down this fundamental principle, as having self-evident validity, 'that rational insight must prepare the way for faith, since without that faith is not sure of its truth' [Ueberweg, vol. i. p. 387]. 'My disciples,' he says, 'asked me for arguments drawn from Philosophy such as Reason demanded, begging me to instruct them that they might understand, and not merely repeat what was taught them; since no one can believe anything until he has first understood it, and it is ridiculous to preach to others what neither teacher nor pupil understands.' The wide popularity of Abelard, the multitude and zeal of his disciples, and the manifest truth of his leading utterances on this subject, originated and perpetuated within the Church a strong opposition to the extreme doctrine of Scholasticism, and prepared the way for its final overthrow.

The rise of experimental studies, and the open opposition of not a few of the Scholastic dogmas to forms of demonstrated truth, contributed much to ensure the same result. Roger Bacon, one of the greatest thinkers the world has known (1214—1294), really commenced the work which Francis Bacon did so much to consummate near the beginning of the seventeenth century. The former was confined in prison for ten years on account of his heretical teachings in the Natural Sciences. In the early days of the Reformation, his writings, as containing such heresies, were committed to the flames. The impulse given to such studies, however, could not be checked. The wonderful advance in experimental knowledge which followed the discovery of the magnet and of the telescope, the discovery of America and the circumnavigation of the globe, together with the demonstrations of such thinkers as Galileo and Copernicus, and their associates, in subsequent ages, so absolutely exposed the false teachings of Scholasticism in the sphere of scientific thought, as to assure the downfall of the system.

This consummation was hastened and completed by the revival of letters which followed the discovery of the art of printing, and the influence of the Greek scholars who fled from Constantinople to Italy, and other parts of Europe, on the fall of the Eastern Empire. The general introduction of classic literature, and with it the wide diffusion of free and independent thought, gradually weakened and finally broke the shackles of authority.

The Dogma that Doubt is a Pre-requisite Condition of Knowledge.

Abelard not only opposed the dogma, '*Credo ut intelligam*,' by affirming that 'faith has certainty only so far as it is transformed into science,' but also taught the doctrine that *doubt* is the necessary pre-requisite of real knowledge. 'By doubting,' he says, 'we are led to inquire, and by inquiring we perceive the truth.' To this principle, he affirms, Christ refers in the injunction, 'Seek, and ye shall find; knock, and it shall be opened unto you.' 'Dubitando enim ad inquisiorum venemus; inquirendo veritam percipimus; juxta quod et Veritas ipsa *Quærite*, inquit, *invenietis; pulsat, et aperietur vobis.*' This principle of doubt as the condition of attaining to a valid knowledge of truth, the condition first announced by Abelard, was introduced into the sphere of modern science by Des Cartes, and has since been the guiding light of Transcendental thought in all its forms. The Transcendental philosopher, 'when he begins to philosophize, puts himself into a state of not-knowing,' and 'assumes all his previous knowledge to be uncertain,' his avowed object being thereby to 'find a knowledge which shall be certain, or be rendered such.' In respect to this assumption, Des Cartes thus speaks: 'I do not in this imitate the Sceptics, who doubt for no other purpose but that they may doubt, and seek for nothing but incertitude. My whole endeavour in this matter is that I may find that which is certain.' 'This purification of the mind [from all forms of previous knowledge, this state of universal doubt] is effected,' says Coleridge, 'by an absolute and scientific

Scepticism to which the mind voluntarily determines itself for the specific purpose of future certainty.' This 'prudential doubt' of all existing certitude is presented in all schools of Idealism as the immutable and certain condition of attaining to 'all wisdom and all knowledge.' Let us, for a few moments, consider this 'prudential doubt,' and see if we cannot find its true and proper place in the sphere of science.

Let us first consider the motive which, in the form now under consideration, doubt presents for diligent research for truth and 'future certainty.' In 'assuming all our previous knowledge to be uncertain,' we of course assume, in the same form and to the same extent, the invalidity of the faculties which have furnished us with this knowledge. But all the faculties of which we are in conscious possession have been most diligently and honestly employed in our previous search for truth and certitude, and all to no purpose. These twenty, fifty, or seventy years, men may say, have we 'come to,' and employed these faculties, seeking truth and certainty by and through them, and have found nothing but incertitude. Where is the motive for their still further use 'for the specific purpose of future certainty?' All mankind, we remark again, have for thousands of years employed these same faculties for this one specific purpose, and have obtained nothing through them but the 'wild grapes' of incertitude. This miscalled 'prudential doubt,' takes away totally every rational motive for a further use of the Human Intelligence in a search for truth and certitude, and renders such hope in their use perfectly absurd. The only rational motive which can be presented to the mind for searching for truth and certitude, is found in the doctrine that truth and conscious certitude both lie within the reach of our intellectual faculties, and that in their honest and earnest use both are attainable; and this, in opposition to the gross perversion of Abelard, is the real meaning of our Saviour in the admonition, 'Ask and ye shall receive; knock and it shall be opened unto you.' The basis of faith, as set forth by reason and revelation both, together with all rational motives for searching for truth and certitude, is not doubt, but present rational conviction.

It is admitted by all these philosophers that by means of the faculties under consideration—the perceptive and reflective faculties common to the race, we can attain to neither truth nor real certitude. This high attainment is reached by a special faculty, not possessed by the masses, nor, in the language of Coleridge, by many 'even of the most learned and cultivated classes,' a special faculty born in philosophers of certain schools, a faculty which goes by different names, as Reason, 'the Inner Sense,' 'the Vision and Faculty Divine,' the Vernunst, and Intellectuelle Anschauung. Of this faculty the Oriental Yogees claim an exclusive possession. Plato affirmed that it was possessed but 'by the Gods and a very small portion of mankind.' 'There are many among us,' says Coleridge, 'and some who think themselves philosophers, too, to whom the philosophic organ is entirely wanting.' Hence, he tells us, 'Philosophy cannot be intelligible to all, even of the most learned and cultivated classes.' 'To remain unintelligible to such a mind' [a mind in whom the Intellectuelle Anschauung has not been inborn], exclaims Schelling, 'is an honour and a good name before God and man.'

What shall we think of the authority of this new and special faculty? Can we rationally hope to attain through it to real knowledge and conscious certitude? How can these philosophers assure to *themselves* the validity of this faculty? They have taken away from themselves and the race the Intelligence as it exists in all minds in common, and with it all the knowledge and certitude obtained through its use and action, and neither we nor they can tell where they have located either. How can they know that this new-born faculty is not, like its predecessors, 'a liar from the beginning?' Do they say that by 'this Vision and Faculty Divine' they have a consciously direct and immediate aspect of the Absolute? This is all that any faculty of intuition can yield us. But we do have in the use of other intuitive faculties a knowledge as consciously direct, immediate, and absolute, of Matter and Spirit as real entities. If intuition consciously direct and immediate is of doubtful validity in one case, why not in the other? 'The scientific Scepticism to which the mind voluntarily determines itself,' in respect to the action of the common intuitive faculties, must, in all reason, pass over to the intuitions of this 'Inner Sense.'

Besides, the former class of intuitions have infallible characteristics of validity which are totally wanting in the latter. In all minds, as we have formerly demonstrated, there exist the same identical apprehensions and convictions in respect to the essential characteristics of Matter and Spirit; whereas the intuitions of this especial faculty are not only totally wanting in the mass of mankind, but absolutely and palpably contradictory, as given forth by different philosophers in whom, if in anybody, this faculty has been fully 'inborn.' Who will deny that we have equal evidence of its existence and action, for example, in Plato, Kant, Fichte, Schelling, and Hegel? Yet, if we credit the revelations of this faculty in any one of them, we must as fully discredit them in all the rest. If we are to doubt intuitions identical in all minds, on what authority can we be bound to credit those—which, to say the most, exist but in the brains of certain philosophers, and are here as revelations of absolute truth, to be sure, but are at the same time as contradictory as are the 'responses of Chaos and Old Night'? While these philosophers can by no possibility verify to themselves the validity of this in-born faculty, which has had even imaginary birth but in their own brains, we who occupy the 'cis-Alpine' regions of thought, are in a bad fix truly. Having assumed all our existing forms of knowledge to be uncertain, having seen that these philosophers cannot verify to themselves, much less to us, the validity of this special faculty, and having found that in different philosophers in whom, if anywhere 'it is inborn,' its revelations of the Absolute are absolutely contradictory; and having no criteria by which we can distinguish the real Absolute from the unreal, we are out at sea in deep and perilous midnight, with no chart or compass to guide us in our researches after truth and certitude. So much, and no more, and no less, do we gain by means of this 'prudential doubt,' 'that scientific Scepticism to which we voluntarily determine ourselves.'

Still further, we have only to do what these Idealistic philosophers do, assume that we have and can have no valid intuitions through external perception, and that we do and can have through consciousness a valid knowledge of Spirit or its operations, and all the forms and systems of Idealism ever developed will rise up before us in their perfected entireness, and that through the proper action of the common faculties of the Intelligence, without the aid of any special faculty at all. This we have already demonstrated. The idea of the existence of any such faculty in any class of thinkers is one of the wildest dreams of a crazy philosophy. No new and special faculty was ever 'inborn' in Vayasa, Gautama Buddha, Pythagoras, Plato, Plotinus, Kant, Fichte, Schelling, Hegel, or Coleridge. They were born, grew, ate, drank, lived, and died, like other men, had the same faculties as other men, no more and no less than they, and reasoned like other men, excepting when they made fools of themselves in their methods of philosophizing. We dementate ourselves, when we give the remotest credit to their self-assumed possession of a 'special faculty of intellectual intuition,' an 'Inner Sense,' a 'Vernunst,' an 'Intellectuelle Anschauung,' not common to the race. Give us the assumptions which lie at the basis of Idealism, assumptions for the validity of which no reason whatever can be assigned, give us these assumptions, we say, and without any new faculty of any kind, and with just the faculties common to the race, we will manufacture to order, and that in full completeness, any system which any Transcendental thinker has ever developed. We will not only give the origin and complete form of the system, but will demonstrate the source from which all its principles and elements were derived, and the reason why they occupy the identical places in the system which they do occupy. We will then, as we claim to have done already, and will do hereafter, render equally evident the fact that such system has and can have no more claim to our regard, as a valid solution of the problem of being and its laws, than has the wildest creations of Dreamland.

The Real Place of 'Prudential Doubt' in Science.

What, then, is the real place and function, of 'prudential doubt' in the domain of scientific research? It pertains not at all, we answer, to the reality of truth itself, to the possibility of our finding the truth, nor to the validity of our faculties as interpreters of truth. In the sphere of science, every intellectual faculty has its proper and exclusive place and function, and in that place and in the legitimate exercise of that function, has absolute and exclusive authority. To doubt the validity of the Intelligence renders all research for truth absurd and ridiculous. Nor can the validity of any faculty within its proper and exclusive sphere be questioned, but for reasons which necessarily throw equal doubt over the action of all the other faculties, and thus render all the principles and deductions of all the sciences chimerical. Absolute faith in truth, and in the validity of all our intellectual faculties, is an immutable condition of any rational procedure in science.

In connection with the Intelligence, however, we have other faculties, the Sensibility and Will, whose aspirations and sentiments are everywhere intermingled with the real dicta of the Intelligence. Hence, intermingled with forms of valid knowledge, we have numberless forms of opinion, belief, conjecture, guessing, assumptions, and vain imagining; some of which may or may not be true, and more, perhaps, are utterly false, or but half-truths. Here, then, is a wide sphere for 'prudential doubt.' An affirmed system of knowledge is before us. If we were absolutely certain that we have here nothing but the exclusive action of the unperverted intelligence, we may rationally embrace the system as the exclusive embodiment of pure truth. We call to mind, however, that most systems are based upon mere assumptions in the place of self-evident and necessary principles, and that in the rearing up of systems, opinions, beliefs, conjectures, guessing, and assumption, have place, where nothing but logical deductions should appear. 'Prudential doubt' here comes in, and induces careful and rigid scrutiny in all places where error, in the forms designated, may appear.

A system of religion is before us—a system embodied in a given volume, claiming to be of divine origin and authority. We call to mind the fact that many such systems are in the world—systems which have, undeniably, their origin in mere superstition and imposture. From such facts, the spirit of Infidelity assumes, without examination, that this is one among the many other creations of falsehood—an infinite leap in logic, a leap in which infinite and eternal interests are suspended upon mere conjecture. 'Prudential doubt' which pertains equally, prior to examination, to positive belief or disbelief, induces the most careful and candid examination of all the forms of evidence, external and internal, on which the claims of this religion are based, and a decision in perfect accordance with the *weight* of that evidence. Faith, or dissent, in such a case, and on no other condition will have a rational basis. Suppose that research is refused, or conducted under the control of a doubt of the validity of the Intelligence in the research for truth in such cases. We then doubt, that we may doubt, and suspend infinite concerns upon lawless assumption.

For ages prior to Sir Isaac Newton, mankind had generally believed in ghosts. When the question came before him, he neither affirmed nor denied the common faith; but holding his mind in a state of 'prudential doubt' between belief and disbelief, carefully examined the real facts bearing upon the subject. The result of the examination was a rational denial of that faith. If Infidelity existed as the result of such an examination of the real evidences of the Christian religion, such unbelief would be without sin. Such are the express teachings of our Saviour.

'Prudential doubt,' then, rightly understood, has an important place and use in scientific research, and its absence always results in the credulity of superstition or unbelief, which are twin sisters of one common mother—infidelity of will to rational conviction. This form of doubt is equally antagonistic to the spirit of Scepticism which doubts the Intelligence in its entireness, or to that of Materialism and Idealism, which doubt the same Intelligence in one or the other of its essential functions. No chimera of false science is more absurd than the idea that the condition of rational certitude in any form is 'a scientific scepticism to which the mind voluntarily determines itself.' Voluntarily determined doubt, in all its forms, is wilful blindness, in the place of the integrity of truth.

HETERODOX TEACHINGS AND SYSTEMS OF THE MIDDLE AGES.

The highest authorities among the Schoolmen admitted the distinction between science and religion, and that each had its own exclusive method of induction and deduction. What they claimed was, that the doctrines of the Church should be held as absolute truth in both spheres in common. The endless conflicts of thought, both in science and religion, induced at length a general doubt of the possibility of scientific verification of religious truth. This state of doubt originated the dogma, that, of two palpably contradictory doctrines, each might be held as absolutely true, the one as a truth of theology, and the other as a verity of science. Under the influence of this dogma, all forms of Materialism, Idealism, and Scepticism, were taught in the schools and universities, as being scientifically true, and accordant with right Reason, but as being, at the same time, theologically false. Such teachings were at length condemned by the ecclesiastical and civil authorities, as forms of the grossest heresy and hypocrisy. Finally, the irreconcilable antagonism between religion and science was admitted and affirmed, and the claims of the Christian Religion were repudiated on the grounds of the higher claims of science. We will give a few examples of these heretical teachings.

Among the Arabians, as we have seen, we find the systems of Idealism, Materialism, and Scepticism in all their forms, and developed in full accordance with the Oriental and Grecian methods of philosophizing. The Mohammedan Soufis answer perfectly to the Christian Mystics. Among Mohammedan theorizers, also, we have repeated, in fact and form, the dogma affirmed by the Schoolmen—that what is true in science may be false in theology. Averroes, of the 12th century, gave professedly a scientific basis for this distinction—what was not attempted among Christian thinkers. 'He distinguished in man the intellect and the soul. By the intellect man knows universal and eternal truths; by the soul he is in relation to the phenomena of the sensible world.' Religion pertains to the soul, and has relation to what is phenomenally true. Science pertains to the intellect, and gives us what is true in itself. As the phenomenal may not correspond with the real, so scientific and theological truth may be contradictory, the one to the other.

In the heterodox teaching among Christian nations during the Middle Ages, we find philosophic thought moving round in its old circles, and repeating over and over again, the ancient dogmas of Idealism, Materialism, and Scepticism, with no change of method, and no new deductions. Scotus Erigina, for example, in the ninth century, after laying down and repeating, almost word for word, the principles of science as affirmed in the Rarika, an ancient document of the Sankhya Philosophy, gives us the Pantheism of the Vedanta School simply modified in detail in conformity to Christian ideas. 'Scotus Erigina,' says the Abbé Gerbert, 'effected the construction of a system which, in grandeur, in gigantic character, rivalled the bold assumptions of the Philosophy of India. He set out, like that Philosophy, with the primary unity, that unity represented, according to him, by the word nature, which comprehends the universal whole. This starting-point taken, what would the office of Philosophy be? Its object would be to explain how variety has proceeded from the radical unity, and hence the title of his book, *De divisione Naturæ*.' But under all phenomena, all diversities, he acknowledges nothing real but God, 'because His intelligence embraces all things, and intelligence in all things.' This cognitive power knew all things before they existed, and knew them not as out of itself, since out of itself there is nothing, but in itself, and as a part of itself. Everything thought and felt is but the apparition of something which in itself appears not, the comprehension of the incomprehensible, the name of the ineffable, the approach of the unapproachable One, the form and the body of that which has neither form nor body, the incarnation of spirit, the number of the innumerable, the localization of that which has no place, the temporary duration of that which is eternal, the circumscription of the uncircumscribed, the apparent boundary of the infinite.' 'Everything proceeds from this unity, everything will one day return thither, according to the law of a progress which will spiritualize all things.'

In Scotus Erigina, Schelling finds himself, in fact and form, anticipated in respect to his doctrine of 'the potence of reflection,' in which 'the Infinite embodies its own infinite attributes in the Finite,' and in 'the potence of subsumption,' in which there is 'a regress of the Finite into the Infinite.'

Amaury, born near the close of the twelfth century, set forth, as stated by Gersau, the following system : 'Everything is God, and God is everything. The Creator and the creature are one and the same being. *Ideas are at once creative and created.* God is the end of all things, in the sense that all things must return to Him, in order to constitute with Him an immutable individuality. Just as Abraham and Isaac are nothing but individualizations of human nature, so all beings are only individual forms of one sole essence.'

Giordano Bruno suffered martyrdom at the stake in Rome, February 17th, 1600, for teaching the doctrine of Pantheism in the pure Idealistic form. As stated by Mr. Lewes, the principle of his system was 'the identity of Subject and Object, of Thought and Being.'

In such thinkers as David de Dinant, of the thirteenth century, we have developed the doctrine of Material Pantheism. 'God,' he taught, 'is universal matter; the forms, that is, everything not material, are but imaginary accidents.'

We have given the above as examples in illustration of the validity of a statement made in the commencement of this treatise, that but a specific number of philosophical systems are possible to human thought. If we admit the validity of our knowledge of Spirit and Matter, and consequently of that of Time and Space, we must be Theists, and with Theism admit the doctrine of Immortality and Retribution. If we deny the validity of our knowledge of Spirit or Matter, or of both in common, then scientific thought must move in the direction of Idealism, Materialism, or Scepticism, and must generate, in all essential particulars, the same identical systems. The following statement of Mr. Lewes, in regard to Scepticism, is equally applicable to each of the other systems. 'It is worthy of remark that modern Sceptics have added nothing which is not implied in the principles of the Pyrrhonists. The arguments by which Hume thought he destroyed all the grounds of certitude, are differently stated from those of Pyrrho, but not differently founded; and they may be answered in the same way.' If the reader expects, in our advance into the sphere of the Modern Evolution in Philosophy, to find, Theism excepted, any new systems—systems which are not, in their principles, methods, and substantial forms, as old as Vayasa, Kapila, Kanada, Gautama Buddha, Pythagoras, Zeno, Democritus, Epicurus, Protagoras, and Pyrrho, he will find himself very much mistaken. He will find nothing of which it can truly be said, 'See, this is new.' 'The thing that hath been, it is that which shall be; and that which is done is that which shall be done; and there is no new thing under the sun.' Error has its fixed laws as well as truth. When Philosophy runs mad, there will be method in its madness, and always the same method and the same eternally repeated forms of Logical Fictions.

SCIENTIFIC PROBLEMS DISCUSSED IN THE MIDDLE AGES.

While the faith of the Church was set forth during the Scholastic Era as absolute truth, the *objects* of faith were also propounded as objects of thought and inquiry. 'As the right order demands,' says Anselm, 'that we first receive into ourselves, believing the mysteries of Christianity before subjecting them to speculative examination, so it seems to me the part of negligence if, after having been confirmed in the faith, we do not endeavour to understand what we have believed.' In the sphere of revealed truth, science, as the subject was then understood, has two missions—exposition and proof from facts of nature known to mind. Here was opened a wide field for thought, inquiry, diversity, and conflict of opinion, argument, and discussion. Within this sphere thought was not inactive among the Schoolmen, particularly in the western portion of Christendom. The *methods* of teaching and study then common in the schools and universities, was most favourable to the highest forms of independent thought and intellectual development. The pupil was not then, as is too commonly the case now, a mere recipient of thought through a text-book or lecture, but was in the presence of his teacher, to argue and discuss with him the great problems of universal truth. It has been well said that thinkers then *argued* themselves into mental greatness. There were, indeed, 'giants in those days.' When the great bodies of rival sects would confront each other before the pupils of the varied schools and universities with their conflicting *Theses*, and when the pupils would take part in the high debates, thought could but move in the sublimity of power. Hence it is that the world has known but few thinkers superior to such men as Anselm, Thomas Aquinas, and Roger Bacon.

Puerility of the Questions agitated by the Schoolmen compared with those common in other Eras.

Not a few of the questions which these great thinkers agitated, as involving problems of world-interest, were indeed very useless and puerile in character; as, for example, how many angels can stand together upon the point of a needle; or whether such being can transfer himself from one point in space to another, without passing the intermediate points. Such puerility is commonly regarded as peculiar to Mediæval thought, and has not unfrequently been presented as a reproach of the Christian Religion. Individuals who speak thus forget that deep thought expended upon questions of like puerility, the building up of world-systems from mere 'imaginary substrata,' the most wide-sweeping deductions with no form of proof, and infinite leaps in logic, have constituted the chronic infirmity and distemper of philosophers from the commencement of science to the present time. How much thought and discussion were expended by the greatest thinkers of Greece, for example, over such problems as this. A single pebble, for example, is in a given vessel. We say that there is one pebble there. A second one is put in. We now say that there are two pebbles in that vessel. What *made* the two instead of the one? Did the putting in of the last one do this? If so, the first one cannot be reckoned, and we have but a single pebble there. Did the one first in the vessel make the one two? Here we have the same conclusion as before. The final deduction was that the idea of making, by addition, one into two is a chimera. In a similar manner every object of thought, and every form of belief, was involved in inexplicable puzzles and perplexities, until Socrates affirmed that he did not know that he knew anything at all, even whether he himself did or did not exist. Which is the most important or least puerile question—what *made* the two, in place of the one, or how many angels can stand together on the point of a needle? Which is the most puerile or least important, attempted proofs in such cases, or the attempt of a great leader of the New Philosophy in our age, to PROVE by argument that *all* proof by argument is impossible? Was there ever a greater solecism or absurdity than is involved in a deduction from premises formally laid down, that all deduction from such premises involves the vicious error of *petitio principii*, and said production presented to the world as valid proof? One of these world-renowned scientists promises to 'demonstrate to us' that 'a unity of power or faculty, a unity of form and a unity of substantial composition, does pervade the whole living world,' and then, as a necessary inference from said affirmed demonstration, asserts that all mental and spiritual Phenomena do in fact arise from, and consist of, 'molecular changes in this matter of life.' He then in the process of the same article affirms just as absolutely that it is, 'in strictness, true that we know nothing about the composition of any body whatever as it is,' and that 'it is certain that we can have no knowledge of the nature of either Matter or Spirit.' For ourselves, we should regard ourselves as being quite as rationally employed were we engaged in a serious attempt to prove that 50,000 angels can or cannot stand together on the point of a needle, as we should be in an endeavour to 'demonstrate' 'a unity of form and a unity of substantial composition' in that of 'the composition' and 'nature' of which we affirm ourselves absolutely ignorant. The 'New Philosophy' is throughout characterized by just such puerilities and absurdities as these—a formal attempt to demonstrate 'the composition,' 'nature,' and 'laws' of a nature of which absolute and necessary ignorance is affirmed. We took up, some time since, a book designed to 'demonstrate' the place of man in creation. On a certain page in that book is a line of skeletons, commencing with the lowest form of the monkey, and ending with that of man. Between each two members of the series quite a similarity of structure appeared. From this mere fact of skeleton similarity, the inference is gravely drawn that man is lineally descended from the monkey. Why was not the opposite inference deduced, namely, that the monkey was begotten by the man? Degeneracy is a fact as real and almost as common in this world as progression from the least toward the more perfect. The argument is just as valid in one direction as in the other, and has not even the appearance of validity in either form. Humanity does degenerate, but never descends so low as to touch or approach brute irrationality. There is also progression in brutism, but never towards, much less across, the gulf which separates unreason from rationality. We might as reasonably and logically affirm that the Finite originates the Infinite, as that brutism begets rationality.

Mr. Lewes very justly ridicules one of the problems of the Schoolmen, namely, 'Whether God knows all things through *apprehensions* of them, or otherwise?' We apprehend that he finds superlative wisdom in the attempt of Mr. Herbert Spencer to develop a valid system of universal being and its laws, after affirming absolutely, that all our knowledge is 'exclusively phenomenal,' mere appearance in which no reality appears as it is, and 'that the reality existing behind all appearance is, and ever must be, unknown;' and especially, in his attempt to tell us just how and why matter, of the nature of which we know and can know nothing, first becomes organized from chaos, then vital in vegetables and animals, and finally rational in man.

The Main Problems agitated by the Schoolmen not Puerile.

The *main* problems about which these Scholastic thinkers occupied their thoughts, however, were by no means of the puerile character above indicated. To his disciples who stood weeping and praying for him around his death-bed, Anselm, for example, when, as it has been well said, 'infinite truth was soon to be unfolded to him in clear vision,' made this remark, 'I should have been glad before my death to have committed to writing my ideas upon the origin of evil, for I had got some explanations which will now be lost.' While Anselm maintained the doctrine of faith as the proper ground of certitude, he still affirmed that the 'human mind should aim to unfold itself in another mode, that of science.' The condition of unity in science, he asserted, is the development of a principle which will explain all facts of matter and spirit as they are in themselves, and as given in the universal intelligence. This principle, he affirmed, is found nowhere else than in the idea of an infinite and perfect personal God. The reality of the object of this idea explains the possibility and reality of the universe as it is. The presence of this idea in the Intelligence enables it to explain the facts of the universe as they are known to the universal mind. These two undeniable facts absolutely evince the validity of this idea. That this great thinker failed in the form in which he argued from the existence of the idea of God in the mind to the reality of the Divine existence, we readily admit. That he has here developed the great central doctrine of universal truth, and indicated the method of demonstrating its validity, we will now proceed to show. Anselm is undeniably right in affirming that rational mind cannot exist without becoming possessed of the idea of an infinite and perfect personal God, and that in the presence of that idea, the mind has an intuitive conviction of its validity. What is the ground of this conviction? Here we may fail as he did. Anselm sought this ground in the nature of the idea itself, and here he was, no doubt, wrong. We find this ground in the conscious relations of universal mind to this idea. Let us see if we have not found the true solution. It is self-evident, that no form of valid disproof, positive evidence, or even antecedent probability, exists against the validity of this idea. If we cannot prove that such a being does exist, no one, as all will admit, can present the most shadowy form of disproof of this doctrine. Whenever, on the other hand, this idea takes distinct form in the mind, every department and law of our moral and spiritual nature is in conscious harmony with that idea, and in equally conscious antagonism to every opposite idea and sentiment. We violate no law of our moral and spiritual nature, but consciously conform to every such law, when we admit the validity of that idea, and act accordingly. If, on the other hand, we repudiate that idea as representing a non-reality, and move and act accordingly, darkness visible encircles us, and all our moral and spiritual activities become lawlessly disordered. Universal mind, in all the higher departments of its nature, is a lie, or the doctrine of an infinite and perfect personal God is true. In the absence of all evidence to the contrary, such high proof as this has absolute validity. The unbelief of the present, and of all ages, is merely a relentless war upon human nature itself. The idea of a Godless universe can have place in no mind which does not ignore all the conscious intuitions, and promptings, and laws of its own moral and spiritual nature. When the idea of an infinite and perfect personal God lifts its Divine form, as it must do, before the mind, rational mind must deny its own being, and conscious nature and laws, or admit the validity of that idea, and this fact does furnish a basis and principles of infinite importance for the scientific prosecution of our inquiries on the subject.

There is, also, connected with this argument, a form of evidence of the highest weight in favour of the Theistic hypothesis. While all do and must admit the reality of an ultimate reason, or cause, why the facts of the universe are what they are and not otherwise, it is undeniably manifest, as Kant acknowledges and affirms, that no idea so fully and naturally and adequately represents our conception of that cause as that of an infinite and perfect personal God. As this idea fully explains *all* the facts of the universe just as they are, it absolutely excludes all possible proof, positive evidence, or antecedent probability in favour of any opposite hypothesis. The Theistic hypothesis, as we have before shown, accords fully with the intuitive convictions of the race, and a conviction thus universal is, as Cicero has truly affirmed, a law of nature, universality being the immutable and infallible test of such law. Now an hypothesis against which no form or degree of real proof, positive evidence, or antecedent probability can be adduced, which more naturally, fully, and adequately represents our necessary idea of ultimate causation, and which perfectly accords with the intuitive convictions of the race, such an hypothesis we must admit to be valid, or openly ignore and repudiate a known law of nature. Such is the undeniable state of the Theistic argument in the sphere of thought and inquiry in which we now are. We must admit the validity of the doctrine of God, or hold an hypothesis of some kind—an hypothesis in favour of which not a shadow of evidence of any form or degree can be adduced, on the one hand; and on the other place ourselves in open antagonism to an absolute law of the Universal Intelligence, the intuitive convictions of the race.

END OF VOL. I.